MW01039745

The Last Circle

Danny Casolaro's Investigation into The Octopus and the PROMIS Software Scandal

Cheri Seymour

THE LAST CIRCLE — DANNY CASOLARO'S INVESTIGATION INTO THE OCTOPUS AND THE PROMIS SOFTWARE SCANDAL

COPYRIGHT © 1994, 2000, 2009, 2010 CHERI SEYMOUR. ALL RIGHTS RESERVED.
PRESENTATION COPYRIGHT © 2010 TRINE DAY, LLC

References to Internet websites (URLs) were accurate at the time of writing. Neither the author nor Trine Day is responsible for URLs that may have expired or changed since the book was prepared.

Published by:
TrineDay LLC
PO Box 577
Walterville, OR 97489
1-800-556-2012
www.TrineDay.com
publisher@TrineDay.net

Library of Congress Control Number: 2010932355

Seymour, Cheri — Author
The Last Circle — Danny Casolaro's Investigation into the Octopus and the PROMIS Software Scandal—1st ed.
p. cm. (acid-free paper)
(ISBN-13) 978-1-9362960-0-2 (ISBN-10) 1-9362960-4
1. Political corruption — United States — History — 20th century. 2. United States — Politics and government — 20th century. 3. United States. -- Dept. of Justice. 4. United States. — National Security Council. 5.. Organized crime — United States. 6. Drug traffic — California. 7. Music Corporation of America – History. 8. Casolaro, Daniel, -- 1947-1991. I. Seymour, Cheri. II. Title

FIRST EDITION
10 9 8 7 6 5 4 3 2 1

Printed in the USA
Distribution to the Trade by:
Independent Publishers Group (IPG)
814 North Franklin Street
Chicago, Illinois 60610
312.337.0747
www.ipgbook.com

But if my words be seed that may bear fruit
Of infamy to the traitor whom I gnaw ...

Publisher's Foreword

My soul is not a palace of the past,
Where outworn creeds, like Rome's gray senate, quake,
Hearing afar the Vandal's trumpet hoarse,
That shakes old systems with a thunder-fit.
That time is ripe, and rotten-ripe, for change ...

— James Russell Lowell, "A Glance Behind the Curtain"

Be patient, spread the word among friends, do your little bit.
The system will self-destruct because it is founded on corruption and untruth.

— Antony Sutton, *Fleshing Out Skull & Bones*

The *system*, like a worried Titan eating its young, devours our humanity while slowly excreting an empire, transforming golden tomorrows into yokes of servitude, corruption and venal banality.

Isn't it time for a swaddled stone?

The Last Circle is a tale of our time: an era of "high crimes and misdemeanors." These acts are not more heinous, but are simply committed by personages in "lofty" positions, for preeminence bestows deeper responsibilities, stricter standards, and demands honest transparency, especially while dedicating our common weal.

Jesus said to pluck out your eye if it offends. Krishna told us to stand up, fight for justice – to make things right in the world – no matter the consequences to the established order. *It is our duty.*

Finding Antony Sutton's books in the late '80s finally gave me some perspective on what my former-OSS/G2/CIA father had originally told me some twenty years earlier about a hidden world behind the curtain: of intelligence agencies, secret societies, war, propaganda, the drug trade, unlimited budgets and the attending undercurrents of corruption. Hubris plumped for a fall.

The fact that, Cheri Seymour, a reporter for a small newspaper in a remote idyllic community on the doorstep of the majestic Yosemite Valley became part of numerous attempts to expose this malfeasant malignancy, demonstrates the breadth, depth and scope of the rot within our civic institutions.

My father tried to explain to me the enormity of the illegal drug trade and its effects upon our society and body politic. I had no context to fathom his words. Seymour supplies us with context and then some. Presenting all facets of a complicated story, supplying background, a large cast of characters, drama and intrigue, murder and mayhem, Cheri takes us on an amazing journey wherein the storyteller becomes part of the tale. She is the courageous reporter, following the story no matter where it leads, laying her cards on the table, letting the chips ride.

The Last Circle has won a strong following since an initial draft of the first fifteen chapters was put up on an Internet server at Cornell University in 1996. The work has been reposted on dozens of websites, become heavy blog fodder and been used as a source for books and countless newspaper, magazine, and Internet articles. TrineDay is honored to be publishing ... "the rest of the story."

Let us hope this leads to more than a small press releasing a book that simply gets ignored. TrineDay has brought many stories of contemporary corruption to press, only to see the system deftly sidestep astounding revelations with disdain, malice and fluffery.

Thomas Jefferson declared, "The people cannot be all, and always, well informed. The part which is wrong will be discontented, in proportion to the importance of the facts they misconceive. If they remain quiet under such misconceptions, it is lethargy, the forerunner of death to the public liberty."

Venturing on the Internet you find the long-suffering aren't remaining quiet, yet the hubbub is kept at bay through spin, lies, and a compliant media, leaving us wandering through a foggy soporific fraud.

In 1959, my father quit his profession of over twenty years, intelligence gathering and analysis, because he would not be involved in a nascent authorized narcotics trafficking operation. They tried to keep him in the fold by offering a bribe, he said no, and then later told me some truths I didn't understand. Comprehending his words have brought me here – to tell you. And also to ask these questions: Where is our Republic? Can we cease our current masquerade and correct this mess? Is there the understanding and political will?

What we have is terribly broken and causing trouble.

Our children deserve better.

Onwards to the Utmost of Futures,
Peace,
Kris Millegan
Publisher
TrineDay
August 18, 2010

To Danny Casolaro and the other fallen warriors who did battle with the Octopus.

"Let Justice Be Done, Though The Heavens May Fall"

Fiat justitia, ruat coelum.

Contents

Acknowledgements ix

Preface 1

Prologue 3

1. The Awakening - Mariposa 17

2. D.I.G. [Decency in Government] 29

3. The Wizard 35

4. Wackenhut Corporation 43

5. Danny Casolaro 49

6. The Trade 61

7. FIDCO [First Intercontinental Development Corporation] 95

8. The Lebanon Drug Connection 107

9. Files in the Mojave Desert 115

10. Covert Operations 135

11. Bio-Technology 149

12. Rendezvous with the Underworld 165

13. The Investigators 195

14. The Cali Cartel 211

15. The Old Boy Network 215

16. Nugan Hand Bank 243

17. The Inslaw Affair 247

18. The Benefactor 257

19. The Internet 275

20. Enter RCMP 283

21. Spookloop 297

22. The Octopus Exposed 337

23. The Wiretaps 375

24. Robert Booth Nichols 383

25. Rachel's Resolution 393

Epilogue 443

Documents 447

Photographs 558

Appendix — Corporate Structures - Joint Ventures.. 583

Index 587

Acknowledgements

Grateful acknowledgement is made to the following people for their valuable contributions, their insight, and the honor of their friendship during the writing of this book. (In alphabetical order):

Rachel Begley – Curt Butler – John Cohen – Steve Hager – Bill Hamilton – Dave Hendrix – Scott Lawrence – Garby Leon – Dave Massey – Sean McDade – Dan Moldea – Kelly O'Meara – John Powers – Marvin Rudnick – Richard Stavin – Sue Todd.

Special thanks to Paul Rodriguez, editor of *Insight* magazine, and Kelly O'Meara, former reporter at *Insight,* for their 4-part investigative series: "Nothing is Secret" (1-29-01) – "The Plot Thickens in PROMIS Affair" (2-5-01) – "PROMIS Trail Leads to Justice" (2-12-01) – "PROMIS Spins Web of Intrigue" (2-19-01).

Appreciation is also extended to Steve Hager, editor at *High Times* magazine for permission to reprint from "The Ghost of Danny Casolaro" by Cheri Seymour. Copyright @ August, 2001.

A singular acknowledgement to *Los Angeles Times* reporter, Henry Weinstein, for his contribution relating to the *Los Angeles Times* story on March 21, 1993 entitled, "Trial Offers Murky Peek Into World of Intrigue" by Henry Weinstein and Paul Feldman.

I am forever indebted to publisher Kris Millegan of TrineDay for his professionalism and courage in bringing quality, long-awaited suppressed books [including *The Last Circle*] into print and making them available to book stores and the general public.

Special acknowledgement is also extended to the following individuals for their generous contributions from all points of the spectrum: (In alphabetical order):

Gene Gilbert – George Granby – Ted Gunderson – Robert Booth Nichols – Michael Riconosciuto – Jimmy Rothstein – Peter Zokosky – and others who wish to remain anonymous, but whose contributions were equally appreciated [names withheld] in the book.

And finally, gratitude is especially extended to the late Daniel Casolaro for blazing the first trail to the layer of the Octopus.

Preface

Journalist Danny Casolaro's death was like a stone hurled into a pool of water. Ever expanding circles of shock-waves rippled from the epicenter in Washington D.C. to the furthest reaches of the nation's consciousness. When *the last circle* wave crashed upon the West Coast, its psychological effects prompted California journalists to seek answers to what had been contained in Casolaro's files, stolen on the eve of his death. This book attempts to follow the trail of his investigation which he termed "The Octopus."

This book is also a comprehensive historical account of the various tentacles of the Octopus, an anatomy of an investigation narrated by the author, which includes the inside story of reputable law enforcement investigators and prosecutors who probed various aspects of the Octopus and were ultimately obstructed and betrayed by the Justice system that they worked for.

Some of them risked reprisals to contribute to *The Last Circle.* Most of the information they provided has never been made public to this day, except in *The Last Circle.*

Danny Casolaro

Prologue

High Times magazine, August 2001 issue, Vol. No. 313 - Headline; "The Ghost of Danny Casolaro," by Cheri Seymour. (Copyright, *High Times*, 2001). Reprinted below in its entirety [with updates]:

Danny Casolaro, a Washington D.C. investigative journalist, dubbed his probe of organized crime, drug trafficking, money laundering, pirated software and other nefarious activities "The Octopus." Just prior to his death on August 10, 1991, Casolaro ecstatically told friends he would be traveling to Martinsburg, Va. to bring back the head of the Octopus. Instead, his body was found in a blood filled bathtub at a Martinsburg hotel, his wrists slashed deeply ten or twelve times. No papers were found in his hotel room or in his car, though he was known to cart an accordian file folder everywhere he went. The room was cleaned and his body was embalmed before relatives were notified; authorities had assumed it was a suicide.

Danny's brother, Dr. Anthony Casolaro, publicly stated his disbelief that his high spirited, gregarious brother could have committed suicide. Danny was so afraid of blood, he said, that he refused to allow samples to be drawn for medical purposes, and would never have chosen to slash his veins a dozen times. Moreover, Danny had a life filled with friends and a close-knit Italian Catholic family. He was known in private circles as an upbeat, golden-haired, Gatsby-esque romantic who loved to quote poetry, raised Arabian horses, and was adored by women.

Friends later told investigators, and Casolaro's notes at home confirmed that he had traced the tentacles of his Octopus back to a

CIA [Central Intelligence Agency] 'Old Boy' network that had begun working together in the 1950's around the Albania covert operations. Reportedly these men had gotten into the arms and drug trade back then and had continued in that business ever since.

Ten years later, Casolaro's Octopus is a visible reality. He was the first investigator to put the pieces of the puzzle together, but others followed in his wake. Most recently, Sean McDade, a national security investigator from the Royal Canadian Mounted Police [RCMP] secretly entered the U.S. in February 2000 to investigate evidence that the Canadian government was using a computer software program called PROMIS which allowed the U.S. to eavesdrop on Canadian intelligence secrets through a modified "back-door."

The software in question was a revolutionary case management system developed in the early 1980's by Inslaw Corporation for use by the U.S. Department of Justice. According to Bill and Nancy Hamilton, owners of Inslaw, a version of the PROMIS software was pirated and sold to Canada. Canadian authorities denied this, but never actually investigated the Hamiltons' claim --- until last year when RCMP found an invoice for the purchase of PROMIS from Strategic Software Planning in Cambridge, Massachusetts.

RCMP investigator Sean McDade, 33, soon arrived in the U.S. to conduct a classified investigation code-named Project Abbreviation. The RCMP probe resembled a James Bond novel; McDade's e-mail handle was simorp, that's PROMIS spelled backwards. In his briefcase was a bound printout of this writer's manuscript taken off the Internet entitled, *The Last Circle*, which basically outlined Casolaro's findings, the people he interviewed, and the investigators who wrestled with the many tentacles of the Octopus.

In Southern California on February 19th, 2000, at this author's home, the stalwart, soft-spoken Mountie explained that high-ranking Canadian officials may have unlawfully purchased the PROMIS software from officials in the Reagan-Bush administration. RCMP had reportedly traced some banking transactions that supported this claim. If his investigation was successful, he said, "it could cause the entire U.S. Republican Party to be dismantled and more than one presidential administration would be exposed for their knowledge of the [PROMIS] software transaction."

Sue Todd, an attractive, petite Police Detective from Hercules, California, had accompanied McDade to the meeting. Their demeanor was serious and both were armed with 9mm police guns bulging under their jackets. Todd explained they had hooked up in early January when they discovered they shared the same "source." Todd had been investigating a three-year-old double homicide, which coincidentally had occurred on February 19, 1997, and had reason to believe her case was connected to the PROMIS case. Also present at the meeting was an impartial observer invited by this writer.

With full British decorum, in the straight-forward manner that became characteristic of the big Mountie, McDade made it clear his investigation was authorized at the highest level of RCMP, and well funded. He was deeply committed to ascertaining whether the Canadian government's computer system had been compromised, and if indeed it contained a "back door."

He said a meeting had been held in December 1999 at the Los Alamos facility in New Mexico which was attended by the heads of the intelligence divisions of the U.S. [CIA], Britain [MI6], Israel [Mossad], and CSIS [Canadian Security Intelligence Service] relative to questions about upcoming Y2K computer problems. The topic of discussion was labeled "Unique Elements." The meeting had been called after a glitch was found in the British computer system which caused the loss of six months of "historical case data."

A source who attended the Los Alamos meeting had suggested to McDade that it appeared all four allied countries shared the same computer system, possibly PROMIS, presumably because PROMIS was the only system developed years ago which could be mutually integrated by these allies. McDade had been told by another source that the Israeli Mossad may have modified the PROMIS software so it became a "two way" backdoor, thus allowing the Israelis access to top U.S. weapons secrets at Los Alamos and other installations. He hinted that the Israelis may now possess all the nuclear secrets of the United States. This was four months *before* Associated Press reported in June that hard drives and discs containing nuclear secrets were discovered missing at Los Alamos.

For three days McDade xeroxed thousands of supporting documents to *The Last Circle*, then returned to RCMP headquarters in Ottawa to set up a "war room." It was here that the RCMP probe morphed into an eight-month saga of interviews with former investigators, witnesses, undercover-informants and law enforcement people across the U.S.

With the assistance of Detective Sue Todd and others, McDade learned that his U.S. predecessors had found themselves on a collision course with the Justice Department when their investigation of PROMIS inevitably led to drugs and money laundering. Some investigators were fired, some suspended, others quit their jobs when they were directed by the DOJ to shut down.

The proportions of the cover-up are astounding by today's standards. Investigators from the FBI, U.S. Customs, Judiciary Committee, police, and even the Royal Canadian Mounted Police [RCMP] still fear punitive action if they come forward, despite the fact that many of them are now employed in the private sector.

Nevertheless, they all left an investigative trail, whether by design or accident. Danny Casolaro's tragic death essentially opened a Pandora's Box which the DOJ was never able to close. During the last week of his life, Danny had discovered a connection between Mike Abbell, a former director of international affairs for the Justice Department, the Cali Drug Cartel, and Robert Booth Nichols, an international intelligence operative whom he had been interviewing extensively for months. Danny's last phone bills indicated he'd spent hundreds of hours on the phone with Nichols, most of the calls averaged one to two hours. This in effect, was one tentacle of the Octopus.

Danny had confronted Nichols about Mike Abbell and the Cali Cartel while staying in Martinsburg. It was the last conversation Danny ever had with Nichols, and with Bob Bickel, a friend whom Danny confided in. Bickel subsequently confirmed the conversation, but for reasons unknown, the Abbell - Cali Cartel connection was never published in any of the official investigative reports on Danny's death. These included the DOJ report of September 27, 1994.

In fact, a note handwritten by Danny four days before his death, found by relatives, read as follows: "Bill Hamilton - August 6. MR ... also brought up '*Gilberto*.'" Unknown to anyone outside the DOJ at that time, a FBI investigation of Mike Abbell was underway at the time of Danny's death. Years later, an indictment unsealed in Miami on June 6, 1995 charged Abbell with laundering money for the Cali Cartel. Surveillance reports indicated he'd made frequent visits to the home of *Gilberto* Rodriguez, leader of the Cali Cartel in Bogota, Colombia. Abbell was prosecuted and served a prison term.

Robert Booth Nichols was reportedly in Vietnam, working for a wealthy U.S. businessman in the private sector. During a recent Valentine's Day interview at the home of Nichols' close friend and former business partner, it was revealed that Nichols worked as a contract operative for the NSC [National Security Council] at the time of Danny's death. Nichols had been on the Board of Directors of First Intercontinental Development Corporation [FIDCO], reportedly a NSC cutout used in Lebanon to arrange the release of a prisoner.

Letters written in the summer of 1983 between FIDCO directors Michael McManus, then assistant to President Ronald Reagan at the White House, and George Pender, president of FIDCO, established that FIDCO had an important role to play in Lebanon. A follow-up letter, dated July 12, 1983, from Pender to Amin Gamayel, the president of Lebanon, indicated that all transactions should be telexed to "652483 RBN ASSOCS LSA," Nichols' telex address at his Marina Del Rey condo in Calif. The Arab Bank Limited in Amman, Jordan, responded that there would be no problem taking care of the "US$ three billion or more" financial transaction. The release of the prisoner was successful.

Others on the Board of FIDCO included Robert Maheu, former CEO for Howard Hughes operations in Las Vegas, and Clint Murchison, Jr., of the Dallas oil family, to name a few. According to Nichols' friend, who does arms consulting for the British government and lives part of the year in London, these were all intelligence people working for the NSC. It is likely these powerful men headed one tentacle of Danny's Octopus, and comprised the "CIA 'Old Boy' network" Danny referred to in his notes. Some of them served under General Douglas MacArthur during WWII and Clint Murchison, Sr. helped fund MacArthur's presidential campaign. Senator Joseph McCarthy, Richard Nixon, and J. Edgar Hoover were often seen at Murchison's Hotel Del Charro in La Jolla, California during the 1950's. Murchison often picked up the tab.

At the time that FIDCO was arranging the release of the prisoner in Lebanon, Robert Booth Nichols was under investigation by the Los Angeles FBI as a suspected "international launderer of money derived from both narcotics and organized crime activities." An FBI report obtained by Nichols through "special" contacts, and provided to his friend, indicated Nichols' telex number was 652483, the same as that sent to the president of Lebanon.

Though Nichols has no known source of income in the U.S., the background check within the report stated Nichols resided nine months of the year at a 3.5 million dollar villa in Italy, and his name "was associated with the illegal transportation of narcotics through the Golden Triangle." Once again this tied in with Danny Casolaro's final inquiry of the Golden Triangle. The FBI report concluded that "Robert Booth Nichols should be considered armed and dangerous."

FBI agent Thomas Gates in Los Angeles had frequent conversations with Danny Casolaro until three days before his death. Danny had told Gates that Nichols warned him to drop his investigation of the Octopus. Nichols had even flown to Martinsburg to convince Danny of the danger of his probe. Gates had conducted a wiretap of Music Corporation of America [MCA] under the supervision of U.S. Attorney Marvin Rudnick, who subsequently lost his job when he refused to drop the investigation. [Subsequent interviews in 2009 revealed that DOJ prosecutor Richard Stavin supervised the FBI wiretaps].

The wiretap had recorded Robert Booth Nichols communicating with Eugene Giaquinto, then president of MCA home entertainment division. Giaquinto was a board member on Nichols' holding company, Meridian International Logistics [MIL], under investigation by the FBI as a "source of funding for the purchasing of narcotics/controlled substances and the allocation and use of the proceeds from its trafficking," according to the wiretap application.

MIL was reportedly a NSC cutout, used for the purpose of "funneling money to pay the board of directors," according to Nichols' friend who was once on the board. He explained that the NSC is a "profit-making entity; funding is unlimited and no accountability is required because of national security."

He further explained that all business conducted covertly today relates to two things: "money and/or drugs." Drugs are used as international currency, commonly called "gold." Drugs are a business at the highest levels of corporations because there is a huge market and demand for drugs. Entire countries and banking institutions are now dependent on the drug trade for income, he said. Presumably these include Colombia, Mexico, Lebanon, Afghanistan, and other drug-dependent economies.

Another tentacle of the Octopus involved La Cosa Nostra. Wrote Gates in his affidavit in support of the wiretap of Giaquinto, Nichols, et al: "I have become familiar with how some union officials, alleged labor consultants and La Cosa Nostra (LCN) members and associates manipulate, extort, and corruptly influence companies and/or individuals associated with the production of films and television shows and how stockbrokers associated with the LCN, LCN members and associates use deceptive and fraudulent practices in the buying and selling of stocks."

The LCN members specifically related to members of the Gambino and Bufalino crime families, many of which were reportedly picked-up in the FBI wiretaps. Marvin Rudnick, Thomas Gates, and Richard Stavin, a member of the Organized Crime Strike Force, all believed MCA had been penetrated by organized crime, based on the wiretaps.

It was reported that the MCA Board of Directors at that time included Howard Baker, a former U.S. Senator, Eugene Giaquinto, Lew Wasserman and others. Giaquinto and his partner in MIL, Robert Booth Nichols, both had a close working relationship with the Justice Department, according to the wiretaps. Nichols' friend alluded to this as well.

MCA was being offered in a leveraged buyout to the Japanese, and a FBI investigation could effectively ruin the sale. The wiretaps were subsequently sealed by the DOJ and no prosecutions were forthcoming. The Los Angeles Organized Crime Strike Force was disbanned, Richard Stavin quit his job, Thomas Gates closed the FBI investigation, and the Japanese bought MCA, the largest reported corporate sale in U.S. history. [After the loss of his job, Marvin Rudnick ultimately got part of his story told in a 1993 book entitled, *Stiffed: A True Story of MCA, The Music Business, and the Mafia* by William Knoedelseder].

Robert Booth Nichols had undoubtedly told Danny Casolaro about this leveraged buyout, just as he had told this writer in a face-to-face interview on February 13, 1992, six months after Danny's death. Nichols was aptly described in magazine articles as "Clark Gable without the ears." He was tall with probing brown eyes, his demeanor simultaneously controlled and dramatic with an international flavor. He'd been the weapons technical advisor for Steven Seagal's movie, *Under Siege*, and it was apparent why Seagal gave him a cameo appearance as a military colonel in the movie. On his application to carry a concealed weapon, Nichols wrote: "I am involved in the research and development of weapons systems, ranging from the basic blow-back automatic weapon to various advanced destructive devices ---" He listed residences in Italy, France, England, Australia, and the U.S.

Nichols believed Danny Casolaro had been murdered and wrote a manuscript entitled, "Danny Casolaro's Octopus," dated November 22, 1991, which he copyrighted at the Library of Congress. In the manuscript, Nichols relates a meeting in which Danny and a man who worked closely with the DIA met [with Nichols] at a restaurant in McLean, Virginia. Another scenario depicted Danny's demise at the Martinsburg hotel in August 1991. The last paragraph in the manuscript describes a military man placing a medal at the location of Danny's coffin. It is noted that the only agency that does this is the NSA [National Security Agency].

But Nichols testified under oath in a Los Angeles courtroom in March 1993 that he worked quietly and selflessly for nearly two decades on behalf of shadowy CIA keepers in more than 30 nations from Central America to Southeast Asia. Nichols' friend and former partner explained recently that Nichols adeptly provides "service for money" to any government agency that requires his services. He showed a photo of Nichols with Arab leaders during the Gulf War, noting that Nichols is considered a valuable asset and well respected in U.S. intelligence circles. "He gets the job done," said the friend.

The FBI [Federal Bureau of Investigation] report which Nichols shared with his friend corroborates his ability to move large sums of money around the world, as follows: "RBN assisted Ignacio Paz, Deputy Chief of Staff, Intelligence, Philippine government, with removing large sums of money from the Philippines by investing with RBN who placed the money in Swiss bank accounts."

Like a many tentacled octopus, this ties in with what John Cohen, a House Judiciary Committee investigator on Inslaw, said about the theft of the PROMIS software: "You see, I've had a side theory about why PROMIS was taken. It was that PROMIS could be modified to track money laundering. And it could be used as an active information gathering, or an active moving software program that can go into other data bases. And it could be modified to control hundreds of accounts and move money through the international banking system."

Cohen added, "What a lot of people don't realize is that there are two international banking systems. There's CHIPS and SWIFT. And the word Swift Chips has been spread throughout this whole [Inslaw/PROMIS] investigation. CHIPS is a referral to the Clearing

House Interbank Payment System and its European counterpart, SWIFT. And they do $2 billion dollars worth of banking transactions a day. And if one was able to move accounts through there, you could move money invisibly around the world ---"

Cohen felt there was a narcotics connection to this. As a former Los Angeles police officer, he had worked international narcotics conspiracies with the DEA [Drug Enforcement Administration] and FBI and learned about Southeast Asian heroin and the rise of the Cartels in Latin America. "I ran into quite a few law enforcement professionals who were pretty irritated because of the intelligence agency, drug dealer connection," he said.

Bill and Nancy Hamilton, owners of Inslaw, ultimately sued the DOJ for non-payment on a version of PROMIS called Modification 12, and for allegedly modifying the software for sale to foreign governments, including Israel and Canada. Michael Riconosciuto, 44, a West Coast computer scientist, had sent them an affidavit in March 1991 claiming he installed a "back door" in PROMIS so the U.S. could access intelligence data of foreign countries.

Danny Casolaro began interviewing Riconosciuto during this time. The patient, amenable wizard with the dark, weary eyes, opened a window for Danny into a netherworld of real life players in Dungeons & Dragons, where scientific genius is employed in nefarious activities, and spooks jump on and off the board at will.

Riconosciuto had been a child prodigy at the age of 10, when he wired his parents' neighborhood with a working, private telephone system that undercut Ma Bell. As a teenager, he had won so many science fairs with exhibits of laser technology that he was invited to be a summer research assistant at Stanford's [University] prestigious Cooper Vaper Laser Laboratory. Dr. Arthur Schalow, a Nobel laureate, remembered him: "You don't forget a 16-year-old youngster who shows up with his own argon laser," he told Casolaro.

Riconosciuto and Robert Booth Nichols joined forces in a 1981-83 Joint Venture between Wackenhut Corporation and the Cabazon Indian tribe in Indio, California. They were partners in Meridian Arms, a subsidiary of MIL [Meridian International Logistics], and provided technical assistance to Wackenhut in the proposed development of esoteric armaments at the reservation.

Riconosciuto was having difficulty getting security clearances, however a letter written by Patrick Cannan, Director of Relations for Wackenhut Corporation in Coral Gables, Florida, confirmed Riconosciuto's scientific value to the Venture. In 1981, Riconosciuto and Robert Frye, Vice President of Wackenhut in Indio, had met with Dr. Harry Fair, chief of propulsion technology at the U.S. Army installation in Dover, New Jersey. Riconosciuto conducted a highly technical theoretical blackboard exercise on a railgun for Army personnel at the arsenal. Afterward, Dr. Fair commented that it would be a shame if Riconosciuto, whom he termed a "potential national resource," couldn't be used for military/research projects.

Danny's interviews with Riconosciuto inevitably turned to Robert Booth Nichols. But Danny learned more than he bargained for. Seven days after providing Inslaw with the affidavit about the modifications to PROMIS, Riconosciuto was arrested for operating a methamphetamine lab in Tacoma, Washington. In an apparent attempt to trade information on Nichols' alleged drug activities to authorities, Riconosciuto reached out to Bill Hamilton and Danny Casolaro in August 1991 to quietly research Mike Abbell's connection to the Cali Cartel. Riconosciuto warned Hamilton that getting the information might be dangerous. Danny jumped on this, and within five days was found dead in Martinsburg. His handwritten note, "Bill Hamilton - August 6. MR ... also brought up '*Gilberto*'," corroborates this.

In January 1992 Riconosciuto disclosed to his wife, Bobby Riconosciuto, that he had been present when Nichols met with Abbell in Washington D.C. about "crow-barring" the extradition to the U.S. of Cali Cartel leaders Gilberto Rodriguez, Jose Londono and Miguel Rodriguez because they were "intelligence people." At Riconosciuto's request, the information was passed to an FBI agent who spoke directly with Riconosciuto about a possible trade into the Witness Protection Program. The trade never materialized, but Riconosciuto continued to send taped messages to the agent in an attempt to prove his veracity. One tape related to a drug/sting operation in Lebanon in which Riconosciuto claimed to have participated through Euramae Trading Company in Nicosia, Cyprus, yet another NSC cutout, according to Riconosciuto.

Also in early 1992, Judiciary investigator John Cohen began communicating closely with FBI agent Thomas Gates. As noted earlier, Gates had been speaking with Danny Casolaro until three days prior to his death; Danny had been desperate to communicate his findings to someone in authority, even a representative of

FinCen [Financial Crimes Enforcement Network], to no avail. His elation at identifying the head of the Octopus must have become deeply depressing when he could find no one to believe him. At the time, Mike Abbell was a prestigious lawyer with offices in Washington D.C. and Miami. Who would have believed he was laundering money for the Cali Cartel? Or that Robert Booth Nichols was connected to the highest levels of government allegedly in collusion with organized crime?

In October 1992 John Cohen and Thomas Gates learned about Riconosciuto's statement to the FBI. An excerpt from the transcript read as follows: "Bob Nichols runs Glenn Shockley. Glenn Shockley runs Jose Londono ... and the bottom line here is Bob Nichols and Gilbert Rodriguez, and Michael Abbell, who's now an attorney in D.C., but he was with the criminal section of the Justice Department ... are all in bed together."

Riconosciuto said before his arrest he had been handling gold transfers, money laundering, "virtual dead drops," altered ACH daily reconciliations and other transactions for various underworld figures including Cali Cartel leaders Gilberto Rodriguez and Jose Londono - and Bob Nichols and Glenn Shockley, both board members on FIDCO and MIL together. Riconosciuto's statement was made over three years before the Abbell indictment was unsealed.

After reading the statement, Cohen remarked, "Now that corroborates some information that I got in the past which talked about one of the reasons PROMIS was stolen." Apparently it all boiled down to money laundering, possibly with the use of PROMIS, if in fact Riconosciuto had possessed the software.

In February 1993 Scott Lawrence, a U.S. Customs internal affairs investigator from Boston, obtained a copy of the statement on Abbell that had been provided to Cohen the year before. Lawrence was investigating Peter Videnieks, a U.S. Customs contract specialist detailed to the DOJ in the early 1980's to develop the PROMIS software. However, within a short time, like the investigators before him, Lawrence was soon following the drug trail.

It was not until February 2000 that Lawrence's investigation of corruption within U.S. Customs was described to this writer by Sean McDade, the RCMP national security investigator, who briefly outlined Lawrence's deep-cover drug investigation code-named THE INDO-CHINA PROJECT on the Maine/Canadian border. It is unknown who or what McDade's source was for this information. However, a former New York police officer who assisted with the case told *Insight* magazine ["PROMIS Spins Web of Intrigue" - 2/19/01] that Lawrence's investigation was abruptly shut down after he and his supervisor, John (Tim) Kelly, requested to impanel grand juries in several states to depose officials from the CIA. The DOJ declined the request and Videnieks was never charged with any wrongdoing.

To date, no official report has ever been written on Danny Casolaro's findings or how they related to his death. Robert Booth Nichols has no arrest record, according to a law enforcement officer who viewed his file. The National Security Agency [NSA] is now spying on Canadian citizens while Canada spies on American citizens, both using ECHELON technology and trading data back and forth. This according to Sean McDade, who found himself a target of ECHELON during his investigation in the U.S. and was forced to take extraordinary measures to communicate with Detective Sue Todd and this writer.

The Department of Justice has sealed all files on the MCA - organized crime investigation. The L.A. FBI agent, U.S. Customs agents, U.S. Attorney, L.A. Organized Crime Strike Force, Judiciary investigator, and RCMP investigator who directly or peripherally investigated the alleged theft of the PROMIS software, were *all* abruptly shut down when they plugged into high-level organized crime, drugs and money laundering. Only two remain in law enforcement today. Scott Lawrence is still in U.S. Customs, and though Sean McDade reportedly left RCMP following the exposure of his investigation in the *Toronto Star* in August 2000, Detective Sue Todd says he ultimately returned to police work in his home-town.

Each of these men confronted Danny Casolaro's Octopus. In a perfect world they would have banned together and testified before Congress, and the tentacles would have been trimmed temporarily. Meanwhile, the Octopus has reached Jules Verne proportions and grows daily --- or was it a squid? It is likely Danny derived his "Octopus" title from Dan Moldea's 1986 book, *Dark Victory: Ronald Reagan, MCA, and the Mob,* in which Moldea labeled MCA "The Octopus." But even Moldea couldn't have known in 1986 that his creature had tentacles in the NSC.

••••••••

Dante's Inferno

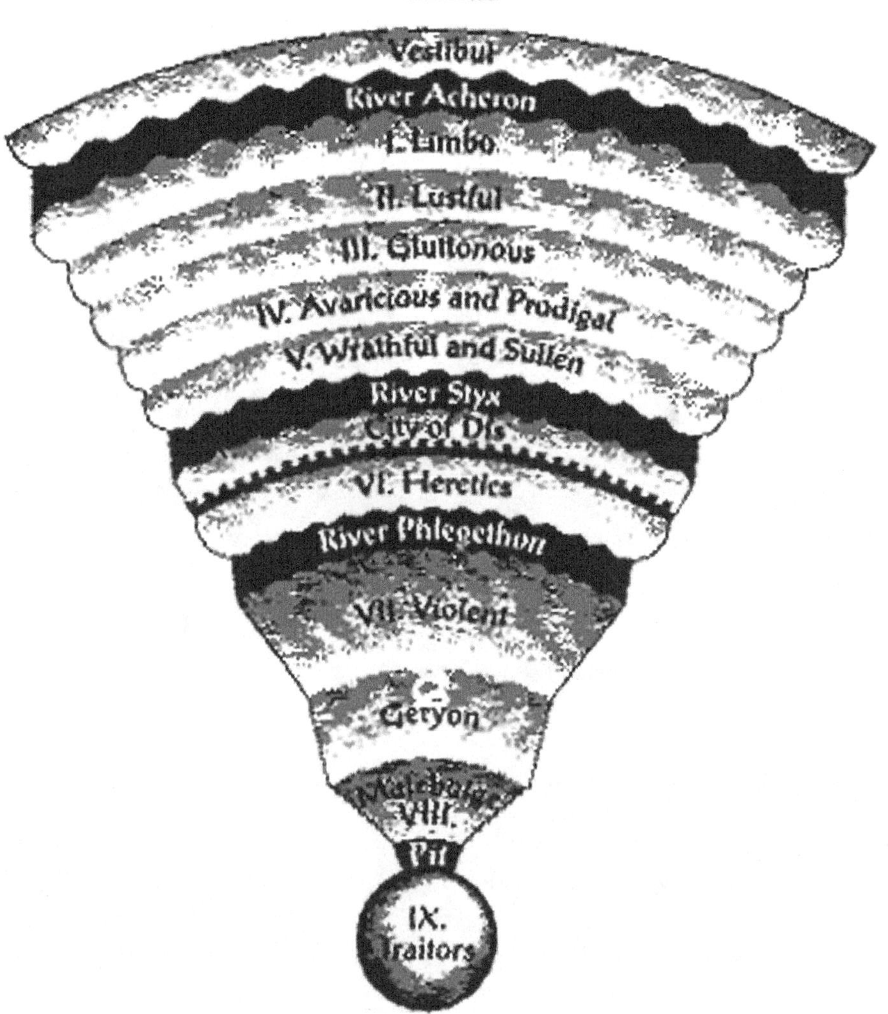

The last circle in Hell is reserved for traitors.

Mariposa County — The Gateway to Yosemite

— 1 —

The Awakening

The historic *Mariposa Gazette* offices resembled an old-time black and white Spencer Tracy movie, except the newspaper was older than Spencer Tracy, older than movies with sound tracks. The typesetting and printing equipment was ancient, there was no central air-conditioning or heating so the employees sweltered in the summer and froze in the winter, and the pay was low but no one complained because they had ink in their blood and it was a privilege to have a job in a town of only 1,500 people.

To flatlanders, Mariposa County might have been situated in outer Siberia. Nestled in the foothills of Yosemite National Park, it was the smallest *county* in California with a population of 15,000 mostly retired folks. The old western town consisted mainly of small businesses; a couple of gas stations, mom and pop restaurants and markets, a courthouse and a history center. The residents of Mariposa were obliged to entertain themselves. There were two saloons in town and no theatre, the county fair was the biggest event of the year. The nearest metropolis was Fresno, approximately 80 miles down a 2-lane highway to the south.

Across the street from the *Gazette* loomed the old courthouse, a relic from the California gold-rush days, but still operational as the hub of county government. The ruling faction congregated here, a clique of county officials and sheriff's deputies who controlled the life's blood of Mariposa.

In the Fall of 1986 I received a note at the *Gazette* office from a sheriff's deputy who had relocated from Los Angeles a few years earlier. The note read: "Cheri, meet me in the back room of the Gold Coin Saloon after work. Don't tell anyone about this meeting.

Come alone." This was uncommon since my reporter's beat ordinarily covered Board of Supervisors meetings at the courthouse. I shared a small cluttered office with the managing editor, who frequently interacted with the sheriff's commander, the district attorney, or Board members daily, but the note had asked me not to apprise her of this meeting.

That afternoon, in the back room of the Gold Coin Saloon, I listened to a chronology of long-standing corruption, murder, threats and harassment. For the deputies of the Mariposa Sheriff's Department, the awakening occurred on June 24, 1980, when Ron Van Meter, a fellow deputy, drowned in an alleged boating accident on Lake McClure. Those whom he confided in believed he was murdered after uncovering and reporting drug trafficking within the sheriff's department.

The dilated fear in the deputy's eyes as he told the story, the way he'd looked under the table to search for listening devices, convinced me that this story was way off my beat, and the *Mariposa Gazette*, a family newspaper, would never publish it. As I emerged from the dusky saloon into the Fall sunlight, I felt no warning bells for the deputy's plight, just pity that his idyllic life in Mariposa had turned ugly with intrigue and murder conspiracies. These things didn't happen in Mariposa. As I drove home, my mind wandered to more pleasant thoughts; the planned afternoon horse ride with members of the Mariposa Mountain Riders, the creak of the saddle, the cool breeze and the scent of pines wafting through the valley.

But the seed had been planted. The following week I found myself rummaging through old news stories and files. Official reports listed Ron Van Meter's death as a drowning from a boating accident on Lake McClure. The search party consisted mainly of three divers, deputies Dave Beavers, Rod Cusic and Gary Estep. In subsequent interviews with these deputies, I learned that adjacent counties had offered additional divers, but Sheriff Paul Paige refused outside help, even a mini-submarine offered by Beavers' associate.

Van Meter's widow, Leslie, had been at home baking cookies when she was notified of her husband's disappearance. She was an Indian girl who had no affinity with sheriff Paul Paige. The horror began for her that day also. Her home was ransacked and her husband's briefcase and diary were seized by the Mariposa Sheriff's department. Only she and a few deputies knew what Van Meter's diary contained. He'd told his wife he'd taken out a special life insurance policy two weeks before, but after the search that was missing also.

The story surfaced one tiny bubble at a time. On March 23, 1984, Leslie Van Meter filed a Citizen's Complaint with the Mariposa County Sheriff's department alleging that the Sheriff's office had been negligent and unprofessional in their investigation of her husband's disappearance. His body had still not been found, despite private searches by Sergeant Beavers and other friends of the missing deputy. She wanted the case re-opened.

Paul Paige was no longer sheriff, but newly elected Sheriff Ken Mattheys responded by re-opening the investigation. Deputies Frank McCoy and Lonnie Hammond, both former cops from the Southern California area, were appointed to handle the internal affairs aspect of the case.

In October 1984 Sheriff Mattheys also recruited private investigator Raymond Jenkins, a former Merced College Police Chief, and retired FBI agent Tom Walsh from Merced, to investigate the Van Meter disappearance and help him clean up the Sheriff's Department. These investigators subsequently concluded that Ron Van Meter was murdered when he obtained evidence of drug trafficking within the sheriff's department.

Their investigation also led them straight to the doorstep of MCA (Music Corporation of America), parent company to Curry Company, the largest concessionaire in Yosemite National Park. A major drug network had surfaced in the park, compelling one park ranger, Paul Berkowitz, to go before the House Interior Subcommittee on National Parks and Recreation to testify about drug distribution by Curry Company officials.

Ed Hardy, then president of Curry Company, was closely associated with Mariposa County officials, in particular, Mariposa District Attorney Bruce Eckerson, County Assessor Steve Dunbar, and Congressman Tony Coelho, whose district encompassed Mariposa and the Park. The annual camping trips that the three men took together was encouraged by the local townsfolk because much of Mariposa's tax base emanated from Curry Company. Coelho and Hardy were regular fixtures around town, seen at most of the social events. Coelho even cooked and served spaghetti dinners for the whole town annually at the Mariposa Fair Grounds, and purchased property in partnership with one member of the Mariposa Board of Supervisors. In fact, Mariposa was one of the first places Coelho bid farewell to after resigning from Congress to avoid an investigation of his finances.

On July 6, 1985, Mrs. Van Meter filed a "Request for Official Inquiry" with the State of California Department of Boating and Waterways stating that no satisfactory investigation was ever conducted into the matter of her husband's disappearance.

That same month, shortly after a meeting at Lake McClure with Mrs. Van Meter, Sheriff Mattheys mysteriously resigned from his position at the Mariposa Sheriff's Department. Mattheys revealed to reporter Anthony Pirushki that he had been ordered by two county supervisors and the county's attorney "to stay away from the Van Meter investigation." But that was not the reason he resigned. The whole story would not surface until seven years later when a reporter from the *Mariposa Guide* interviewed him.

However, while still in office, Mattheys and his internal affairs investigators had learned the reason for Van Meter's disappearance. A few weeks prior to his death in 1980, Van Meter had driven to the Attorney General's office in Sacramento and reported drug dealing and other forms of corruption within the Mariposa Sheriff's Department. This, according to his friends whom he had confided in, deputies Dave Beavers, a fifteen year veteran of the sheriff's department, and Rod Cusic, a seventeen year veteran. Both deputies were ultimately forced out of the department and retired on stress leave.

On that same day, reserve deputy Lucky Jordan had driven to the Fresno office of the FBI to report similar information. According to Jordan, they had split up and reported to separate agencies in the event "something" happened to one of them. The crux of the story was the State Attorney General's response to the requested investigation by Ron Van Meter. When Ron returned home from Sacramento, he was confronted by Sheriff Paige. Paige had received a call from the Attorney General informing him of the visit and its contents, and the sheriff was livid about Van Meter's betrayal. Van Meter had been photographing and journalizing drug activity by deputies at Lake McClure. He was part of a California State Abatement Program which involved harvesting and eradicating marijuana fields in Yosemite National Park and adjacent counties. Instead, the harvested marijuana was being stored in abandoned cars and towed out of town by a local wrecker under contract with the sheriff's department. It was also being distributed at a hidden cove at Lake McClure.

On June 24, 1980, frustrated and angry at the Attorney General for betraying him, Van Meter had borrowed a boat and was on his way to arrest the deputies at Lake McClure himself. He never returned.

♦♦♦♦♦♦♦♦

In September 1990, in the shallow, placid waters of Lake McClure, Van Meter's body was finally recovered. His torso, wrapped in a fish net and weighted down by various objects, including a fire extinguisher, had washed ashore a few hundreds yards from where Sergeant Roderick Sinclair's houseboat had once been moored.

It was at this juncture that I joined forces with investigator Ray Jenkins. I was no longer working as a reporter at the Mariposa Gazette, but working on a book. Through Jenkins I learned that the investigation of Van Meter's 1980 "accident" had initially been handled by Sergeant Roderick Sinclair, who could not have known on that fateful day that in exactly three years, three months, and nineteen days, he would enter the Twilight Zone where his own private hell awaited him.

♦♦♦♦♦♦♦♦

The first substantial hint that a tentacle of the Octopus had slithered into Mariposa County occurred on March 5, 1983 when a Mariposa County Sheriff's vehicle scouting Queen Elizabeth II's motorcade route rounded a curve in the Yosemite National Park foothills, crossed a highway and collided head-on with a Secret Service car, killing three Secret Service agents. CHP (California Highway Patrol) Assistant Chief Richard Hanna reported that the collision occurred at 10:50 A.M. between Coulterville and La Grange on Highway 132 about 25 minutes ahead of Queen Elizabeth's motorcade. CHP Sergeant Bob Schilly reported that Mariposa County Sheriff's Sergeant Roderick Sinclair, 43, was driving with his partner, Deputy Rod McKean, 51, when "for some reason, [he didn't] know why," Sinclair crossed the center line and hit the second of the three Secret Service cars, which went tumbling down a 10-foot embankment.

The three Secret Service agents killed in the collision were identified as George P. LaBarge, 41, Donald Robinson, 38, and Donald A. Bejcek, 29. Sinclair, who had sustained broken ribs and a fractured knee, was first stabilized at Fremont Hospital in Mariposa, then transported several days later to Modesto Memorial Hospital.

Years later, several nurses who had been present when Sinclair was brought into Fremont Hospital confided that Sinclair had been drugged on the day of "the Queen's accident" as it became known in Mariposa. For months Sinclair had been receiving huge daily shots of Demerol, "enough to kill most men," according to one billing clerk. Some former deputies who had feared punitive measures if they spoke up, later corroborated the story of the nurses.

Meanwhile, Assistant U.S. Attorney James White in Fresno ordered Dr. Arthur Dahlem's files seized to prove Sinclair's alleged drug use. Sinclair's Mariposa doctor and close friend had been prescribing heavy sedatives to him for years. When White attempted to prosecute Sinclair for criminal negligence, he was called into chambers during the federal probe and told by U.S. District Court Judge Robert E. Coyle to "drop the criminal investigation" because Sinclair's drug problem was not relevant to the prosecution and the drug records could not be used in court. Judge Coyle's reasoning was that no blood tests had been taken on Sinclair at the Fremont Hospital on the day of the accident, therefore no case could be made against him.

In fact, the blood tests *had* been taken, but later disappeared. A significant piece of information relative to Judge Coyle's background was passed to me during my inquiry of the Queen's accident by retired FBI agent Thomas Walsh. Allegedly, the Judge was once the attorney of record for Curry Company (owned by MCA) in Yosemite National Park

Relative to the Queens accident, in the civil trial that followed the tragic accident, Judge Coyle ruled that both Sinclair and the deceased Secret Service agents were at fault. Mariposa County was ordered to pay 70 percent of the claim filed by the widows, and the Secret Service to pay 30 percent. The county's insurance company paid the claim, and ironically, Sinclair was subsequently promoted to Commander of the Mariposa Sheriff's Department.

In an interview on March 7, 1988, at Yoshino's Restaurant in Fresno, former U.S. Attorney James White related that the original

CHP report on the Queens accident was sent to the State Attorney General's office (Van De Kamp) in Sacramento. The report was first received by Arnold Overoye, who agreed with White that Sinclair should be prosecuted. But when the report crossed Van De Kamp's desk, he told Overoye and his assistant to discard it – trash it.

Van De Kamp then appointed Bruce Eckerson, the Mariposa County District Attorney, to take charge of the investigation and submit a new report. Coincidentally, Bruce Eckerson's disclosure statements on file at the Mariposa County Courthouse indicated that he owned stock in MCA Entertainment Corporation. White added that *all* of the crack M.A.I.T.S. team CHP officers involved in the original investigation either resigned or were transferred (or fired) afterward. The CHP Commander and the Deputy Commander who supervised the M.A.I.T.S. investigation also resigned as did Assistant U.S. Attorney White himself after the cover-up took place.

However, White noted that before he resigned, he quietly filed with Stephan LaPalm of the U.S. Attorney's office in Sacramento the transcripts of the trial and an affidavit which listed the "hallucinatory" drugs Sinclair had used prior to the accident. I privately continued with the Queen's accident investigation, interviewing deputies Dave Beavers and Rod Cusic who had been privy to Sinclair's drugged condition on the day of the accident.

Beavers, who was the first deputy to arrive on the scene, maintained four years later, in 1987, that he was cognizant of Sinclair's condition, but when he was questioned by James White he was *not asked* about the drugs. (James White had by then been ordered to drop the criminal investigation and stay away from the drug aspect of the case).

In January 1988, deputy Rod Cusic strode into the offices of the *Mariposa Guide,* a competitor newspaper to the *Mariposa Gazette,* and stated that he was "told by Rod Sinclair to lie to a Grand Jury" about Sinclair's drug addiction and the resulting Queen's accident. Cusic added that he officially disclosed this to the Fresno FBI on April 26, 1984 and again on October 9, 1987. In 1987, Cusic also noted that he witnessed a booby-trapped incendiary device explode at Rod Sinclair's home during a visit to his residence. Additionally, earlier on, Sinclair allegedly barricaded himself inside his home and booby-trapped the property, as witnessed by numerous deputies who tried to persuade him to come out.

While reviewing old newspaper clippings from the Mariposa Gazette, I discovered an odd sidebar to the story. In December, 1984, during the Queen's accident civil trial in Fresno, U.S. Attorney James White had introduced testimony that Sinclair's vehicle contained "a myriad of automatic weapons including a booby-trapped bomb" when the collision occurred on March 5, 1983. It was not until 1991 that I discovered the depth of the cover-up.

A CBS television executive and Ron Williams, a Secret Service agent who had ridden in the third car of the Queen's motorcade in 1983, arrived in Mariposa to enlist my help in putting the pieces of the puzzle together on the Queen's accident. The Secret Service agent's best friend had been the driver of the car in which all three agents were killed. I signed a contract with the television executive then drove them to the site of the accident, then to the site of where the damaged vehicle was stored near Lake McClure. The Secret Service agent broke down at the sight of the vehicle, remembering the gruesome appearance of his dead friend in the front seat. He turned, tears welling in his eyes, and said, "His heart burst right through his chest and was laying in his lap when I found him."

Dave Beavers joined us the next day, as did former sheriff Ken Mattheys. Beavers did not recognize that the same Secret Service agent whom he was sitting with in my car was the man who had tried to pull Sinclair out of the sheriff's vehicle on the day of the accident. There had been a scuffle, Beavers insisting that Sinclair go to the hospital with "his own people," and the Secret Service ultimately conceding. The Secret Service agent reflected sadly that they didn't know to ask the hospital for blood tests on Sinclair that day, didn't know of his drug use. By the time the case went to court, the records at the hospital were gone.

I subsequently obtained a file containing copies of Sinclair's drug records for three years prior to the accident. They were the same records that U.S. District Court Judge Robert Coyle had disallowed in the Queen's accident trial. But it was not until producer Don Thrasher, a ten-year veteran of ABC News *20/20*, came to town, that I learned of Sinclair's background, or the extent of his drug treatment.

By chance, at a book signing engagement at B. Dalton Bookseller I had mentioned to the manager, Shaula Brent, that my next book contained information about the Queens accident. Surprised,

Shaula blurted out that she had worked at Fremont Hospital when Sinclair was brought in from the accident. Shaula recounted the following: Rod Sinclair was brought into Fremont Hospital and placed in a room with an armed guard outside the door. Sinclair had been receiving huge shots of Demerol in the arm every day prior to the accident, by order of Dr. Arthur Dahlem. Shaula noted that Sinclair was a big man and the amount of Demerol he had been receiving would have killed most men. After the Queen's accident, all drugs were withdrawn from Sinclair, and employees, including Shaula, could hear him suffering aloud for days from his hospital room. The employees at the hospital were instructed not to speak about or repeat what took place at the hospital while Sinclair was there.

Because Shaula and her friend, Barbara Locke, who also worked at the hospital, were suspicious about Sinclair's hospital records, they secretly took photostats of the records "before they were destroyed by the hospital." Blood *had* been drawn on Sinclair on the day of the Queen's accident, and he *had* been under the influence, according to Shaula. Shaula gave the names of six nurses who were witness to Sinclair's condition at the time he was brought into Fremont Hospital. When his body was finally drug-free, Sinclair was transported, against his wishes, to Modesto Hospital.

♦♦♦♦♦♦♦♦

In January, 1992, the final pieces to the puzzle fell into place. Sinclair's background had been the key all along. Producer Don Thrasher had interviewed Ron Williams, the Secret Service agent, and although the information he obtained would not be used in his production, he advised me to follow up. The Secret Service corroborated the following profile: Sinclair's father had been a military attache to General Douglas MacArthur during World War II. (I had privately mused how many of MacArthur's men later became arms of the Octopus). In Japan, after the war, Colonel Sinclair (Sr.) supervised the training of selected Japanese in intelligence gathering operations.

According to the Secret Service, he was an "international figure," highly regarded in the intelligence community. Rod Sinclair, Jr. attended school in Japan during this time. He later reportedly worked in the Army C.I.D. in a non-military or civilian capacity, allegedly receiving training at Fort Liggett in San Luis Obispo, a training center for military intelligence operations.

Could it have been possible for Colonel Sinclair, Sr. to have called upon old friends in high places to rescue his son, Rod, from the Queen's accident investigation? Did the Octopus have enough power to alter an investigation of the death of three Secret Service agents? According to the Secret Service agent in Los Angeles, it did. And he intended to tell the story after he retired.

••••••••

In the months that followed, investigator Raymond Jenkins followed the drug trail from Yosemite National Park back to the Mariposa airport, where sheriff's deputies had been observed loading and unloading packages from planes in the dead of night.

One Indian girl complained bitterly about deputies using the Sara Priest land allotment (reservation) to grow marijuana and operate methamphetamine labs. Jenkins, now investigating for a private citizens group, was called in to interview the Indian girl. That same day, as a favor, he provided me with copies of his notes. I followed up with a tape-recorded interview at her home in Bear valley. Her father and uncle operated a small auto dismantling business on the reservation in Midpines, and after locating them and gaining their confidence, the uncle drove me out to Whiskey Flats, the site of the marijuana and methamphetamine lab operations.

That week I borrowed a horse and rode down into the rocky, isolated valley of Whiskey Flats. Brush and shrubbery tore at the saddle on the horse and at the end of the dirt path I encountered three snarling Rottweiler dogs who put the horse into a frenzied lather.

Nevertheless, I managed to photograph the irrigation system, artesian spring and pond from which the water was supplied as well as various points of identification for future reconnaissance. I later returned in a four-wheel drive pick-up truck and managed to view the trailer and lab shack.

The tape recorded interview with the Indian girl, the photos and notes from my discovery were provided to the Stanislaus County Drug Task Force, but jurisdictionally, they couldn't enter Mariposa County without authority of the Mariposa Sheriff's department. It was a catch 22 situation. Ultimately I provided the same information anonymously to several related agencies. It was not until 1993 that the fields were eradicated, and 1994, before the labs were raided.

However, no arrests of any deputies were ever forthcoming. In fact, no arrests occurred at all, except for a few non-English speaking Mexican nationals who had handled the "cooking." The head of the Los Angeles Drug Enforcement Agency noted to a local newspaper that the meth lab was part of a large California drug network, but they were unable to identify the kingpins.

Ronald Reagan

— 2 —

D.I.G.

By this time three consecutive grand jury foremen had sought help from the California Attorney General, to no avail. It came to pass that one of the deputies, Dave Beavers, was having trouble obtaining his "stress leave" pay and hired a Jackson, California lawyer to represent him in the case. The lawyer, Ben Wagner, not only interviewed Beavers, but began interviewing other deputies who corroborated Beavers' story. Most of them, at least a dozen, had at one time or another testified before the grand jury – and subsequently been forced out of the department. Interestingly, none of the deputies knew "why" the others had been placed on stress leave or resigned until Wagner finally assembled them together and the story was aired.

At that point some of the former grand jury members were called in to confirm the testimony of the individual deputies. Most refused to speak up, but a few corroborated the deputies' story. Ultimately, after numerous meetings, the group of deputies and grand jurors formed and later incorporated an organization they called D.I.G. (Decency in Government).

By now, Wagner was carrying a gun inside and out of Mariposa for the first time in his life and writing letters to the Attorney General, the FBI, and even President Ronald Reagan. One response was forthcoming, from a special agent at the Fresno Department of Justice, Division of Law Enforcement. This agent listened to Kay Ritter, a former grand jury foreman and several deputies after reviewing Wagner's evidence.

Wagner was contemplating a huge civil rights lawsuit against the county of Mariposa, but it was imperative that he first understand *why* the attorney general refused to help these people. When the special agent drove to Sacramento and reviewed the files within the attorney general's office emanating from Mariposa, and talked to some of the office staff there, he learned that everything pertaining to Mariposa was automatically "trashed" when it crossed the A/G's desk.

Disgusted, the agent called Ben Wagner and told him "Go ahead with the lawsuit." He had no idea why all the grand jury documents had been trashed, but he was convinced no help would be forthcoming from the attorney general's office.

On November 20, 1987, Wagner filed with the U.S. District Court in Fresno the first of two lawsuits, later revealed in a Sacramento newspaper to be the largest civil rights lawsuits ever recorded in California history. Newspaper reporters and television crews flocked to Wagner for interviews. In one instance, Wagner, former Sergeant Dave Beavers and others stood in front of the Fresno FBI building while being interviewed by Channel 3 Sacramento News.

On camera, without hesitation, Beavers recalled observing deputies carrying packages of drugs from the Gold Coin Saloon, a notorious drug hang-out, and placing the packages in the trunk of their patrol car. A subsequent raid indicated the drugs had been stored by the owner in a historic underground tunnel once used by the infamous bandit, Joaquin Murietta, to escape the sheriff's posse.

Meanwhile, on February 10, 1988, attorney Wagner filed at the U.S. District Court in Sacramento a Writ of Mandamus against John Van de Kamp, the State Attorney General; George Vinson, regional director of the Fresno FBI; George Deukemejian, then Governor of California, and David F. Levi, United States Attorney for refusing to investigate corruption in Mariposa County.

The citizens of Mariposa were choosing sides, writing letters to the editor, arguing amongst themselves, and being interviewed on the sidewalks by news media. D.I.G. was the talk of the town. On February 17, 1988, Capitol News Service in Sacramento ran a story entitled, "Law & Order Failing on Hill County," by Jerry Goldberg. The article noted that Capitol News Service had had discussions with several Attorney General staff members who "stonewalled questions about any investigation of charges or direct answers on the willingness of Van de Kamp to meet with the citizen's group [D.I.G.]."

Goldberg mentioned the "Queen's accident" in his article: "The Fresno case charges destruction of records on individuals [Commander Rod Sinclair] involved in the case. This includes possible information about the fatal accident which occurred in the area [of Mariposa County] when an escort vehicle involved in the visit of Queen Elizabeth in 1983 [crashed.]"

Goldberg went on to note that "several people had received threats about dangerous things happening to them if they continued to stand up to the sheriff and district attorney." A San Joaquin County official, who asked not to be named, told Goldberg that a key element to the problems in Mariposa County "related to the fatal accident which occurred to Queen Elizabeth's escort vehicle."

On February 19, 1988, Ben Wagner's wife, a legal secretary, sent a letter to President Ronald Reagan at the White House. The Wagners did not live in Mariposa County, indeed, lived far away in Jackson County, unfettered by corruption, yet they saw fit to take it upon themselves to write for help. That emotionally gripping letter was headed, "Restoring Equal Rights to the Citizens of Mariposa County." It read as follows:

> Dear President Reagan: I am writing to you not only as the wife of an attorney, but as a citizen of the United States. My initial concern is that you personally receive this letter and enclosures, as many residents of Mariposa County have literally placed their lives, and the lives of their families in jeopardy by coming forth to expose the local government corruption detailed herein. I understand that your time is at a premium, however, your immediate attention regarding these matters is of the utmost importance, and respectfully requested.
>
> In August, 1987, our office was approached by several ex-deputies and individuals from Mariposa County requesting assistance in redressing unlawful and corrupt activities by officials and departments within their local government, and failure on the part of the State Attorney General John Van De Kamp, the Office of the Attorney General, and our Federal agencies, to investigate these alleged activities.
>
> What we found through our initial investigations and accumulation of evidence into these allegations was appalling. It took us time to realize that in fact, the Constitution of the United States had been suspended in this county.
>
> The organization, Decency in Government [D.I.G.], was formed, and on November 20, 1987, the first multi-million dollar Civil Rights suit was filed in Fresno. We felt media coverage

would lay a solid ground of personal safety for other complaintants to come forth. This coverage proved to be successful, and on February 11, 1988, the second Civil Rights suit was filed, along with the filing of a Writ of Mandamus in Sacramento.

I have enclosed copies of these suits, including several newspaper articles regarding the situation. Since 1979, many residents, including individuals, sheriff's deputies, groups, organizations, members of Grand Juries and Grand Juries have taken their complaints to the Office of the Attorney General, State Attorney General John Van De Kamp and Federal authorities for investigation.

These agencies have continuously and blatantly failed to redress the grievances of these citizens. What appears to be a consistent procedure of one Arnold O. Overoye, of the State Attorney General's Office, is to refer the complaints directly back to the local agencies to whom the complaints were made.

Over the years, this has perpetrated threats, intimidation and fear by these local officials to the complaining individuals. There has also been questions regarding the disappearance of citizens possessing incriminating evidence, and the incompletion or failure to investigate `homicides' and `suicides.'

Further, it has recently come to our attention, that Mr. Overoye's `procedure,' and the inaction of State Attorney John Van de Kamp and Federal agencies is not limited to Mariposa County, but in fact, expands to a number of foothill counties who are experiencing the same types of local corruption.

The grievances of these citizens, as you will note in paragraph IV of the WRIT are: (1) Violation of Individual Civil Rights (2) Abuse of discretion in the prosecution of criminal complaints (3) Intentional obstruction of the due course of Justice (4) Malicious prosecution (5) Bribery (6) Intimidation of Grand Jury members and witnesses (7) The deprivation of property (8) Illegal and unlawful land transaction (9) The failure to arrest and prosecute those involved in illegal drug sales, including individuals employed by the County of Mariposa (10) Violation of Property Rights (11) Conspiracy to impede and obstruct criminal investigations (12) Homicide (13) Attempted homicide (14) Rape (15) Battery (16) Perjury.

Why Mr. President, are we bound to the laws of this country, and our officials are not? Life in Mariposa is as if the citizens were being held in detention, and the local agencies, the criminals, were running the county.

Needless to say, residents feel it is a way of life to literally arm themselves and their homes against their government! I have been in these people's homes, and have witnessed the arsenal of weapons they feel they must possess to protect themselves and their families.

My husband must travel in, around and out of this county [Mariposa] with an armed escort. He is transported during `the midnight hours' to interview Plaintiffs and witnesses.

I ask you, Mr. President, what country are we living in? We should certainly make sure that our backyard is clean before we boast to the Soviets regarding the Civil Rights of Americans.

On January 19, 1988, my husband took two witnesses, Kay Ritter, a former Mariposa Grand Jury Forewoman and Robert Ashmore, an ex-deputy, to Mr. [George] Vinson, the Regional Director of the FBI in Fresno. The testimony, both oral and documentary, took approximately 3 hours to present. To this date, the FBI has failed to redress the grievances of these complaintants, and Mr. Vinson did not even have the courtesy to return my husband's phone calls. It came to our understanding, through a reliable source, that Mr. Vinson felt the complaints had `no substance.'

Mr. President, my husband has been a trial attorney for 14 years. He certainly wouldn't waste his time or expertise, or the time of these witnesses, if he felt there was `no substance' to the contents of their testimony. However, this attitude by Attorney General Van de Kamp, his office, and Federal agencies is typical and consistent.

Shortly after this incident, a major drug dealer contacted our office with valuable information detailing the sale of illegal drugs to county officials, and wanted information regarding the Federal Witness Program. Mr. Vinson, knowing this by telephone messages, again failed to return my husband's inquiries.

There is evidence by another credible witness, who was informed by the FBI, that should they get involved now, it would be `bad publicity,' and `they have let the problems in Mariposa get too far out of hand.'

You may wonder why my husband and I became dedicated to the citizens of this county. We certainly don't foresee large amounts of money at the end of this case. Our investment in time and expenditures exceeds $40,000 to date. What we do see are people, just like you and I, who have been suppressed by their own `elected ' officials, with no help or assistance from Attorney General Van De Kamp, his office, or Federal agencies. If someone doesn't help them, they will continue to live under these conditions, which I could never imagine would exist in America.

My husband is not a righteous individual, nor is he perfect. None of us are you know. He also doesn't believe that he can solve the problems of the world. However, being an attorney, he is an officer of the Court, and he feels a professional obligation to uphold the laws of the State, and to maintain the freedom of the citizens of this country.

This is, however, more than I can say about a number of `representatives' and officials, who have failed to perform their appointed duties of their office, and are paid by the taxpayers. Through my involvement in this case, I have found, to my repulsion, that my lifelong conception of our government's representation of the `people,' its vested authority and ability to uphold Civil Rights, and its duty to maintain the laws and the Constitution, has been only an shattering illusion.

Our system has failed, Mr. President. And by its failure, has crushed and destroyed the lives of many innocent, law-abiding people. Why? There is an answer. And we will utilize every legal avenue to find it. We will not be discouraged, or give up in our effort to restore the Constitution of the United States in Mariposa County, and other foothill communities. We will continue until the answer is found. Even if it means presenting the problem to you, Mr. President, on the steps of the White House.

Our best regards to Mrs. Reagan.

Respectfully yours,
Vivian L. Wagner.

••••••••

Shortly before Ben Wagner's first scheduled appearance in U.S. District Court in Fresno on behalf of D.I.G. (Decency in Government), Wagner received an obscure response from "Chuck" at the Reagan White House. Wagner excitedly called Kay Ritter and Dave Beavers, me and a few others to note that a meeting with "Chuck" was scheduled that week. It was to be a somewhat secret meeting as requested by the White House.

However, the day after meeting with "Chuck," Wagner unplugged his phone and walked out on his law practice and his home in Jackson, California, taking nothing with him except his clothes and his wife, never to be seen again. I was later told that Jerry Goldberg of Capitol News Service did the same, on the same day, and I was never able to locate either of them again.

— 3 —

The Wizard

The last remnants of the D.I.G. group were beginning to call themselves "The Loser's Club," resembling forlorn characters out of a Stephen King novel. They had squared off against a labyrinthine evil so incomprehensible, they didn't know what they were fighting. It was time to bring in some outside help.

During a strategy meeting in Jackson, California, Ben Wagner had received an impressive 700-page report commissioned by the Tulare City Council. The report, compiled by Ted Gunderson, a former Los Angeles FBI agent, was in-depth and straightforward about deputies receiving payoffs and distributing drugs in the small farm town of Tulare. Wagner had given me a copy for my files.

On an impulse, I picked up the phone and called Gunderson's telephone number listed at the top of the attached resume. He'd worked as SAC (Senior Special Agent in Charge) at Los Angeles FBI headquarters, Washington D.C. headquarters and in Dallas, Texas. It would be two years before I would grasp the significance of the Dallas connection. After retiring from the FBI, he'd worked for F. Lee Bailey, Esq., then formed his own investigative agency in Los Angeles County.

I left a message with the answering service and he returned the call a few days later. His voice was open, attentive, devoid of the bureaucratic hollowness I had come to expect from FBI agents. We talked briefly, mostly about the problem DIG was experiencing in Mariposa. I said I needed help, anticipating his next question. But none came forth. Instead, a clipped knowingness entered his tone, as if nothing more should be said on the phone. He agreed to meet with me at his home a few weeks later and we hung up.

Unknown to me at the time, I had taken a quantum leap in the direction of the Octopus when I contacted Ted Gunderson. The mystery of the Mariposa cover-ups would soon be divulged through an associate of his, a former member of "The Company" in nearby Fresno, California.

••••••••

On November 30, 1991, Ted Gunderson opened the door at his Manhattan Beach home and ushered us into a small living room cluttered with toys. He made no explanation for the toys scattered around the floor and the couch, but offered coffee and donuts, then proceeded to eat most of the donuts himself. I had expected someone dripping with intrigue, instead he was classic in the sense of an investigator; rumpled shirt and slacks, nervous movements, distracted behavior. We sat on the couch bunched together amongst the toys. Gunderson pulled a kitchen chair up in front of us, leaned over and began stuffing his mouth with cheese and crackers, all the while talking, his body in perpetual motion. He was a big, handsome man with an aging face and tousled silver hair. He seemed entirely unaware of his appearance or the appearance of his home, but his pale eyes were intelligent and probing. Intuitively, I knew he was more than he appeared to be.

Ray Jenkins recounted the Mariposa story for several hours, with my husband and I digressing to insert a fact here or there. The investigation had led beyond Mariposa into MCA Inc., and various State and Federal levels of government. I noted that Danny Casolaro's research had started at the eastern end, in Washington D.C., yet he had been preparing to travel to California for the rest of the story, before his highly publicized death in August, three months past.

Gunderson listened carefully, occasionally interrupting to ask questions, then motioned us to follow him to the backyard. There we stood in a circle in the middle of his yard while he surveyed the area. Satisfied that he was not being surveillanced, he agreed to come to Mariposa, with media, and perform a citizen's arrest on the corrupt officials. He pulled a frazzled piece of paper from his pocket and gave me a list of telephone numbers to write down. They were numbers to telephone booths at various locations in the vicinity of his home. Each booth had been coded 1, 2, 3, 4, or 5. He instructed that the next time I called him, he would give me the code number of the booth and a time to call. I would then call him at the designated booth.

Eight hours later, I handed him a copy of my first book, as a courtesy, then left Manhattan Beach loaded with newspaper clippings and documents, mostly relating to Casolaro's investigation of the Octopus. One packet was titled, "The Wonderful Weapons of Wackenhut," others related to the Inslaw affair, Iran/Contra and various savings and loan scandals.

In the van, reviewing the documents, I wondered what relationship they had to Mariposa County and why I was given the packet? The documents were far ranging, beyond anything I had heretofore imagined. But within days of my visit to Gunderson, I would be introduced to the Octopus.

♦♦♦♦♦♦♦♦

The following morning, December 1, 1991, at 7:30 A.M., I received a collect call from a man who identified himself as Michael Riconosciuto (pronounced Ricon-o-shooto), calling from the Pierce County jail in Tacoma, Washington. He had been informed by Gunderson that I was investigating a corruption/drug ring in Mariposa County. For 45 minutes Riconosciuto related the names of those in charge of methamphetamine operations in Mariposa, Madera and Fresno counties.

A ton of methamphetamine had been seized in the area of my investigations, according to Riconosciuto. Richard Knozzi was a high level "cooker" and Jim DeSilva, Ben Kalka, and others were medium level distributors or lieutenants. Kalka was currently serving time in a Pleasanton prison; 900 pounds of methamphetamine had been seized under his control.

"Who's behind this ring?" I asked. Riconosciuto paused for a moment, then took a deep breath. "It's The Company. Arms get shipped to the Contras, the Afghanistan rebels [Mujahaden], the Middle East. You know, to fight the Soviet influence. But the Contras and the Mujahaden don't have money to pay for arms, so they pay with drugs, cocaine or heroin. The Company handles the drug end of it in the U.S. ..."

"What's The Company?," I asked. Riconosciuto interrupted, "Wait a minute. It's a long story. You have to start at the beginning."

Concerned that Riconosciuto might have to hang up, I hurriedly pushed for answers. "Arms for drugs, do you have proof?"

"Oh, yeah. It's a self-supporting system, they don't have to go through Congress ..."

"Michael," I pressed, "who ships the arms?" Riconosciuto quieted for a moment, gathering his thoughts. "Let's start with Wackenhut. I didn't play ball with Wackenhut so they poisoned the well for me. I'm in jail because I worked for Wackenhut. The government has put together a very simple drug case against me ... as if that's what I'm about, just a druggie."

"Tell me about Wackenhut."

"It's a security corporation headquartered in Coral Gables, Florida. Wackenhut provides security for the Nevada nuclear test site, the Alaskan pipeline, Lawrence Livermore Labs, you know, all the high security government facilities in the U.S. They have about fifty thousand armed security guards that work for minimum wage or slightly above.

"On the other hand, on the Wackenhut board of directors, they have all the former heads of every government agency there ever was under Ronald Reagan and George Bush; FBI, CIA, NSA, Secret Service, etc.

"You know, they've got retired Admiral Stansfield Turner, a former CIA director; Clarence Kelley, former FBI director; Frank Carlucci, former CIA deputy director; James Rowley, former Secret Service director; Admiral Bobby Ray Inman, former acting chairman of President Bush's foreign intelligence advisory board and former CIA deputy director. Before his appointment as Reagan's CIA director, the late William Casey was Wackenhut's outside legal counsel ..."

I interrupted him, wanting to know where *he* fit into the picture?

"Well, I served as Director of Research for the Wackenhut facility at the Cabazon Indian reservation in Indio, California. In 1983-84 I modified the PROMIS computer software to be used in law enforcement and intelligence agencies worldwide. A man named Earl Brian was spearheading a plan for worldwide use of the software, but essentially, the modified software was being pirated from the owners, Bill and Nancy Hamilton."

I asked, "So how did that cause your arrest?" Michael was articulate, but his story was becoming complicated. He continued.

"I signed an affidavit for the Hamiltons stating that I had been responsible for the modification. The House Judiciary Committee on Inslaw was investigating the theft of the software and I was afraid I would be implicated since I had performed the modification. Eight days later, in an attempt to discredit my testimony, I was arrested for allegedly operating a drug lab."

I didn't want to push Riconosciuto on the subject of a drug lab at that point, but voiced my foremost concern. "Will the House Judiciary Committee be bringing you in to testify?"

"Eventually, yes."

"Are you in any danger where you are right now?" I was unaware at the time that Riconosciuto had been recruited at Stanford University into the CIA nearly twenty years earlier, and danger was a matter of fact in his life.

"Oh, you bet! Several of the jail guards here moonlight for Wackenhut here in Tacoma." Riconosciuto went on to discuss the Wackenhut setup. "Basically, what you have is a group of politically well connected people through Wackenhut who wanted to get juicy defense contracts when Ronald Reagan got elected president. And they did! They also preyed on high tech start up companies, many of them out of Silicon Valley in California.

"They saw technology that they wanted and they either forced the companies into bankruptcy or waited on the sidelines, like vultures, and picked them up for pennies after they were bankrupt."

I made profuse notes as Riconosciuto spoke, not knowing where he was leading, but assuming his narrative would eventually intersect with my investigation of government sanctioned drug operations. Finally it did. According to Riconosciuto, people at Wackenhut Corporation "made inroads" into the methamphetamine operation. A man named [withheld] allegedly headed major government sanctioned meth laboratories in Fresno, Madera and Mariposa counties. A man named [withheld], a former Israeli intelligence officer with U.S. citizenship, was the liaison or connection between the [withheld] operation and the U.S. government.

In subsequent documents obtained from Michael's secret hiding place in the California desert, I located documents which indicated Michael had first been recruited into government operations by Al Holbert. However, during this first of many phone conversations with Riconosciuto, I found myself searching for a beginning, something concrete to get a foothold. "Michael, is there any proof that you worked at Wackenhut?"

Michael responded diffidently. "CNN recently ran a piece, and they filmed a location shot from the parking lot of the casino. Then they aired another location shot on the [Cabazon] reservation of just an expanse of bare land, blue sky, sand and sagebrush. Then the narrator says, `Here on the Indian reservation is where Michael Riconosciuto claims to have modified the PROMIS software.' They didn't show the tribal office complex, they didn't show the industrial park. They showed a bare expanse of land, like I had a computer out in a teepee in the middle of the desert! The government is doing a character assassination on me. I'm fair game now that I'm in jail, because I've raised too many provocative questions, you know, and they're trying to relegate me to the area of delusion ..."

••••••••

For three months Riconosciuto called daily from the Pierce County jail in Tacoma, Washington. At his request, I attached a tape recorder to my phone and unraveled a complicated web of illegal overseas arms shipments, espionage, CIA drug trafficking, biological warfare development, computer software theft, money laundering and corruption at the highest levels of government.

Throughout this time span, I also obtained every newspaper and magazine article I could lay my hands on relative to Riconosciuto's background and contacts. Riconosciuto had been a child prodigy at the age of 10, when he wired his parents' neighborhood with a working, private telephone system that undercut Ma Bell. As a teenager, he had won so many science fairs with exhibits of laser technology that he was invited to be a summer research assistant at Stanford's [University] prestigious Cooper Vaper Laser Laboratory. Dr. Arthur Schalow, a Nobel laureate, remembered him: "You don't forget a 16-year-old youngster who shows up with his own argon laser," he told Danny Casolaro, a Washington D.C. journalist.

Casolaro began interviewing Riconosciuto prior to his arrest on March 29, 1991. The patient, amenable wizard with the dark, weary eyes, opened a window for Danny into a netherworld of real life players in Dungeons and Dragons, where scientific genius is employed in nefarious activities, and spooks jump on and off the board at will.

On August 10, 1991, Danny's nude body was found in the bathtub of room 517 of the Sheraton Hotel in Martinsburg, West Virginia. His wrists had been slashed ten or twelve times. No papers were found in his hotel room or in his car, though he was known to cart an accordian file everywhere he went. An X-Acto blade found in the bathtub was not sold locally and his accordian file is still missing to this day. Casolaro was working on a book entitled, "Behold, A Pale Horse," which encompassed the October Surprise story, the Inslaw computer software case, the Iran/Contra affair, the B.C.C.I. scandal, and M.C.A. entertainment corporation, all overlapping and interconnecting into one network which he dubbed, "The Octopus."

He told friends that he "had traced the Inslaw and related stories back to a dirty CIA `Old Boy' network" that had begun working together in the 1950's around the Albania covert operations. These men had gotten into the illegal gun and drug trade back then and had continued in that business ever since.

Before his death, Danny had made plans to visit the Wackenhut Corporation in Indio, California, and even considered naming his book, "Indio."

Through an investigator in Indio I was able to obtain a copy of a letter written on Wackenhut letterhead by Patrick F. Cannan, Director of Wackenhut Corporate Relations, dated January 31, 1992, which confirmed Riconosciuto's scientific value and involvement with Wackenhut.

A Joint Venture agreement between the Cabazon Band of Mission Indians and Wackenhut Corporation was formalized on April 1, 1981 by a prestigious Washington D.C. law firm headed by ex-Senator James Abourezk and his associate, Glen M. Feldman, representing the Cabazons. The main purpose of the Joint Venture was to establish a production facility, called "Cabazon Arms," on the one square mile of Cabazon-owned desert land near Indio.

One excerpt from the 11-page letter referred to a meeting in May 1981 at the U.S. Army installation at Dover, New Jersey between Robert Frye, Vice President of Wackenhut in Indio; Michael Riconosciuto; John P. Nichols, Cabazon administrator; Peter Zokosky, former president of Armtec [in Indio] which produced combustible cartridge cases for the Army; and Dr. Harry Fair, the Army's lead engineer on the Railgun Project at Picatinny Arsenal. Cannan noted that Riconosciuto and several Army personnel conducted an "extensive and highly technical theoretical blackboard exercise on the Railgun, and afterwards, Dr. Fair commented that he was extremely impressed with Riconosciuto's scientific and technical knowledge in this matter."

Cannan further wrote: "Dr. Fair had apparently been apprised by Nichols that Riconosciuto had been convicted and served time for stabbing a DEA agent whom he purportedly caught in bed with Riconosciuto's wife. Dr. Fair had commented that Riconosciuto would probably not be able to ever get a government security clearance because of his past, but it would be a shame if Riconosciuto, whom he termed a *'potential national resource,'* could not be used for military/research projects in his field of expertise."

The Wackenhut/Cabazon Joint Venture was terminated on October 1, 1984 after Robert Frye suffered a heart attack. What transpired at the Cabazon Indian Reservation while the Joint Venture was in effect subsequently became the subject of investigations by the U.S. Department of Justice, the House Judiciary Committee on Inslaw, U.S. Customs, the Royal Canadian Mounted Police, police agencies and media worldwide.

— 4 —

Wackenhut Corporation

The history of Wackenhut Corporation is best described from its own literature. An outdated letter of introduction typed on Wackenhut letterhead once sent to prospective clients provided me with the following profile: (excerpted)

> Wackenhut Corporation had its beginnings in 1954, when George R. Wackenhut and three other former Special Agents of the Federal Bureau of Investigation formed a company in Miami, Special Agent Investigators, to provide investigative services to business and industry.
>
> The approach was so well received that a second company was formed in 1955 to apply the same philosophy to physical security problems. In 1958 the companies were combined under the name of Wackenhut Corporation, a Florida company. From the outset, George Wackenhut was President and chief executive officer of the enterprise. Wackenhut established its headquarters in Coral Gables, Florida in 1960, extending its physical security operations to the United States government through formation of a wholly-owned subsidiary, Wackenhut Services, Incorporated. This was done in order to comply with federal statute prohibiting the government from contracting with companies which furnish investigative or detective services.
>
> In 1962, Wackenhut operations extended from Florida to California and Hawaii. On January 1, 1966, the company became international with offices in Caracas, Venezuela, through half ownership of an affiliate.
>
> The Wackenhut Corporation became public in 1966 with over-the-counter stock sales and joined the American Stock Exchange in 1967. Through acquisitions of subsidiaries and af-

filiates, now totaling more than 20, and expansion of it contracts into numerous territories and foreign countries, the Wackenhut Corporation has grown into one of the world's largest security and investigative firms.

In 1978 acquisition of NUSAC, a Virginia company providing technical and consulting services to the nuclear industry, brought Wackenhut into the fields of environment and energy management. In 1979, Wackenhut acquired Stellar Systems, Inc., a California company specializing in outdoor electronic security.

The executive makeup of the company reflects the stress Mr. Wackenhut placed on professional leadership. The Wackenhut Corporation is guided by executives and managers with extensive backgrounds in the FBI and other military, governmental and private security and investigative fields.

The principle business of the company is furnishing security and complete investigative services and systems to business, industry and professional clients, and to various agencies of the U.S. Government.

Through a wholly-owned subsidiary, Wackenhut Electronic Systems Corporation, the company develops and produces sophisticated computerized security systems to complement its guard services.

Major clients of Wackenhut's investigative services are the insurance industry and financial interests. These services include insurance inspections, corporate acquisition surveys, personnel background reports, pre-employment screening, polygraph examinations and general criminal, fraud and arson investigations.

The wide variety of services offered by Wackenhut Corporation also includes guard and electronic security for banks, office buildings, apartments, industrial complexes and other physical structures; training programs in English and foreign languages to apply Wackenhut procedures to individual clients needs; fire, safety and protective patrols; rescue and first aid services; emergency support programs tailored to labor-management disputes, and pre-departure screening programs widely used by airports and airlines.

The company now has some 20,000 employees and maintains close to 100 offices and facilities with operations spread across the United States and extending into Canada, the United Kingdom, Western Europe, the Middle East, Indonesia, Central and South America and the Caribbean."

••••••••

On the surface, Wackenhut Corporation seemed innocuous enough, but through documents I later obtained, I learned there was another, darker side to Wackenhut operations at the Cabazon Indian reservation.

Because Indian reservations are sovereign nations and do not come under federal jurisdiction, Wackenhut International had formed a partnership and entered into a joint business venture with the Cabazon Indians to produce high-tech arms and explosives for export to third-world countries. This maneuver was designed to evade congressional prohibitions against U.S. weapons being shipped to the Contras and middle-eastern countries.

In the early 1980's, Dr. John Nichols, the Cabazon tribal administrator, obtained a Department of Defense secret facility clearance for the reservation to conduct various research projects. Nichols then approached Wackenhut with an elaborate "joint venture" proposal to manufacture 120mm combustible cartridge cases, 9mm machine pistols, laser-sighted assault weapons, sniper rifles and portable rocket systems on the Cabazon reservation and in Latin America. At one point, he even sought to develop biological weapons.

I later obtained inter-office memorandums and correspondence relating to biological technology, but more on that in a future chapter. Meanwhile, in 1980, Dr. John Nichols obtained the blueprints to Crown Prince Fahd's palace in Tiaf, Saudi Arabia, and drafted a plan to provide security for the palace.

The Saudis were interested enough to conduct a background check on the Cabazons. Mohammad Jameel Hashem, consul of the Royal Embassy of Saudi Arabia in Washington, D.C., wrote former South Dakota Senator James Abourezk at his offices in Washington D.C. and noted, "According to our black list for companies, the Cabazon Band of Mission Indians/Cabazon Trading Company and Wackenhut International are not included." Translated, that meant that neither the Cabazons or Wackenhut were Jewish-run enterprises.

George Wackenhut's political leanings were once described in a book entitled, *The Age of Surveillance, The Aims and Methods of America's Political Intelligence System*, by Frank J. Donner (Knopf, 1980), pp. 424-425 as such:

> The agency's [Wackenhut] professional concerns reflect the political values of its director, George Wackenhut. A rightist of the old blood, he selected as his directors an assortment of ultras prominent

> in the John Birch Society, the ASC, and other right-wing groups. The agency's monthly house organ, the 'Wackenhut Security Review,' systematically decried the subversive inspiration in virtually all the protest movements of the sixties, from civil rights to peace. This vigilance earned the publication the accolade of right-wing organizations, including (in 1962) the George Washington Honor Medal and the Freedom Foundation Award at Valley Forge, Pennsylvania; and (in 1965 and 1966) the Vigilant Patriots Award from the All-American Conference to Combat Communism.

••••••••

Of all the articles written about Wackenhut Corporation, probably the most provocative was written by John Connolly for *SPY* magazine, published in September 1992, pp. 46-54. Connolly, a former New York police officer turned writer, began his story with the following introduction: "What? A big private company – one with a board of former CIA, FBI and Pentagon officials; one in charge of protecting nuclear-weapons facilities, nuclear reactors, the Alaskan oil pipeline and more than a dozen American embassies abroad; one with long-standing ties to a radical right-wing organization; one with 30,000 men and women under arms – secretly helped Iraq in its effort to obtain sophisticated weapons? And fueled unrest in Venezuela? This is all the plot of a new best-selling thriller, right? Or the ravings of some overheated conspiracy buff, right? Right? *wrong*."

Connolly highlighted George Wackenhut as a "hard-line right-winger" who was able to profit from his beliefs by building dossiers on Americans suspected of being Communists or left-leaning "subversives and sympathizers" and selling the information to interested parties. By 1965, Wackenhut was boasting to potential investors that the company maintained files on 2.5 million suspected dissidents – one in 46 American adults then living.

In 1966, after acquiring the private files of Karl Barslaag, a former staff member of the House Committee on Un-American Activities, Wackenhut could confidently maintain that with more than 4 million names, it had the largest privately held file on suspected dissidents in America.

Connolly wrote that it was not possible to overstate the special relationship that Wackenhut enjoys with the federal government. Richard Babayan, claiming to be a CIA contract employee, told SPY that "Wackenhut has been used by the CIA and other intelligence agencies for years. When they [the CIA] need cover, Wackenhut is there to provide it for them."

Another CIA agent, Bruce Berckmans, who was assigned to the CIA station in Mexico City, but left the agency in January 1975 (putatively) to become a Wackenhut international-operations vice president, told *SPY* that he had seen a formal proposal submitted by George Wackenhut to the CIA offering Wackenhut offices throughout the world as fronts for CIA activities. In 1981, Berckmans joined with other senior Wackenhut executives to form the company's Special Projects Division. It was this division that linked up with ex-CIA man Dr. John Phillip Nichols, the Cabazon tribal administrator, in pursuit of a scheme to manufacture explosives, poison gas and biological weapons for export to the Contras and other communist fighting rebels worldwide.

SPY also printed testimony from William Corbett, a terrorism expert who spent 18 years as a CIA analyst and is now an ABC News consultant in Europe. Said Corbett, "For years Wackenhut has been involved with the CIA and other intelligence organizations, including the DEA. Wackenhut would allow the CIA to occupy positions within the company [in order to carry out] clandestine operations." Additionally, Corbett said that Wackenhut supplied intelligence agencies with information, and it was compensated for this – "in a quid pro quo arrangement" – with government contracts worth billions of dollars over the years.

On page 51, in a box entitled, "Current and Former Wackenhut Directors," *SPY* published the following names: "John Ammarell, former FBI agent; Robert Chasen, former FBI agent; Clarence Kelly, former FBI director; Willis Hawkins, former assistant secretary of the Army; Paul X. Kelley, four-star general (ret.), U.S. Marine Corps; Seth McKee, former commander in chief, North American Air Defense Command; Bernard Schriever, former member, President's Foreign Intelligence Advisory Board; Frank Carlucci, former Defense Secretary and former deputy CIA director; Joseph Carroll, former director, Defense Intelligence Agency; James Rawley, former director, U.S. Secret Service; Bobby Ray Inman, former deputy CIA director."

Danny Casolaro

— 5 —

Danny Casolaro

August 10, 1991, Martinsburg, VA – Danny Casolaro's body was found at 12:30 P.M. in a blood-filled bath tub by a hotel maid who called the Martinsburg police. The body contained three deep cuts on the right wrist and seven on the left wrist, made by a single edge razor blade, the kind used to scrape windows or open packages. At the bottom of the bath water was an empty Milwaukee beer can, a paper glass coaster, the razor blade and two white plastic trash bags, the kind used in wastepaper baskets. On the desk in the hotel room was an empty mead composition notebook with one page torn out and a suicide note which read:

> *"To those who I love the most, please forgive me for the worst possible thing I could have done. Most of all, I'm sorry to my son. I know deep down inside that God will let me in."*

Casolaro was a Catholic whose religion teaches that it is a sin to commit suicide. Friends wondered if the words *"God will let me in"* was a coded message that he did not take his own life? And why would a writer who loved language leave such a short, cryptic note?

There were no other papers, folders, documents of any sort, nor any briefcase found at the death scene. Danny's wallet was intact, stuffed with credit cards. The body was removed from the tub by Lieutenant Dave Brining from the Martinsburg fire department, and his wife, Sandra, a nurse who works in the hospital emergency room. The couple, who often moonlighted as coroners, took the body to the Brown Funeral Home where they conducted an examination. Charles Brown then decided to embalm the body that night and go home, rather than come back to work the next day, Sunday.

No one in Danny's family had been notified of his death at that time, nor had they requested the body be embalmed. When Casolaro's family learned of the death, they insisted it was not a suicide and called for an autopsy and an investigation. Danny's brother, Dr. Anthony Casolaro, publicly stated his disbelief that his high spirited, gregarious brother could have committed suicide. Danny was so afraid of blood, he said, that he refused to allow samples to be drawn for medical purposes, and would never have chosen to slash his veins a dozen times. Moreover, Danny had a life filled with friends and a close-knit Italian Catholic family. He was known in private circles as an upbeat, golden-haired romantic who loved to quote poetry, raised Arabian horses, and was adored by women.

Though Danny's body had already been embalmed, an autopsy was performed at the West Virginia University Hospital by a Dr. Frost. The findings indicated that no struggle had taken place because there were no recent bruises on the body. The drugs found in Casolaro's urine, blood and tissue samples were in minute amounts but they were also unexplainable by his brother, Tony, who is a medical doctor.

According to Tony Casolaro, Danny did not take drugs or have any prescriptions for the drug traces of Hydrocodone and Tricyclic antidepressant that were found in the body. No pill boxes or written prescriptions were found. Dr. Casolaro searched through his brother's Blue Cross records and found no record of the prescriptions or doctor visits.

During the autopsy of the body, Dr. Frost had found lesions within the brain which were characteristic of Multiple Sclerosis. It was possible that Danny was having blurring of vision, but Dr. Frost downplayed the possibility that this contributed to any suicide. Of particular interest, was Frost's observation that the deep razor wounds on Danny's wrists were inflicted "without any hesitation marks." However, the lack of hesitation did not indicate one way or the other whether they were or were not self-inflicted. Investigators and police never found Danny's missing briefcase.

On August 6, 1991, Casolaro's housekeeper, Olga, helped Danny pack a black leather tote bag. She remembered he also packed a thick sheaf of papers into a dark brown or black briefcase. She asked him what he had put into the briefcase and he replied, "I have all my papers ..." He had been typing for two days, and as he left the house, he said, "Wish me luck. I'll see you in a couple of days."

By August 9th, Casolaro's friends were alarmed. No one had heard from him and Olga was receiving threatening phone calls at Danny's home. On Saturday, August 10th, Olga received another call, a man's voice said, "You son of a bitch. You're dead." After learning of Danny's death, Olga recalled seeing Danny sitting in the kitchen on August 5th with a "heavy man ... wearing a dark suit. He was a dark man with black hair – he turned towards the door, I saw he was dark-skinned. I told police maybe he could be from India."

At 3:00 P.M. on Friday, the day before Danny's death, Bill Turner, a friend and confidante, met Danny in the parking lot of the Sheraton Hotel to deliver some papers to him. The papers allegedly consisted of two sealed packages which Turner had been keeping in his safe at home for Danny, and a packet of Hughes Aircraft papers which belonged to Turner who had been let go from Hughes for whistleblowing.

Danny had appeared exuberant to most of his friends before his death, noting that he was about to "wrap up" his investigation of The Octopus. He had originally been trying to prove that the alleged theft of the Inslaw computer program, PROMIS, was related to the October Surprise scandal, the Iran-Contra affair and the collapse of BCCI (Bank of Credit and Commerce International).

Turner later admitted to police that he had indeed met with Danny on August 9th, but at that time he refused to specify what time and would not describe what was in the papers he delivered to Danny. I later learned that Turner had been investigating discrepancies involving his former employer, Hughes Aircraft Company. The documents he had delivered from his safe to Danny had been sealed, with Casolaro's name written across the seal, and he claimed not to have known what they contained. Nevertheless, it is feasible to assume that Turner may have known who Danny was preparing to meet that evening at the Martinsburg Hotel because, for reasons of his own, Turner apparently wanted Danny to show the Hughes Aircraft documents to whoever he was meeting with.

Turner later noted to reporters that he was "scared shitless" about information he had seen connecting Ollie North and BCCI. "I saw papers from Danny that connected back through the Keating

Five and Silverado [the failed Denver S & L where Neil Bush had been an officer]," he said.

To his friend, Ben Mason, Danny showed a 22-point outline for his book. Included in the information he shared with Mason were papers referring to Iran-Contra arms deals. *Photocopies of checks made out for $1 million and $4 million drawn on BCCI accounts held for Adnan Khashoggi, an international arms merchant and factotum for the House of Saud, and by Manucher Ghorbanifar, an arms dealer and Iran-Contra middleman, were presented.*

"The last sheet," noted Mason, "was a passport of some guy named Ibrahim." Casolaro had emphasized that Ibrahim had made a big deal of showing him (Casolaro) his "Egyptian" passport. Ibrahim was obviously the informant whom Olga, Casolaro's housekeeper, had seen sitting in the kitchen with Danny on August 5th. Hassan Ali Ibrahim Ali, born in 1928, was later identified as the manager of Sitico, an alleged Iraqi front company for arms purchases. Casolaro had obtained these papers from his confidant, Bob Bickel, who in turn obtained them from October Surprise source Richard Brenneke.

Neither Danny or Bob Bickel were aware at that time of a document from the U.S. Department of Justice, dated May 16, 1985, written by William Bradford Reynolds, Assistant Attorney General in the Civil Rights Division, to William F. Weld, United States Attorney in Boston, Massachusetts, advising Mr. Weld that the PROMIS(E) software was being provided to an Arab Sheik for resale and general distribution in his region. The letter read as follows:

> Dear Mr. Weld: As agreed Messrs. *Manichur* [sic] *Ghorbanifar, Adnan Khashoggi, and Richard Armitage* will broker the transaction of Promise software to Sheik Klahid bin Mahfouz for resale and general distribution as gifts in his region contingent upon the three conditions we last spoke of. Promise must have a soft arrival. No paperwork, customs, or delay. It must be equipped with the special data retrieval unit. As before, you must walk the financial aspects through Credit Suisse into National Commercial Bank. If you encounter any problems contact me directly. Sincerely, WM. Bradford Reynolds, Assistant Attorney General, Civil Rights Divison.

Bill Hamilton, owner of INSLAW, said he had had received this document in the mail in November 2004 from a consistently reliable U.S. intelligence source. He said Donald Carr showed the document to Bradford Reynolds in 2005. Carr was writing a biography of Elliot Richardson and served with Reynolds in the Edwin Meese and Richard Thornburgh Justice Departments as a Republican political appointee. Reynolds authenticated the document. He told Carr that Lowell Jensen's secretary brought the letter to him for signature because Jensen was out of the building, the letter needed to be sent that day, and it needed to be signed by someone in Edwin Meese's inner circle. He said he signed the letter but did not draft it. Reynolds said he had a vague recollection that Meese recused himself on PROMIS when he became Attorney General in February 1985 and Jensen had, therefore, to handle PROMIS. Reynolds told Carr that he had an independent memory of Armitage, Khashoggi, and Ghorbanifar working together on PROMIS.

Hamilton said it was a very important letter. The source who sent it to him in November 2004 told him that all copies were supposed to have been destroyed but obviously were not.

Adnan Khashoggi's sister, Samira Khashoggi Fayed, was the mother of Dodi Fayed, an Egyptian multi-millionaire film producer who was romantically involved with Diana, Princess of Wales. In the early hours of August 31, 1997, the couple died in a car crash in a Paris underpass.

A shrewd businessman, Khashoggi covered his financial tracks by establishing front companies in Switzerland and Liechtenstein to handle his commissions as well as developing contacts with notables such as CIA officers James H. Critchfield and Kim Roosevelt and US businessman Bebe Rebozo, a close associate of former US President Richard Nixon. He was considered the richest man in the world in the 1980s. His sister married Mohammed Al-Fayed, father of Dodi Fayed. His yacht, *Nabila,* was the largest in the world at the time and was used in the James Bond film "*Never Say Never Again.*" http://en.wikipedia.org/wiki/Adnan Khashoggi

Adnan Khashoggi was implicated in the Iran–Contra affair as a key middleman in the arms-for-hostages exchange along with Iranian arms dealer Manucher Ghorbanifar and, in a complex series of events, was found to have borrowed money for these arms purchases from the now-bankrupt financial institution the Bank of Credit and Commerce International (BCCI) with Saudi and US backing. In 1988, Khashoggi was arrested in Switzerland, accused of concealing funds, held for three months and then extradited to the United States where he was released on bail and subsequently acquitted. In 1990, a United States federal jury in Manhattan acquitted Khashoggi and Imelda Marcos, widow of the exiled Philippine President Ferdinand Marcos, of racketeering and fraud.

Ari Ben-Menasche, a self proclaimed Israeli military intelligence officer, was responsible for the tip-off to an obscure Lebanese magazine about what later became known as the Iran-Contra scandal. After Casolaro's death, Menasche called Bill Hamilton, the president of Inslaw Company and creator of the PROMIS software. (Hamilton had been in daily contact with Casolaro until about a week prior to his death).

Menasche claimed that two FBI agents from Lexington, Kentucky, had embarked on a trip to Martinsburg to meet Casolaro as part of their investigation of the sale of the PROMIS software to Israel and other intelligence agencies. Ben Menasche told Hamilton that one of the FBI agents, E.B. Cartinhour, was disaffected because his superiors had refused to indict high Reagan officials for their role in the October Surprise. Ben Menasche claimed the agents were prepared to give Casolaro proof that the FBI was illegally using PROMIS software.

It is highly unlikely that the two FBI agents were en route to Martinsburg to *give* anything to Casolaro, but they may well have been on their way to obtain *his* documents and those belonging to Bill Turner. If, in fact, Danny had disclosed to any one of the many "sources" he had developed during his investigation, that he was turning over his documents to the Lexington FBI, that may well have alarmed a few of them.

I was able to validate that Casolaro had contacted the FBI in Lexington, Kentucky through an inquiry to that office. They said they had been en route to meet with Danny, but turned around and went back to Lexington when they learned of his death.

A source of information which Danny may have read, *Dark Victory: Ronald Reagan, MCA, and the Mob*, by Dan E. Moldea, could have been the inspiration behind Danny's identification of "The Octopus," and it would have corroborated some of Danny's findings in his own investigation. Dan Moldea called this unholy alliance "The Octopus" in his 1986 book.

Casolaro was also investigating Colonel Bo Gritz's expose of CIA drug trafficking in the Golden Triangle, and had requested to meet with a former police officer who had information on Laotian warlord Kuhn Sa's Golden Triangle drug trade proposal to the U.S. Gritz had staged several expeditions to Laos in search of missing POW's, but reportedly stumbled upon a "massive drug network in Southeast Asia and American POW's were intertwined in that network," he told the *Sacramento Bee* [June 6, 1987]. Gritz had been indicted in May 1987 for using a false passport in the name of Patrick Richard Clark from Vancouver, Canada, but at his arraignment before a U.S. Magistrate in Las Vegas he said he had "proper authorization" for his travels.

Casolaro also learned through a *Sacramento Bee* newspaper article, dated June 2, 1990 that Patrick Moriarty, the Red Devil fireworks magnate convicted of laundering political contributions and bribing city officials in Sacramento, had been subpoenaed to testify on behalf of Gritz at his trial in Las Vegas. Gritz was acquitted of the charges.

Moriarty's lawyer, Jan Lawrence Handzlik, told the *Bee* that Moriarty had paid Gritz to make business trips to China, Singapore and other parts of Asia. Gritz said his business trip to Asia in July 1989 was for the purpose of negotiating an oil interest that he and Moriarty had set up between the People's Republic of China and Indonesia.

At the time of Gritz's trial, Patrick Moriarty was the long-time (30 years) partner of Marshall Riconosciuto, Michael Riconosciuto's father. They owned several California businesses together, two of which were Hercules Research Corporation, of which Michael was a partner, and Pyrotronics Corporation.

I privately mused after reading the *Bee* article that Michael Hand, before he founded Nugan Hand Bank in Australia with Frank Nugan and officials of the CIA-owned Air America, had been a highly decorated Special Forces Green Beret soldier in Vietnam. Colonel Bo Gritz was also a highly decorated Green Beret in Vietnam, and both Gritz and Hand had special knowledge of intelligence operations in the Golden Triangle. After his first stint in Vietnam, Hand moved to the clandestine CIA war in Laos, according to a former station chief in Indo-China, Ted Shackley.

The Nugan Hand bank, a primary CIA operation in the Pacific area, reportedly laundered profits from drug trafficking in the

Golden Triangle which, in turn, financed subversive paramilitary activities in Southeast Asia. In 1980 the Nugan Hand bank collapsed, $5 billion in debt, and Michael Hand disappeared.

In the book *The Crimes of Patriots* by Jonathan Kwitny, Michael Hand reportedly fled Australia under a false identity on June 14, 1980 on a flight to Fiji. He was helped to escape by an American code-named "Charlie", identified by Kwitny as a former member of the U.S. Special Forces and ex-CIA operative.

In 1991, top Australian journalist Brian Toohey reported in his *The Eye* magazine that Michael Hand had a postal drop at a suite in NE Bellevue, Washington State. Hand's wife was reportedly living with him there. I found this particularly interesting because Michael Riconosciuto had been living near Tacoma, Washington State when he was arrested in 1991. During our subsequent phone conversations, he said he had been in direct communication with Michael Hand before and after Hand's disappearance, and that he had handled money transfers for Hand when he fled Australia.

••••••••

Another tentacle of Casolaro's Octopus investigation involved the Wackenhut/Cabazon Joint Venture. At one time he considered the title of "Indio" for the book he was writing. His death occurred just days before he planned to visit the Cabazon Indian reservation near Indio, California. Though his notes did not divulge what role the Cabazons may have had in the conspiracy, Casolaro listed Dr. John Phillip Nichols, the Cabazon administrator, as a former CIA agent.

Numerous publications reporting on Casolaro's death corroborated that one of his sources included Michael Riconosciuto, dubbed a "44-year-old former high-tech scientist who had connections with Wackenhut Corporation ..." What brought Casolaro to Riconosciuto was an affidavit signed by Riconosciuto claiming that when he worked on the Wackenhut-Cabazon project, he was given a copy of the Inslaw software by Earl Brian for modification. Riconosciuto also swore that Peter Videnieks, a Justice Department official associated with the Inslaw contract, had visited the Wackenhut-Cabazon project with Earl Brian.

Earl Brian was a businessman and Edwin Meese crony who served in Governor Ronald Reagan's cabinet in California. The $6 million in software stolen from William and Nancy Hamilton, co-owners of Inslaw Company, was allegedly sold by the Justice Department through Earl Brian to raise off-the-books money for covert government operations.

On May 18, 1990, Riconosciuto had called the Hamiltons and informed them that the Inslaw case was connected to the October Surprise affair. Riconosciuto claimed that he and Earl Brian had traveled to Iran in 1980 and paid $40 million to Iranian officials to persuade them *not* to release the hostages before the presidential election in which Reagan became president of the United States.

Riconosciuto's information created a domino effect in Washington D.C., opening numerous investigations and causing a media blitz. At that time, Casolaro was involved in the Hamilton's private investigation of the theft of their software and he had regular communication with Riconosciuto.

Former U.S. Attorney General Elliott Richardson, the Hamilton's attorney, subsequently sent Riconosciuto an affidavit to sign, to be filed by Inslaw in federal court in connection with Inslaw's pending Motion for Limited Discovery. The affidavit, dated March 21, 1991, Case No. 85-00070 entered into court records, resulted in Riconosciuto's arrest within 8 days. It read as follows:

> I Michael J. Riconosciuto, being duly sworn, do hereby state as follows:
>
> (1) During the early 1980's, I served as the Director of Research for a joint venture between the Wackenhut Corporation of Coral Gables, Florida, and the Cabazon Band of Indians of Indio, California. The joint venture was located on the Cabazon reservation.
>
> (2) The Wackenhut-Cabazon joint venture sought to develop and/or manufacture certain materials that are used in military and national security operations, including night vision goggles, machine guns, fuel-air explosives, and biological and chemical warfare weapons.
>
> (3) The Cabazon Band of Indians are a sovereign nation. The sovereign immunity that is accorded the Cabazons as a consequence of this fact made it feasible to pursue on the reservation the development and/or manufacture of materials whose development or manufacture would be subject to stringent controls off the reservation. As a minority group, the Cabazon Indians also provided the Wackenhut Corpo-

ration with an enhanced ability to obtain federal contracts through the 8A Set Aside Program, and in connection with Government-owned contractor-operated (GOCO) facilities.

(4) The Wackenhut-Cabazon joint venture was intended to support the needs of a number of foreign governments and forces, including forces and governments in Central America and the Middle East. The Contras in Nicaragua represented one of the most important priorities for the joint venture.

(5) The Wackenhut-Cabazon joint venture maintained close liaison with certain elements of the United States Government, including representatives of intelligence, military and law enforcement agencies.

(6) Among the frequent visitors to the Wackenhut-Cabazon joint venture were Peter Videnieks of the U.S. Department of Justice in Washington, D.C., and a close associate of Videnieks by the name of Earl W. Brian. Brian is a private businessman who lives in Maryland and who has maintained close ties with the U.S. intelligence community for many years.

(7) In connection with my work for Wackenhut, I engaged in some software development and modification work in 1983 and 1984 on the proprietary PROMIS computer software product. The copy of PROMIS on which I worked came from the U.S. Department of Justice. Earl W. Brian made it available to me through Wackenhut after acquiring it from Peter Videnieks, who was then a Department of Justice contracting official with responsibility for the PROMIS software. I performed the modifications to PROMIS in Indio, California; Silver Spring, Maryland; and Miami, Florida.

(8) The purpose of the PROMIS software modifications that I made in 1983 and 1984 was to support a plan for the implementation of PROMIS in law enforcement and intelligence agencies worldwide. Earl W. Brian was spearheading the plan for this worldwide use of the PROMIS computer software.

(9) Some of the modifications that I made were specifically designed to facilitate the implementation of PROMIS within two agencies of the Government of Canada; the Royal Canadian Mounted Police (RCMP) and the Canadian Security and Intelligence Service (CSIS). Earl W. Brian would check with me from time to time to make certain that the work would be completed in time to satisfy the schedule for the RCMP and CSIS implementations of PROMIS.

(10) The proprietary version of PROMIS, as modified by me, was, in fact, implemented in both the RCMP and the CSIS in Canada. It was my understanding that Earl W. Brian had sold this version of PROMIS to the Government of Canada.

(11) In February 1991, I had a telephone conversation with Peter Videnieks, then still employed by the U.S. Department of Justice. Videnieks attempted during this telephone conversation to persuade me not to cooperate with an independent investigation of the government's piracy of Inslaw's proprietary PROMIS software being conducted by the Committee on the Judiciary of the U.S. House of Representatives.

(12) Videnieks stated that I would be rewarded for a decision not to cooperate with the House Judiciary Committee investigation. Videnieks forecasted an immediate and favorable resolution of a protracted child custody dispute being prosecuted against my wife by her former husband, if I were to decide not to cooperate with the House Judiciary Committee investigation.

(13) Videnieks also outlined specific punishments that I could expect to receive from the U.S. Department of Justice if I cooperate with the House Judiciary Committee's investigation.

(14) One punishment that Videnieks outlined was the future inclusion of me and my father in a criminal prosecution of certain business associates of mine in Orange County, California, in connection with the operation of a savings and loan institution in Orange County. By way of underscoring his power to influence such decisions at the U.S. Department of Justice, Videnieks informed me of the indictment of these business associates prior to the time when that indictment was unsealed and made public.

(15) Another punishment that Videnieks threatened against me if I cooperate with the House Judiciary Committee is prosecution by the U.S. Department of Justice for perjury. Videnieks warned me that credible witnesses would come forward to contradict any damaging claims that I made in testimony before the House Judiciary Committee, and that I would subsequently be prosecuted for perjury by the U.S. Department of Justice for my testimony before the House Judiciary Committee."

♦♦♦♦♦♦♦♦

Danny Casolaro was, of course, intent on interviewing Peter Videnieks. A strange coincidence occurred during the week prior to his death. While sitting in a pub, having a beer, a man named Joseph Cuellar approached him and they began talking. At some point during the conversation, Danny disclosed the contents of his investigation and expressed a desire to interview Peter Videnieks.

To Danny's astonishment, Cuellar, claiming to be a Special Forces operative, said he could arrange a rendezvous between Peter Videnieks and Casolaro. Cuellar's connection to Peter Videnieks allegedly came through Videnieks' wife, Barbara, who was the executive assistant to the powerful West Virginia Democratic Senator, Robert Byrd. Byrd played a major role in the effort to have the CIA move some of its administrative offices to Charlestown, 20 miles from Martinsburg, on the Virginia border. It was apparently through Barbara Videnieks that Cuellar intended to arrange the interview.

Casolaro confided to friends that he was unnerved by this supposedly chance meeting. He met with Cuellar at other times that week, but it is unknown whether he ever spoke with Videnieks. To date, that question remains unanswered.

Significantly, Elliot Richardson, the respected former U.S. Attorney General representing Inslaw, called for the appointment of a special counsel to look into the death of Casolaro. That did not occur, but some of the positive fallout from Richardson's request came back in the form of sources who allegedly knew Cuellar. One source said Cuellar was a U.S. army Major, Army intelligence unit, who went to work for a company that was a DIA (Defense Intelligence Agency) cutout. One FBI agent said Cuellar reportedly spoke Arabic fluently and had spent time in Iraq.

The Trade

At Michael Riconosciuto's trial in Tacoma Washington, Peter Videnieks testified that while working for the Justice Department he had contact with the PROMIS software. He "conducted the competitive contract – competitive procurement for acquisition of the services to implement PROMIS." Under cross-examination he testified that "it required preparation of a request for proposals issuance of that document to industry ... negotiating, selecting, and awarding the contract. Then after award, administering the contract to see that the work that the government paid for was properly performed."

So, essentially, Videnieks administered the Inslaw contract with the government. His employment record included work with the Internal Revenue Service as a revenue officer from 1964 to 1967. From 1967 to 1972 as a contract specialist with NASA. From 1972 to 1973 with Customs as a contract specialist. From 1973 through 1975 back at NASA as a contract specialist. From 1975 through 1981 as a contract specialist with Customs, supervisory at this time. From 1981 through September, 1990, with the Department of Justice as a contract specialist. And from September 1990 through present (January 1992) as a supervisory contract specialist at Customs again.

Thomas Olmstead, Riconosciuto's attorney, showed Videnieks the Inslaw affidavit signed by Riconosciuto. Videnieks said he had seen the affidavit prior to court, but testified that he'd never heard of the Wackenhut-Cabazon joint venture and never visited the Wackenhut-Cabazon facility in Indio, California. He also testified that he'd never met Earl Brian.

Olmstead asked Videnieks if he knew Robert Chasen [Executive Vice President of Wackenhut]? Videnieks testified that he knew him "by name since he was head of Customs for about a three-year period, from about 1977 through 1980. I met him once in the line of my duties."

Interestingly, according to his resume, Robert Chasen was Commissioner of Customs in Washington D.C. from 1969 to 1977, then Executive Vice President of Wackenhut from 1981 to present (1991). And Peter Videnieks, a contract officer at Customs in Washington D.C. from 1972 to 1974, then again at Customs from 1976 to 1981, said he did not know Robert Chasen. How could that be? Videnieks had worked in the same department with Chasen, off and on, for at least three years.

Videnieks also testified that he met Chasen in the line of his duties sometime between 1977 and 1980. Yet, Chasen no longer worked at Customs between 1977 and 1980?

Thomas Olmstead had done his homework on Inslaw. He pressed Videnieks to disclose under oath whether he supervised a Hadron contract within the same time frame that he was administering the Inslaw contract? Though it was unstated in court, the significance of this query related to Hadron's aborted attempt to purchase Inslaw Corporation during the development of the PROMIS software, but Bill Hamilton had refused to sell. This had created a domino effect; Hamilton ultimately sued the DOJ for allegedly stealing a version of his software. In court, Videnieks was evasive pertaining to Hadron. As follows:

> Olmstead asked Videnieks to reiterate his position with the PROMIS software. "I worked on the [PROMIS] contract. The procurement was assigned to me by a lady named Patricia Rudd. My function was to conduct a competitive procurement, negotiate an award of contract, and then administer the contract."
>
> Olmstead: "What time frames are we talking when you were ...?"
>
> Videnieks: "We're talking about from the day that I reported for duty at Justice, which was in September 1981, through about 1985."
>
> Olmstead: "Are you familiar with Hadron Company?" (This was a loaded question because Earl Brian, who Videnieks testified he did *not* know, owned Hadron Company at the time of the court proceedings.)

Videnieks responded, "Yes, I am."

Olmstead: "Have you done work for Hadron Corporation in your procurement contract?"

Videnieks: "I supervise currently a contract specialist who is administering a contract with Hadron."

Olmstead: "Prior to supervising someone, did you personally handle that particular contract?"

Videnieks: "I have administered well over a hundred contracts, maybe a couple hundred or several hundred over my career, and I don't recall whether I have or not."

Olmstead: "And you have never given a deposition in regards to the Inslaw matter?"

Videnieks: "My recall is not that good. Like I said, I have administered hundreds of contracts, and I may or may not have administered one with Hadron."

Again Olmstead asked Videnieks if he knew Earl Brian? Videnieks responded, "No, sir."

Olmstead: "Do you know who owns Hadron?"

Videnieks: "I really don't. I've heard -- I mean, I don't want to speculate now. He may be an officer with Hadron. He may be."

Olmstead: "You don't recall any questions in any depositions at all regarding that?"

Videnieks: "I do recall questions along these same lines. But again, from general knowledge, I think he is an officer or has been an officer with Hadron."

Olmstead: "In fact, in your deposition, you admitted you knew that he was an officer of Hadron, didn't you?"

Videnieks: "I would like to see my transcript from my deposition as to what I said ..."

Olmstead went on to question Videnieks about "Modification No. 12" of the PROMIS software. Videnieks stated that he knew what Modification No. 12 was, but repeatedly refused to discuss it until someone produced the original Inslaw contract. Finally, under pressure to give a general recollection, he said it dealt with the twelfth modification to the PROMIS software.

Olmstead asked, "Were you personally chastised as a result of Modification No. 12 in the way you handled that?"

Videnieks: "Please define `chastised.'"

Olmstead: "Were you told that you took, converted, and stole six million dollars worth of Inslaw software through the way you handled Modification No. 12?"

Videnieks: "A judge in the bankruptcy court ruled that. Since then the record was erased. And that language should not be -- the way a non-lawyer like me understands, it is no longer in existence ..."

••••••••

It is necessary to digress here to disclose the magnitude of the apparent government cover-up at Riconosciuto's trial. About two weeks before his trial began, I had received a call from Michael asking me to contact Brian Leighton, a former assistant U.S. Attorney in Fresno, whom Michael claimed to have provided information to on a drug operation called "The Company." Michael was lining up his ducks. Essentially his defense rested on his ability to prove he worked for the U.S. government in intelligence and undercover operations, but his lawyer was behind schedule in making the contacts.

Brian Leighton had been instrumental in prosecuting 29 members of a drug/arms organization called "The Company." The Company had been written up in the *San Francisco Chronicle* on April 28, 1982 under the heading "Story of Spies, Stolen Arms and Drugs." According to reporter Bill Wallace, The Company consisted of (quote) "about 300 members, many of them former military men or ex-police officers with nearly $30 million worth of assets, including planes, ships and real estate."

The article went on to say that "federal drug agents said the organization had imported billions of dollars worth of narcotics from Latin America, and was also involved in gunrunning and mercenary operations." Specialized military equipment consisting of nine infrared sniperscopes, a television camera for taking pictures in darkness, 1500 rounds of small arms tracer ammunition for night combat, a five-foot remote-control helicopter, and secret components from the radar unit of a Sidewinder guided missile were stolen from the U.S. Naval Weapons Station at China Lake in the Mojave Desert.

Federal agents said some of the stolen equipment was going to be used to make electronic equipment for drug smugglers and some was traded to drug suppliers in Colombia. Twenty-nine members of the Company were indicted by the Fresno federal grand jury in 1981. Amongst those indicated was Andrew "Drew" Thornton, 40, a former narcotics officer.

On September 13, 1985, the *Los Angeles Times* published the story of Thornton's death, entitled, "Former Narcotics Officer Parachutes Out of Plane, Dies with 77 Pounds of Cocaine." The article said Thornton was indicted in 1981 for "allegedly flying a plane to South America for a reputed drug ring known as `The Company.'" In an interview with the *Los Angeles Times*, Brian Leighton said, "I'm glad his parachute didn't open. I hope he got a hell of a high out of that ..."

Thornton's mysterious death was discussed at length in a book written by Sally Denton entitled, *The Blue Grass Conspiracy*. Part of The Company was headquartered in Lexington, Kentucky. Prosecutors in Lexington, Fresno, California (Brian Leighton), and Miami, Florida were working together in a joint effort to bring down The Company.

Journalist Danny Casolaro had been communicating regularly with Michael Riconosciuto and obviously learned about The Company. It is not to be overlooked that coincidentally or not, Ari Ben-Menashe (a former Israeli intelligence agent who lived in Lexington, Kentucky) told Bill Hamilton that two Lexington FBI agents had been en route to meet with Danny at the Martinsburg Hotel on the day of his death. The Company was headquartered in Lexington. Danny may have scheduled a meeting with the Lexington FBI relative to drug trafficking by The Company.

Ben-Menashe further told Hamilton that one of the agents, E.B. Cartinhour, was angry that the Justice Department was not pursuing Reagan administration officials for their role in the October Surprise.

Bill Hamilton mentioned to me years later for insertion into the manuscript that he believed "the main role of the Joint Venture was connected to government-sanctioned drug trafficking and money laundering by organized crime groups like the Gambino Family and groups like the Contras, and that Riconoscuito's job was to help these groups avail themselves of NSA's bank surveillance version of PROMIS to launder the proceeds from the drug sales."

Hamilton added, " I assume that the bad guys kept some of the proceeds for themselves and contributed the rest to a fund for covert intelligence operations not authorized by Congress. If that is even roughly accurate, it could explain why Riconosciuto and Robert Booth Nichols played important roles in the Joint Venture and why nobody, including Riconosciuto, has ever told the whole truth about what took place under the auspices of the Joint Venture."

Hamilton said he had received an affidavit from William (Bill) Turner on "highly classified computer printouts on off-shore accounts that he claimed Casolaro intended to use the night he died in a planned meeting with Peter Videnieks and Joseph Cuellar and others." (More on that later).

••••••••

Meanwhile, it was necessary to contact Brian Leighton to corroborate Riconosciuto's story that he had been instrumental in helping Leighton identify members of The Company.

I did not directly contact Leighton, who had resigned from the U.S. Attorney's office shortly after the prosecutions and entered into private law practice, but asked the Secret Service agent in Los Angeles who had visited my home regarding the "Queen's accident" in Mariposa (mentioned in the first chapter of this book) to run a check on Riconosciuto.

Instead, he called Brian Leighton and when I checked back with him, he acknowledged talking to Leighton about Riconosciuto. Leighton confirmed to the Secret Service agent that he recalled a three-hour face-to-face meeting with Riconosciuto and remembered him well. He gave specific details of Riconosciuto's cooperation with the U.S. attorney's office. I thanked the Secret Service agent and hung up.

I next contacted a retired police officer and colleague in the Mariposa investigation, and asked him to put me in touch with someone trustworthy in government who could corroborate Leighton's information. The contact was made and this individual agreed to call Brian Leighton to see if he could glean further details of Michael's cooperation with the U.S. attorney's office. For purposes of anonymity, this source will be identified as "J.H." (I originally identified him as "R.J." in the Internet version of *The Last Circle*, but in this book I have used his *real* name initials for historical accuracy, and because he is now retired). When I checked back, he confirmed that Leighton did indeed remember Michael's help with the case and, in fact, said Michael led law enforcement officers to a marijuana cache belonging to members of The Company.

At that point I was satisfied that Michael had been operating within the framework of The Company and had spoken accurately about his cooperation with Brian Leighton. I called Thomas Olmstead, Michael's attorney, and related the above information.

Two weeks later, on January 15, 1992, at Michael's trial in Tacoma, Washington, Brian Leighton testified that the case in question [The Company] involved the theft of military equipment from the China Lake Naval Weapons Center in California. "The FBI and Naval Intelligence Service began the investigation," he said, "and there were several people that were targets of the investigation. One of those targets began cooperating with us and then it became a DEA and FBI investigation. The thefts occurred in 1979 and 1980, and the case continued on for a couple of years."

Leighton testified that he "could not recall ever meeting personally with Mr. Riconosciuto and he didn't know if he spoke to him personally or spoke to him through a government agent." Under cross-examination, Leighton testified that he thought Riconosciuto was brought to him by an agent Barnes from the Oakland or San Francisco office of the FBI, but he couldn't remember exactly ..."

After Leighton's testimony, Michael called me and asked, "What happened?" I was astonished at Leighton's testimony. What was at stake here? Michael speculated that Leighton was operating out of fear. He said Leighton retired from the U.S. Attorney's office shortly after prosecuting members of The Company, and recalled that the prosecuting attorney in Florida had been shot in the head.

I called the Secret Service officer and J.H. individually and asked them to repeat what Leighton had told them before the trial. They both repeated verbatim what Leighton had told them the first time about Michael Riconosciuto. I said it appeared Leighton had withheld information in court. Neither could understand why?

♦♦♦♦♦♦♦♦

In August 1994, I received from a friend of Bill Hamilton's (President of Inslaw) a Declaration, signed by Hamilton, which stated that " ... On or about April 3, 1991, I spoke by telephone with Mr. Brian Leighton, an attorney in private practice in Fresno, California. He stated that during the early 1980's, while serving as an Assistant United States Attorney in Fresno, California, he had investigated a nationwide criminal enterprise known as 'The Company,' which was engaged in illegal drug trafficking on a massive scale.

"Mr. Leighton told me that (A) Michael Riconosciuto had furnished Mr. Leighton 'valuable intelligence' on illegal drug activities and The Company; (B) Mr. Leighton had been unable to use the information in prosecution but (C) the failure to use Mr. Riconosciuto's intelligence information was not because of any fault of Mr. Michael Riconosciuto."

Also mentioned in the affidavit was corroboration of Riconosciuto's work in the defense and national security fields. Section six of the affidavit noted that during the course of a telephone conversation with Robert Booth Nichols on or about April 18, 1991, Hamilton learned that Nichols had attended a meeting that had been organized by a Colonel Bamford, an aide to General Meyer, then Chairman of the Joint Chiefs of Staff. Others participating in the meeting were department heads from Department of Defense scientific facilities.

Michael Riconosciuto was the principal presenter to this group of senior-level national security research and development officials. According to Nichols, Riconosciuto made a day long presentation to this meeting of scientists lasting from approximately 9 A.M. until approximately 4 P.M., answering questions from the participants and filling the halls of the conference facility with his hand-printed notes on the scientific and technical issues that arose in the course of his presentation.

I was able to locate in Riconosciuto's files, a letter written on July 20, 1983 from Tom Bamford, Vice President of Research and Development at FMC Corporation in Santa Clara, California to William Frash in Escondido, California. At that time, Frash, a retired USMC Colonel, was Chairman of the Board and Chief Executive Officer of Lilac Corporation.

Essentially, the letter expressed enthusiasm for the potential application of technologies being proposed to FMC Corporation by Meridian Arms, and called for a list of all active participants in the joint venture. At that time Riconosciuto was vice president of Meridian Arms. Bamford added, " ... You may want to do this only for Mike at this stage."

Frash hastened to respond to Bamford on July 27, 1983 to apprise him of a meeting between himself and Michael Riconosciuto, Robert Booth Nichols, Peter Zokosky and Patrick Moriarty (Michael's father's business partner) regarding "energy transfer phenomena." A proposal was underway to outline technology in the form of patents applied for jointly between Meridian Arms and FMC. Frash noted that the technology would "supercede all existing world patents in the field."

"Had we patented previously, it would only have announced our `edge' in the field," he wrote. Three of the four major patents that would be forthcoming were (1) the application of Perturbation Theory to enhanced energy transfer, (2) the application of stationary methods with powders and aerosols to enhanced energy transfer and (3) the application of Perturbation Theory to hydrodynamic flow regimes.

It is noteworthy that the submarine propulsion system depicted in the movie, *Hunt for Red October* utilized this theory. Frash concluded, "Tom, as you well know, Mike's tried and true value is in the field of high voltage and electrostatics and their application. The meetings in San Jose highlighted application of this technology in over one hundred areas that are in-house FMC." He added, " ... Per your reference to meetings in Washington, D.C., I assume the meetings with Dr. Fair, Admiral Renkin and the ACCOM people will suffice in this matter. In closing we are very enthused, Tom, and we look forward to an expeditious closing. Sincerely, William Frash."

Frash's payment for putting together the above referenced joint venture, if successful, would be $500,000 for the first fifteen million invested, or $166,666.66 for only five million invested, a one-hundred-thousand-dollar per year salary for a period of 20 years, and a 2% share in the gross profits. This, according to a Letter of Understanding sent to and signed by Robert Booth Nichols and Michael Riconosciuto in July, 1983.

In questioning Michael Riconosciuto about the FMC agreements, he said he attempted to break away from Robert Nichols in 1984. "The guy nearly got me terminated," declared Riconosciuto.

> At the time I was working with Nichols on a proposal to FMC Corporation, which is Food Machinery Corporation, they produced

the Bradley Personnel Carrier. I've got a complete paper-trail on the technology that was being presented. We conducted a test demonstration of an enhanced airfield device which I developed. We also conducted a test of a hydro-dynamic implosion type of explosive device.

The implosion device settled the Nevada Test Range by about 30 feet. The Lawrence Livermore Labs and the Gallup Ordinance people built a prototype of the device, but they overbuilt it because they wanted an impressive demonstration. It created an international incident because the demonstration was picked up by Soviet monitoring satellites.

Anyway, the bona fides were established. The next thing was to get the business done and get me into harness in a program. I was all for it, but Bob [Nichols] started getting spooky on me. He wanted to receive the set-up of our end off-shore, in Singapore. He wanted to receive $20 million dollars in cash in Singapore, and he wanted to use certain of the technology overseas, namely in Australia, OK?

Bob started drinking a lot. He was obviously under a lot of pressure from somewhere, and his facade of respectability started to crack. About that time Bob began pressuring me to do things a certain way. We'd already been approved at the executive level by FMC. But we still had to go through the legal department and FMC is a publicly held stock corporation. So we still had to go through the share-holders for about eight months, which put us about a year away from consummating the deal.

So, I asked Bob for some extra money to meet my everyday expenses, but Bob said, `Hurry up and get the business done and then you'll have plenty of money.' I tried to explain to Bob that there was no way he could expedite this thing, and so on and so forth. Well, Bob became really overbearing. And that's when he demanded that I state things in the contract proposal to FMC which would have been mis-statements, to the point of being illegal. That's when I started having second thoughts about it.

There were other people involved in the development of that technology. Bob wanted me to pay him out of my share and make no reference to the other people in the agreement. But when you've got the University of California and the University of Chicago having 16 percent of your company, having 16 percent of Hercules Research and Interprobe, you know, how could I mis-represent the interests of my dad, Moriarty and [Admiral] Al Renkin in a deal with a U.S. publicly held corporation [FMC]?

At that time, Riconosciuto had been Vice President of Meridian Arms, a subsidiary of Meridian International Logistics. But he was also technical advisor for FIDCO (First Intercontinental Development Corporation) of which Nichols was on the Board of Directors. Noted Riconosciuto,

> I walked into FIDCO in equal good faith. And that also turned sour because Bob wanted me to take embargoed technology out of the United States, to run an operation with embargoed armaments and high technology outside of the United States.
>
> So I walked out on Bob. And Bob put the heat on me and they wouldn't leave me alone. When I got re-married [to Bobby Riconosciuto], they continued to harass me by putting out false intelligence reports on me to law enforcement ..."

I asked Michael why he didn't fight back? Michael responded, "You don't seem to understand. All my involvements were under closely controlled situations. There's only one time in my life when I was planning on doing something off-color, and it never went anywhere. All the rest of the time, everything was under complete controls. I never took any elective actions. Everything was, you know, on direct orders. And I got to the point where I balked with Bob Nichols and that's when he went ballistic on me."

Riconosciuto said he was in the process of cleaning up his life in Washington State when a private investigator from Inslaw contacted him. "I didn't want to get nailed for piracy of that software, so I talked to my attorney, who talked to the Inslaw attorneys, and I gave them a declaration. Seven days later I was arrested on drug charges."

♦♦♦♦♦♦♦♦

Ted Gunderson was one of the few "cooperating" witnesses at Michael's trial. Through his affidavit and testimony, Gunderson hoped to supply the defense with needed corroboration of Michael's covert government sanctioned activities. Unfortunately for Michael, Ted could not disclose numerous activities which had included Robert Booth Nichols. At one time Gunderson, Nichols and Riconosciuto had been inseparable, like the three musketeers. But, Nichols was currently under investigation by the Los Angeles FBI for alleged involvement in organized crime in the U.S. and abroad.

Gunderson's handwritten affidavit, submitted to Michael's lawyer on September 27, 1991, read as follows (excerpted):

> I, Ted L. Gunderson, make the following free and voluntary statement. No threats or promises were made to get me to make this statement. I was born 11/7/28 at Colorado Springs, Colorado.
>
> In early 1986, I met one Ralph Olberg through a friend of mine, Bill Sloane. Sloane is a former official with HUD. Sloane was appointed by President Ronald Reagan to the HUD position after the president was elected in 1980.
>
> Olberg is a prominent American businessman who was spearheading procurement of U.S. weapons and technology for the Afghanistan rebels.
>
> In late Spring or early summer of 1986, Ralph Olberg, one Tim Osman, Michael Riconosciuto and I met in a room at the Hilton Hotel, Ventura Blvd., Sherman Oaks, California. I accompanied Michael Riconosciuto, and Osman and Olberg were together. We were there to discuss Olberg's role with the worldwide support network involving the Mujahideen, Afghanistan Resistance Movement against the Soviets.
>
> In particular we discussed the ability of the Mujahaden's willingness to field test weapons, new and esoteric in the field and to return a research report, complete with photos.
>
> We also discussed the capture and/or defection of high ranking Soviet military personnel who had sensitive compartmentalized information and the availability of their briefings. We discussed one person who was a Soviet defector and was a communications officer who had detailed information of the highest levels of Soviet military C-3I (Command Control Intelligence and Communications).
>
> We also discussed the Soviet directed weapons system referred to in the conversation as `Blue Death.' Michael and I were told by Olberg that witnesses stated the corpses did not decay even after being exposed and unburied for six months.
>
> We discussed the possibility of Michael analyzing one of these units captured in the field by the Afghan rebels for the purpose of having Michael help their technical experts develop effective counter-measures.
>
> We discussed a military joint venture in Turkey to produce specialized ammunition. We discussed a lobbying effort to legally obtain Stinger II missiles as well as the various Stinger post and Stinger alternates. Michael was to formulate a plan to sanitize the

electronics of any Stingers that would be at risk of Soviet capture so any information gained from a captured Stinger could not be effectively used against the U.S. or NATO forces.

This report was to be presented to a Congressional position as support for the lobbying effort to convince Congress to legally sanction the shipment of these missiles to the Afghan rebels.

We discussed Michael's proposed modification of Chinese 107 MM rockets and how to reconfigure the package into a back-pack portable effective artillery counter battlery system.

We discussed Michael's connection with the Chinese weapons position, Norinco, to provide the basic components for the unassembled rocket system. We discussed the modification and assembly of these 107 MM rockets and their launchers at a facility in Pakistan known as the Pakistan Ordinance Works.

It was my understanding from the discussion that we were working on a legally sanctioned arms assistance project to the Afghan rebels and that Ralph Olberg was working through the Afghan desk at the State Department as well as through Senator Humphrey's office. This was subsequently confirmed by journalist Danny Casolaro who was recently `suicided.'

Olberg indicated a potential turf battle problem with certain factions of the CIA and his group MSH (Management Science For Health). In negotiations and/or lobbying efforts with Congress, the CIA-MSH people were arguing that Ralph and Tim Osman's group did not truly represent the leadership of the Afghan rebel resistance.

Tim and Ralph proposed calling their people and having an unprecedented leadership meeting in Washington D.C. to prove that their group did in fact represent the full leadership of the Mujahaden.

When I recently called Ralph, he denied that the above meeting had taken place and then after prodding, he finally admitted to it and he asked me not to talk about it. This five-page statement is true and correct to the best of my knowledge.

Ted L. Gunderson.

♦♦♦♦♦♦♦♦

Michael's trial was not going well. He called and asked me to contact J.H. (FBI agent in Fresno) and bring him to my house. Michael was ready to talk – he wanted me to set up a phone conversation in which he could preliminarily open negotiations for entry into the Federal Witness Protection Program. I was out of my depth here.

I had no idea whether J.H. would cooperate with such a request. Nevertheless, I called him and related Michael's proposal. He said he had no authority to approve such a request, but he would take the information and pass it along.

He arrived at my home early the following week and Michael called as scheduled. Excerpts from that first tape-recorded conversation went as follows: (Michael did most of the talking)

> ... In the Fresno area, there was a group of people known as the Fresno Company and all of these people seemed to have charmed lives ...
>
> The Company was originally out of Lexington, Kentucky and Mena, Arkansas. Brian Leighton was the assistant U.S. Attorney who was the most effective person in formulating a strategy in the Justice Department to go after these people.
>
> We recognized what they were, for what they were, at that time, and there were a few ATF guys down in Los Angeles that recognized them for what they were, OK? Here was a group of over 300 people, most of them ex-law enforcement and ex-military, ex-intelligence people involved in a major drug and smuggling operation. And they were involved in compromising activities. The bottom line was espionage.
>
> And all Leighton served to do was vaccinate the group against further penetration. Just hardened them. And all the major sources that were developed from inside turned up dead. A federal judge in Texas turned up dead.
>
> ... This is a nasty bunch of people. And they're still alive and well. Now where that dovetails into my current situation, is in 1984 I was involved with Robert Booth Nichols who owns Meridian Arms Corporation and is a principle in FIDCO, First Intercontinental Development Corporation. The CEO of FIDCO is George Pender and Bob Maheu was Vice President ...
>
> FIDCO was an NSC [National Security Council] corporate cut-out. FIDCO was created to be the corporate vehicle to secure the financing for the reconstruction of the cities of Beirut and Damour in Lebanon. And they were working out of an office in Nicosia, Cyprus.
>
> ... And here I got involved with a group of people that were all high profile and should have been above reproach. FIDCO had a companion company called Euramae Trading which operated throughout the Middle East. I came in contact with the PROMIS software (unintelligible). Euramae had a distribution contract

with several Arab countries and I was asked to evaluate the hardware platforms they had chosen. That was IBM/AS400 stuff ...

... That had come from IBM Tel Aviv but it came through a cut-out, Link Systems, because they couldn't deal directly with the Arabs.

And I came across a guy named Michael T. Hurley and I thought he worked for the State Department but it turned out he was in-country attache for the DEA in Nicosia, Cyprus. [Nicosia is the capital of the island of Cyprus, off the coast of Lebanon]. Now, the DEA had no real presence in Lebanon. Neither did anybody else, including the Israelis. They had their usual network of contacts but it was very ineffective. The only way to penetrate that situation, was to get into the drug trade.

Euramae got into the drug trade and I was told that it was a fully sanctioned NSC directed operation, which it turns out that it was ... All those operations were bona fide and all the people who were in them were definitely key government people, although they were not who they said they were.

They all worked for different agencies other than was stated. Probably part of the normal disinformation that goes with that. And I was technical advisor for FIDCO and we had auspices through the government of Lebanon to get in and out of Lebanon.

But as far as going to the eastern part of Lebanon, unless you were connected with the drug trade, your chances were slim coming out unscathed ... They built a network throughout the Bekaa Valley, and [Robert Booth] Nichols ... he is under Harold Okimoto from the Hawaiian Islands.

Harold Okimoto was represented to me as being an intelligence person, which he is. He has worked under the auspices of [Frank] Carlucci for years. [Carlucci was former CIA deputy director and former Defense secretary]. Apparently Harold performed services for the U.S. government during World War II. He's of Japanese ancestry. I guess he was rewarded for services well done.

When FIDCO was wheeling and dealing on financing for the reconstruction of the infrastructure of Beirut, they were making sweetheart deals with Syrian mobsters and the brother of the president of Syria, Hafez Assad.

... The intelligence people in their infinite wisdom decided to capitalize on the long-standing battle between Rifat Assad and his group and the Jafaar family. Selectively they were backing both people, but they were also playing them off against one another, developing networks. They got a bunch of prominent Syrians thoroughly compromised and they were in tow in the intelligence game. And they had people that could get me in and out of the Bekaa Valley, even out of certain areas of Syria.

From an intelligence standpoint, it was a success. But to maintain the credibility of those intelligence operations the heroin had to flow. To make it real. And the stuff was starting to accumulate in a warehouse outside of Larnaca. "I personally was in a warehouse where ... there was upwards of twenty-two tons. And even though it was packaged for shipment, the smell of it in that closed warehouse was overpowering. You know, white heroin like that has a certain odor because of the way it's processed.

They had authorization for what they called `controlled deliveries' into the United States. And they would target certain cities and then follow the stuff out, ostensibly unmasking the network and conducting prosecutions.

However, the operation became perverted at the U.S. end of the pipeline. Controlled heroin shipments were doubled, sometimes tripled, and only one third of the heroin was returned to the DEA.

At a certain transfer point at the airport in Larnaca, the excess baggage from the original controlled delivery would be allowed to go through. I was given the names of the narcotics people who were handling that. But there were a couple of agents who were on the up and up, and they had suspicions.

An intelligence agent who worked with DIA is now deceased. His name was Tony Asmar and he got on to the operation early on, and started going toe to toe with Hurley [DEA]. He died in a bomb blast and it was ascribed to terrorists. And it actually was terrorists who did it, but his cover was deliberately blown ...

••••••••

After researching Michael Riconosciuto's information, J.H. noted to me that Michael gave mostly valid information, but he could not prove that Michael had been involved. He did, however, verify (through Customs) that Michael *had* been in Lebanon, but he could not verify the details of the drug operation.

Michael responded (on a taped message to J.H.) by visually recounting the DEA apartment/condo in Nicosia, Cyprus:

"The DEA had a condo, I think it was on Columbra (phonetically spelled) Street, in Nicosia, Cyprus [off the coast of Lebanon].

"They had a ham radio station there. It was an I-COM single side band amateur radio set-up, with a linear ..."

"Were you actually there?" I asked.

Michael quipped, "Yes, I was there," then continued. "I can describe the antenna system, on the top floor and the way it's wired up and everything. Unless you were there, you wouldn't know it was I-COM equipment.

"Now, the game plan with Euramae and Hurley's operation ..." Pause. " ... You need to understand that the airport in Lebanon was closed down. I took the ferry from Larnaca to Jounieb. Now Jounieb was slightly south of where the casino city was and the casino city was intact. Beirut was a nightmare, and so was Damour, because the PLO destroyed the infrastructure by burrowing bunkers, and there was no water, electricity or phones. It was a combat zone.

"The Syrian mob controlled the Casino du Liban in a little city north of Beirut. It was used as a front by narcotics people. Island Tobacco, owned by Harold Okimoto, sells all the cigarettes there. Now, I could give you the names of the families. They pitted them off against one another. FIDCO was to finance the reconstruction of the infrastructure of the cities of Beirut and Damour. Deals were cut as to who got what concessions. There were certain families, like the El-Jorr family that had to be placated. And there was Rifat Assad and his group.

"Tony Asmar figured out what was going on with Hurley, that they were shipping `non-controlled' loads of heroin back to the U.S.. They killed Tony ..."

"What were the names of the people you were working for over there?," I asked. Michael's time was always limited on the phone.

"OK, there was a man named Maurice Ganem. He had a relative, either a brother or a cousin, who is a senior DEA official with Michael Hurley. I can't remember his name right now. Anyways, Maurice was agency, you know, in country, in Lebanon. And Maurice and I and George Pender worked together."

"Which agency? CIA or DEA?," I asked.

"CIA." Michael continued. " ... And then there was Danny Habib. Danny Habib and Bob Nichols worked out of Cario (phonetic spelling) and Italy."

"And Bob was NSA or ..." "No, Bob was NSC at that time."

I asked, "What was your involvement with that particular operation?"

"I handled communications protocol. All the communications and financial transactions. If I could get my records on line I could show all the money flows, everything."

••••••••

Michael called back later that day, on January 9, 1992, and we continued our conversation. He was intent on talking to someone in FinCen: (excerpted)

" ... The keystone cops are working on my defense. You know it's really an ordeal. Have you talked to J.H. again?"

"No Mike, he's not giving much information."

"Listen, tell him that not only am I willing to polygraph, but I need some expert help and I think he needs some expert help. In the league we're playing in, the only guys we can get that have the where-with-all are with FinCen. That stands for Financial Crimes Enforcement Network. Get me a technical guy that speaks my language."

"Alright, Mike ..."

"I'm talking about Swift Chips. That stands for Clearing House Interbank Payment System, OK?"

"Right."

"I'm mad, OK?"

"Uh huh."

"I'm real mad. The government has all my files and records. They've got all of my optical storage disks. Each of those optical storages, 130 of them, contains 20,000 plus pages. They jacked me around so bad ..."

"Mike ..."

" ... Get an expert that speaks my language, and I'll tell him everything I know and he can do so much damage, they won't need my testimony or anything else."

"Mike, everything you know about what?"

"Tell J.H. it goes all the way back to the Cayman Islands and the Bahamas and Castle Bank ... Resorts International Bank ..."

"How'd you get this stuff?"

"I handled the money for them, OK?"

"For who?"

" ... For the Wackenhut people. Now, there was the Workers Bank in Colombia. I can't pronounce the Spanish name for it, I just know it as Workers Bank. I set up their virtual dead-drops ..."

"What's that?"

"It's a way to get around A.C.H. reconciliations on a daily basis. It'll take an expert, you know, I can't even talk to a normal human being about this ..."

"OK"

" ... And the bottom line here is Bob Nichols and Gilbert Rodriguez, Michael Abbell, whose now an attorney in D.C., but he was with the criminal section of the Justice Department – and Jose Londono are all in bed together. [Three years after this conversation, Michael Abbell was indicted for laundering money for the Cali Cartel].

"This took place in 1983. I have correspondence on the things we were doing. But I was in fear of my life because Bob was starting to act irrational. The guy was getting drunk all the time, waving a gun out of the car window, shooting in the air, you know, just really doing a mind trip on me. I've been on the run ever since ..."

"Listen, Mike, what do you need from FinCen?"

"If I had help from the FinCen people, I could reconstruct my files. Tell them that I need two types of computers. I need a VAX 11-730 set up with two RLO II disks; one RA-80 and a TU-80 tape drive. That's one package. And then I need a VAX 3900 computer. Now the reason why I need the older, slower VAX – and I know where to get all this stuff, no problem, I've got the VAX's in Southern California, but I need a place to set them up and somebody to operate them, and just follow my instructions."

"Alright."

"Now, the VAX Series 3900 machine ... it's too complicated to go into what mass storage devices, but those are the two levels of machines I need.

"OK, I'm thinking about going to visit your wife in Southern California, do you want us to bring those computers up here?"

"No, No! No, leave them where they're at. Tell J.H. to find someone at FinCen. If we move them around, we're going to wreck them. I'm not trying to talk down to J.H., but this is too far above him."

"Mike, Raymond Lavas turned some of your disks over to the Jack Brooks investigative committee (House Judiciary Committee on Inslaw)."

"Yeah, I know. There's no data on those disks. What that is, is that is a sub-set of VAX VMS, OK? What I do is I modify some of the VAX VMS routines to activate a one time pad encryption scheme. That's why I have to have two RLO-2 drives on the VAX 11-730, because one RLO-2 Platter is a system planner, the other one is the one time pad. The data is on a 1625 BPI 9 track tape on the TU-80 tape drive. That's the system configuration."

"If you say so."

"Now, J.H. needs to put me in touch with somebody he trusts at FinCen. There's about 120 experts there. There are a few guys there that speak my language.

"What's the encryption key?"

"Well, they're ten digit numbers ... it's a one time pad, but it has a pseudo-random, prime number expansion system ..."

"Mike, do you have access to PROMIS through this system?"

"What? Oh, I've got access to PROMIS, I've got access to FOIMS ..."

"Well, PROMIS is the one that's going to get you off the hook in court."

"OK, I understand that. But PROMIS and FOIMS are one and the same. Now they will say no, that's not true, but in Virginia where the FBI has their center, and where the Justice Department has a center in D.C., they're both Amdahl mainframes, OK?"

"Yes."

" ... You see, I want that RLO II Platter out of the hands of the Brooks Committee and into the hands of somebody who'll do with it what I tell them to do. I don't want somebody to run it up without first getting my instruction."

"Does it have to be that particular one?"

"Yes, either that or it will take me six months to re-write the sub-set. They want me to give them the codes to unravel everything. If I did, they wouldn't know what to do with it anyway. They'd make a mess out of things."

"Mike, what are you going to provide to FinCen?"

"I'm going to show them how these boys handled the life blood of the cash flow on a day to day basis. I'm going to unmask the whole operation ..."

"Anything specific on Robert Booth Nichols?"

Mike: "Nichols is Harold Okimoto's god-son. He's also Renee Hanner's (phonetic sp.) boy, and Wolfgang Fosog's (phonetic sp.) boy."

" ... And who are they?"

"The FinCen people will know. There's also Octon Potnar --"

"Alright. Well, if I'm going to play around with this, I don't want to be in the dark ... I could end up like Danny. I've got to know what I'm dealing with ."

"If you get the right guy at FinCen, he'll jump at this, OK? We've got to start right now. We're talking about some time getting things up and rolling to where we're fluid and flexible and functional in their system internationally. They'll be able to watch the daily transactions ..."

••••••••

Michael continued to request of J.H. that he be connected with someone "trustworthy" at FinCen, to no avail. He also requested to be placed into a Witness Protection Program, again offering to assemble his computer equipment in a secret location and provide FinCen with a day by day view of alleged Mob (and MCA Corporation) illegal banking transactions.

According to Michael, before his arrest, he had been handling gold transfers, money laundering, "virtual dead drops," altered ACH daily reconciliations and other transactions for various underworld figures including Robert Booth Nichols, (names withheld) ... Gilbert Rodriguez, Jose Londono, and others.

Michael continued to call and give me tape-recorded (at his request) messages to pass on to J.H. The man accepted the messages, but they just went down the big, black hole and never emerged again.

One message in particular later became significant to me. The message from Michael to J.H. went as follows: (Quote)

> There are three dozen C-130's down at the Firebird Lake Airstrip on the Gila Indian Reservation in Arizona. Check out J & G Aviation, it's an FBO. The Fresno Company is alive and well down there.
>
> The real activity is not at Mirana, it's at Firebird Lake Airstrip. Other airlines operating at Firebird are Beigert, Macavia International, Pacific Air Express, Evergreen and Southern Air.
>
> Question to J.H.: How much cocaine or heroin can be transported in a C-130? Do you want the C-130, or do you want the guys who orchestrate it?
>
> Do a matrix link analysis, then sit down and pick the targets. Otherwise, you will tip off the others and the proof will dry up.
>
> ... Brian Leighton made 29 arrests out of five hundred within the Fresno Company. All Leighton succeeded in doing was to `vaccinate' the Fresno Company against further penetration."

Riconosciuto said he had a fragile window into this organization (The Company), but Leighton and others were causing the window to close by being too public about their investigation.

The message continued regarding Robert Booth Nichols:

> Bob Nichols runs Glenn Shockly Shockley runs Jose Londono. I [Michael] sat with Bob Nichols and Mike Abbell. Bob handed him $50,000 cash to handle an internal affairs investigation that the Justice Department conducted which would have led to the extradition of Gilbert and Miguel Rodriguez and Jose Londono.
>
> Bob Nichols told me [Michael] that it was necessary to `crow-bar' the investigation because they were `intelligence people.'"

Michael wanted to hand The Company and Bob Nichols over to FinCen in exchange for entry into the Witness Protection Program, but nothing was forthcoming from J.H.

It was two years before I learned who Mike Abbell, Gilbert Rodriguez and Jose Londono were. Abbell had worked in the criminal division of the Justice Department, according to Bill Hamilton. Hamilton added that, to his knowledge, Abbell had left the DOJ in 1984 and went directly into the Bogota, Colombia law offices of Kaplan and Russin.

Abbell's background was obtained from library directories: From 1973 to 1979 Abbell was staff assistant to the Assistant U.S. Attorney General. From 1979 to 1982 he was the Director of the Office of International Affairs of the Criminal Division of the Department of Justice.

After leaving the Department of Justice in 1984, Abbell became counsel at the law firm of Kaplan, Russin and Becchi, with offices in San Francisco, California – Bogota, Colombia – Santo Domingo in the Dominican Republic – Bangkok, Thailand – Tapai, Taiwan – New York – Madrid, Spain – and Miami, Florida.

Abbell was listed as working in his own firm with a partner named Bruno Ristau (Ristau and Abbell) in Washington D.C. Ristau was also formerly with the law firm of Kaplan, Russin and Becchi. And from 1958 to 1963 he was an attorney in the Internal Security Division and Civil Division of the Department of Justice. He was also with the DOJ from 1963 to 1981 where he was Director of the Office of Foreign Litigation. Ristau speaks German, Polish, Spanish and French. He was Chairman of the Division of International Law of the Washington D.C. Bar from 1971 to 1973. In the American Bar Association from 1981 to 1984, he was Chairman of the Committee of Private International Law Practice. He is also a member of the American Society of International Law. Ristau is obviously a heavyweight in the field of international law.

A *Time* magazine article, dated July 4, 1994, described Gilbert Rodriguez as a "leader of the Cali [Colombian drug] cartel, which controls 80% of the world's cocaine trade." The newly elected president of Colombia, Ernesto Samper Pizano, was accused of taking $3.7 million in campaign funds from Rodriguez, which in effect, put Samper in league with Colombia's drug lords.

Three audio tapes of conversations between Rodriguez and Samper's campaign manager, Santiago Medina, had been handed over to U.S. State Department officials before the election, but nothing was done. DEA officials were furious, stating to *Time* that "No one did anything. They [the State Department] allowed this travesty to take place. Everybody, including the U.S. government, is participating in this cover-up."

The State Department responded, "We can't interfere with elections."

I pulled out a book from a dusty corner of my library entitled, *Cocaine Politics* by Peter Dale Scott and Jonathan Marshall, and looked up the name Gilbert Rodriguez. On page 83, Gilberto Rodriguez Orejuela and Jose Santacruz Londono were mentioned as part of the early leadership of the Cali Cartel. On page 88 it was noted that the "Cali-based Ocampo and Gilberto Rodriguez had been the principal targets of a major DEA Centac investigation that resulted in indictments of Rodriguez in Los Angeles and New York in 1978."

At that time, President Jimmy Carter's Human Rights foreign policy in Latin America distanced the CIA under Stansfield Turner (later a Wackenhut Board Director) from any death-squad interdiction. The Carter administration was also reportedly reluctant to go after Ocampo because of its determination in 1977 to sign a Panama Canal treaty with General Torrijos, even though Torrijos and family members were heavily involved at the highest levels of the world cocaine trade.

The Cali Cartel, described in a 1983 Customs report, laundered its profits through Miami banks, one of which was Northside Bank of Miami, owned by Gilberto Rodriguez. Rodriguez popped up again as the leader of a delegation to the "cocaine summit conference" in Panama City in the early 1980's. Yet, Rodriguez's name was subsequently removed from DEA reports under the Ronald Reagan administration. In fact, according to disgruntled DEA agents, some of whom suspected they were stumbling into a CIA connection, the case was never pursued past the indictment level and the Centac 21 task force was totally dismantled when Reagan and Bush came to office.

So, Gilbert Rodriguez and Jose Londono were revealed to be high ranking members of the Cali drug cartel in Colombia. I wondered if they were also CIA intelligence operatives? Or CIA drug operatives? Or both, as Manuel Noriega had been? Noriega had ultimately been ousted when he chose to back the violent Medellin cartel, George Bush's target. If in fact Gilberto Rodriguez had been compromised and forced to cooperate with U.S. officials after his 1978 indictment, and taking into account his strategic position of leadership in the Cali Cartel and his alleged funding of the newly elected president of Colombia in 1994, it would indeed place the U.S. government in a powerful controlling position within Colombia and the cartels at that time. In fact, it would place CIA drug operatives behind the election of the president of Colombia! The implications were earthshaking.

♦♦♦♦♦♦♦♦

It is important to point out here that, on August 5, 1991, Michael Riconosciuto had called Bill Hamilton at Inslaw and asked him to obtain information on former DOJ official Mike Abbell. Riconosciuto planned to trade information on Abbell, Rodriguez, Nichols and others to the FBI in exchange for entry into a Witness Protection Program.

But Hamilton, pressed for time and not comprehending the significance of the "drug" connection, had turned the investigation over to Danny Casolaro. Riconosciuto had stressed to Hamilton that Abbell's activities might be risky to track and he should not take the information lightly.

That same day, August 5, Casolaro called Bob Bickel, the Texas oil engineer who once worked as an informant for the Customs Bureau, to discuss Mike Abbell. Bickel later confirmed that Casolaro had in fact discussed Abbell, Nichols and Rodriguez at length during that last phone conversation. And he added, "Danny confronted Robert Booth Nichols about his relationship with Mike Abbell."

Hamilton and Casolaro secretly devised a plan whereby Danny would conduct an inquiry with the Department of Justice, but would couch a number of other inquiries in with the Mike Abbell inquiry to avoid alerting authorities to the real "focus" of their search.

An October 15, 1991 *Village Voice* investigative piece, entitled "The Last Days of Danny Casolaro," by James Ridgeway and Doug Vaughan, shed further light on Casolaro's investigation during those last five days: (Note that most of Danny's last calls focused on "drug connections.")

> **On Monday, August 5th:** "Riconosciuto called Bill Hamilton from his jail in Tacoma. He wanted some information about a former Justice Department attorney [Mike Abbell], and warned Hamilton that getting the information might be dangerous. Hamilton called Casolaro to help him find out about the attorney.
>
> That same day, Danny called Bob Bickel to say that he was "getting close to the source, and he would soon go to Martinsburg and bring back the head of the Octopus."
>
> **Tuesday, August 6:** Casolaro had been typing steadily since Monday, and by afternoon, he'd finished. Olga, his housekeeper, helped him pack a leather tote bag. She also remembered him packing a thick sheaf of papers into a dark brown or black briefcase. Danny walked out the door saying, "I have all my papers ... Wish me luck. I'll see you in a couple of days." That was the last time Olga saw Casolaro alive.
>
> **Wednesday, August 7:** According to Inslaw records, Casolaro called the Hamiltons in the afternoon, and was put on hold. Before Hamilton could get free, he had hung up. At some time on that same day, Riconosciuto called Hamilton again to ask for the information about the Justice Department lawyer [Mike Abbell]. Hamilton called Casolaro, but he had already left for Martinsburg.
>
> **Thursday, August 8:** Casolaro called Danielle Stalling and asked her to set up appointments for him the next week with a former police officer, now employed as a private investigator, to learn more about the Laotian warlord Kuhn Sa's proposed Golden Triangle drug trade.
>
> **Friday, August 9:** By now Hamilton was starting to worry. "I talk to Danny everyday," Hamilton said. "I had never [gone without

speaking to him for so long] before, so I called Bob Nichols in Los Angeles and asked whether he had heard from Danny recently."

Nichols told Hamilton "Yes," he had spoken with Danny late Monday night [August 5th] and he had been "euphoric." Nichols told Hamilton he (Nichols) was taking off for Europe that evening.

It was at that point that Olga, Danny's housekeeper, received four or five threatening phone calls. The first was about 9 A.M., a man's voice, in good English, said, "I will cut his [Danny's] body and throw it to the sharks."About a half-hour later, another call came in. "Drop dead," the man's voice said.

Saturday, August 10: At 12:30 that afternoon, a maid knocked on the door of room 517 at the Sheraton Martinsburg Inn. Nobody answered, so she used her passkey to open the door; though it had both a security bolt and a chain lock on the inside, neither one was attached. When she glanced into the bathroom, she saw a lot of blood on the tile floor and screamed. Another hotel maid came into the bathroom and saw a man's nude body lying in the blood-filled tub. There was blood not only on the tile floor but splattered up onto the wall above the tub as well. The police were called to the scene.

At 8:30 P.M. that night, unaware that Danny's body had been found, Olga, Danny's housekeeper, returned to Casolaro's house to look for him. The phone rang. A man's voice said, "You son of a bitch. You're dead." It was not until Monday, August 12, that authorities notified family and friends that Danny Casolaro was dead.

Had Danny in fact called Robert Booth Nichols on Monday, August 5th, and confronted him about his relationship with Mike Abbell? Had he told Nichols he planned to meet with FBI officials from Lexington, Kentucky? And what about FBI agent Thomas Gates, Nichols' antagonist? *SPY* magazine's article on Danny Casolaro indicated that he spoke with Gates three days before his death, relating a conversation in which Nichols had warned him to abandon the investigation.

Riconosciuto later conceded that he had tried repeatedly to reach Hamilton and Casolaro between August 5 and 10th to warn them *not* to mention Abbell or Rodriguez to Nichols, but it had been too late. Bill Hamilton told one investigator that he didn't know why Riconosciuto was inquiring about Mike Abbell - until *after* Danny's death.

Bob Bickel's confirmation that Danny *was* trailing Mike Abbell in the last days before his death indicate that Danny may have unknowingly stepped into the largest narcotics trafficking/intelligence operation the world.

••••••••

Another in-depth article came to my attention which further corroborated Danny's investigation of Gilberto Rodriguez. "The Strange Death of Danny Casolaro," by Ron Rosenbaum in *Vanity Fair's* December 1991 issue included an interview with Michael Riconosciuto. According to Rosenbaum, Danny's investigations were taking him into areas that involved dangerous knowledge and dangerous characters. It was Danny's habit of "bouncing" Riconosciuto's stories off Robert Nichols that put him in peril, Riconosciuto told Rosenbaum. One of the things he reportedly "bounced" *involved a major heroin-related sting operation.*

Another involved Riconosciuto's claim about an "*effort by the Cali cocaine cartel to derail the extradition of an alleged Colombian kingpin called Gilberto*."

Nichols "went ballistic," according to Riconosciuto, when Danny bounced the Gilberto (Rodriguez) matter off him. Riconosciuto said he tried to warn Danny. "I called from that day on – it was on a late Monday – Tuesday, Wednesday, all the way through the weekend when they found Danny [dead]," he said. "Every day I was calling the Hamiltons, asking if anybody had heard from Danny. And I was frantic."

Labeled by Rosenbaum as the "resident demon of the labyrinth," Riconosciuto said "Danny's theory was different from the typical mega-conspiracy theory. Danny was dealing with real people and real crimes."

Rosenbaum asked Riconosciuto about the germ warfare technology he had found in Danny's notes. Riconosciuto admitted that he had learned about "horrible things" going on at the Cabazon Indian reservation but did not elaborate on the subject. Wrote Rosenbaum, "This is the labyrinth [that] Riconosciuto was leading Danny into – the one he died in."

Just days before his death, Danny had planned to visit the reservation. In his notes were cryptic references to slow-acting brain viruses like Mad Cow Disease, which could be used against targeted people by slipping the virus into meat pies. Riconosciuto told Rosenbaum that Danny was "concerned" that he may have been a target of this virus. "That was one of the reasons he [Danny] had such an obsession with this story. He felt he had been hit by these people."

Accordingly, Riconosciuto filled Danny's head with allegations of Robert Booth Nichols' sinister, international covert-world connections. He painted a picture linking Nichols to organized crime syndicates, the fearsome Japanese Yakuza, and various CIA and British intelligence plots emanating from Nichols' friendship with "a legendary Bond-ish Brit known as `Double Deuce' [Sir Denis Kendall]."

Riconosciuto said Nichols was the key to Danny's Octopus. But Danny was receiving warnings from Riconosciuto's counterpart as well. Robert Booth Nichols had flown to Washington D.C. from Puerto Rico to warn Danny to stay away from Riconosciuto.

Danny's girlfriend, Wendy Weaver, had been present at one of the meetings at the Four Seasons Hotel bar when Nichols issued the warning: "You don't know how bad this guy Riconosciuto is ... he might not get you today, he might not get you next month. He might get you two years from now. If you say anything against him he will kill you."

Nichols repeated the warning several times, said Weaver. "At least five times." Weaver described Nichols as "very charming, very handsome," but said "it [the meeting] was a weird night, so weird."

Another friend of Danny's met Nichols at a luncheon at Clyde's in Tysons Corner where Nichols allegedly informed them that he had just been asked to become "minister of state security" on the island of Dominica. Reportedly, the island was going to be transformed into a CIA base. The friend, who spoke to Rosenbaum on condition of anonymity, said Nichols was "very slick, very civilized-appearing" ... "oozing intrigue," but he added that he had never witnessed a performance like the one that ensued.

After lunch Danny had pulled his friend aside and showed him a purported FBI *wiretap summary on Nichols.* The summary was part of FBI agent Thomas Gates's affidavit in Nichols' slander suit against him. *The summary linked Nichols to the Yakuza and to the Gambino crime family as a money launderer.*

Danny's friend had been shocked. "You just put me in a meeting with this man and didn't tell me, what the hell – why didn't you tell me before?," he asked Danny. Danny said he wanted to see how Nichols would react. The friend told Rosenbaum, "In other words, he gaffed me with a hook and tossed me in the water to see if the Octopus would move!"

Danny *had* in fact been receiving death threats on the phone. One threat reported by his housekeeper, "You're dead, you son of a bitch," which came hours *after* Danny's body had been found, ruled out Danny himself as a possible source of the threats. And his prophesy to his brother, Tony Casolaro, "If anything happens to me it won't be an accident," made it unmistakably clear that Danny did, indeed, feel threatened.

Nevertheless, Danny appeared upbeat to most of the people he talked to prior to his death. Dr. Tony Casolaro, a specialist in pulmonary medicine, told *Vanity Fair* that he didn't believe his brother committed suicide because Danny was so excited and upbeat about his investigation on that last Monday when he saw him.

The autopsy examination of Danny's brain had revealed possible symptoms of Multiple Sclerosis, but friends and family dismissed this as irrelevant because Danny had never complained of symptoms or, to their knowledge, known of the disease, if he had it.

Tony was also troubled by a number of facts, one of which was Danny's current papers and files which he took to West Virginia were missing from his motel room. His body had been embalmed even before family members were notified of the death, and the motel room had been commercially cleaned before any type of investigation, other than a cursory look at the death scene by police, could occur.

In his *Vanity Fair* article, Ron Rosenbaum wrote that he had obtained one of Casolaro's surviving notebooks and found mentioned under the heading of August 6, four days before Danny's death, the name "*Gilberto.*" It read: "Bill Hamilton – August 6. MR ... also brought up `*Gilberto.*'" Rosenbaum did not speculate publicly who Gilberto might be, but it was obviously Gilberto Rodriguez, head of the Cali Cartel, at that time deeply involved with Michael Abbell, formerly of the Department of Justice.

••••••••

A dozen or so drafts of Casolaro's proposed manuscript along with notes and phone bills had been sent to the Western Historical

Manuscript Collection at the University of Missouri by his brother, Dr. Tony Casolaro. Tony had sent the material to the University because, at one time, the IRE (Investigative Reporters and Editors) Association, headquartered at the University, had researched the fatal car-bombing of reporter Don Bolles in Arizona.

Bolles had been researching a mob-connected gold smuggling operation in that state. Through Tracy Barnett at IRE, I learned that a graduate student at the University had been assigned to catalog all Danny's material for eventual insertion into a data-base. In contacting the graduate student, who by then (September 1994) worked for ABC in Houston, Texas, I learned that few if any journalists had inquired about the notes.

But, interestingly, Chief Assistant U.S. Attorney Steve Zipperstein from Los Angeles, working for the Department of Justice, had requested copies of Danny's notes, but declined Danny's phone records. The graduate student noted that the notes and drafts of Danny's proposed manuscript focused on a Cabal of intelligence people who, originally consisting of numerous names, were subsequently narrowed down to about eight. One of those names was Glen Shockley. Shockley, of course, was listed on the Board of Directors of FIDCO along with Robert Booth Nichols. Shockley was also a corporate partner in Meridian International Logistics, headed by Nichols.

I purchased everything of any significance pertaining to Danny's writings and documents, including the FBI wire-tap summaries which corroborated everything I had learned to date.

In reviewing the summaries, it became apparent that the FBI had inadvertently stumbled onto a government drug trafficking operation which included high ranking La Cosa Nostra figures, the Gambino crime family and the Japanese Yakuza.

One affidavit in support of an application to intercept wire communications over the telephone listed names of those to be intercepted: Robert Booth Nichols, Eugene Giaquinto (then President of MCA Corporation Entertainment Division, and corporate partner with Nichols in Meridian International Logistics), Angelo Commito, Edward Sciandra, Michael Del Gaizo, Joseph Garofalo, and others.

The purpose of the interceptions was to determine "source, type and quantity of narcotics/controlled substances, methods and means of delivery, and the source of funding for purchasing of narcotics/controlled substances."

The intercepted conversations read like a "Who's Who" of organized crime. It was also apparent that Eugene Giaquinto enjoyed a special relationship with John Gotti.

••••••••

Ann Klenk, a long time friend of Danny Casolaro's and former associate of Washington D.C. columnist Jack Anderson, held all his personal notes which were not sent to the University. In a September 14, 1994 phone interview, she noted that the last time she talked to Danny, that last Monday before his death, he told her he'd cracked the Inslaw case.

I asked her, "Do you think he resolved that?"

Ann responded, "Oh, yes. I know he did. He told me he did. He said, `Ann, I broke Inslaw.' And I said, `Geez, Danny that's great!' But, I never asked him what he found because he was very despondent about it. He said, `You can have it. You and Jack [Anderson] can have the story. I don't even want it.'"

Ann said Danny was disgusted and related their last conversation: "I said, `Danny, you worked on this [so long] and now you don't want it?' He said, `It's just a little piece of the puzzle anyway.' See, Inslaw led him into this, but Danny quickly became more involved with the *drug aspects* ... with the CIA aspects, with the Wackenhut aspects."

I mused, "I know what you mean, because I followed the same trail."

••••••••

Danny's proposed drafts and notes obtained from Western Historical Manuscript Collection at University of Missouri revealed information never published in mainstream media. Typewritten and handwritten lists of contacts included names and telephone numbers of Ted Gunderson, Raymond Lavas, Robert Nichols, Peter Zokosky, Bob Bickel, Fahim Safar, Earl Brian, Peter Dale Scott, Art Welmas, John Vanderwerker, Jack Blum, Dr. Harry Fair, Bill Hamilton, Bob Parry, Bill McCoy, and numerous others.

Most of Danny's drafts focused on the Southeast Asian heroin connection, CIA drug money used to finance the Contras, and the ability of terrorists to send missiles containing dangerous chemicals and biological diseases into the U.S.

One typewritten draft, entitled, "Behold, A Pale Horse," described an "international cabal [in Southern California] whose freelance services covered parochial political intrigue, espionage, sophisticated weapon technologies that included bio-toxins, *drug trafficking, money laundering* and murder-for-hire, that emerged from an isolated desert Indian reservation ..." According to Danny, the cabal continues today, "its origins spawned thirty years ago in the shadow of the Cold War."

Though there were no dates on his drafts, it appeared that his list of names in the cabal, or those whom he believed headed The Octopus, grew as his investigation progressed. Such names as Richard Helms, Howard Hunt, Kim Philby, Robert Chasen, Ray Cline, Edwin Wilson, and others were scribbled throughout his notes.

The backgrounds of these men is discussed in a future chapter, but Danny left clues in his notes. One clue read as follows: " ... While a few of these eight men actually came together as an 'impossible mission' force in the fifties to make sure that an initiative in Albania failed, almost every one of them were used to frustrate the Cuban Bay of Pigs invasion."

Casolaro's June – July (1991) phone bills told a story of their own. Having followed Danny's investigative trail for three years, I had an entire directory of phone numbers relating to his inquiries. Most obvious were Danny's numerous calls prior to his death to Robert Booth Nichols in Los Angeles. Most of the calls from Washington D.C. to Los Angeles lasted an average of one to two hours, invariably in the wee hours of the morning – 1:50 A.M. 12:36 A.M. 1:13 A.M. 12:18 A.M. etc.

It was also apparent that Danny was riding a see-saw with Nichols and Riconosciuto. He would talk to one, then the other, often on the same day, back and forth for months. Then suddenly, he cut off Riconosciuto and his calls to Nichols increased in frequency.

Other phone numbers matched those of Ted Gunderson, Alan Boyak, a lawyer in Utah, Bo Gritz, Heinrich Rupp and Chuck Hayes, a self-professed (on the Internet) CIA operative. Oddly, Hayes never came forward during the official investigation of Danny's death to disclose the content of those conversations.

••••••••

Within six months of Casolaro's death, Riconosciuto was again attempting to trade information in exchange for entry into a Witness Protection Program. But this time, instead of using Casolaro or Bill Hamilton, he was using me to make the contacts.

At Riconosciuto's request, I contacted a man whom I will identify as N.B. at the BATF (Bureau of Alcohol, Tobacco & Firearms) in San Francisco. Michael had advised me to call this agent because the BATF was "Treasury Department" – as was FinCen.

I set up the phone meeting and Riconosciuto called the San Francisco BATF collect, as scheduled. N.B. listened attentively to Michael, then ran a check on him through the departmental computer system. Shortly thereafter, I received an unnerving phone call.

N.B. advised me in strong terms to "get out of this" while I still could. He said I would end up getting subpoenaed as a witness if I didn't discontinue my investigation. He added that sometimes people got killed or committed suicide when they got involved with Michael Riconosciuto or Robert Booth Nichols.

N.B.'s computer inquiry had bounced back on him. His superior in the BATF had been notified by someone from another agency, he didn't say who, who had instructed N.B. that he was to have no further contact with Michael Riconosciuto or me.

When I related this conversation to Michael, he indicated no surprise, but immediately wanted to be put back in touch with J.H. He needed someone in the government with access to his files to verify his credibility and get that information back to Tom Olmstead, his attorney. Regarding the computer inquiry, Riconosciuto explained as follows: "I know what's happening here. Tell J.H. if he uses FOIMS, Field Office Information Management System, and if he leaves an audit trail, he's going to be exposed. There are all sorts of different levels of flags on my name. Whenever the computer gets a hit, the issuing agency is notified as to who made the request and from where it came."

"Mike," I asked, "how can he get around that? I don't understand ..."

"Listen, whenever there's a hit on one of those flags, whether it's a want or [a] warrant, or whether it's simply an administrative interest, unbeknownst to the user who's making the request, his access is audited. Tell J.H. before he starts making inquiries, no matter how discreet he thinks they are, that he should have someone totally uncoupled from him to enter into FOIMS."

"Alright."

"Now," Michael continued, "if he goes into NCIC or NADDIS, ah, NCIC is the least dangerous as far as making inquiries, because NADDIS can track just like FOIMS ..."

"Alright."

"Now, on NCIC there is a `non-electric' filing on me and he can make the request that way without alerting anyone. If he has trouble checking anything out, tell him I can help him along."

"He can't call you at the jail. How can he get in touch with you?"

"Through my attorney. The minute he [J.H.] gets a line on me, ask him to notify my attorney. Tell him he can check my attorney out through the government. Tom has excellent records with the government."

"Alright."

"Explain to J.H. that I know PROMIS, I know FOIMS inside out. I helped develop that internal tracking audit trail ..."

I had lost all hope of J.H. rescuing Michael Riconosciuto, and I think in his heart, Michael knew that too, but I passed the information along as requested. J.H. politely accepted the information as he always did, then I never heard from him again.

— 7 —

FIDCO

I was subsequently able to obtain the corporate documents on FIDCO Corporation (First Intercontinental Development Corporation). This formidable organization led me straight to the head of The Octopus. The Board of Directors of FIDCO consisted of the following principles:

(1) Robert Maheu, Sr, Vice President, Director – former FBI agent, former CEO of Howard Hughes Operations, senior consultant to Leisure Industries.
(2) Michael A. McManus, Director, Vice President and General Counsel to FIDCO – former Assistant to the President [Reagan] of the United States at the White House in Washington D.C.
(3) Robert Booth Nichols, Director, Sr. Vice President and Chairman of Investment Committee – Chief Executive Officer of R.B.N. Companies, International, a holding company for manufacturing and development of high technology electronics, real estate development, construction and international finance.
(4) George K. Pender, Director – former Director of Pacific Ocean area of Burns & Roe, Inc., an international engineering & construction corporation with active projects on all seven continents of the world. Senior engineer consultant to Burns & Roe, Inc.
(5) Kenneth A. Roe, Director – Chairman and President of Burns & Roe, Inc., International engineers and Constructors, a family corporation owned by Kenneth Roe and family. Major current project of the company is the engineering design and construction of the U.S.A. Fast Breeder Nuclear Reactor Plant in conjunction with Westinghouse Electric Corporation which is responsible for the nuclear system supply of steam. Construction value

of present business backlog of Burns & Roe, Inc. is in excess of six billion U.S. dollars.
(6) Frances T. Fox, Vice President and Director – former General Manager of L.A. International Airport, former Director of Aviation for Howard Hughes Nevada operations, now called Summa Corporation, City Manager of San Jose, California.
(7) Clint W. Murchison, Jr. Director – Owner of the Dallas Cowboys NFL football team.
(8) William M. Pender, Director and Sr. Vice President – licensed contractor, State of California.
(9) Glen R. Shockley, Director – Consultant to Fortune 500 Companies in business management. Internationally known as financial consultant in funding.

The list of directors was accompanied by a letter dated January 11, 1983 on FIDCO letterhead originating out of Santa Monica, California addressed to Robert Booth Nichols in Marina Del Rey, California. The letter, signed by George K. Pender, briefly referenced a copy of a resolution resulting from a meeting of the Board of Directors of FIDCO.

On April 13, 1983, Robert Booth Nichols wrote a letter to Joseph F. Preloznik in Madison, Wisconsin, outlining proposed arms projects, one of which was to build a two story building of approximately 7500 square feet with concrete walls and floors to house the "R & D position." (I later found the R & D facility referenced in a 1981 Wackenhut Inter-office memorandum as a companion facility to Wackenhut to be constructed on the Cabazon Indian reservation for the assembly of shell casings, propellants, war heads, fuses, combustible cartridge cases and other weapons systems).

Nichols wrote to Preloznik, "Should there be any questions with regard to my credibility, verification can be made through F.I.D.C.O. I have enclosed a copy of that appointment."

If in fact, FIDCO was a vehicle of The Octopus, then the tentacles of its Board of Directors lead straight to the head. Clint Murchison, Jr. of Dallas, Texas was the son of Clint Murchison, Sr. who, according to Dick Russell, author of the book, *The Man Who Knew Too Much*, (pp. 521-523) was cut from the same political cloth as H.L. Hunt.

Wrote Russell: "Back in 1951, after General Douglas MacArthur was relieved of his Korean command by President Harry Truman,

H.L. Hunt accompanied MacArthur on a flight to Texas for a speaking tour. Hunt and Murchison were the chief organizers of the pro-MacArthur forces in Texas. They would always remember the general standing bareheaded in front of the Alamo, urging removal of the `burden of taxation' from enterprising men like themselves, charging that such restraints were imposed by `those who seek to convert us to a form of socialistic endeavor, leading directly to the path of Communist slavery.'"

According to Russell, Hunt went on to set up a MacArthur-for-president headquarters in Chicago, spending $150,000 of his own money on the general's reluctant 1952 campaign, which eventually fell apart as MacArthur adopted the strident rhetoric of the right wing.

> Still, connections were made, Charles Willoughby, for example, was a regular part of the MacArthur-Hunt entourage and undoubtedly was acquainted with Murchison as well." Both [the Hunts and the Murchisons] cultivated not only powerful people on the far right, but also J. Edgar Hoover, Richard Nixon, organized crime figures, and Lyndon Johnson, whose rise to power emanated directly from his friends in Texas oil.
>
> Like Hunt, Murchison was an ardent supporter of Senator Joseph McCarthy's anti-communist crusade. McCarthy came often to the exclusive hotel that Murchison opened in La Jolla, California, in the early 1950's. So did Richard Nixon and J. Edgar Hoover.
>
> In 1961, after Nixon had lost the presidential election to JFK the previous year, Murchison sold Nixon a lot in Beverly Hills for only $35,000 – a lot Murchison had financed through a Hoffa loan – which Nixon sold two years later for $86,000.

When Hoover visited the (Murchison) Hotel Del Charro, as he did every summer between 1953 and 1959, Murchison picked up his tab. That amounted to about $19,000 of free vacations for the FBI Director over those years.

Whether Hoover knew it or not, almost 20 percent of the Murchison Oil Lease Company in Oklahoma was then owned by Gerardo Catena, chief lieutenant to the Genovese crime family.

By the autumn of 1963, a major scandal was brewing around Bobby Baker, whom Vice President Lyndon Johnson had made secretary of the Senate Democrats in 1955, when LBJ was majority leader. LBJ called Baker "my strong right arm, the last man I see at night, the first I see in the morning."

On October 8, 1963 Baker was forced to resign, as a Senate investigation of his outside business activities began producing sensational testimony on numerous questionable deals. "Baker's deals were tightly interwoven with the Murchison family – and the Mob," wrote Dick Russell.

> What first attracted the attention of Senate investigators was a lawsuit brought against Baker in 1963 by his associates in a vending company, alleging that he failed to live up to certain bargains. Those associates were, for the most part, Las Vegas gamblers; one of them, Edward Levinson, was a lieutenant of Florida mobster Meyer Lansky, whose Fremont Hotel in Vegas was financed through a Hoffa loan.
>
> Baker, it later turned out, did considerable business with the Mob in Las Vegas, Chicago, Louisiana, and the Caribbean. Through Baker, Levinson had also gotten to know Clint Murchison."
>
> Clint Murchison, Jr. [listed on the Board of Directors of FIDCO] tried to persuade the Senate Rules Committee in 1964 that his real estate dealings with Jimmy Hoffa in Florida were `hardly relevant' to the Baker investigation."

Robert Maheu (Senior Vice President and Director of FIDCO), was also mentioned in Russell's book, *The Man Who Knew Too Much*, (pp. 190). Wrote Russell:

> Back in 1960, with then vice president Richard Nixon serving as the White House's liaison to the CIA's Cuban operations, the CIA had initiated its long series of assassination attempts against Castro. The 'cut-outs' in the operation started with Las Vegas billionaire Howard Hughes's right-hand man, Robert Maheu, who got in touch with organized-crime leaders Sam Giancana, Johnny Rosselli, and Santos Trafficante, Jr. They in turn enlisted the direct assistance of Cuban exiles ..."

In August, 1994, I managed to obtain three significant letters with the signatures of Michael A. McManus and George Pender (FIDCO) on them. The following letters on FIDCO confirmed its presence in Lebanon:

Letter No. 1 – Written on White House letterhead stationary, dated, June 29, 1983, from Michael A. McManus, Assistant to the President (Reagan) to George K. Pender in Santa Monica, California:

> Dear George: It was good to see you again. I appreciate the update you and your associates gave me concerning the status of your efforts in the rebuilding of Lebanon.
>
> Without question FIDCO seems to have a considerable role to offer particularly in the massive financial participation being made available to the government of Lebanon.
>
> As you are aware, the United States government is providing financial aid. We are very interested in the success of the rebuilding effort in Lebanon. I will appreciate your continuing to keep me posted. Best personal regards. Sincerely, Michael A. McManus, Assistant to the President.

It is interesting to note that in 1982, one year before the above letter was written, Israel invaded Lebanon in a bid to crush the PLO strongholds there and install the Gamayel family in power. At that time Tel-Aviv was supporting the ultra-right Christian Phalange militia. It was the Christian Phalangist militia which first brought Lebanon into the heroin trade. And it was the powerful Christian Gamayel family which led the way in turning to outside forces for money, guns and political support. Foremost among those sources was the international heroin trafficking network. This according to Bill Weinberg, editor of *High Times* magazine, who wrote the in-depth article, "The Syrian Connection" in March 1993.

Weinberg also noted that as far back as 1955, U.S. Senate Judiciary Committee hearings learned that Sami el Khouri, the Gamayel's chief of finances, was importing raw Turkish opium into Lebanon, where it was processed into heroin and then shipped to Sicily for re-export throughout America and Europe.

El Khouri controlled the Gamayel family's shipping lines, trading, trucking and air freight companies. El Khouri's machine was the Lebanese wing of the French Connection – the wing that continued to do business with the Sicilians in a bid to propel the Gamayel family to power.

After the Israeli invasion, the Lebanese Parliament elected to the presidency Bashir Gamayel – who had long been on the CIA payroll. But before he could take office, Bashir was killed by an assassin's bomb, and Bashir's brother, Amin, was installed as president. Bashir was also known as "Bachir" Gemayel.

The following letter from George Pender, President of FIDCO, to President Amin Gamayel in Beirut is printed in its entirety here.

Letter No. 2 – Written on FIDCO letterhead stationary, dated July 12, 1983, from George K. Pender, President of FIDCO, to President Amin Gamayel, Presidential Palace, Beirut, Lebanon:

> Dear Mr. President: I had visited Beirut in February and May, 1983 to discuss FIDCO participation in the redevelopment of Lebanon. These meetings were held with the Chamouns, Maurice Ghanem and Mourad Baroudy. Of particular interest is the fact that FIDCO offered to arrange the financing of projects considered, provided they were in the government sector. Unfortunately, the response, to date, is dragging and a golden opportunity for Lebanon is slowly dying.
>
> I had made no effort to see you at that time as I thought it more prudent to delay until I had something more tangible to present. I expressed specific interest in the rebuilding of Damour and Alkhyam. FIDCO has presented these projects to an international Trust with whom we have a close relationship, and we are very confident that we can arrange the funding under International Chamber of Commerce format, provided FIDCO can negotiate turn-key contracts on both projects. We are ready, willing and able to proceed immediately on this basis.
>
> I understand you will be at the White House on July 22nd. Would it be possible for me to meet with you in Washington, D.C. on July 21st briefly so that I may personally present our interest in Lebanon? As per copy of attached letter, the White House is actively interested in our efforts.
>
> For your personal information, I was a good friend of Bechir. I was with him in Beirut in 1976 when the Syrian Army came in to police. When he later visited the United States on a speaking tour, my wife and I went to Framingham, Massachusetts to meet with him. I miss him tremendously.
>
> I would appreciate your reply as soon as possible. You can also reach me via telex 652483 RBN [Robert Booth Nichols] ASSOCS LSA.
>
> Thank you for your time and consideration.
> Sincerely yours,
> George K. Pender."

I cannot stress enough the importance of this letter From George Pender to Amin Gamayel. In the very first paragraph of Pender's letter he noted that "Maurice Ghanem" participated in the meetings held in Beirut in May 1983 to discuss FIDCO's participation in the redevelopment of Lebanon.

Michael Riconosciuto had stated to J.H. in the attempted trade into Witness Protection in 1991 that he had worked directly under "Maurice Ghanem" and George Pender in Lebanon! Riconosciuto had explained that Maurice had a "relative, either a brother or a cousin, who was a senior DEA official with Michael Hurley."

Then, in a 1993 book entitled, *Trail of the Octopus* by Donald Goddard with Lester Coleman, on page 152, I stumbled across the name of Fred Ghanem in the following context: "The number of DEA-controlled deliveries of heroin down the pipeline to the United States had increased noticeably during the winter as a result of Fred Ganem's special knowledge of the Lebanese communities in Detroit, Houston and Los Angeles."

This was independent corroboration of a link between FIDCO (George Pender and Michael McManus) and the very same heroin operation in Nicosia, Cyprus which Riconosciuto had described in detail to me in December 1991!

It also directly connected George Pender with Michael T. Hurley. Goddard and Coleman recounted how "members of the Jafaar clan and other DEA couriers would arrive at Larnaca with suitcases full of high-grade heroin, white and crystal, and be met off the boat ... by officers of the Cypriot Police Narcotics Squad, who then drove them up to the Euramae office in Nicosia."

In his interview with J.H., Riconosciuto had maintained that "FIDCO had a companion company called Euramae Trading ..." Three years later, *Trail of the Octopus*, described Euramae as such:

> Coleman was given a desk at the Euramae Trading Company., Ltd., a DEA/CIA 'front' newly set up by the Cypriot Police Narcotics Squad in a luxury three-bedroomed penthouse apartment down the street from the US Embassy. It gave him the creeps from the start.
>
> Intended as a place where DEA and CIA agents could meet unobserved with informants and clients, as a message drop for CIA arms dealers supplying Iraq and the Afghan rebels, as a waiting room for DEA CI's and couriers from Lebanon, and as

> a transit point, not just for heroin, but for cash, documents and bootleg computer software moving to and fro along the Beirut-Nicosia-US pipeline, Euramae, as run by El-Jorr, was more like a low-life social club than a secret intelligence centre.

Coleman had complained to Hurley, but Hurley had just brushed it aside.

It is noteworthy that George Pender listed Robert Booth Nichols's "telex" number at the bottom of his letter to Lebanon President Amin Gamayel. See letter No. 2 where Pender asked Gamayel to respond to "652483 RBN [Robert Booth Nichols] ASSOCS LSA." During that time span, Nichols and Pender (when they weren't in Lebanon) were operating a NSC listening post from a condo at Marina Del Rey. It was allegedly the U.S. end of the Nicosia, Cyprus operation.

Next, was the Lebanese response to George Pender's aforementioned letter (No. 2):

Letter No. 3 – Written on Arab Bank Limited letterhead, dated November 23, 1983, from Abdul Majeed Shoman, Chairman/General Manager of Arab Bank Limited in Amman, Jordan to George K. Pender in Santa Monica, California:

> Dear Mr. Pender: Mr. Ahmad has talked to me about the fund to reconstruct Lebanon and we the Arab Bank together with a group of other banks will be glad to cooperate with you concerning this respect.
>
> We shall discuss, in future, how this cooperation will be made and on what conditions and plans.
>
> You have mentioned in your letter to Mr. Ahmad on September 27th that this fund amounts to US$ three billion or more. There is no problem to take care of this by the Arab Bank and the other group of banks as stated above. The terms and conditions will be discussed with you provided the condition is clear in Lebanon and subject to the approval and counter guarantees of the Lebanese Authority. Yours sincerely, Abdul Majeed Shoman, Chairman/General Manager.

It is unlikely any "reconstruction" (funded by FIDCO) ever took place in Lebanon. Only a Congressional investigation could determine what the US$3 billion dollars was actually used for. However in a subsequent interview with Peter Zokosky, he maintained that

FIDCO was a NSC front corporation and the money was used to purchase the release of a hostage in Lebanon. Zokosky had briefly been a director in FIDCO, thus in a position to know such details.

The next document, pertaining to Robert Booth Nichols, Senior Vice President of FIDCO, originated from an interview between Jeffrey Steinberg, a writer for *Executive Intelligence Review*, and Allan Boyak, an attorney in Utah. The following "Memorandum for the File," dated 6-25-91, was written by Steinberg after his interview with Boyak: (excerpted)

> I met at length Saturday, June 22, 1991 with Allan Boyak, an attorney from Utah who is representing Michael Riconosciuto in his pending drug case. Boyak is not the lead attorney and will not apparently be making court appearances in the case.
>
> Boyak recounted the following personal background information: He was in the U.S. Army in Special Forces and apparently did some contract work for the CIA during the 1960's and early 1970's. At some point in the early 70's, he worked briefly for the Drug Enforcement Administration (or its antecedent agency), being stationed in California.
>
> Boyak had some falling out with the DEA and left the government service altogether, entering law school. While in law school, Boyak became friendly with Jim Nichols, a classmate. Nichols told him that he had a brother who was heavily involved in organized crime and had been disowned by his family.
>
> Once out of law school, Boyak joined a Hollywood law firm and became involved in criminal defense work, representing a number of well placed West Coast drug traffickers. At some point, Boyak moved to Utah (he is a practicing Mormon), while retaining his California law practice on a part-time basis.
>
> In addition to his o.c. [organized crime] clientèle, Boyak also maintained contacts and apparently did some legal work for some of his old buddies from his Green Beret and CIA days. One such pal was Art Suchesk, who ran a CIA proprietary company called Hoffman Electronics.
>
> ... At some point in the late 1970's, one of Boyak's clients, a Mormon old boy named Cap Kressop, who was a technical wizard, was approached by Robert Nichols and asked to manufacture a prototype laser site for a rifle. Kressop was offered a $200,000 contract for the job but he became suspicious when Nichols wanted to pay him in cash.

Boyak contacted Nichols at his Marina Del Rey, California home/office [apartment "007"] and the two had a lengthy meeting there. Boyack's description of that meeting is that it was continuously interrupted by telephone calls and telex messages. Boyak came away convinced that Nichols was involved in large scale illegal drug operations.

After consulting with one of his close friends from Green Beret days, then an assistant U.S. Attorney named Dexter Leitenen (now the Miami U.S. Attorney), Boyak went to the Los Angeles FBI office with the suspicions about Nichols' activities.

The FBI background check [conducted by Ted Gunderson] on Robert Booth Nichols (born 1943 or 1944 – he couldn't remember for sure) revealed that he was `squeaky clean.' In fact, he had a Class I machine gun license.

Boyak did discover, however, that one of the people Nichols referenced as a business associate and personal friend, Harold Okimoto, was believed by some of his sources to be a top Japanese organized crime figure based in Hawaii. Okimoto was described as a top agent in the Yakuza overseas.

Over the next two year period, after the L.A. FBI had dropped any interest in the Nichols matter, Boyack's friend, [Arthur] Suchesk, repeatedly ran into Nichols in such places as Singapore, the Philippines, and Taiwan. Suchesk was based out of Zurich, Switzerland during this period, apparently still doing his front man work for the CIA.

Boyak says that information developed during this period, through Suchesk and others, [indicated] that Nichols was indeed a bigtime drug dealer who was very well insulated from any U.S. law enforcement problems. Nichols operated exclusively overseas. Whenever he came to the United States, he never engaged in any illegal activities.

However, Boyak described Nichols' rum importing business as a cover for bigtime heroin trafficking from the Golden Triangle. Nichols was also named as `Mr. Big', according to Boyak, in the Medellin Cartel, in drug prosecutions in Utah and Los Angeles.

Three to four years ago, Boyack received an out of the blue telephone call from Michael Riconosciuto. Michael identified himself as a former employee of Robert Nichols. He also referenced Ted Gunderson as a `mutual friend.' Boyak had only met Ted once very briefly when he was pressing the L.A. FBI to look into the Nichols dope suspicions ..."

... Then in April 1991, Boyak received a phone call from Ted Gunderson, informing him that `Michael was in trouble. He was caught in a government frame-up.'

Boyak returned to his background profile of Bob Nichols, parts of which were apparently provided by Bob's estranged brother, Jim Nichols. It seems that as a young man, Robert Nichols wound up in Hawaii functioning as a hitman for the Tongs. He was `adopted' as the Yakuza godson of Harold Okimoto, a 67-year-old car dealer in Hawaii.

Nichols grew up to be a big business front man for the Far East syndicate. He reportedly laundered between $50-200 million for Ferdinand Marcos. He now owns an estate in Hawaii, a feudal castle outside of Milan, Italy and the referenced Marina Del Ray home in California.

Nichols has an office in Zurich. At one point, he was reportedly involved in the smuggling of China White heroin into Mexico where it was treated to look like the Mexican brown heroin which was more popular at the time.

It should be emphasized that all of this information about Robert Nichols comes exclusively from Allan Boyak. None of it has yet been independently corroborated to my knowledge. Bill Hamilton and some other people involved in tracking the Inslaw story have all spoken to [Robert] Nichols and report that he has been straightforward with them and has provided leads and documents re: Michael Riconosciuto.

Nichols is listed on the board of directors of First Intercontinental Development Corporation (FIDCO) along with George Pender and several officials of the Howard Hughes linked Suma Corporation."

Lester Coleman

— 8 —

The Lebanon Drug Connection

In March, 1993, two years after Michael Riconosciuto had attempted to trade information on the FIDCO/Euramae drug/intelligence operation in Lebanon to the government, the aforementioned magazine article printed in *High Times* magazine by Bill Weinberg, entitled, "The Syrian Connection," exposed CIA penetration into the Bekaa Valley drug trade in Lebanon.

Essentially, this article validated much of Riconosciuto's earlier information. The following are some excerpts:

> ... Many of Lebanon's armed factions depend on the international drug trade for funds," wrote Weinberg. "Each paramilitary group controls its own port in or around Beirut – which serves as a transfer point for drugs on the way out of Europe and America and weaponry on the way in from the international market. Whoever holds the fertile Bekaa [Valley] holds the ticket to power. As the war escalated in the late 1970's, hashish, the traditional mainstay of the Bekaa, started to be replaced by the more lucrative heroin. Marijuana fields were converted to opium fields, hashish production compounds converted to heroin labs.
>
> Heroin production exploded in the Bekaa Valley under the Syrian occupation. However, the Syrian occupation forces didn't touch the drugs, but "profited from the trade and protected it." It was estimated that up to $2 billion in protection money was paid annually by dope plantation operators to Syrian occupation forces.

> DEA official Felix Jimenez told a reporter in 1990 that the Syrian occupation received $10,000 per kilogram of Bekaa heroin. With the valley producing over 20,000 pounds a year, that was a lot of money.
>
> Bekaa also became a center for processing Colombian cartel cocaine for re-export to European markets.
>
> In 1988, two Syrians arrested with large quantities of heroin and coke in Milan [Italy] claimed to be working for a Syrian colonel in Bekaa. Prior to Desert Storm, Syria's president Hafez Assad and Iraq's Saddam Hussein were rival factions in the Arab nationalist Ba'ath Party. Syria was the only Arab nation to back Iran in the long and brutal war against Iraq in the 1980's. So when President George Bush invited Syria to join the Arab coalition against Saddam after Iraq's invasion of Kuwait, Assad accepted.
>
> After Desert Storm, Assad closed ranks with the White House and even softened his stand against Israel. President Bush and Secretary of State James Baker peddled a post-war peace plan for the region and Syria and Israel were encouraged to recognize each others' Lebanese occupation zones.
>
> Under a 1990 accord, Christians and Muslims were finally granted equal representation, officially bringing the civil war to an end. A new Syria-backed Muslim-led government came to power. Under the accord, Syria maintained control of the Bekaa Valley. Among the areas still under Syrian control were the notorious drug ports north of Beirut.

High Times maintained that there were long standing back-channel relations between Washington D.C. and Damascus. According to a 1987 Pentagon memo leaked to the Chicago paper, *In These Times,* Lt. Col. Oliver North was personally notified that Syrian intelligence in Lebanon was willing to negotiate with the White House for release of the hostages held by Lebanese terrorists.

The *Washington Jewish Week* reported that Bush himself had made secret visits to Damascus for hostage negotiations. But there were other reasons for the U.S. to be in Lebanon. In 1988, when Pan Am Flight 103 exploded over Scotland, Pan Am hired the private investigative firm of Interfor to look into the bombing. The owner, Juval Aviv, was reportedly a former Mossad agent.

Interfor maintained that the Syrian-backed Popular Front for the Liberation of Palestine-General Command (PFLP-GC) was behind the bombing. The PFLP-GC had been able to get their bomb on board the 747 because the flight was part of a heroin smuggling route run by a drug trafficking ring connected to the Syrian regime and protected by both the U.S. DEA and the CIA.

Interfor claimed the ring was overseen by Syrian kingpin Monzer Al-Kassar – often known as the world's biggest arms dealer. The CIA was protecting the Al-Kassar operation because he was cooperating with efforts to free U.S. hostages in Lebanon.

Reporter Bill Weinberg added that "the CIA and DEA had apparently both instructed Germany's internal intelligence agency, the BKA, to allow certain suitcases to pass uninspected onto US-bound flights at the Frankfort airport, where Flight 103 originated."

Apparently, unknown to anyone except the PFLP-GC and Al-Kassar, a suitcase which was supposed to be full of the usual heroin was covertly substituted with a suitcase full of explosives.

A *London Times* news article, dated July 22, 1991, entitled, "US Drugs Sting Gave Pan Am Bomber Cover," noted that the DEA admitted that the protection program had existed. The explanation for this operation, which was code-named Khourah, was provided by Ronald Caffrey, acting assistant administrator of the operational division of the DEA. In a U.S. government submission, dated March 20, 1991, Caffrey said the drug operation was a "controlled delivery."

According to Caffrey, in a controlled delivery, a law enforcement agency permits and monitors shipments of contraband, including drugs, to move from a source or transit location to its intended destination. Use of this technique is sometimes essential to enable law enforcement agencies to identify and arrest high-ranking members of trafficking organizations, rather than simply arrest low level couriers.

Pan Am argued in court that it had been the pawn of an international intelligence operation, but still lost the case and was forced into bankruptcy.

In 1990, when the White House started to woo Syria as a partner in the Allied coalition, blame for the Pan Am bombing suddenly shifted from Assad's Syria to Qaddafi's Libya, and that is pretty much where it stands today.

Meanwhile, Al-Kassar was alleged to have provided Oliver North with drug profits to purchase arms for the Nicaraguan Contras. The U.S. Tower Commission probe into Iran-gate revealed that Al-Kassar had been paid $1.2 million by Oliver North's co-conspirator General Richard Secord to move weapons from Israel to the Contras.

In her book *October Surprise*, former Reagan White House aide Barbara Honegger alleged that Al-Kassar's heroin smuggling network in Italy was used to launder NATO arms stocks for diversion to Iran with the help of corrupt Italian intelligence officials linked to the secretive fascist Masonic lodge, P2.

It is noteworthy that Al-Kassar was reported to hold large tracts of land in the Bekaa Valley. The PFLP-GC also has camps in the Bekaa – which were the target of Israeli air strikes in 1989.

••••••••

The U.S. government's presence in Lebanon is not to be taken lightly according to Lester Coleman, a self-employed freelance writer, editor and security consultant who once moonlighted as a DIA (Defense Intelligence Agency) covert intelligence officer when he was called to serve. Coleman, age 47, told the *London Times* that for six years he worked as an intelligence officer with the secret unit, Middle East Collection 10 (MC-10) in Cyprus, running a network of agents in Beirut whose mission was to find American hostages held by extremists.

Coleman was paid in travelers checks sent from the Luxembourg branch of the now collapsed Bank of Credit and Commerce International (BCCI). Two senior MC-10 members, Matthew Kevin Gannon and Major Charles Dennis McKee, had been on Pan-Am flight 103 and had just returned from a mission in Beirut.

Coleman explained that the DEA, with the narcotics squad of the Cypriot national police, the German BKA police and British customs, ran a "drug sting operation" through Cyprus and airports in Europe, including Frankfurt.

The operation involved delivering heroin from the Bekaa Valley in Lebanon to the United States; the operation was code-named "Khourah." Coleman maintained that Pan Am Flight 103 was being used by the DEA as a "controlled delivery" flight.

After the explosion, the Beirut end of MC-10 had obviously been "blown." There were five key members of the MC-10 cell in Cyprus and Beirut, one of whom was Lester Coleman. Another was Werner Tony Asmar, a German Lebanese, who was killed in a bomb explosion at his office in east Beirut on May 26, 1988.

Another member of MC-10 was Charlie Frezeli, a Lebanese army officer, who was shot dead at his home in east Beirut in November 1989. When Asmar was killed, the DIA ordered Coleman home.

Danny Casolaro had contacted Coleman in Sweden on August 3, 1991, seven days before his death in Martinsburg, West Virginia. They talked about the sale of the PROMIS software by the U.S. Government to foreign governments, the Bank of Credit and Commerce International (BCCI), and the Iran-Contra scandal.

After Coleman learned of Danny's death on August 10th, 1991, he provided Inslaw president Bill Hamilton with an affidavit in October 1991. That affidavit read as follows:

> Affidavit of Lester K. Coleman, being duly sworn, do hereby state as follows:
>
> (1) I am currently self-employed as a freelance writer, editor, and security consultant. I am a United States citizen and am temporarily outside of the United States.
>
> (2) In November 1984, the Defense Intelligence Agency (DIA) offered me a position in human intelligence operations in the Middle East. I was raised in the Middle East, where I lived in Iran, Libya and Saudi Arabia. I speak three dialects of Arabic and some Farsi. I accepted the position and received training from the DIA. I was assigned to a Middle East intelligence unit.
>
> (3) Between February and September 1987, I was seconded by DIA to the Drug Enforcement Administration (DEA) in Nicosia, Cyprus, reporting to the DEA Country Attache, Michael T. Hurley.
>
> (4) After a cover assignment in the United States, I was again seconded to the DEA in Nicosia, Cyprus, in early 1988.
>
> (5) During April and May 1988, I worked in the office of Euramae Trading Company, Ltd. in Nicosia, Cyprus, a DEA proprietary company. On or about May 29, 1988, because of my concern about poor security in the DEA operation in Cyprus, I returned to the United States, having previously obtained the concurrence of DIA.
>
> (6) During my two stints as a DIA covert intelligence officer seconded to the DEA in Nicosia, Cyprus, I became aware of the fact that DEA was using its proprietary company, Euramae Trading Company, Ltd. to sell computer software called PROMISE or PROMIS to the drug abuse control agencies of various countries in the Middle East, including Cyprus, Pakistan, Syria, Kuwait and Turkey.

"(7) I personally witnessed the unpacking at the Nicosia, Cyprus, Police Force Narcotics Squad of boxes containing reels of computer tapes and computer hardware. The boxes bore the name and red logo of a Canadian corporation with the words `PROMISE' or `PROMIS' and `Ltd' in the company name.

"(8) The DEA objective in inducing the implementation of this computerized PROMIS[E] system in the drug abuse control agencies of the Middle East countries was to augment the drug control resources available to the United States Government by making it possible for the United States Government to access sensitive drug control law enforcement and intelligence files of these Middle East governments.

"(9) It is also my understanding that third-party funds were generally made available for the purchase of these computer software and hardware systems. One third-party funding source was the United Nations Fund for Drug Abuse Control in Vienna, Austria.

"(10) As DEA Country Attache for Cyprus, Michael T. Hurley had overall responsibility for both the Euramae Trading Company, Ltd. and its initiative to sell PROMIS[E] computer systems to Middle East countries for drug abuse control.

"(11) In 1990, DEA reassigned Hurley to a DEA intelligence position in Washington State.

"(12) I became aware in 1991 that Michael Riconosciuto, known to me as a long-time CIA asset, was arrested in Washington State by DEA for the manufacturing of illegal chemical drugs. I had also become aware of the fact that Riconosciuto had made a sworn statement, prior to his arrest, about his participation in a covert U.S. intelligence initiative to sell Inslaw's PROMIS software to foreign governments.

"(13) In light of Hurley's personal involvement in the U.S. Government's covert intelligence initiative to sell PROMIS[E] software to foreign governments and his reassignment to a DEA intelligence position in Washington State in advance of the DEA's arrest of Riconosciuto, the arrest of Riconosciuto should be regarded as suspect. I do not believe that Hurley's posting to a drug intelligence position in Washington State in advance of Riconosciuto's arrest on drug charges is merely coincidental. Rather, the probability is that Hurley was reassigned to Washington State to manufacture a case against Riconosciuto in order to prevent Riconosciuto from becoming a credible witness about the U.S. Government's covert sale of the PROMIS software to foreign governments.

"(14) The investigative journalist Danny Casolaro contacted me in Europe on August 3, 1991. Mr. Casolaro had leads and hard information about things that I know about, including Department of Justice groups operating overseas, the sale of PROMIS[E] software by the U.S. Government to foreign governments, the Bank of Credit and Commerce International (BCCI), and the Iran-Contra scandal. I subsequently learned of Mr. Casolaro's death in Martinsburg, West Virginia, one week later, on August 10, 1991. I contacted Inslaw in October 1991, after learning about Mr. Casolaro's death under suspicious circumstances."

Michael Riconosciuto

— 9 —

Files in the Mojave Desert

Village Voice newspaper ran an article entitled, "The Last Days of Danny Casolaro," by James Ridgeway and Doug Vaughan on October 15, 1991 which gave a brief profile of Michael Riconosciuto's background:

> The 44-year-old Riconosciuto is – to put it mildly – a colorful character, wilder than anything in `The Falcon and the Snowman.' He was a gifted child. When he was just 10 years old, Michael wired his parents' neighborhood with a working, private telephone system that undercut Ma Bell; in the eighth grade, he won a science fair with a model for a three-dimensional sonar system. By the time he was a teenager, he had won so many science fairs with exhibits of laser technology that he was invited to be a summer research assistant at Stanford's [University] prestigious Cooper Vaper Laser Laboratory. Dr. Arthur Schalow, a Nobel laureate, remembered him: `You don't forget a 16-year-old youngster who shows up with his own argon laser,' he told Casolaro.

••••••••

Bobby Riconosciuto lived with Michael Riconosciuto at the time of his arrest in Washington state. Immediately upon learning of his arrest, she had fled to California with her four children, the youngest of which, Elizabeth, had been fathered by Michael.

Bobby was well situated in an exclusive suite at the Embassy Suites Hotel in Orange County, California. Her suite contained a living room and bar overlooking lush indoor tropical gardens and water fountains, marble walkways over bridge-covered ponds and a gazebo where free breakfasts were cooked and served to order.

Within the room, she had at her disposal office equipment, phones in every room, answering machines, room service and anything else she needed for herself and her children. Patrick Moriarty, Marshall Riconosciuto's business partner of 40 years, was paying the bills.

Moriarty and the Riconosciutos, father and son, had once owned Hercules Research Corporation together in Hercules, California. An old Contra Costa County newspaper article, dating back to April, 1981, gave the story of Hercules. The sub-heading of the article pretty much said it all, "Device Could Make Hercules a Silicon Valley."

In 1981, Hercules had developed a small electronic power supply the size of a tissue box, designed to specifically feed 30,000 volts of electricity to another device, a METC (Modular Energy Transfer Catalyzer) unit, that would cut the heating and cooling time in food processing and of making glass, metal and other products by 40 percent.

The METC unit, patented by Interprobe of Chicago, worked by electrostatically exciting air molecules by moving them through a charged field. This removed a boundary layer of molecules that inhibited the exchange of thermal energy. Hercules' high-voltage power supply was essential to the application of Interprobe's METC unit, so both companies were in the process of working out a merger in order to market both technologies as a complete system.

Admiral Henry Rankin, vice president of Interprobe, was a longtime family friend, and was very enthusiastic about incorporating the Hercules power pack with Interprobe's high voltage electrostatic technology.

Patrick Moriarty and Marshall Riconosciuto had funded research for 15 years and spent about $1 million of their own money on the project.

By 1983, things were not looking so good for Patrick Moriarty. The *Los Angeles Times* newspaper reported in a series of articles that "fireworks magnate W. Patrick Moriarty, his business and associates spent nearly half a million dollars in the last three years to influence government decisions throughout California."

Moriarty's relationships with several key state legislators and his campaign contributions to elected officials from Anaheim to Sacramento had made him a powerful force in state and local politics. His association with the notorious Robert Ferrante, head of Consolidated Savings and Loan which failed in 1985, and who was the subject of a disorganized, on-again off-again FBI investigation, was written up in the book, *Inside Job*, by Mary Fricker.

Patrick Moriarty was described as "the manufacturer of Red Devil fireworks, who founded the Bank of Irvine. The bank failed in 1984, the victim of fraud and mismanagement, according to regulators." In 1985, Moriarty pleaded guilty to mail fraud in a case that became the biggest political scandal in California in 30 years. Over 10 prominent politicians, including one state senator, were indicted for taking bribes from Moriarty.

Though I'd spoken with her on the phone numerous times, I first met Bobby Riconosciuto face-to-face on January 15th, 1992. On the day I visited her hotel suite, I hauled my Mita copy machine on a cart up to her room and we talked and made copies of documents all morning. Bobby was young, buxom and attractive in a natural, mother earth sort of way. Her long blond hair hung loosely around her shoulders, she wore no makeup, and her nose and mouth had an impish upturn that made her appear to be smiling even when she was not.

We became friends as the day progressed. Bobby confided that some of the more sensitive material was stored at Michael's hidden trailer in Trona, California.

While working at Wackenhut, Michael had anticipated a future need to have a hiding place for himself and his files in the event that things got out of control. Bobby, who had met Michael in Washington State *after* he left Wackenhut, had been instructed by Michael to stay away from the trailer in case she was being surveillanced.

The files and computer equipment stored there were Michael's last ace in the hole. Nevertheless, Bobby said she was frustrated by the slow progress of Michael's court defense, by J.H.'s lack of response to Michael's request for Witness Protection, and she had been barraged by reporters who wanted documented proof of Michael's statements.

I offered to drive her out to Trona, near Death Valley, to retrieve Michael's files and she agreed. However, when we walked to the parking lot, Bobby decided to drive her own vehicle, and invited me to ride with her and the children. My husband, Roland, followed us in our van. We arrived at the isolated trailer at dusk and began sorting through documents that could substantiate Michael's claim that he worked for the government.

The electricity had been shut off and as it became dark, we were forced to use flashlights. Bobby was terrified that we might get caught in that God-forsaken place. The children were cold and tired, and from sheer exhaustion, she offered to turn all the boxes and documents over to me to make copies at home, rather than at her hotel suite.

We threw everything helter-skelter into large plastic trash bags, dumped the bags into my Chevy van, and quickly headed back to civilization.

It is noteworthy that before we left, Bobby pointed the flashlight towards another, smaller trailer situated on a knoll overlooking the property, which she claimed contained Michael's hidden computer equipment.

It was several weeks before Michael learned that Bobby had turned the documents over to me. She never told him, nor did I. She asked me not to mention it to Michael because she would tell him in her own good time. Ironically, it was through Jonathan Littman, a *San Francisco Chronicle* reporter whom I had confided in, that Riconosciuto learned of our secret.

Upon arriving home from my trip to the desert, I had xeroxed round-the-clock for five days with help from friends. The documents corroborated everything Michael had related over the phone, and more.

It was an exciting time. Boxes and boxes of documents provided me for the first time with a window into the CIA corporate structure, arms deals, drug operations, money laundering, biological technology, all the connecting tentacles of Danny Casolaro's "Octopus."

After making copies, I squeezed the originals into eight large packing boxes, sealed them tightly, and called Bobby to find out where she wanted them shipped to? She gave me Marshall Riconosciuto's business address and said to ship them there. Shortly afterward, she called back and said *not* to ship them, she would have someone pick them up. At that time, Bobby was temporarily staying with a woman in the Bay Area. The woman and her husband subsequently arrived at my home and loaded the boxes into their vehicle, then drove back to the Bay Area. Bobby later said she intended to drive to Marshall Riconosciuto's business in Southern California and store the documents there. (Marshall Riconosciuto was Michael's father, but was reportedly very ill at that time).

Michael Riconosciuto seemed almost relieved when he learned that Bobby and I had driven to Trona and retrieved his files, with no mishaps. Now that Bobby had the original documents, she could provide Michael's lawyer with needed documents. Later, Michael said Marshall shipped them to Ian Stuart Spiro for safekeeping. I was never able to prove that and placed no significance on it until I read an April 1993 Associated Press news story entitled, "Deaths Linked to Spy Network," published in the *Merced Sun Star* newspaper, outlining the death of Ian Stuart Spiro, 46, who was found dead of cyanide poisoning in the Anza-Borrego desert on November 8, 1992, one week after his wife and children were found shot to death in their Rancho Santa Fe home.

The news story, originating from the *Oceanside Blade-Citizen*, noted that "documents and U.S. intelligence sources implicated Spiro in the Iran-Contra arms-for-hostages affair and an alleged Justice Department conspiracy to pirate software from a private company and sell it to foreign intelligence agencies."

Spiro's name also appeared in Lt. Col. Oliver North's personal notebooks documenting the Iran-Contra affair, according to the National Security Archives in Washington D.C.

Former hostage David Jacobsen told the *Blade-Citizen* shortly after Spiro's death that Spiro helped negotiate the release of hostages in the Middle East.

After obtaining a copy of a follow-up *Blade-Citizen* article dated June 3, 1993, entitled, "Spiro Probers Want to Talk to North" by Wade Booth, Stacy Finz and Michael Williams, I learned that Ian Spiro lived in Beirut, Lebanon during the 1970's and 1980's where he "made contacts with Lebanese religious leaders and the Islamic Jihad."

Greg Quarton, Spiro's brother-in-law, told reporters at the *Blade-Citizen* that Spiro maintained communication with Lebanese business associates until the time of his death, but investigating officers had possession of Spiro's phone bills, and as of this writing, they had not released them.

San Diego sheriff's Capt. Jim Marmack said detectives were investigating allegations by Spiro's relatives that his file cabinets and business papers were missing. I later learned from a Hercules Police Detective who communicated with Marmack that the San Diego Sheriff's Department destroyed the Spiro files when the case was closed. Spiro allegedly committed suicide, he had no connection to the PROMIS software, and the *Oceanside Blade Citizen* newspaper had been misinformed on that issue.

The week of the Spiro family's death, Robert Corson, a business associate of Spiro's indicted in a savings and loan scam, was found dead in an El Paso, Texas, motel room. Corson, who reportedly worked for the CIA, died of a heart attack, officials said. The *Blade-Citizen* reported that Corson once carried money to South America in a deal to deliver covert weapons. Corson also allegedly associated with California investor Wayne Reeder who was seen at a Wackenhut/Contra meeting in Riverside County (See Chapter 10).

The newspaper article went on to say that Alan Michael May, age 50, [a former Northern California field director in Richard Nixon's presidential campaign and attorney for Nixon's brothers Donald and Edward] was found dead in his San Francisco home on June 19, 1991, four days after a newspaper story in the *Napa Sentinel* outlined his role in an alleged plot by Republican Party officials to bribe Iranian officials to delay the release of U.S. hostages until after President Reagan's inauguration.

Immediately after May's death, Raymond Lavas, Ted Gunderson's former associate, (and a former protege of Robert Maheu according to Michael Riconosciuto) wrote a letter to one of Michael's friends, expressing his professional opinion about the death of Michael May. A copy of that letter was faxed to me and the following excerpts quickly captured my attention:

> ... I don't understand why it's going to take two weeks to determine May's cause of death. Did you know that certain chemical assassination methods will have been evaporated out of the body by that time?
>
> Then, the cause of death would be ruled as natural, since the chemical agents are the primary cause that result in a secondary action such as heart failure, kidney or liver damage, etc.
>
> Some examples of these agents include BZ-2, Ricin, Tropodotoxin, shellfish toxia and a variety of methlamine based neurotox-

> ins that affect the central nervous system and cause failure of one or more organs in the human body.
>
> Some, if not most of these toxins are solvent based [DMSO] and may be introduced in minute quantities through the skin. Their effect [may] vary – and some toxins take weeks to months to take effect. Others take moments to damage the nervous system, then evaporate within hours.
>
> Unless the body is immediately refrigerated, the toxins are quickly evaporated, leaving only one or two parts per million in quantity. Unless there are suspicious circumstances surrounding the death, a trained forensic expert would never detect any traces of the toxin.
>
> So there you have it. [Michael] May is dead and they are dragging their asses to find out how! What is next? A statement that May died of natural causes? Let me predict this now ... and we'll see.
>
> Regards, Ray."

Michael May also apparently attended briefings connected with Lawrence Livermore Labs in California according to an official listing of Lawrence Livermore employees at a "Briefings and Discussions" document obtained from Riconosciuto's files.

The document, stamped, "Official Use Only," listed Edward Teller along with nine other names, including Michael May, under the heading "Lawrence Livermore Laboratory." Other headings with names listed underneath included the Department of Energy, Department of State, Defense Nuclear Agency and Naval Research Laboratory. There were no other pages accompanying the document, so it was impossible to determine from what manual it came from.

May's name also popped up in a letter Michael Riconosciuto wrote to Dr. John Phillip Nichols at the Cabazon Indian reservation when he was being screened for security clearances to work on the Cabazon/Wackenhut joint venture.

The letter focused primarily on Al Holbert, an Israeli intelligence officer who allegedly recruited Riconosciuto into the CIA, and May's name was mentioned only once, in connection with members of "The Company." That one sentence read as follows: "Ben Kalka's relationship with Holbert and `May' will give the proper authorities the necessary auspices to come in and swiftly clean it [The Company] up."

Other portions of the letter gave a history of Riconosciuto's experience with Al Holbert: (excerpts)

> ... My problems stemmed from my association with Al C. Holbert. I first met Holbert when I was still in high school and I was led to believe that he was an `unofficial' representative of the Israeli government. I was further led to believe that his interests were not contrary to those of the United States. It was not until July of 1981 that I learned the truth about Holbert. It came directly from him to me personally in what I will call a confrontational situation.
>
> August of 1981 was when I first brought Holbert to your [Dr. John Nichols] attention. At that time, I still did not know much and I was still in a sort of state of shock from my `new awareness' of Holbert. I was in deep with this guy and so was Paul [Morasca].
>
> At first Paul thought that I was off base and over-reacting and then by degrees he started to come around. Much of the incredible account of Paul's doings (money transfers, gems, weapons, drugs) were the result of his relationship to Burt and Jensen. Burt, Jensen and Kalka all met Paul through his brother Joe. I was the one who introduced Al Holbert to Paul, and Paul was the one who introduced me to Burt, [Bill] Jensen and Kalka. This was in early 1967.
>
> I was introduced to [Al] Holbert through the Stanford crowd at the home of [name withheld] in Portola Valley, California. Interesting enough, [name withheld] is a former State Department employee ..."
>
> ... The realization of who and what Holbert is, and Paul's death, have taken me some time to adjust to. And that required professional help. I now have a clear idea and good perspective on what has really happened in my life.
>
> I am in awe of Holbert and his group's power [The Company]. During the last year, I have forced this structure to rear its ugly head in many different times and places, and in ways that can't be covered up. I have also spread far and wide what knowledge I have with the intent to first protect others involved and secondly to chisel the story in stone.
>
> Where it all stands now is that no matter who the group attempts to silence or what ruse they attempt to perpetrate, the truth cannot be destroyed. This is now in the hands of a competent attorney. My direct involvement is finished except to be available to answer questions.

> ... I feel that Holbert and his group represent a current national security nightmare to this country. I feel that I have been extricated from the hold of this group. But I also feel that the destruction by legal means of this group ranks in importance with my scientific and engineering skills to the overall picture.
>
> Ben Kalka's relationship with Holbert and May will give the proper authorities the necessary auspices to come in and swiftly clean it up. I would now like to start out where we should have been a year ago. The first point I will start with is a recap of our visit to Picatinny Arsenal ...

It is noteworthy that two of the people mentioned in the above letter are now dead: Paul Morasca and Michael May.

The bizarre circumstances of Morasca's death are detailed in the next few pages. Ben Kalka of The Company, is now serving time in prison for having 900 pounds of methamphetamine in his possession at time of arrest.

Through one of Michael's contacts, I managed to locate the current (1991) whereabouts of Al Holbert and confirm his identity. A letter written on "Solomon Investigations" letterhead, dated June 13, 1991, to a client requesting payment for the services of Holbert read as follows: (excerpted) " ... I enlisted the services of my electronic countermeasures expert, A.C. Holbert, for an immediate survey and sweep of the premises. Mr. Holbert is highly regarded as the best electronics man in the [San Francisco] Bay Area and has recently worked with Israeli intelligence services in the field of electronic countermeasures. He agreed to take on this job. I have enclosed a copy of Mr. Holbert's faxed report ..."

The mystery of Al Holbert was further uncovered in a 1983 transcript in which Michael stated, "After Paul's [Morasca] death, Holbert admitted to me that he was a Soviet backed agent, and they had a home, or he had a home for me, and I could be treated like royalty, and he reiterated that offer in the latest meeting, and he said, `He was prepared to deliver some five-hundred-thousand dollars cash to me us a show of good faith ..."

The transcript, originating from a series of tape recorded interviews between Michael Riconosciuto, Ted Gunderson and Robert Booth Nichols at Nichols' "007" apartment in Marina Del Ray, provided a window into the entire drug scene in California from the early 1960's through the 1980's, mostly relating to methamphetamine operations in the Bay Area. It had been typed by Ellen Nichols, Robert's wife.

Riconosciuto's relationship with Ted Gunderson dated back at least as far as 1982. Michael and Nichols dated back to 1967. In reading the transcript, it appeared that Gunderson and Nichols were interviewing Riconosciuto for recruitment into a drug/sting operation.

Riconosciuto later verified that he was, in fact, being recruited into the overseas Lebanon drug operation by Gunderson and Nichols because of his (Riconosciuto's) undercover experience in the drug trade.

It is noteworthy that Al Holbert, the Israeli intelligence agent who originally recruited Michael into the CIA, is mentioned extensively throughout the 71-page transcript.

Riconosciuto's relationship with Holbert had lasted from 1966 to 1981, a span of fifteen years. Most of that time had been devoted to complex drug activities in California. In one passage, Riconosciuto stated that "Ben Kalka was one of [Al] Holbert's lieutenants. The other lieutenant with Kalka was Charlie Weinberg, who set up the Vortex Chemical Company in Berkeley, California for Holbert."

Holbert was also interested in technology. "I really confided in him. I was constantly steering him to various people in the Silicon Valley, you know, for requests that he made which were very sophisticated technical requests."

In the transcript, Ted Gunderson asked Michael, "Holbert had a technical mind for that sort of thing?"

Michael responded, "Absolutely! [He had] a firm grasp of physics, mathematics, chemistry, military hardware ..."

Gunderson asked, "Let's go back to '66 to '81, you were close to him?"

Michael: "Not on a regular basis. He would get in contact with me when he needed consultation in certain areas. I made some good money. I designed communications equipment for them. I did a lot of software development ..."

Ted: "And then he gave it to the Israelis?"

Mike: "Yes."

Ted: "And he admitted this?"

Mike: "Oh yeah, none of it was really classified. I did software for the analysis of radar change data. It was based on mathematical models that the Department of Defense wasn't using – you know, my approach was new and different from theirs, but it wasn't connected with any of their projects, so technically it wasn't classified."

Michael developed other technology along the way and subsequently attracted the attention of Dr. John Phillip Nichols at Wackenhut/Cabazon who wanted his services. But Michael's association with Al Holbert was hindering Michael's security clearances. Through the screening process and Dr. John Nichols, Michael had learned more about Al Holbert.

Ted: "Well, how could he [Holbert] be a Soviet agent and an Israeli agent?"

Mike: "Your guess is as good as mine. I talked to Major General Peratt on that subject last May and he said, `You don't understand the ways of the world.' Regarding Al Holbert, I said, `That man has done more damage to my generation and my country [drugs] – How can you people say that you're friends of the United States, when you send us a guy like that?"

Michael continued ..."You know, Holbert came to the United States and he went to work for the Treasury Department out of Philadelphia and ..."

Ted interrupted. "In what way? As an agent?"

Mike: "I don't know what the relationship was. The Treasury Department wouldn't tell me. They wouldn't comment at all except to acknowledge that, `Yes, he was involved at very high levels, giving special training.'

" ... Holbert taught courses in interrogation techniques. He taught touch-kill techniques – you know, with the thumbs on the temples and various scare areas like that. He moved around to a lot of different agencies. He got involved with the FBI, and he was involved with the Drug Enforcement people ..."

Ted: "He indicated to you for fifteen years [that] he was with the Israelis?"

Mike: "Israelis. Yes."

Ted: "And then you realized through Dr. Nichols that he was a Soviet?"

Riconosciuto explained that he thought it was John Ammarell at Wackenhut who had "zeroed in on Holbert."

Gunderson continued to press Riconosciuto about Holbert being a double agent. Michael responded: "Well, he was with the Soviets, but he was also with the Israelis. Holbert definitely is connected with Israeli intelligence. I mean there's no ifs, ands, buts, or maybes ... He was decorated in combat for them."

Riconosciuto further recounted a visit to Israel in April 1982. He had met a man (name unspecified) who was the assistant Secretary of Defense of Israel for a number of years and was in charge of defense production for the Israeli government. This man was a friend of Ariel Sharon and he had introduced Riconosciuto to Sharon. It was through this man and a man named "General Peratt," that Riconosciuto confirmed Holbert's position with the Israelis.

"Holbert definitely is one of their boys. I got an admission out of General Peratt that Holbert was funny, that he's a Trotski-ite, and they knew about it, and I couldn't understand why they kept a guy like that around? I was told that I just didn't understand the ways of the world!"

Ted asked, "Who does Holbert report to?"

Mike: "Jean Pierre Boegner."

At this point in the transcript, Robert Booth Nichols interceded and provided Boegner's address: " ... His address in Paris is 114 Champs Elysees, Paris 8, France. That goes into my territory ..."

Mike added, "Jean Pierre reports directly to Colonel Stefan Uznanski of the Ukraine ..."

Nichols noted, "I have strict files on him."

Ted asked, "And is he GRU?"

Mike answered, "No KGB."

Nichols added, "As high as you can go ..."

Ted asked, "And where is he, in the Kremlin?"

Mike answered, "No, he's in Vienna."

Nichols interjected, " ... Out of Salzberg. He has a home twenty minutes from Salzberg. His hobby is boar hunting. He has about a twenty man contingent."

Gunderson asked, "Is Boegner a Canadian?"

Nichols responded, "Boegner is French. Boegner was involved in the assassination attempt on de Gaulle. Boegner served time."

Ted: "He's KGB?"

Nichols: "Oh yeah, a Colonel."

Ted: "Okay, anything else. Anything more on Holbert that we should bring up?"

Riconosciuto noted that Holbert was very disappointed that he couldn't "turn him" (Riconosciuto) in August of 1981. Ted asked Michael if Holbert admitted at that time that he was KGB?

Michael corrected Ted, "GRU, he was GRU. He told me that he was GRU and he bragged that there were over thirty-five thousand GRU agents active on the North American continent. And I checked with John Ammarell and with Robert Frye [executives at Wackenhut Corporation] and they told me it was about half that number.

" ... He [Holbert] wanted me to leave the United States, through Canada, and go to Israel."

Riconosciuto added, "You know, he's touched the Central Intelligence Agency, the Treasury Department, the Secret Service and various local law enforcement agencies all over the country ..."

The above-mentioned transcript was mailed by one of three people to the "prosecutor" at Michael Riconosciuto's trial in Washington state where it was entered into evidence.

••••••••

At that time, to Michael's knowledge, only Robert Booth Nichols, Peter Zokosky and Jonathan Littman, a *San Francisco Chronicle* reporter, had possession of it.

I subsequently received a copy of it from Jonathan Littman, who coincidentally, I learned later, happened to be Ben Kalka's "cousin" (Kalka belonged to The Company, according to Riconosciuto, and had been arrested with 900 pounds of methamphetamine in his possession). Littman had obtained the transcript from Peter Zokosky, Robert Booth Nichols' partner.

Riconosciuto believed Littman had given the transcript to Kalka during one his visits with him at the Pleasanton prison, and Kalka had sent it on to the prosecutor at Michael's trial.

Nichols later confirmed to me that he (Nichols) had indeed interviewed Riconosciuto with Ted Gunderson in 1983 and the transcript was legitimate, though he wouldn't state the purpose of the interview.

••••••••

It is significant that a passage in the 1983 transcript mentioned Michael May as "one of the top three guys in the Lawrence Livermore Laboratory management structure" who was associated with Riconosciuto.

••••••••

Michael and Bobby Riconosciuto had been communicating with Jonathan Littman for months, as had Danny Casolaro before his death, and they wanted me to connect with him. At that point, Littman had written a series of in-depth articles on the Cabazon Indians and Dr. John Nichols, and I hadn't been interested in talking to him ... until he wrote about the death of Michael's partner, Paul Morasca.

The article, entitled, "Bizarre Murders Puzzle Cops," published on the front page of the *San Francisco Chronicle* on December 30, 1991, noted that the body of Paul Morasca, 31, had been found by Michael Riconosciuto. Morasca's arms had been lashed behind his back as he was hog-tied with a telephone cord from his curled-up legs to his neck. Police believed he died when his legs finally gave out and the cord tightened like a bow-string, drawing the noose around his neck until he slowly strangled.

Before his death, Morasca and Riconosciuto had planned a business venture with Cabazon administrator John Phillip Nichols to develop high-technology military hardware. Morasca was also described as a "San Francisco entrepreneur suspected of being a money launderer involved in a major Northern California drug ring."

Oddly, when Riconosciuto found Morasca's body, he drove 500 miles to the Cabazon reservation and told John Nichols about the death. Nichols then called his Los Angeles attorney, who telephoned the San Francisco police.

Just three days after Morasca's death, Mary Quick, a 63-year-old school teacher was shot in the face and her purse stolen as she was about to enter Fresno's American legion Post 509, where she was president of the Woman's Auxiliary.

At first, police assumed it to be a routine mugging murder, until it was discovered that her nephew, Brian Weiss, who had been living at his aunt's house in Fresno, was a business associate of Michael Riconosciuto's. (Brian Weiss was also mentioned in the above-mentioned 1983 "drug transcript").

Riconosciuto explained to police that he told Paul Morasca that he had given Mary Quick a card containing secret bank account code numbers because "she had no connection to any of the principles and could be trusted." She had been instructed to give the code numbers over the phone only to Paul Morasca or Michael Riconosciuto.

It was not until I obtained Michael Riconosciuto's "desert" files that the above story affected me personally. Within one of the boxes was an envelope containing eight coded computer cards with large sums of money handwritten next to the account numbers. One card, containing ten account numbers, indicated sums of upwards of $3.5 million dollars. That was just one card of eight.

In my next conversation with Michael Riconosciuto, I inquired of him the "real" story behind Paul Morasca and Mary Quick's death. I did not reveal to him that I was in possession of his bank cards, but referred to the *Chronicle* newspaper story.

Michael remorsefully indicated that he had not, in fact, given any cards to Mary Quick as he had told Paul Morasca he did. Michael had kept them (and obviously hidden them at his desert trailer). Nevertheless, Morasca believed, and under torture revealed, that one of the cards was being held by Mary Quick and the rest were stored in a safe deposit box. As we know, Mary Quick died three days later.

After that conversation I immediately took the cards to a professional photographer, had close-up photographs taken of them, and returned the originals in a separate envelope to Bobby Riconosciuto. I never knew what she did with them.

During subsequent phone conversations, Riconosciuto often referred to his former partner, Paul Morasca. During his attempted trade into the Federal Witness Protection Program, he had made a statement which caught my attention, and which I later inquired about. While relating his background in the electronics field, he had mentioned that he once worked at Tyme Share, Inc.

Noted Riconosciuto, " ... And at the time of Paul Morasca's death, the biggest loss I received was a big bag of bearer shares of original Tyme Shares stock. And that was the main reason why Paul got killed."

Riconosciuto had stressed that only the FinCen people would understand the significance of that. I later learned that the computer cards which Paul Morasca and Mary Quick had died for belonged to the Tyme Shares on-line financial clearing house used worldwide by banking institutions. Essentially, the cards were provided to a subscriber or "user" who rented time on the computer for conducting banking transactions.

Riconosciuto chose not to elaborate on his operation at Tyme Shares from a "jail" phone, nevertheless, I was able to decipher that he and Paul Morasca had accessed bank accounts using the computer cards in conjunction with a "password" determined by the user. Michael had created the passwords from the "pets" named in Phyllis Riconosciuto's (Michael's ex-wife's) diary.

He did, however, randomly discuss his background with Tyme Shares: "I developed the modem, error trapping routines for Tyme Share used on the original network. I developed the protected mode memory for the scientific data systems, SDS, Sigma 7 computers. And I developed the capital P-E-R-T, Pert Software, which was the next generation of critical path method. That's a Programmed Evaluation Review Technique that Tyme Shares, for years, was the leader in.

"And then Electronic Data Systems bought a license from them, and you know, EDS's story is legendary. Now, PROMIS is an outgrowth of PERT. The Hamiltons had a woman programmer who was self-taught and she's the one, her signature is in the code structures of PROMIS. It's just like her signature because she was out of the mainstream and did things her own way ..."

Shortly thereafter, while reviewing Riconosciuto's documents, I came across a copy of an obscure statement reportedly submitted by Riconosciuto in February 1984 to the San Francisco Grand Jury on the death of Paul Morasca. It cryptically tied Morasca to Wackenhut and appeared to have been transcribed from a tape recorded interview.

Bill Hamilton had provided the two-page statement to Garby Leon, identifying it as Riconosciuto's "Grand Jury statement." Garby had forwarded it to me. However, it was not until years later, in an interview with Peter Zokosky, that I learned (according to Zokosky) that the statement had actually been typed by Ellen Nichols, wife of Robert Booth Nichols, after Riconosciuto met with Zokosky and Bob Nichols to provide an explanation.

The statement in its entirety read as follows:

> February 16, 1984 Statement of Michael J. Riconosciuto.
>
> I first heard of Phil Porath in December of 1981. John Phillip Nichols [Cabazon administrator] told Paul Morasca and myself that we needed Phil Porath as a consultant to Recovery Technology, Inc. Porath was represented by John P. Nichols as being able to smoothly handle metals transactions for RTI on a large scale. Phil Porath was one of the contacts that John Phillip Nichols had

committed to arrange for Paul as part of our deal. Paul Morasca's body was found after he failed to contact Porath for that scheduled meeting in January 1982.

After Paul's death, JPN [John Phillip Nichols] came to me with a request. He asked me if I could recover some of Ben Kalka's LSD because he had a sale for 5 lbs. of it to someone in Romania. John Phillip Nichols claimed that this was an authorized covert intelligence operation and the proceeds would be used to purchase George Wackenhut's yacht, *Top Secret.*

Military electronics equipment to be delivered to South Africa was also to be purchased according to JPN and delivered by the yacht. I went along with the program because JPN told me that the `agency' was involved through WSI. I did some checking on my own and became suspicious of JPN. Then JPN met with myself and Raoul Arana of Central Caribbean Research, Inc.

At this meeting, the details were plainly discussed by Mr. Arana. At that point, JPN directed me to have PAT (Phillip Arthur Thompson) recover [all] of Kalka's assets. I then contacted DeSilva, who had control of Kalka's assets and he agreed to release them to me. DeSilva later called the Indian reservation and gave the location of the assets which included: one bobtail semi-truck with power lift gate loaded with amphetamine production chemicals; one red Datsun truck with a portable refrigerator containing the acid.

I accompanied PAT and Steve Finley to the locations of these vehicles in the Oakland area. The keys, title and registration were with each vehicle. PAT and SF drove the vehicles off and I reported to JPN that the vehicles had been located and picked up.

"I also reported to my attorney, DW (Don Wager), the details. I contacted JPN a few days later and he complained to me that PAT had made off with everything.

... with George Wackenhut in Las Vegas. JPN told me that my problems would be over with if I went along with the program. Brian Weiss [Mary Quick's nephew] drove me to Palm Springs where I rented a car. JPN, myself and Brian Weiss then drove to Las Vegas.

We arrived in Las Vegas late in the afternoon. We checked into the hotel. After we checked in, I was then introduced to Phil Porath by JPN. Porath seemed a little nervous and upset with JPN. JPN seemed desperate to have Phil Porath stall George W. on the sale of the yacht. Phil Porath seemed reluctant to go along with JPN.

JPN, myself and Porath then went to a private section of the dining room and met with GW [George Wackenhut] and JA[John

Ammarell]. During dinner, JPN outlined my situation. [Al] Holbert, [Ben] Kalka, [Richard] Knozzi, [and] the Fresno Company were covered in detail.

A cutaway, sectioned high security lock was also shown to JA and GW [George Wackenhut]. JA said that this should be presented to his personal friend, Bud Miller, for action and that I would be contacted.

The sale of the WH [Wackenhut] yacht then came up. Porath gave GW a story [at] JPN's prompting. GW was impatient and asked where the `South African' Thompson could be reached? I then asked GW [George Wackenhut] if he was referring to PAT [Phillip Arthur Thompson] and he said, `Yes.'

I then demanded to know what was going on? I laid out to GW what PAT had done, including murdering PM [Paul Morasca]. JPN interrupted me and told GW that I was mistaken and it was a different PT that I was talking about. It was at that point that GW [George Wackenhut] said he had a hearing problem and the dinner broke up.

I went immediately to make telephone calls. I spread the word that I felt my life was in danger and that JPN, WH, and PAT had conspired to kill PM [Paul Morasca]. I then went back to the dining area where I saw PP [Phil Porath] and GW [George Wackenhut] at a small two-person table talking about the yacht deal. JPN and JA were standing up and they asked me to come to JA's room.

At JA's room, everybody acted like nothing had happened. There we talked for an hour or so about hi-tech projects. JPN and I then went to PP's room and talked [about] P's missed meeting with Paul M., Bill Jensen, Burt Gardener and metal projects. We then went to bed. The next morning JPN, BW [Brian Weiss] and I drove back to Indio. At no time did JPN mention the problem that came down at dinner."

••••••••

In John Connolly's *SPY* magazine article on Wackenhut, September 1992 issue, on page 54, a brief notation mentioned Riconosciuto's meeting in Las Vegas with George Wackenhut and John Ammarell, a Wackenhut board member and consultant to George Wackenhut. *SPY* contacted Ammarell regarding the meeting, and Ammarell confirmed that such a meeting did indeed take place in Las Vegas. "I don't remember any specific conversations," Ammarell said, "but I think we were there to discuss the sale of George's

[Wackenhut] yacht, the Top Secret. I think Nichols said he had a potential buyer."

Wrote *SPY*, "So, the wealthy president of a large security company with CIA ties and one of his board members meet with a drug dealer turned electronics expert and a spook turned arms supplier – and all they discuss is the sale of a boat?"

••••••••

After reading the newspaper article on the death of Paul Morasca, I contacted Jonathan Littman at the *San Francisco Chronicle.* Littman jumped in the car and drove from San Francisco to Mariposa (near Yosemite National Park) when he learned I had obtained Michael's hidden documents.

Interestingly, when he arrived at my home he thumbed through piles of documents, but seemed to be looking for something specific. I later learned he was searching for Phyllis Riconosciuto's (Michael's first wife's) diary.

While Michael had worked at Wackenhut, Phyllis had been treated psychiatrically by the Cabazon administrator, Dr. John Phillip Nichols. Part of her treatment included writing a "diary" of her life with Michael. Michael later broke into Nichols' office at the reservation and stole the original diary before fleeing to Washington state.

The original diary was in fact included in the documents I had obtained in the desert, but I decided to withhold specific pages from Littman until I could determine what his purpose for wanting them was. An incident which I have enumerated in Chapter 10, confirmed that my instincts had been subliminally correct.

Meanwhile, I attempted to satisfy Littman with a few documents sent to me by Henry Weinstein, court reporter for the *Los Angeles Times.* I had contacted Weinstein in early March to inquire if he had written anything on Robert Booth Nichols' (unrelated to Dr. John Phillip Nichols) lawsuit against the Los Angeles FBI, specifically FBI agent Thomas Gates?

Weinstein had not heard of the lawsuit, but immediately investigated at the Los Angeles courthouse. Shortly thereafter, he sent a package of documents relating not only to Nichols' lawsuit against Thomas Gates, but also relative to Nichols' corporate minutes on the facilitation of biological technology to Japanese institutes, copies of his weapons permits, and documents indicating that Eugene

Giaquinto, Vice president of MCA Entertainment Division, was on the board of directors of Nichols' corporation, Meridian International Logistics.

Marvin Rudnick, now a Pasadena lawyer, once tried to prosecute MCA Corporation for organized crime involvement, but got shut down at the highest level, and the Organized Crime Strike Force was disbanned. One member of that investigative team was Richard Stavin, who talked to Danny Casolaro shortly before his death.

Eugene Giaquinto and Jack Valenti played heavily in Stavin's investigation of MCA, as did Curry Company (a subsidiary of MCA) in Yosemite National Park. Rudnick was written up in American Lawyer for his explorations through the MCA labyrinth, and at some point, worked parallel with Thomas Gates during his investigation of Robert Nichols. Gates and Weinstein were also well acquainted with Mariposa County government's relationship with Curry Company.

In return for sharing copies of these documents with him, I asked Littman to collaborate with me on a story concerning the government sanctioned (10 years!) methamphetamine operations at Whiskey Flats, on the Sara Priest Indian reservation in Mariposa. I was still intent on forcing the arrest of deputies involved in the meth lab at that location. Littman instructed me to put together a detailed synopsis which he would submit to the *San Francisco Chronicle.*

— 10 —

Covert Operations

Through Michael Riconosciuto, Danny Casolaro had compiled a sizable list of former CIA officers and arms dealers, the most noteworthy of whom was Robert Booth Nichols, described in various publications as a James Bond type who jetted around the world trading arms and other products.

At the time of Danny's investigation, Nichols headed Meridian International Logistics (M.I.L.), a California-based company that conducted extensive business in Australia and Japan. M.I.L. also controlled Meridian Arms Corporation of which Riconosciuto was briefly Vice President.

Out of the Wackenhut-Cabazon endeavor grew a business partnership between Nichols and Riconosciuto, both interested in developing new, high-tech sub-machine guns and powerful explosive devices that, like a nuclear blast, could produce an electromagnetic pulse that could wipe out an enemy's communications and electronics.

The secretive Nichols chatted with Casolaro frequently. Casolaro's July phone bills indicated that he called Nichols fifteen times that month, often in the wee hours of the morning. Several of those phone conversations lasted for more than two hours. Before his death on August 10th, Danny Casolaro told his brother, Tony, and Bill Hamilton that Nichols warned him that his investigations were risky.

According to FBI statements, Nichols is not a man whose warnings should be taken lightly. Special Agent Thomas Gates of the Los Angeles FBI had been investigating the activities of Robert Booth Nichols and his corporation, Meridian International Logistics, through Japanese and Australian legal attaches abroad.

According to a subsequent deposition filed by Gates, the bureau suspected Nichols of being involved in a $500 million stock fraud and of maintaining ties to the Gambino crime family and organized crime in Japan.

Gates's deposition was part of a 1987 wire-tapping on the phone of Eugene Giaquinto, an official of the MCA entertainment corporation with reputed *mob* links. Nichols was one of the people whose calls the bureau intercepted. According to the wiretap application, Nichols was allegedly an international money launderer for money generated through narcotics trafficking and organized crime activities.

In June, 1989, Nichols sued Thomas Gates in a California state court for libel, slander, and interference with contractual relationships when he (Gates) allegedly acted outside the scope of his employment by initiating contacts with the Australian Federal Police and various individuals in Australia and Japan. The complaint asked for damages in the amount of $11,000,000.

Ted Gunderson submitted an affidavit on Nichols' behalf, stating that he believed Gates *had* acted outside the scope of his employment when investigating Nichols abroad; the suit was subsequently dismissed through the Ninth Circuit Court of Appeals.

Robert Booth Nichols was depicted in one eastern publication as a "handsome, dashing figure, frequently described as `Clark Gable without the ears' ..." His friendship with movie actor Steven Seagal brought him a cameo appearance in the movie, "Under Siege," but his real purpose for being on the set was to act as technical advisor for the weaponry used in the movie.

The son of a prominent Los Angeles surgeon, Nichols is the inventor of a submachine pistol that he maintained was superior to the MAC-10.

Nichols' weapons permit application, dated January 28, 1985 from the Santa Clara County Sheriff's Department, indicated that he was born on March 6, 1943 at Loma Linda, California. In addition to his residences in California, he maintained residences in Italy, France, Australia and London, England for "business purposes for twenty years."

His medical doctor was listed in Zurich, Switzerland. He had worked for Harold Okimoto in Hawaii for four years, from 1968 to 1972 as Vice President of Preventor Security Center, an intruder electronics firm.

The four guns registered to him included two Colt .45 automatics. His purpose for carrying a concealed weapon was listed as such: "I am involved in the research and development of weapons systems, ranging from the basic blow-back automatic weapon to various advanced destructive devices. As I have detailed knowledge of the workings of these systems, I feel it is imperative to have personal protection for myself and for the good of the community."

Nichols' corporation, Meridian Arms, a subsidiary of Meridian International Logistics, was licensed in California in 1987 to posses and/or transport machine guns, Permit No. 01678, and to sell machine guns, Permit No. 01677. A 1985 Statement by Domestic Stock Corporation filed with the Secretary of State in Sacramento listed Harold Okimoto, Peter Zokosky, and Glen Shockley as Directors in addition to Nichols' family.

Okimoto, Zokosky and Shockley are also listed as Directors on Meridian International Logistics, Inc. (MIL). Eugene F. Giaquinto, president of MCA (Music Corporation of America) Home Entertainment Division in Universal City, was also a Director of M.I.L. until May 31, 1988, when he resigned and returned his 10,000 shares of stock as a result of the Los Angeles Organized Crime Task Force investigation, at that time headed by Thomas Gates and Richard Stavin.

The May 25, 1988 Minutes of an MIL Board meeting reflected Robert Booth Nichols concern with the investigation: " ... Upon meeting with Agent Gates on March 8, 1988, our legal counsel, Judge Mark Robinson, interpreted the line of questioning of Agent Gates as having a main focus on the relationship between Robert Nichols and MCA, Inc. (of which Mr. Giaquinto is an officer).

" ... Therefore, due to Mr. Nichols' concern, which Mr. Giaquinto understood and thus stated he would submit written resignation within two days; it was the unanimous decision of the Board to remove Mr. Giaquinto from the position of Director of MIL forthwith ..."

Nichols' concern with such an investigation can well be justified when you review the Minutes of an MIL board meeting held in Sherman Oaks on August 26, 1988. The following business was discussed and voted upon: (excerpted)

> It was the unanimous decision of the Board to draft a letter to the President of an internationally recognized Medical School in

> Japan (as referenced in our corporate minutes of April 24, 1988) with regard to our corporation's intention to make available a grant of funds to said School, as the funds become available to our corporation, and under specific terms and conditions.
>
> ... The phenomenal success in the field of immunotherapeutics by the Immunology Department of said Japanese Medical School has convinced the Board [of MIL] that the EXCLUSIVE training of qualified physicians under contract to and the direction of Meridian International Logistics, Inc., would be of great value and benefit to our company and it's shareholders.

While reading these documents, I couldn't help wondering why an "arms" dealer, allegedly tied in with organized crime, wanted to fund the exclusive training of physicians at a Japanese medical school?

The Minutes of MIL dated September 20th, 1988, referred to an agreement executed on September 14th, which discussed the three-way, equal ownership between MIL, Dr. Shigeyoshi Fujimoto, and Ajinomoto Co. Inc., of certain patented biological technology identified as "a newly devised technology for induction and activation of cytotoxic T-lymphocytes (T-cells), referred to as CTL, directed to autologous cancer cells in vitro with high efficacy utilizing a serum-free medium."

A Power of Attorney was issued to attorney Fujio Kubota in Japan to file patents and registrations on the technology entitled "The Method for Induction and Activation of Cytotoxic T-Lymphocytes."

The signatories on the Agreement to file Registrations and Patents on September 14, 1988 were listed as Dr. Shigeyoshi Fujimoto; Takasha Miyamae (Ajinomoto Co., Inc.); Hidetoshi Onogi (representative of MIL); Kanehiro Ishida (International Service Center, Inc.); and Takashi Kumakawa (American Embassy).

Hidetoshi Onogi was granted full power of attorney to negotiate and execute an equity position for Meridian International Logistics related to the filings and "any other documentation pertaining to the technical knowledge and the mechanical and/or chemical processes for the production of T-Cells as are present in the immune system of the human body or any other organism."

In and of itself this transaction seemed innocuous enough. But again I asked myself, why was an international arms dealer on the Board of F.I.D.C.O (First Intercontinental Development Corporation), a CIA-NSC front corporation, which offered three billion dollars to rebuild Beirut to President Amin Gamayel of Lebanon, whose chief of finances (Sami el Khouri) was shipping tons of heroin to Sicily for re-export to America, want to invest in "a method for induction and activation of cytotoxic T-Lymphocytes"?

Was this technology being developed with the authority of the U.S. government, or independently? If Nichols' operations were in fact government sanctioned, then it must have been frustrating for him to be investigated by the FBI. The concept of the FBI inadvertently investigating the CIA was ironic. And what had Danny Casolaro learned about this technology?

I found a possible answer in an obscure letter written on Wackenhut/Cabazon letterhead, dated January 20, 1983, addressed to Dr. Harry Fair at Tactical Technology in Arlington, Virginia, from Dr. John P. Nichols, Cabazon Administrator. The letter noted that on February 15th, 1983, Dr. Nichols would be forwarding to Dr. Fair "a unique list of agents and production techniques related to biological warfare."

The letter went on to say that the Storemont Laboratories business plan Dr. Nichols mailed to him was to prepare him for what was to be sent in the area of biological warfare. Added Dr. Nichols: "[These] products could be utilized in small countries bordering *Albania* or large countries bordering the Soviet Union. You will be amazed at the scope ..."

I could not help recalling the *Village Voice* article ("The Last Days of Danny Casolaro," October 15, 1991) which had stated, tongue in cheek, that "Casolaro had traced the Inslaw and related stories back to a CIA `Old Boy' network that had begun working together in the 1950's around the ALBANIA covert operations ..."

The hybridoma technology discussed in attached documents (in Michael Riconosciuto's files), centered around the ability to reorganize and synthesize genetic structures – and to modify "lymphocytes" (immune cells).

Under the heading "Possible Military Applications Utilizing Hybridoma Technology" was the notation that "gene-splicing technology provides the ability to produce pathogenic (harmful) agents, i.e. viruses."

"In fact," noted the writer, "biological warfare weaponry of this nature (both production and supply) is limited only by the imagination of the scientist."

Included in the above mentioned documents (attached to the Dr. Harry Fair letter), was a proposal to develop monoclonal antibody kits to detect the presence of such harmful biological agents in a field (combat) environment. In other words, develop a laboratory created vaccine for a laboratory created virus. The very same proposal had been submitted to Peter Zokosky in December 1982 by John P. Nichols.

I wondered, was THIS the same technology that Robert Booth Nichols and the Directors of MIL, including Peter Zokosky, Glen Shockley and Harold Okimoto, were fronting to the Japanese? What kind of "weapon" was this?

Other weapons discussed in the same letter included the Cabazon Arms CA 9 SMG which "Peter Zokosky had the British interested in." The CA 9 SMG could be produced for $75.00 per unit on the reservation and sold for $100 to $125.00. "It meets all the needs of a small, poor democracy for 9MM parabellum," said Nichols.

"They can afford to purchase this one. We have fired over 50,000 rounds with the test model using South Korean ammunition without jamming. We could begin manufacturing within two weeks in a country like Guatemala, Chile, etc., utilizing USA produced dies and Swedish extrusion machinery." ... Peter Zokosky has fired both the Viper and the CA 9 SMG and was impressed with both, but particularly with the CA 9 SMG. Kuwait has been particularly interested in financing the production of the CA 9 SMG ..."

Dr. Nichols concluded: "We would initially manufacture on the reservation. We can purchase an existing small company with all the licenses to manufacture and export. [Meridian Arms?] We are ready. We are continuing to experiment with the combination sniper rifle (9MM) equipped with microprocessor vision enhancement (no tubes) (night vision). Michael Riconosciuto and some friends of the reservation have been working cooperatively on this project. Within another 90 to 120 days we should have a working model to use on the CA 9 SMG and the sniper rifle."

The ongoing projects listed in research and development were a second 9MM calibre machine pistol, an assault rifle with laser sighting, a long-distance sniper rifle, and a small portable rocket system which could be attached to the assault rifle.

Three months later, on April 13, 1983, Robert Booth Nichols wrote to Joseph Preloznik in Madison, Wisconsin, recapitulating exactly the same weapons proposal as outlined above by Dr. John Nichols to Dr. Harry Fair.

I never found out who Joseph Preloznik was, but Dr. Harry Fair's name popped up in a Wackenhut Inter-Office Memorandum in Michael's files. Dated May 25, 1981, from Robert Frye, a Vice President of Wackenhut in Indio, to Robert Chasen, a Vice President of Wackenhut in Coral Gables (and former Commissioner of U.S. Customs) the memorandum detailed a May 12-13 visit to Dr. Harry Fair, Chief of Propulsion Technology, Applied Sciences Division and others at Picatinny Arsenal in Dover, New Jersey.

The arsenal was listed under the official heading of "U.S. Army Armament Research & Development Command, Large Caliber Weapon Systems Laboratory" or ARRADCOM.

The five-page memo not only outlined the depth of Wackenhut's commitment and involvement at the Cabazon reservation, but it delineated Peter Zokosky's importance to the projects underway there. One of those projects included proposed construction of an "R & D" (Research and Development) facility on the Cabazon Indian reservation for the manufacture of 120 mm. combustible cartridge cases for sale to the U.S. Army, with sales also to NATO, and especially to the Federal Republic of Germany which at that time, was adopting the use of such cases in their Leopard tanks.

Wrote Frye: "The obvious key to any such endeavor is [Peter] Zokosky. He is reportedly one of only 6-7 personnel in the world who have had any significant experience in the development and manufacture of the slurry process involved in combustible cartridge cases. He is under present non-compete agreement with Armtec, his former company, until August 1981. Armtec is the present sole source supplier of 120 mm. combustible cartridge cases to the U.S. Government. Zokosky is also serving as a consultant to the British Government ..."

It is noteworthy that the Cabazon Indians had enlisted the aid of other Indian tribes to join in their endeavor. Use of adjacent tribal lands as a location for a large caliber weapons range test site was obtained from a sister tribe, the Torres Martinez, involving some 30,000 acres of very remote and desolate land near the Salton Sea. Potential use of a test firing range for the "railgun" on the Santa Rosa Mountain, under the control of the Santa Rosa Indians, had also been pledged to the Cabazons and the U.S. Government.

A notation in the Wackenhut memorandum referred to the proposed purchase of Valleyfield Chemical Products Corporation in Valleyfield, Quebec, near Montreal, Canada. Valleyfield was formerly owned by Gerald Bull, assassinated in March 1990, who had developed the original Project Babylon super rail gun for the Iraqi government. The Wackenhut memorandum outlined an interest to purchase Valleyfield Chemical by Dr. John Nichols with a Barry Zuckerman and Charles F. Agar, both Canadian citizens, who were involved in a Canadian firm called Mineral Resources International Limited, as well as both being involved in Canadian financial institutions.

"Dr. [John] Nichols envisions that the role of the Cabazon/Wackenhut Joint Venture should the Zuckerman-Agar group be successful in so purchasing this plant, would be to serve as the foreign marketing representative for the plant; to have this group possibly finance the establishment of the casing/loading facility on the Cabazon reservation; and to have the capability to conduct R&D [Research and Development] for the group in the armament industry," according to the memorandum.

A meeting had been set up in Ottawa, Canada at 9:00 A.M., May 26, 1981 involving Dr. John Philip Nichols, Frank Agar, F. Thornburg, A.R. Frye and members of the Canadian Munitions Board to discuss capital investment in the Valleyfield plant.

Another notation was included in the lengthy memorandum to "firm up the deal between the Joint Venture and John Vanderwerker, President of Intersect Corporation, [in] Irvine, California, who had the exclusive rights for foreign marketing" with the Litton Electron Tube Division in third world countries.

Mention of John Vanderwerker in the Wackenhut memorandum was singularly important in my investigative leap from overt arms operations to "covert" intelligence operations.

According to Peter Zokosky, Vanderwerker was on the CIA payroll. In Riconosciuto's files, I located a letter dated April 11, 1983, written to Vanderwerker at Intersect Corporation from Glenn Shockley, a Board Director of both FIDCO (First Intercontinental Development Corporation) and MIL (Meridian International Logistics), under investigation for organized crime activities. Robert Booth Nichols was also on the Board of both corporations.

The Octopus trail gets a little complicated here, but it is a significant trail. Both Vanderwerker and Shockley were allegedly on the

CIA payroll. Documents to that effect will be noted in future pages. In the afore-mentioned letter, Shockley was offering to Vanderwerker forty-two AH1-S Cobra Helicopters at a unit price of seven million eight hundred thousand U.S. dollars each.

The rest of the letter read as follows: (Note: a few words had been damaged while Xeroxing)

> The price offered is F.A.S. location at Seller's option Europe. The price is net to Buyer possessing the proper documentation and does not include any government considerations (taxes), if any, all of which (indecipherable) to the Buyer's account.
>
> For verification of the existence of these products, you are requested to refer to telex transmission occurring during the Spring of 1981 between Union Bank Suisse of Zurich, Switzerland, and Omega Industries of Long Island, New York. The transmissions were addressed to Mr. Parvis Lavi at Omega and were signed by Mr. N.A. (indecipherable) bank officer. Your immediate response to this offer would be greatly appreciated. Sincerely, Glenn. R. Shockley.

Attached to this letter was a handwritten memorandum, obviously taken from the above referenced "telex" transmission. The memo delineated the procedure for "airframe I.D. number acquisition." The buyer's bank officer was instructed to telephone Seller's bank officer at 8:00 A.M. Tuesday morning to relay the following Seller's bank data: "Bank – Credit Suisse, Geneva. Officer – Mr. Eucomun. Telephone number – 011-41-22-36-53-80. Account Number – 02746590 5482-1 Reference Code – J.H."

If the connection was missed, then it was to be repeated Wednesday at 8:00 A.M. $10 million U.S. dollars was to be exchanged at the bank for [a] Frame I.D. No. on Wednesday. If all was ready to proceed in Geneva in 5 banking days, then the $10 million would be credited to the buyer's account toward acquisition of all craft. If not, then $10 million was to be forfeited.

The bank officer's follow-up monologue as noted on the memorandum read as follows: "Acting on behalf of our client, I confirm that he has on deposit the sum of $10 million U.S.D. Upon receipt of one airframe identification number, the price of one craft will be set aside irrevocably for your client. If our client does not present to you within 5 banking days in Geneva, Switzerland, all necessary data, documents and fund commitments, he has agreed to forfeit the price of one craft to your client's account."

Also attached to these documents, was a sheet of handwritten notes obviously related to the above transaction. The names of various banks and their locations, along with the name of a bank officer, notations about metric tons of gold, and a code name, "Messenger Boy," were cryptically scrawled on the sheet.

I inquired of Michael Riconosciuto what the story was on the sale of the Cobra helicopters? Riconosciuto briefly related the following story. The forty-two Cobra helicopters had been ordered by/for NATO, then after the helicopters were built, the funding was not available. Nichols and Glenn Shockley, working for the CIA, were contracted to "get rid of the helicopters." John Vanderwerker was brought into the operation and the helicopters were shipped to a warehouse in Europe, destined for North Korea, then Iraq.

It is important to note here that North Korea was a conduit for arms to Iraq from both the United States and the Soviet Union. In essence, the United States was forced to "compete" with the Soviets in providing arms to Iraq.

This is discussed in further chapters, but in summary, what it all boiled down to was Oliver North supplied arms to Iran. The CIA supplied arms to Iraq. And Wackenhut supplied arms to the Contras. All under the authority and supervision of the U.S. Government.

I asked Michael Riconosciuto if Danny Casolaro had knowledge of the "helicopter" deal? Michael responded, "I gave him the names of the people that were involved and Danny went out and confirmed it."

I asked him to elaborate. "Well, Danny went and talked to Roy Furmarc (phonetic sp.), William Casey's ex-right hand man, and Furmarc admitted that he had contact with them [the helicopters]. And when the NATO stuff disappeared, Bob [Nichols] disappeared with it. They weren't going to pay Bob and his accomplices what they wanted, per the original deal, and Bob got angry and just walked away with it all. But Bob got help from some people in the White House, and they cut a certain group of guys in the agency [CIA] out."

I asked, "Who was involved with the helicopter sale besides Nichols?"

"Well, Glen Shockley, Parvis Lavi (phonetic sp.), he's an Iranian, but he worked with the Israeli (indecipherable word) Mission out of New York ..."

Riconosciuto paused, remembering, then continued with his story: " ... I brought in Stan Singer, former deputy Israeli Defense Minister, to try and take all those helicopters off everybody's hands. I would have made a nice, tidy sum of money for myself ..."

"Who were the helicopters originally destined for?"

Mike: "NATO. During the Carter administration, there was a slip up on some funding, they were really screwy in the way they handled certain things ..."

"Was this some kind of an undercover operation?"

Mike: "It was on the up and up, regular deliveries from the United States to NATO, but there was some kind of a misunderstanding between the upper reaches of the Carter Administration and some of the other NATO countries, so while they were having high-level discussions, no financial instruments exchanged hands.

"They finally came to terms on the financial end of it, but by that time the stuff [helicopters] had been removed from the loading docks and warehouses."

"So, they were gone?"

Mike: "They were gone."

"To North Korea?"

Mike: "Into storage in Europe. Later they got sold to North Korea, and other places. It was hotter than hell ..."

"Where in Europe, do you know?"

Mike: "Well, I don't want to go into it on the phone [from jail], but I know the whole story behind it. While it was in storage, everybody and their brother was trying to buy the stuff and the price got jacked way up. Casey's faction and Carlucci and those guys, they wanted it all, wanted to screw Bob and his guys, and Bob made an alliance with somebody else for the stuff ..."

"Who?"

"Well, later with Mike McManus in the White House." (McManus was assistant to President Reagan, and on the Board of Directors of FIDCO with Nichols).

"Why did they call upon Nichols to do this? What was his connection?"

Mike: "Bob had been doing errands for them for years ..."

"Was he working for the NSC at that time?"

Mike: "Just the CIA. He was just doing contract type work. He was good at what he did. Whatever objectives were given to him,

Bob always achieved them. You know, he has an impeccable track record ..."

In a subsequent interview with Robert Booth Nichols, I asked him about the helicopter deal. Nichols confirmed that he had, indeed, participated in the shipment of the helicopters to Europe through the CIA.

In news interviews, Wackenhut had denied association with Michael Riconosciuto, yet in Michael's files, I found a letter written on Meridian Arms letterhead, dated February 10, 1984, from Robert Booth Nichols to Dr. Harry Fair referring to the Wackenhut visit to Picatinny Arsenal in May, 1981. Nichols reminded Dr. Fair of the demonstration at Picatinny in which "Michael Riconosciuto [had] discussed electrostatic heat transfer augmentation in a wide range of applications ... and demonstrated control of heat in electric discharge."

This letter was significant in that it confirmed that Riconosciuto *had* in fact accompanied Peter Zokosky and Robert Frye, Vice President of Wackenhut, to the Picatinny Arsenal to demonstrate the above mentioned technology.

••••••••

The crux of the Wackenhut involvement in arms development and shipments through various sources, including Peter Zokosky, Robert Booth Nichols, John Vanderwerker, and others, was tied irrevocably to the Reagan administration's efforts to aid the Nicaraguan Contras.

A Special Operations Report emanating from the Riverside, California, District Attorney's office which was sent to John Cohen, investigator for the House Judiciary Committee on Inslaw, provided indisputable proof that Wackenhut sold arms to the Contras.

The Special Operations Intelligence Report entitled, "*Nicaraguans and Earl Brian at Lake Cahuilla – 9/10/81*" described a meeting held between two groups, the Nicaraguans and Wackenhut/Cabazon officials, at a county-owned police firing range at Lake Cahuilla in Riverside County.

According to the surveillance report, the purpose of the meeting was "to test a new night vision device and weapons. All [the] weapons tested were semi-automatic. [A] new sniper rifle tested was a 50 caliber with a 308 bullet."

The report went on to note that "some automatic weapons were present, but all had necessary permits through Meridian Arms.

Meridian Arms [is] owned by Michael Riconosciuto, Robert Booth Nichols (no relation to John Phillip Nichols), and Don Oliver – former Undersheriff of San Diego County. Meeting and testing took about one hour, then all parties left."

Police officers had been placed around the surrounding area in a surveillance/protection type mode. Each of the six Indio police officers participating in the range surveillance were named individually in the report.

The license plate numbers of each car that arrived on the scene was included in the Report along with the names and identification of everyone who attended the demonstration. Some of those names and I.D.'s were:

"Michael Riconosciuto – Researcher for Cabazon Indians."

"Peter Zokosky – President of Armtech – Coachella."

"John D. Vanderwerker and a couple of his friends – Vanderwerker, CIA Research Director – for CIA [for] 8 years."

"Earl Brian – Wisconsin businessman and CIA employee."

"Two Nicaraguan Generals – Eden Pastora, Commander Zero and Jose Curdel, Commander Alpha."

"Raul Arana – Central Caribbean research procurement front for liberation of Nicaragua (Pre-Contra days)."

"John Phillip Nichols – Cabazon Indian Manager."

"Wayne Reeder – Builder/Developer""Jimmy Hughes – Security Chief – Cabazon Indians"

"Art Welmas – Tribal Chairman of Cabazon Indians."

"Scott Wesley – United States Army."

"Honduran Telephone Company – Military connection network in Southern Hemisphere." And others.

The surveillance report indicated that Wayne Reeder and Earl Brian arrived together in a 1981 White Rolls Royce, License Plate Number OK 2XG2302. The two Nicaraguan Generals arrived in a 1981 Honda, License Plate Number AZ AFM877.

A newspaper article in the *Los Angeles Times*, dated May 16, 1991, entitled, "Noriega Papers Claim CIA Sent Him Millions," by Mike Clary, reported that General Manual Noriega, Panama's former strongman leader, was paid more than $11 million from a CIA slush fund. A 107-page Noriega defense document contended that Noriega once warned the CIA to put an end to cocaine shipments to the United States that were being used to raise funds for the Contras in Nicaragua.

Noriega, who was scheduled to go on trial for drug smuggling on July 22, maintained that planes carrying arms to Nicaraguan rebels returned to the United States loaded with illegal drugs. It was clearly a guns for drugs policy, he said.

The article concluded that "Noriega served as a conduit for cash payments from the CIA to onetime anti-Sandinista leader EDEN PASTORA."

So, in 1981, Eden Pastora attended the Wackenhut night-vision goggles demonstration in Indio with numerous CIA employees in attendance, and ten years later, the L.A. Times reported that Pastora was a recipient of cash payments, via Noriega, from the CIA.

••••••••

I believe it is safe to theorize at this point that the various tentacles of the Octopus heretofore outlined were used to develop and ship arms to various countries such as Nicaragua, Afghanistan, Lebanon, Pakistan, and other third world countries in exchange for cocaine and heroin. These countries certainly didn't have the funds to pay with cash. And it is possible that The Company was in fact the mechanism used to distribute the drugs after entry into the United States.

The reader may be wondering how I obtained a copy of the above-mentioned "Special Operations [surveillance] Report." I had requested a copy of it from both the Riverside District Attorney's office and John Cohen, investigator for the House Judiciary Committee on Inslaw, but the report was confidential and neither would send me a copy.

I then called Peter Zokosky and asked him to corroborate the report's existence. He not only corroborated it, but he offered to send me a copy. When I asked how HE had obtained a copy, he said, "I asked a friend in Washington D.C. to go into the [House Judiciary] vault and make a copy for me."

I received a copy shortly thereafter from Peter Zokosky. When I called John Cohen and mentioned I'd obtained a copy, he said he was aware that "someone" had gotten past the guards and into the House vault. He didn't know what had been taken, but he validated the document in my possession.

— 11 —

Bio-Technology

Michael Riconosciuto had some, if not all, of the answers to the gene splicing technology that Zokosky and Wackenhut had attempted to sell to the Army weapons division in 1983, and later fronted to the Japanese, through Meridian International Logistics, in 1988.

I felt that time was of the essence in uncovering the nature of this technology, so I pushed Riconosciuto to talk about it. "It looks like Earl Brian, Sir Denis Kendall, Hercules Research, Wackenhut, Zokosky and Bob Nichols were all involved in the same bio-technological agenda ..."

Michael answered, "You got it."

I asked, "Are they connected, or are they all individually working on their own projects?"

Michael: "Yes."

"How?"

Michael: "Check out Bio-Rad Laboratories. Their international headquarters are on half of the property that used to be the Hercules plant, in Hercules, California. Do you understand what I'm saying? Bio-Rad makes the most toxic biological and radioactive compounds known to man. And they're now located in the town of Hercules. Bio-Rad Industrial Park.

"See, Bio-Rad was the flagship company, and then they [Earl Brian] started Info-Tech, and then they got mired in lawsuits and then Hadron was formed to be a cut-out parent corporation, you know, just to be a firewall from law suits ..."

I asked, "What do they do at Bio-Rad?"

"Well, they make the most hazardous biological and nuclear chemicals in the world, for medical research."

"Who do they sell it to?"

"Well, front line researchers all over the world. Bio-Rad is the single source for this stuff ... actually Aldrich Chemical sells it, there's about 100 companies, but Bio-Rad is head and shoulder above all of them by a factor of ten on many things like Cyto-toxins."

I remembered reading about Cyto-toxins in the Wackenhut/Cabazon biological warfare letters to Dr. Harry Fair.

Michael continued ... "You look at Cytotoxic T-Lymphocytes. You go ask any medical professional what they're doing on the leading edge of research there? What the full implications to humanity are, OK?"

I wanted clarification from Michael, so I answered, "It looks to me like research on a cure for cancer."

Michael took the bait. "Go ask a professional. I'd rather have you hear it from a collateral source other than from me."

"Well, give me some indication ..."

Michael responded hesitantly, "It would have been Hitler's wet dream. It's selective to such a degree that it's awesome. With the appropriate genetic material, you can wipe out whole segments of humanity. There's no stopping it."

"I asked, "You mean you could selectively wipe out certain races of people?"

"Sure."

"Jeez."

Mike continued ..."And, also, from the beneficial side, you can very specifically wipe out disease cells, cancer cells. Look at the patents. Look at Immunix (phonetic sp.) Corporation, look at the patent portfolios on Bio-Rad."

"Who's Bio-Rad's main buyer?"

"Well, the National Institute of Health, you know, every hospital in the world buys Bio-Rad products."

I had read about Sir Denis Kendall, the famous MI6 British intelligence officer during World War II, in "Who's Who in America," 1989 issue. Kendall had worked with Michael in some, as yet, undefined capacity. Bobby Riconosciuto had noted to me that Kendall and Ted Gunderson had counseled Oliver North prior to his testimony to Congress. Kendall was also heavily involved in arms and biotechnology, according to Michael Riconosciuto.

"Who's Who" described Denis William Kendall as a "medical electronic equipment company executive," born in Halifax, Yorkshire, England on May 27, 1903. Kendall came to the United States in 1923, was naturalized in 1957. His background included being a consultant to the Pentagon on high velocity small arms from 1940 to 1945. He was listed on Churchill's War Cabinet Gun Board from 1941-45. He was later executive vice president of Brunswick Ordnance Plant in New Jersey from 1952 to 1956. From 1961 to 1973, became president of Dynapower Medonics in Los Angeles, and chief executive of Kendall Medical International, Inc. in Los Angeles in 1973.

In 1983, the same year that Wackenhut was offering biological warfare agents to the Army, Sir Denis Kendall was the chairman of Steron Products, Inc. His club membership listings indicated he was a 32 degree Shriner in the Pacific Palisades (California) Masons and a member of the Religious Society of Friends (Quaker), amongst other things.

I asked Riconosciuto, "What was Sir Denis Kendall's connection ...?"

Michael broke in ..."He's involved in all of it. You might be able to get a handle on Kendall through Tiny Roland, a subsidiary of which is Penguin Books. And the other good-ole-boy in the nail work is Octav Botnar. Then there's Wolfgang Fosog (phonetic sp.), Renee Hanner, Count Otto Linkee (phonetic sp.) ..."

"How did you meet these guys?"

"I was introduced through Joe Snell and Norman Davis. Snell was considered the father of industrial design. He was an industrial design artist who did the logos for Coca Cola, Chanel No. 5, *Life* magazine. Norm Davis owned (unintelligble) brewery until he sold to Carling. My dad was his advertising and public relations man. My dad didn't know Kendall personally, but Norm Davis did. I met Kendall through Davis."

"Do you know what Kendall is into currently?"

"Sure."

"What would that be?"

"There's a pharmaceutical company in Los Angeles. There's a medical electronics company ... Ted Shannon in Los Angeles supervises all the production for that stuff. It's very exotic, far out stuff. And he's still in a controlling position in Brunswick [Ordnance] Corporation."

I asked Riconosciuto, "How close was Bio-Rad to your father's plant, Hercules?"

Mike answered, "It's on the same property!"

"Mike, when you were conducting research at Hercules, you were incubating something in fish tanks there. What was it?"

Michael's response had a nervous edge to it. "Where ... where are you getting this?"

Riconosciuto was unaware at that point that his hidden files were in my possession. "I'm just thumbing through some old documents ..."

" ... Those documents aren't supposed to exist any more. They've all been destroyed."

"By whom?"

"Well, it was a matter of routine, you know ... they COULDN'T exist ...'""

"Uh, huh."

"That's what they're doing with all this stock manipulation, you know. The biologicals are what got them in the door at such a high level in Japan ..."

I sensed Riconosciuto's possible involvement in the project, his reluctance to discuss it. But he believed I had "all" the records and he stammered on. " ... That paperwork trail shouldn't exist. I mean it was kept in a safe place, and then it was shredded. And the only people that had any direct knowledge of it was [Peter] Zokosky and Earl Barber, John Nichols, Bob Nichols, you know, those people ..."

Michael was attempting to disengage himself from any responsibility for the research.

" ... If there are any records left, those are their records, not any of ours [at Hercules], because I'm sure all of ours were destroyed."

I asked, "Why did you destroy them?"

"Well, do you understand the nature of this technology? You're talking in vague, general terms."

I answered, "I have an idea ..."

Michael interjected, " ... Horrible things. You know, it makes what the Nazi's did to the Jews look mild. The Romanian Project, do your homework on that project, you know it's a horrible germ warfare project ..."

"Uh, huh."

" ... And the Soviets were involved in it, and we countered it with our own methods."

I noted to Michael that Bill Turner, the man who had met Danny Casolaro in the parking lot of the Sheraton Martinsburg Inn (with Hughes Aircraft documents) on the day before his death, was currently in jail. Turner had written a letter in which he talked about an Iraqi from the Iraqi Embassy who was facilitating the transportation of biological warfare items to Iraq.

Michael responded, "Listen, Saddam Hussein introduced chemical and biological warfare agents to all his top military leaders. And he became enamored with this technology. He's been on a binge of sorts. Even when he was in the secret police of Iraq, he used chemical means on a wide scale ..."

I asked, "But none of these various entities that I've just named were dealing directly with Iraq, were they?"

"No, no. Not directly. All they needed was a VENDORS LIST."

Riconosciuto noted that the shipments were all ITAR (International Trafficking of Armaments) regulated chemicals, electronics, communications equipment, anything that was on the ITAR list.

♦♦♦♦♦♦♦♦

In August, 1991, the *Financial Post* ran a story on Dr. Earl Brian. At that time, Brian's main company, Infotechnology Inc. of New York was bankrupt, and its subsidiary United Press International (UPI) was on the verge of collapse.

According to the *Financial Post,* the Securities and Exchange Commission and the FBI were investigating Brian, and a flurry of affidavits filed in the Inslaw Inc. scandal accused him of selling bootleg copies of the computer company's case-tracking software (PROMIS) to the intelligence services of Canada, Israel, and Iraq.

Brian was referred to as "Cash" in the intelligence community and reportedly had a close relationship with the CIA. He was a highly decorated combat surgeon in the Vietnam war in the late 1960's, allegedly working in the controversial Phoenix Program. This, according to a 1993 *Wired,* premier issue, entitled "INSLAW, The Inslaw Octopus" by Richard L. Fricker. Wrote Fricker, "After a stint in Vietnam, where he [Brian] worked as a combat physician in the unit that supplied air support for Operation Phoenix, Brian returned to California ..."

In 1970, Ronald Reagan appointed Brian director of the California Department of Health Care Services. He was only 27 and destined to remain a part of Reagan's inner sanctum. U.S. and Israeli intelligence sources linked Brian's name to the sale of weapons to Iran in the 1980's. "He was serving U.S. intelligence people, " said Ari Ben-Menashe, a former Israeli intelligence officer who claims he met Brian several times, once in Tel Aviv. Brian allegedly had more to do with the financial end of the transactions.

Other publications listed Brian's holdings in the rapidly developing biotechnology field. The high-tech empire of Dr. Brian was a grab bag of fledgling companies involved in all the hot areas – lasers, cancer detection kits, blood-testing products, genetic engineering, computer programs, telecommunications and investment databases.

One of Brian's companies, Hadron, Inc. of Fairfax, Virginia, which, incidentally, both Michael Riconosciuto and Robert Nichols maintained Peter Videnieks was involved in, was a laser manufacturer and computer services company.

According to Bill Hamilton, president of Inslaw, Hadron had attempted to buy Inslaw in 1983. Dominic Laiti, Hadron's chairman at the time, had phoned Hamilton out of the blue and said Hadron intended to become a dominant vendor of software to law enforcement agencies. Would Hamilton like to sell? Hamilton demurred. "We have ways of making you sell," Laiti is said to have replied.

Laiti, in an interview in 1988 with the Senate Subcommittee on Investigations, said he didn't remember calling Hamilton. Nevertheless, Hamilton said he believes his rejection of Hadron on that day in 1983 triggered an attempt by the Department of Justice to put Inslaw out of business, or at least bankrupt the small, Washington-based software maker.

At that time, Peter Videnieks was the administrator of the contract between Inslaw and the DOJ. Within a few months of Hadron's call, the Department of Justice, citing contract violations, stopped making payments on Inslaw's $10 million deal to install PROMIS software in its 20 largest U.S. attorney's offices nationwide. (PROMIS stands for Prosecutor's Management Information System.)

Inslaw, starved of cash, was forced into Chapter 11 bankruptcy protection in 1985. Hamilton sued the DOJ for theft of property in 1986.

In February 1988, Federal Bankruptcy Court Judge George Bason ordered the DOJ to pay Inslaw $7 million in licensing and legal fees. The DOJ, Bason ruled, had "stolen PROMIS from Inslaw through trickery, fraud and deceit," then tried to put the company out of business.

The DOJ appealed Bason's ruling, but it was upheld. However in May, the U.S. Court of Appeals reversed the decision on a technicality. Hamilton believed Dr. Brian and his old crony, former Attorney General Edwin Meese, were behind the attempt to bankrupt and liquidate Inslaw. When Inslaw refused to sell to Hadron, Hamilton believed the DOJ tried to bankrupt and liquidate Inslaw to force the sale of its assets, perhaps to Hadron, at firesale prices.

Several journalistic publications accused Dr. Brian of profiting from the Justice Department's theft of the PROMIS software. According to a number of sources, Brian traveled the world during the mid-eighties, selling the data management program to intelligence and law enforcement agencies the world over.

Brian's role, if any, in the October Surprise was less well publicized. The primary source thus far for the allegations that Brian was involved, is former Israeli intelligence officer Ari Ben-Menashe. Menashe alleged that Earl Brian helped make one of the first contacts between Republicans and the government of Iran in 1980. Ben-Menashe claimed Brian accompanied Robert C. "Bud" McFarlane to Tehran in late February 1980. The trip came shortly after the New Hampshire primary, when insiders knew that there would be a Reagan-Bush ticket.

Earl Brian and McFarlane, then an aide to Senator John Tower (R-TX), allegedly contacted Iranians with whom Brian had conducted business prior to the fall of the Shah. According to Ben-Menashe, one of these was Mehdi Bazargan, one-time Prime Minister, and in February 1980 still closely connected to the Iranian leadership.

An old 1975 Sacramento Bee newspaper article, dated January 12, 1975, reported that Earl Brian, called the Genius Doctor by his friends, was out to get a little "of that Middle Eastern oil money." The article went on to say that Brian was "helping to write a proposal on health care for Iran."

Brian, then at the University of Southern California, was working with Samuel Tibbetts of the California Lutheran Hospital Association, which in turn was working with a Chicago group. The Chicago group was not named and details of the proposal were not known. It is significant that Brian left his post one year before this proposal was written, in 1974, as Governor Ronald Reagan's Health and Welfare secretary. It was not known whether the contract with the Iranian government was ever consummated.

Another interesting facet of Brian's background included his relationship with Senator Terry Sanford (D-N.C.). Prior to his election, Sanford had been the attorney representing Earl Brian in his 1985 takeover bid for United Press International (UPI). Sanford was also instrumental in winning Brian an appointment to the board of Duke University Medical School. At that time, Sanford was the president of Duke University.

Dr. Brian ultimately directed his energies towards biological technology. Another of his companies, Biotech Capital Corporation of New York, became 50% owner of American Cytogenetics, which was planning in 1982 to create a subsidiary to engage in genetic research. One notable investor in Biotech, when it went public in 1981, was Edwin Meese. Today, American Cytogenetics in North Hollywood, California, conducts Pap tests for cervical cancer. It also tests tissue samples for cancer and related diseases. Sales in 1985 were $3.4 million.

Hadron, of which Dr. Brian was a director, provided engineering and computer consulting services, along with telecommunications products. Sales were $25.7 million in 1985. Clinical Sciences, Inc. sells biochemical products used for diagnostic tests and antibody analysis. Dr. Brian was also a director of this company. Sales in 1986 were about $4 million.

••••••••

Michael Riconosciuto had stated that he believed Earl Brian held a financial interest in Bio-Rad Laboratories in Hercules, California. I was unable to locate Brian's name in Board directories, but obtained some documents on an OEM agreement between California Integrated Diagnostics, Inc., a wholly owned subsidiary of the InFerGene Company, ("Manufacturer") a Delaware corporation, and Bio-Rad Laboratories, Inc. ("Customer") a Delaware corporation, which listed the terms under which the manufacturer would provide the customer with various products.

Various exhibits outlined the product price list, delivery schedules, engineering specifications, etc. What made this agreement significant was a newspaper article published in the *San Francisco Chronicle* on May 31, 1991, entitled, "S.F. Firm Faces Toxics Charges." A criminal complaint had been filed against a law firm, an investment banking house and several lawyers and financiers involved with InFerGene Company for abandoning its toxic wastes after filing for bankruptcy.

According to an affidavit filed by the Solano County District Attorney's office at the Fairfield Municipal Court, after InFerGene was evicted from the premises, a county inspector found several hundred containers including petri dishes and vials marked "chlamydia, herpes, and HSV-2." Many others contained "bacteria of unknown etiology."

A Vacaville newspaper reported that on December 7, an environmental health inspector found 36 55-gallon drums of radioactive Butanol containing "beef mucosa." They were improperly stored and lacked labels showing content, hazard warning or the owner's business address. A follow-up report made by the environmental health office noted that a Halloween 1990 investigation into a smell was traced to a door with a radiation warning on it. The department had recommended that the lab doors be sealed and the pipe opening sealed.

In all, the county Environmental Health Department had responded four times to complaints about smells from the InFerGene labs in the Benicia Industrial Park well before it shut down in February. One complaint listed persistent smells causing nausea, a problem also cited by others still working in the area.

Founded in 1983, InFerGene specialized in DNA technology, making diagnostic test kits for AIDS, hepatitis and other diseases.

My research led me to another article on Bay Area bio-labs. In June, 1991, the *San Francisco Examiner* published a story entitled, "Germ War Lab Alarms Berkeley" which noted the community of West Berkeley "was home to the Defense Department's one and only supplier of anti-plague vaccine." On December 28, 1990, four maintenance men made an unauthorized entrance into a room at Cutter Biological which housed Yersinia pestis, commonly known as "The Black Plague," which once killed a quarter of the population of Europe 650 years ago.

There was no harm to the workers and no release of the live bacteria, but if an accident had occurred, all of Berkeley would have been wiped out.

••••••••

It is impossible *not* to compare the two incidents in the San Francisco bay area with the Wackenhut proposal to develop biological warfare viruses on the Cabazon Indian reservation in Indio, California. In order to develop vaccines, which sounds innocuous enough, the virus must first be created. In the case of biological warfare viruses, the disease would have to be highly sophisticated indeed, if it were to be used in military applications. Certainly nothing that would be easily recognizable, if it escaped the laboratory, to a layman medical doctor in Indio, California, or for that matter at any Indian reservation in the United States.

Any type of biological research on an Indian reservation would not be subject to scrutiny by the federal government because Indian reservations are sovereign nations. Nevertheless, if a virus DID escape a secret government installation at an Indian reservation, the reservation would provide an ideally "isolated environment" for further study (by a government entity) of affected subjects or victims under quarantine. Not a very pretty picture. Yet this was the exact nature of the proposal by Wackenhut to Dr. Harry Fair of the Army weapons division.

For the first time, I began to notice various "mysterious" illnesses cropping up in the media. I'm sure there have been unidentified diseases throughout history, but for the first time, I was conscious of what was written about them.

The first to capture my attention was the sudden deaths of twelve Navajo Indians in New Mexico and Arizona. A June 3, 1993, Department of Health Services inter-office memorandum distributed to public health laboratory directors throughout California labeled the virus a "Mystery Illness in New Mexico and Arizona." The memo asked, "Is it in California too?"

On June 2, 1993, New Mexico officials had reported a total of 19 cases, summarized as follows: Of the 19 cases, 12 were Native American Indians. Twelve died. All of the victims were residents within a 100 mile area in northwest New Mexico and Northeast Arizona. The symptoms included fulminant respiratory distress which killed within hours. There was "NO IDENTIFIABLE CAUSE." This was printed in capital letters.

Under "Etiology" (origin), the memorandum noted, "[The illness] remains a mystery despite extensive testing at University of New Mexico Hospital, New Mexico Department of Health, and CDC. If etiology were plague, anthrax, tularemia, some cases should have been identified by cultures/stains ..."

Oddly, nationwide media printed stories stating that the illnesses were caused by rat droppings, yet the actual documents from the Department of Health Services in Berkeley, California, confidentially given to me by a laboratory director in June 1993, mentioned nothing about rat droppings.

I later read about a mystery illness in *Time* magazine, November 22, 1993 issue entitled, "The Gulf Gas Mystery," which reported that American troops in the Persian Gulf, upon returning home, were complaining of chronic diarrhea, aches in all the joints, and difficulty breathing. Several veterans and their families testified before a congressional committee that the Defense Department had ignored their complaints, and the Veterans Affairs Department downplayed the affair. The veterans themselves were convinced they had been exposed to "disease-causing chemical agents" while in the Persian Gulf. Eight-thousand veterans registered their symptoms with the U.S. government, thus labeling the disease "Gulf War Syndrome" (GWS).

Ultimately, the disease was determined by Major General Ronald Blanck, commander of the Walter Reed Army Medical Center, to be "multiple chemical sensitivity," syndrome. A board of inquiry was created headed by Joshua Lederberg of Rockefeller University, a Nobel-prizewinning expert on rare and emerging diseases. But, noted *Time*, "It is up to the Pentagon to bridge the credibility gap that seems to have sprouted over the strange new syndrome." It was not until 1996 that the Pentagon admitted GWS may have been caused by exposure to bombed chemical/biological plants in Iraq.

By far the most provocative incident occurred in February, 1994. The *Spokesman-Review*, out of Spokane, Washington, printed a story on August 9, 1994, entitled, "Victim of Mysterious Fumes Seeks Investigative Reports." In Riverside, California, the county in which the Cabazon Indian/Wackenhut facility is located, Dr. Julie Gorchynski, an emergency room doctor, was overcome by mysterious fumes while examining a woman who later died.

"This is a bona fide, genuine medical mystery, and we intend to solve it," said Russell S. Kussman, attorney for Dr. Gorchynski. Gorchynski suffered from osteonecrosis, avascular necrosis of bone, post-traumatic stress disorder, shortness of breath, restrictive lung disease and other ailments, as a result of exposure to the dying cancer patient on February 19th. Coincidentally, her symptoms matched those of GWS.

Later, in the same newspaper, dated September 3, 1994, another article emerged regarding the Riverside mishap. The bizarre episode had sent six emergency room workers to hospitals after being exposed to fumes emitting from patient Gloria Ramirez's blood samples drawn on February 19, 1994.

According to the state's 15-page report, 11 people reported smelling an unusual odor after blood was drawn from Ramirez. After five collapsed and the emergency room was evacuated, 23 people complained of at least one symptom, most commonly headache, dizziness, and nausea. More serious complaints included muscle spasms and breathing disruptions. "Despite extensive epidemiologic, toxicologic and environmental investigations, the cause of the outbreak of symptoms among emergency room staff members ... remains unknown," the report concluded.

Dr. Gorchynski's lawyer stated that it could only be a toxin. "It's physically impossible for Julie to have had the symptoms, and not just the symptoms, the laboratory findings and test results that showed ... clearly Dr. Gorchynski was poisoned that day."

But epidemiology experts could find no culprit to explain the bizarre episode. The Department of Health Services ultimately described the incident as an outbreak of "mass sociogenic illness," perhaps triggered by an odor.

I could not help wondering if the deceased Gloria Ramirez was an Indian, or had ever been on the Cabazon reservation in Indio? I later learned she had been receiving experimental cancer treatments at a clinic in Mexico.

••••••••

In February 1993, I was contacted by Scott Lawrence, a senior special agent, U.S. Customs internal affairs, headquartered in Boston, MA. Lawrence was conducting an inquiry into the whole Inslaw, Peter Videnieks, Wackenhut affair. The agent had flown in to California from Boston to interview Mike and Bobby Riconosciuto and other witnesses associated with the Inslaw case. Someone, whom he would not identify, advised him to contact me.

On February 5th, agent Lawrence and Mark Peter Dankel, special agent, U.S. Customs internal affairs in San Francisco, drove to my home in Mariposa and spent the day. I provided Lawrence with an affidavit relative to Riconosciuto's attempted trade into the

Witness Protection Program. The affidavit contained mostly drug-related information on The Company and Robert Booth Nichols' connection to Michael Abbell (DOJ) and the Cali Cartel. The agent also obtained a tape-recorded verbal statement, under oath, relative to my findings and left with an armload of documents. (Two years later, in 1995, Abbell was indicted for money laundering for the Cali Cartel and drug related charges).

Lawrence called frequently after that (1993), to compare notes on some of his investigative findings. We subsequently struck up an investigative collaboration of sorts. On September 3, 1993, I received a call from him in Palm City, Florida. He had interviewed Robert Chasen, former Executive Vice President, Systems and Services Group, of Wackenhut Corporation in Coral Gables. Chasen, 70, was still senior consultant at the Florida facility, but was allegedly dying of cancer and weighed less than 100 pounds at the time of the interview.

Because he (Chasen) had once been Commissioner of Customs in Washington D.C., he felt a rapport with this young agent and spoke candidly about his experience with Wackenhut in Indio.

Of significance, was Chasen's confirmation of the horrendous properties of the "virus" which he encountered at the Indio facility. He said, "Wackenhut was running amuck." Robert Nichols and Peter Zokosky had attempted to sell the biological warfare technology (developed in cow uteri) through Wackenhut, using Robert Frye, Vice President of the Indio facility, as the front man.

According to Chasen, Frye went behind his [Chasen's] back in facilitating the project; when Chasen learned of the project, he shut it down. (Chasen supervised the Indio facility from Coral Gables, Florida.) Because of the projects underway at the Cabazon reservation, Chasen chose not to step foot on the property, but instead met with the Indio executives in Palm Springs.

In other respects, Chasen was not so candid. Though the Customs agent said Chasen "said a lot of derogatory things about Wackenhut in Indio," he did not admit to knowing Peter Videnieks. The agent's investigation had led him to believe that the PROMIS software WAS stolen but he did not have enough evidence to take his case to court.

Chasen was evasive on the subject of PROMIS, though his background would indicate that he must have been knowledgeable about it. He had been a Special Agent in the Washington D.C. Federal Bureau of Investigation from 1943 to 1952. From 1952 to 1968, he was Vice President and President, respectively, of ITT Communications Systems in Chicago, Illinois and Paramus, New Jersey. He became Commissioner of U.S. Customs in Washington D.C. from 1969 to 1977 – the same time span that Peter Videnieks was in and out of Customs.

I called Dick Russell (author of *The Man Who Knew Too Much*) to act as a "cut-out" for me and interview Chasen. At that point, I didn't want to expose myself to Wackenhut, so Russell agreed. When Russell called back, he said Chasen didn't trust Robert Booth Nichols. Wackenhut had "run a check" on Nichols and couldn't learn anything about his background. This had bothered Chasen, but, he said, Robert Frye and Dick Wilson were "dazzled" with Nichols.

Chasen believed Nichols worked for the CIA, said he was a "slippery guy," and couldn't understand why Frye and Wilson were dazzled by Nichols for such a long time. Reportedly, George Wackenhut liked Frye and Dick Wilson, but did not trust Riconosciuto or Nichols. Michael Riconosciuto had been introduced to Chasen as a "specialist engineer in weapons."

Chasen acknowledged the biological technology introduced by Nichols and Zokosky, saying it had been presented to him as something that could "create anything from chicken soup to long range missiles." When he learned of the properties of the technology, he halted it immediately. When pressed for further details, he added reluctantly, "It was the kind of thing your mind erases."

Regarding the Cabazons, Chasen said he felt an affinity with Arthur Welmas, Chairman of the Cabazon Band of Mission Indians, because his [Chasen's] wife is part Cherokee. He noted that he sympathized with their situation and wanted to protect them.

Perhaps he protected them more than he realized when he shut down the Wackenhut proposal to the Army to develop biological viruses (and vaccines) on the Cabazon reservation.

••••••••

One year later, on September 5, 1994, *Time* magazine published an article on page 63 entitled, "A Deadly Virus Escapes," in which a Yale University researcher was exposed to the deadly Brazilian "Sabia" virus when a container spinning on a high-speed centrifuge cracked, causing the potentially lethal tissue to spatter. Fortunately, the researcher was wearing a lab gown, latex gloves and a mask, as required by federal guidelines.

Every surface of the area was scrubbed with bleach, all instruments were sterilized, then wiped down again with alcohol. Having decided the danger was over, he didn't bother to report the accident, and a few days later he left town to visit an old friend in Boston. Soon after the researcher returned to Yale, he began running a fever that reached 103° F.

An experimental antiviral drug eventually stopped the illness, but the man had exposed five people, including two children, before being confined to a hospital isolation ward, and another 75 or so health-care workers after that.

The Sabia virus is particularly frightening because it kills in such a grisly way. Characteristic symptoms are high fever, uncontrolled bleeding in virtually every organ and finally shock. The liver turns yellow and decomposes. Blood can leak from literally every bodily orifice, including the eyes and the pores of the skin. Sabia was never seen before 1990, when a female agricultural engineer checked into a hospital in Sao Paulo, Brazil, with a high fever. Within days she was dead.

Fortunately, in the Yale University incident, none of the potential victims died or showed any evidence of symptoms. A book and movie on the Sabia virus's counterpart, the lethal Ebola virus from Central Africa, which is as deadly and as gruesome as AIDS, yet has an incubation period of only one week, was underway at the time and was later released in 1994.

The book, *The Hot Zone,* described a victim who contracted Ebola. *Time* wrote, "His eyes turn red and his head begins to ache. Red spots appear on his skin and, spreading quickly, become a rash of tiny blisters, and then the flesh rips. Blood begins to flow from every one of the body's orifices. The victim coughs up black vomit, sloughing off parts of his tongue, throat and windpipe. His organs fill with blood and fail. He suffers seizures, splattering virus-saturated blood that can infect anyone nearby. Within a few days the victim dies, and as the virus destroys his remaining cells, much of his tissue actually liquefies ..."

The Ebola virus, found in the rain-forest regions of Central Africa, once caused an outbreak in 1976 through villages near the Ebola River in Zaire, killing as many as 90% of those infected. Such dangerous viruses may seem a distant menace, wrote *Time*, but *The*

Hot Zone details a 1989 Ebola crisis that occurred in the Reston, Virginia Primate Quarantine Unit, run by a company that imports and sells monkeys for use in research laboratories.

When an unusual number of monkeys originating from the Philippines died, tissue samples were sent to a U.S. Army research center. There a technician identified the strands as either Ebola Zaire or something very close. Even more alarming, the virus found in Reston, Virginia, unlike the African one, could be transmitted through the air. Frantic phone calls were made to Virginia health authorities and to the Centers for Disease Control in Atlanta. An Army team, wearing space suits, went into the Reston building and killed 450 surviving monkeys, then placed them in plastic bags for safe disposal. Before the building was boarded up, the Army sterilized every square inch of the interior. No humans were infected with the virus, but Richard Preston, the author of *The Hot Zone*, wrote, "A tiny change in its genetic code, and it might [have] zoomed through the human race."

A rival 1995 film on the same subject entitled, *Outbreak*, directed by Wolfgang Peterson, also focused on the Ebola virus.

— 12 —

Rendevous with the Underworld

It was time to interview Robert Booth Nichols. While communicating with Ted Gunderson one day, on an impulse, I asked him for Nichols's telephone number. Gunderson hesitated, then gave me the telephone number of a "relative" of Nichols' in Los Angeles, stating that he really couldn't give out Robert's home number without first consulting him.

I called the relative and left a message for Nichols to return my call. The call came back on December 31, 1991. There was an intriguing international flavor to Nichols' voice. The tone was hostile but polite, and inquiring. Essentially, Nichols wanted to know why I was communicating with Michael Riconosciuto?

I explained to him that I was writing a book on government sanctioned drug trafficking and Michael had information to offer on local corruption. During the conversation, which lasted about 45 minutes, Nichols admitted that he worked for FIDCO and used the code word "Wa Latteral" for the operation in Lebanon.

The following are some excerpts:

> CS: "Do you know anything about Michael Riconosciuto in Lebanon?"
>
> Nichols: "Never."
>
> CS: "He [Michael] talked about an interesting operation in Lebanon."
>
> Nichols: "What was it called, the operation? I've heard of quite a few projects in Lebanon. If I've heard of it, I'll tell you."
>
> CS: "Well, what was the code name of the one that you heard about?"
>
> Nichols: "Wa Latteral."

CS: "Wa Latteral? And what type of operation was that?"

Nichols: "Well, it was trading in two directions. Now what's yours?"

CS: "Same thing."

Nichols: "Wa Latteral? Yours is the same name?"

CS: "No. I've never heard that name before."

Nichols: "Well, what was the code word of the one Michael said he was involved in?"

CS: "I would have to go over all of my notes, to tell you the truth. It didn't seem important at the time, so I don't have it off the top of my head ..."

Nichols: "What the project was, I can tell you very clearly, there's nothing secret about it now, was to develop an agenda whereby all sides, the Muslim and the Christian sides, would come to an agreement on a redevelopment project to where their respective areas would have the same capitalization, and the same benefit to stop the fighting."

CS: "Did this include rebuilding of the infrastructure of Beirut?"

Nichols: "Very definitely."

CS: "Did this have anything to do with FIDCO?"

Nichols: "Uh, FIDCO was involved in it, right. That was an effort by that company, as I understood it ... the project was to make sure that both sides developed building programs that were initiated concurrently and the development was fair and equitable to all sides, to stop the fighting." (I wondered why an "arms dealer" wanted to stop the fighting in Lebanon?)

CS: "Was there ever any subsidiary of that corporation called Euramae?"

Nichols: "I never heard that name before."

CS: "Ted Gunderson gave me a huge manual on The Octopus ..."

Nichols: "In my opinion, to research anything of that magnitude you are looking at -- it would require a lot of money and a lot of travel and a lot of patience. I don't think Ted Gunderson knows anything, personally. He's domestic. It's not his area."

CS: "Did you operate a telex company with him during the Olympic Games?"

Nichols: "Absolutely not. A telex company. Absolutely not. Oh, jeez. Did you ask Ted Gunderson that?"

CS: "Well, no, I didn't ..."

Nichols: "Well, you can't be shy. You have to ask questions, or else how do you know?"

CS: "What did Danny Casolaro spend so much time on the phone with you for?"

Nichols: "Danny used to ask me different things. But Danny was more into the names in Paris and Switzerland and -- Danny was investigating the whole international situation. You have to spend a lot of money and do a lot of traveling. Danny had said to me that he had a whole agenda worked out, you know, where he was going to go and who he was going to see. And I mean it was literally a global trip ..."

Nichols said he believed Danny was murdered and did not commit suicide. He believed Danny's death had to do with the international scene, someone Danny had contacted overseas.

I asked him, "Do you suppose his death had anything to do with the Justice Department?"

Nichols answered, "I would say, `Time will tell. Time will tell.'"

I pressed Nichols about his civil suit against FBI agent Thomas Gates:

Nichols: "The activities that I've been involved with, I can tell you very clearly, an effort was made for many years to benefit a lot of people that were involved in the corporation. That effort was destroyed by certain moves [by agent Gates]. And it caused a great deal of hardship to myself and quite a few other people who are very angry about it. And we'll deal with that matter in court."

CS: "What was Gates investigating?"

Nichols said he wrote two stories for some Italian movie producers. "They were `sensitive' stories, about overseas. What I did, was I took two little, very brief parts of two stories to copyright in the United States. And so they're very diluted, but enough for the copyrights.

"That's when I met the guy from Universal [studios], because he wanted the stories. And the French wanted the stories ... in 1987, but the stories haven't changed, they're still pertinent."

Gates had overheard the "pertinent" parts on the wiretap and initiated an investigation. I made a mental note to try to convince Nichols at a later date to provide me with the manuscripts. But I didn't want to push him during our first conversation.

••••••••

I later asked a friend in Washington, D.C. to research Nichols' copyrights at the Library of Congress. There were indeed two stories copyrighted by Robert Booth Nichols under the pseudonym of R.N. LeDevoilier. Perhaps he was unaware that a cross-reference would reveal his true identity.

The 20-page manuscript entitled "Acceptable Casualty," essentially outlined gays and I.V. drug users as targets of bio-war by a cabal of military intelligence officers. In the story, a secret file, "C-911-Tuhnekaw," revealed the origin of the first AIDS infection. Field research dated November 12, 1977 originated from a Bay Area laboratory destroyed by fire in December 1975. Assorted bio-labs were mentioned, one in Palo Alto, California. The hero of the story obtained the secret cure from "the Chosen Ones" and escaped to Singapore with his family.

Interestingly, the names of those involved included "Yutaka Okimoto" and "Lawrence Zokosky," the last names of which match those listed on Nichols' "real life" corporation, Meridian International Logistics (MIL).

Nichols also copyrighted a 90-page James Bond type treatment entitled, "Decision of Conscience," which described state-of-the-art electromagnetic technology (launchers) used to demolish a two-story concrete building. I later found the words, "Decision of Conscience," written in Danny Casolaro's handwritten notes also.

Nichols' secret desire to write about his exploits in the CIA had led him to contact Jack Valenti, president of the Motion Picture Assn. of America, through his (then) corporate partner Eugene Giaquinto. The three met at the Beverly Hills Hotel where Nichols attempted to sell Valenti manuscripts disclosing top secret CIA technology.

Nichols later said Valenti refused the manuscripts because they contained "classified national security information." (Valenti once served as assistant to President Lyndon B. Johnson).

••••••••

During several phone conversations with reporter Jonathan Littman, I learned that he had communicated with Danny Casolaro on a regular basis prior to Danny's death. At the time, I wondered why Littman hadn't written a story on Danny, since he was one of the few reporters to have spoken extensively with him?

I would have that answer soon enough. My confidence in Littman nearly cost me my life. An incident which I am about to relate forced me to document the following events, which I titled, "Vortex," and subsequently turned over to John Cohen, investigator for the House Judiciary Committee on Inslaw. Cohen had strenuously advised me to send it to him as he feared for my life. "Vortex" was also the "affidavit" I supplied to the Customs Agent who interviewed me in February 1993.

During the course of our conversations, Littman had noted to me that he had a close relationship with Robert Booth Nichols, Peter Zokosky and Ben Kalka of The Company. Littman also verified to me that he was in fact, Kalka's cousin, but he (Littman) was a secretive, non-communicative individual and I didn't press him for explanations. Kalka was currently serving time in prison for possession of 900 pounds of methamphetamine.

Littman did, however, confide that Kalka hated Michael Riconosciuto because Riconosciuto was responsible for Kalka's imprisonment. I described how former Assistant U.S. Attorney Brian Leighton appeared to have perjured himself at Michael's trial, and asked Littman's opinion of that. Littman stated simply that it didn't matter if Leighton had perjured himself, nothing should be done to get Michael out of jail. There should be no mistrial or acquittal or anything of that nature because Michael was probably guilty of the crime for which he was incarcerated. I didn't pursue the matter further at that point.

Meanwhile, Littman offered to arrange an interview with Robert Booth Nichols and Peter Zokosky for me. In exchange for this, he wanted me to arrange an interview with Tony Patterson and Raymond Lavas (Ted Gunderson's former forensics expert) through Bobby Riconosciuto. Tony Patterson had allegedly served with Robert Booth Nichols in Vietnam, and Raymond Lavas had access to Michael Riconosciuto's hidden computer tapes.

Both men were watching over Bobby Riconosciuto while Michael was in jail. I said I would do the best I could to arrange the interviews. Bobby was the only person communicating with these individuals and only she knew how to contact them. I never mentioned to Littman that I had been communicating with Robert Nichols on the phone. I can't say what my reasoning was at the time. Intuition, I suppose.

Bobby Riconosciuto reluctantly agreed to set up the interviews with Patterson and Lavas, though she pointed out that neither man trusted journalists. I naively assured her that Littman would be okay. It is noteworthy that Littman had been communicating with Bobby and Michael for several months prior to my introduction to them, yet, they didn't completely trust him at that stage of their relationship. When they learned of his relationship with Ben Kalka, they didn't trust him at all.

Elizabeth Riconosciuto's fifth birthday party was scheduled to be celebrated at the La Mirada Gateway Holiday Inn on February 14, 1992 at 11 A.M. Reportedly, Patrick Moriarty and Marshall Riconosciuto had a financial interest in the hotel and they were paying the bills.

Littman and I decided that would be a good weekend to confidentially interview Robert Booth Nichols and Peter Zokosky in Los Angeles, and it would give Littman the opportunity to meet Bobby Riconosciuto face-to-face. We would also squeeze the Patterson/Lavas interviews in during that time.

Michael Riconosciuto was cooperative about allowing his wife to be interviewed by Littman because it would give the journalist a close-up view of Michael's "family" in action. Tom Olmstead, Michael's lawyer, was scheduled to attend the birthday party as was Patrick Moriarty and Marshall Riconosciuto. After the luncheon celebration, the children and those adults who wanted to tag along would go to Disneyland.

Michael Riconosciuto had dual motives for wanting Littman in attendance. Olmstead had been instructed to pressure Littman to reveal "who" had sent the incriminating 1983 "drug" transcript to the prosecuting attorney in Michael's trial - only Littman knew if it had been Ben Kalka or Littman himself. (Littman had obtained it originally from Peter Zokosky).

On Tuesday evening, February 11th, Littman confirmed a Thursday appointment with Robert Booth Nichols. However, he stressed that Nichols had insisted that the meeting be kept absolutely confidential. No one in media or Michael Riconosciuto's circle was to know of the interview.

I agreed, but explained that I had already mentioned briefly to Michael that I "planned" to interview Nichols at some future date. Michael had said he understood the importance of interviewing Nichols and he would cooperate. I even asked Michael to notify Tony Patterson and Raymond Lavas, via Bobby, that Littman and I would be interviewing them during our trip to Los Angeles.

Littman said that was alright, but I was to tell no one else associated with Michael. I noted to Jonathan that he might want to inform Nichols that I had already mentioned to Michael that I "intended" to interview Nichols at some time in the future. Littman said leave it at that. No problem.

Littman spent the night at my home in Mariposa on Wednesday night. The following morning, on February 13th, 1992 at 7 A.M., we departed for Los Angeles. Strangely, at the last moment, Littman decided to follow us to Los Angeles in his own car. I rode intermittently with Littman, then with my husband, during the five-hour drive. At hour intervals, Littman pulled off the freeway to report to Nichols – and to a police officer in San Francisco whom he did not identify, but described as his "security."

At noon, we arrived at Nichols' Sherman Oaks apartment building. Littman punched in #68 and spoke briefly to Nichols, who buzzed the door open. At Nichols' apartment, #103, Littman pointed out the electronic security system on the front door, then at the last moment, instructed my husband to wait in the van. We owned a 1991 Chevrolet conversion, so he napped and watched television the rest of the afternoon. Towards the end of the five-hour meeting, Nichols invited him up for coffee and cake.

Peter Zokosky and his wife (former Mayor of Indio), Robert Booth Nichols and his wife, Ellen, were present inside the apartment. Littman had previously warned me that the apartment was electronically wired to detect any listening devices I might be wearing on my body. I said I had none.

Littman had also warned me that I would be seated on a couch next to a stuffed lion which had a tape recording device (bug) under its tail. Sure enough, when I entered the apartment, I was seated on a white couch near the lion. A giant anaconda skin hung stretched across the wall. European and African relics decorated the apartment. It was instantly obvious that Nichols and his wife didn't live in the apartment, it was a meeting place.

Nichols smoked cigarettes and as a result, kept the upstairs windows in the apartment open, allowing a cool February breeze to flow through the apartment. Nerves, and the cool air induced me to keep my light coat on during most of the interview. At first, Peter Zokosky, a friendly, congenial man, did most of the talking. As the conversation warmed up, Nichols entered intermittently, then took over completely.

A formal gourmet luncheon was served of curried soup, salmon and turkey finger sandwiches, wine and home-made strawberry cake. Ellen Nichols was the perfect hostess, but rarely said a word.

At one point during lunch, Nichols instructed Ellen to get the camera and snap a front and side picture of me, which she carried out silently. There was no explanation given for the picture.

After lunch, Nichols often stood or sat at the open window while he talked and smoked. It was cold and rainy, and I wondered why he kept glancing down at my van. Littman frequently left the room to attend to something in the back of the apartment. I was unable to determine what he was doing, but noticed that he took no notes and never once joined in the conversation.

Nichols was aptly described in magazine articles as "Clark Gable without the ears." But his mannerisms were intense, simultaneously controlled and dramatic. I intuitively sensed the violence in him, but only through his eyes. He studied me intently as I spoke, making every effort to throw me off balance by continuously correcting me. He also would not speak while I wrote on my notepad, stopping mid-sentence each time I put pen to paper.

It worked in some cases, but I finally rallied. I was in HIS apartment, with women present, though they were busy in the kitchen, and my husband was parked outside the apartment. I was certainly in no physical danger, so I gathered myself and bluntly asked the questions I had driven 350 miles to ask.

Referring to the U.S. currency and gold transfers into Swiss bank accounts, Nichols admitted that he was contracted by the government to "handle" the 42 Cobra helicopters which Michael had said were stored in Europe, then shipped to Iraq via North Korea.

At first he would not say what he did with the helicopters, but then revealed the entire operation. John Vanderwerker at Intersect Corporation in Irvine, California, had been the CIA facilitator. It was a "classified" CIA operation, though Nichols would not give the name of the White House official behind it. I assumed it was Michael McManus, but didn't push it. Glenn Shockley had brought Nichols into the operation. At least I had verbal confirmation of the operation, and unknown to Nichols, I had the entire paper trail.

Regarding Danny Casolaro, Nichols and Zokosky both insisted that Danny had been "murdered." Danny's book research had progressed to a point where he was looking overseas for answers and

Nichols had offered to direct him to certain connections that would have completed his investigation.

Nichols confirmed that he was privy to Danny's findings on a regular basis, but chose not to elaborate on the content of his last conversation with Danny.

I continued to press him for information on the "cause" of Danny's death; what had he discovered that caused him to be murdered? Nichols responded defiantly that he knew why Danny died, but he said "no journalist or investigator had done enough work to be deserving of that information yet."

It was not until the end of the meeting, when we had established a tentative rapport, that Nichols offered to take *me* to Europe, as he had Danny, to find the answers to my investigation of the Octopus. But, he stressed it would be very expensive and I would be gone for several months. I remember the probing look on his face as he made the offer. I had nodded slowly, stating I would give it some thought. I wondered fleetingly if he was trying to recruit me into the CIA? Or create a new Manchurian Candidate?

Regarding the stolen PROMIS software, Nichols said he believed Michael Riconosciuto had been contracted by the government to "derail" Bill Hamilton at Inslaw. According to Nichols, Michael *did* have the PROMIS software codes. Allegedly, Peter Zokosky's "brother" sold copies of the software to Israel. Zokosky nodded in agreement at that statement.

Nichols said Michael *had* to know he was going to be arrested for operating a meth lab, but he (Michael) thought the FBI would bail him out again. Someone named (Admiral) Al Renkin allegedly "covered Michael's drug act."

I never knew what that meant and didn't pursue it, as I wasn't there to learn about Michael Riconosciuto. While we were on the subject of drugs, I took the opportunity to question Nichols's involvement. I led in by describing the drug situation in Mariposa county, adding that the entire country seemed to be economically dependent on the drug trade. Nichols nodded in full agreement, then noted that Europe's economy was completely dependent on drug money. Without drugs, banks and whole countries would collapse financially.

We moved into another area of discussion. Peter Videnieks was an associate of Earl Brian, according to Nichols. Other names were tossed around such as Senator Terry Sanford, a family friend of Earl Brian. Sanford was Nichols' link with Earl Brian. And, noted Nichols, Videnieks was associated with Earl Brian through Hadron Corporation.

Allegedly, all of these fellows had met at Nichols' "007" Marina Del Ray condo at one time or another, including Videnieks.

It is noteworthy that at the time of this meeting, neither Nichols or I could have foreseen the importance of this information. The issue of Videnieks' connection with Earl Brian or Terry Sanford, or even Nichols himself, had not been raised publicly yet. At the time, I didn't place any particular significance on Nichols' relationship with Earl Brian or Peter Videnieks, I just took the information at face value and wrote it in my notes.

Nichols reacted violently when I asked him if he had any business dealings with Brunswick Corporation in New Jersey. He jumped up from his chair by the window and yelled, "Absolutely not!"

I quickly explained that I had looked up Sir Denis Kendall (the famous MI6 World War II British officer) in *Who's Who in America* and learned that he had once been associated with Brunswick. Nichols said he did not know Sir Denis Kendall. His eyes told me otherwise.

I noted that was strange since Michael Riconosciuto seemed to know him well. Nichols and Zokosky exchanged glances. I further explained that Bobby Riconosciuto said she had been to Kendall's home on Doheny Drive in Beverly Hills with her children once. She had often called Kendall when she was trying to locate Michael, and within hours of calling Kendall, Michael always called her back. Nichols and Zokosky seemed disturbed by that statement. I didn't mention that Riconosciuto had stated Kendall was Nichols' supervisor ("handler").

I had obtained all of the documents pertaining to Nichols' current lawsuit against Thomas Gates of the Los Angeles FBI, his corporate activities and his weapons permits. Nichols had been investigated by Gates for allegedly turning over sensitive information to organized crime figures in America and the "Yakuza" crime syndicate in Japan.

Nichols' corporation, Meridian International Logistics, Inc. (MIL), the parent company to Meridian Arms, had filed a lawsuit against Gates for contacting Nichols' European and Japanese business associates.

As a result, not only were Nichols' weapons permits cancelled, but his associates were allegedly intimidated by the investigation, thus damaging Nichols' ability to transact business.

I was curious about how far Nichols would take the lawsuit, and exactly what the nature of the research was that MIL fronted to the Japanese. I started out by asking Nichols if he had provided a "grant" to a Japanese facility for biological research? Nichols said he had provided no grant to any Japanese facility and attempted to change the subject.

Nichols was not evasive, but aggressively direct when he did not want to discuss something. Michael Riconosciuto had once commented to me that the biological technology which Nichols was involved in was "Hitler's wet dream." According to Michael, who was uncharacteristically hesitant about discussing the subject, "biotechnology was the weapon of the future, making all other weaponry obsolete."

In Michael's files in the desert, I had retrieved a small cylindrical canister, about six inches in length, with a cap on it. The metal canister had not been marked, and instinctively, I had not opened it, but had placed it on a shelf in our empty guest house in Mariposa.

It was not until months later, after Michael learned I had copies of his documents, that I had asked him what the canister contained. Michael had become distraught, explaining that the canister contained genetic material in a hybridoma base, a military concept, only to be used for military applications. Michael had stolen the canister from a shipment at Wackenhut destined for King Fahd of Saudi Arabia and placed the sample in his files in the desert. (Proposals had also been underway with King Fahd to provide "security" for his palace).

His voice had been fraught with worry. He implored me to remove the canister from my property immediately, take it to a "class 4 facility" where it could be disposed of. I was absolutely NOT to open the canister as it contained lethal toxins.

Later, at the meeting with Robert Booth Nichols, I again wondered why arms dealers such as Peter Zokosky and Robert Nichols would be interested in genetic research? Five years earlier, Zokosky and Wackenhut Corporation had attempted to sell "biological warfare viruses" and vaccine kits to the U.S. government to be used against small countries bordering Albania or large countries bordering the Soviet Union.

I did not openly confront Nichols at his apartment about the above documents, but asked him if he had sold or facilitated the research of specific biotechnology to the Japanese? Nichols adamantly denied any involvement in any such research.

When I re-phrased the question, and he realized I knew about the MIL agreements, he admitted that he had in fact facilitated the research of methodology and induction of cytotoxic T-Lymphocytes through "five offshore [out-of-country] research institutes." But, he added that the research was "classified" by the sponsoring governments and "secret" and he could not discuss it.

When I pressed for the names of the sponsoring governments, he clammed up. Had I known more about the technology at the time, I would have pointedly questioned him about the properties of the virus, but in retrospect, my ignorance opened doors that otherwise wouldn't have been opened.

I did, however, mention to Nichols and Zokosky that Michael Riconosciuto had allegedly worked on the same technology at Hercules Research in the early 1980's, reportedly using fish for incubation purposes.

Zokosky responded, embarking upon a lengthy discourse on the processes by which "they" had incubated the virus in cow uteri and udders in bio-labs twenty floors beneath the ground. But Nichols interjected, discontinuing the narrative. It was obvious that both men were becoming agitated, so I dropped the subject for the time being.

Regarding Thomas Gates, Nichols expressed real anger and noted he would take the lawsuit against Gates as far as it would go. He said he didn't care if he was awarded any money (he was suing for $11 million), but he would ruin Tom Gates, no matter what it took.

A thought crossed my mind that he was about to say that he would kill him, but instead, he sat silently glaring, waiting. I asked him how much the lawsuit had cost him so far, and he said not a dime. Originally, Michael McManus had advised Nichols, but then the case was handled by John Rowell.

It was already apparent that Nichols was warming to the interview, in a disarming, contentious sort of way. We were reaching a common ground, a netherworld of danger and intrigue. The room became his stage, the people his audience. He never took his eyes from mine, making every effort to distract me from my notes.

Unquestionably, he was a "game" player. The more I entered the game, the better he liked it. It was a trade off, I gave him a little information, he gave me a little. But he gave as much as he took ...

I asked him about his relationship with MCA corporation. He said Eugene Giaquinto, President of MCA Home Entertainment Division, had resigned from his company, MIL, after the FBI investigation was underway.

But Giaquinto was a smart man, noted Nichols. He had learned much from the man. Giaquinto drove an older car, as did Nichols. They hid their assets, living modestly when in the U.S., keeping a low profile. The FBI would "prove" nothing, said Nichols. He added that MCA Corporation was "going broke," and the only division that was making a profit was the home entertainment division, which Giaquinto headed.

I recalled privately the conversation in which Michael Riconosciuto had told J.H. that MCA was currently facilitating the largest leveraging scam ever conceived of in this country. MCA was subsequently sold to the Japanese, but I had no idea what connection that had to the above referenced conversation.

Nichols continued to lead the conversation towards Riconosciuto. Nichols and Zokosky could not understand why Ted Gunderson testified for Michael at his trial in Washington state. At a previous dinner party at Nichols' apartment in Sherman Oaks, Ted reportedly told the two men that Michael had loaned him (Gunderson) $60,000 for a joint business venture. Ted still owed Michael the money.

It is noteworthy that Ted also supplied Robert Booth Nichols an affidavit for HIS lawsuit against Thomas Gates.

Ellen Nichols had mentioned during lunch that Michael often buried secret documents and equipment. Obviously, they were trying to learn what documents I had acquired. I had not uncovered any "buried" documents, but had obtained his private files from the trailer in the California desert. I did not reveal this to Nichols, assuming that Littman had kept my secret.

However, as the conversation progressed, I came to realize that Nichols did, indeed, know I had obtained Michael's files. One statement which Nichols said in the presence of Jonathan Littman surprised me. Littman continued to leave the room to attend to something in the back of the apartment. When he returned, I asked Nichols to repeat what he had just said. Nichols obliged by reiterating that "Michael Riconosciuto would kill me if he learned that I had obtained his private documents."

I asked him "why" he believed Michael would kill me over that? Nichols seemed to want confirmation of something I'd obtained, something specific, but wouldn't define what it was – and I had no intention of revealing anything to him at that point.

He randomly discussed the (coroner's grand jury) affidavit in which Riconosciuto had accused Phillip Arthur Thompson of killing Paul Morasca (Michael's partner) in San Francisco. Thompson had worked for the FBI under the code name of "Jason" in some capacity which Nichols would not define.

But, according to Nichols, it was Riconosciuto who had tortured and killed Paul Morasca. Peter Zokosky corroborated Nichols' comment. Both men said the torture of Paul Morasca was Michael's "style" – that Michael had discussed torture techniques of that nature to Nichols prior to Morasca's death.

They added that "Jason," Phillip Arthur Thompson, was not so creative in his killing style. Thompson had allegedly killed many people in his career, but he chose to use a gun and get the job done quickly. Nichols also said at lunch, with Ellen listening, that he knew who killed Mary Quick. Ellen rolled her eyes at her husband and beseeched him to change the subject. I asked Nichols to name the killer or at least give me a clue. Nichols said the killer of Mary Quick had been arrested and released. Obviously they were talking about "Jason," who *had* been arrested and released.

Nichols and Zokosky both agreed in a conversation between themselves that Michael Riconosciuto had caused the death of other people also. Nichols repeated at least three times to my face, with Zokosky and Littman nodding in agreement, that he believed Michael would kill me.

I privately wondered why Nichols was making such an issue of this? I would understand soon enough. Meanwhile, Nichols continued to press his point. He said Michael was a patient man and would wait as long as necessary to accomplish this. I did not respond, as I had become somewhat immuned to the threat by then.

Littman had made similar statements on the drive up to Sherman Oaks. I simply did not perceive Riconosciuto as a killer. Nevertheless, I asked Nichols how Michael would kill me if he was in jail? Nichols said it would be done by one of Michael's "drug flunkies." He said Riconosciuto *had* worked for the government, and had been "rescued" by the FBI for years. He added that Michael could get away with murder.

I was becoming unresponsive to the game, so I presume Nichols decided it was time to "set the hook." It was not until two years later that I understood the significance of this incident. At one point during our conversation, and completely out of context with what we were discussing, Nichols played a video tape of the assassination of President John F. Kennedy. The southern wall of Nichols' apartment contained a six-foot-wide screen on which I watched a blown-up (enlarged), slow motion "uncut" version of the famous Zapruder film.

I watched what appeared to be the standard media version of the film, seen so many times in film clips over the years, but then Nichols slowed the camera even more, and on the six-foot screen, I observed the driver of the limousine turn to his right, first looking at Connolly, then at Kennedy. The driver's left hand came over his right shoulder, and he was holding a long barreled gun. Smoke and a bullet emerged from the gun, traveling ever so slowly across the screen into Kennedy's head, blowing brain tissue into the air as he fell back against the seat.

Stunned, I watched Jacqueline Kennedy open her mouth in horror as she glanced at the driver, then try to climb over the back seat of the car.

Littman and Zokosky and I stared at the scene in silence, unable to believe what we were seeing. Nichols then changed the tape and showed what he described as the "media" version of the Zapruder tape. In the media version, the driver continued to drive, unflinching, as the shots rang out. Then the scene switched to the back part of the limousine.

At this point, Nichols stopped the frame and pointed with a stick at a tree in the background behind the limousine. From the middle of the tree to the ground, there was no trunk, just air. The top part of the tree was growing in air!

I demanded that my husband be allowed to see the film. I felt I must have been hypnotized. When he arrived, he viewed both films up close, in slow motion, and saw the same thing. Nichols played both tapes backwards and forwards as often as we demanded, until the memory of it was burned forever into our minds.

I assumed the video had been tampered with. I asked Nichols where he had obtained the original "un-cut" version? He would not say. I had no idea at that time that his FIDCO partner, Clint Murchison, Jr.'s father had had instant access to the Zapruder film immediately after the assassination in Dallas, Texas.

Nichols studied me for the longest time, then walked over to the window and lit a cigarette. He finally commented that the CIA can cover up anything it wants, even a president's murder. He wanted to show me the power of the Octopus. "Nothing is as it appears to be," he said.

Somehow, that statement rang true. He then noted that he'd read my first book, the one I had sent him, then handed me a book entitled, *The Search for the Manchurian Candidate*. He told me to read it, appraising me silently. Inwardly, I recalled a conversation with Ted's live-in partner (name withheld by request), in which she related a conversation she'd had with Ted after a dinner engagement with Nichols. Nichols had reportedly stated to Ted that he headed a 200-man assassination team. Ted's partner had been too frightened to elaborate on this conversation, but had pointed out that Nichols once worked in the MK-Ultra (Manchurian Candidate) program during the Vietnam war. This program was part of the "Phoenix Project." Interestingly, numerous publications had mentioned that Earl Brian had also participated in the Phoenix Project during the war.

Nichols' sister was allegedly a professional hypnotherapist, and Nichols himself was reportedly trained in the art of hypnotism. According to Riconosciuto, they all called themselves "The Chosen Ones," wore skull and crossbones rings, and shared a common interest, if you could call it that, in the old German SS occultism, its tribal and inner circle rites.

As I was preparing to leave, Nichols pointed his finger at me and reminded me of the agreement I had made with him through Littman. I asked him what agreement? He said the agreement that I would tell no-one about this meeting. I again assured him that I would mention it to no-one. He said I had better not or I would end up like the rest ...

••••••••

When we finally left Nichols' apartment around five P.M., I told Littman I did not intend to accept any more collect calls from Michael Riconosciuto at the Tacoma jail. I might even wrap up the whole investigation at that point, because I had more than enough material for a story or a book.

Littman proceeded to issue a warning which I recorded in my notebook in the car. It read as follows: "Littman warned me today to watch out. No-one gets out of this alive. No one walks. If I cut them off, it would be very dangerous." I was completely numb at that point, and unresponsive to any further threats. We agreed to meet at 11:00 A.M. at the La Mirada Gateway Holiday Inn in La Mirada the following day to attend Elizabeth Riconosciuto's birthday party. Tom Olmstead, Michael's lawyer, would be flying in for the meeting, Ted Gunderson would be there, Patrick Moriarty would be picking up Olmstead at the airport, Raymond Lavas would be there and possibly the elusive Tony Patterson, if Bobby could arrange it. Also expected was Janice Wynogradsky, the Australian reporter who produced the news story for Australian TV.

I was exhausted and looked forward to a restful evening, but first I drove to the nearest toy store and purchased some birthday presents for Elizabeth.

That evening, I mentally reviewed the day's events. Nichols and Littman were undoubtedly screwing with my head. The doctored Zapruder tape gave them deniability. The information I had obtained at the meeting may or may not have had value, but I knew one thing, the deaths surrounding Riconosciuto and Nichols were real enough.

Behind the smoke and mirrors labyrinth was a story, one they were working very hard to conceal. I felt sure the corporate and government connections were little more than "fronts" for large scale drug trafficking.

••••••••

At 7:30 A.M. the following morning, Bobby Riconosciuto called the hotel where we were staying (the La Mirada Gateway Holiday Inn) and informed me that the luncheon meeting had been changed to a new location and Jonathan Littman was not going to be allowed to attend. I explained that I had not heard from Jonathan, did not know where he was staying, and could not get in touch with him to tell him about the change. Bobby and I argued about the inconvenience to Littman. I told her that Jonathan and I were not puppets to be manipulated by her or Michael. Bobby argued back that Olmstead had not shown up at the airport, Ted and his partner were having a tiff, and she did not trust Littman because of his relationship with Ben Kalka and Robert Booth Nichols.

She did not want her daughter's birthday turned into a "circus." I agreed with that aspect of the meeting, however, Bobby still had not arranged an interview with Raymond Lavas or Tony Patterson. Bobby argued that she did not think Lavas or Patterson would talk to Littman. I implored her to arrange the appointments for Littman's sake, since he had driven from San Rafael for that purpose. I explained to her that it was important that Littman be present at the interviews with Lavas and Patterson because I was working on the Mariposa story with him and we had made an agreement.

Bobby asked me directly if I had interviewed Robert Booth Nichols? I said I had not. I felt it was really none of Bobby's business. I qualified that, however, by saying that I expected to interview Nichols at some time in the future. Bobby said she understood and would attempt to arrange the interviews with Lavas and Patterson for the following day, Sunday.

It is noteworthy that Littman wanted to interview Tony Patterson because Patterson "claimed" to have been in Vietnam (Phoenix/MK-Ultra) with both Earl Brian and Robert Booth Nichols. I doubted that. To my knowledge, Nichols had never served in the military.

Patterson had a rather provocative story to tell about Nichols. Allegedly, Nichols had smuggled several gold icons out of Vietnam into the U.S. Nichols' activities in Vietnam also allegedly included drug trafficking for the CIA, which both Bobby and Michael Riconosciuto maintained was still operational today. *That* sounded closer to the truth.

Bobby called me back and instructed me to arrange a dinner meeting with Littman that evening (Saturday) and she would show up to be interviewed, then if Littman agreed to provide her with the name of the person who had sent the 1983 "drug" transcript to the prosecutor at Michael's trial, she would call Patterson and Lavas for interviews on the following day.

I was becoming stressed at that point. The whole weekend was spinning out of control and I was caught in the middle. I noted to

Bobby that I would wait for Littman to show up at the La Mirada Gateway Holiday Inn and tell him the meeting had been changed to a new location, but that he was not invited. I would then give him the new meeting time – 7:00 P.M. at the Belle Isles restaurant in Anaheim. Bobby agreed to that arrangement.

My husband and I waited at the hotel until 11:30 A.M., but Littman never showed. He also never called to say he would be late. At 11:40 A.M., I left a message for Littman at the front desk apologizing for the sudden change in plans, and said we would meet him at the Belle Isles at 7:00 P.M..

Bobby had changed the luncheon to the hotel where she was staying with her children in order to be able to sign the tab on Patrick Moriarty's bill. Janice Wynogradsky was present, along with Ted Gunderson, his partner and her two children. Neither Olmstead, Moriarty nor Marshall Riconosciuto showed up at the birthday party. Elizabeth opened her presents, we ate lunch and cake and caravanned over to Disneyland. We had a good time with the kids until six P.M.

At 6:30 P.M., Ted, Bobby and all the children returned to Bobby's hotel suite. I drove directly to Belle Isles. At 7:00 P.M., neither Bobby nor Littman had appeared for dinner. It turned out that Littman had left a message at the restaurant that he was sorry he missed us at the La Mirada hotel, but there was no mention of whether he would be joining us for dinner or not.

I called Sheri Littman, his wife, and she said Jonathan was on his way home. She did not know why.

Bobby Riconosciuto sat with Ted Gunderson and his partner in her hotel suite and ate pizza. When I called her, she said Ted had detained her at the hotel, she couldn't get away. My husband and I finished our dinner and drove to San Diego to see my mother.

I had no contact with Bobby or Michael Riconosciuto until one week later when I learned Bobby had requested the return of Michael's boxes of original documents. My husband had dropped me off at my mother's home and returned to Mariposa. For days he had been receiving urgent messages from Bobby requesting that I call her. He simply told her that I was tired and needed a rest.

Michael Riconosciuto called and asked him if we had interviewed Robert Booth Nichols? My husband said, "No."

When I returned home, I called Bobby and we arranged to have her boxes of documents returned to her via a friend who would drive from the Bay Area to pick them up. She had originally wanted them shipped to Marshall Riconosciuto's business address, but changed her mind at the last minute.

Bobby noted that Jonathan Littman had told Michael Riconosciuto all about the meeting with Robert Booth Nichols. Bobby wanted to know why I had lied to her about the Nichols meeting? She explained that Littman had also told Michael that he had dug through Michael's private documents at my home which I had obtained from Michael's secret trailer in the desert. Bobby had never told Michael about this because Michael had instructed her to stay away from the trailer.

I told Bobby that I did not believe Littman would do such a thing. I added that if I *had* interviewed Nichols, and he requested confidentiality, I would keep my word to him. There was no reason to discuss such an interview with Bobby or Michael. Bobby accepted that.

However, to convince me that Littman had in fact told Michael about the contents of the meeting, she recounted that Michael had told her that the meeting took place on Thursday, it lasted five hours, and I would not take my coat off during the entire meeting, which allegedly made Nichols nervous.

Bobby also stated that I had been seated in a location where I could be scanned for electronic devices, and since I was not "bugged," Nichols could not understand why I didn't take my coat off.

I immediately hung up from Bobby and called Littman. There was no answer at his home, so I called Robert Booth Nichols. Upon answering the phone, Nichols immediately accused me of "breaking my word to him." There was a sinister edge to his voice. I explained to him that, to date, I had not spoken to Michael Riconosciuto since two days prior to the Sherman Oaks meeting on February 13th.

Nichols countered that Littman had called him and told him that "I" had immediately reported to Michael the entire contents of the meeting, because Michael knew all about it. His tone was accusing, attentive, but devoid of anger. Then silence, waiting. I was indeed caught in the tentacles of the Octopus, and I felt the weight of it at that moment.

I told Nichols that I would have Bobby Riconosciuto call him and repeat what she had said to me, that Littman had betrayed both Nichols and me.

Nichols laughed. "Why should I believe anything Bobby says? I don't want to talk to her, and I don't want her to have my telephone number. Did you tell her where we met?" His voice was deeper, throatier, and I felt like a fool. Why should he believe her? I was grasping at straws and I had no answers. Why would Littman betray me, with so much at stake?

I said I would get to the bottom of this and let him know the results. Nichols said he was leaving for Australia the next day, would not be back for three months. (He had said the same words to Bill Hamilton when Hamilton was searching for Danny Casolaro on August 5th).

Nichols said he was *very* interested in hearing the results. "For my sake." He added that I should keep Peter Zokosky apprised of the results of my inquiry, then he hung up.

I called Jonathan Littman and asked him, "What's going on?" His voice was withdrawn, cautious. "I don't know. What is going on?" I decided to tape-record the conversation. My life was in danger as a result of Littman's actions, and I needed a lifeline to save it.

I explained that I had been in San Diego visiting my mother, and when I returned, Bobby Riconosciuto related the details of my interview with Nichols. "She said *you* told Michael everything."

Littman said, "Michael knew the truth."

"I haven't talked to Michael since before the interview with Nichols! How did he know about it?"

Littman's voice took on a slow, malignant tone. "What I'm saying is, you told him beforehand, and you can't play games with people like Michael."

I was astonished. And somewhat flustered. But I wanted to give him every opportunity to explain himself. "No. No. Something has happened. Something's wrong. Bobby just told me that YOU told Michael all about the meeting. And I told her I didn't believe that. I told her I *didn't* have an interview with Robert Booth Nichols ..."

Littman quickly responded, "You shouldn't lie to Michael ..."

I thought to myself, why should I have to report who I interview to Michael or Bobby? It was none of their business. But instead, I said, "Bobby told me she knew I interviewed Robert Booth Nichols on Thursday, for five hours, and I wore my coat through the entire meeting. And she said, `That made Nichols paranoid.' Now, how in the hell could she have known that?" Littman answered in an eerie, robotic voice, "I want to tell you something ..."

I interrupted, " ... And how did she know that I allowed you to look at Michael's documents, Jon?"

Littman began again, "She didn't. She only knows you have them ..."

Littman was being evasive, outright lying. I was becoming increasingly frustrated. I hated being reduced to that level of conversation. But so much depended on it. "Jon, Bobby said Michael called her. Michael *never* knew I had those boxes until *you* told him. Bobby said *you* revealed to him that you had seen the documents, seen the diary, seen everything."

I had withheld portions of the diary from Littman, amongst other things. I had no intention of ever showing it to anyone. It was a private part of Michael's life that belonged to him alone. I couldn't understand why Littman would have alarmed Michael about the diary, or lied about having it. Michael had risked his life at Wackenhut to obtain the only copy, broken into Dr. John Nichols' office to retrieve it, and fled to Washington state to begin a new life. He had thought it was secure in the desert. Now I had it. And Michael knew Bobby and I had kept the secret from him. And Littman had betrayed us both.

I continued ... "How would Michael have known that I didn't take my coat off in the meeting with Nichols? Nobody knew that except you, Jon."

Littman stayed cool as ice. "Let me get one thing straight with you. I gave you the conditions under which you were to meet with Nichols ..."

"Absolutely."

" ... And you betrayed those conditions by telling Michael that we were going to interview Nichols. And that put all of us in an awkward position ..."

I was astonished at how twisted the whole situation had become. I stammered, "Jonathan, I didn't know I *had* an appointment with Nichols at the time I told Michael that. I simply told him I *planned* to interview him at sometime in the future. I haven't spoken with Michael since the interview with Nichols? But *you* have ..."

Littman continued his train of thought, disregarding what I had said. "Once you told Michael you planned to interview Nichols, then you had to tell him everything. You had to tell the truth."

I asked pointedly, "Did *you* tell him the truth?"

Perversely, he confessed, "I told him the truth exactly. Because he knew we'd been there. And I'm not going to lie to Michael. He knew we'd been there ..."

I interjected, "But you gave your word to Robert Booth Nichols that you would never divulge the contents of the meeting to anyone. How could you do that?"

Littman attempted to change the subject, to put me on the defensive. "*You* are now the fly in the spider's trap ... You gotta be straight with all these people. With Michael, with Zokosky, with Nichols, these people can figure these things out. They're not dumb people."

"John, I've been straight with all of them. Every one of them. I have never betrayed any of them, other than to provide you, as a journalist, with some documents you requested ..."

He interrupted me, still speaking meticulously, ever so slowly. "You cannot fool people like Michael and Bobby and Ted Gunderson. Michael knew the meeting was going to take place. And it's not a good idea to go back and tell him a story that something didn't happen when it did happen."

There was a monotonous sing-song to his voice. He sounded like a tape recording. I was incredulous. Why was I defending myself to this man? I tried once again. "Michael doesn't control my life. I didn't tell him the meeting never took place. *I never spoke to Michael after the meeting with Nichols!* I didn't lie to him because I haven't spoken with him. I was in San Diego. I still haven't spoken to Michael. Why can't you understand that?" Littman: "Well, you're in the middle of it, because you're involved with Bobby and ..."

" ... Well, I'm not. That's the point, I'm not. It's a dangerous game and I want no part of it. I made that very clear with Bobby today when I spoke with her, which is the first time I've spoken with her since the meeting in Sherman Oaks."

" ... You told Michael that you were going to have a meeting with ..."

I was determined to get a confession from Littman. My life might depend on it. "Jonathan! Jonathan! You stood in that room with Robert Booth Nichols, and you heard him say aloud in front of both us, that if Michael ever found out what I have [the documents], he would kill me. I would be dead. Do you remember when he said that?"

"Sure."

" ... Yet you told Michael you had come to my home and seen his documents from the desert? Why?"

Littman repeated over and over the same words. "You lied to Michael. That was very stupid ..."

I wondered if he was intoxicated. I cut in, "You set me up. You called Nichols immediately after YOU told Michael about the meeting. Then you called Nichols and told him that "I" told Michael about the meeting. Now, Nichols just told me that today. Why did you do that, Jonathan?"

Jonathan did not deny setting me up, but stammered lamely, "I ... I did not appreciate your phone call to Nichols earlier today. You have placed me in an awkward position with Zokosky and Nichols ..."

So, Nichols had informed Littman of my phone call! Had he accused Littman of betraying him to Michael? I would probably never know the answer to that. I responded, "I called Nichols and asked him what was going on? How in the world could this have come about? I told Nichols what Bobby had said."

Littman was outraged that I had called Nichols and conveyed what Bobby had said. He was also outraged that Bobby had called me and confronted me about the Nichols meeting. Obviously *this* had not been in the scheme of things. Littman had obviously *not* expected Bobby to confront me.

After the Los Angeles fiasco, I had been fed up with her treatment of Littman and was cooling off in San Diego for a week. I had told Littman that I wouldn't be speaking with either Bobby or Michael again. Littman had underestimated Bobby's determination to speak to me, and my assertiveness in calling Nichols. His plan had backfired. Perhaps he had expected me to be dead before I had an opportunity to talk to anyone?

I was immediately alarmed about the synopsis and back-up documents I had turned over to Littman on the Mariposa drug lab. It had included the names of the Indians who had confided in me. We had planned to do a story together for the *San Francisco Chronicle*. "Jon, can I ask you one more question? Did you ever send the Mariposa information to the *Chronicle*?"

He answered curtly, "No."

"You asked me to send it to you. Why didn't you send it to the *Chronicle*? Why did you even ask for it?"

Jonathan hissed at me. "You lied to Riconosciuto's wife, or your husband did [regarding the Nichols meeting], and as a consequence of that, you're in hot water. I warned you about this whole thing ..."

"I'm in hot water because *you* betrayed me to Michael," I countered.

Again he repeated, "I told him *exactly* what happened. You're a fool, and you better start getting smart ... I think you should think twice about continuing with this ..."

The Indians who had turned in the drug lab were at risk. Jonathan had their names, including detailed information on two deputies implicated in growing marijuana and distributing methamphetamine on the Indian reservation in Mariposa. I wanted my paperwork back.

"Jonathan, there's something I need to know right now. This is important. You have information on Mariposa ..."

Jonathan hung up. I paced the floor of my office for a moment, then called him back. He didn't answer, but I knew he was standing by the phone while I talked into his answering machine. I informed him that I intended to document everything that had transpired at the Nichols meeting, including his betrayal of me to both Nichols and Riconosciuto, and that he had attempted to set me up to be killed by one or both of these men.

I said I was taking the report to the nearest U.S. Attorney and sending a copy to his editor at the *San Francisco Chronicle*. And, I wanted my Mariposa paperwork returned.

I then called Robert Booth Nichols, but there was no answer at his home, so I called Peter Zokosky. Zokosky, as always, was friendly and congenial, and confirmed that Nichols was very interested in the results of my inquiry. I recounted the conversation I'd had with Littman, in which he had confessed his betrayal, and offered proof of the conversation.

Zokosky said that would be fine and he would pass the information along to Nichols. On Sunday, February 23rd, I again talked to Bobby Riconosciuto. We again discussed what Littman had done and why he had attempted to convince Nichols that I had betrayed him [Nichols] to Riconosciuto.

Bobby and I both acknowledged that Michael had knowledge of Nichols' government and drug activities over a twenty-year time span. Unquestionably, Nichols wanted to discredit Michael in any way he could ... or deter anyone from obtaining Michael's information.

Suddenly, Bobby said she believed I was being "set up for a hit." I said I thought Michael was being set up with Robert Booth Nichols.

Someone, whoever was controlling Littman, was trying to create friction between Michael and Nichols, and attempting to use me to do it. My friendship with Bobby had unexpectedly thrown a monkey-wrench into their plans.

Bobby confided that Michael had tape-recorded the conversation in which Littman had reported the contents of the Nichols meeting. Michael had called a "friend," and had the friend patch Michael through to Littman. The conversation had then been monitored and tape recorded by the third party (obviously Ted Gunderson who performed this function often). Bobby agreed to send me a copy of the tape-recording.

I asked her why Littman would try to turn both Nichols and Michael against me. Professional jealousy? Bobby said, "No, the same thing happened to Danny Casolaro."

Littman had been talking to Danny Casolaro regularly, as well as Nichols and Riconosciuto at the time of Danny's death. Yet, Littman had never written a single word about Danny – or Robert Booth Nichols!!

We both agreed that someone was being set up, but Bobby insisted that it was me. She said she needed to check something out and she would call me back. Shortly thereafter, Bobby called back and breathlessly stated she had confirmed that I was about to die. She would not say who she had talked to, but intuitively, I felt it was Ted Gunderson.

Bobby said if I died, Michael would be held responsible. I had received collect calls daily from him for three months, then cut off all communication with him after meeting with Nichols. I had obtained *all* of Michael's documents in the desert without his knowledge, until recently. Bobby said Michael was not upset about our trip to the desert because we had survived it unscathed, and he was glad the *original* documents were now in her possession. He needed them for his case. However, I held in my possession copies of the bank cards which Paul Morasca and Mary Quick had allegedly died for.

It was a perfect set up, noted Bobby. Everyone, including my own husband, would believe Michael had contracted my death. Inwardly, I recalled the numerous statements by Nichols and Littman and Zokosky that "Michael would kill me."

Undoubtedly, they had expected me to repeat those statements to others, perhaps other reporters, or friends, or relatives. Who, in turn, would have repeated it to the police "after my death."

In fact, I hadn't repeated it to anyone, but it *was* scattered throughout my notes. Bobby advised me to get out of the house immediately, then call the FBI, the U.S. Attorney, the police or anyone else I could think of immediately. "They're going to kill you, if you don't *run*!" she yelled.

She said she was going to hang up, and when she called back, she didn't want me to be in the house. I became somewhat alarmed because of the various deaths surrounding Michael Riconosciuto. Regardless whether anyone believed him or not, the deaths were *not* make-believe. To name just a few: Mary Quick; Paul Morasca, Michael's former partner; Michael May who had visited Riconosciuto in jail two weeks before his death; Dennis Eismann, a lawyer Michael tried to hire; and of course, Danny Casolaro who had been introduced to the Octopus through Michael Riconosciuto. There were others with less direct connections.

Just three months after Danny's death, I had been approached by Riconosciuto, and the game of Dungeons & Dragons had begun again, this time with a new player. It seemed as if Nichols and Michael and Ted, and others, played a real life game, and when one of the players got "accidented" or "suicided" (as Ted called it), they simply recruited new players.

Oddly, Michael had once said that anyone could leave "the game" by simply dropping out while they were still alive. Once it was known they had dropped out, they were left alone - if they kept their mouths shut.

Michael had used journalists to gather information he needed to stay abreast of the game. It was a subtle form of blackmail he used on Nichols and Ted and, indeed, the government whom he had worked for. I had once asked him why "they" didn't just kill him. He had answered that they didn't want to kill him. They wanted his technology. The FMC deal was, in fact, still on hold. The deaths around him were allegedly "punishment" for his indiscretions, and to keep a lid on their biological warfare, high-tech weaponry, and large-scale heroin and cocaine operations worldwide. But who would believe it all? There were hundreds of dead-end gopher trails ... dried up corporations, discredited witnesses, dead bodies. Nichols had said only days before, in Littman's presence, that my death would be brought about by one of Michael's "drug flunkies." Who would believe otherwise?

Littman had seemed adamant, even outraged, that I *hadn't* reported the contents of the Nichols meeting to Riconosciuto. Why? When it was Littman who originally warned me not to? When I didn't, Littman reported it himself.

Somehow, the success of the scheme had hinged upon Riconosciuto having knowledge of the meeting. I had unexpectedly kept my word to Nichols. Of course I had. My life depended on it. And, why had Nichols made a point of showing me the Zapruder film? What possible significance could that have on my investigation?

(Two years later, after speaking with Dick Russell, author of *The Man Who Knew Too Much,* a 17-year investigation of the Kennedy assassination, and Garby Leon at Silver Pictures, we theorized that the film had been shown to provide Nichols with "deniability." If I had mentioned the showing of the film to anyone in media, and placed any credibility on it, it would have invalidated everything else that took place at that meeting.)

The phone rang again, and it was Bobby Riconosciuto. She was even more agitated than before – and furious that I was still in the house. I assured her that I was leaving and hung up. I called Ray Jenkins and Roger Imbrogno and asked them to come to my home in Mariposa. Ray was a former Chief of Police of Merced College and a good friend. His companion, Roger, was in the State Guard with him. They arrived 45 minutes later carrying military rifles and a bullet-proof vest.

I sat at my computer and documented the whole event, entitled, "Vortex." It was a 17-page diary of sorts which began as follows: "The following is a detailed account of an investigation which I began on December 1, 1991 and continue to work on intermittently as time allows. In all my years as an investigator and journalist, I have never encountered anything as bizarre or as alarming as this story. The purpose of this diary is to document these occurrences for my own safety ..."

I did not send the report to the U.S. Attorney as I had threatened to do. Nor did I send it to Littman's editor, Michael Yamamoto, at the *San Francisco Chronicle,* though I should have. I simply kept it and sent a copy to J.H., where I'm sure it disappeared, as always, down the big, black hole.

At that point in time, my sense of reality was diminishing. I couldn't tell if I was over-reacting to Bobby Riconosciuto's warning, or if my lack of experience might cause my death by staying at home. Ultimately, I decided to disappear for a while.

I drove to Fresno to stay with a friend, who subsequently accompanied me to Galveston, Texas where we stayed with her mother for three months. Walking the beaches of Galveston, I found some measure of balance within myself, and returned home in June, rested and ready to resume my life. For several months after that, I had no contact with any of the principles in my investigation until October, 1992.

John Connolly

— 13 —

The Investigators

Sometime in mid-October 1992, at the offices of the *Mariposa Guide*, I received a hurried phone call from Dave Massey, standing in the lobby outside the Washington D.C. offices of ABC's *20/20* news bureau. I had asked Massey to pick up key documents at the offices of producer Don Thrasher at *20/20* who had been holding them there as a safety precaution for me. (*20/20* had aired an in-depth piece on the corruption in Mariposa County and I had developed a friendship with Thrasher at that time).

After Massey emerged from Thrasher's office building, he'd met with John Cohen, investigator for the House Judiciary Committee on Inslaw. They talked for a few minutes, then Cohen asked Massey if he would turn over my documents to him? Massey excused himself and hurriedly called me at my office in Mariposa. I instructed him *not* to hand over the documents. Most of them were my originals and I had no copies. (Thrasher had flown into California to pick the documents up, but we hadn't had time to make copies. He was considering producing a segment on Danny Casolaro).

However, I mentioned to Massey that he was welcome to give Cohen my telephone number if he wished. Shortly thereafter, Cohen called me at my home and we had numerous conversations during the next several weeks. It was my understanding that he was the lead investigator in the House Judiciary Committee's three-year investigation of the Inslaw stolen software. The final Investigative Report, dated September 10, 1992, titled "The Inslaw Affair," had already been published and I wondered why he bothered to call me?

After much coaxing, I finally agreed to send him some sort of an affidavit. I was working as a reporter for the local newspaper and didn't have time to put together a detailed report, so I simply attached a notarized cover sheet to "Vortex" and mailed it off to him with a few supporting documents.

On October 28, 1992, Cohen called back. He was very excited about Vortex. "There's some great information here," he observed. "You did a very good investigative job, I have to commend you on that. I realize it's only a fraction of everything you have. What you have done, you have put the pieces of the whole thing together. Little bits and pieces of things that I have known about, that I had theorized about, you have found the answers to those specific questions." I explained to Cohen that I planned to publish a book on the subject and his professional opinion was valuable to me.

He added, "You've done some good investigative work here. It puts me in a position to say, `Yeah, this stuff is good, and this is some stuff you may want to get out.' In fact, I can put myself out as being available to these media people to be an inside source, for background only, which would also add credibility to your project."

Cohen hesitated, seemingly uncomfortable with what he was about to say. He drew a deep breath, then proceeded. "You are actually a key witness to this thing now. And you might want to consider talking to a couple of the honorable law enforcement people that are still working on this. I do know there are currently some FBI investigations that are in place on this ..."

Cohen hesitated again, gathering his thoughts. " ... There has been coordination on this." He waited for a response, a signal that I understood what he was trying to say. I said I understood.

"It's been unofficial, but there has been coordination. So, I'd like to know whether ... maybe it would even keep you out of the limelight, whether you would mind, as long as I talk about it and clear it with you first ..."

Cohen was leading up to something, but having trouble getting to the point. " ... There is a certain sharing of information. Some of the leads and some of the stuff [in Vortex] (pause) ... Because I'll tell you, one of the biggest hits (pause) ... I always felt that there was a narcotics connection in this ..."

I laughed aloud. Cohen continued ... "regarding international narcotics distribution. And I've sort of made my expertise in my years in law enforcement, international narco-terrorism, the weapons-dope connections in the intelligence agencies ..."

I could only say, "Yes, yes, yes."

" ... And when I was in Los Angeles I did a lot of undercover work with Colombians, where I worked international narcotics conspiracies with DEA and FBI and, being a local police officer, I didn't really get caught up in their systems, I just made some great contacts in these agencies. But I also learned quite a bit about Southeast Asian heroin and the rise of the Medellin Cartels and the other Cartels in Latin America."

"Yes." By then, I knew Cohen had grasped the significance of the information Michael Riconosciuto had attempted to trade to the FBI, as well as Danny Casolaro's fatal inquiry about Mike Abbell of the DOJ and his connection to Gilbert Rodriguez and Jose Londono of the Cali Cartel.

Cohen continued ... "And I also ran into quite a few law enforcement professionals who were pretty irritated because of the intelligence agency, drug dealer connection."

"Yes. Right."

"Well, the thing that is interesting is, one of the most interesting things in the whole report, was the article on The Company."

"Yes."

" ... Because that immediately answered, or confirmed, what my suspicions had been. And I know the exact, right channel to push to get this thing hooked up. And he's a big-time ... (pause) See this is a very good time for people like us, who are out for purposes of good, to ...(pause) You see, right now the FBI is in a war with the Department of Justice. So, the time is ripe to feed this stuff to the right people." (I would later learn in early 2001 that the "war" between the FBI and the DOJ was the entire *key* to the Octopus story).

I agreed that the drug operations needed to be cleaned up, because the drugs were filtering into the smaller communities. But, thinking of Mariposa, I added that there were law enforcement people involved in the drug trade.

Cohen agreed. "I'm very careful with who I deal with. And I think when these people contact you, you'll be somewhat surprised."

Reluctantly, I said, "OK, I will work with them."

Cohen concluded by saying, "You said some real interesting things. I like the section where you said `Bob Nichols runs Glen Shockley, Glen Shockley runs Jose Londono.' Now that corroborates some information that I got in the past which talked about one of the reasons PROMIS was stolen. You see, I've had a side theory about another reason why PROMIS was taken. And it was that PROMIS could also be modified to track money laundering.."

"Oh, absolutely."

"... And it could also be used as an active information gathering, or an active moving software program that can go into other data bases. And it could be modified to control hundreds of accounts and move money through the international banking system."

I interjected, "This is what Michael Riconosciuto was trying to trade to the FBI and to FinCen ..."

Cohen added, "What a lot of people don't realize is that there are two international banking systems. There's CHIPS and SWIFT. And the word Swift Chips has been spread out throughout this whole [investigation]. And a lot of people don't realize what that meant. Well, Swift Chips is a referral to those two clearing house systems. The clearing house interbank payment system and then the European counterpart, Swift. And they do $2 billion dollars worth of banking transactions a day."

"Yes ..."

" ... And if one was able to move accounts through there, you could move money around the world ..."

••••••••

I was subsequently contacted by Thomas Gates of the Los Angeles FBI, and John Connolly of *SPY* magazine. Gates was somewhat cryptic and non-communicative about his investigation. It was understandable since he had been sued by Robert Booth Nichols in a civil court for taking his investigation "out of country" to Australia and Japan.

Just before Gates called me, I had spoken with Gene Gilbert for the first time, the investigator at the Riverside District Attorney's office, and learned that drug activities at Wackenhut had been investigated for years, but a certain FBI agent, a Fred Reagan, had always shut the local investigations down.

I related this information to Gates, who seemed not particularly interested in that avenue of approach. "I'm mostly interested in Robert Booth Nichols," he said.

I explained to Gates that Nichols had made it very clear that I was not to discuss the meeting I'd had with him to anyone."

Gates inquired, "Why would he tell you that?"

I responded, "I have no idea. But I think he was serious. He had his wife take my picture front and side, and he wouldn't allow my husband into the interview. My husband had to sit downstairs in the van."

I summarized the interview briefly, then noted that I had obtained, through Bobby Riconosciuto, eight boxes of Michael's documents in the Mojave Desert near Death Valley. I believed those documents had caused Nichols and/or Jonathan Littman to want me out of the picture.

"Michael didn't know that we had done this," I noted. "Michael had instructed his wife not to go near the trailer out there. However, Bobby and I *did* go out there. It was dark and it was cold and the kids were hungry, so rather than go through all those documents, she just gave them all to me. I put them in my van and I came home with them. All the originals. And I spent a week copying all this stuff, then I shipped the boxes back to her father-in-law." [Actually, Bobby had sent a friend to pick the boxes up, saying she was going to store them at her father-in-law's business in Orange County].

Gates had a habit of saying nothing when I finished my sentence. So I continued ... "Some of this stuff was incredibly incriminating for all of them. And this is why they're all concerned. They're really afraid that I'm going to send some of this material to someone, somewhere. And, I did send a 17-page summary ("Vortex") to John Cohen, but not the material itself. There's too much to send. Additionally, I have reams of notes. I kept notes on all the calls I received."

Gates asked what "Vortex" contained? I replied that it pretty much summarized everything that had transpired from the first day. "I had contacted Ted Gunderson regarding a problem here in Mariposa. He had compiled a 700-page report on Tulare County and I wanted to know if he had anything on Mariposa county, where I live. We had a meeting for about eight hours [November 30, 1991] and I discussed the things that were going on in our community, which is close to Fresno. And, the very next morning, Michael Riconosciuto called me. I'd never heard of the man before, but he proceeded to give me all the names of the people involved in The Company out of Fresno, which he was working within the framework of."

Again Gates said nothing. I waited, but there was no response. So I added, "Now, all of this starts to get real involved at this point. I don't know if you're interested in this, or not ..."

Gates replied, "The Company?"

"Yes."

Gates noted, "At a future date. I'm more interested in what Nichols had to tell you right now."

Nichols had sued Gates and lost his case quite recently. I wasn't sure I wanted to walk into a situation where I would be caught in the middle. I asked, "Well, I need to find out from you - I'm not real thrilled about playing with this guy, you know ..."

Gates: "I don't want you to play with him."

"Do you want me to come in as a witness on your behalf, or what?"

Gates explained, "The civil suit is finished. This is a criminal proceeding. I want to know what he said to you."

I responded, "Well, I want to know where this is going to go. I want to know who's listening in ..."

"Nobody's listening in ..."

" ... I want to know what you're going to do with it. Where it's going to go."

"Well, what do you *want* me to do with it?"

"Well, if I'm going to get involved in it, and once I tell you what I know, I'm going to be involved. I want to know in what capacity I'm going to be involved?"

Gates was evasive. "Well, I don't know what you have to say. As far as looking at the gross amount of evidence we have, we're getting ready to do that real soon. We have a lot of people out there talking to us, but we need to find the substance of the criminal act."

"Yes."

Gates continued ..."And you may have the key to some of that."

I was surprised. "So, you're putting together a `criminal case.' You're going to have to level with me to a certain point. I understand that you're FBI, and everything goes in and nothing ever comes out again, but still you're going to have to level with me to a certain point, because I need to know where I stand."

Gates drawled, "Well, if there's information that would be needed for criminal prosecution, then we'd have to talk to you about the use of that material. And if you decide you don't want to use it, or don't want to relinquish it, then we can't compel you to get on as a free witness and talk about this."

"Uh,hmmm."

" ... So, we would hope that you would do it. Whatever information you provide at this point will remain confidential."

"Uh, hmmm."

" ... You know what I'm saying?"

"Uh, hmmm."

" ... That's your choice."

"Yes, well I'll have to think about it."

"Well, if you could give me an idea as to what was mentioned, I could tell you, basically, how we can handle it."

I didn't know where to begin, what he wanted, so I asked, "May I ask what are the charges that you're going to bring against Nichols? Would this have to do with the government aspect of what he's been involved in, such as arms shipments, or would it have to do with drug trafficking ... murder, or what?"

Gates chuckled, "Well, that sounds like a pretty good package to me."

I laughed. "I'm just curious about what you're specifically focusing on."

He answered, "I'm focusing on any criminal activities that Nichols is involved in. Obviously, the most significant areas of interest are the drugs, the murders and the gunrunning."

I explained that it was very complex. I didn't have my notes or "Vortex" at my home, so I summarized as briefly as possible from memory what I had obtained from the boxes in the Mojave desert.

Gates listened attentively. When I concluded, he noted, "Do you have these things [referring to the documents] put away where nobody else can get at them?"

"Yes. They are not in my home or anywhere on my property."

Gates asked, "Does anybody else know where they are?"

I wondered if he thought I might NOT be around in the near future. "The person whose house they're at. Nobody else."

His next question confirmed my suspicion. "What if something happens to you? Where do we find them? How do we find them?"

I noted that I had copies out with two people. Gates asked, "Are they trustworthy?"

I said, "Absolutely."

Gates pressed further. "The place where the original documents are, can you trust that individual?"

"Yes. Absolutely."

Gates seemed satisfied that the documents were safe for the time being. He reiterated that I would have to be debriefed extensively and the information would be maintained under the Attorney General guidelines for confidential sources.

The word "Attorney General" struck a cord in my consciousness. "You said `Attorney General,' you mean through the DOJ [Department of Justice]?"

Gates answered carefully, "Yeah."

I laughed sardonically. "This is getting funny ..."

Gates hurried to explain that it was only through the DOJ "guidelines." He added, "It's their rules, but they don't have access to the information."

I pointed out that I might consider talking to him, because I knew of his commitment to busting the drug cartels and finding Casolaro's murderer. I added that I would never talk to "the FBI, quote, unquote," and Gates said that was okay. He understood. So I said, "We'll go on from there then ..."

I proceeded to describe the interviews with Robert Booth Nichols. When I was finished, Gates asked me what I was going to do with the information? I explained that I planned to write a non-fiction book about it because much of the information I had obtained through my investigation had been independently substantiated by the recently published House Judiciary Committee Report on Inslaw.

However, I had not decided what the focus of the book would be - the story still had to develop. A thought occurred to me. "I would be very interested in what you've experienced in your investigation right from day one. That's what the public wants to read about."

Gates agreed, "It would make a hell of a book." Then he added, "So, how do we put Nichols and his group away?" I answered simply, "I don't know, Tom, that's your department."

I never sent the documents and never spoke to him again until two years later when I was hot on the trail of Mike Abbell.

••••••••

John Connolly, a former New York police officer turned writer, was also researching the death of Danny Casolaro. Through sources unknown to me, he learned of my investigation, and after several conversations, I agreed to send him documents which he needed for his "Octopus" investigation. But first, I demanded that he fax me a letter protecting my copyrights and giving due credit.

Connolly faxed back the following letter, dated October 22, 1992: "I hereby agree that any and all information, documents, etc. sent to me from you will be treated confidentially. Any information supplied by you will not be used by me without your express permission. Furthermore, in the event that I publish a future story and use any of the information supplied by you, you will receive the proper reporting credits or bylines. Sincerely, John Connolly."

Connolly was a gung-ho journalist, and apparently found it impossible to withhold such provocative information. The January, 1993 issue of *SPY* included much of the information I had sent him in a story entitled, "Dead Right," by John Connolly.

He had not obtained my permission nor given me a byline, but I didn't hold it against him. The story was well written, and gutsy, and I had to respect that. Essentially, the story focused on the death of journalist Danny Casolaro, but pages 63-65 gave an in-depth profile of Robert Booth Nichols, who was portrayed as Danny's "dangerous friend" ... "The Lethal Robert Booth Nichols."

Wrote Connolly, "By the late Spring of 1991, Robert Booth Nichols had become one of Danny Casolaro's most important sources. They spoke frequently and at length ...

"We know Nichols was a man as comfortable in the underworld as in the intelligence community and that he was associated with people who treated killing as an ordinary part of doing business."

FBI agent Thomas Gates had identified Nichols in his sworn affidavit as a drug trafficker and money launderer stemming from a 1987 investigation of Mob activities in Hollywood. Interestingly, Nichols had been identified by the FBI as early as 1978 as being involved in drug trafficking, the very same year that Gilbert Rodriguez was indicted in Los Angeles. I wondered if Nichols and Gilbert Rodriguez had been connected in the FBI investigation?

In 1989, Nichols represented a group of unknown investors who wanted to take over Summa Corporation, the holding company of Howard Hughes' empire. Hughes had just died, and Nichols had convinced a Saudi company called Ali & Fahd Shobokski Group to become partners in the (failed) takeover attempt.

Joseph Cicippio, who was later taken hostage in Lebanon, was at that time the London manager of Ali & Fahd. Cicippio told *SPY* he specifically remembered Nichols telling him he was representing interests in the U.S. Government and had been shown *U.S. Justice Department identification by Nichols.*

By 1981, Nichols had become partners with retired arms manufacturer Peter Zokosky and they formed Meridian Arms, which in turn joined up with Wackenhut Corporation in a scheme to manufacture arms on the Cabazon Indian reservation.

In Meridian's quest to provide guns for the Contras, Nichols had obtained all the required California permits to possess and sell machine guns – using recommendations from CIA official Larry Curran.

Connolly pointed out Nichols' listing of Harold Okimoto as a former employer on his application to carry a concealed weapon, describing Okimoto as "believed by intelligence sources to be a high-ranking member of Japan's Yakuza crime syndicate."

Eugene Giaquinto, president of MCA's Home Entertainment Division, was mentioned as one of M.I.L.'s board directors. (Nichols' Meridian International Logistics corporation). Noted Connolly, "[FBI] agents caught Giaquinto and Nichols lunching at Le Dome, the swank Los Angeles show business restaurant, and afterward transferring a box from Giaquinto's car to Nichols's. The [wire] taps caught them discussing possible takeovers of MCA, and the effect on stock prices. It was also evident from the wire-taps that Giaquinto enjoyed a special relationship with John Gotti ..."

Thomas Gates testified before the House Judiciary Committee on Inslaw that he had twice heard from informants that Nichols had put a contract out on his life. In July 1991, Danny Casolaro became somewhat alarmed and began confiding in Thomas Gates. Nichols had flown from Puerto Rico to Washington D.C. to meet with Casolaro, staying several days.

SPY didn't know what they talked about, but after Nichols left, Casolaro told Agent Gates that Nichols had warned him, "If you continue this investigation, you will die." Three days before his death, Danny had asked Gates whether he should take Nichols's warnings seriously?

On July 31, 1991, Casolaro had also spoken with Richard Stavin, a former special prosecutor for the Justice Department who had been assigned to the MCA case. In his investigation of MCA, Stavin had unearthed documents implicating Nichols as a money launderer with ties to the Gambino crime family and the Yakuza.

Connolly wrote, "Danny must have thought he hit the jackpot." Six days after speaking to Stavin, Danny Casolaro, "who still had a young man's vision of his immortality," had a long phone conversation with Robert Booth Nichols, but the contents of that conversation were unknown to Connolly.

SPY also interviewed Allan Boyak, a former CIA operative now practicing law in Utah, who had known Nichols for 15 years. Boyak told *SPY*, "Nichols is lethal." A transcript of a conversation between Boyack, Michael Riconosciuto and former FBI agent Ted Gunderson, (which I had sent Connolly a copy of) described an occasion in which Nichols wanted to deliver a message to a mobster from Chicago. Nichols hung a man upside down on a hoist in an airplane hangar in front of a prop plane, then started the engine of the plane and revved it up, so that the man hanging on the hoist was sucked toward the propellers. According to Riconosciuto, "By the time Bob got finished with him, he wanted to die."

••••••••

What Connolly failed to report in his article was the name of the man who had been "hung up." His name was Sam Marowitz, a professional hit man, who had been "the trigger man" in the non-fatal shooting of Robert Ferrante, head of Consolidated Savings and Loan.

Ferrante had been involved with Patrick Moriarti, Marshall Riconosciuto's partner of 40 years. It is important to remember that Robert Booth Nichols and Michael Riconosciuto had been close associates since 1967. Ted Gunderson had located, through his sources, the "trigger man" in the Ferrante shooting, and Nichols and Riconosciuto had forced Marowitz to confess to his crime by hanging him upside down in front of the airplane propeller.

Riconosciuto recalled, " ... So he [Marowitz] starts talking ... and Bob goes out of the room like this: `Oh my God, I don't want to hear anymore,' covering his ears. This Marowitz starts confessing to every hit he's ever done, including the Dorfman killings in Chicago. ... I mean, all hell breaks loose. All of a sudden Ted has found the torpedo in the Dorfman killings ..." After the "hanging" incident, Marowitz fled to Israel.

The transcript was taken from Riconosciuto's first (tape-recorded) meeting with Alan Boyak on May 5, 1991 at the attorney visiting room of the Tacoma, Washington house of incarceration.

Riconosciuto had been arrested on March 29, 1991 by DEA agents, reportedly under the supervision of Michael T. Hurley, who had been transferred from Nicosia, Cyprus to Washington state shortly before the arrest. It is significant that this arrest took place exactly eight days after Michael had signed the Inslaw affidavit on March 21, 1991.

Michael already had a law firm representing him, John Crawford and John Rosalini, but Ted Gunderson had brought Boyak into the case because of the intense political ramifications. In other words, they needed someone to put together a case against the government officials involved, "so they could buy out cheap."

Danny Casolaro had obtained a copy of that transcript from Boyak, according to Ted Gunderson and Bobby Riconosciuto. Bobby noted that Danny had taken the transcript to people in the *Department of Justice and confronted them with it.*

Michael Riconosciuto later added that Robert Nichols had flown to Washington D.C. and "followed Danny's trail through the DOJ, doing `damage control' and repudiating the transcript."

This may well be the encounter (per SPY magazine) that Danny had with Nichols in Washington D.C. less than a month before his death in which Nichols had said, "If you continue with this investigation, you will die."

Danny had a unique habit of fearlessly "bouncing" information from one person to another, particularly between Michael Riconosciuto and Robert Booth Nichols. After the "transcript" incident, it undoubtedly created a hostile climate between Nichols and Riconosciuto. (Riconosciuto was attempting to trade information on Nichols' activities in exchange for his freedom).

Numerous passages in the transcript openly named narcotics traffickers allegedly working under Robert Booth Nichols. On page 53, just one of many named was Bryce Larsen, currently (1991) operating a hotel for "one of Harold Okimoto's people in Thailand," who smuggled China White heroin into the U.S.. "The DEA seized two Lear jets from him the last time they busted him," noted Riconosciuto.

"Skip Jahota (phonetic sp.) was here trying to recruit people to go to work in Thailand, and to off-load the boats when they bring the stuff in [to the U.S.]. They've got some heroin coming in the next few weeks, a rather large ..."

Boyak interrupted, " ... There's a big case in Miami where a female black Assistant U.S. Attorney is handling this gal I was telling you about, but that's ... I don't want to go into details on that because she's in a witness protection program ..."

Riconosciuto added, "Well, she's probably working against the Martin brothers ..."

Boyak interjected, "No, it's against Larsen!"

On page 63, Riconosciuto brought Al Holbert, the Israeli intelligence agent, into the picture. " ... Now the other area where I can do some real damage is Al Holbert's procurement of chemicals nationwide. He has a mail-order chemical company that is mailing out chemicals right now. What they do is they mail out large multiple orders under threshold limit value for the reporting requirements under the new DEA regulations. Like with Phenol acidic acid, it's one kilo a month, so they mail out 800 grams per month to one customer. And they've got fifty customers ..."

Boyak asked, "Where are they doing that?"

Mike answered, "In Miami, Florida."

But, Riconosciuto added, in the California operation, Holbert and Richard Knozzi weighed their drugs on U-Haul trucks! "When they do their meth lab, they usually do 1,500 to 2,000 pounds."

Holbert's address was listed at Ft. Mead. Riconosciuto informed Boyak that Holbert was a former Israeli intelligence officer who came to the United States to give special education classes to law enforcement agencies. "He's dirty as the day is long," he added. "He's out of OMV now. I don't know what OMV is doing at Ft. Mead."

Boyak had interjected, "Just so you know, because it may click with you. Ft. Mead has headquarters ISCOM (Intelligence Security Command) which has part of the intelligence network for the Delta Force."

In another section of the 65-page transcript, Riconosciuto detailed his operation with Tyme Share Inc. – something he had been unable to discuss with me on the jail phone. "Barry Smith, who is an associate of Bob Nichols, had done some research on some interlocking directorates with the board members of Wackenhut, and I started to realize how deeply involved in the Nugan Hand Bank the Wackenhut people were.

"Paul Morasca and I were very close to Michael Hand [former President of Nugan Hand Bank of Australia]. Now he's on the run, in Canada. I had a complete set of all the records for Nugan Hand that had not been destroyed."

Boyak: "What function were you doing for them?"

Mike: "I set up the data processing base. See, I was a principle in Tyme Share, Inc. Do you know what Tyme Share is?"

Boyak: "No."

Mike: "This is a giant computer communications company, and all the Justice Department field offices communicate via Tyme Net. FO-

IMS (Field Office Information Management System) for the FBI is all done via Tyme Net. Okay? Most of your big banking institutions ..."

Boyak interrupted, "I'm not even a user friendly person ..."

Mike continued, "I had the Nugan Hand records and I analyzed the situation and I looked at the Saudi position. They were taking people's paychecks, you know, foreign workers, and giving them unbelievable deals just to put their money in the bank ..."

Boyak: " ... And they were skimming the interest?"

Mike: "Yeah, oh yeah. So, what I did ... I was looking at block transfers on Swift Chips, and reconciliations ..."

Boyak: " ... You've lost me there."

Mike: "Anyway, what I did was I screwed up everything with the automated clearing house between Nugan Hand ..."

Boyak: " ... So nothing could be liquidated."

Mike: "No, what I did was I created a virtual bank on the automated clearing house system and I funneled all that money into it, and then I funneled it out of there into blocked currencies ..."

Boyak interrupted again: "I can't track the technical paper trail. What I'm trying to do is get to the bottom line ..."

••••••••

The bottom line was, Danny Casolaro *allegedly carted the above transcript around the Department of Justice, demanding answers.* Less than a month later he was dead. The transcript gave details of the Cobra helicopter shipments to Iraq, via North Korea, corporate structures, under-cover operatives, espionage activities, advanced weapons technology tested at the Nevada Nuclear test site, and much more.

"Something" in the transcript pushed some buttons at the DOJ, but at that time I could only theorize as to what that was.

••••••••

In all fairness, it is necessary to relate Robert Booth Nichols' response to Alan Boyak's accusations about him. The following narrative originated from a phone conversation with Nichols in which he said "Boyak was unbelievable."

> (Nichols speaking): "I know what he said about me, and that's all well and dandy. But I don't know why he said it. It's all totally

false. The guy could not be doing this unless he was under the orders of someone. Or he's crazy.

The thing with this Boyak, he said I was involved in BCCI, he said narcotics trafficking, he said money laundering ... as did the FBI.

The point is, I know people inside the bureau [FBI], I know people inside the agency [CIA], I know people inside government who are very responsible people. I speak to people as individuals, not as initials. In other words, I wouldn't talk to the FBI, I would talk to an agent that I knew in the FBI who was honest. Or I would talk to an agent in the company, or the CIA, who I know is honest, but I wouldn't talk to them as a whole, or someone I didn't know. Because I think they've become so corrupt and polluted that they don't know what they're doing half the time ...

Some people in government are extremely concerned about it. They're very much involved with it. I mean, the honest ones are the biggest critics ...

With regards to the Yakuza, I don't know them. To my knowledge, I've never been around them. With regard to the Mafia, I don't know them. To my knowledge, I've never been around them. With regards to narcotics, I hate narcotics. And anyone who's known me for any length of time, and my friends are all old friends, knows that I hate narcotics, have never been around them, have never seen heroin in my life ... except on television. So, it makes me wonder and many other people that are friends of mine, wonder what agenda ... who's up to what? Right?

The Tong, I don't know them, nor have I ever been around them to my knowledge. One story [newspaper article] said [I was] a hit man for the Tong. That was one story. I've never been a hit man for anything, including Tong, which is the Chinese mafia.

Ask yourself this. I sued them [the FBI], right? We were told, 'Don't sue them,' by a lot of people. 'Kill everybody, don't sue them.' But the point is, there are a lot of people overseas that said pursue them anyway, and that's it, period. So, it comes down to one thing, really. When we get to the courtroom, we are not going to say, 'This is this, and that is that, and trust us.' We're going to document everything we say ..."

When I asked Nichols if Michael Riconosciuto had worked for the CIA, he said, "Why don't you call the CIA and ask them. I'm sure they're listed in the phone book."

••••••••

Nichols' lawsuit against Thomas Gates and the Los Angeles FBI was dismissed twice in federal court. However, he also filed a lawsuit against the Los Angeles Police Department for alleged false arrest stemming from a 1986 incident at the Palomino nightclub in North Hollywood.

On March 21, 1993 the *Los Angeles Times* published a story entitled, "Trial Offers Murky Peek Into World of Intrigue" by Henry Weinstein and Paul Feldman

Nichols stated on the witness stand that he worked for the CIA for nearly two decades. His lawsuit charged that as a result of his detainment by the LAPD, the Santa Clara County Sheriff's Department rescinded his concealed weapons permit. That action, Nichols claimed, resulted in the loss of Swiss financing for a multi-million dollar deal to manufacture machine guns in South Korea.

Nichols also testified that he had no visible income for more than 15 years except for the living expenses he received from the CIA. He said he was recruited into the CIA while living in Hawaii in the late 1960's by a man named "Ken." Ken had told him that instead of joining the U.S. military, he could serve his country in other ways. He was instructed to take a job with a Hawaiian security firm (Okimoto?) and later to move to Glendale, California to join a construction company (Pender?).

From that point until 1986, Nichols worked intelligence gathering operations in more than 30 nations from Central America to Southeast Asia. To prove this, Nichols' lawyer, John F. Denove, supplied the court with a list of Washington D.C. personages to be subpoenaed which ultimately caused Judge Thomas C. Murphy to declare a mistrial. No record was ever made public of that list of names, though Thomas Gates (FBI) and Henry Weinstein of the *Los Angeles Times* respectively confirmed its existence over the phone, but neither would divulge the names.

— 14 —

The Cali Cartel

In August 1994 I placed several calls to John Cohen, former investigator for the House Judiciary Committee on Inslaw, to follow up on Cohen's investigation of Mike Abbell and Casolaro's findings on him prior to his death. Cohen was now stationed at the Office of National Drug Control Policy at the Executive Offices of the President (Clinton) in Washington D.C.

I also made calls to Special Agent Thomas Gates at the Los Angeles Joint Drug Intelligence Group, who originally testified before the House Judiciary Committee on Inslaw. Gates had spoken with Casolaro during the week before his death and I felt he might help me to identify what Casolaro learned about Abbell. Both men were congenial, but hesitant to talk about Abbell at that point in time.

I then called the young Customs Agent, Scott Lawrence, to whom I had given the affidavit mentioning Mike Abbell in February 1993. His supervisor said he was stationed in Miami, Florida and put me in touch with him. He too was cryptic and uncommunicative about Mike Abbell.

I soon discovered why. A few weeks later, on September 9th, 1994, the FBI raided the law offices of Michael Abbell in Washington D.C. The raid was the result of a Miami federal grand jury probe of the Cali Cartel. As of that date no criminal charges had yet been filed against Abbell.

I had also placed a call in September 1994 to Steve Zipperstein, Chief Assistant U.S. Attorney in Los Angeles, who *conducted an investigation for the DOJ* on Inslaw and Casolaro in 1994. Zipperstein was uncooperative and defensive when approached about Casolaro's investigation of Michael Abbell and Gilberto Rodriguez.

Less than two weeks later, the DOJ report was released to the public with no mention of Mike Abbell, Gilberto Rodriguez, Robert Booth Nichols, or any of the afore-mentioned information in this manuscript, including FIDCO, though it was available for scrutiny through many sources.

••••••••

In November, 1994, *Time* magazine reported that the 56-year old Gilberto Rodriguez was "stressed out" and seeking to surrender to the Colombian justice system in exchange for reduced jail time, perhaps three or four years, and his fortune left intact. In a Colombian jail, this would inevitably amount to a quiet vacation.

However, Gilberto insisted that any deal would have to be endorsed by the United States. In return, the Rodriguez brothers, Gilberto and Miguel, would guarantee that a large percentage of Colombian drug dealers would be willing to get out of the drug business and dismantle their infrastructure, their labs and their routes. The estimated net effect would be a 60% reduction in the drug supply to the U.S. alone.

Prior to Rodriguez's offer, President Samper had announced that it would be necessary to dismantle the Cartels rather than incarcerate their leaders. An aide to Samper noted that the door was open to a surrender program.

In light of everything I had learned to date, I could not help wondering what price did the U.S. government pay to bring the Cartels to the point of surrender?

••••••••

On June 6th, 1995, the *Washington Post* broke the news about Mike Abbell in a front page story entitled, "Ex-Prosecutors Indicted in Cali Case." Three former federal prosecutors, including Michael Abbell, who served "as a top ranking Justice Department official, were named in an indictment [on June 5th] in Miami along with 56 others as part of a broad racketeering case against the Colombia-based Cali Cartel ..."

Jose Londono, a founder of the Cali Cartel, and Donald Ferguson, an assistant U.S. attorney in Miami were also charged. Former assistant U.S. attorney Joel Rosenthal pled guilty in the case to charges of money laundering. Abbell and other lawyers faced charges of money laundering, drug conspiracy and racketeering. The indictment charged them with obstruction of justice, preparing false affidavits and conveying warnings to arrested cartel members that they should not cooperate with government investigations.

The *Washington Post* noted that, ultimately, it was not expensive cocaine interdiction on the high seas, but detective work by a team of Miami-based U.S. Customs agents and the Drug Enforcement Administration that compiled the evidence necessary to bring the 161-page indictment.

Tracking cartel shipments, authorities found cocaine hidden inside 40-foot cargo containers used to ship frozen vegetables, lumber, *concrete posts* and coffee. The smuggling system effectively evaded U.S. radar planes and naval vessels deployed in the Caribbean. The racketeering case began when a load of *cement posts and cornerstones* arrived in the Port of Miami on August 23, 1991. DEA and Customs agents found 12,250 kilos of cocaine hidden inside their hollow cores.

♦♦♦♦♦♦♦♦

Significantly, in early March 1995, *three months before* the Miami indictment was unsealed, I had received a letter from Michael Riconosciuto who had learned of the initial raid on Mike Abbell's law offices. He wrote as follows: (Referring to his trial in 1991)

> ...[During] pretrial I made an on the record proffer in an attempt to dispose of this case. The U.S. Attorney rejected it as garbage. That was in 1991. Now in 1995, it is a major case. In my proffer, I outlined a sophisticated smuggling scheme. It involved plastic items and *concrete products. I named both* [Harold] *Ackerman and Abbell.*
>
> The DOJ now has evidence seized from attorney's offices. The cement items were handled through TRANCA Corporation. The specialized equipment to make concrete posts and beams came from Tacoma, Washington. The aircraft came from a Canadian brokerage known as THABET Aviation in Quebec City, Canada.
>
> Raymond Thabet is Lebanese and has special contacts that give him privileged access to Canadian military surplus. Fourteen (14) of these planes were handled through Abbell and Laguna. All the paperwork was handled by Ed Smith in Darrington, Washington state. These were ex-submarine patrol planes. Specialized electronics were provided.

> An insider in Customs was involved – Richard Cardwell.
>
> This is heavy stuff. The fact that I detailed it in 1991 demands an explanation. Forty (40) tons of coke [cocaine] would have been stopped. I want a direct explanation from Teresa Van Vlet.
>
> Signed "Mike R."

Van Vlet reportedly worked in the drug enforcement administration of the Department of Justice.

••••••••

— 15 —

The Old Boy Network

–When the ill born soul comes before him, it makes a full confession, and that connoisseur of sins sees what place in hell is fitting to it; he wraps his tail around himself as many times as the number of circles he wishes it to be sent down"

–From: *The Divine Comedy* by Dante Alighieri – 1265-1321 A.D.

I was never able to rectify the purpose behind the biological technology that Robert Booth Nichols was involved in developing with the Japanese. Why did his patents stress the "Method for Induction and Activation" of Cytotoxic T-Lymphocytes? It is noteworthy that Harold Okimoto, Nichols' godfather and a member of his Board of Directors, had allegedly been a high-ranking intelligence officer during World War II.

While reading Dick Russell's book, *The Man Who Knew Too Much,* I came across a chapter referencing Japanese biological experiments conducted during World War II. In one passage (pp. 125-126), Russell noted that, at the end of World War II, Charles Willoughby, General Douglas MacArthur's chief of intelligence, had seized Japanese lab records on germ warfare. When the Pentagon determined that the biological research might prove useful in the Cold War, the Japanese responsible for the experiments received immunity from prosecution in exchange for their cooperation.

At least three thousand people died as a result of those experiments, including an unknown number of captured U.S. military personnel. "Only in 1982 did this seamy story come to light, including the Pentagon's 1947 acknowledgement of Willoughby's 'wholehearted cooperation' in arranging examination of the human pathological material which had been transferred to Japan from the biological warfare installations," wrote Russell.

Another book, *Unit 731* by Peter Williams and David Wallace, gave a detailed background on bacteriological warfare experiments conducted by all of the major combatants during World War II. When the United States government determined that the Axis Powers, including Russia, were evaluating this weapon, it became necessary to study the possibilities. This led to the thought that if one prepared for offensive bacteriological warfare, then one must also prepare for defensive bacteriological warfare.

However, history shows that reasoning broke down with the first use of nuclear weapons by the United States in Japan to finish the war in the East quickly. That action saved American lives if a land attack on the islands had been effected, but the principle is obvious. Would the U.S. do the same thing with viruses and bacteria?

In 1939 the Rockefeller Institute for Medical Research in New York studied the virulent, unmodified strain of yellow fever virus, ostensibly for the purpose of developing a cure for the disease. The laboratory at that time was under the direction of Dr. Wilbur Sawyer. It was in 1939 that a Japanese Army doctor, Dr. Ryoichi Naito, visited the laboratory with credentials from the Japanese military attache in Washington to obtain a sample of that strain of the Yellow Fever virus.

A report of that incident was subsequently sent to the Army Surgeon General and after evaluation of similar incidents, it was determined by Army Intelligence that Japan was interested in the yellow fever virus for bacteriological warfare purposes.

Based on that information, along with other corollary information, the decision was made to build Fort Detrick near Frederick, Maryland to provide a secret laboratory for the study and development of defensive and offensive capability to wage bacteriological warfare (BW).

The secrecy of the project was of the same magnitude as the nuclear work done within the Manhattan Project. From the writings and speeches given by the military men associated with this project, it is apparent that they were genuinely concerned for the security of the United States, but inside this organization and within the government at large, was a potential for ulterior motives. (More on that later).

By 1944, more than sufficient evidence had been gathered by American intelligence units to indicate that Japan was deeply involved in bacteriological warfare. Thirty-thousand bombs, manufactured at the Osaka Chemical Research Institute in Japan, containing typhus, diphtheria and bubonic plague were sent to the Chinese front.

By then, overwhelming evidence was coming in, particularly regarding research being conducted by Major General Shiro Ishii who was awarded a Technical Meritorious Medal with highest degrees. After the war, American intelligence learned that General Ishii, through an organization called "Unit 731," conducted his more serious research at a camp in northern Manchuria. It was here that General Ishii experimented on human beings.

The experiments conducted on those human beings made Japan the world's leading authority on offensive and defensive bacteriological warfare systems. No other country, Ishii reasoned, would have equivalent technical data on how epidemics spread and how to protect against them.

Japan's fascination with biological warfare dates as far back as 1932, when experimentation on prisoners already sentenced to death was conducted at Harbin, but later during the war with China, the Japanese used prisoners of war. White Russians, caught in the area of Japan's war with China were also used, according to an interrogated Japanese army officer.

Each prisoner was placed in a closely guarded cell where the experiments were conducted. After each prisoner died, they were cremated in an electric furnace to remove all evidence of what had occurred. Starting in 1935, motion pictures of the experiments were taken and these were shown to senior army officers. It was reported that 3,000 were sacrificed at a separate test site called Pingfan. Why was it required to use so many humans?

The Japanese had learned that epidemics occurred naturally but the method for inducing and activating them artificially was more difficult. In order to find the most efficient method of transmittal, many experiments were needed to find the lethal doses required to spread the agent. What would work with animals might not necessarily work with humans. Also, a method was needed for immunization and only humans could be used for that purpose.

General Ishii thought that the West's moral codes would not allow for such experimentation and that alone would put Japan on the leading edge of such technology. Healthy humans were needed, so extensive medical tests were even conducted on prospective prisoners. Diseases were forcibly injected or administered with a special stick-shaped gun. Some prisoners were infected through food or drink. Cholera, anthrax, TB, typhoid, rickettsia and dysentery were but a few of the bacteria used in the tests.

Live human prisoners were also exposed to chemical warfare agents such as mustard gas, hydrogen cyanide, acetone cyanide and potassium cyanide. Hydrogen cyanide was given extensive study because of its potential for ease of delivery into water supplies. In some instances, live human victims were actually opened up to observe the progress of various diseases and chemicals.

At one point, American intelligence learned that Japan had developed techniques for efficient delivery of Botulinus, a germ that attacks the central nervous system followed by paralysis and rapid death. Vast quantities of Botulinous germs were developed at Fort Detrick and a vaccine was hurriedly injected into all military personnel involved in the invasion of Europe.

What the United States subsequently did with the technical data from the Japanese experiments, under the direction of General Charles Willoughby, was shocking. During the War Crimes Trials in Japan following World War II, "sweetheart deals" were arranged between the United States and Japan to secure that data. Colonel Murray Sanders was assigned to General Douglas MacArthur, along with General Charles Willoughby (Chief of Intelligence) and Karl T. Compton (Chief of Scientific Intelligence). General MacArthur specifically assigned these men to investigate the Japanese bacteriological warfare experiments.

During the war, Lt. Col. Sanders, a medical doctor, had been responsible for investigating and analyzing the capabilities of the Japanese in bacteriological warfare. He had also overseen the Fort Detrick experiments. When the Legal Section of the U.S. government tried to obtain the Japanese lab records on human experimentation from General MacArthur's staff, they were stonewalled. MacArthur's staff reasoned that if the U.S. Army's investigative evidence was given to the Legal Section in Washington D.C., the Russians would have access to the records. This sounds logical on the surface, but the resulting memorandums tell another story.

The State-War-Navy Coordinating Committee (SWNCC) responsible for coordinating and overseeing the war crimes trials in Japan, made an extraordinary statement which conclusively supported the intelligence community's stance on the matter. One excerpt read as follows:

> Data already obtained from Ishii and his colleagues has proven to be of great value in confirming, supplementing and complementing several phases of U.S. research in BW, and may suggest new fields for future research. This Japanese information is the only known source of data from scientifically controlled experiments showing direct effect of BW [bacteriological warfare] agents on man. In the past it has been necessary to evaluate effects of BW agents on man from data through animal experimentation. Such evaluation is inconclusive and far less complete than results obtained from certain types of human experimentation.
>
> It is felt that the use of this information as a basis for war crimes evidence would be a grave detriment to Japanese cooperation with the United States occupation forces in Japan. For all practical purposes an agreement with Ishii and his associates that information given by them on the Japanese BW program will be retained in intelligence channels is equivalent to an agreement that this Government will not prosecute any of those involved in BW activities in which war crimes were committed. Such an understanding would be of great value to the security of the American people because of the information which Ishii and his associates have already furnished and will continue to furnish.

The astounding conclusion went as follows: "The value to the U.S. of Japanese BW data is of such importance to national security as to far outweigh the value accruing from `war crimes' prosecution. In the interests of national security it would not be advisable to make this information available to other nations as would be the case in the event of a `war crimes' trial of Japanese BW experts. The BW information obtained from Japanese sources should be retained in intelligence channels and should not be employed as `war crimes' evidence."

Communications between Washington D.C. and General MacArthur's headquarters in Japan were very revealing. One excerpt read as follows:

> *... The feeling of several staff groups in Washington, including G-2, is that this problem is more or less a family affair in the Far Eastern Command.*

No mention was ever made during the war crimes trials in Japan about bacteriological warfare or chemical warfare experiments being conducted on human test specimens. No indictments were ever handed down against those who had perpetrated these crimes. Colonel Sanders was ordered back to the United States to brief scientists at Fort Detrick but shortly thereafter became ill with tuberculosis and spent the next two years in bed. Oddly, the expert who was sent to replace Colonel Sanders, Arvo Thompson, committed suicide following his work for the Far Eastern Command and the scientists at Fort Detrick.

What happened to all of the Japanese officers and scientists who worked in the Manchurian labs during World War II? The military officers were retired on sizable pensions and the civilian scientists continued their work with some of the largest chemical and medical companies in Japan. Some became presidents and professors at leading universities, others became a part of the industrial complex which so successfully competed with the West for international trade.

Numerous board directors of FIDCO, of which Nichols was also a director, had been closely associated with General Douglas MacArthur. In fact, Clint Murchison, Sr. had helped finance MacArthur's presidential campaign.

♦♦♦♦♦♦♦♦

The December 1991 *Vanity Fair* article by Ron Rosenbaum, "The Strange Death of Danny Casolaro" had noted on page 98 that not long before his death, Danny Casolaro had reportedly approached a nurse he knew and asked her closely about the symptoms of multiple sclerosis and brain diseases.

Rosenbaum had asked himself what had been going on in Danny's head as he was being whipsawed between the shadowy Riconosciuto and Nichols and their death warnings? In Danny's notes, Rosenbaum had found references to germ warfare and slow-acting brain viruses like Mad Cow Disease which could be used against targeted individuals. Had Danny thought *he'd* been targeted?

A subsequent conversation with Michael Riconosciuto confirmed Rosenbaum's suspicions. According to Riconosciuto, Danny had not only been concerned, but had an obsession with the story because he suspected he'd been "hit by these people." A source had allegedly told Danny that he, among others, had been targeted with a slow acting virus. Riconosciuto had advised him to go to a doctor and get tests. The tests had been inconclusive. "Now, what he probably had was the genesis of a naturally occurring ailment," said Riconosciuto to Rosenbaum.

Rosenbaum had described the entire Inslaw/Casolaro affair as "Kafkaesque weirdness." Indeed, after Nichols had handed me the book, "The Search for the Manchurian Candidate" at his Sherman Oaks apartment, I had obtained a copy and recalled the author, John Marks, referring to the CIA MK-Ultra (Manchurian Candidate) interrogation methods as Kafkaesque in nature. Though Danny's notes mentioned nothing about "mind-control," and Bill Hamilton later noted that Danny had spoken mainly about the biologicals, I found it difficult to believe that he was not subjected to some form of mind control either subliminally or otherwise by someone in the field.

♦♦♦♦♦♦♦♦

The Search for the Manchurian Candidate (1979) by John Marks gave significant background on the history of biological warfare and mind-control research by the CIA. The author, John Marks, obtained much of his material from seven boxes of heavily censored MK-Ultra financial records and another three or so Artichoke (CIA behavor-control program), documents supplemented by interviews.

As early as 1943, the CIA, or actually its predecessor, the OSS, initiated "humanistic psychology," or studies of what the brain can do, during World War II when a "truth drug" committee headed by Dr. Winfred Overholser conducted experiments with marijuana and mescaline to find a way to induce prisoners to confess. A parallel OSS group had also investigated the use of "quietus medications" – lethal poisons – for possible use against Adolf Hitler.

The original program was headed by General William "Wild Bill" Donovan, a burly, vigorous Republican millionaire who had started as White House intelligence advisor even before Pearl Harbor. A former Columbia College and Columbia Law Graduate, Donovan early on recruited Richard Helms, a young newspaper executive who had gained fame for interviewing Adolf Hitler in 1936 while working for United Press. He would subsequently become the most important sponsor of mind-control research within the CIA, nurturing and promoting it throughout his steady climb to the top of the Agency.

Despite harsh condemnation at the Nuremberg trials after World War II of Nazi scientific experiments, U.S. investigators found the research records from the Dachau prison camp to be "an important complement to existing U.S. knowledge." Doctors connected to the S.S. and Gestapo had conducted experiments that led to the testing of mescaline on prisoners at Dachau. Their goal had been to "eliminate the will of the person examined."

The Japanese, for their part, had stockpiled chemical and biological warfare substances during World War II and even went so far as to drop deadly anthrax germs on China during the early stages of the war. OSS responded by individualizing CBW (Chemical and Biological Warfare) and creating methods of secretly disorienting, incapacitating, injuring or killing an enemy at Fort Detrick.

The CIA's post-World War II mind-control program was headed by Dr. Sidney Gottlieb, who presided over investigations that ranged from advanced research in amnesia caused by electroshock to dragnet searches through the jungles of Latin America for toxic leaves and barks. Gottlieb's office not only found ways to make Fidel Castro's beard fall out, but he personally provided operators with deadly poisons to assassinate foreign leaders like the Congo's Patrice Lumumba.

Other areas of CIA sponsored research included explorations of personalities. Henry Murray, a former Donovan protege, devised a battery of tests which could size up the personality of potential CIA recruits as well as predict future behavioral patterns. "Spying is attractive to loonies," wrote Murray. "Psychopaths, who are people who spend their lives making up stories, revel in the field." The program's prime objective, according to Murray, was to weed out the crazies, as well as the "sloths, irritants, bad actors, and freetalkers."

Murray's assessment system subsequently became a fixture in the CIA and some of his assistants went on to establish CIA-like systems at large corporations, starting with AT&T.

It is important to remember that at the beginning, the OSS (precursor to the CIA) researchers from Security and Scientific Intelligence shared jointly the literature and secret reports seized from the Germans and the Japanese after World War II. They had theorized that in order to build an effective defense against mind control and CBW, it was necessary to understand the "offensive" possibilities. But as the years went on, the line between offense and defense – if it ever existed – soon became so blurred as to be meaningless.

In 1947 when the National Security Act created not only the CIA, but also the National Security Council – in sum, the command structure of the Cold War – a warlike posture was developed against the new perceived enemy, the Soviet Union. The men in the CIA took this job seriously. "We felt we were the first line of defense in the anticommunist crusade," recalled Harry Rositzke, an early head of the Agency's Soviet Division. "There was a clear and heady sense of mission – a sense of what a huge job this was."

A contingent of the CIA behavior-control program, code named "Artichoke," developed a program whereby guinea pigs for mind-control experiments were obtained from the flotsam and jetsam of the international spy trade: " … individuals of dubious loyalty, suspected agents or plants, subjects having known reason for deception, etc," as one agency documents described them. Artichoke officials looked upon these people as unique research "material" from whom meaningful secrets might be extracted while the experiments went on.

As one CIA psychologist who worked in the mind-control program put it, "One did not put a high premium on the civil rights of a person who was treasonable to his own country …" Thus the Artichoke teams were given mostly the dregs of the clandestine underworld to work on.

In one experiment in the early 1950's, an alleged Russian double agent was brought to a safe house and plied for information with a mixture of drugs and hypnosis under the cover of a "psychiatric-medical exam." A professional hypnotist had accompanied the team, giving his commands to an interpreter through an elaborate intercom system, who, in turn, was able to put the Russian into a hypnotic trance.

Afterward, the team reported to the CIA's director that the Russian had revealed extremely valuable information and he had been made to forget his interrogation through hypnotically induced amnesia. The Russian was also used in a subsequent experiment where he was given Seconal, Dexedrine and marijuana in combination in a beer delivered during the cocktail hour. There were little, if any, positive results.

Nevertheless, the CIA was still consistently on the cutting edge of specialized behavioral research, sponsoring the lion's share of the most harrowing experiments. One CIA psychiatric consultant provided a small personal glimpse of how it felt to be a soldier in the mind-control campaign. The psychiatrist, who insisted on anonymity, estimated that he made between 125 and 150 trips overseas on Agency operations between 1952 through his retirement in 1966. "To be a psychiatrist chasing off to Europe instead of just seeing the same patients year after year, that was extraordinary," he said.

Later, due to bureaucratic squabbling, the CIA transferred its behavior work to a (CIA) outfit with Ph.D.'s called the Technical Services Staff (TSS). Under TSS's Chemical Division, research was conducted on the use of chemicals and germs against specific people. LSD had been used extensively between 1951 and 1956 by Dr. Sidney Gottlieb, a native of the Bronx with a Ph.D. in chemistry from CalTech; Gottlieb continued to oversee most of TSS's behavorial programs up to and including 1973.

At the top of the Clandestine Services (officially called the Directorate of Operations but popularly known as the "dirty tricks department"), Sid Gottlieb had a champion who appreciated his qualities, Richard Helms. For two decades, Gottlieb moved into progressively higher positions in the wake of Helms' climb to the highest position in the Agency.

Under the TSS leadership of Gottlieb and Helms, research on the covert use of biological and chemical materials progressed under the code name of "MK-Ultra." The operational arm of MK-Ultra was labeled MK-Delta, the purpose of which was to "investigate whether and how it was possible to modify an individual's behavior by covert means." Hashish had been around for millennia, but LSD was roughly a million times stronger by weight. A two-suiter suitcase could hold enough LSD to turn on every man, woman, and child in the United States.

But the CIA was concentrating on individuals. TSS understood that LSD distorted a person's sense of reality and they felt compelled to learn if it could alter a person's basic loyalties. Could the CIA make spies out of tripping Russians – or visa versa?

Suddenly there was a huge new market for grants in academia, as Sid Gottlieb and his aides began to fund LSD projects at prestigious institutions. Author John Marks (*The Search for the Manchurian Candidate*) identified the Agency's LSD pathfinders as: Bob Hyde's group at Boston Psychopathic, Harold Abramson at Mt. Sinai Hospital and Columbia University in New York, Harris Isbell of the NIMH-sponsored Addiction Research Center in Lexington,

Kentucky, Louis Jolyon West at the University of Oklahoma, and Harold Hodge's group at the University of Rochester.

The Agency disguised its involvement by passing the money through two conduits: The Josiah Macy, Jr. Foundation and the Geschickter Fund for Medical Research, a Washington D.C. family foundation, whose head, Dr. Charles Geschickter, provided the Agency with a variety of services for more than a decade.

Beginning in 1952, TSS had an agreement with the Special Operations Division (SOD) of the Army's biological research center at Fort Detrick, Maryland, whereby SOD would produce germ weapons for the CIA's use with the program called MK-Naomi. Under MK-Naomi, the SOD men developed a whole arsenal of toxic substances for CIA use.

Wrote Marks: "If Agency operators needed to kill someone in a few seconds with say, a suicide pill, SOD provided super-deadly shellfish toxins." Agency operators later supplied pills laced with this lethal food poison to its Mafia allies for inclusion into Fidel Castro's milkshake.

In other instances, "If CIA officials wanted an assassination to look like a death from natural causes, they could choose from a long list of deadly diseases that normally occurred in particular countries," wrote Marks. When CIA operators merely wanted to be rid of someone temporarily, SOD stockpiled for them about a dozen diseases and toxins of varying strengths. "At the relatively benign end of the SOD list stood `Staph enterotoxin,' a mild form of food poisoning – mild compared to botulinum," noted Marks.

Even more virulent in the SOD arsenal was "Venezuelan equine encephalomyelitis" virus which usually immobilized a person for 2 to 5 days and kept him in a weakened state for several more weeks. If the Agency wanted to incapacitate someone for a period of months, SOD provided two different kinds of "brucellosis." This incapacitating agent was allegedly placed on the monogrammed handkerchief of an Iraqi colonel in 1060 who was said to be promoting Soviet-bloc political interests, but the colonel was shot by a firing squad before the handkerchief arrived."

SOD was forever developing more virulent strains," wrote Marks. Perhaps the most important question was whether a germ could be covertly delivered to infect the right person. One branch of SOD specialized in building "delivery systems," the most notorious of which was a dart gun fashioned out of a .45 pistol which ex-CIA Director William Colby once displayed at a 1975 Senate hearing.

The Agency had long been after SOD to develop a "non-discernible microbioinoculator" which could deliver deadly shots that, according to a CIA document, could not be "easily detected upon a detailed autopsy." One high Detrick official noted that the best way to infect people was through the respiratory system. SOD rigged up aerosol sprays that could be fired by remote control, including a fluorescent starter that was activated by turning on the light.

A former newspaper journalist turned narcotics agent, George White, was recruited by MK-Ultra chief Sid Gottlieb to test drugs on unsuspecting subjects at a San Francisco "safe house" on Telegraph Hill. The apartment was bugged with four DD-4 microphones disguised as electrical wall outlets hooked up to two F-301 tape recorders which agents monitored in an adjacent "listening post."

The San Francisco safe house specialized in prostitutes who brought unwitting victims back for study. In addition to LSD, TSS officials gave White even more exotic experimental drugs to test. One TSS source noted, "If we were scared enough of a drug not to try it out on ourselves, we sent it to San Francisco."

According to a 1963 report by CIA Inspector General John Earman, in a number of instances, the test subject became ill for hours or days and, in one case, hospitalization was needed. Wrote Marks, "The Inspector General was only somewhat reassured by the fact that George White maintained close working relations with local police authorities which could be utilized to protect the activity in critical situations."

At another safehouse located in Marin County, TSS scientists tested such MK-Ultra specialties and delivery systems as glass ampules that could be stepped on to release itching or sneezing powders, a fine hypodermic needle to inject drugs through the cork in a wine bottle, and a drug-coated swizzle stick.

At one point, an attempt was made to spray LSD from an aerosol spray can at a house party, but the heat of the summer caused all the windows and doors to be open. "Years later," wrote John Marks, "George White wrote an epitaph [in a personal letter to Sid Gottlieb] for his role with the CIA: `I was a very minor missionary, actually a heretic, but I toiled wholeheartedly in the vineyards because it was fun, fun, fun. Where else could a red-blooded American boy lie, kill, cheat, steal, rape, and pillage with the sanction and blessing of the All-Highest?'"

Not every scientist cooperated with the CIA. While conducting experimental studies on monkeys at the National Institute of Health, Dr. John Lilly discovered a method of inserting electrodes into the brain to stimulate precise centers of pleasure, pain, fear, anxiety and anger. As Lilly refined his brain "maps," officials of the CIA and other agencies descended upon him with requests for briefings.

Lilly insisted that all briefings remain unclassified, completely open to outsiders. Other scientists ordinarily had their work officially classified, which meant that access to the information required a security clearance. But Lilly's imagination had conjured up pictures of CIA agents on deadly missions with remote-controlled electrodes strategically implanted in their brains, and so he withdrew from that field of research. By 1958 he had finally concluded that it would be impossible for him to continue working at the National Institute of Health without compromising his principles, so he resigned.

MK-Ultra officials were clearly interested in using grants to build contracts and associations with prestigious academics. The CIA-funded Society for the Investigation of Human Ecology, later known as the "Human Ecology Fund," (HEF) supported such publications as the "Research in Mental Health Newsletter" published jointly at McGill University by the sociology and psychiatric departments.

Similarly, HEF gave grants of $26,000 to the well-known University of London psychologist, H.J. Eysenck, for his work on motivation. Marks noted that the MK-Ultra documents acknowledged that this research had "no immediate relevance for Agency needs, but it would lend prestige to the Human Ecology Fund."

A whole category of HEF funding, called "cover grants," served no other purpose than to build the organization's false front. A TSS source explained that grants like these "bought legitimacy" for the organization. Nevertheless, one small grant to a psychologist from the University of Pennsylvania provided valuable information on "confidence men." The CIA was intrigued with the ability of con men to manipulate human behavior. As one CIA official put it, the psychologist unwittingly gave them "a better understanding of the techniques people use to establish phony relationships" – a subject of interest to the CIA.

Marks wrote that at one point, the CIA took the "Svengali" legend to heart. In 1954, Morse Allen, the CIA's first behavioral research czar, simulated the ultimate experiment in hypnosis: the creation of a "Manchurian Candidate," or programmed assassin. Allen's "victim" was a secretary whom he put into a deep trance and told to keep sleeping until he ordered otherwise.

He then hypnotized a second secretary and told her that if she could not wake up her friend, "her rage would be so great that she would not hesitate to kill." An unloaded pistol was placed nearby. Even though the second secretary had expressed a fear of firearms of any kind, she picked up the gun and "shot" her sleeping friend. After Allen brought the "killer" out of her trance, she had no recollection of the event, denying she would ever shoot anyone.

Some of the CIA's experiments wandered so far across ethical borders of experimental psychiatry that Agency officials ultimately conducted much of the work outside the United States. The CIA's Human Ecology Fund provided financing to foreign researchers and American professors to collect information abroad. The MK-Ultra men realized that ninety-percent of their experiments would fail to be of any use to the Agency, but the "behaviorists" continued to search for the elusive answer to human control.

Unbound by the rules of academia, the CIA took stabs at cracking the human genetic code with computers and finding out whether animals could be controlled through electrodes placed in their brains.

Within the Agency itself, the one significant question remained to be answered: Will a technique work? CIA officials zealously tracked every lead, sparing no expense to check each angle many times over, yet no foolproof way was found to brainwash another person. Specific methods worked "fantastically" on certain people, but not on others. It wasn't predictable enough, noted one official."

In the aftermath of the Bay of Pigs, President Kennedy reportedly vowed to splinter the CIA into a thousand pieces," wrote John Marks. In the end, he settled for firing Allen Dulles and his top deputies. Until that point, the TSS (Technical Services Staff) had been the Agency's largest scientific component. Under the new head of CIA, John McCone, TSS was stripped of its main research functions – including the behavioral one – and Seymour Russell, a tough covert operator, was brought in as the new chief. But the highest deputyship at TSS went to Sid Gottlieb, who became number-two man under Russell.

In his new job, Gottlieb kept control of MK-Ultra. His emphasis switched back to chemical and biological substances – "not because he thought these could be used to turn men into robots," wrote Marks, "but because he valued them for their `predictable' ability to disorient, discredit, injure, or kill people." A $150,000 a year contract was signed with a Baltimore biological laboratory which provided TSS a private place for "large-scale production of microorganisms" for biological weapons without the Army's germ warriors knowing about it.

Dr. James Hamilton, the San Francisco psychiatrist who worked with George White in the original OSS marijuana days, was brought back to MK-Ultra by Gottlieb to conduct "clinical testing of behavioral control materials" on prisoners at the California Medical Facility at Vacaville. Hamilton worked through a non-profit research institute connected to the facility to conduct his research. Marks estimated that he experimented on between 400 to 1,000 inmates between 1967 and 1968.

In July 1977, after receiving notification that the CIA had located seven boxes of MK-Ultra financial records, author John Marks held a press conference in which he criticized then CIA Director Admiral Stansfield Turner (later a Wackenhut Board member) for several distortions in describing the MK-Ultra program. Turner had described MK-Ultra as only a program of drug experimentation and not one aimed at behavior control to President Carter and the Senate Select Committee on Intelligence.

Marks responded by releasing a score of CIA documents to reporters that indicated the flavor of the CIA behavioral efforts. The documents set off a media bandwagon that had the story reported on all three network television news shows as well as others. The Senate Select Committee on Intelligence and Senator Edward Kennedy's Subcommittee on Health and Scientific Research soon announced they would hold public hearings on the subject. The CBW program at Fort Detrick was subsequently shut down.

In 1979, Marks concluded that he could not be positive that the CIA never found a technique to control people. CIA officials actively experimented with behavior-control methods for another decade *After* Sid Gottlieb and company lost the research action.

The Office of Research and Development (ORD) picked up the ball by creating its own latter-day version of the Society for the Investigation of Human Ecology.

Located outside Boston, it was called the Scientific Engineering Institute and had originally been used by the CIA as a proprietary company to conduct radar research. In the early 1960's, ORD officials built a new wing to the Institute's modernistic building for "life sciences" or human behavior research.

According to Marks, one scientist from the institute recalled a colleague joking, "If you could find the natural radio frequency of a person's sphincter, you could make him run out of the room real fast."

"Just as the MK-Ultra program had been years ahead of the scientific community, ORD activities were similarly advanced," wrote Marks. One researcher noted that MK-Ultra looked at the manipulation of genes and gene splintering as early as 1965, eleven years before the rest of the world even thought about it. Added the scientist, "Everybody was afraid of building the supersoldier who would take orders without questioning, like the kamikaze pilot. Creating a subservient society was not out of sight."

••••••••

The above research was conducted thirty years ago! What had been developed along those same lines by 1994? Even the most rampant imagination could not conceive of what might be underway in CIA laboratories today.

With today's cutting and splicing techniques, scientists can attach any genes they choose to certain carrier genes. These linked genes, called "recombinant DNA," are then conveyed inside a host cell, which virtually adopts the new gene as one of its own. The object of most current experiments is to transplant genes from the host to bacteria. These tractable, microscopic cells proliferate faster than rabbits. On a simple cheap diet a single bacterium makes a few billion copies of itself overnight. Its DNA, including that of the transplanted gene, is reproduced at the same rate.

Biochemists at Stanford University have found a technique for combining DNA from "two different sources" and putting it into a common bacterium. The bacterium they chose was "E.coli bacteria," commonly found in the intestine of every living person. Modified E.coli, containing certain cancer genes, could become a biological bomb. The bacterium carrying its little package of cancer genes, could then be passed as easily as the common cold from one human to another.

The U.S. is not the only country to have this technology. A classified report prepared for the National Security Council (U.S.) and obtained by the *Washington Times* claimed "the Soviet Union was using genetic engineering to create virulent new biological weapons that could be deployed as early as 1989 - if in fact some had not already been deployed." Robert H. Kupperman, a chemical warfare expert at Georgetown University's Center for Strategic and International Studies, told the *Times* that "it's like making designer drugs."

A report was prepared by the CIA and the Arms Control and Disarmament Agency which outlined extensive violations by the Soviets of two anti-biological warfare treaties. The report noted "the Soviets were using recent advances in biotechnology, such as genetic engineering, to develop a new class of CBW [chemical, biological warfare] agents that can be rapidly produced for deployment."

Recent scientific findings on the Gulf War Syndrome (GWS) indicate genetic material common to Gulf War-era veterans could provide a clue as to why so many became sick after serving in the 1991 war. In a study presented to Gulf War veterans at a conference in Tampa, Florida, microbiologist Dr. Howard Urnovitz said the genetic marker could point to the existence of a "virus." The virus, in turn, could make veterans exposed to chemical agents or other toxins more susceptible to illness, he added.

Beginning on Veterans Day, November 11, 1996 and continuing through November 17th, KREM-TV out of Spokane, Washington, an affiliate of Northwest News in Seattle, telecast a series on Gulf War Syndrome (GWS). Reporter Tom Grant interviewed numerous doctors, one of which was Dr. Garth Nicholson, a microbiologist, who maintained that GWS contains "altered genetic structures" similar to AIDS. He suggested GWS is a genetically engineered biological warfare organism, and it's contagious.

Dr. Larry Goss, in Walters, Oklahoma, not only confirmed Nicholson's findings, but said on public TV that he and his wife "caught" GWS while treating Gulf War veterans. Dr. William Baumzweiger, a neurologist/psychiatrist at the V.A. hospital in Los Angeles found brain-stem damage in GWS vets, and noted the virus turns the immune system against itself.

GWS veterans were warned NOT to have unprotected sex or have any more children. The vets themselves were interviewed along with their families. Tragically, their wives and children were now suffering from the same GWS symptoms. Pictures were shown of the children, providing indisputable proof of the infectiousness of the disease.

Doctors warned the public that GWS could soon enter the general populace, and it could be terminal. However, on November 17th, Dr. Nicholson noted that treatment was available through antibiotics.

••••••••

Scientists have long suspected the existence of a "lab-created" virus which attacks the immune system. In January 1986, the French-born and trained biologists Professor Jakob and Dr. Lilli Segal, published a pamphlet entitled, "AIDS: USA-Home Made Evil; Not Imported from Africa." The two scientists, a biophysicist and a biologist affiliated with the Humboldt University in Berlin, pointed out that examination of the genes making up the HIV retrovirus revealed it "could not have come about by a natural way known to biologists." They called the virus a "chimera," originally created in 1977 at Fort Detrick, Maryland.

The Segals were not the only researchers to suggest that "genetic engineering" was involved with AIDS. John Seale, M.D., a London venereologist, also stated that the molecular structure of HIV suggested "manipulation of viruses" rather than a natural mutation from known retroviruses. And Dr. Robert Strecker, M.D., a Los Angeles internist, has made the same assertion.

These advocates of the artificial HIV theory all note the structural similarities of HIV to visna virus, a pathogen found in sheep with similarities to AIDS. The scientists argue that the visna virus was artificially combined with the HTLV-I virus, another retrovirus which causes human lymphoma, a cancer of the white blood cells.

Today designer viruses are limited only by the imagination of the scientist creating them. Thus, bio-labs in both the U.S. and abroad are in a race to find vaccines which build the human immune system - or search out and destroy killer T-Cells.

A new study, recently released by Dr. Jeffrey Leiden, director of a research team at the University of Chicago, showed that genes can be injected directly into "muscle tissue" to cause production of proteins needed to correct some blood disorders, such as anemia. Genes in the injection are taken into the nucleus of cells in the muscle tissue and become, in effect, a pharmaceutical factory, increasing red blood cell levels as high as 64%. In the past, gene therapy involved using "viruses" to transfer genes into the body, a technique that was "poorly controlled," according to Dr. Leiden.

And another finding by Arthur Vandenbark, of the Veterans Affairs Medical Center in Portland, Oregon noted the discovery of a new vaccine which enables the human immune system to churn out more T-Cells, thus preventing multiple sclerosis patients from becoming sicker.

The ultimate irony of the 21st century could be the development of vaccines, in response to the threat of biological warfare, which boost the human immune system to such a degree that people become completely disease resistant. The question is, with overpopulation looming on the horizon, would the U.S. government release such a vaccine to the general populace – if not, who would have access to it? The Chosen Ones?

Interestingly, Robert Booth Nichols' manuscript, entitled "Acceptable Casualty," copyrighted at the Library of Congress in May 1987, outlined an identical scenario.

♦♦♦♦♦♦♦♦

Within Michael Riconosciuto's secret files in the Mojave Desert, I had found a box marked "Ted Gunderson," which I had dragged home along with the rest of the material.

This particular box had contained records of most of Gunderson's investigations, but one report particularly caught my attention. It was titled, "From PSYOP to MindWar: The Psychology of Victory" by Colonel Paul E. Vallely with Major Michael A. Aquino.

The 12-page Army report was undated but it outlined the use of "Psychotronics," intelligence and operational weapons systems employing the use of mind control, commonly known as Psychological Operations (PSYOP).

Wrote Aquino, "In 1967 and 1968 alone, a total of 29,276 armed Viet Cong/NVA (the equivalent of 95 enemy infantry battalions) surrendered to ARVN or MACV forces under the Chieu Hoi amnesty program – the major PSYOP effort of the Vietnam War. At the time MACV estimated that the elimination of that same number of enemy troops in combat would have cost us 6,000 dead."

Aquino argued that the U.S. lost the war in Vietnam "not because we were out-fought, but because we were out-PSYOPed. Our national will to victory was attacked more effectively than we attacked that of the North Vietnamese and Viet Cong, and perception of this fact encouraged the enemy to hang on until the United States finally broke and ran for home."

The lesson, according to Aquino, was not to ignore U.S. PSYOP capability, but rather to change it and strengthen it "so that it can do precisely that kind of thing to our enemy in the next war." To begin, there would be a name change from Psychological Operations to "MindWar." Noted Aquino, "We must reach the people *before* they resolve to support their armies, and we must reach those armies *before* our combat troops ever see them on battlefields."

Aquino went on to compare his proposal with the definition of Psychological Warfare first introduced by General William Donovan of the OSS in his World War II-era "Basic Estimate of Psychological Warfare" in which Donovan discussed the need to destroy the will of the enemy. But an attendant 1947 letter stressed the need for a "synonym which could be used in peacetime that would not shock the sensibilities of a citizen of democracy."

Aquino indicated contempt for the U.S. Army's inability to accept PSYOP in its "most effective configuration," adding that "the reluctance with which the Army had accepted even an `antiseptic' PSYOP component" was well documented.

Having read about General Donovan's "behavioral control" program in the MK-Ultra book, I didn't perceive it to be exactly "antiseptic." Aquino's report, obviously written after the Vietnam war, suggested that future MindWars should be fought through "skillful use of communications media."

"MindWar," noted Aquino, "states a whole truth that, if it does not now exist, will be forced into existence by the will of the United States ... A MindWar message does not have to fit conditions of abstract credibility as do PSYOP themes; its source makes it credible."

Aquino continued, " ... The MindWar operative must *know* that he speaks the truth, and he must be *personally committed* to it. What he says is only a part of MindWar; the rest – and the test of its effectiveness – lies in the conviction he projects to his audience, in the rapport he establishes with it."

As I read the document it was difficult not to recall Oliver North's diary in which he called his associates, "The True Believers." Aquino noted that the recipient of the statement by the MindWar operative would judge such messages not only by his conscious understanding of them, but also by the mental conditions under which he perceived them. "For the mind to believe its own decisions," wrote Aquino, "it must feel that it made those decisions without coercion. Coercive measures used by the MindWar operative, consequently, must not be detectable by ordinary means ..."

Aquino's basis for his report came from various publications which were listed at the back of the document. "More effective configurations" of MindWar as noted by Aquino may well have included the following (taken from the back of the document):

"ELF (extremely low frequency) waves (up to 100 Hz) ... are naturally occurring, but they can also be produced artificially ... ELF-waves are not normally noticed by the unaided senses, yet their resonant effect upon the human body has been connected to both physiological disorders and emotional distortion. Infrasound vibration (up to 20 Hz) can subliminally influence brain activity to align itself to delta, theta, alpha, or beta wave patterns, inclining an audience toward everything from alertness to passivity. Infrasound could be used tactically, as ELF-waves endure for great distances; and it could be used in conjunction with media broadcasts as well."

So, the human brain can be aligned to infrasound through media broadcasts. Was that technology used on Manuel Noriega when he was forced to surrender in Panama under blaring radio broadcasts? And hadn't the Branch Davidians been subjected to loud music and chants for extended periods of time?

Another section of the Aquino report noted that "ionization of the air" could be used to control an individual's emotions. "An abundance of negative condensation nucleii (air ions) in ingested air enhances alertness and exhilaration, while an excess of positive ions enhances drowsiness and depression. Calculation of a target audience's atmospheric environment will be correspondingly useful."

After his retirement from the Army, Lieutenant Colonel Michael Aquino, an ex-Green Beret, was later written up in the *San Francisco Chronicle* as the head of the Temple of Set, a satanic, devil-worshipping church. The November 1987 headlines read as follows: "Army Says Constitution Lets Satanist Hold Top-Secret Job," by reporters John Whittinger and Bill Wallace. The story went on to say that "the high priest of a San Francisco-based satanic church is able to keep his top-secret security clearance because his activities are constitutionally protected, Army officials said yesterday. "Lieutenant Colonel Michael A. Aquino, a highly decorated Vietnam veteran, is the founder and president of Temple of Set, a satanic church headquartered in Aquino's Russian Hill home ...

"Aquino, a psychological warfare officer who has worked in military intelligence, holds a top secret security clearance that allows him to handle information whose release would gravely damage U.S. security, according to Defense Department regulations.

"He maintains the clearance even though he has performed Nazi occult rites and has described himself as the `Anti-Christ' in literature published by the Temple of Set ..."

Temple of Set literature described a coming apocalypse in which only followers of Satan would be saved. Readers were encouraged to read such works as "Mein Kampf," "Hitler: The Occult Messiah," and "The Occult Roots of Nazism."

Aquino conducted occult rituals patterned on ceremonies performed by Nazi leader Heinrich Himmler in a German castle once used by the Nazi SS for black magic ceremonies during the Third Reich. Nazis considered the black arts and satanic worship part of an ancient Germanic tradition.

Aquino, in his book, "Crystal Tablet of Set," wrote that he performed the rituals to recreate an order of Knighthood for followers of Satan. He even encouraged his followers to study the beliefs of the Nazi terrorist group, the Vehm, the Thule Gesselschaft, and the Ahnenerbe, two fanatic right-wing Aryan groups that existed before and during Hitler's reign.

When the two reporters from the *Chronicle* inquired about Aquino's security clearances, Major Rixon declared that "to the best of his knowledge, there was no part of the liturgy of his church that caused any (security) problem." Aquino admitted to being involved in devil worship for 22 years.

Ted Gunderson's box contained reams of literature written by Aquino along with other documents pertaining to identical subject matter. It was no secret that Gunderson lectured on the subject of

Satanism, as I learned from a July 1993 Colonel Bo Gritz newsletter which advertised Gunderson as a featured speaker on one of Gritz's national radio broadcasts.

But it was not the Satanic aspect of Aquino's writings that caused me to scrutinize his earlier writings for the Army. Shortly after the Waco incident in Texas, a secret "classified conference" was held at the Los Alamos National Laboratories in New Mexico. Through a friend in Maine, I was able to obtain an official copy of the speaking agenda for the November 1993 conference and, oddly, the subject matter under discussion correlated with not only the original Aquino Army report, but also with the MK-Ultra behavior research underway during the 1950's and 1960's.

The title of the conference was "Non-Lethal Defense" and just a few of the speakers included such dignitaries as the Honorable U.S. Attorney General Janet Reno; Dr. Edward Teller who had helped develop the nuclear bomb; Dr. Milt Finger from Lawrence Livermore National Laboratory; Mr. Andy Andrews, Non-Lethal Project Leader at Los Alamos National Laboratory; LTG William H. Forster from Army Research, Development and Acquisition; Dr. Clay Easterly from the Oak Ridge National Laboratory; Dr. Henry Brisker from U.S. Army Research Laboratories; Ms. Astrid Lewis from the U.S. Army Chemical Research & Development Command; Lt. General Richard G. Trefry, former Military Advisor to President George Bush; and many more.

The most noteworthy "non-lethal" technology presentations included the following: "High Power Microwave Technology" – "Application of Extremely Low Frequency Electromagnetic Fields to Non-Lethal Weapons" – "Voice Synthesis" – "Incremental Aggression: Requirements for the Future" – "Chemical/Biological Anti-Terrorism" – "Biological Challenges" – "Non-Lethal Research: Fracture & Dynamic Behavior, Biotechnology & Structural Ceramics," and many more.

Interestingly, the opening address was given by General E.C. Meyer (Ret.), former Chief of Staff of the U.S. Army – the very same General Meyer who had set up the Department of Defense conference in which Michael Riconosciuto had been the principal speaker from 9 A.M. to 4 P.M. to a group of senior-level national security research and development officials.

The objective and scope of the 1993 Los Alamos conference included exploring a non-lethal approach to apply force against not only war-time enemies (the Soviet Union had already fallen) but against "terrorists" and "international drug traffickers" as well.

The introduction noted that the purpose of the conference was to bring together "industry, government, and academia to explore the potential of non-lethal defense and identify requirements so that the defense community can work together in leveraging the non-lethal concept."

"Industry [law enforcement], particularly, will benefit from a more precise understanding of requirements and operational constraints regarding non-lethal defense technologies," noted the conference's sponsors, The American Defense Preparedness Association.

Additionally, non-lethal defense was described as "an emerging technological option being developed conceptually with a sea of technical opportunity."

Based upon the technical presentations listed in the brochure, it didn't appear to me that such technology as acoustical, high-power microwave, laser, ELF/RF weapons and "psychotronic" systems were particularly *new* in the field of military or intelligence applications. Obviously, what was occurring at this conference was the presentation of these formidable weapons to law enforcement for domestic (U.S.) applications.

In late November 1993, a letter came to my attention which discussed the above-mentioned conference. The letter had been written to U.S. Attorney General Janet Reno by a former CIA employee, Julianne McKinney, on letter-head stationary originating from the "Association of National Security Alumni, Electronic Surveillance Project, P.O. Box 13625, Silver Spring, Maryland 20911-3625."

Portions of the letter read as follows: " ... In December 1992, when `Microwave Harassment and Mind-Control Experimentation' was published, U.S. Government representatives routinely took the position that directed-energy technologies were nothing more than mere figments of physicists' imaginations, still on the drawing boards. Shortly following publication of this report, information concerning these technologies began to appear in such noteworthy organs as The *Wall Street Journal, Defense News, Aviation Week & Space Technology, Tactical Technology, Defense Electronics* and, most recently, the *Washington Post.*

In a flurry of activity these past 10 months, directed-energy-based surveillance and anti-personnel systems have suddenly leaped off

> of physicists' drawing boards into the world of reality, thus obviating the criticism, it would appear, that the attached publication [Los Alamos conference brochure] concerns non-existent technologies.
>
> Indeed, directed-energy technologies appear to have evolved at such a rapid rate that they are now being promoted as the "Final Solution" to crime – preliminarily, at a classified conference sponsored by the Los Alamos National Laboratory ...

McKinney's concern focused primarily on future law enforcement application of "psychotronic" tools, or directed-energy weapons technologies. "What, so far, has prevented this government and its contractors from testing these technologies on U.S. citizens under involuntary circumstances?," she asked.

The letter went on to outline various instances in which people had complained to her organization of alleged symptoms of directed-energy technologies in such areas as the United States, England, Canada and Australia.

♦♦♦♦♦♦♦♦

After reading *The Search for the Manchurian Candidate*, I couldn't help wondering if Danny Casolaro had been subjected to some form of hypnosis.

Any such far-reaching scenarios were outside the boundaries of normal human experience, indeed no main-stream journalist would pursue such a theory. But, then Robert Booth Nichols, Michael Riconosciuto and the CIA were not within normal human experience. And, who would have believed, ten years ago, that the CIA would be investigated by Congress in 1996 for drug trafficking in Los Angeles?

At one point in time Danny had signed an agreement with Nichols in which Nichols was to give Danny a $25,000 loan against his home in Fairfax, Virginia. Nichols had offered to take Danny overseas to find the answers to his questions and Danny had needed the money to make the trip. Where had they planned to go? What possible motive could Nichols have had for enticing Danny to go overseas for several months?

During one of my conversations with Bobby Riconosciuto, she had mentioned a private installation at Alice Springs, Australia which Michael had visited with Nichols. The tour of the installation had upset Riconosciuto to such a degree that he had become ill and cut the trip short. Nichols later confirmed the trip, and recalled that Michael had indeed become anxious and ill, but would not discuss the purpose of the trip.

When I subsequently questioned Michael about the Australian installation, he first asked where I had learned of it? When I noted the information came from Bobby, he explained that the underground facility had been built during World War II to be used as a bomb shelter. It was capable of housing thousands of people and was completely self-contained.

I asked Riconosciuto if he had been inside the facility? He said he had, it was owned by a private corporation; inside was a city of sorts, containing sophisticated communications equipment, laboratory equipment and other items which he would not define. He chose not to discuss it further, but concurred that what he saw made him realize that it was time to terminate his relationship with Robert Booth Nichols.

Both men had confirmed to me that the Australian trip marked the end of their 20-year association. I later contacted a journalist in Alice Springs to gain more knowledge of the mysterious "installation." I was able to confirm that the installation existed, that it was leased by a private corporation, and that it was heavily guarded, but no-one seemed to know what it was being used for in 1992.

••••••••

On November 22, 1992, I received a call from Michael Riconosciuto. It was the first time I had spoken with him in nine months. The first thing he asked me was, "Did Bob Nichols threaten you?"

I explained to him that I had nothing to fear from Nichols as long as I didn't reveal the contents of the meeting. Michael pressed further.

"Did he attempt to destroy my credibility, or did the meeting pertain to *his* activities?"

"Well, essentially, I asked him questions specifically about what he was doing with his corporation in Japan and overseas ..."

Mike knew I was referring to the genetic engineering project. Michael interjected, "That is so heavy. I've got a full paperwork trail on that."

I answered, "I have the paperwork trail on it."

Michael: "He didn't like that, did he?"

CS: "No, but after he knew I had information on it, he came right out and talked about it."

Michael: "Did he tell you what it was for?"

CS: "I think he did."

Michael: "Isn't that a `Dr. Strangelove tale'?"

CS: "Yes, I need to ask you some things ..."

Michael cut in. "Let's not talk about that over this phone."

Once again, Michael became evasive when confronted with the biological technology Nichols was involved in. This seemed to be one of the few subjects he refused to discuss over the phone.

His next question caused me some alarm. "Where did you send the metal canister you found in my files in the desert?"

I replied, "I sent it out to have it analyzed. I haven't received the results yet ..."

Michael: "Oh, Jesus. Where ... If they don't know how to handle it ..."

I stammered, "... I haven't heard from them yet ..."

Michael took a deep breath. "Oh, God." Then silence.

I was alarmed. "What is it? Tell me the truth."

Michael seemed shaken. "It's a military concept where you can genetically engineer these biological agents ... you see, a specific penetration group can be immunized, and everbody else dies. Now, whoever you sent that to, if they're not set up ... if they're not a class-4 facility, they better call someone who can handle it and get rid of it ..." Mike stopped abruptly. "Has anyone opened or touched the canister?"

I responded that it had not been opened. He drew another deep breath and seemed to relax somewhat. "Alright, it's not your problem anymore. As long as it's off your property."

I had provided the canister to J.H. in Fresno, who sent it to Quantico, VA to have it tested, but I never received a satisfactory response as to what the canister contained.

••••••••

Frank Nugan

— 16 —

Nugan Hand Bank

One very long tentacle of journalist Danny Casolaro's Octopus extended from Sydney, Australia to San Francisco, California where a pair of unsolved murders have been traced to looted CIA money from the Sydney-based Nugan Hand Bank.

Casolaro's earlier notes, the ones that weren't taken from his hotel room at the time of his death, were provided by his brother,Tony, to the Western Historical Manuscript Collection at the University of Missouri-Columbia. Throughout dozens of these handwritten drafts, Casolaro cryptically referred to Nugan Hand and the cast of characters associated with the scandal-ridden bank.

He also allegedly made the connection between the twin 1982 unsolved murders of Paul Morasca and Mary Quick in San Francisco and the looted CIA money. Morasca was described in the *San Francisco Chronicle* [12/20/91] as "a San Francisco entrepreneur suspected of being a money launderer involved in a major Northern California drug ring."

Morasca's partner, Michael Riconosciuto, told Casolaro and other journalists in 1991 that Morasca was tortured by his murderer to obtain secret bank code cards containing account numbers where CIA monies had been hidden, including funds from Nugan Hand bank. He also claimed that he and Morasca had transferred millions of dollars for Michael Hand when he fled Australia.

Nugan Hand Bank was founded in 1973 by Michael Hand, Frank Nugan and officials of the CIA-owned airline, Air America. Michael Hand had trained with U.S. Special Forces at Fort Bragg before being posted to Vietnam, where he was awarded the Distinguished Service Cross for bravery. After his first stint in Vietnam, in the mid-1960's Hand moved to the clandestine CIA war in Laos, according to a former station chief in Indo-China, Ted Shackley.

While in Laos, Hand reportedly worked with the US backed mercenary armies drawn from the Laotian Meo hill tribes who dealt in the currencies of gold, guns, and opium. In 1968 Hand arrived in Australia where he formed Australasian and Pacific Holdings, comprised mostly of shareholders from the CIA's covert airline in South East Asia. Around 1970 Hand and Frank Nugan officially teamed up.

According to the Australian Royal Commission, Nugan Hand was the principle conduit for laundering money from major narcotics transactions from the Golden Triangle and importing heroin into Australia in the 1970's. In short time the bank expanded into Germany, Malaysia, the Philippines, Saudi Arabia, Argentina, Singapore, Taiwan, Thailand, Hawaii, Washington D.C., Maryland and London. One office was located in Chiang Mai, Thailand, in the heart of the Golden Triangle heroin trade.

In addition to drugs, Nugan Hand was involved in various arms deals with Indonesia, Thailand, Malaysia and Brazil. During this time William Colby was director of the CIA. After his retirement in 1976 he served as Nugan Hand's attorney in Sydney. Other Nugan Hand officers included a network of U.S. generals, admirals and CIA employees. Their identities officially surfaced two decades later in Texas, when a judge unsealed classified CIA internal documents in response to an appeal filed in a Houston federal court.

The appeal was filed by Edwin Wilson, a former CIA agent convicted in the U.S. of selling C-4 high explosives to Libya and charged with supplying trained men, arms, and technology to Libya and other military buyers. He had served 17 years of a 25-year sentence and was eligible for parole.

At his 1983 trial Wilson never identified his compatriots within the Nugan Hand galaxy, but David Adler, his appeal lawyer in 1999, reviewed hundreds of CIA documents confirming Wilson's relationship with William Colby, Thomas Clines, Bernie Houghton, and others involved with Nugan Hand Bank.

The *Texas Observer* had reported in September 1991 that CIA officials Theodore Shackley, chief of clandestine operations in the Far East in the mid-1970's, and Thomas Clines, along with their subordinate Edwin Wilson, utilized secret bank accounts at Nugan Hand to fund a variety of covert operations, including the destabilization of Australia's Labour Party in 1975. Both Shackley and Clines would later resurface as key figures in the Iran-Contra scandal.

Maurice Bernard Houghton, the closest friend and advisor to Michael Hand, had daringly traded goods all over the Southeast Asia war zone in the 1960's. The mysterious Texan played an active role in Nugan Hand's affairs since its inception in 1973, according to the *Wall Street Journal* [8/24/82].

The *Journal* identified nine top-ranking U.S. military and intelligence officers who worked for Nugan Hand Bank. A few of these included:

- Admiral Earl "Buddy" Yates, former commander of the aircraft carrier USS John F. Kennedy and chief of staff for plans and policy of the U.S. Pacific Command. Yates became president of Nugan Hand in 1977 after his retirement from the military.
- Three-star General Leroy J. Manor, former chief of staff of the entire Pacific Command. He occupied the bank's Manila branch.
- General Edwin F. Black was former commander of OSS [Office of Strategic Services which evolved into the CIA] in Berlin and wartime boss of Richard Helms, who later headed the CIA. In 1977 General Black became the president of Nugan Hand in Hawaii.
- William Colby, the U.S. director of central intelligence from 1973-1976, handled most of Nugan Hand's legal matters after his retirement. He was succeeded at the CIA by George Bush of Texas.

The fraud-ridden bank collapsed in June 1980, six months after its co-founder, Frank Nugan, 37, was found shot to death in his Mercedes Benz on a quiet road outside Lithgow. Police found a business card from William Colby in his pocket and a rifle clutched in his left hand. In April 1980 a Hong Kong financial newsletter exposed Nugan Hand's cover, requiring the CIA to loot the bank's assets and transfer them to other CIA proprietaries.

According to Jonathan Kwitney, author of the book *Crimes of Patriots,* Michael Hand fled Australia under a false identity on June 14, 1980 on a flight to Fiji. He was reportedly helped to escape by an American code-named "Charlie," identified by Kwitny as a former member of the U.S. Special Forces and ex-CIA operative.

In 1991, top Australian journalist Brian Toohey reported in his *The Eye* magazine that Michael Hand had a postal drop at a suite in NE Bellevue, Washington State. Hand's wife was reportedly living there with him.

William Hamilton

— 17 —

THE INSLAW AFFAIR

Danny Casolaro, Michael Riconosciuto, Robert Booth Nichols, and others were mentioned rather prominently in the final House of Representatives Report #102-857 released to the public on September 10, 1992. The Investigative Report, put together by the Committee on the Judiciary headed by Congressman Jack Brooks of Texas, "The Inslaw Affair," summarized a three year investigation into the theft of the PROMIS software from Bill and Nancy Hamilton, owners of Inslaw Corporation in Washington D.C. (The investigators who handled the three-year probe were listed on the Report as James E. Lewin, Chief Investigator, and John D. Cohen, Investigator.)

Two federal court judges and the House Judiciary Committee ultimately concluded that "the Department of Justice acted willfully and fraudulently" and "took, converted and stole" Inslaw's enhanced PROMIS software by "trickery, fraud and deceit."

The story of INSLAW is unparalleled in U.S. history, but it is far from over. The pendulum is swinging back and the world has not heard the last from the Hamiltons.

For that reason I have recorded notable facts from the "The Inslaw Affair" investigative report as well as Bill Hamilton's personal account in this chapter for purposes of historical relevance.

The Hamilton's nightmare began in the 1970's when the Law Enforcement Assistance Administration (LEAA) an agency of the U.S. Department of Justice, funded Inslaw to develop a standardized management information system to assist local and state law enforcement offices across the country in recordkeeping and tracking of criminal cases. PROMIS (Prosecutor's Management Information System) was subsequently developed to meet criminal prosecutor workloads of large local prosecution offices; and by 1980, two of the largest U.S. Attorney's Offices were also using PROMIS software for both criminal and civil cases.

During the 1970s, Inslaw was a non-profit, tax-exempt corporation called the Institute for Law and Social Research and which was funded almost entirely through government grants and contracts. When President Carter liquidated LEAA, the Hamilton's Inslaw created a successor profit-making corporation, INSLAW, Inc., bought the assets of the predecessor Institute, and, in 1981, developed significant, privately-financed improvements to PROMIS and began commercially marketing the enhanced version of the software.

In March 1982, the Justice Department awarded Inslaw Inc. a $10 million, 3-year contract to implement in the 22 largest U.S. Attorneys Offices an earlier version of PROMIS that the predecessor Institute had licensed in 1980 for two other large U.S. Attorneys Offices. However, the three-year contract became embroiled in controversy when the government demanded that INSLAW deliver under the contract a version of PROMIS that the new INSLAW, Inc. had developed in 1981 with private funds.

"The Inslaw Affair" report outlined the conflict on the question of whether Inslaw had ownership of its privately funded "enhanced PROMIS," which was installed at numerous U.S. Attorney's Offices after a 1983 modification to the contract. Justice officials initially recognized Inslaw's proprietary rights to any privately-funded enhancements to the original version of PROMIS, and even provided a letter to INSLAW to that effect in August 1982 following five months of meetings between Justice and INSLAW's lawyers. The bankruptcy court ruled, however, that by November 1982, ignoring its own August 1982 letter to INSLAW, Justice had launched a scheme fraudulently to induce INSLAW to deliver under the contract a later, privately-financed version of PROMIS.

Inslaw attempted to resolve the matter several times through negotiation but was met largely with indifference or hostility by Department officials. At the start of 1984, Justice cancelled part of INSLAW's contract for its own convenience while withholding payments due INSLAW on the remaining part of the contract. By February 1985, Justice had withheld at least $1.6 million in payments, forcing INSLAW to file for Chapter 11 protection from its creditors. Both the bankruptcy and district courts ruled that Justice then sought "unlawfully and without justification" to convert INSLAW from Chapter 11 reorganization into Chapter 7 liquidation to incapacitate the Company from litigating. Department officials steadfastly claimed that the Inslaw controversy was merely a contract dispute that INSLAW had mischaracterized to the media.

As a result of media exposure, Inslaw's owners, Bill and Nancy Hamilton, received information that eventually led them to believe that the Department's actions were part of a high level conspiracy within Justice to steal the "enhanced" version of PROMIS.

Inslaw alleged that former Attorney General Edwin Meese and Deputy Attorney General Lowell Jensen forced Inslaw into bankruptcy by intentionally creating a series of sham contract disputes which provided a pretext for Justice to put financial pressure on INSLAW by withholding increasingly larger amounts of money due INSLAW for its work under the three-year PROMIS Implementation Contract with U.S. Attorneys Offices.

The Hamiltons maintained that, after driving Inslaw into Chapter 11 in February 1985, Justice officials immediately attempted to force the conversion of Inslaw's status to Chapter 7 (Liquidation). Such a change in bankruptcy status could have forced the sale of Inslaw's assets, including "enhanced" PROMIS, to a rival computer software company such as Hadron, Inc. which had approached INSLAW in 1983 about buying the Company for the stated purpose of obtaining the PROMIS software so it could obtain federal contracts from its claimed friendship with then Presidential Counselor Edwin Meese. According to Hamilton, Hadron's Chairman threatened him in 1983, when he declined any interest in INSLAW's acquisition by Hadron, by saying ominously "we have ways of making you sell."

Hadron, Inc. was controlled by the Biotech Capital Corporation, the holding company of Dr. Earl Brian, a Ronald Reagan crony. In his deposition to the House Judiciary Committee, Brian testified that Hadron had approximately 40 computer system contracts with U.S. intelligence agencies and the U.S. Department of Justice.

Attorney General Edwin Meese had previously worked with Dr. Brian in the cabinet of former California Governor Ronald Reagan and later at the Reagan White House, where Brian reported to

Meese as the unpaid chairman of the White House Task Force on Health Care Cost Reduction during the first couple of years of the Reagan Administration. According to the Hamiltons, the Meese Justice Department launched Project EAGLE, the largest procurement in the Department's history to provide uniform case management systems to every litigation office and investigative agency of the Justice Department, without explaining where the case management software was expected to come from. If Justice had succeeded in its unlawful 1985 scheme to force INSLAW into liquidation, PROMIS would have been sold at a liquidation auction, placing the buyer in an advantageous position for winning the huge Project EAGLE contract.

The Inslaw Affair report noted that information obtained by the Hamiltons through sworn affidavits of several individuals, including Ari Ben-Menashe, a former Israeli Mossad officer, and Michael Riconosciuto, who claimed to have ties to the intelligence community, indicated that one element of the Justice Department's malfeasance against INSLAW was the modification of the 'enhanced' PROMIS software by individuals associated with the world of covert intelligence operations. The Hamiltons claimed that unauthorized, copyright-infringing modifications to PROMIS, including the insertion of a so-called "trap-door," was part of a scheme by U.S. and Israeli intelligence to steal the intelligence secrets of foreign governments by selling them a trap-door version of PROMIS.

The Hamiltons also presented information indicating that PROMIS had been distributed to U.S. intelligence and law enforcement agencies such as the CIA, NSA, DIA, FBI, and DEA.

The House Judiciary Committee focused its investigative efforts on two principal questions: (1) Did high level Department of Justice officials convert, steal or otherwise misappropriate Inslaw's PROMIS software and attempt to put the company out of business? And (2) did high level DOJ officials, including Attorney General Edwin Meese and then Deputy Attorney General Lowell Jensen, and others conspire to sell, transfer, or in any way distribute Inslaw's "enhanced" PROMIS to other federal agencies and foreign governments?

The Judiciary Committee concluded that there was strong evidence to indicate that the Justice Department *"fraudulently took, converted and stole Inslaw's 'enhanced' PROMIS by trickery, fraud and deceit,"* and that the actions taken against Inslaw by the Justice

Department's project manager had been undertaken at the direction of top officials of the Justice Department.

Two federal court decisions were mentioned in *The Inslaw Affair* report: Bankruptcy Court Judge George Bason found that Mr. C. Madison "Brick" Brewer's [the government's PROMIS project manager] recommendation that the Inslaw contract be cancelled at a meeting on April 14, 1982 of PROMIS Project Team members, when the three-year contract was only one month old, "constituted a smoking gun that clearly evidenced Brewer's intense bias against Inslaw, [and] his single-minded intent to drive Inslaw out of business ---."

By his own admission, Mr. Brewer had become upset when Inslaw claimed that it had made enhancements to the earlier version of PROMIS using private funds. In his view, the government was entitled to use every version of PROMIS without having to pay license fees to INSLAW.

The Judiciary Committee added that it was clear from the record that Mr. Brewer and Mr. Peter Videnieks (the government's PROMIS contracting officer), supported by high level Justice officials, continued to confront Inslaw at every turn.

Senior U.S. District Court William Bryant, Jr. subsequently stated in the second ruling: "There was unending contention about payments under this contract and the rights of the respective parties – what is strikingly apparent from the testimony and depositions of key witnesses and many documents is that Inslaw performed its contract in a hostile environment that extended from the higher echelons of the Justice Department to the officials who had the day-to-day responsibility for supervising its work."

Over the life of the contract, Inslaw made several attempts to reach an agreement with the Department over its proprietary rights to the "enhanced" PROMIS software. The Department, however, steadfastly refused to conduct any meaningful negotiations and exhibited little inclination to resolve the controversy. Meanwhile Inslaw had installed PROMIS at the 20 largest U.S. Attorney's offices across the nation as required by the contract.

Mr. Brewer and Mr. Videnieks knew that Inslaw had installed "enhanced" PROMIS in 20 of the largest U.S. Attorneys Offices, yet without notice, and certainly without permission, the Department of Justice illegally *copied* the privately-financed version of PROMIS and installed it in 25 more U.S. Attorneys Offices.

The bankruptcy court ruled that *"[The Department] engaged in an outrageous, deceitful, fraudulent game of cat and mouse, demonstrating contempt for both the law and any principle of fair dealing."* (Finding No. 266 at 138).

It is worth noting that Deputy Attorney General Lowell Jensen, who headed the Department's PROMIS Oversight Committee, and who kept a close watch over the administration of the contract as well as being involved in every major decision, had also once worked with Attorney General Edwin Meese in the Alameda County District Attorney's Office. Jensen later became a U.S. District Court Judge in San Francisco, after serving at the Justice Department between 1981 and 1986 successively as Assistant Attorney General in charge of the Criminal Division, Associate Attorney General, and Deputy Attorney General.

Mike Abbell, the attorney whom Danny Casolaro had been investigating during the last week of his life, had served as Director of the Office of International Affairs of the Criminal Division of the Justice Department until *1984* when he left to become counsel at the law firm of Kaplan, Russin and Becchi – so Jensen and Abbell had served in the Criminal Division of the DOJ at the same time between 1981 and 1982.

••••••••

Bill Hamilton, President of INSLAW, Inc., had become "the Keeper of the Flame" in this never-ending saga: Through interviews and e-mail communications, I was able to glean his personal behind-the-scenes account of what had transpired. This is a summary of what Hamilton provided, as follows:

In May 1988, just a few months after the federal bankruptcy court in Washington, D.C. issued fully-litigated findings that the Justice Department had stolen the PROMIS legal case management software from INSLAW, Inc. in the early 1980s "through trickery, fraud and deceit," and then attempted to drive INSLAW out of business so the Company would be unable to litigate, Ronald LeGrand, the Chief Investigator for the Senate Judiciary Committee, telephoned Hamilton, to pass on information from someone he described as a trusted senior Justice Department career official who had been in the Criminal Division of the Justice Department since the time of the Watergate scandal under President Nixon.

Hamilton had recently explained to LeGrand his belief that the Reagan Administration had stolen PROMIS with the intention of using the stolen software as the basis for the award of a massive Justice Department computerization contract to a friend of the Reagan Administration. LeGrand told Hamilton that his source had asked him to tell Mr. and Mrs. Hamilton the following: "*What you think happened, did happen. You are not crazy. But you do not know squat about how dirty the INSLAW case really is. If you ever learn even half of it, you will be sickened. INSLAW is a lot dirtier for the Department of Justice, in its breadth and depth, than Watergate. The Justice Department has been compromised at every level on the INSLAW case.*"

The source also sent word to INSLAW that the Criminal Division had served as the nerve center for the scheme to drive INSLAW out of business by engineering sham contract disputes. INSLAW had no idea in 1988, when the Chief Investigator of the Senate Judiciary Committee passed on the information, what the government had done with the PROMIS software that this senior career prosecutor viewed as *sickening.*

Senior U.S. District Judge William Bryant, Jr. affirmed the bankruptcy court's findings a year later, in November 1989, in a separate opinion of almost 50 pages, following a *de novo* trial. Notwithstanding these two strongly worded federal court decisions, the Justice Department failed to settle with INSLAW, and its Office of Professional Responsibility promptly cleared of any wrongdoing every Justice Department official criticized by the bankruptcy court. Moreover, the Justice Department exhibited no interest in investigating indications that the malfeasance against INSLAW might be even more widely-ramified.

After writing letters to Attorney General Richard Thornburgh twice about the need to investigate such indications but without receiving any reply, INSLAW's Counsel, and former U.S. Attorney General, Elliot Richardson, filed a lawsuit against Thornburgh in federal district court in Washington, D.C. for failing and refusing to carry out his clear duty to enforce the federal criminal laws in the INSLAW case. The court ruled, however, that it did not have the legal authority to intrude into the exercise of prosecutorial discretion, no matter how questionable the attorney general's exercise of his discretion might appear to be.

It was not until early 1991 that INSLAW obtained the first evidence, in the form of affidavits, about a much broader PROMIS. Several individuals, each of whom claimed under oath to have worked for U.S. or Israeli intelligence, testified that the Justice Department had been covertly disseminating PROMIS since the early 1980s for various intelligence-tracking applications.

INSLAW Counsel Richardson asked retired four-star Admiral Daniel Murphy, who had served as Richardson's Military Advisor when Richardson was Secretary of Defense under Nixon, and who later held two of the top U.S. intelligence posts (Deputy Director of the CIA under Ford and Undersecretary of Defense for Intelligence under Carter), to review the plausibility of the claims about the covert dissemination of PROMIS for intelligence-tracking applications, and also to give his opinion on whether the claimed intelligence uses could explain Attorney General Thornburgh's otherwise inexplicable failure to enforce the federal criminal laws.

After reading the affidavits and the INSLAW lawsuit against Thornburgh, Murphy told Richardson and Hamilton that he was sorry to say that there was nothing implausible about any of the claims, including the claim by Michael Riconosciuto that he had modified PROMIS for U.S. intelligence on an Indian reservation in southern California; that the available evidence made it look like an NSA operation; and that if it were an NSA operation, it would explain Thornburgh's behavior because Thornburgh would not have needed to receive a call from the White House to know that his job was to stonewall "until the cows come home".

Elliot Richardson passed away at the end of 1999. In 2001, Hamilton contacted Admiral Murphy again and gave him an approximately 50-page INSLAW summary of evidence revealing that the Justice Department began misappropriating PROMIS in 1982 for three separate intelligence projects: (1) NSA's deployment of PROMIS to banks to enable NSA to track wire transfers of money and letters of credit; (2) Israeli intelligence's sale of a trap-door version of PROMIS to foreign governments so Israel and the United States could covertly intercept their intelligence secrets; and (3) the CIA's deployment of PROMIS throughout the U.S. Government as the standard database software for the gathering and disseminating of U.S. intelligence information.

Murphy told Hamilton that the INSLAW summary eliminated any doubt about what had happened and that the INSLAW case needed to be settled. He warned Hamilton, however, that government officials would "regard it as their patriotic duty to look INSLAW's lawyer in the eyes and lie", making it essential that INSLAW find another outstanding lawyer like Elliot Richardson to represent the Company in seeking compensation.

Shortly before introducing Mr. and Mrs. Hamilton to C. Boyden Gray one week after the September 11, 2001 terrorist attacks, and asking Gray "to become the John Adams of the INSLAW case" and represent INSLAW simply because it was the right thing to do, Murphy said something to Hamilton that Hamilton now suspects may have been an allusion to the use of *the NSA bank surveillance version of PROMIS to launder drug profits.*

In September 2001, Murphy, who had served as Chief of Staff to Vice President Bush during the first term of the Reagan Administration when the PROMIS misappropriations began, told Hamilton that it was his "hunch" that there was still another use of PROMIS that INSLAW had not yet discovered, that it "involves something so seriously wrong that money alone cannot cure the problem," and that the government might never compensate INSLAW unless the Company discovers that additional use of PROMIS.

Unfortunately, Admiral Murphy passed away suddenly several days later on September 21, 2001, and Hamilton was never able to obtain clarification from Murphy where his *hunch* had originated from relative to "still another use of PROMIS that INSLAW had not yet discovered."

♦♦♦♦♦♦♦♦

As a postscript, Bill Hamilton later mentioned to me that, in retrospect, he had come to believe that the "other" use of PROMIS involved laundering money from drug profits. He said he believed that "the main role of the Cabazon/Wackenhut Joint Venture was connected to government-sanctioned drug trafficking and money laundering by organized crime groups like the Gambino Family and groups like the Contras, and that Michael Riconoscuito's job was to help these groups access NSA's bank surveillance version of PROMIS to launder the proceeds from the drug sales."

Garby Leon

— 18 —

The Benefactor

Garby Leon, Director of Development at Joel Silver Productions at Warner Brothers Studios in Burbank, California had been investigating the death of Paul Wilcher, Danny Casolaro and others associated with the Octopus story. On July 14, 1993 Garby wrote a letter to the U.S. Attorney General to influence her to investigate the death of Paul Wilcher, a Washington D.C. attorney who had been investigating the October Surprise incident based on the claims of his client, Gunther Karl Russbacher.

On or about May 21, 1993, attorney Paul Wilcher had hand delivered a letter to the Department of Justice claiming holdover DOJ employees from the Reagan-Bush era were responsible for a number of government cover ups, unbeknownst to the Attorney General and President Clinton. The 100-page letter was addressed to Janet Reno. On or about June 11, Wilcher was interviewed by her public relations man, Carl Stern, formerly of NBC, regarding the contents of the letter. Later, after days of not hearing from him, worried friends contacted the police, who went to Wilcher's apartment on June 23. His decomposing body was found propped on a toilet.

Sarah McClendon, a White House correspondent and close friend of Paul Wilcher, wrote in her *Washington Report* on July 4, 1993, entitled "Death of a Friend," that Wilcher believed Gunther Russbacher to be a political prisoner, that Russbacher was being persecuted because he allegedly flew former President George Bush to Paris to meet with leading Iranians to make a deal to supply Iran with weapons in exchange for that government keeping the 52 American hostages until after the November election so that former President Jimmy Carter would not get a boost by bringing home the American citizens held there. Instead the deal was that the hostages would be delivered to Ronald Reagan as soon as Reagan was inaugurated in 1981, wrote McClendon.

Wilcher was working daily for Russbacher. "Wilcher wanted to ask the new Attorney General, Janet Reno, to grant immunity from prosecution to Russbacher so that he might testify to the government about the goings on inside the CIA."

McClendon had called local police for 24 hours imploring them to check up on Wilcher. Finally they found he had been dead for several days. McClendon concluded, "I believe Wilcher to be a casualty of good citizenship and patriotism. I tried to get possession of the papers and tapes he left behind, but his family, who did not know how to assess these things, took them away. "

Garby Leon had been friends with both Sarah McClendon and Paul Wilcher, so he wrote a letter to Janet Reno on July 14, 1993 which later became highly publicized on the Internet. Garby's letter read as follows:

> TO: The Honorable Janet Reno, Attorney General of the United States, Department of Justice - Room 4400, Tenth and Constitution Ave N.E., Washington, DC 20530.
>
> Dear Madame Attorney General,
>
> I am writing because I feel the death of Paul Wilcher deserves your most serious attention, and should be investigated by your most trusted officials in the Department of Justice.
>
> Paul Wilcher, like Danny Casolaro, was investigating possible government involvement in a variety of questionable activities, including the controversial October Surprise allegations and the INSLAW case, his researches leading him into areas that Casolaro had covered earlier. In his quest Wilcher made himself known in and around Capitol Hill as a persistent gadfly, trying to spur inquiries into possible government malfeasance in several areas. He had contacts with, among others, Lee Hamilton, William Webster, Elliot Richardson and Ross Perot.
>
> By late May, Wilcher said his information had gone beyond Casolaro's and he felt this made him a "danger signal." In three weeks, he was dead.
>
> I feel that the two deaths, Casolaro's and Wilcher's, offer disturbing parallels, outlined below.

On the 23rd of June, 1993, the body of Paul Wilcher was discovered in his Washington DC apartment. This is not a certainty, since to my knowledge no evidentially identification--no fingerprint or dental x- ray matching-- was made before the body's reported cremation two weeks ago.

Present at the scene after Wilcher's death was noted White House correspondent Sarah McClendon, who knew Wilcher well and who had alerted authorities that he was missing. McClendon was unable to identify the body as Wilcher after viewing the remains.

McClendon has been told that preliminary autopsy results have found "no natural cause of death, and no other cause of death" to explain Wilcher's demise. Given that Wilcher, in his 40s, was in apparent good health, this seems fairly astonishing.

A much larger issue is also implied here: if critics of our government are found dead in their bathrooms from obscure causes, and the government itself doesn't take steps to find out why, then our freedoms themselves are threatened--as well as the activities that protect those freedoms.

If individual investigation and criticism of government activities is chilled or intimidated into silence, then democracy loses its most important protection.

To put it another way, if Danny Casolaro's death was a message of some kind, then Wilcher's death is an even grimmer message--it suggests that Casolaro's death was not a fluke. Anyone inspired to follow Casolaro or Wilcher's path now has a strong added reason to fear doing so.

And a real investigation into Wilcher's death might not be an academic exercise. One person who is extremely close to and knowledgeable about the Casolaro case has said in private that the mystery of Casolaro's death could be resolved by a Grand Jury investigation, with sworn testimony, subpoena power, etc. This suggests Paul Wilcher's death may not have to remain a mystery either.

Paul Wilcher was an acquaintance of mine. He was not a perfect person; he made mistakes like anyone else but he was also, at times, a man of unusual energy and altruism. A seminary student who considered becoming a priest, he later became an attorney is his efforts to accomplish some good in this world.

Overall, I feel he was a good man. He didn't deserve to die.

Personally, I don't believe he died of natural causes.

•••

In the following pages are brief remarks regarding A) disturbing parallels between the Casolaro and Wilcher cases; B) Police, FBI and CIA presence at the scene; C) other information about Wilcher's death; and D) possible further forensic investigation.

Mme. Attorney General, I feel the death of Paul Wilcher offers too many questions and inconsistencies to be ignored. I am writing because I feel this matter deserves your most serious attention,and hope this letter will bring some action on your part to answer some of the many, very troubling questions raised by Paul Wilcher's death.

Sincerely,
Garby Leon (PhD, Harvard University)

Disturbing Parallels Between The Wilcher And Casolaro Cases:

Both were investigating possible government involvement in illegal activities.

Each was acting on his own, with dogged persistence, over a long time period.

Both Casolaro and Wilcher expressed fears, shortly before their deaths, that their lives were in danger because their investigations had led into sensitive territory. Casolaro was known to have received direct phone call threats, and told his brother shortly before he died, "If something happens to me, it won't be an accident."

As stated, Wilcher told at least one other person at the end of May that he feared he'd become a "danger signal" because his information on government malfeasance had gone beyond Casolaro's. In three weeks he was dead.

Both decedents' bodies were found in bathrooms, in bizarre circumstances (Casolaro a supposed suicide though forensic evidence cast substantial doubt on this; Wilcher, a man in good health, propped up on a toilet but showing no discernible cause of death).

In both cases, the scene of death was sealed off and made inaccessible, then cleaned, preventing any further official or independent investigation (the motel room where Casolaro was found was industrially cleaned the next day; Wilcher's apartment was sealed off and no one was allowed to enter; it was also cleaned the next day. I am unaware of any subsequent, serious investigation or crime report released to the public in either case).

In both cases, personal records, documents, computer files and/or other information belonging to the decedents are apparently not officially accounted for. Casolaro's briefcase and personal records were not found at the scene of his death. While Wilcher's family reportedly has taken possession of some personal belongings, the location of Wilcher's complete files, the result of years of hard work, is not publicly known.

In both cases, rapid alterations were made to the corpse making further forensic study difficult or impossible. Casolaro was embalmed shortly after death without family consent; Wilcher was cremated, as remarked above, without fingerprint or other evidential identification of the body, and without complete forensic examination to determine cause of death.

In both cases, forensic evidence relating to the corpses is scant.

In neither case was any kind of inquest held, no official testimony taken under oath, nor was any thoroughgoing official investigation undertaken (at least publicly). Nor has any official report been released in either case.

Police, FBI & CIA Presence At The Scene, June 23, 1993:

According to Mr. MASON O. LIDELL JR., superintendent of Wilcher's building, a Lieutenant and a Sergeant from the DC Police (with the help of firemen to force the door) entered Wilcher's apartment at about 11:30 AM on June 23rd. Three detectives from DC Police entered and found Wilcher's computer was turned on. When they read what was on the computer screen, they summoned the FBI. There is no further information on what the screen actually said.

After entering the apartment and getting a brief glance at the body and the apartment, Lidell was ordered to leave. The apartment was sealed off for the rest of the day, except for official personnel. The body was removed at about 12:30 according to Lidell (who didn't witness this), though he did mention that when he entered the apartment later, there was blood on the floor and on the commode which wasn't present earlier. He was told that this was because of measures taken to move the body.

At about 4:30 in the afternoon FBI Agents arrived. Sarah McClendon was also present, though not allowed in the apartment itself. She says two groups of four FBI Agents - eight FBI Agents in all – arrived and asked questions. McClendon checked their identification, which seemed convincing. According to Lidell at least three FBI Agents entered the apartment during the 4:30 to 7:30 time period.

Then, according to Lidell, one man appeared and said he was CIA (without offering identification). He joined the FBI agents in the Wilcher apartment during the 4:30 to 7:30 time period. More people could have entered during this time Lidell says "he returned to his own apartment and didn't keep track."

Lidell says that an NBC camera crew was prevented from entering the apartment. Aside from firemen, medical personnel to remove the body and the above Government agents, no one was allowed in the apartment for the entire day - no reporters, friends, media crews, etc. This raises a question: why no other observers, since police okayed cleaning of the apartment the very next day?

Ms. McClendon phoned the FBI to ask about the presence of FBI Agents; later MR. JAMES V. DESARNO JR., Assistant Special Agent in Charge from the D. C. Metropolitan Office, arrived. Mr. Desarno also asked questions, but strongly denied that the FBI was interested in or involved in the case. "We are not interested in this case," he told McClendon, Lidell and others repeatedly.

This seems curious. If Wilcher was a "nobody" why the official presence and vehement expression of non-involvement "ironic" with so many agents present? How could Desarno know the FBI would or wouldn't be involved without an investigation or known cause of death? Why all the secrecy and denial? Why the presence of the CIA?

Other Information About Wilcher's Death:

Only a few slight pieces of information have filtered down about public officials and others involved in the Wilcher matter:

Two FBI Agents present at the scene were JAMES V. DESARNO, as remarked, and CRAIG OLSON, both of the D. C. Metropolitan Office: 1900 Half Street SW, Washington DC 20535. (202) 252-7801, both at same address and office.

The DC police officer in charge of investigating the Wilcher death is named BRIAN HENRY, (202) 727-4347.

Coroner for the government is a DR. KIM, who performed the autopsy, the results of which have not been released.

Building superintendent MASON LIDELL was questioned by Desarno and others, and has kindly provided information in this letter.

One friend of Wilcher's phoned apartment 302 in Wilcher's building (across from his) and got a taped answer message on the telephone intercom. The message said (paraphrasing) "This is a government telephone line, no longer in service" or words to that effect. Phone records, occupancy etc. from this address should be investigated.

Possible Further Forensic Investigation:

Given the inconclusive autopsy results, further testing of the forensic evidence would seem to be crucial. Wilcher's body fluids, sent by the D. C. Medical Examiner to the Armed Forces Institute of Pathology at Walter Reed Hospital, haven't yielded any clue as to cause of death. Apparently coroner Dr. Kim is still in possession of Wilcher's heart.

Sarah McClendon is petitioning Dr. JOYE CARTER of the D. C. Medical Examiner's office to submit this forensic evidence for further study. Dr. Carter hasn't moved with alacrity to permit or facilitate this.

McClendon would like to submit the evidence to a DR. MASON, one of the top forensic toxicologists in the U. S. (Dr. Mason: 2300 Stratford Ave, Willow Grove, Pennsylvania, 215 657-4900). Dr. Mason feels it is extremely significant that no cause of death has been found, a rarity in his experience.

••••••••

Perhaps, Mme. Attorney General, you can aid in investigating this and other crucial aspects of Paul Wilcher's death. Thank you for any consideration in response to this request

Garby Leon.

To my knowledge, Janet Reno never responded directly to Garby's letter.

While at Joel Silver Productions, Garby developed the movies *The Matrix,* with Larry and Andy Wachowski, *Exit Wounds* with Chris Bertolini, *Lethal Weapon IV,* and the *Manchurian Candidate* in association with Tina Sinatra, as well as overseeing a slate of over seventy projects. Yet, despite his busy schedule, Garby found time to communicate with me regularly from late 1993 through 1995.

By 1994 my husband, Roland, and I had moved to the North Idaho Panhandle National Forest where we were building a vacation home on Lake Pend Oreille, the largest lake in Idaho. I was still investigating material for *The Last Circle* and sharing it with Garby. At one point, Garby earnestly encouraged me to get all the material *into writing,* and send my progress to him weekly.

The logistics of writing a manuscript at this time were complicated. Roland and I were living in a trailer on our property while we constructed our vacation home; at that point it was only in the framing and roofing stages, so I dragged the boxes of Riconosciuto's files into the 8x11 framed walk-in *closet* and converted that portion of the house into an office with a folding table and computer. The site was comical – I had strung electrical cords from the closet through the entire house to the outside temporary electric pole. Every time more than one person used a skilsaw, my computer blinked and experienced a brownout, so I had to be notified in advance by my husband when he was preparing to use the saw. In addition I was not impervious to the constant hammering above my head as the roof was being installed, and the sawdust falling into my hair.

Nevertheless, Garby was relentless, encouraging me to *write* and generously providing me with his phone card so I would continue interviews to fill in the gaps in the manuscript. He called at least every other day and we exchanged information on the progress of our respective investigations and the manuscript.

Meanwhile, Garby was communicating regularly with Bill Hamilton, owner of INSLAW in Washington D.C., and probing the death of Danny Casolaro amongst other PROMIS issues. Garby made notes on all his phone conversations with Hamilton and sent them to me, and also shared info that I sent to him with Hamilton, though Hamilton never knew my name at that time.

One NOTES memorandum, written by Garby Leon, dated January 21, 1994, entitled "Hamilton Phone Call," indicated the scope of Bill Hamilton's probe (excerpted from a 4-page letter), as follows:

> Concrete things for *60 Minutes* to do: Nazis from Vendors List – Met with retired FBI agent on our case; nice guy. Sharing with him some of the raw info from one of our sources – that the FBI did do an investigation after Danny's death. Maid in [Martinsburg] hotel; she describes a guy, thirty, dressed, that she saw come out of Danny's room the morning he was dead. It would fit the description of Joseph Cuellar.
>
> Cuellar worked, before he went to Desert Storm, worked for same security firm. He's a full time covert government agent. I asked my friend, Suggestions for *60 Minutes*: Take Cuellar's picture down to the maid.
>
> I've been wondering if there's something Elliot [Richardson] can do ...? There's a retired FBI agent, Scott Erskine, interviewing people about Danny's death. Seems to be honest. What can we do to help him?

> Called Nichols [Robert Booth Nichols] last night about OSI: He knows that it is OSI, an intelligence agency. He's (RBN) leaving for the far-east, few months, and said 'I told Danny to be careful and it got misconstrued that I threatened him, I didn't. I was with a friend in British Intelligence who told me, 'It's a good thing you're not going to be in the U.S. in a few months, because the PROMIS matter is going to get very nasty.'

Garby wrote that "a guy from military intelligence told B.H. [Bill Hamilton] last month that two things happened that prove his stuff is true. I've learned, don't dismiss anything you hear; don't believe it all, but don't be sure it's not true. Time and time again it proves to be true, but you didn't understand [at the time]."

Garby further quoting Hamilton: "In retrospect, stuff I was hearing from both sources in April, I now think was probably accurate. There was an approved effort to kill me, that didn't happen because maybe someone was there to intercept it.

"MI gives me details on Rafi [Eitan], can only come from having under surveillance in the United States. That doesn't surprise me, and also makes sense to me that it's not a monolithic corrupt intelligence empire. When I worked at NSA, I found those people with high moral values. If there were awful things going on, I wasn't exposed to them. All very decent people there, given toward intellectual stuff. You couldn't corrupt all those people; it's impossible, too many nice people. But you can have an agency within an agency where not everybody knows what's going on."

The notes memorandum, in a section dated, January 18, 1994 went on to discuss information obtained by Hamilton from someone identified as "Witness 9," as follows: (excerpted) " --- A close friend, we have never found anything from that witness that has been inaccurate, an extremely high level source. The person said: 'First authorized use of PROMIS is on nuclear submarines.' I never had an inkling of that ... I didn't necessarily believe it; I'm in an insane asylum. Submarines have a heavy intelligence mission. What a computerized data base for that mission is, I don't know ... source said it's installed in every nuclear sub owned by the U.S. and Great Britain."

Hamilton had asked the high level witness to meet with anyone in Congress or government, or Elliot Richardson, Hamilton's legal counsel for the INSLAW case, but the witness declined with the following explanation: "It will hurt you; reason is people in CIA have spent a lot of money trying to get the evidence we need for INSLAW, maybe millions of dollars. There are a lot of people in that agency who don't like what's been going on; it's guerilla warfare."

Elliot Richardson was former Attorney General of the United States in 1973 under President Richard M. Nixon. His integrity became legendary when Nixon ordered him to fire Watergate Special Prosecutor Archibald Cox; Richardson resigned rather than fire the prosecutor. Prior to being appointed U.S. Attorney General, Richardson had served as Secretary of Defense under the Nixon administration.

While representing Inslaw on the PROMIS software case, Richardson wrote of Bill Hamilton's "witnesses:" "*Why in the world would this one group of informers ever have come together and cooked up all this stuff? How did they keep it consistent from day to day among themselves as to who told what to whom? There is a hell of a load of stuff they've told to various people, including staffers, journalists, the Hamiltons, me. The picture they paint is relatively coherent and consistent ... and then you add the stonewalling by the Department of Justice. I have never understood why.*"

Before Elliot Richardson could solve the mystery of the PROMIS software case, he died at 79, on December 31, 1999. Meanwhile, in early 1994, Garby Leon, who has a Ph.D. from Harvard, shared with Bill Hamilton (and me) a proposal that he and Jim Hougan had developed, to send to KPFK suggesting a one-hour weekly program centered upon telephone interviews, discussion, and possibly on-air call-ins from viewers. The focus of the program would be National Security issues. Hougan, a former Washington editor of *Harpers Magazine* and author of two books about the intelligence community – *Spooks* and *Secret Agenda*, his 1984 book about Watergate, aptly wrote to Garby: "*What very few historians or other people have grasped is that intelligence has been institutionalized in our country. When CIA was invented in 1947, we began to encrypt our history. The CIA charter says it shall be an 'engine of conspiracy' – that's why they have a $30 billion budget. But everything about it is unknowable, secret. I think a case can be made that a democracy is incompatible with an intelligence capacity of that size, breadth and clandestinity. How can we make any informed decisions politically if we can't know anything that's pertinent?*"

The proposed guest list for the KPFK program included several notables from Garby's writer's network: Jim Hougan, Bill Hamilton,

Norman Mailer, Julian Holmes, Jack Colhoun, Dick Russell, Robert Parry, Don Delillo, Noam Chomsky, Sarah McClendon, Seymour Hersh, Tom Blanton, James Rothstein, David Massey, and others less known.

One memorandum, entitled " Phone Calls – Log and Notes" sent to me from Garby Leon included excerpts from various conversations with Bill Hamilton (BH) in which Garby would individually ask BH a question, then later ask me the same question, then compare the two answers side-by-side in a memorandum. This was especially interesting to Garby because BH and I had only spoken to each other briefly in one phone conversation years before, so there was no "echo effect;" we had obtained information independent of each other.

For instance, Bill Hamilton confirmed to Garby that Michael Riconosciuto had requested that Hamilton check out Mike Abbell, formerly with the Department of Justice, and his relationship with Cali Cartel leaders. Hamilton: "MR told me to ask about the case of proposed extradition of a leader of one of the Cartels - three Spanish names - vis-à-vis Abbell, never extradited. He [MR] said we ought to find out what happened; I asked Danny, MR had emphasized it was very dangerous. Danny [said]: 'Oh, I can find out about that,' a few days before he died."

Equally interesting was Abbell's computer software expertise. Wrote Garby, quoting Bill Hamilton: "I [Hamilton] knew Mike Abbell in DOJ, before MR [Michael Riconosciuto] mentioned him to me, slightly. He's also a computer lover. Knew of him through MR. He'd been over here once; he was head of the Criminal Division Office of International Affairs. He was a computer software guy before he became a lawyer.

"Whenever they'd discuss big computer projects in those days, they'd bring him [Abbell] in. I think he was here once. *MR said that Abbell had been present at a meeting between him and Nichols in a Georgetown restaurant where Nichols handed him a satchel of cash."*

Mike Abbell had worked within the U.S. Department of Justice for 17 ½ years until his resignation in 1984. At that time he was Director of International Affairs, Criminal Division of the DOJ. *Newsweek* magazine published the story of his criminal indictment and outlined some history of his career below (article dated June 26, 1995), as follows: http://www.newsweek.com/id/117642

"A Turncoat in The Drug War" by Michael Isikoff, *Newsweek*, June 26, 1995: Lawyers: How A Nerdy Former Fed Sold Out To The Cali Cartel: (excerpted)

> --- He [Mike Abbell] joined Justice in 1967 and in 1978 was named to head the department's newly created Office of International Affairs, whose mission was coordinating with foreign governments on law-enforcement issues. The rise of big-time drug smuggling in the early 1980s raised the stakes. Abbell suddenly became a key player in Ronald Reagan's drug war--negotiating extraditions, among other legal business, with countries like Mexico. By some reports, he played his new role to the hilt. "He was always trying to be a big shot," a former DOJ official says. "But he did it in a clumsy way." Some colleagues, mindful of his appetite for foreign travel, mocked him as "the Ugly American." Others, deriding his habit of laughing at his own jokes, called him "the braying ass--" behind his back. In 1982, the department concluded that Abbell wasn't star material and demoted him to the number-two job in his own section. He endured it for a while, but quit in 1984 to go into private practice ---

During Mike Abbell's illustrious career within the DOJ, Edwin Meese was Counselor to President Ronald Reagan from 1981 – 1985, then served as the seventy-fifth Attorney General of the United States under President Reagan and Vice President George Bush from 1985 – 1988.

So both Mike Abbell and Edwin Meese simultaneously served in a legal capacity under President Reagan for at least three years, from 1981 to 1984. Clearly these lawyers must have had a close working relationship during that time span.

As noted, Abbell was considered a *computer nerd* by close associates, according to Bill Hamilton and *Newsweek*, and was involved with the Cali Cartel. Edwin Meese, during this *same* time span was legal Counselor to the President, and subsequently investigated for being implicated in the PROMIS software scandal in which the DOJ was accused of pirating a version of the software and selling it to foreign countries.

Within a 122-page investigative report, "The Inslaw Affair," published by the Committee on the Judiciary on September 10, 1992, former Attorney General Elliot Richardson, counsel to Inslaw at the time, stated on page 7 of the report that the circumstances involving the theft of the PROMIS software system constituted a "possible criminal conspiracy involving Mr. [Edwin] Meese, Judge[Lowell] Jensen, Dr. [Earl] Brian, and several current and former officials at the Department of Justice."

In the affidavit that Michael Riconosciuto sent to Bill Hamilton, dated March 21, 1991, reproduced in the above report, he claimed he modified the PROMIS software during 1983-1984, the same time span that Abbell and Meese were operating within the Reagan administration. Section 7 of the affidavit read as follows:

> In connection with my work for Wackenhut, I engaged in some software development and modification work in *1983 and 1984* on the proprietary PROMIS computer software product. The copy of PROMIS on which I worked came from the U.S. Department of Justice. Earl W. Brian made it available to me through Wackenhut after acquiring it from Peter Videnieks, who was then a Department of Justice contracting official with responsibility for the PROMIS software. I performed the modifications to PROMIS in Indio, California; Silver Spring, Maryland; and Miami, Florida.

Both Mike Abbell, a computer nerd within the DOJ, and Edwin Meese had direct access to the PROMIS software. In an article copyrighted in 1993 by *Wired* magazine, entitled "The Inslaw Octopus," author Richard Fricker wrote that Edwin Meese was well aware of the potential of PROMIS: (excerpt)

> ... Edwin Meese was apparently quite taken with PROMIS. He told an April 1981 gathering of prosecutors that PROMIS was 'one of the greatest opportunities for [law enforcement] success in the future.'
>
> In March 1982, Inslaw won a $9.6 million contract from the Justice Department to install the public domain version of PROMIS in 20 U.S. Attorney's offices as a pilot program. If successful, the company would install PROMIS in the remaining 74 federal prosecutors' offices around the country ---
>
> Designed as a case-management system for prosecutors, PROMIS has the ability to track people. 'Every use of PROMIS in the court system is tracking people, said Inslaw President Hamilton. 'You can rotate the file by case, defendant, arresting officer, judge, defense lawyer, and it's tracking all the names of all the people in all the cases.

> But the real power of PROMIS, according to Hamilton, is that with a staggering 570,000 lines of computer code, PROMIS can integrate innumerable databases without requiring any programming. In essence, PROMIS can turn blind data into information. And anyone in government will tell you that information, when wielded with finesse, begets power. Converted to use by intelligence agencies, as has been alleged in interviews by ex-CIA and Israeli Mossad agents, PROMIS can be a powerful tracking device capable of monitoring intelligence operatives, agents and targets, instead of legal cases.
>
> At the time of its inception, PROMIS was the most powerful program of its type. But a similar program, DALITE, was developed under another LEAA grant by D. Lowell Jensen, the Alameda County (Calif.) District Attorney. In the mid-1970's, the two programs vied for a lucrative Los Angeles County contract and Inslaw won out. (Early in his career, Ed Meese worked under Jensen at the Alameda County District Attorney's office. Jensen was later appointed to Meese's Justice Department during the Reagan presidency).

Garby Leon continued to mail his "Notes Memorandums" to my home in Idaho. In one page of typewritten notes, Garby noted that Bill Hamilton had talked to Robert Booth Nichols about a book that Nichols was doing on Danny Casolaro, allegedly in cooperation with Jonathan Littman. This, in a way, explained to me why Littman never wrote any newspaper articles about Casolaro or Nichols in the *San Francisco Chronicle*.

Hamilton added, "Nichols I think tape records all the calls to his house. He told me he had a hundred hours of talks with Casolaro. We wouldn't know how many hours. But if you record them all, you would. Nichols did the first draft on the book; Littman worked on it. They couldn't get a publisher. Nichols told me it's going to make a lot of people look like idiots, because C [Casolaro] knew what he was talking about, well informed, right on top of it. Littman said he wasn't free to talk about it – he never told me anything about it except he was supposed to be co-author.

... I wanted access to Danny's stuff to see what he was saying and I'd think his family would love to see it also. But Nichols always sends tapes overseas so USG can't get them ---

••••••••

Then in June 1994, I received a letter from Garby Leon, dated June 7, 1994, originating from Silver Pictures, Warner Bros., 4000

Warner Boulevard, Burbank, CA 91522. The letter noted that Tina Sinatra had read the draft manuscript of *The Last Circle* that I had sent to Garby in installments. The letter read as follows:

Dear Cheri, Thanks for the great letter and lovely enticements to travel to remote Idaho. Looks like you're reliving the lives of the pioneers ... must be a lot of fun, work, exhilaration, tiredness, the whole lot! But I envy your natural surrounding; it must be beautiful and I feel starved for nature here in sunny L.A. where only a dusty palm at the end of the street slakes one's thirst for the color green.

Quite a lot of stuff; I left a message at your old number about two weeks ago, fairly urgent because ... well, in short, I gave your book introduction to Tina Sinatra, in confidence of course. She's quite the fireball: she read it and instantly wanted to meet Robert B.N. [Robert Booth Nichols] see the Z. tape [Zapruder] and read his script right now! Hell I got the phone # from BH [Bill Hamilton] and she grabbed the phone and dialed it! All this was taking me by storm, but, well, you've spoken of having the proper back-up to go into this thing. After two seconds thought, I realized we couldn't be much safer than to go in with the chairman's [Frank Sinatra] daughter, possibly her attorney, and you and me.

"But the RBN number is out of service. You know, that annoying beep-beep-beep, the taped 'out of service' announcement, and nothing more. BH tried it too, and even called zokosky [Peter Zokosky], who thinks our topic is in Vietnam (and wife in Hawaii) doing business for [Ross] Perot. Will he return? No real answer.

So maybe that's all moot for the time being, but I wanted you to know you lit a fire here.

We're ready to roll.

We've got a big gun behind us.

She wants to meet you.

She also wants to read your book, whatever further pages you've written by now. She's thinking seriously about the possibility of setting it up. This means a potential TV or movie project for you.

If you have any more pages you can send, don't hesitate. It will remain completely confidential. It may result in good things.

I think you know me well enough by now to know that I don't make promises or suggestions that aren't serious, and I don't string anyone along. I'm ringing the alarm bell now.

--- Second arena: Bill Hamilton asked me to ask my 'investigator' (and I know he's not wise since he refers to you in the mascu-

> *line gender) about a couple of things, urgent now since the Hubbell report is finished (though Reno [Attorney General Janet Reno] may not get to it for a few months!) and because the Independent counsel law is going to be passed tomorrow, and Jack Brooks has promised a statement from the House floor, demanding an Independent Counsel for Inslaw. He's apparently immovable on this topic.*
>
> *Bill said with sharp irony, 'God bless him for doing his job!'*
>
> *Still it's a big breakthrough.*
>
> *He asked me to ask you if you have any of the following ...*

To summarize, essentially Hamilton wanted to know if (1) I had any documentary proof that the PROMIS software had been illegally sold to any US or foreign agency, (2) did I have anything on Jackson Stephens, Systematics, and/or Beverly Enterprises? Garby pointed out that Systematics is the largest vendor of banking software in the U.S. and has clients in 17 countries. Ben Menasche told Hamilton that they were selling PROMIS for the US/Israel intelligence.

Garby added that the connections were bizarre: "*Stephens owns 48% of Systematics. He bankrolled Bush, then loaned Clinton 3.5 mil (crucial to launch the presidential candidacy). Hubbell handled both Systematics and Beverly from the Rose Law firm. BH thinks he personally profited from illegal PROMIS sales.*

Bill ran this all by Cohen [John Cohen] last week, your pal, and he was fascinated, said this could be the missing link in the case, why the Clinton Adm. has stonewalled Inslaw.

This means PROMIS money may have funded Clinton's campaign.

It also may mean that Hubbell was installed at DOJ to keep Inslaw under control.

It also means we aren't crazy; Stephens is the link between Reagan/Meese/Bush and the Clinton gang. He plays both sides. Cute and sweet, but why not. Cheap at the price, a few hundred grand.

Garby then listed five banks that Bill Hamilton said bought PROMIS from Systematics, with Robert Maxwell allegedly representing Israel helping to negotiate the sales, as a joint venture. Most of the banks were swiss banks.

In conclusion, Garby wrote: "*Very best, Cheri; it's been an exciting time, and I hope you'll send us some (or all) of your work. There's a major producer interested, the kind of outcome I've been quietly working toward, in your behalf, for some time now. I'm excited. And, if you have anything for BH, or even a lead, let me know. Don't eat too many bass. Best to Roland, and to you, Garby Leon.*"

The Last Circle was never produced at Warner Brothers, because, reportedly, the "chairman's daughter," Tina Sinatra, showed it to her father, Frank Sinatra, "the chairman of the board," and the project fell into a very deep hole, probably the Labyrinth in my estimation. And, Tina was working on the movie "*The Manchurian Candidate*" at that time, which was probably why she was so intent on interviewing Robert Booth Nichols!

Nevertheless, I appreciated Garby's efforts on my behalf, and our friendship continued. By end of 1995 I had accumulated a three-inch thick file of communications from Garby relative to *his* findings on the Octopus. Garby was providing most of his material and mine to Julio Thompson, an attorney in the prestigious law firm of Tuttle and Taylor in Los Angeles. Julio was editor of *Law Review* and had an impressive background in law. Garby said Julio was placing all our mutual material on CD-ROMS and microfilm, for safekeeping.

The Internet's free-flow of information creates hope for solutions to the corruption.

— 19 —

The Internet

The Internet World-Wide Web was first introduced in 1991, but it was not until 1993 that the first proper web-browser, Mosaic, took the Internet by storm having been developed at the National Center for Supercomputer Applications (NCSA). Services were set up for domain registration and sites began turning up all over the Web, running on very basic HTML. The WWW was quickly the most popular service on the Internet.

Then sometime in 1995, the first large ISP's like AOL and CompuServe began offering Internet access to the masses.

On September 17, 1995 I subscribed to AOL and created the screen-name of Stormbird8@AOL.com. I created the name Stormbird from the poem *The Ancient Mariner*, published in 1798. Essentially, in ancient times, when a mariner on a long sea voyage observed a seabird landing on his ship, he considered it *a warning of a coming storm*, and the seabird theoretically led the crew to safer waters, thus they were called "stormbirds." The number "8," I read somewhere, is the number of Christianity, the Father and Son connected in two never-ending circles.

I thus continued peddling *The Last Circle* dog and pony show under the name of my deceased sister, Carol Marshall, to people whom I believed had integrity and commitment to making the world a better place to live. My sister had been a victim, indirectly, of the Octopus, and I was motivated to put forth whatever resistance I could to this growing criminal enterprise.

For this reason, I faxed a two-page letter to Rep. Maxine Waters on September 25, 1996 at the Cannon House Office Building in Washington D.C. This was one month after Gary Webb's expose,

"The Dark Alliance," was published [August 22, 1996] in the *San Jose Mercury News* alleging that the CIA sold tons of cocaine to street gangs in South-central Los Angeles and funneled millions in profits to a CIA-run guerrilla army in Nicaragua. It was reported that Rep. Waters was investigating these claims and I felt she had the capability and interest to digest the complexities of the material I had acquired, and I wanted the documents entered into the Congressional Record while hearings were taking place.

On September 27th I subsequently faxed documents to Joseph Lee, assistant at her office, followed up with hard copies sent Priority Mail, and was put in touch with Rep. Donald Payne. Because of the complexities of the material, I was asked to find a journalist who could condense the story into a newspaper article, then send a copy of that article immediately to Maxine Waters.

I was staying in Post Falls, Idaho at that time, so I contacted David Bond, a journalist who worked for the *Coeur d'Alene Press* in Idaho. Bond reviewed the draft manuscript and supporting documents, but after reading the FBI wire tap summaries naming organized crime figures in collusion with intelligence operatives and Reagan administration officials, he decided he needed "backup" to write the story.

On October 10, 1996 I received an e-mail from Bond inviting me and my husband to meet with him and his "Green Beret buddy" at the Thai Café on the Northwest corner of Appleway and Highway 95. At the meeting on Friday, my husband, Roland, and I were introduced to Bruce Bell, a former Green Beret (Special Forces) who said he was deeply involved in private investigations with Senator John McCain, attorney James H. Warner, and Bob Dole. James Warner was former Senate Counsel, later the Assistant General Counsel for the NRA (National Rifle Association). Bell noted during conversation that John McCain and James Warner had shared adjacent POW cells at the "Hanoi Hilton" in Vietnam for approximately 5½ years.

Bruce Bell, at that time working as comptroller at Olympic Arms in Olympia, Washington, requested I hand over the manuscript and explained that it would be sent to his brother who worked for the CIA in Langley, VA. The manuscript would also be sent to Senator John McCain, James Warner and Bob Dole.

When Bell had mentioned his brother in the CIA, my self-preservation instincts kicked in and I terminated the meeting. The idea of turning the manuscript over to an arms manufacturer with a brother in the CIA seemed ludicrous. My husband, Roland, had served in the U.S. Marine Corp., Charlie Company, 1st Battalion, 1st Marines, 3rd Marine Division called the "Tip of the Spear" in those days. During 1961-1962, he had served in the special weapons RECON platoon in Cambodia, in an advisors and information gathering unit, so he had a pretty good idea of the underlying issues plausibly related to Bruce Bell and the CIA.

I later e-mailed David Bond that the whole thing was off, but I wanted to remain friends with him. I said I was going to put the manuscript on the Internet because a friend had received an offer from (name withheld) saying they would provide me with a free homepage to get the manuscript out. (My friend had become alarmed at the CIA connection at the Thai Café meeting).

On October 15, 1996 I received a forwarded e-mail from David Bond, originating from Bruce Bell as follows:

> Talked to DC – they can guarantee that she will be anonymous and also an immediate Congressional inquiry (which is in progress quietly). They think she would be foolish to put on Internet for number of reasons we discussed ---.

Basically Bruce Bell's group was concerned that the manuscript would not be taken seriously, considered just another anti-government conspiracy, if it was placed on the Internet. I responded directly to Bruce Bell about concerns that the manuscript might fall into the wrong hands in D.C.

On October 24th, he wrote back that he had forwarded information about my investigation to his people, presumably John McCain, James Warner, et al. He wrote:

> I think your concerns are valid and approach is reasonable. They are among the few seriously honorable people left and I trust them with my life (and have before). Will keep you posted. The level of corruption and emphasis on the ends justifying the means attitude is beginning to astound even me. Fortunately, we peasants now have our own e-mail and fax networks, and the mushrooms can't hide too well anymore. Take care ---

Again on October 24, 1996, I received a follow-up transmission from Bruce Bell in which he wrote:

> Spoke with man in DC. He can guarantee to do whatever you want. He is an attorney [James Warner] and therefore anything that comes to him as a cutout means he is able to invoke privilege vis-à-vis access to you, me, etc. Can get immediately all matl's en masse to launch investigation with committee and/or Congressperson (Senate or House) of your choice. He is very familiar with Inslaw, Fostergate, Casolaro, Mena, etc., and participation on both sides of aisle. He spent 6 years in the cell next door to John McCain and would be willing to call and discuss with you ---

In the above transmission, Bruce Bell gave a code-name that would be used by any of his friends who called me:

> Anyone who uses my name, etc., will give you code-name [withheld here] in Vietnamese, and if they do not know me, and very well for lots of years, they will not have this word in reference to me and do not talk to them. Perhaps these procedures will not be necessary and someday we can all laugh about it, but better safe than sorry ---

On October 25, 1996, I received a transmission from Bruce Bell inviting me to join him and his friends in a private chat room on the Internet at a prearranged time. I got an idea of what would be discussed in the chatroom by what he wrote in the e-mail, as follows: (excerpted)

> --- If you have been following events in Clinton's administration closely, I will give you a scenario to think about. Willie re-elected Nov. 5, Electoral College does not vote until Jan. 1. In between, wife indicted, he faces possible impeachment, while Republicans in control of Congress. Things could get very messy in a hurry! Even to point of declaring constitutional crisis and Willie invokes national emergency powers passed by Reagan. Just something to think about I suppose ---.

Bruce Bell used his code name in the chat room, and informed me that if I found myself in any danger, I could enter a special code word [withheld here] used within this Special Forces group when someone is in trouble or in danger. He said that codeword, *would trigger immediate disposition by others in the vicinity or region of the sender.*

A few other e-mail transmissions arrived, then on October 26, 1996, I received an e-mail directly from James Warner noting that he had attempted to reach me by phone, and providing me with phone numbers at his home and office. I was particularly interested in this portion of his e-mail:

> *I have a contact in the office of the member of Congress to whom you had addressed your draft letter.* The member of Congress is eager to receive whatever you may wish to transmit. I am an attorney, licensed in Michigan, and any communications with me are subject to the attorney client privilege. Please let me know how you wish to proceed. I look forward to hearing from you, and am eager to assist. James H. Warner.

During subsequent phone conversations, James Warner did not provide the name of the individual in "the office of the member of Congress [presumably Maxine Waters] to whom I had addressed my draft letter," though he talked about his relationship with John McCain, their history together, and what they were attempting to achieve.

I was becoming frustrated by all the secrecy at the Congressional level, and let off some steam in a letter to all concerned, then apologized later. Bruce Bell responded patiently:

> No problem – in 1st Cav our motto was to get pissed on, pissed off, and then continue mission (for what that is worth). If you ever want to read some interesting history, look up the first LRP units in Vietnam and you will know what I am talking about.

Some further e-mails indicated the group's extraordinary concern for security:

> "Had talk with Jim [James Warner] – he is determined this country will not become another Mexico [drugs] – he also knows much of the story, how deep it goes, but needs documents, etc. that you are working on – we both agree on that. When I get what you are working on – overnight copies will go to him, me, 2 of my close people from way back, and 2 of his [McCain and ?] for safekeeping. You keep copy and give one to db. Our security lies in knowing that others have it and have ability to disclose if something happens. If, for some reason, you think there are real difficulties, send or say words [code word withheld]. This will stop all contact until you get ahold of me or Jim. If no word in reasonable

> amount of time (24-48 hrs?), then this will trigger immediate disposition of others. I-Net should be last resort, but have ready to go on it if needed. Let me know what you think."

On November 5th, Bruce Bell notified me that the manuscript and documents had been received:

> Catalogs received by all and being perused intently. Expect some large orders and will keep you posted. Thanks.

On November 10th, he followed up with:

> Great catalog – will be ordering soon. Response so far has been that people want to place orders, but are still absorbing the extent of the product line. Lots of stuff, so don't fret. Kinda a learning curve thing due to technical nature of product. Distributors have to market it correctly and hit market running.

At this same time, in early November 1996, I had been keeping some of my friends apprised of the above transactions. One friend, who expressed deep concerns that the manuscript was allegedly floating around a Congressional office in Washington D.C., and no Congressperson had made contact with me to date, felt I was a sitting duck waiting for the hunter to arrive. He even wanted to stay at my home to guard me. (My husband worked during the day and couldn't stay home).

I laughed at that. I envisioned the Special Forces veterans bivouacked around my home, along with my friends, and the entire middle-class neighborhood where I lived becoming a secret armed military encampment with everyone using Vietnamese code-names.

Realistically, I didn't feel the need for extravagant security measures, but appreciated Bruce Bell and James Warner's (and my friend's) concerns. They were all true gentlemen, and kindly, despite their affinity for guns. (At that time, James H. Warner was the Assistant General Counsel for the NRA [National Rifle Association], and Bruce Bell worked for Olympic Arms, an arms manufacturing company).

••••••••

Unknown to me at that time, however, my friend had sent a copy of the first 15 chapters of *The Last Circle* draft to [name withheld] at Cornell University. He wanted someone with access to an Internet website to have a copy.

On November 20, 1996 I received an e-mail from the individual at Cornell noting:

> I think you have an excellent piece of journalism here – so good in fact that my loved ones around me do not want me connected directly with its publication – and so I am going to rely on a distributed group to release it ---

He added that his group's preliminary assessment of the manuscript was as follows:

> --- If it is false, we could get sued, if it is true we could get killed, and there is certainly enough information here for any good journalist to verify everything and make a big difference in the affairs of the nation and the world – or so we all hope.

The Cornell webmaster offered to place the manuscript on the Internet in such a way that if it was shut down at the university, it would be automatically re-created elsewhere, within hours.

By then, I still had not heard from anyone in Congress. My friend wrote an e-mail on November 20 imploring me to authorize publication on the Internet:

> Cheri, there are two compelling reasons to put this on the Internet. You are responsible for this truth coming out. The scarier it is, the more important it is. Please believe me, if you try to hide from this, they're going to get you. They always go after rabbits – always. That's the key here. Get it on the Internet, wait for response and then hold a press conference. Be cheerful, fatalistic and up-front. Smile and say they're going to try to kill you – name names and put the burden on them! Safety (relative) lies in publicity – always!

I didn't want any publicity. But I had lost faith in Congress to accomplish anything of value with respect to my manuscript, or the issues therein.

On December 7, 1996 I received a transmission emanating from Cornell University notifying me that *The Last Circle* was now on the web at www.lycaeum.org/books/books/last_circle/0.htm

As the author of the manuscript, I had used the pseudonym of Carol Marshall, in honor of my deceased sister who would have wanted to see this book in print.

Sean McDade, RCMP

— 20 —

Enter RCMP

It was really Danny Casolaro's story, he had died trying to write it. On August 10, 1991, his body had been found in a blood-filled bathtub by a maid at the Martinsburg Sheraton Hotel in West Virginia. Nine years later, whether his death was murder or suicide, it was still a mystery and an outrage.

When I placed *The Last Circle* on the Internet, I'd had no idea there was a last circle represented in Dante's *Inferno*, but in retrospect it seems fitting. In 1306 A.D., Dante poeticized nine circles, the ninth being the last level before the final descent into Hell. "The last circle housed those souls who had been traitors to their country, their friends, and their Lords."

This indeed was Danny's "Octopus," a CIA 'Old Boy' network that had begun working together in the 1950's around the Albania covert operations. These men had gotten into the illegal gun and drug trade back then and had continued in that business ever since.

People didn't just read the Octopus story, they participated in it, like pawns being moved across a game board by a powerful and deadly chess-master. Over a span of years, some survived, others got accidented, suicided, or just plain murdered, but anyone could jump on and off at will. Only those who survived on the board longest, knew the story best. Danny was the first investigator to enter the labyrinth, but not the last.

In January 2000 the story came back to haunt again, like some thorny bottom-feeder, stealthily sucking its prey into a cavernous labyrinth, then settling back in the sand and muck to await the next intruder.

The next intruder's presence on the board was announced in the form of a clandestine e-mail, dated January 19, 2000, addressed to

Stormbird8@aol.com from "Dear Hunter." It read as follows: "Good afternoon. I'm looking to contact Carol (Cherie) regarding a matter that has surfaced in the past. If this e-mail account is still active, please reply and I will in turn forward a Canadian phone number and explain my position and reason for request." The e-mail came from simorp@yahoo.com., which was actually PROMIS spelled backwards. And of course Cherie means dear or dearest in French.

Dear Hunter subsequently identified himself as Sean McDade of the National Security Section of the Royal Canadian Mounted Police (RCMP). During our first phone conversation on January 24, McDade explained he was investigating allegations that a stolen version of the PROMIS software was in use by RCMP and a back-door or Trojan Horse may have been installed allowing the United States and Israel to eavesdrop on Canadian intelligence secrets.

I asked McDade what he wanted from me? The PROMIS software [Prosecutor's Management Information System] was ancient history, a dinosaur by today's standards, though the technology had been revolutionary when it was developed - and it was the forerunner of all the sophisticated systems in use today.

He referred to *The Last Circle* on the Internet (which contained only 15 first-draft chapters). One aspect of the manuscript referred to the theft of PROMIS in the early 1980's by employees of the U.S. Department of Justice (DOJ). The software had been the center of a major scandal a decade ago when Bill and Nancy Hamilton, owners of Inslaw Inc., the company that developed PROMIS, alleged the U.S. government had stolen their software and pedalled pirated versions to intelligence agencies around the world.

McDade noted he had inadvertently stumbled upon a paper-trail leading to Strategic Software Company in Cambridge, Massachusetts which reportedly facilitated the sale of PROMIS to Israel and possibly the RCMP. He'd contacted Massimo Grimaldi, formerly associated with Strategic Software, and learned the CIA also purchased all its software from this now defunct company.

I explained to McDade I had obtained a vast accumulation of material on covert operations and scientific technology from a trailer in the Mojave Desert near Death Valley in 1992. The documents had been stashed at this secret location for years by Michael Riconosciuto [pronounced Ric-ono-shooto], the scientist who allegedly installed the back door in PROMIS. Seven days after sending an affidavit to Bill Hamilton claiming he'd modified the software, Riconosciuto was arrested for operating a methamphetamine lab in Tacoma, Washington. Ironically, Riconosciuto had contacted Hamilton to exonerate himself and obtain immunity from Hamilton's lawsuit against the DOJ [for pirating the software], but the DOJ retaliated by arresting him.

No official investigator to date had actually seen the boxes containing twenty-years of Riconosciuto's records, but numerous agents had followed the same trail and their findings had been suppressed at the highest level of government. McDade was hot to see the documents, but I knew he would be opening a Pandora's Box where spooks climbed out of the woodwork, the labyrinth as I called it, where he would meet real life players in Dungeons and Dragons, and the stakes were high. Some jumped off the board and survived, others died gruesome deaths.

McDade said he'd been communicating with Sue Todd, a homicide detective in Hercules, California, who was investigating the execution-style murder of Neal Abernathy and his 12-year-old son, Brenden, in Hercules on February 19, 1997. He'd joined forces with her in 1999 when a Canadian source informed him that Neal Abernathy was murdered because he was holding papers belonging to Riconosciuto.

I told McDade I didn't believe that. Todd had contacted me years before, in 1997, after reading *The Last Circle*, and I'd told her the same thing. The evidence connecting Riconosciuto to Abernathy just didn't hold water. But McDade was not dissuaded. He and Sue Todd arrived at my home at 12 noon on February 19, 2000, the third anniversary of the Abernathy homicides.

They looked good together. It was apparent they'd melded, a phenomenon investigators experience, regardless of gender, when they're focused intensively on a case of this magnitude. In other words, they lose the egos. McDade, 33, was a big, stalwart Mountie with an incongruous baby-face and soft eyes. He seemed quiet and introspective, displaying what Americans characteristically refer to as British decorum, but in reality he was just a gentleman through and through. I liked his accent.

Todd was petite, animated, blond and elegant. She looked like she belonged at a country club social. Her entire demeanor was feminine and un-cop-like, and it put me instantly at ease. I would subsequently learn that persona belied the fact that she was a relentless investigator who would swim through the federal bureaucracy like a shark in her obsession to catch the killer of the Abernathys.

I had invited a friend, J.M., to attend the meeting with McDade and Todd that day. I felt the need to have a witness to the meeting besides myself, and I was glad he had come. We sat at the dining room table, getting acquainted, sipping coffee. I had no idea where this was going. I was used to asking questions, not answering them, I'd jumped off the board when the manuscript hit the Internet, so I had nothing new to offer --- or so I thought. I relaxed and waited to hear why McDade had flown in from Canada? He began to give some background on his investigation ---

In December 1999, a meeting was held at the Los Alamos facility in New Mexico which was attended by the heads of the intelligence divisions of the U.S. (CIA), Britain (M16), Israel (Mossad) and CSIS (Canadian equivalent of the CIA). The topic of discussion was labeled "Unique Elements," relative to upcoming Y2K computer problems. The meeting had been called by M16 after a glitch was found in the British computer system resulting in the loss of 6-months of "historical case data." McDade's unnamed source in CSIS confided to him that information surfaced during this meeting suggesting all four allied countries shared the same computer system, possibly PROMIS, because PROMIS was the only system developed years ago which could be shared mutually by these allies.

Additionally, McDade offered a scenario: "The Israeli Mossad may have modified the original PROMIS modification, or back door, so it became a 'two-way' back door allowing the Israelis to access top U.S. weapons secrets at Los Alamos and other installations." He hinted through innuendo that the Israelis may now possess all the nuclear secrets of the United States.

I stared at McDade in undisguised amazement. In a space of fifteen minutes I had been transported into international espionage and stolen nuclear secrets at Los Alamos!

I asked, "What do you plan to do with this information?"

McDade hesitated, eyes flickering briefly at Sue Todd. She was watching him cautiously. He didn't answer my question, which in the months to come, I would ask many times. As if finishing a thought he said, "The Jonathan Pollard case is insignificant by comparison to this current crisis. The Israelis also secretly sold U.S. AWAC secrets to the Japanese."

I remembered that Pollard, an Israeli, was serving time in prison for stealing U.S. secrets and it had almost developed into an international incident. McDade's expression was searching, but otherwise devoid of expression. His demeanor was calm, reassuring, but a worm of doubt crawled to the frontal lobe of my brain. Maybe McDade was not from RCMP, maybe he was a spook. I made a mental note to obtain further credentials from him. I nodded, encouraging him to continue.

When he spoke again, it was in the tone of an idle academic remark. "High ranking Canadian government officials may have lied about the purchase of the PROMIS software when it was originally investigated in the early 1990's."

I asked, "You mean when the Inslaw case was being investigated?"

He said, "Yes."

"Who are you investigating, the U.S. officials who stole it, or the Canadian officials who bought it? Did someone in RCMP buy it?

His reaction was swift. "Oh, no, no. No one in RCMP bought it. I'm investigating Canadian government people outside of RCMP, very high level people. They're no longer in office." He said he had several sources in Canada cooperating with his investigation, some of which were U.S. citizens and some were Israelis.

I asked who had authorized this investigation? Did the Prime Minister know about it? He stressed that only the national security section of RCMP knew about the investigation, not CSIS [Canadian Security Intelligence Service], and not any of the political branches.

"How high up did you get authorization at RCMP?"

There was no hesitation to answer these questions. "Oh, I have authorization at the highest level of RCMP, but no one else knows about it." It was reassuring to have an American cop present, for the first time I understood why he brought Todd. She knew about it, so that made it okay --- I hoped.

A sparkle of certainty was too swift to be identified, but it was clear he was asserting the full authority of his agency when he reported, almost cheerfully: "The details of my findings in Canada could cause a major scandal in both Canada and the U.S. If my investigation is successful, it could cause the entire U.S. Republican

Party to be dismantled, and more than one presidential administration will be exposed for their knowledge of this."

He didn't say for their knowledge of "what?" And actually at that moment, I didn't think to ask. The implications were confounding. Were we really talking about PROMIS software here? This was an election year. Maybe RCMP had a political agenda. Maybe they didn't like the Republicans, or the Israelis. The room was deadly silent. The dog was yapping in the back yard, rain clouds had parted outside allowing sunlight to filter through the potted tree in front of the window. Everything seemed normal --- but it wasn't. The dining room and its occupants were being sucked through some ethereal vortex into another dimension. At any moment someone would say, "Beam me up Scotty." Every instinct I had developed from years of investigative experience told me something was amiss here. For the time being there was nothing left to do but play it out.

I responded as if playing a part on cue, biting back my uneasiness, "Well, I know very little about the PROMIS software theft, my investigation focused on peripheral criminal activities of the parties involved. The cast of characters is incredible. Have you familiarized yourself with these guys?"

He pulled a bound copy of *The Last Circle* printed off the Internet from his briefcase, indicating he knew the characters. The pages of interest were identified with brightly colored tabs. It was apparent he had spent time with the manuscript. It made me recall his U.S. predecessors and the way this case had ransacked their lives. I inquired, "Have you interviewed any of the law enforcement agents who investigated this case?"

He looked away, debating something in his mind. The muscles in his face constricted briefly. Then he confided that he had obtained a U.S. Customs report, code-named the "Indo-China" project, which included an internal affairs investigation of Peter Videnieks, a former Customs specialist contracted by the DOJ to oversee the development of PROMIS at Inslaw in the early 1980's.

It was common knowledge that Videnieks administered the Inslaw contract for the DOJ. The DOJ, aware that its case management system was in dire need of automation, had funded Inslaw to develop PROMIS. Designed as a case-management software for federal prosecutors nationwide, PROMIS had the ability to combine disparate databases, and track people by their involvement with the legal system. Bill Hamilton, owner of Inslaw, subsequently sued the DOJ, claiming the Justice Department modified PROMIS to monitor intelligence operations, agents and targets, instead of legal cases.

McDade would not describe details of the Indo-China investigation, or how he obtained the report, but stated that certain high-ranking officials under investigation along with anti-narcotics and anti-organized crime strike force members were allegedly found to be involved in illegal drug-related activity during this investigation.

I nearly jumped out of my seat. This confirmed everything I had learned in my investigation! It was of immense importance! I'd always believed, and indeed all the evidence pointed to the use of PROMIS for money laundering and drug trafficking, but no one had ever published it! And amazingly, all the official investigators connected with the Inslaw case had suspected the same thing, but their findings had been suppressed too.

No matter how hard I pried, I couldn't get McDade to discuss the Indo-China project further. Nevertheless, it was a momentous turning point. I realized I was hooked again, and had just jumped back on the board.

I asked McDade, "Have you talked to Scott Lawrence about this?" Lawrence had conducted a U.S. Customs internal affairs investigation of Videnieks in the early 1990's. In fact he had come to my home on February 5, 1993 from Boston to obtain an affidavit I had provided to John Cohen, lead investigator for the House Judiciary Committee on Inslaw, in October 1992. The 17-page affidavit, named "Vortex," had contained information from Michael Riconosciuto on the use of PROMIS to launder drug money through Swift-Chips, the Clearing House Inter-bank Payment System. Riconosciuto also claimed an associate, Robert Booth Nichols, paid a former DOJ official, $50,000 to "crowbar" the extradition of Cali Cartel leaders Gilbert and Miguel Rodriguez and Jose Londono into the U.S. for prosecution. Noted Riconosciuto, "Bob Nichols told me that it was necessary to 'crowbar' the investigation because they were 'intelligence people.'" Additionally, Riconosciuto described related CIA operations in the United States, Lebanon, Latin America, and Afghanistan, all under the auspices of U.S. government officials.

McDade looked surprised, as if he had no conception of the depth of the issue confronting him, and a hint of dread, as if subliminally he had always had full knowledge of it. At this juncture, we were both wondering who the other one was? He couldn't grasp how I knew of this, and I couldn't understand what a National Security investigator from RCMP was doing in my home? Despite this discomfiture, it was apparent everyone at the table felt an odd, lighthearted self-confidence, as if we had glimpsed a trail destined to lead us to the truth. McDade further explained that he had located numerous banks around the world which had been used by U.S. officials to launder money from the sale of the PROMIS software, but also noted there had been numerous deaths associated with this case, many of them still unsolved.

I chose not to discuss the deaths at this first meeting because it might have added a dimension they weren't ready to address. Sue sat silent and remote, finding refuge in private thoughts. Sean sat staring at a page in the manuscript long after he had finished reading it. It was a relief when he announced, "let's get to work."

We stood inside my tiny office observing several boxes of documents, perhaps 6,000 copies in all. It is noteworthy that after the RCMP probe ended, eight months later, I would have 10 boxes of documents. Meanwhile, the first day was spent preliminarily reviewing the files; I explained the contents, outlining the cast of characters and their inter-locking connections to each other, the Mob and the U.S. government. They hadn't actually read the files yet, but they listened, often eyeing each other, clearly realizing for the first time that their investigation had expanded beyond the borders of PROMIS. At the same time, they were still in cop mode, serious, reserved, unresponsive to what I was saying. I smiled wryly, the worm had turned. Their investigative instincts were being assaulted, just as mine had been at the dining-room table a few hours earlier. I was glad they were suspicious, I wanted them to scrutinize the facts as subjectively as they could.

In spite of this, their actions gave them away. Sean wouldn't let me put any of the files away, inadvertently taking them from my hands and piling them next to the copy machine. Sue rummaged through them as fast as he could stack them. By the end of the day they had hundreds of files scattered all over the office.

On day two, February 20, they arrived at 7:00 A.M. and began copying everything in the boxes, including handwritten notes. On the wall above the copy machine was an antiquated Marine Corps poster depicting a grizzled Marine drill instructor nose-to-nose with a young recruit at boot camp. The caption read, "We don't promise you a rose garden." Sean kept looking at the poster, as if it held a message. It would be a day none of us would forget. Though we didn't know it then, we would embark on a journey in the months to come that would take us into the darkest depths of the labyrinth.

I live three miles from the Pacific Ocean so the weather is generally mild, but on that day the wind howled, rain beat on the windows and patio furniture flew across the back yard. My office was claustrophobic with three people jammed in it, so I kept the window open for air, despite the rain splashing on the windowsill.

Sean stood at the copy machine, hour after hour, while Sue sat on the couch painstakingly reviewing the files. At first they rarely spoke except to ask questions, mostly about the chronology of events or details of the intricate corporate web developed by our cast of characters over a twenty-year time span. One corporation, First Intercontinental Development Corporation (FIDCO), had played a role in funneling $3 billion dollars to Amin Gamayel, the president of Lebanon in 1983. The Board of Directors of FIDCO included Michael A. McManus, then Assistant to the President at the White House; Robert A. Maheu, former CEO for Howard Hughes Nevada Operations; Clint W. Murchison, Jr., owner of the Dallas Cowboys NFL football team; George Pender; Glen Shockley and Robert Booth Nichols, both known CIA operatives; and other notables in the shadow government.

A letter dated June 29, 1983 written on White House stationary from Michael McManus to George Pender, president of FIDCO, noted FIDCO had a considerable role to offer in the massive financial participation being made available to the government of Lebanon for the re-building of the cities of Damour and Alkhyam. Pender then wrote President Amin Gamayel on July 12, 1983 asking him to respond to this offer via telex at 652483 RBN [Robert Booth Nichols] ASSOC LSA. The Arab Bank Limited in Amman, Jordan responded in November 1983 that it would be "no problem to accept the US$ three billion or more" at their bank. It was signed by Abdul Majeed Shoman, Chairman/ General Manager. To my knowledge no "reconstruction" (funded by FIDCO) ever took place in Lebanon. Michael Riconosciuto had said it was a cover for a DEA/CIA drug –sting operation in Lebanon. Only a Congressional investigation could determine what the US$ three billion dollars was actually used for.

In 1981 Robert Booth Nichols had been partners with Michael Riconosciuto in Meridian Arms which played a role in supplying arms to the Nicaraguan Contras. But all of this would become clear to the investigators in the months to come as the story unfolded.

By noon we had transformed into a team, working purposefully as investigators do when they're engrossed in a case. I had shown them my private investigator's credentials and by now they had acknowledged the quality of the documents. But I wondered why they were intently reading and copying documents that had nothing to do with PROMIS?

I broke to make sandwiches, but they were too intent to eat in the dining room, preferring to eat as they worked. As I handed them turkey sandwiches, I noticed for the first time the condition of the office. They were both young and I had somewhat adopted them by then, so I felt compelled to chuckle at the trust they now displayed. They had stripped their holstered guns from their bodies and the guns were lying conspicuously on the table and the couch as they read scattered stacks of files and copies.

As the day wore on, the trajectory of their emotions became more pronounced. At one point, they used the phone to call their respective supervisors in Canada and Hercules to obtain permission to cancel their plane flights and stay another day. Sean had found handwritten notes written by Michael Riconosciuto before his arrest which listed Rafi Eitan's phone number. Eitan was a former Israeli intelligence officer, written up in *Gideon's Spies* by Gordon Thomas, who asserted that he oversaw the installation of the pirated PROMIS software into Israeli computer systems. Other notes on the same page referred to "Ackerman," a business partner of the very same former DOJ official, Mike Abbell, whom Riconosciuto had connected to the Cali Cartel.

One handwritten note referred to the Canadian Communications Branch of the National Resource Council, along with cryptic references to a command headquarters center in Cheltenham, England, the Australian Defense Sig. Div., MI6 and some undecipherable computer language. Other notes named banks where monies were presumably deposited, as well as names of connecting individuals involved in drug trafficking and money laundering which subsequently surfaced in FBI wire tap summaries involving Mob penetrations into MCA Corporation. These notes had been buried undisturbed in a "miscellaneous" file since 1992.

Sean stood galvanized at the copy machine, unspoken thoughts narrowing his eyes, unconsciously gripping the "notes" file. I grabbed a pad of sticky notes and began placing them on the notes he had suddenly become so possessive of. I wasn't going to be left out of the loop any longer. "Explain to me, Sean, what's the significance of these notes?"

He wanted to hold back, but his hesitation broke in a blast of shifted perspective: "The Canadian branch mentioned in Riconoscuito's notes is the same entity that purchased PROMIS for RCMP and CSIS! No one could have known that except me, no one, yet here it is in these notes!" he lamented. He was thousands of miles from home, standing in an obscure office in Southern California, gripping a file of notes that had been innocuously buried for eight years. I sympathized with his confusion, but the revelation was anticlimactic for me. Sue Todd explained it was standard police procedure to attempt to disprove evidence before it was accepted as truth. In fact, they had come to "disprove" the documents in *The Last Circle*, but instead everything they found was valid. This was disconcerting to them, clearly he'd been distracted by the find. Ironically, until Sean's arrival, I'd had no understanding of their significance anyway.

I decided it was time to see Sean's credentials. He'd handed me a card when he arrived, but that didn't suffice anymore. I was about to say, "Hey, Sean, we gotta talk," when I noticed Sue's hand had begun to tremble, yet she was wearing a jacket. She was holding a letter dated January 27, 1999 written by Riconosciuto from Coleman prison to a scientist at Stanford University outlining some theories on cryptographic applications. Riconosciuto had once been dubbed a "potential national resource" by Dr. Harry Fair, an Army scientist at Picatinny Arsenal in Dover, New Jersey.

Dr. Fair was mentioned in a Wackenhut letter, which outlined a May 1981 meeting between Riconosciuto and Dr. Fair at ARRADCOM (U.S. Army Armament Research & Development Command, Large Caliber Weapons Systems Laboratory). Riconosciuto had conducted an extensive and highly technical theoretical blackboard exercise on a Railgun. Dr. Fair, who was Chief of the Propulsion Technical and Applied Sciences Division at ARRADCOM, had commented that he was extremely impressed with Riconosciuto's scientific and technical knowledge of weapons systems, and thus termed him a "potential national resource" to Vice President Frye.

I really hadn't discussed Riconosciuto in depth with the investigators yet; we would get to that soon. This would take several pots of coffee and I didn't want to introduce them to the labyrinth until they were ready to deal with it. However, it appeared they had found it all by themselves. I emphasized that spooks abound in Riconosciuto's realm, they flocked around him like bats in the night, and it was necessary to screen the smoke and mirrors from the truth.

I asked Sue what she had found that interested her? Within Riconosciuto's January 1999 sixteen-page letter was mention of Neal Abernathy. I had never actually read the 16-page letter in its entirety before. It contained pages and pages of scientific jargon, beyond my ability to understand. An obscure paragraph on page 6 mentioned that Neal Abernathy was attempting to help Riconosciuto on his case, and had possession of some of his files and records.

Sue left the office and stood outside on the patio, clutching her coat at the collar. I followed her outside. The wind and rain immobilized us against the wall, shocked into silence by the maelstrom. I waited, but she made no move to explain, eyes still haunted by the memory of something I couldn't fathom.

None of us smoked then, but I asked if she wanted a cigarette? There had to be a pack of my husband's cigarettes lying around somewhere. At first she said no, then changed her mind and accepted a cigarette. We lit up and smoked silently together. I finally asked why the letter had significance? The letter proved nothing, it had been written two years after the Abernathy homicides. She explained that something Riconosciuto wrote about Abernathy corroborated "other sources." She couldn't discuss the details, but it had something to do with an organization called "The Company." It had rattled her to find this after three years of investigation. She described the death scene of a 12-year-old boy shot in the head by a killer so remorseless that he probably executed the son while the father watched. The memory of it haunted her.

I realized these two investigators were absorbing the full brunt of the "story" in one day, no wonder they were surprised. It had taken me years to assimilate it, slowly.

Sean peered around the corner of the patio door, undecided whether to intrude or join us, as if we'd been caught smoking in the girl's restroom. But he surprised us and asked for a cigarette. The three of us "non-smokers" huddled, smoking and de-stressing in the windblown patio. An unspoken prescience passed between us that destiny had placed us together that day, and we would share many hours in the months to come unraveling the mystery of the labyrinth.

On the day they left, February 21, I snapped some photos of them in the dining room to prove they'd actually been there. I also asked Sean for validation of his credentials and the RCMP investigation. He was hauling approximately 6,000 documents back to Canada and I still didn't have proof of who he was or who authorized him to be here, other than his business card. I knew he had 6,000 copies because Sue had purchased an ink cartridge at Office Depot for my Cannon copier and it produces 3,000 copies per cartridge. They used two cartridges. She had told him to cough up the credit card, winking at me, and reminding him that he had an "unlimited" expense account for this trip, up to $100,000!

By then Sean was so pleased with what he had in the satchel, he decided to trust me. Sue was stunned when he handed me a classified authorization form signed by the heads of OIC "A" Division - RCMP and OIC Special Projects – ANSIS, in Canada. One section of the form pertained specifically to my documents, excerpted as follows: " ... The investigator believes that the documents may also corroborate information related to an investigation being conducted in Canada by the RCMP, National Security Investigations Section, under Project 'ABBREVIATION.' Cst. [Constable] McDade will provide assistance in the interpretation and understanding of the documents to be researched which are currently in the possession and control of a source ..." The classified document was dated February 8, 2000, eleven days before Sean arrived at my home, but due to the extreme secrecy of Project ABBREVIATION, it was not being provided to the FBI by the RCMP Liaison officer in Washington D.C. until Sean gave the go ahead to do so. (Project ABBREVIATION = PROMIS).

My husband and I barely slept that night, worrying that Sean might be intercepted before he reached Canada. He and Sue had decided to drive back to Hercules, rather than fly, and it was a long way from Southern California to Hercules, then back to Canada. To date, he was the only person who had a complete set of the documents, and if coincidentally something "happened" to him or his cargo between my house and RCMP headquarters, well, it would leave me out in the cold too. I'd been dragging the documents around for years, hidden in storage units, garages, and other places, and it was a relief to know someone trustworthy in law enforcement had copies. In a way it insured my safety --- or so I thought at the time.

My concern for Sean's safe return to Canada was assuaged when I received an e-mail from Sue Todd on February 23rd. It read as follows: (excerpted)

> Hello Stormy - We got home at about 11 P.M. last night, then got up early this morning --- rushing around pulling some last minute info together. I'm exhausted! I put S on the plane this afternoon, so he is off and away as I write. I can't tell you how much help you have been. What you have done is awesome! You are an ace investigator. I hope sometime in the near future I can tell you everything about my investigation, then clearly you will see how helpful you were. I don't know how we can ever repay you --- thank you for everything. Stay safe. Sue.

A few days later, Sean called from RCMP headquarters to say they had set up a "war room" at headquarters, pulling tables together to sort and catalogue the documents. I knew his cargo would create a dynamic catalyst; before long the residents of the labyrinth would discover he had jumped on the board. He would be contacting them in the months to come, and I wondered if he would comprehend what Danny Casolaro had learned, that the secret of the PROMIS software was not whether it had been stolen, that was impossible to prove at this late date, but rather what PROMIS was used for, i.e., money-laundering. The RCMP investigator had come to Southern California for PROMIS, but left with Danny Casolaro's secret.

— 21 —

Spookloop

Sean and Sue subsequently interviewed Michael Riconosciuto, their shared witness, during Easter 2000 at the Federal Corrections Center at Coleman, Florida, in addition to dozens of other case-related witnesses, journalists and investigators who had preceded them. Sean called it the "Spookloop." Their combined eight-month investigation also took them into the hallowed halls of law enforcement agencies nationwide, where, with hindsight as an advantage, they harvested the dossiers of related probes dating as far back as the 1980's.

On August 26, 2000, detective Sue Todd called me to discuss the abrupt closing of the RCMP investigation. She said the *Toronto Star* newspaper had reported on Friday, August 25, that the RCMP National Security Division was investigating the use of the PROMIS software for spying by the United States and Israel.

As a result of this exposure, some high-ranking officials from CSIS and RCMP had conducted an internal meeting in which they apparently decided to shut down the PROMIS investigation. After eight months of intense work, both Todd and McDade were not only disturbed by what they had learned about the Octopus's far-reaching tentacles, Sean had told me that he was being monitored or surveilled by an Israeli Mossad agent, this according to Sean's source at RCMP. I don't know if Sue was aware of this, or not?

Nevertheless the longest phone conversation in my life began on that day, August 26, at approximately 10:00 A.M. until 3:00 P.M., then picked up again from 5:00 P.M. until approximately 10:47 P.M. The conversation comprised a total of approximately 10 hours. Todd said if anything happened to her as a result of her investigation, and the RCMP findings, she wanted me to publish what they learned. I readily agreed to that.

I did not take this lightly, because Sue Todd was not easily rattled. Before she reached the rank of homicide detective, she had been a police officer for more than 15 years and prior to that had worked on a California Department of Justice /Bureau of Narcotics Enforcement Task Force as an undercover narcotics officer. She had served as an intelligence consultant for numerous state and federal law enforcement agencies and held numerous certificates in specialized training. In her spare time, Sue liked to race her Corvette up to maximum speed, when she could. This was not a woman who shied away from danger.

Today, Todd is alive and well. However, she and McDade shared their findings with me throughout their investigation with the full understanding that at the conclusion of their probe, that data would be included in *The Last Circle* book. And what a prodigious exploration it was ---

The following information was derived from the above phone conversation, and from my own follow-up work to validate the data provided to me that day. The RCMP investigation began as follows: Through a mutually shared Canadian source, John Belton (a banker who claimed he lost a great deal of money regarding the sale of PROMIS to Canada, and alleged that his bank financed the purchase of PROMIS from Earl Brian), McDade and Todd had been brought together and ultimately joined forces in their respective investigations.

Later, in 1996, in an unrelated scandal, Earl Brian was indicted, arrested, and convicted on ten of thirteen counts of falsifying company finances during 1989 to obtain $56 million in bank loans. At the time of the alleged fraud, Brian was the chairman of two companies specific to the charges: United Press International and Financial News Network. He was then sentenced to four years and nine months in federal prison, but was free on bail during his appeal. On October 14, 1998, a federal appeals court upheld his fraud convictions. Brian soon entered prison. The following year, the U.S. Supreme Court refused to hear his case. (He was released on November 1, 2002, after having served his complete sentence.) http://en.wikipedia.org/wiki/Earl_Brian

Sue had followed a long and tangled road to discover that the Abernathy murders were *not* connected to Michael Riconosciuto;

whether he knew them or not was irrelevant. A former reporter from the *San Francisco Chronicle* had told her that the Abernathys in Hercules, father and son, were murdered because the father was "holding documents for Michael Riconosciuto." And, of course, the connecting factor to McDade's investigation was also Michael Riconosciuto, who claimed to have installed a back door, or Trojan Horse, in the PROMIS software which RCMP was allegedly in possession of.

In the end, the two investigators *did* solve the mystery of PROMIS and RCMP, but not the Abernathy homicide. Essentially, the former reporter from the *San Francisco Chronicle* who had originally provided Sue in May 1997 with the lead that Neal Abernathy was holding documents for Michael Riconosciuto, had been misinformed, and so her homicide investigation of the Abernathy execution-style murders in Hercules was being closed as well.

Nevertheless, Todd and McDade's joint 8-month investigation produced results beyond anyone's wildest expectations relative to the Octopus. Anyone who had observed the RCMP investigation up close in the United States would have realized that the pattern of witnesses who were questioned by the Mountie, the information for which they were asked and which they provided, revealed that the alleged theft of the PROMIS software was not, in fact, always the focus of the investigation, but rather *how* the software had come to be used. McDade and Todd clearly focused on drug trafficking and money laundering, and Michael Riconosciuto was at the top of their list.

Riconosciuto was a scientific genius, but he also had familiarity with drug operations worldwide and had secretly provided Sean and Sue with information relating to Ben Kalka's arrest in California, in which 900 -1000 lbs. of methamphetamine and $1 million in cash had been seized in Kalka's possession. It's important to point out that in the beginning, few investigators of the Octopus saga ever realized the significance of the *drug angle*, but in the end they always discovered that it was a key piece to the puzzle.

Ben Kalka's San Francisco defense attorney, Chris Cannon, explained that the chemical precursors necessary to make that much meth would require all the precursor sold in one year in the United States on the *open market*. And that was just one shipment. Kalka said he obtained all his precursors from Michael Riconosciuto, who was originally a co-defendant in Kalka's case. Riconosciuto told Mr. Cannon that he had records that would prove that the precursors Kalka used to make the drugs were provided by the U.S. government. Riconosciuto told investigators McDade and Todd that [name withheld] Chemical Company was cooperating with the FBI and reporting all the chemicals that Riconosciuto ordered for his chemical companies in Washington State. Riconosciuto then provided the precursors to Ben Kalka.

Reportedly the precursors were laundered through [name-witheld] in Los Angeles, and cleared by FBI agent Robert Barnes. The money (millions) was laundered through the principality of Liechtenstein, the smallest German-speaking country in the world which is bordered by Switzerland to the west and south and by Austria to the east. It has an estimated population of 35,000.

According to the Trivia-Library.com, Liechtenstein is a tiny, wealthy tax haven, which owes much of its prosperity to the fees paid by some 20,000 to 30,000 foreign corporations that maintain letter-box "offices" there. Other moneys were laundered from the U.S. to Canada, then to Israel, then to Switzerland. This operation lasted 1½ years, ending in 1981. Other companies were named in Illinois.

Ben Kalka was released from prison in April 2000. His lawyer, Chris Cannon, struck a deal and got his sentence overturned, contingent upon Kalka signing a letter (in April 2000) stating that he did *not* obtain his precursors from the U.S. government. The letter was reportedly written by U.S. Attorney William Shockley in San Francisco. Detective Sue Todd found the letter buried in the *Di Giorgio Extradition File – Case No. CR89-0603 VRW, U.S. verses Di Giorgio.*

The criminal indictment of John Di Giorgio had been filed under seal by the INS on October 26, 1989, and remained secret for nearly a decade. At a news conference on November 17, 1989, former California State Attorney General John Van de Kamp had touted the case as the "biggest methamphetamine seizure in the world," and reportedly displayed the 1,022 pounds of methamphetamine and $1 million in cash according to the *San Francisco Daily Journal.*

Pam MacLean, a reporter for the *San Francisco Daily Journal*, had spent thousands of dollars to get the Di Giorgio file unsealed. The unsealed documents revealed that the U.S. government was looking for an alleged $13 million in laundered drug funds believed to be in Switzerland, Germany and Israel. Ben Kalka reportedly said that he was able to purchase, *from government supplies*, enough precursor chemicals to produce four tons of methamphetamine.

As of August 2000 the file was located at the U.S. Federal Court on Golden Gate Avenue in San Francisco. John Di Giorgio, a former Austrian citizen, was allegedly an undercover informant working against Ben Kalka for the California Department of Justice. The methamphetamine precursors were reportedly supplied to Kalka in a "reverse sting" operation headed by FBI agent Robert Barnes.

Doug Bricker, from the IRS Treasury Dept. in Walnut Creek, California had followed Ben Kalka out-of-country during his investigation, and he had a copy of the DOJ investigative file. Ben Kalka had a brother in Israel; between 1967 and 1970, Kalka was involved in undercover work with the Israelis. Kalka was also close to Al Holbert, a former Israeli intelligence agent, and to Paul Morasca, who was found murdered in San Francisco on January 14, 1982, during the time these sting operations were underway.

(Sue Todd provided some of her typewritten notes at the end of her investigation that stated that the motive for the [unsolved] murder of Paul Morasca was as follows: *"Morasca was a trustee to several estates, including Riconosciuto's family. The San Francisco Police Department lead investigator told me [Todd] that Morasca was killed because he had a computer disc which identified these estates and the off-shore banks/codes to access them. A copy of this disc was found at [Cheri] Seymour's house."*)

Also involved in the government drug-sting operation was Philip Arthur Thompson (PAT) AKA Jason Smith, who worked as an undercover informant for FBI agent Robert Barnes at the San Francisco Bureau. In an interview with Detective Sue Todd in June 2000, retired FBI agent Barnes admitted that PAT had worked for him. Philip Arthur Thompson was originally sent in by Patrick Moriarty to be Michael Riconosciuto's bodyguard. (Patrick Moriarty was Michael's father's partner of 40 years. They also owned the Hercules Corporation at one time). Moriarty paid PAT $10,000 per month to bodyguard Michael Riconosciuto, but did not know that Thompson was an undercover informant for agent Barnes. PAT was arrested on June 16, 1983 for an unrelated murder and is incarcerated for life in a prison in California.

During a prison interview with Detective Sue Todd, Thompson talked about "kick-backs" to powerful people being handled by Riconosciuto on his computer.

Sean McDade came across information relating to Ben Kalka's *former* attorney, David Mayer of Marin County, California, who also represented Calvin Robinson, dubbed the "drug tug" captain by local media. McDade had interviewed Robinson in prison. Robinson reportedly had some connection to a former U.S. Customs official and the Cabazon reservation, but McDade's investigation was closed before he could prove the connection.

Calvin Robinson's tug was seized in the San Francisco Bay in the Spring of 1988 and was found hauling a barge containing 157 tons of hashish and marijuana. On December 12, 1991, Robinson filed a "Pro Per" affidavit in the U.S. District Court, Northern District of California (Case No. C-90-2839-VRW-JPV) requesting that Judge John Paul Vukasin, Jr. be recused from Robinson's case because "*Vukasin is a long-time associate and political ally of Edwin Meese III,*" and Robinson believed that "*Vukasin was appointed to the district court bench as a damage control agent for Meese and the United States Department of Justice ---*"

Robinson summarized in his Affidavit for Recusal of Judge Vukasin that he obtained the assistance of attorney David Mayer to represent him at his 1989 trial, but on the night before Mayer was to appear in court to defend Robinson, he died from a gun-shot wound. Robinson wrote in his affidavit:

> ... On February 6, 1989, Mr. Mayer died of a gun-shot wound. A suicide tape was found. His death was ruled a suicide. I learned of Mr. Mayer's death on the morning of February 7, 1989, the day Mayer was to appear [in court] to defend me.

Robinson also wrote:

> ... In Mayer's attorney/client files existed documentary evidence from Mayer's client, *Ben Kalka,* as to Kalka's business ties with one Michael Riconosciuto at R & R Research, at the extensive laboratory facilities at Hercules, CA and Doctor John Philip Nichols ---

I had learned that Dr. John Philip Nichols, administrator at the Cabazon Indian reservation, had met with Riconosciuto at the Hercules plant on more than one occasion, along with Philip Arthur

Thompson and others in the "spookloop" at that time. Investigators reported that they uncovered evidence that a chemical or drug operation had been going on at the Hercules plant *which contaminated the entire property.* This was at the time that PAT was hired at $10,000 per month by Patrick Moriarty to guard Michael Riconosciuto.

Detective Todd found evidence of money laundering exploiting the Cabazon operations in a two-page letter dated January 28, 1985 written to President Ronald Reagan from former Cabazon Tribal Chairman Joseph R. (Mike) Benitez in which he requested an investigation of the Cabazon Casino and the Indio Bingo Palace because "non-Indian investors" had not provided them with financial statements for 4 years and withheld information from the tribal members. Benitez said that tribal members had been assessed taxes by the IRS on income of $270,000 each, but they never received any of this money.

On November 22, 1998, an article published at the Post-Gazette.com website http://www.post-gazette.com/win/day2_3b.asp by Bill Moushey, entitled *"Federal Sting Often Put More Drugs on the Street,"* provided an insightful synopsis of the drug operation that former California State Attorney General John Van de Kamp had touted in 1989 as the "biggest methamphetamine seizure in the world." Most of the article is excerpted here:

> There's another problem with government drug stings: They sometimes create a drug problem where none existed.
>
> Ben Kalka had been a bit player in the San Francisco drug world off and on for most of his life — mostly scoring small hits of cocaine — but at the time of his arrest in 1982, he'd become a major supplier of methamphetamine on those same San Francisco streets. Cheaper than cocaine and heroin, it induced many of the same sensations, including quick addiction.
>
> Federal agents had set Kalka up in a sting. But by the time Kalka began manufacturing the drug, the Drug Enforcement Administration insists the sting had ended, an argument Kalka finds bizarre.
>
> By the time the government caught up with him, Kalka figures he'd produced 8,000 pounds of drugs worth $10 million, using ingredients federal agents had arranged for him to buy.
>
> Kalka should have been suspicious of his good fortune in 1980.

A chemist friend had asked him to find a barrel of phenyl acetic acid, a key precursor for the manufacture of methamphetamine. Kalka had a contact at a chemical company who said there was no way he could get him the chemical. While it wasn't illegal, the government scrutinized who bought and sold the chemical.

A week later, this contact called to say he could get Kalka a semi-truck load of the chemical precursor weighing 25,000 pounds. All Kalka needed was the money — $250,000.

What Kalka didn't know was that in the interim, the contact, Paul Palmer, had become an informant for the government after being busted for selling the very precursors Kalka had bought.

By now, Kalka was hooked. He set up a partnership with another drug dealer, Paul Morasca, to get the money, then began his search for the last ingredient he'd need for the speed — monomethylamine. Palmer put him in touch with Michael Riconosciuto, whose past included shadowy connections with various U.S. intelligence agencies, unbeknownst to Kalka.

Riconosciuto greeted Kalka like a long, lost brother. He claimed Kalka had once talked him out of suicide when they were imprisoned in the 1970s at Lompoc federal prison. Kalka vaguely remembered Riconosciuto.

Riconosciuto said in a recent interview that he was working for the FBI when he connected with Kalka and the agency told him to find the monomethylamine for Kalka as part of the sting operation. When the chemical was delivered, the FBI planned to bust Kalka and various subordinates.

The plan failed miserably, an array of court documents show. Kalka, naturally mistrustful of almost everyone, managed to divert the tractor-trailer truck carrying the chemicals away from federal agents who were tailing it.

Even so, Kalka wonders today why the FBI didn't track him down once the methamphetamine began hitting the streets. The agency maintains it eventually stumbled across Kalka's drug enterprise during another undercover operation.

Soon, he had produced what might have been the largest batch of methamphetamine produced in this country.

And it was all with chemicals supplied with the help of federal agents.

When he was finally arrested, Kalka gave the government $1 million and 1,000 pounds of methamphetamine, all that remained of the 8,000 pounds of the drug he'd produced, in exchange for a promise that he would serve no more than 10 years in prison.

A judge ignored the prosecutor's request and slapped Kalka with a 20-year sentence. In the meantime, Riconosciuto was arrested and convicted on a methamphetamine manufacturing charge. From his prison cell in Coleman, Fla., he described the role of federal agents and their authorization for him to sell Kalka the final ingredient needed to make the methamphetamine.

Kalka says the government's complicity in supplying the drugs might yet win him release from prison if he can convince a court to hear him.

In the meantime, he has been moved from one prison to another because of his repeated attempt to sue the government over his case and the conditions of his incarceration ---"

••••••••

In 2000, Detective Eddy Erdelatz, a former San Francisco Police inspector, provided a valuable lead about an obscure file, long forgotten at the San Francisco Police Department, which opened a window back in time to what was going on at the Cabazon reservation in the early 1980's. The file was labeled the "Paul Morasca Homicide Investigation File – Case No. 82-1052505" and it had never been computerized, so unless you knew it existed in the police department archives, it was essentially inaccessible unless you walked into the police department and signed for it. Only law enforcement personnel could access the file, it was unavailable to the public.

In 1981 Detective Erdelatz had investigated suspected drug trafficking and money laundering, then investigated Paul Morasca's gruesome homicide in January 1982 and placed a comprehensive report within the file relative to Philip Arthur Thompson's suspected connections to the murder.

It is noteworthy that the Morasca murder occurred just six months after the June 29, 1981 execution-style triple homicide of former Cabazon Tribal Council vice-chairman Fred Alvarez and his friends, Ralph Boger and Patricia Castro in Rancho Mirage, California.

As of August 2000 only one law enforcement officer had accessed the Morasca file in a decade, but the contents of the 1980's file, consisting of a thousand pages of police reports from the Riverside County Sheriff's Department, Riverside County D.A.'s office, and Indio Police Department, along with numerous other agencies in California, became significant not only to Sue Todd and the RCMP investigators, but to *future* investigators in the years to come; it was instrumental in solving a 28-year-old homicide case (Chapter 25).

Morasca had been chosen to manage the Cabazon Casino shortly before his murder, so this might explain why the Cabazon-related investigative reports had been inserted into the Morasca file in San Francisco. Many of the Alvarez triple-homicide reports, including those written in Riverside relating to the Octopus, no longer existed in Riverside twenty years later, so it was fortunate that someone inexplicably inserted them into the Morasca file for safekeeping.

Within the huge file, was a report entitled, "Interim Overview --," dated February 1982, which included a document from the Indio Police Department dated August 21, 1981, relating to the investigation of the Cabazon Indians in Indio, California. This document included a surveillance report in which Cabazon Administrator Dr. John Philip Nichols was observed visiting and meeting with various La Cosa Nostra underworld figures such as Tommy Marson, a known Gambino family associate who lived in a sprawling mansion in Rancho Mirage near Indio in the 1980's. Other alleged mobsters mentioned in the report included Vincent Caci Bologna, Anthony Fratianno, Daniel Magano, and other LCN figures.

Another report within the Morasca file contained information about Al C. Holbert, who was trained in military intelligence in Israel and the U.S. In 1965 Holbert attended a Marine (Sea) training school in Atliet, Israel. Also in 1965 Holbert attended a U.S. Army school of military intelligence. Beginning in June 1971, Holbert lived in Israel, Egypt and Syria, working respectively as a cryptographer and other capacities. In August 1972, Holbert operated in Central and South America. In 1977 Holbert worked in a state public defender's office as Chief of Criminal Investigations. In 1982, Holbert reportedly lived in Belize (formerly British Honduras, bordered by Guatemala to the south and west in Central America) working with a noted ex-British Army officer.

After Morasca's death, evidence was seized from his (Morasca's) briefcase relating to Sertec Corporation and /or RTI Research Tech Corporation. Some of the documents contained the names of Earl Barber, Chuck Emmert, and Al Holbert.

A December 2, 1982 FBI report noted that beginning on March 15, 1978 Robert Booth Nichols came under investigation by the

FBI for money laundering, drug smuggling, and related activities, including money laundering for Ferdinand Marcos.

One large report on Ben Kalka was written by Gene Gilbert, criminal investigator for the Riverside D.A.'s office at that time. Detective Sue Todd noted that, oddly, none of the alleged drug traffickers mentioned in the police reports, i.e., Ben Kalka, Michael Riconosciuto or Philip Arthur Thompson, were ever convicted of *any* drug-related charges during a ten-year time span while they were working as undercover informants or intelligence operatives for the government. Todd said Ben Kalka had been arrested several times in the past, but the FBI always took possession of him away from the arresting officers. She had come to the conclusion that Ben Kalka was an undercover operative, and the entire drug operation was sanctioned by the U.S. government.

In May 2000, Sue Todd and Sean McDade were given access to Michael Riconosciuto's storage unit in Vallejo, California by Bobby Riconosciuto. Michael had told them during their Easter visit to him at Colman Prison in Florida that they could find proof of the PROMIS software modification within the storage unit. The RCMP paid $1,500 back storage fees for two large storage units in Vallejo. They flew Bobby from Washington State to Vallejo to access one of the storage units which Michael directed them to search.

Sean, Sue and Sean's partner, Randy Buffam, searched the storage unit and found Marshall Riconosciuto's phone book which reportedly contained the phone number of Peter Videnieks. They also found six RL02 back-up magnetically sealed tapes that Riconosciuto said were the PROMIS modification updates – the boot-up system for PROMIS he claimed to have created. He said the data was backed-up from a computer located at Bobby's mother's house in Tonasket, Washington. This house was not searched by authorities during the raid on Riconosciuto's Tacoma property when he was arrested. The computer was subsequently sold to a police detective in Huntington Beach, California (name-withheld). Philip Arthur Thompson independently told Sue Todd that Riconosciuto used this computer at his mother-in-law's home to process "kickbacks" to five powerful people.

Bobby Riconosciuto argued that the back-up tapes contained actual mirror drive images of the upgrades that Riconosciuto made to the PROMIS software. Riconosciuto ultimately agreed, at Bobby's urging on a tape-recorded message, to provide RCMP with the source codes for the boot up system. Sue Todd said she photographed the six tapes and deposited them into her personal safe deposit box because she was concerned they might get de-magnetized inside the Hercules Police department. She subsequently turned the tapes over to Sean McDade and he flew back to Canada with them.

Sue said the RCMP was careful not to contaminate the evidence (tapes) by accessing them prematurely. They protected the tapes from contamination until such time as a computer expert familiar with PROMIS could boot up the tapes, using Riconosciuto's codes, and view them. Sean McDade planned to fly Bill Hamilton [developer of the PROMIS software] to the RCMP headquarters to access the PROMIS tapes, but when the *Toronto Star* article broke on August 25 in Canada, McDade backed off.

Sometime after the September 11, 2001 terrorist attacks on the World Trade Center in New York, Randy Buffam mailed the Riconosciuto/PROMIS tapes back to the Hercules Police Department, according to Sue Todd. (Years later, Todd explained that the computer equipment that would be needed to access the tapes today does not exist anymore. It is too outdated).

During her investigation, Sue said that both she and Sean could call Riconosciuto at the prison at any time and talk for as long as they wished. At that point Riconosciuto had been moved to Allenswood Federal Care Facility in Pennsylvania. She had viewed Riconosciuto's Central Inmate File containing his psyche papers, visitor's list, correspondence list, and other information. She noted that Frederick Whitehurst, the FBI forensic lab whistleblower, had visited Riconosciuto in prison.

(Dr. Frederic Whitehurst joined the FBI in 1982 and served as a Supervisory Special Agent in the FBI crime lab from 1986-98. He achieved a great deal of media attention during the 1990s for blowing the whistle at the FBI Lab.

While employed by the FBI crime lab, the FBI officially rated Dr. Whitehurst as the leading national and international expert in the science of explosives and explosives residue. He investigated, uncovered and reported scientific misconduct which reportedly caused the FBI crime lab to institute forty major reforms).

Todd had initiated various internal data base searches on hundreds of "volumes" of case files relating to her investigation and the RCMP investigation. She searched NCIC, the Police Records Management System, DOJ data banks, internal data banks, BNE data banks (Bureau of Narcotics Enforcement), and through her experience as a former undercover narcotics officer, she was able to identify informants by how the BNE logged their informants through a "CR#." She then tracked down the informants and interviewed them. Two of them were Philip Arthur Thompson (PAT – AKA Jason Smith) and Ben Kalka, amongst others (whom she did not name). She had even identified who the informant used against Robert Booth Nichols was, but didn't share that name with me either. (PAT and Kalka had already been made public on the Internet, so she wasn't revealing anything that wasn't already in the public domain).

When Sue Todd contacted retired FBI agent Robert Barnes in early June, 2000, he said that PAT, who worked undercover for him, had provided him with three of the computer coded cards that belonged to Michael Riconosciuto. Barnes had sent them to Quantico.

PAT told Sue at an interview that he had withheld one of the cards for himself. These were some of the computer cards that were mentioned in the *San Francisco Chronicle* newspaper story on the death of Paul Morasca, entitled "Bizarre Murders Puzzle Cops," dated December 30, 1991, which reported that Morasca died because he was allegedly in possession of the computer cards. I had subsequently found the *original* cards in Michael Riconosciuto's files in the desert which I had photographed and Xeroxed before sending them to Bobby Riconosciuto, along with the rest of Michael's original documents. Michael called them the "Tyme Shares" cards.

Because Sue and Sean were investigating organized crime activities connected to the PROMIS software, they accessed, reviewed and sometimes copied volumes of computerized investigative reports on money laundering, drug trafficking, extradition cases, homicide cases, software theft, payoffs, kick-backs, and related activities. Sue found three volumes in Oakland, California and hundreds of volumes in Los Angeles.

Again, no portion of the Paul Morasca file was on computer, thus it couldn't be accessed through any of the data banks. Sue said few people were aware that the file existed.

On July 31 and August 1, 2000, Sean McDade, Randy Buffam, and Sue Todd visited Gene Gilbert, investigator from the District Attorney's office, Indio branch. They were given access to several boxes of old documents relating to the activities at the Cabazon reservation in the 1980's. They validated the Lake Cahuilla S.O.P. "Contra" Report, and obtained a copy of an 11-page letter written by Patrick F. Cannan, director of corporate relations for Wackenhut Corporation, to Jonathan Littman at the *San Francisco Chronicle*, which provided a chronology of Wackenhut's "Joint Venture" at the Cabazon reservation beginning in April 1, 1981 and ending on October 1, 1984.

During the first few months of the Joint Venture Agreement, a number of proposals were prepared by Wackenhut on behalf of the Cabazon/Wackenhut Joint Venture and submitted to various U.S. government agencies which have been outlined in previous chapters. Cannan wrote that John P. Nichols had first introduced Michael Riconosciuto to A.R. "Bob" Frye, executive V.P. of Wackenhut, in May 1981 during a trip to the U.S. Army installation at Dover, N.J. where Dr. John Philip Nichols, Peter Zokosky, Frye and Riconosciuto met with Dr. Harry Fair and several of his Army associates who were the project engineers on the Railgun Project.

"Riconosciuto and these Army personnel conducted an extensive and highly technical 'theoretical' blackboard exercise on the Railgun and afterwards, Dr. Fair commented that he was extremely impressed with Riconosciuto's scientific and technical knowledge in this matter. Dr. Fair had apparently been apprised by [Dr.] Nichols that Riconosciuto had been convicted and served time for stabbing a DEA agent whom he purportedly caught in bed with Riconosciuto's wife. Dr. Fair had commented that Riconosciuto would probably not be able to ever get a government security clearance because of his past, but it would be a shame if Riconosciuto, whom he termed a 'potential national resource,' could not be used for military/research projects in his field of expertise.," wrote Cannan.

The letter said that A.R. Frye saw Riconosciuto "hanging around" the Cabazon office in 1981-1982 without any apparent purpose. The Cabazons operated a Casino on their reservation in Indio, which pre-dated the Cabazon/Wackenhut Joint Venture. Frye recollected that Paul Morasca may have been the person initially hired by the Cabazons to manage the Casino, and thus Frye was briefly introduced to Morasca at the Casino.

In early April 1983, A.R. Frye suffered a heart attack and was hospitalized with a by-pass operation. He never traveled to California to meet with J.P. Nichols or the Cabazons again subsequent to that time. "Wackenhut's involvement with the Cabazon Joint Venture thereupon virtually ceased.... In October 1984, Wackenhut formally terminated the Joint Venture Agreement," Cannon concluded.

On August 2, 2000, Sean McDade and Randy Buffam accompanied Sue Todd to the FBI headquarters in Los Angeles. McDade and Buffam dropped Sue off and toured the area. Detective Todd was given access to various FBI files, including and particularly the Robert Booth Nichols file. She obtained some copies and tagged other documents to be copied and sent to her because the file was huge. Afterward, the three investigators drove to my home and I served them a B.B.Q.'d salmon dinner. In the warm summer night, we sat at the table in my patio and they related what they had learned during the past three days (which has already been outlined in this chapter).

Sean McDade had discreetly summarized his concerns about the ECHELON technology being used to monitor his and Todd's investigation in the United States. I noticed that Randy Buffam remained silent, despite the fact that he was a Middle Eastern Terrorist Specialist in the Canadian intelligence services and probably very familiar with ECHELON.

Buffam *did* acknowledge, however, that RCMP had requested information on Robert Booth Nichols and received a significant report from the FBI. He said the report noted that Nichols was suspected of money laundering in connection with the Royal Bank of Canada, a Caribbean branch, which had originally funded Hercules Corporation (owned by Marshall Riconosciuto, Michael Riconosciuto, and Patrick Moriarty).

The three investigators also discussed the role of CSEC (Communications Security Establishment) in Canada which they said is used by the NSA to spy on American communications. In return, the U.S. government spies on Canadian communications. They said the entire operation is overseen by the military.

I asked why the U.S. would spy on Canada, an ally? They explained that Canada is a gateway for terrorists and spies to enter into the U.S., and U.S. authorities routinely spy on Canadian intelligence operations because Canada has access to intelligence from foreign countries that the U.S. cannot obtain. They said the U.S. is considered corrupt by foreign powers, the U.S. has a bad reputation, and Canada can access those countries.

After doing some research on CSEC and ECHELON, it appeared they are either closely integrated, or they are one and the same system. According to wikipedia.org, under a 1948 UK-USA agreement, CSEC's intelligence is shared with the NSA (U.S. National Security Agency) as well as GCHQ (the British Government Communications Headquarters); DSD (the Australian Defense Signals Directorate); and GCSB (New Zealand's Government Communications Security Bureau.

CSEC is believed to form the ECHELON system. Its capabilities are suspected to include the ability to monitor a large proportion of the world's transmitted civilian telephone, fax and data traffic. The intercepted data, or "dictionaries" are "reported linked together through a high-powered array of computers known as 'Platform.'" http://en.wikipedia.org/wiki/Communications_Security_Establishment_Canada

I subsequently looked up ECHELON on the Internet and this is what I found: (excerpt)

http://en.wikipedia.org/wiki/Echelon_(signals_intelligence)

ECHELON is a name used in global media and in popular culture to describe a signals intelligence (SIGINT) collection and analysis network operated on behalf of the five signatory states to the UK-USA Security Agreement (Australia, Canada, New Zealand, the United Kingdom, and the United States, known as AUSCANZUKUS). It has also been described as the only software system which controls the download and dissemination of the intercept of commercial satellite trunk communications.

ECHELON was reportedly created to monitor the military and diplomatic communications of the Soviet Union and its Eastern Bloc allies during the Cold War in the early 1960s, but since the end of the Cold War it is believed to search also for hints of terrorist plots, drug dealers' plans, and political and diplomatic intelligence.

The system has been reported in a number of public sources. Its capabilities and political implications were investigated by a committee of the European Parliament during 2000 and 2001 with a report published in 2001, and by author James Bamford in his books on the National Security Agency of the United States.

In its report, the European Parliament states that the term ECHELON is used in a number of contexts, but that the evidence

> presented indicates that it was the name for a signals intelligence collection system. The report concludes that, on the basis of information presented, ECHELON was capable of interception and content inspection of telephone calls, fax, e-mail and other data traffic globally through the interception of communication bearers including satellite transmission, public switched telephone networks (which carry most Internet traffic) and microwave links.
>
> Bamford describes the system as the software controlling the collection and distribution of civilian telecommunications traffic conveyed using communication satellites, with the collection being undertaken by groundstations located in the footprint of the downlink leg.
>
> In 1999 the Australian Senate Joint Standing Committee on Treaties was told by Professor Desmond Ball that the Pine Gap facility was used as a ground station for a satellite-based interception network. The satellites are said to be large radio dishes between 20 and 100 meters in diameter in geostationary orbits ---

During one interview with Sue Todd, she had noted that she had obtained some phone numbers which Robert Booth Nichols had called from Los Angeles. She provided three of those numbers and hinted that they were government agencies and one of them went into the White House, but she wouldn't explain further.

I sent the numbers to a couple of computer-expert friends and asked them to identify who the phone numbers belonged to? This is what one of them wrote back: "I searched each of the three telephone numbers on the reverse search capability at www.switchboard.com and found that the first number is a U.S. Government number in Reston, Virginia, the second number is an unpublished number in Atlanta, and the third number is an unpublished number located right next to or at the White House." The other friend wrote back that one of the phone numbers connected to the U.S. Department of Commerce – Technology Administration, and the other number connected to the White House.

I decided not to call the numbers due to concerns it might raise flags that I was snooping, and I could end up being snooped upon myself. In fact, Todd and Sean McDade and already told me the first day they arrived at my house that my phone was bugged, which surprised me. He had learned it through RCMP headquarters. I'd always enjoyed anonymity, never been arrested in my life, and had committed no crime by researching material for my book. However, McDade had not followed normal protocol (had not notified the FBI) when he entered the United States, so perhaps that explained the reason for the bug.

Nevertheless, I wasn't particularly concerned about what I was saying on the phone until one day I mentioned to a reporter friend that RCMP said my phone was monitored. The reporter laughed and began making obscene remarks to the "listeners," and both our phones simultaneously went dead for a relatively long period of time. My husband, Roland, subsequently complained to the phone company about the incident, and they notified us later that our phone security had been "temporarily compromised," but they had no idea what had caused that. To this day I will never know if the incident was a coincidence or a deliberate response from some individual who was actually listening to my conversations.

In late August, Sue Todd remarked that she had not received the copies she had flagged in the Robert Booth Nichols file at the FBI in Los Angeles. She called "Steve," the FBI lawyer, to inquire about her copies. She was told that the copies she requested had to be authorized by Washington D.C. first due to "national security reasons." Todd said that was odd, she didn't need authorization at the Oakland FBI offices? The FBI lawyer struggled to find a logical answer, but could not.

Sue said she suspected that the FBI federal building *cameras* in Los Angeles had videotaped Sean McDade when he came to pick her up at approximately 5:30 P.M. on August 2. She had called Sean on her cell phone from the FBI building, but when she didn't come out of the building right away, Sean had come up the walkway to find her. He had been on the verge of entering the building when she emerged and they departed together. (As mentioned earlier, Sean was covertly inside the U.S. investigating whether the United States government had placed a back door in Canada's PROMIS software system. Protocol dictated that he was supposed to have notified the FBI of this before he entered the U.S.)

Sue had also been dismayed when she drove out to the Hercules plant and located the walk-in vault where she found boxes of documents and returned with them to the Hercules police department. The commander told her to throw them away, trash them, the case was closed – so they went into the dumpster.

Sean sent an e-mail in late August outlining how the *Toronto Star* had compromised his investigation. A number of people whom McDade had interviewed began communicating with each other, the "Spookloop" as Sean called it. Sue Todd called it the "Board," and some of them, one in Ireland, one in Canada, and one in Washington D.C., had independently arranged for the *Toronto Star* to begin probing Sean's investigation, according to Sean.

In addition, Sean wrote, "This is now involving Rafi Eitan in Israel, whom [name withheld] has been speaking to, and is familiar with my ongoing status. Cheri, the s--t's going to hit the fan soon. Nothing will be said to any reporter. I can't due to National Security matters. SRM."

The *Toronto Star* called me for an interview after their initial story broke, and I provided them with what I could relating to the U.S. end of the story, but they weren't interested in that aspect, and I didn't want to talk about Sean and Sue. They weren't giving interviews to reporters at that time.

♦♦♦♦♦♦♦♦

During the eight-month long RCMP investigation, I had provided Dave Hendrix, editor at the *Press Enterprise* newspaper in Riverside, California, with packages of documents and typewritten notes in manila envelopes for safekeeping. People investigating the Octopus often felt the need to do this, and I was no exception. Dave was as trustworthy as anyone I had ever known, and he was not only my friend, but had an illustrious career as a journalist and newspaper editor.

When the story about RCMP's probe in the U.S. broke in the *Toronto Star* (Canada) on August 25, 2000, I asked Dave to put me in touch with a publication that would have the integrity and power to run an *in-depth* story. Dave said he would contact his long-time friend, Kelly O'Meara, a reporter at *Insight* magazine. He explained that before Kelly became a reporter, she had served four members of Congress on Capitol Hill for 17 years. During her tenure, she was Chief-of-Staff to Congressman Michael Forbes (R-N.Y.) and had been responsible for the investigation into the 1996 downing of TWA 800 off the coast of Long Island.

Kelly subsequently made preliminary inquiries with me, then offered to do the story if it would remain exclusive with *Insight* magazine. She stipulated that if *Insight* sent a reporter from Washington D.C. to California to do a 4-part investigative piece, the expense and time spent in California warranted exclusivity. I agreed, and Kelly and I began communicating daily.

On September 14, 2000 I received an e-mail from Kelly notifying me that she would be flying out to California shortly. Kelly checked into the Best Western motel at the bottom of the hill, near where I lived, and we met for the first time. She followed me in her rented car up to my home and we began the first of dozens of interviews that preceded months of investigative work.

On the first day we met, I realized I had caught a tiger by the tale. Kelly was a dynamic, Irish whirlwind with natural long blond hair and blond eyelashes that emanated a kind of white light energy as she grilled me for hours, on tape, and reviewed hundreds of documents. She didn't want to buy into any conspiracy theory, so she was suspicious at first of the magnitude of the story.

At night at the motel, in the wee hours of the morning, she sent reports on her laptop to her editor, Paul Rodriguez, at *Insight* magazine, with copies to me. I wondered if she ever slept. At 7:30 A.M. each morning she arrived at my home and worked until dark. It was exhausting, but inspiring to be so challenged. I instinctively knew I had entered into the big leagues with this reporter. I did not know, however, how big that league really was! In the months to come, Kelly would solve the mystery of the labyrinth, and forever lay to rest the reason why so many souls had died in their quest to tackle the head of the Octopus.

Kelly flew back and forth from Washington D.C. to California several times, focusing on following the trail of the RCMP investigation. Because I was the only individual outside of law enforcement who knew the dynamics of that investigation, she allowed me to accompany her on the interviews in California.

But, before the interviews began in earnest, she wanted to take photographs of the various sites that connected to the story. On the first of many photo excursions, she decided to drive out to Trona, near Death Valley in the Mojave Desert, and photograph Michael Riconosciuto's secret mobile home where Bobby and I had originally obtained his documents nine years earlier. (Sean McDade and Sue Todd had visited the site also in February 2000, at the beginning of their investigation and found Riconosciuto's phone book there).

Dave Hendrix and Kelly were long-time friends who had worked together on projects in the past, so she invited Dave to accompany us to the desert for a reunion of sorts. My husband, Roland, drove the car and the conversation inside was boisterous until, as we left civilization behind and entered the land of desert rats, everyone became introspectively hushed. The single-wide mobile home was situated approximately 78 miles from Death Valley, at the end of a narrow gravel road surrounded by hundreds of miles of barren desert. Our intrusion into the small settlement of scattered dwellings along the road was conspicuous and vulnerable, but Kelly was determined to obtain proof that the documents in my files had actually been obtained from this site. For some reason, the RCMP investigators had found this site important too, but I never knew why.

We located Riconosciuto's trailer at the top of a knoll, visible to the settlement below. We stood outside and photographed the dwelling and surrounding desert, then departed hurriedly just as a sheriff's vehicle turned off the highway and headed in our direction.

♦♦♦♦♦♦♦♦

On October 17, 2000, Kelly O'Meara and I drove from my home in Southern California to Detective Sue Todd's home in the San Francisco Bay Area. RCMP investigator Sean McDade's investigation had been shut down, and Todd's investigation of the Abernathy double-homicide had collapsed as well due to premature exposure in the Canadian media.

In an e-mail on August 28, 2000 Todd had written that their respective joint investigations were "all over the media," and would most likely end her investigation. She wrote: "They are breathing down our necks and even calling witnesses in the U.S. on my case.... Thousands of hours of work down the drain thanks to one reporter in a foreign country. And there is no recourse.... Viva la Freedom of the Press!"

Kelly O'Meara offered to set the record straight; now that Todd and McDade's cases had been closed, they were in a position to talk about their findings. At Todd's luxury waterside home in Solano County, we met her husband and her beautiful daughter. Sue's personal and professional life was a study in contrasts. Her home was gracious, filled with light and polished oak, in sharp divergence from the somber landscape of her homicide investigation. Her husband was athletic and striking with a lucrative career in the field of polygraphy and held the position of Senior Inspector in the District Attorney's Investigative Unit. I wondered how two such high-powered people could live under the same roof peaceably, but their attraction to each other was palpable when they were in the same room together, and in the months to come I learned how deeply devoted they were to each other and to their family.

Sue confirmed to Kelly and I during that nine-hour visit at her home that Michael Riconosciuto (MR) had in fact laundered money on a computer at Bobby Riconosciuto's mother's house in Washington State. She believed Riconosciuto had been using the PROMIS software to launder the money; that house was not raided – only MR's house in Tacoma was raided.

Sue said she had spoken with FBI agent Thomas Gates on July 11. She promised to ask Gates to call Kelly. She had no difficulty getting Gates to talk about Robert Booth Nichols. She wouldn't say what they discussed, but she hinted, "When you talk about RBN, you talk about drugs, money laundering and stock fraud." And she insinuated that Nichols was hooked up with the Department of Justice. I asked, "Did Gates tell you that?" Sue looked carefully at my face, and nodded affirmatively.

Sue had gone to the Oakland FBI office and reviewed the RBN case file. They allowed her to make copies and told her the rest of the file was at the Los Angeles FBI headquarters. The Oakland office had called Thomas Gates and he called Sue back. He gave her permission to review the Nichols file at the L.A. FBI offices, and obtained authorization for her.

Sue had found that RBN was investigated by the FBI as far back as 1971 in Australia. He did not work for the CIA based on what she saw in the file. She took notes and obtained *some* copies at the Los Angeles bureau, but the file was so big she put stickies on the pages she wanted copied and sent to her, but never received all of them because the *Toronto Star* story broke in Canada that same month. Sue believed she was under investigation by the FBI as a result of her visit to Indio with Sean McDade.

At that first face-to-face meeting between Sue and Kelly, they had figuratively circled each other like two cats sizing each other up. Sue was not particularly fond of reporters at that time, and Kelly was about as far removed from being a "police groupie" as a reporter can get. In the evening we went to an upscale restaurant on the bay and ordered expensive steaks, compliments of *Insight* magazine. Kelly began to push Todd about Sean McDade's findings during his investigation, but Todd was uncooperative on that level. The two women barely touched their food, still sparring, until finally late into the evening, the barrier broke, the conversation loosened up about *Todd's* findings relative to the Octopus, and the two women became friends in the months ahead.

The following is taken from Kelly O'Meara's notes: Riconosciuto had also purportedly been working on the CRYPTX software, a powerful data security/encryption program, and the TRELLIS software, before he assertively became involved with PROMIS and the Cabazon/Wackenhut weapons proposals. Ben Kalka was allegedly involved in the CRYPTX project also in 1981-1982.

Sue said, "We got further than anyone else ever got on this case ... Nobody outside of law enforcement will ever know what we found because no one in law enforcement can ever tell anyone what they found." "Who controls the flow of money controls countries. PROMIS was tailored by Riconosciuto for banking and money laundering," she added. She also believed that ECHELON has PROMIS in it and there is a treaty between the U.S. And Canada to share the data from that spy apparatus.

Kelly asked, "What did Sean want when he visited Indio on July 31 – August 1, 2000?" Sue admitted that she and Sean went to Indio to meet with Gene Gilbert, investigator for the Riverside D.A.'s office, to confirm the validity of the SOP Contra report about the September 1981 weapons demonstration at Lake Cahuilla with the Contra leaders but they also wanted to see the warrants that were issued against the Cabazons that Gene Gilbert had been filing for years.

Dr. John Philip Nichols had asked for security around the perimeter of the gun range and that's why the police were there. Sue and Sean reviewed the entire back-up documents folder and she said all the documents were dated and coincided with the SOP report that they obtained from my files. Gene Gilbert was very shocked when he saw that they had a copy of the report and he said that John Cohen told him that the document was stolen from the Judiciary vault, but the copy that Sean showed them was the correct one.

Sue said she went to the San Francisco Police Department and looked at the Paul Morasca file, spent five days looking at it. She said there is some forensic information in the file that is of interest. She said Eddy Erdelatz was the detective on the Morasca case and she has worked with him.

On October 18, Sue Todd met with Scott Lawrence for lunch. By that time, Scott worked at the U.S. Customs building on Montgomery Street in San Francisco, California. Neither Sue nor Scott would reveal what they talked about, but during a brief phone call from Kelly O'Meara, Scott remarked, "It's a good thing that you're working on this; it's a good thing to follow."

I subsequently obtained a detailed 12-page "Memorandum for the Files" document relating to the Indo-China Project which discussed some U.S. Customs Internal Affairs findings during their far-ranging investigation. The memorandums outlined a dark tale of U.S. intelligence activities dating back as far as World War II when the OSS (Office of Strategic Services, the predecessor of the CIA) was conducting secret intelligence operations against the Nazis on the European continent. A major international money laundering infrastructure was involved, and a European-wide "private" intelligence network running through Britain, Germany, Monaco and other points with very close ties to the International Monetary Fund, according to the report.

Of particular interest to me was one Memorandum dated 5/3/91 which stated that one official closely related to the former Reagan administration appeared to be "in the middle of a major heroin transaction involving the Gambino family, dirty elements of the U.S. and British intelligence and others ---"

The report said that a UK-German-Japanese consortium which handled the off loading of containers from ships in New York were on the mob payroll and were used to smuggle drugs into the United States. Reportedly, one or two of the containers were specially constructed to conceal large shipments of heroin. The 8'x40' model No. 150 668-1A was rebuilt with a lighter weight false floor so that the weight of the container would conform to that of an empty container, while actually holding 350 kilos of pure China White heroin. As long as the containers arrived manifested empty, they would not be searched by port Customs officials.

The heroin shipment was part of an overall guns-for-drugs transaction. The assassination of John Gotti's chauffeur, according to the Customs source, was linked to some missing containers of heroin.

The chauffeur was in some way directly responsible for securing the safe delivery of the heroin, and there was suspicion that the shipment was somehow bungled by him, the report noted.

Another memorandum dated June 22, 1991 estimated that one heroin load contained 1,500 pounds of pure heroin. Accordingly, the report said that the combined Gambino-Gotti-Castellano families were involved in putting up the cash for the heroin shipment, and several recent murders were a fallout of the problems with that shipment.

••••••••

In a subsequent adventure two days later, Kelly and I drove to the desert to interview Gene Gilbert, senior investigator for the District Attorney's office in Indio, California. We met with Gilbert on October 19, 2000 at the IHOP restaurant in Palm Springs for lunch.

Gilbert had been a police officer in Indio for 18 years before moving over to the D.A.'s office in 1989, so he had valuable historical information that was key to Kelly's story. (Gilbert later became Mayor of Indio). However the main purpose of the meeting was to validate a document, referred to as "the Contra report" by investigators.

Kelly asked Gilbert to validate the Special Operations [Surveillance] Report, entitled "Nicaraguans and Earl Brian at Lake Cahuilla – 9/10/81" in which several high-level people from Wackenhut, the Cabazons, and CIA met with two Contra generals, Edin Pastora Gomez (Commander Zero) and Jose Curdel (Commander Alpha), at the Lake Cahuilla Gun Range in Indio. The purpose of the 1981 meeting had been to test night-vision goggles and to fire semiautomatic rifles with special night scopes.

Gilbert was surprised we had a copy of the document, but he validated it, noting that he had written it himself. He said he had originally sent it to John Cohen, but later learned it had gone missing from the Judiciary Committee storage vault. (I had obtained my copy from Peter Zokosky in 1992). I later learned that the Judiciary Committee had wanted information on the weapons demonstration at Lake Cahuilla and Gilbert had compiled the report for John Cohen after-the-fact by talking to the individuals who had attended the September 10, 1981 meeting, as well as obtaining whatever back-up documents were still available.

Under questioning from Kelly, Gilbert related what had transpired between him and Sean McDade, Sue Todd, and Randy Buffam (from RCMP) when they visited his office on July 31, August 1, 2000, (derived from Kelly's notes) as follows: Sean asked Gilbert if he knew there was a "backdoor" in the PROMIS software? Sean added that his government (Canada) had just acknowledged that they had PROMIS. Gilbert said he believed RCMP was doing damage control.

Michael Riconosciuto, according to Gilbert, might have done the PROMIS modification in the back of two vans on the Cabazon Reservation. Computer equipment was in the vans, with electric cords running into the administration building.

Gilbert allowed the trio to go through five or six file boxes containing information on the Cabazon operations; they seemed particularly interested in any Canadian connections. Sue Todd reviewed the files on Phillip Arthur Thompson (PAT). In 1978, Gilbert had seized entire file cabinets from the Administration Building at the Cabazon Reservation; some of the files contained diagrams of Michael Riconosciuto's "fuel-air" bomb technology.

Gilbert noted that he possessed photos of Dr. John P. Nichols and Mob figures taken in Indio. (He agreed to send Kelly copies, but never did).

He said Peter Zokosky and Wayne Reeder were investors in the Cabazon Casino and a skeet range. But he said the Mob built the Casino for the Cabazons.

Gilbert had written a two-page report on the visit from Sean, Sue and Randy and provided it to his boss, who condensed it into two paragraphs and turned it over to FBI agent Joe Shaw in Palm Springs. He admitted that he had just met with Shaw prior to *our* meeting as well. We all suspected we were under surveillance inside the restaurant.

Gilbert confided that Joe Shaw had told him that the State Department was "on their ass" because McDade and Buffam were in the U.S. illegally; protocol dictates that an FBI agent should accompany them wherever they go in the country.

He said the NSA told the FBI to "get out of the Cabazon investigation" because they were out of their jurisdiction (sovereignty issues).

Reportedly, Allan Boyak travelled with Gilbert to interview Riconosciuto (MR) in early 1991 in Missouri. He said Boyak introduced himself as MR's lawyer. At 12:30 A.M., Boyak and Gilbert met with MR in the prison. Boyak said he was an ex-DEA agent.

Bobby Riconosciuto and her friend had eight boxes of MR's *original* documents, and they asked Gilbert to drive to the Bay Area to pick them up. These were the same boxes that Cheri sent back to Bobby, via the friend. Gilbert never picked the boxes up.

Gilbert said most of the events that occurred at the Cabazon Reservation occurred in 1983-1984. He added that all the evidence of the Fred Alvarez triple murders was missing from the Sheriff's Department.

♦♦♦♦♦♦♦♦

On January 29, 2001, the *first* of four articles on Kelly's investigation was published in *Insight* magazine under the heading, "Nothing Is Secret," by Kelly Patricia O'Meara. For purposes of clarity and educational value, I have excerpted most of it below:

> **Nothing Is Secret**
> January 29, 2001
> By Kelly Patricia O'Meara
> Good morning, Mr. McDade. The Royal Canadian Mounted Police has reason to believe that the national security of Canada has been compromised. A trojan horse, or back door, allegedly has been found in computer systems in the nation's top law-enforcement and intelligence organizations.
>
> "Your mission, should you decide to accept it, is to establish whether this is the PROMIS software reportedly stolen in the early 1980s from William and Nancy Hamilton, owners of Inslaw Inc., and reportedly modified for international espionage. As always, should you or any of your associates be caught, the governments of Canada and the United States will disavow any knowledge of your actions. This recording will self-destruct in five seconds. Good luck, Sean."
>
> Sounds like the opening taped message from an episode of the 1960s TV action series *Mission Impossible*. But just such a mission was offered - and accepted - by two investigators of the National Security Section of the Royal Canadian Mounted Police (RCMP). The Mounties then covertly entered the United States in February of last year and for nearly eight months conducted a secret investigation into the theft of the PROMIS software and whether and by whom it had been obtained for backdoor spying.

PROMIS is a universal bridge to the forest of computer systems. It allows covert and undetectable surveillance, and it and its related successors are unimaginably important in the new age of communications warfare.

In this exclusive investigative series Insight tracks the Mounties and explores the mysteries pursued by the RCMP, including allegations involving a gang of characters believed to be associated with the suspected theft of PROMIS, swarms of spies (or the "spookloop" as the Mounties called them), the Mafia, big-time money laundering, murder, international arms smuggling and illegal drugs - to name but a few aspects of the still-secret RCMP probe.

But the keystone to this RCMP investigation is PROMIS, that universal bridge and monitoring system, which stands for Prosecutor's Management Information System – a breakthrough computer software program originally developed in the early 1970s by the Hamiltons for case management by U.S. prosecutors. The first version of PROMIS was owned by the government since the development money was provided by the Department of Justice (DOJ), but something went awry on the way to proprietary development.

For more than 15 years the story of the allegedly pirated Hamilton software, and how it may have wound up in the hands of the spy agencies of the world, has been hotly pursued by law-enforcement agencies, private detectives, journalists, congressional investigators, U.S. Customs and assorted U.S. attorneys. Even independent researchers have taken on the role of counterespionage agents in a quest to uncover the truth about this allegedly ongoing penetration of security.

But each new U.S. investigation has failed fully to determine what happened. While the Mounties encountered a similar fate, officers Sean McDade and Randy Buffam have been the most successful to date. Last May, with the assistance of Hercules, Calif., Detective Sue Todd, the Mounties walked away with a package of startling evidence that many believe will solve the case of the pirated software and its reported continuing use for international espionage and a host of other illegal activities.

Insight has spent months retracing the steps of the two RCMP officers and interviewing their sources, poring over copies of documents they secured, listening to tape recordings of meetings in which they were involved and reviewing scores of reports and depositions that have been locked up for years.

The result is this first installment of a four-part investigative report about how the Mounties conducted their covert border crossings and investigation that ranged across the United States and back again before returning to Canada where they discovered their cover had been blown. By late summer of 2000 the Canadian press was reporting not only the existence of this secret national-security probe - "Project Abbreviation" - but that if the reported allegations prove true "it would be the biggest-ever breach of Canada's national security." Confusing official comments about the probe added further mystery. But Insight has confirmed many of the details, including the fact that the investigation is continuing. And it's serious stuff.

McDade began his extended trip into international espionage early last year. It began at least on Jan. 19, 2000, with an e-mail that said: "I am looking to contact Carol (Cheri) regarding a matter that has surfaced in the past. If this e-mail account is still active, please reply and I will in turn forward a Canadian phone number and explain my position and reason for request." This communication, from e-mail account simorp (PROMIS spelled backward), was the first of hundreds sent during an eight-month period from "dear hunter," also known as Sean McDade. It reached Cheri Seymour, a Southern California journalist, private detective and author of a well-regarded book, *Committee of the States.*

Seymour became one of the most important of McDade's contacts during the Mounties' continuing investigation. Although she had agreed to remain silent about their probe until McDade filed a report with his superiors, she changed her mind when news of the probe began to leak in the Canadian press. It was then that the Southern Californian contacted Insight and offered to share what she knew about the investigation if this magazine would look into the story. And what a story it is.

A petite, attractive, unassuming middle-aged woman, Seymour looks more like a violinist in a symphony orchestra than an international sleuth. But one quickly becomes aware of the depth of her knowledge not only of the alleged theft of the PROMIS software, but also of other reported illegal activities and dangerous characters associated with it.

Seymour's involvement with PROMIS began more than a decade ago while working as an investigative reporter on an unrelated story about high-level corruption within the sheriff's department of the Central California town of Mariposa, near Yosemite National Park, where deputies reportedly were involved in illegal-drug activity. The dozen or so who were not involved repeatedly had begged the journalist to conduct an investigation. When she learned that one of the officers had taken the complaints to the state attorney general in Sacramento and within weeks was reported missing in an alleged boating accident on nearby Lake McClure, she launched her probe.

The owner of the local newspaper, the *Mariposa Guide*, in time contacted ABC television producer Don Thrasher and the story of the corruption within the Mariposa Sheriff's Department ran in 1991 on ABC's prime-time television news program *20/20*. Seymour's investigation is chronicled in a draft manuscript called *The Last Circle*, written under her pseudonym Carol Marshall but made available anonymously on the Internet in 1997. PROMIS then was only a sidebar to the larger story, but it was this obscure Internet posting that led RCMP investigators McDade and Buffam to Seymour's living room two years later.

According to Seymour: "Nothing [previously] came of the work I did. Even though in October of 1992 I had sent a synopsis of my work to John Cohen, lead investigator on the House Judiciary Committee, looking into the theft of PROMIS and its possible connections to the savage death of free-lance journalist Danny Casolaro. But by then the committee had completed its report and published its findings. It was a closed case. Nothing ever happened with the connections I was able to make among the players involved in the theft of PROMIS and illegal drug trafficking and money laundering." That is, until McDade sent his first cryptic e-mail.

Within a week the Mountie had arranged to meet Seymour at her home to discuss aspects of his own secret investigation and begin the laborious task of copying thousands of documents Seymour had collected from an abandoned trailer in Death Valley belonging to a man at or near the center of the PROMIS controversy, Michael Riconosciuto, a boy genius, entrepreneur, convicted felon - and the man who has claimed that he modified the pirated PROMIS software. The documents provided specific information about Riconosciuto's connections to the Cabazon Indian Reservation, where he claims to have carried out the modification, but they also painted a clear picture of the men with whom Riconosciuto associated, including mob figures, high-level government officials, intelligence and law-enforcement officers and informants - even convicted murderers.

Before McDade focused on a three-day copying frenzy, the Mountie gathered Todd, Seymour and an impartial observer invited by Seymour to corroborate the meeting around Seymour's dining-room table and began to tell a dramatic tale of government lies and international espionage.

[Seymour said] "McDade told us his investigation had to do with locating information on the possible sale of PROMIS software to the RCMP in the mid-1980s. He had found evidence in RCMP files that PROMIS may have been installed in the Canadian computer systems, and he said an investigation was initiated by his superiors at the RCMP."

According to Seymour, "McDade said that the details of his findings in Canada could conceivably cause a major scandal in both Canada and the United States. He said if his investigation is successful it could cause the entire Republican Party to be dismantled - that it would cease to exist in the U.S."

"Then," continues Seymour, "he said something that was just really out there. He stood in my dining room with a straight face and told us that ... more than one presidential administration will be exposed for their knowledge of the PROMIS software transactions. He said that high-ranking Canadian government officials may have unlawfully purchased the PROMIS software from high-ranking U.S. government officials in the Reagan/Bush administration, and he further stated that the RCMP has located numerous banks around the world that have been used by these U.S. officials to launder the money from the sale of the PROMIS software."

Seymour was stunned. Just when she thought things couldn't get any weirder, "McDade detailed a December 1999 meeting at the Los Alamos National Laboratory in New Mexico attended by the heads of the intelligence divisions of the U.S. [CIA], Great Britain [MI6], Israel [Mossad] and Canada [CSIS]. McDade said the topic of the discussion was UNIQUE ELEMENTS, and that during this meeting it allegedly was revealed that all four allied nations share computer systems and have for years. The meeting was called after a glitch was found in a British computer system that had caused the loss of historical case data."

McDade continued with this scenario by telling the astonished group: "The Israeli Mossad may have modified the original PROMIS modification [the first back door] so it became a two-way back door, allowing the Israelis access to top U.S. weapons secrets at Los Alamos and other classified installations. The Israelis may now possess all the nuclear secrets of the United States." According to Seymour, he concluded by saying that "the Jonathan Pollard [spy] case is insignificant by comparison to the current crisis."

Insight has tried repeatedly to contact McDade and his superiors to discuss the Mountie's accounts of espionage and other crimes only to be rebuffed through official channels. But in carefully assembling and independently checking disparate pieces of the McDade story line *Insight* was able to confirm that there was indeed a December 1999 meeting at the Los Alamos National Laboratory and the topic of the meeting was, indeed, codenamed UNIQUE ELEMENTS.

Seymour never learned further details about that meeting, though she tried, alerting several U.S. senators, including Charles Robb, D-Va., Jeff Bingaman, D-N.M., and Richard Bryan, D-Nev., about what McDade had told her in February - nearly four months before the public was made aware of massive computer problems at Los Alamos (see "DOE `Green Book' Secrets Exposed," Jan. 1). Ironically, Congress was probing such lapses, but only Bob Simon, Bingaman's staff director on the Senate Energy and Natural Resources Committee, responded. Simon advised that he would show the letter to the senator and possibly refer "some or all of the information in the letter to Ed Curran, director of the Department of Energy's [DOE] Office of Counterintelligence."

Seymour never had any further communication from Bingaman's office, the DOE or any federal investigator seeking to discover which "foreign agent" had told her of severe computer leakage from Los Alamos long before it became public knowledge.

How McDade knew what he claimed may never be made public. But what is known can be pieced together from the many contacts he had with individuals having historical knowledge of the allegations surrounding PROMIS and a host of other seemingly unrelated criminal enterprises and crimes.

For instance, in January 2000 McDade contacted PROMIS developers and owners Bill and Nancy Hamilton, explaining what his investigation was about; what, to date, had surfaced; and what the implications might be. "McDade said my government made two untruthful statements in 1991 [the year congressional hearings were held on the theft of PROMIS]," Bill Hamilton tells Insight. "The first was that they [Canada] had developed the software in-house. McDade said that wasn't true, it just materialized one day out of nowhere. The second untruth was that they [the Canadian government] had investigated this. McDade said that his investigation was the first."

Hamilton further explained that "McDade believed PROMIS software was being used to compromise their [Canada's] national security." Needless to say, this was interesting news to Hamilton, given that it was "the second time the Canadian government has said they have our software, only to retract the admission later." The first time was in 1991, he recalls. "They contacted us to see if we had a French-language version because they said they only had the English version - which, by the way, we did not sell to them. At first we didn't take it seriously because it was before we were aware that the software was reportedly being used in intelligence. We just knew that the U.S. Department of Justice acted rather strangely, took our software and stiffed us. It never occurred to us that the software was being distributed to foreign governments," Hamilton tells *Insight*.

"When they [Canada] followed up their call with a letter saying PROMIS software is used in a number of their departments – 900 locations in the RCMP, to be exact– Nancy and I said `Hey, wait a minute.'"

Of course, laughs Hamilton, "when one of our newspapers in the U.S. got hold of that information and printed it, the Canadians retracted and apologized for a mistake. They now said the RCMP never had the software."

It is important to note that the alleged theft of PROMIS software was well investigated. However, no investigation by any governmental body, including the U.S. House Judiciary Committee, which made public its findings in September 1992, the Report of Special Counsel Nicholas J. Bua to the Attorney General of the United States Regarding the Allegations of Inslaw, Inc., completed in March 1993, nor the Justice Department's Review of the Bua Report, which was published in September 1993, confirmed that any agency or entity of Canada had obtained and used an illegal copy of the Hamiltons' PROMIS software.

A Justice report commissioned by Attorney General Janet Reno concluded the same but did confirm that a system called PROMIS was being used by Canadian agencies but claimed that this system was totally different – it was just a coincidence that the two software programs had the same unusual name and spelling

So what happened over the course of 10 years to lead the RCMP's top national-security investigators to probe the matter anew and to do so with such secrecy throughout the United States and Canada? Why would McDade, by all accounts a seasoned and well-respected Mountie, tell whopping tales to so many people, including not only Bill Hamilton but strangers Seymour, Todd and others?

The answers may be found in the pattern of people who were questioned by the Mounties. The information for which they were asked and which they reportedly provided, may reveal that the alleged theft of the breakthrough PROMIS software was not, in fact, the focus of the investigation, but was secondary to how the software has come to be used.

In August 2000, McDade told the *Toronto Star's* Valerie Lawton and Allan Thompson, "There are issues that I am not able to talk about and have nothing to do with what you're probably making inquiries about," which centered on PROMIS. Was the Mountie revealing that his investigation had reached the level he had unguardedly revealed to Seymour and friends?

Surprisingly, McDade did not focus his investigation on interviews with government officials who were involved with the PROMIS software. Rather he focused on people who claimed to have knowledge of the purported theft, many of whom also have been connected to other illegal activities, including drug trafficking and money laundering. And Michael Riconosciuto was at the top of McDade's list.

With the help of Detective Todd, who had facilitated the Mounties' meetings with the hope of also obtaining information about the 1997 execution-style double homicide of Neil Abernathy and his 12-year-old son, Brenden, McDade was given access to Riconosciuto and people and information that even few law-enforcement officers in the United States have secured. In fact, the assistance the Mountie received secretly from U.S. authorities was stunning and included access to information from highly confidential FBI internal files and case jackets (including the names of confidential witnesses and *wiretapping information*), U.S. Bureau of Prisons files, local law-enforcement reports and reportedly even classified U.S. intelligence data.

It was with this kind of help that McDade was able to walk away with what many believe to be key material evidence in the PROMIS software legal case - material evidence of which only Riconosciuto had knowledge. After extensive interviews with Riconosciuto in a federal penitentiary in Florida, McDade in May 2000 made a $1,500 payment on a defaulted storage unit in Vallejo, Calif., that belonged to Riconosciuto. Poring through floor-to-ceiling boxes, McDade hit pay dirt when he found six RL02 magnetic tapes that Riconosciuto said were the PROMIS modification updates – the boot-up system for PROMIS he claimed to have created.

Coupling those storage-unit files with the thousands of pages of documents Seymour had obtained some years earlier from an abandoned trailer Riconosciuto had rented in the desert, McDade walked away with the whole kit and caboodle without so much as a peep out of U.S. law-enforcement or intelligence agencies. At least until now.

Today, that evidence is in the hands of foreign agents – our neighbors up north in Canada. When questioned about the magnetic tapes, the RCMP would neither confirm nor deny that they were in its possession. Michele Gaudet, the RCMP spokesman, did tell Insight that the investigation is ongoing and it is very much about the PROMIS software – software that may or may not involve back-door entrance into the most secret computer systems in the Western world.

••••OVERVIEW OF *INSIGHT'S* FOUR-PART SERIES••••

This four-part series is about how a foreign law-enforcement agency, the Royal Canadian Mounted Police (RCMP), covertly entered the United States and for nearly eight months conducted a secret investigation about the alleged theft of PROMIS software and the part it may play in suspected security breaches in Canada, the United States and other nations.

In Part 1, *Insight* tracks the early movements of two RCMP national-security officers - Sean McDade and Randy Buffam - to contacts throughout the United States, including private detective Cheri Seymour, an author and former investigative journalist. Seymour has spent years investigating the alleged theft of PROMIS and illegal activities reportedly associated with it. McDade outlined the nature of his investigation and what is at stake. He described potential security breaches in his country and detailed top-level secret meetings at U.S. national laboratories about similar security problems in the United States. Here, readers also will learn how with the help of a small-town California detective, Sue Todd, the Mounties managed to leave the United States with material evidence that may be crucial to solving a major espionage puzzle.

In Part 2, *Insight* follows the Mounties to the California desert in search of confirmation of allegations made by Michael Riconosciuto, the boy genius who reportedly modified the stolen PROMIS software for international espionage while working as research director of an alleged Cabazon/Wackenhut Joint Venture on the Cabazon Indian Reservation in Indio, Calif. It also is at Cabazon that other "characters" reportedly involved in the theft of the software were revealed and Riconosciuto's connections to them confirmed. It is a strange mix of alleged players - the Wackenhut Corp., government officials, mob-related goodfellows and murderers. Insight also will look at claimed arms deals and government research at the Cabazon reservation, including a secret weapons demonstration in Indio attended by many of the same cast reportedly key to the theft of PROMIS.

In Part 3, readers will watch as the Mounties begin a lengthy review of a U.S. government official, Peter Videnieks, the Justice Department employee overseeing the PROMIS contract, who allegedly made the theft of the software possible. The U.S. Customs Service began an investigation of Videnieks based on its suspicion that he committed perjury when he testified at a 1991 trial of Riconosciuto. Based on documents obtained from federal law-enforcement agencies, Insight looks at a U.S. Customs Service investigation of Videnieks, which ultimately was dropped. The Mounties also probed a Customs investigation of reported drug trafficking and technology transfers over the Maine/Canadian border.

In Part 4, *Insight* will review the numerous investigations conducted by law enforcement, beginning with the Mounties, concerning the alleged theft of the PROMIS software and individuals reportedly associated with that theft. Readers will see how each investigation began with review of the "theft" but quickly led into other suspected illegal activities, including technology transfers. This last part also will review how each new investigation has overlooked key evidence and seen careers threatened.

By Paul M. Rodriguez, Managing Editor, *Insight* magazine

All logos and trademarks in this site are property of their respective owner. FAIR USE NOTICE: This site contains copyrighted material the use of which has not always been specifically authorized by the copyright owner. We are making such material available in our efforts to advance understanding of environmental, political, human rights, economic, democracy, scientific, and social justice issues, etc. We believe this constitutes a 'fair use' of any such copyrighted material as provided for in section 107 of the US Copyright Law. In accordance with Title 17 U.S.C. Section 107, the material on this site is distributed without profit to those who have expressed a prior interest in receiving the included information for research and educational purposes. For more information go to: http://www.law.cornell.edu/uscode/17/107.shtml

Part two of the *Insight* series, entitled "The Plot Thickens in PROMIS Affair," by Kelly Patricia O'Meara, published on February 5, 2001, noted that a lengthy January 1992 tape recorded phone conversation between Michael Riconosciuto and an FBI agent (J.H.) revealed that Robert Booth Nichols "was connected to a high-ranking Justice Department official." It outlined the connection between Mike Abbell and Cali Cartel leaders Miguel Rodriguez and Jose Londono who Nichols had identified as "intelligence people." During his January 1992 trial in Washington State, Riconosciuto had attempted to trade information on large-scale drug operations and money laundering to the FBI in exchange for entry into the Federal Witness Protection Program.

Sean McDade had copied that tape recording at my home, taken it back along with several other tapes to RCMP headquarters and had them transcribed. When McDade's secret investigation began to leak in the Canadian press, and he no longer communicated with me or any other writers, he mailed that particular transcribed conversation to me in a large manila envelope directly from the RCMP office. I later learned it was a message to me; *that transcript was the key to the Octopus investigation.*

Part three of the *Insight* series, entitled, *"PROMIS Trail Leads to Justice,"* dated February 12, 2001, reported that McDade had "plumbed the old Customs probe of [Peter] Videnieks, the former DOJ official who was investigated for possible perjury." An unnamed former high-ranking federal law enforcement official told *Insight* that "Videnieks was under investigation by an internal affairs unit at the Customs Service and the investigation, which included other matters, centered on an allegation that Videnieks committed perjury at the 1992 trial of Michael Riconosciuto."

John "Tim" Kelly, Acting Regional Director of the Office of Internal Affairs at the U.S. Customs Service in Boston, had written to John C. Dwyer, Assistant Associate Attorney General at the DOJ in Washington D.C. on November 15, 1993 asking to impanel federal grand juries in a number of locations relative to the internal affairs investigation of Videnieks. The letter provided a list of 22 witnesses which included employees of the Central Intelligence Agency and Wackenhut Corporation. Tim Kelly was told that impaneling three grand juries would not be authorized by Main Justice in Washington D.C.

Insight wrote, "How this tied into a simple case of suspected perjury by Videnieks is unknown." Jimmy Rothstein, a retired New York City policeman, who worked closely on the case with Tim Kelly and Scott Lawrence (the agent in Customs' Boston office who was in charge of the investigation of Videnieks), confided to *Insight* that "the investigation came to a dead end right after Lawrence interviewed Alexander Haig."

Officially, the probe against Videnieks was shut down because Videnieks no longer worked as an employee of the Customs Service.

Insight questioned why Haig, a former secretary of state, White House official and Army general would be interviewed as part of a Customs investigation? Haig could not be reached for comment.

The *last* article, part four , entitled "PROMIS Spins Web of Intrigue" by Kelly Patricia O'Meara, dated February 19, 2001, again focused on the transcript sent by the Mountie to my house after the RCMP probe was closed in the U.S. "The transcript ... takes on special significance because none of the information in it dealt with the alleged theft and modification of the PROMIS software. Or did it? Was the RCMP sending a cryptic message about a change in the focus of the RCMP investigation, or was it signaling Seymour that the PROMIS software was being used in the international banking system for illegal activities?" wrote *Insight.*

Insight concluded, "The [U.S.] State Department is supposed to have filed a formal complaint with Canada about the secret treks into the United States by the RCMP investigators, and *Insight* has confirmed the FBI has launched a national-security investigation. On orders from Washington, special agents of the bureau quietly have been interviewing people contacted by McDade and Buffam and asking what the Mounties were after and what they got, including computer tapes long sought by prior investigators that could establish convincingly that secret copies of PROMIS indeed were bootlegged, modified and sold illegally."

••••••••

In December 2000, it was officially determined by RCMP that they did not have INSLAW's pirated version of PROMIS with a "back door" or Trojan Horse. McDade said he had simply been protecting the integrity of RCMP and his country by investigating the question of whether his country had been compromised – and ultimately proved it had not been. Case closed.

For historical purposes, to get it on the record, other sources close to RCMP, unrelated to Sean McDade or Randy Buffam or Sue Todd, said that a Canadian government department, outside RCMP or any related law enforcement Department, *does* have the illegal version of PROMIS, but that's another story for another day ....

Edwin Meese

— 22 —

The Octopus Exposed

Meanwhile on February 14, 2001, Kelly O'Meara and I continued on the trail, meeting with Peter Zokosky at his home in Southern California.

Mentally I noted the odd coincidence that so many significant events in my investigation had taken place in the month of February: I had interviewed Robert Booth Nichols at his home on February 13, 1992; U.S. Customs agent Scott Lawrence on February 5, 1993; the Neal Abernathy murders took place on February 19, 1997; and now we were interviewing Peter Zokosky on February 14, 2001. I was sure there were others but couldn't think of them offhand.

The meeting with Zokosky and his wife, Regina, took place in their living room from 10:00 A.M. to 2:30 P.M. Those present at the meeting were Peter Zokosky, Regina Zokosky, Kelly O'Meara and Cheri Seymour. The following summary was taken from the notes of that meeting:

Zokosky and his wife were gracious hosts; the meeting had the ambiance of a bridge party, rather than an inquiry of the Octopus. Zokosky said they would be traveling to London, England in a few days. They also have a home in London. Kelly plowed right in, saying she had heard that Robert Booth Nichols (RBN) was a thug, a drug trafficker, and a money launderer.

Zokosky chuckled and said he is probably all three of those things. He said it is his understanding that RBN works for the NSC, adding, "everything revolves around the NSC." He explained that RBN does "contract work" for the NSA/NSC, but also occasionally does contract work for other government agencies.

He noted that the NSA monitors all phones, faxes, and particularly cell phones. Key words such as "gold, drugs, FBI, and other such words" trigger the NSA listening software to alert the NSA listening center to record the conversation and its source, but landlines are more difficult to monitor, he said.

According to Zokosky, RBN was currently in Vietnam, working for Ross Perot. Kelly asked, "What is he doing?" Zokosky laughed, "What Ross Perot does best." (Presumably making money). Zokosky said he periodically talks to RBN, and can reach him by phone, but did not believe RBN would talk to Kelly for an article. Kelly offered to send Zokosky a copy of her 4-part series which mentioned RBN in it. Zokosky countered, next time he talked to RBN he would ask him to call O'Meara at Insight magazine.

Under questioning, Zokosky said he was told by an NSA employee that the NSA is a "profit" agency and the funding to the NSA is unlimited and no accountability is required because the NSA is "national security" and does not disclose what the money is used for.

Regarding FIDCO [First Intercontinental Development Corporation]: He said FIDCO was a NSA front corporation used in Lebanon. All the FIDCO corporate directors were intelligence people. They "contracted" with RBN to do work for them. This included Robert Maheu, Glenn Shockley and others. Reportedly, Zokosky was once "briefly" on FIDCO.

Regarding the "White House" documents in which Michael McManus, George Pender, and Robert Booth Nichols were mentioned, the $3 billion dollars mentioned in the documents was used to pay the president of Lebanon [Amin Gemayel] for the release of an American prisoner being held in Lebanon. Zokosky couldn't remember the name of the prisoner, but said he would tell us when he thinks of it. He thought the name was mentioned in the documents. [Zokosky didn't mention FIDCO's drug/sting operation in Lebanon].

He added that the prisoner *was* released as a result of FIDCO's efforts. RBN handled the financial transaction. This was a FIDCO/NSA operation in Lebanon. Robert Maheu and the other FIDCO members have respect and good things to say about RBN, according to Zokosky. In addition, he said, the members also fear RBN. He didn't say why.

Zokosky said whenever anyone submits a FOIA [Freedom of Information Act] to the Department of Justice about RBN, he (RBN) is notified.

He sorted through a folder of documents and provided a three-page FBI report on Robert Booth Nichols. He said it was sent to RBN by the DOJ. The title of the report read: *"U.S. Department of Justice – FBI, Los Angeles - December 2, 1982 – Robert Booth Nichols."* The report stated on March 16, 1978 a confidential source alleged that Robert Booth Nichols, AKA Robert Bert Nichols, Robert Nelson, Robert Nioon, is "an international money launderer of money derived from both narcotics and organized crime activities."

The report said the FBI conducted a background check on RBN and wrote the following: That he provided armaments to the Philippine government. He also assisted Ignacio Paz, Deputy Chief of Staff, Intelligence, Philippine government, with removing large sums of money from the Philippines by investing money with RBN who placed the money in Swiss bank accounts.

The FBI report stated that RBN's telex number was 652483. (This was the same telex number that was listed in the White House document sent to President Amin Gamayel of Lebanon in connection with the FIDCO operation in Lebanon).

According to the FBI report, RBN resided nine months out of the year at a $3.5 million dollar villa named "Tenuta Monterosso" in Terme, Italy. (Address withheld).

It stated that RBN ran away from home at the age of 17 and resurfaced in Hawaii where he became involved in organized crime. Harold Tadoo Okimoto took Nichols under his wing in Honolulu. Okimoto was reportedly involved in racketeering since 1962.

The report stated Nichols had permits to develop and sell a submachine gun prototype called the G-77.

In 1973-1977 Nichols began an apprenticeship program with a Swiss Company in dealing in finance and representing various portfolios of *mid-east* companies.

The FBI Report stated that throughout the Los Angeles FBI investigation, RBN's name was associated with the illegal transportation of narcotics through the "Golden Triangle." RBN's code words appeared to relate to drug trafficking.

The report concluded [last sentence] that "Robert Booth Nichols should be considered armed and dangerous."

I photographed the FBI Report while Kelly interviewed Zokosky.

Peter Zokosky played an audio taped conversation with Michael Riconosciuto narrating. The tape referred to the murder of Paul Morasca in San Francisco and Mary Quick in Fresno. The tape provided the names of people involved in the drug operation in Fresno and said they used the Hells Angels in this operation. At some point [unclear] FBI agent Robert Barnes in San Francisco became involved in this investigation. Riconosciuto said Al C. Holbert was working closely with an attorney named Marvin Kahn in the Bay Area. He said Ben Kalka handled the LSD operation in Fresno. Working with Ben Kalka were the names of various alleged drug traffickers.

Peter Zokosky commented on the audio tape after playing it. Zokosky said Paul Morasca was killed because of a "narcotics deal" gone awry, and he was involved in laundering large sums of money from drug profits. He said Morasca wanted his money and got killed because of that.

••••••••

Peter Zokosky said Jimmy Hughes from the Cabazon Indian reservation came to him and he convinced Hughes to talk to authorities. Zokosky drove Hughes to the Riverside District attorney's office. Hughes was required to take a polygraph test. On June 20, 1984 several officials subsequently met at the Riverside D.A.'s office and Hughes took another polygraph and gave a deposition. Present at this meeting were the following people:

- Deputy Attorney General Sanford Feldman, Special Investigations Unit, CA DOJ
- Special Agent Frank E. Brock, Special Investigations Unit, Calif. DOJ
- A black official from San Diego.
- Officers from the Fresno Police.
- Patrick Kenneally, investigator for D.A. of Riverside.
- Mike Trott, D.A. of Riverside.
- Gene Gilbert, investigator for Indio D.A.'s office.
- Others unknown.

••••••••

Peter Zokosky said John Vanderwerker and Glenn Shockley worked for the CIA. Both were involved with the Wackenhut/Cabazon "Joint Venture." He said Meridian International Logistics [MIL], of which he was a board member with Robert Booth Nichols, was a "front company." It was used for the purpose of "funneling money to pay the board of directors of MIL." The payments amounted to "five figures."

Kelly asked, "Where did the money came from?" Zokosky said it came from the NSA. He explained that the NSA does not have to account for money. The NSA makes a "profit." He alluded that some of the money came from drug profits. He said he was told that the "only people that get busted [for drugs] are those that don't have a distribution territory."

Discussion ensued about drug economies worldwide. He said drugs are called "gold" and used as currency worldwide. "Real gold takes up space and is difficult to transport. Payments are made for arms with drugs. Drugs are a business at the highest levels of corporations because there is a huge market and demand for drugs."

Zokosky mused that buying and using drugs are a "voluntary" choice by people who use drugs and the generations today do not have any moral or ethical boundaries with regards to using drugs. Thus the corporations distribute drugs because there is a demand for them. In other words, it's just a pervasive business and everyone is involved in one way or another, including government front corporations.

Kelly asked if RBN was involved in doing "contract" work relative to government narcotics transactions? Zokosky replied that RBN does not use drugs or distribute drugs, he handles the "corporate and government" transactions at a higher level. He said RBN is in the business of "service for money." He added that all business transactions conducted covertly today relate to two things: Money and drugs.

But, he said, when operatives conduct "service for money," it becomes dangerous. He alluded that he [Zokosky] does not accept money or care about money in his dealings with RBN. He was asked by RBN to be on the board of MIL and he agreed, but then asked to be taken off the board later.

Zokosky briefly discussed Michael Riconosciuto and RBN conducting business in Australia – he thought it had something to do with the Nugan Hand bank.

He said he had no knowledge of RBN *ever* being arrested for anything in his life, except once, when he was a young man working for Harold Okimoto in Hawaii. RBN was caught stealing from Okimoto. Afterward Okimoto decided that RBN was so adept at stealing, he decided to bring RBN into his business. They subsequently developed a close working relationship.

Zokosky said a man named Patrick McGuire worked for Wayne Reeder and subsequently joined the Montana Freeman in Jordan, Montana. McGuire was arrested during the Montana Freeman siege and Zokosky reportedly testified on McGuire's behalf as a character witness at the Freeman trial.

Kelly asked, "Why did RBN talk to Danny Casolaro so extensively?" Zokosky said Danny originally called him [Zokosky] about the "Octopus," and Zokosky felt RBN could answer his questions better, so Zokosky introduced Danny to RBN.

Zokosky was somewhat defensive about Danny Casolaro and said he believed Danny committed suicide. Regina Zokosky frowned and said she thought her husband had said otherwise at previous times. She continued to shake her head as Zokosky reiterated that he believed Casolaro had committed suicide.

Peter Zokosky allowed us to review a manuscript written by Robert Booth Nichols about the death of Danny Casolaro. It was dated November 22, 1991. It was entitled, "Danny Casolaro's Octopus."

Within the text of the manuscript it was noted that Danny Casolaro met RBN at Dulles airport and asked him to meet with a man named George Pittaway, the brother of Jim Pittaway, at Cloud's Restaurant in McLean, Va.

Jim Pittaway and George Pittaway both worked closely with the DIA [Defense Intelligence Agency]. They were currently with the Burmese Trade Council.

At the restaurant, RBN noted to George Pittaway that he had recently been asked to be the Cabinet Minister of Security Affairs for the Opposition Party in Dominica. RBN said he had accepted the position with *the approval of the DOJ*.

The manuscript went on to describe how RBN had organized project financing for an oil drilling venture on the Korat Plateau in Thailand.

In a Martinsburg, Va. bar Danny met some attractive girls. Later in his Martinsburg hotel room, he opened the door expecting to see the girls. A cloth containing a chemical was shoved in his face and he passed out on the floor. It was noted that at 5:00 A.M. a couple next door heard Danny say, "Not yet." That same morning, August 10, 1991, Danny's dead body was found in the bathtub by the cleaning maid.

The last paragraph of the manuscript noted that a military man had placed a medal on Danny Casolaro's coffin at the conclusion of the funeral. The last sentence of the manuscript read, "The only agency that does that is the NSA."

••••••••

Kelly asked what branch of the military did he [Zokosky] serve in? He said he had served in ONI [Office of Naval Intelligence] as a young man in the submarines during WWII.

Zokosky said he did "remote viewing" for the military sometime between the 1950's and 1970's. He conducted this work at a special room set up at Hewlett Packard Corporation near the Stanford University area. He said he is also a psychic. He belongs to the Psychic Association of London. He admitted he does readings for friends, and has done a reading for RBN. He said he uses Tarot Cards which his son, a renowned artist, specially designed for him. Each card contains a design which Zokosky Sr. created and the son drew.

He asked Kelly O'Meara if she would like to have a "reading"? Kelly agreed, and Zokosky retrieved a small wooden box from his trophy room. Within the box was a small dried frog, which he said protects the cards and has significance to the focus of his readings. He removed the dead frog, then handed the Tarot Cards to Kelly to view. The cards contained artistic designs of eagles within an eye, and other depictions of personal significance to Zokosky.

He then placed some of the cards on the coffee table and conducted his "reading." He stated a number of personal observations about Kelly which she agreed were accurate. These observations related to Kelly's personal life, her relatives, her travel, her health, and her career. At the end of the reading, Zokosky had obtained considerable information about Kelly (including her fingerprints on the plastic-coated cards).

••••••••

Zokosky said his half-brother, Steve O., is a computer expert who owns a computer company. Steve once talked to Michael Riconosciuto about computer software. Steve later told Zokosky that Riconosciuto had considerable knowledge about computer software. Zokosky said Bill Hamilton also said Riconosciuto is a computer whiz who understands sophisticated computer language.

But Zokosky said Riconosciuto is unreliable, that he is a pathological liar with grains of truth in the tales he spins. He added that Riconosciuto is astute in identifying the interest or focus of those who interview him, then he spins a deeper and deeper web of intrigue around that subject.

Zokosky provided a statement which Robert Booth Nichols asked Michael Riconosciuto to write relative to the death of Paul Morasca. To date I had been identifying this document as a grand jury statement, but Zokosky said it was not a grand jury statement, it was written at the request of RBN to be handed over to Zokosky for his files. Riconosciuto hand-wrote the statement and it was subsequently typed up by Ellen Nichols.

This was the February 16, 1984 statement by Riconosciuto relating to the sale of George Wackenhut's yacht *Top Secret,* in which MR talked about a methamphetamine operation gone awry. As follows:

> ---At that point, JPN directed me to have PAT (Phillip Arthur Thompson) recover [all] of Kalka's assets. I then contacted DeSilva, who had control of Kalka's assets and he agreed to release them to me. DeSilva later called the Indian reservation and gave the location of the assets which included: one bobtail semi-truck with power lift gate loaded with amphetamine production chemicals; one red Datsun truck with a portable refrigerator containing the acid.
>
> I accompanied PAT and Steve Finley to the locations of these vehicles in the Oakland area. The keys, title and registration were with each vehicle. PAT and SF drove the vehicles off and I reported to JPN that the vehicles had been located and picked up.
>
> I also reported to my attorney, DW (Don Wager), the details. I contacted JPN a few days later and he complained to me that PAT had made off with everything ---

••••••••

Zokosky discussed his exploits with Wackenhut at the Cabazon Indian reservation beginning in 1981. He talked about the proposed development of biological warfare "viruses" being developed in cow uteri by Stormont Laboratories. He said RBN and he and others presented a proposal to develop biological warfare technology at Storemont Laboratories, along with anti-toxin kits, and sell it to the Army [Dr. Harry Fair at Picatinny Arsenal]. This technology was also presented for sale to FMC Corporation [Food Machinery Corporation of America] in California.

Zokosky also discussed the September 10, 1981 Lake Cahuilla weapons demonstration in Indio, Calif. [I've identified this meeting as the "Contra meeting."] Zokosky had been present at this meeting. He said Jimmy Hughes and Dr. John Nichols both speak Spanish and they identified the Contra leaders who attended the demonstration. He said Earl Brian was not in attendance at the meeting. Some inexpensive rifles were tested and night vision goggles were tested. He said the rifles could be manufactured at the reservation at a cost of $30 per rifle.

Zokosky said he has in the past, and still does consulting work for the British government, mainly on shell casings. The Zokoskys were nice people, presumably stable, intelligent people. The biggest question in my mind was, why were they involved in all this? Why did they share all the information in the above interview with Kelly and I?

I left with more questions than I came with, unaware that the very next day I would receive the answers to the secret of the Octopus while sitting at my own dining room table!

••••••••

At my home on February 15, 2001, I answered a knock on my door. An individual was standing there with an innocuous bound accordion file brought from Washington D.C. I have assigned a code-name for this individual as "Source" to protect this individual's identity. Source said the documents had been obtained from the House Judiciary Committee on Inslaw archived files. The files were the result of a 3-year investigation by the Committee relative to Inslaw's claim that the U.S. Dept. of Justice stole Inslaw's enhanced PROMIS software under the direction of Attorney General Edwin Meese.

Source noted that the documents involved a lot more than stolen software by the DOJ. They indicated that the Mob was controlling the DOJ. Source had been given access to the documents stored at the National Archives in Suitland, Maryland. Someone in government had ordered the Judiciary Committee files delivered to his/her office and allegedly in the dead of night, source and another person had been given access to the Judiciary files.

Source explained that only Judiciary Committee members are allowed access to these documents. They are reports written by the investigators who worked for the Judiciary Committee and they contain information provided to the investigators by FBI agents, U.S. Attorneys, DEA agents, and other government and law enforcement people.

Source had been allowed to view and copy all 37 boxes of documents, but due to time constraints, had made copies of only two boxes. The two boxes were labeled or code-named "John Cohen-Personal" and they contained statements from and memorandums/reports of conversations with Thomas Gates, Marvin Rudnick, Richard Stavin and others relating to the FBI wiretaps of Robert Booth Nichols, Eugene Giaquinto and others associated with MCA Corporation. Included in the boxes were copies of the FBI wiretap *tapes.* Everything in those two boxes was copied, including the wiretap tapes, according to source.

I had a momentary prescience that this source had connections in very high places. I have inserted below an outline of what was contained in *some* of those documents brought to my house that day. In honor of the short life of journalist Danny Casolaro, it would be a crime in my estimation to withhold such information. In the dedication page of this manuscript, I wrote to Danny Casolaro: "Let Justice Be Done Though the Heavens May Fall." So be it.

The reports which I viewed were written by investigators for the House Judiciary Committee on Inslaw during the time span of August 12, 1991 – January 29,31, 1992 – February 3, 1992 – March 1992 – and May 1992. The investigators who wrote the reports were John Cohen, Ned M. Friece, Jim Lewin, and Richard Newbold. (It is significant that "The Inslaw Affair" investigative Report by the Committee on the Judiciary was published on September 10, 1992 *after* these reports were written, yet none of the information below was included in that publication to my knowledge.)

Most of the reports that I have chosen to outline below were written by John Cohen, based on information received from FBI agent Thomas Gates who clearly was a man of strong integrity and moral courage. I have withheld the telephone numbers and addresses mentioned in the reports. *The following information is accurate almost to the word as it appeared in the reports. Nothing has been* ***added*** *except what was placed in brackets [ ].* Some information in the reports was excluded from this outline due to privacy reasons, or subsequent interviews which conflicted with the information.

Report No. 1 – Conversation between Jonathan Littman and John Cohen: Littman told Cohen that he [Littman] was present at a meeting between Robert Booth Nichols and Robert Maheu, former CEO of Howard Hughes enterprises in Las Vegas. Littman said Maheu and Nichols were "very, very friendly."

Report No. 2 – Conversation between Richard Newbold and Dr. Anthony Casolaro [brother of Danny Casolaro]: Dr. Anthony Casolaro told Newbold that DEA agent Keith Bodine had called him after Danny's death and told him that he [Bodine] had been a "source" for Danny during his investigation of PROMIS, money laundering, drugs, etc. At the time Bodine was communicating with Danny, he [Bodine] was "on detail with FinCen" [Financial Crimes Enforcement Network]. Bodine told Dr. Casolaro ----- (note ended there).

Report No. 3 – The Judiciary Committee interviewed Allan Boyak, who refused to cooperate.

Report No. 4 – The Judiciary Committee interviewed Tara Sonenshine, *ABC Nightline News*. Tara said she had obtained a number of Danny's documents and wanted to know what to do with them?

Report No. 5 - Conversation between John Cohen and Thomas Gates, FBI agent in Los Angeles: Gates stated he had been employed with the FBI for 16 years. Gates said he had been investigating the MCA board members being involved with the Gambino and Bufalino crime families.

Gates said "high level Department of Justice officials" had a close working relationship with the board of directors of MCA Corporation. Gates said he learned this from FBI wiretaps on MCA. He said the wiretaps disclosed that "high level DOJ officials were tied to illegal activities of MCA." Gates advised Cohen to contact Walt Wagner [correct name was Bill Wagner] at the DOJ about this.

Gates said the investigation of Mob and DOJ ties to MCA was shut down by the DOJ and subsequently sealed by the DOJ. Gates explained that the DOJ wanted the case sealed because the Japanese were interested in purchasing MCA, and the DOJ did not want the deal ruined by the wiretaps and FBI investigation.

Gates stated that a confidential informant had visited Robert Booth Nichols' home and observed pictures on the wall of Nichols standing with "high level intelligence and political figures."

Gates stated that three days before Danny Casolaro's death [August 10, 1991], Danny told Gates that Robert Booth Nichols visited Danny in Martinsburg, VA [where Danny was found dead]. Gates said he believed Danny was murdered and Robert Booth Nichols was a prime suspect.

Report No. 6 – Conversation between John Cohen and Thomas Gates, FBI in Los Angeles: Gates told Cohen that "the FBI feels Danny Casolaro's death was an ITAR murder" [Interstate Travel in Aid of Racketeering].

Gates said the FBI wiretap "extensively documents Robert Booth Nichols' connection with the highest levels of the U.S. Department of Justice."

Gates said the wiretap revealed that Robert Booth Nichols was warned by the DOJ that the FBI was investigating him. The conversation between RBN and the DOJ official was picked up on the wiretap.

Gates added that the wiretap revealed that "*there was a close working relationship between the Board of Directors of MCA, Attorney General Edwin Meese, and the White House.*"

Gates said the wiretap revealed a conversation between Eugene Giaquinto [MCA executive and a Gambino associate] and Martin Bacow in which "*Giaquinto told Bacow that he will call Edwin Meese and have the FBI's investigation of MCA stopped.*" [The FBI investigation WAS shut down afterward by the DOJ].

Gates discussed Robert Booth Nichols' influence with the Japanese Yakuza.

Report No. 7 – Internal Memorandum between investigators of the House Judiciary Committee: U.S. Attorney Marvin Rudnick [DOJ lawyer between 1978 and 1989] reported to the House Judiciary Committee that he was called to Washington D.C. by David Margolis, Chief of the Organized Crime Strike Force at the DOJ.

Margolis told Rudnick that he [Rudnick] "was under investigation because of his [Rudnick's] investigation of MCA."

At that time, MCA was being represented by attorney Robert S. Strauss. Assisting Strauss was MCA attorney William Hundley, former Chief of the Organized Crime Strike Force at the DOJ.

The memorandum stated that at this time, during the FBI investigation of MCA, Senator Howard Baker was a member of the Board of Directors of MCA Corp. That Robert Strauss was current Ambassador to Russia, and Lew Wasserman was on the Board as well. Wasserman was connected to organized crime.

The memorandum stated that Marvin Rudnick learned MCA was directly connected to the Reagan White House. That Marvin Rudnick detailed this information in the July 1989 issue of *American Lawyer*. [It was actually the July/August 1988 issue of *American Lawyer* entitled, "Death of A Mob Probe: MCA Charges A Prosecutor with Misconduct, and Justice Kills a Two-Year Investigation. Why?" by Michael Orey].

The memorandum stated that Marvin Rudnick was fired from his position because he refused to drop the MCA investigation. Rudnick detailed how this occurred and who fired him in a deposition to the Judiciary Committee. The Judiciary files contain a transcript of this deposition.

Marvin Rudnick told the Judiciary Committee that Ted Gale, Rudnick's immediate supervisor who became a U.S. Attorney in Rhode Island, resigned from his position because of the DOJ's policies on the MCA investigation.

Richard Stavin, a member of the Organized Crime Strike Force in Los Angeles, also gave a deposition to the Judiciary Committee about the MCA investigation. Stavin said he walked out of his job as a result of the DOJ's policies on the MCA investigation. Transcript in Judiciary files.

Report No. 8 – Conversation between John Cohen and Thomas Gates, FBI in Los Angeles: Thomas Gates stated that he received a phone call from the Assistant Attorney General who advised him to discontinue the MCA investigation. Gates said he dropped the investigation after the phone call because he was concerned he would lose his job.

Report No. 9 - Conversation between John Cohen and a "confidential source" who reports to Thomas Gates, FBI in L.A.: This confidential source called the Judiciary Committee to report information about Thomas Gates. The source said he/she is a confidential source who reports to Thomas Gates.

The confidential source said Danny Casolaro called Thomas Gates a few days before his death and asked Gates to come to Martinsburg, VA to meet with him. Casolaro said he had valuable information relating to MCA and illegal activities. Gates told Danny he could not justify the trip. Danny's body was found in a Martinsburg hotel a few days later. Gates was very upset about this and initiated official authorization to testify to the Judiciary Committee about the death of Danny Casolaro.

Other reports: There were numerous other reports in the packet that source brought from Washington D.C. but they were not as significant, in my estimation, as the personal memorandums written by John Cohen. One report outlined Thomas Gates' efforts to obtain official authorization from the FBI to testify before the House Judiciary Committee on the death of Danny Casolaro. This lengthy report outlined the negotiations between Thomas Gates' FBI superiors and the investigators of the House Judiciary Committee.

Another report was a lengthy chronology written by one of the Judiciary investigators listing dates of contacts and a brief summary of each contact between the investigators and Thomas Gates, Marvin Rudnick, Richard Stavin, Dr. Tony Casolaro, and other people providing information to the Judiciary Committee.

Another document was a printout of data obtained from the RLO-2 platters obtained from Michael Riconosciuto's storage unit by Ned Friece, investigator for the House Judiciary Committee. Source brought just a few pages from this lengthy printout, which allegedly consisted of thousands of pages. All of the pages were printed out at the National Institute of Health in Maryland. The Institute was listed at the top of each printout. I had no idea what this list of names represented.

As of this writing, I have seen only three public references to the documents that source obtained from the National Archives and provided to me relative to the FBI wiretaps in which Eugene Giaquinto, a board member of MCA Corporation, boasted about his lifetime friendship with John Gotti of the Gambino family and assured Martin Bacow that "he would call Edwin Meese and have the FBI's investigation of MCA stopped."

This does not necessarily mean that Meese had agreed to Giaquinto's demand. There is no proof that he agreed --- other than the fact that the investigation was shut down afterward.

Keep in mind that Robert Booth Nichols had mentioned during a meeting with me at his home in Sherman Oaks on February 13, 1992 that MCA was broke and trying to leverage the company for sale to the Japanese. Nichols said that MCA's Home Entertainment Division was the only profit-making division in MCA at that time. Eugene Giaquinto was the President of the MCA Home Entertainment Division, but he was also a corporate partner in Nichols' company, Meridian International Logistics (MIL). When Nichols and Giaquinto learned that they were under investigation by the FBI, Giaquinto resigned from MIL and returned his stock certificates.

Insight magazine conducted follow-up interviews with Marvin Rudnick, John Cohen, Thomas Gates and other investigators who had knowledge of the FBI wiretaps, but those interviews never surfaced publicly after their four-part series was concluded. Thomas Gates had asked *Insight*, "Where are you going with this?" The reporter asked, "What do you know about Cheri Seymour?" Gates derisively responded, "Ask Cheri about her good friend Robert Booth Nichols, how much she talks to him." Gates advised the reporter to contact Robert Maheu, adding that "you'll be contacted by RBN." Gates suggested that there was a "mole" inside the Department of Justice.

Insight was subsequently shut down by its owner, Reverend Sun Myung Moon, a South Korean theocrat who had been one of the Bush family's major benefactors – both politically and financially – for over two decades.

♦♦♦♦♦♦♦♦

I needed to obtain John Cohen's memorandums from the National Archives in Suitland, Maryland through *official* channels, so as not to expose my source who originally showed them to me on February 15, 2001.

After several unsuccessful attempts to access the memorandums through official channels, on September 26, 2001, I finally called retired Congressman Jack Brooks (D-TX), the former Chairman of the House Judiciary Committee on Inslaw. Brooks was full of surprises. He said he knew who I was and called me by my first name.

I explained simply that I wanted to access the Judiciary documents from the Inslaw Affair and needed to know the name of the person who was assigned to store the Judiciary documents. I said I needed the accession number to do this, that Helen at the National Records Center said she would pull them for me if I could give her the accession numbers.

Rep. Brooks responded that he knew the PROMIS software was stolen from Bill Hamilton and the government "treated him very badly." I started to describe what I was looking for in the documents, and Mr. Brooks interrupted me and said, "Yes, I know what you're looking for." I was surprised and said, "You do?" He replied, "I know exactly what you want and I wish you the very best in getting those documents."

Brooks advised me to call Dan Freeman at the Judiciary Committee. He said Freeman was on the original Judiciary Committee with him (Brooks) and was still on the Judiciary Committee. He said Freeman would remember who was assigned to store the Committee on Inslaw's records. Freeman referred my call back to John Cohen and Cohen said he didn't know the name of the person who physically stored the documents.

••••••••

For purposes of accuracy and authenticity, there were no embellishments or prose inserted into the outline of Judiciary Committee reports listed above, so I feel compelled to explain that I excluded the portion in one of the above reports where Thomas Gates told John Cohen that Marvin Rudnick had handled the wiretaps. In subsequent interviews with Richard Stavin, who handled the wiretaps with Thomas Gates, Stavin pointed out that Marvin Rudnick had no involvement in the wiretaps. Marvin Rudnick concurred in an interview that same day. They both had a sense of camaraderie and respect for Thomas Gates' work in the investigation. I advised them that I was attempting to contact Gates to interview him, but neither of them had communicated with him in years and had no idea how to reach him.

When I sent the Judiciary Committee reports to them for comment, at the advice of Dan Moldea who knew them personally, both of these honorable former prosecutors provided detailed accounts of their experience while working for the Department of Justice under Edwin Meese and Ronald Reagan. Their story represents one of the largest cover-ups in American history and is presented here with some background history.

As noted at the end of the Prologue in this book, the first known public reference to The Octopus can be found in Dan Moldea's 1986 book entitled, *Dark Victory,* in which Moldea aptly labeled MCA "The Octopus." There can be no more fitting epitaph than to point out that the answer to the Octopus was hiding in plain sight all along, right under our noses.

MCA had been Ronald Reagan's agent in Hollywood; he subsequently negotiated an exclusive arrangement that enabled MCA to become a multi-billion dollar monopoly.

In the forward of his book, Moldea quoted Ralph Salerno, New York Police Department in 1967, as saying,

> "Organized crime will put a man in the White House someday – and he won't know it until they hand him the bill."

On page 354 of Moldea's book, in a postscript he wrote,

> On February 3 [1987], the Reagan Administration announced that the President would issue an executive order combining all of the federal government's anti-drug programs under the National Drug Policy Board. Selected by President Reagan to head the board – which would be charged with developing budget priorities for every federal agency involved in the war on drugs – was Attorney General Edwin Meese.

Ironically, after the Judiciary Committee's investigation was closed and "The Inslaw Affair" was published in September, 1991, investigator John Cohen became employed as a "policy advisor in the White House's Office of National Drug Control Policy" during the Bill Clinton administration.

Dan Moldea also wrote about the DOJ shutting down Marvin Rudnick's investigation of MCA's relationship with Salvatore James Pisello, an alleged Gambino mobster. In an article published in *Regardie's* in June 1988, entitled "MCA Music & the Mafia: Did the Justice Department cut Reagan's Hollywood pals a break?," Moldea wrote: (excerpt)

> --- One of the industry's giants was being represented by a mobster [Salvatore James Pisello]. How deeply had the industry been

infiltrated? Four years after the convention there's still no answer to that question. But there's a new question: Why has the Justice Department dropped its investigation of the ties between Pisello and MCA?

Last December, according to sources in the Justice Department, the Los Angeles prosecutor who had started the investigation was called to Washington and told by top officials of the Strike Force against Organized Crime to eliminate MCA from the probe. David Margolis, the strike force's chief, and Michael DeFeo, his deputy, told Marvin Rudnick, the prosecutor, that he could pursue a tax case against Pisello, who had earned about $ 600,000 in income from his dealings with MCA, but that he couldn't call several of MCA's executives as witnesses nor could he try to determine the exact nature of Pisello's relationship with MCA.

The action raises a host of troubling questions and has prompted a preliminary investigation by a House subcommittee. While spokesmen for the Justice Department and MCA refuse to comment on the case, the House Energy and Commerce Oversight Subcommittee has interviewed witnesses in an attempt to determine if hearings are warranted and whether Justice Department officials acted properly in killing the investigation.

The case is certainly worth examining. Why, for instance, when the entire record industry is under the scrutiny of grand juries in at least five cities, would one major record company [MCA] be exempted from investigation? Why would a supposedly reputable business get involved in a series of apparently unprofitable deals with a man of dubious background?

One element of the case makes the whole matter even more curious: the names of some of MCA's high-placed friends. These include Robert Strauss, a former chairman of the Democratic National Committee and an MCA board member; Howard Baker, a former U.S. senator and a former MCA board member; and Ronald Reagan, the president of the United States and once one of MCA's most important clients. [On February 27, 1987 Howard Baker resigned from MCA's board and became Reagan's chief of staff].

Interviews with industry sources and law enforcement officials, court documents, and MCA's own records indicate that there's an unusual relationship between the Mafia figure and the Fortune 500 company -- a relationship that seems to be just the sort of thing that the Justice Department is supposed to investigate.

In another excerpt, Moldea wrote:

> --- For 22 of the years that Ronald Reagan pursued a career in show business, MCA was his talent agency. Lew Wasserman, the company's chairman, represented Reagan during the actor's early days in Hollywood. The late Jules Stein, MCA's founder and a longtime political supporter of Reagan's, negotiated the sale of Reagan's California properties at hugely inflated prices. In fact, MCA's help in the real estate transactions made Reagan a millionaire. Wasserman is a major contributor to and currently sits on the board of the Reagan presidential library, along with Attorney General Edwin Meese and seven others. He's helping to raise $ 80 million to build it.
>
> So the biggest question of all, and another one that's still unanswered, is: Did somebody do a favor for Reagan's pals?

So the official head of the Octopus resided in the *U.S. Department of Justice*, supported by an out-of-control presidential administration, its tentacles comprised of a cabal of "Old Boy" cronies, true believers, who held that the end justified the means in their obsession to quell the expansion of communism in neighboring countries and throughout the world. They gave corruption a new meaning as they stampeded through the Constitution, cowboyed the intelligence community, blazed new trails into drug cartels and organized crime, while simultaneously growing *new* tentacles that reached into every facet of criminal enterprise. The theft of high-tech software (PROMIS) for use in money-laundering and espionage, illegal drug and arms trafficking in Latin America, exploitation of sovereign Indian nations, were just a few of these enterprises.

What could be more demoralizing to those men and women who serve and protect, than *to capture on* ***tape*** *(actual voice recordings), members of the Gambino and Bufalino crime families, in collusion with the Department of Justice and U.S. Attorney General, the highest law enforcement authority in the nation, arranging* the *shutdown and sealing of an FBI investigation* of MCA in order to facilitate the largest sale in U.S. history to the Japanese?

Notwithstanding that Ronald and Nancy Reagan were known to celebrate New Year's Eve with their old friends, Edie and Lew Wasserman (Chairman of MCA Corporation), and Howard Baker was on the MCA board of directors before and after he was Reagan's chief of staff.

In November 2009, I contacted Marvin Rudnick, now a practicing attorney in California, and Richard Stavin, a former DOJ Organized Crime Strike Force prosecutor (also a practicing lawyer in California), who investigated Robert Booth Nichols, Eugene Giaquinto and the alleged Mob connections to MCA.

Rudnick explained that there were two simultaneous investigations of MCA at that time, each operating independently of each other. Rudnick and Stavin worked in the same office two doors away from each other. Rudnick's investigation of Salvatore Pisello, a member of the Gambino crime family, focused on Pisello's tax evasion and his strange relationship with MCA, and Stavin and Thomas Gates conducted the wiretaps relating to Meridian International Logistics [MIL] at that time suspected as a "source of funding for the purchasing of narcotics/controlled substances and the allocation and use of the proceeds from its trafficking," according to the wiretap application.

One affidavit in support of an application to intercept wire communications over the telephone listed names of those to be intercepted as Robert Booth Nichols, Eugene Giaquinto, Angelo Commito, Edward Sciandra, Michael Del Gaizo, Joseph Garofalo, and others. These applications were submitted to the DOJ for approval, then to a federal judge for review and approval by Richard Stavin. The affidavits in support of the applications were written by Thomas Gates and Richard Stavin.

Rudnick, who had been a DOJ lawyer from 1978 to 1989, said he had provided deposition testimony to the Judiciary Committee on Inslaw, including a detailed sworn statement to the DOJ defending his termination, which outlined his description of the obstruction by DOJ officials, yet no one in the DOJ sought to follow-up to see if DOJ officials had committed crimes.

Rudnick noted that the *Reagan Diaries* (by Ronald Reagan) mentions the date that Lew Wasserman (Chairman of MCA Inc.) and Reagan met in Los Angeles, it was about two weeks before the FBI wiretaps were *coincidentally* discovered by MCA personnel.

In the 1993 book *Stiffed: A True Story of MCA, The Music Business, and the Mafia* by Bill Knoedelseder, a former reporter for the *Los Angeles Times*, Rudnick discussed the threat made to him in December 1987 by David Margolis, the strike force's chief, and Michael DeFeo, his deputy, who had been present in the room and witnessed

Margolis's conversation with Rudnick. John Newcomer, the new head of the strike force in Los Angeles, had advised Rudnick beforehand that he was under investigation by the Office of Professional Responsibility for including MCA in his investigation of Pisello.

Rudnick believed that Newcomer came into the Strike Force with an agenda to obstruct justice but he was never prosecuted for it, nor was Margolis, according to *Stiffed.* The book's protagonist is Marvin Rudnick, the prosecutor who nailed Sal Pisello twice for tax evasion, and for not reporting income derived from MCA. The villain is the Justice Department. As *Stiffed* tells it, Rudnick's superiors kept him from subpoenaing witnesses and directly ordered him not to investigate MCA.

Dan Moldea's June 1988 article in *Regardie's* gives further details. As follows:

> ... On October 2, 1987 MCA filed a formal complaint against Rudnick "to protest the many unfounded and inflammatory statements (he has made) regarding MCA and its executives and employees." The complaint was forwarded to the department's Office of Professional Responsibility in Washington, which refused to confirm or deny an investigation of Rudnick.
>
> At the same time the company retained William Hundley to plead its case to top Justice Department officials. Hundley, who had headed the department's legendary organized crime division under Attorney General Robert Kennedy, had recently joined Strauss's firm, Akin Gump Strauss Hauer & Feld.
>
> Hundley confirms that he met with Margolis and DeFeo of the strike force. He says that he wanted to tell Justice Department officials that MCA was willing to cooperate in any organized crime investigation. "I said, 'Look, we're going to cooperate,'" Hundley explains. "'Whatever you want from the corporation. You want to talk to people? You want documents? Get in touch with me. I'll see you get them in a hurry.'"
>
> The Washington prosecutors sent Hundley to talk to John Newcomer, the new head of the strike force in Los Angeles. Hundley says that he discussed the Pisello case with Newcomer and asked about MCA's status in the investigation. Hundley says that he inquired, "Are we a target? If you tell me we're a target, maybe my attitude is going to be different."
>
> In mid October MCA received a response from Newcomer. "The allegations (against Rudnick) are a cause of great concern," he wrote to MCA, "and we have taken the necessary steps to en-

> sure that only relevant statements that are factually accurate will appear in pleadings and oral arguments." He concluded by saying, "Neither MCA nor any of its executives or employees are targets of that case and its attendant investigation."

Rudnick pointed out that it was William Hundley's picture on the wall, along with Reagan and Edwin Meese's, in Margolis's office that he (Margolis) pointed to when he threatened him.

The chronology of this incident is interesting: Hundley, a former DOJ Strike Force chief, was now representing MCA - Ronald Reagan had visited Lew Wasserman in Los Angeles and two weeks later the FBI wiretaps were *coincidentally* discovered by MCA - the DOJ looked the other way when MCA blamed Rudnick for illegally wiretapping them, despite the fact that Richard Stavin and Thomas Gates had a legal court order for the wiretaps - and a couple of months later, the DOJ called Rudnick to Washington D.C. to threaten him.

In November 2009, I sent both Marvin Rudnick and Richard Stavin excerpts from John Cohen's memorandums obtained from the Judiciary Committee's archives and asked them for comments. We communicated in an exchange of three-way e-mails back and forth during November; they offered corrections to the Judiciary Committee memorandums, but also set the record straight about why these two seasoned prosecutors either quit or were fired during their respective independent investigations of MCA Corporation.

Marvin Rudnick responded that he did not handle the wiretaps and had no involvement in their management. Richard Stavin confirmed that it was he and FBI agent Thomas Gates who handled the wiretaps, Marvin Rudnick was not involved

I asked a direct question to Stavin which was one of the main reasons I had contacted him. "Mr. Stavin: Can you please confirm that the FBI wiretap revealed a conversation between Eugene Giaquinto [board member of MCA and Gambino associate] and Martin Bacow in which '*Giaquinto told Bacow that he would call Edwin Meese and have the FBI's investigation stopped.*'" Stavin, replying to what is in the public record, ***confirmed it*** in an e-mail.

Stavin had also been called back to Washington D.C. by David Margolis and Michael DeFeo almost a year to the day after Rudnick. When Stavin subsequently quit the Organized Crime Strike Force in May 1989, he was threatened by DeFeo about talking about the circumstances of the case, or "throwing dirt," as he called it.

The wiretaps were shut down around September 1988, and *unofficially* Stavin's investigation was shut down around January 1989 when the first draft of his prosecution memorandum was given to John Newcomer. Officially it was shut down after Stavin left and another FBI agent was assigned to re-interview some of the same witnesses that Thomas Gates had interviewed previously and obtained conflicting information.

The wiretap information and the related investigation reportedly gathered enough evidence to justify seeking an indictment against Detective John St. John of the LAPD-OCID (not to be confused with another LAPD homicide detective of the same name), Eugene Giaquinto, and Martin Bacow for obstruction of justice. Detective John St. John worked for the Los Angeles Police Department's Organized Crime Intelligence Division at that time and had been communicating with Martin Bacow.

In interviews with investigators who worked the case, as well as wiretap information and documents from the Judiciary archives, I had learned that St. John was allegedly Bacow's direct contact at LAPD-OCID. Bacow boasted to Giaquinto that St. John's status within OCID allowed him to obtain intelligence reports on organized crime figures across the nation, and Bacow could then pass that information along to Giaquinto.

A grand jury investigation into the mob's involvement in the motion picture industry was in the process of being opened at that time, which would have included a close look at Giaquinto, Bacow and others. St. John called Bacow on the telephone and told him he would listen and not give up too much, and try to find out what the investigators were looking at and let Bacow know. Bacow then called Giaquinto and related what St. John had said. Giaquinto responded that he would call Meese [and get the investigation shut down].

In the November 2009 interview with Richard Stavin, I asked him who would have had to give authority to pursue an indictment against St. John, Giaquinto, and Bacow? He replied that any indictment would have had to been approved by the then U.S. Attorney, Rob Bonner, and Main Justice including David Margolis and DeFeo. When I asked him to comment whether an indictment against these individuals for obstruction of justice was approved, Stavin would neither confirm nor deny any such approval.

In searching the information I gathered in my investigation and in speaking with investigators involved in the MCA investigation, I determined that no indictment was ever issued against St. John, Giaquinto or Bacow for any criminal violations.

I asked Stavin to comment on why no indictment was issued and he responded,

> I surmise that the prosecution of these suspects never went forward because no one at the DOJ in Washington D.C. wanted all the wiretap affidavits in the case to be released, and any prosecution would have resulted in that.

According to investigators familiar with the case, Stavin's investigation had begun in December 1986 and was being dismantled when he quit in May 1989. Rudnick had been fired in the Spring of 1989. The wiretaps had been shut down in the Fall of 1988.

I sent Stavin and Rudnick a brief outline of my 18-year investigation of the Octopus, including Robert Booth Nichols' transactions during his prolific lifetime career in shadowy undercover operations. Stavin responded, "Quitting and not being able to pursue this investigation was one of the biggest disappointments I had in my 15-year career. I knew we were on to something big. You have done an amazing job in piecing things together." Stavin asked if I had spoken with Bill Weld?

News stories indicated that Weld reportedly left the DOJ because of political influence pedaling in Southern California. Thomas Gates and Stavin believed that the MCA investigation was one of the reasons. I subsequently learned that, indeed, one of the reasons William Weld quit the DOJ in late March 1988 was because of influence peddling at the DOJ involving some cases in Southern California. Weld was interviewed by FBI headquarters, and the 302 Report on that interview was viewed by Thomas Gates. Most of the report had been redacted; the only thing that was mentioned in the report about Weld and MCA was a question to the effect whether "*he (Weld) was ever told by Edwin Meese to not investigate MCA*." Weld reportedly answered "No" to that question. Curiously the two individuals most intimately involved (Stavin and Gates) in the MCA investigation were never contacted by FBI HQ to find out what questions to ask.

I knew from Judiciary reports that Richard Stavin had communicated with Danny Casolaro prior to his death and asked for any comment he could offer. Stavin replied, "I never believed for a moment that Danny Casolaro committed suicide. I spoke to him for about 45 minutes the week before [his death] and this was not a despondent man. The first question he asked me was whether he had to be concerned for his safety because he was going to meet RBN."

Dan Moldea, who was being copied (cc'd) on my three-way e-mail conversations with Stavin and Rudnick, volunteered that he had interviewed William Weld in late April 1988, one month after Weld gave his letter of resignation to Howard Baker, then Reagan's chief of staff and a former member of the MCA board of directors. Moldea offered a transcript of the interview. The cryptic last paragraph of the transcript provided a hint that there was more to the story than we had previously suspected. I have excerpted a portion of that transcript, as follows:

> (Moldea) " --- I told Weld that I was getting ready to come out with a story about a prosecution out in Los Angeles. Again, Weld interrupted me and said, "I can't help you with this one," and started laughing.
>
> I asked him, "Do you know what I'm talking about?" He replied, "I think so." I then said, "The Sal Pisello case." Weld told me to call Jack Keeney or Dave Margolis "and see what you can get. Good luck to you."
>
> He interrupted again when I started talking and said, "You're doing Reagan, Meese, Lew Wasserman, MCA?" "Yeah," I replied.
>
> "I'd wave you cautiously away from that. I'm not as close to it as I might be, but I'd refer you to . . . "
>
> I asked him to listen while I explained. I told him that I liked and respected Margolis and Mike DeFeo. I told him that I had heard that the Justice Department killed the investigation of MCA's role with Pisello.
>
> I added that my concern was that Marvin Rudnick was on a side street and that a truck was coming down the highway. I told him that I didn't want to screw up a Justice Department investigation of MCA. I told him about the OCID situation in Los Angeles.
>
> I then said that I had been told by an FBI source that the investigation of MCA had been killed by Margolis and DeFeo. I was also told that DeFeo would never kill a case unless he was in-

structed to do so. "He wouldn't kill a case even if he was told to, unless there was a reason."

I told Weld that I was told that DeFeo wouldn't kill a case unless Weld told him to and that Weld would only kill the case if he was instructed to do so by the Attorney General. "No, I wouldn't kill a case if I was directed to by the Attorney General," Weld said.

I asked whether the MCA case had anything to do with all the chaos over at the Justice Department. Weld said no and that his resignation was over Bob Wallach and Meese.

I appealed to Weld to point me in the right direction, adding that this case looked bad and that I was on deadline.

Giving Weld some background, I told him about Pisello in MCA and that MCA was turning up on wiretaps of Tommy Vastola and Morris Levy, among others on the East Coast. I told him that I had just been subpoenaed in Vastola and Levy's case.

"There ain't nothing sinister going on here in the department as far as I know. *You probably know that when things are slowed down that means that other things are going on."*

What are the other things?

"Well, the other things, I certainly can't tell you. But it ain't that Ronald Reagan is a friend of Lew Wasserman or Ed Meese is a friend of Lew Wasserman. It's something else. It's a law enforcement thing; it's not a political thing. With that, I've probably told you too much already. But I'd wave you off the sinister explanation . . . It's something else. It's not what you're getting at."

Moldea's 1988 interview with Weld left us all scratching our heads. What was the "something else" that had caused everyone in the Justice Department to create a nightmare for two of their best prosecutors in Los Angeles?

I recalled a document that Bill Hamilton, owner of INSLAW, had received in the mail in November 2004 from a U.S. intelligence source. The letter was dated May 16, 1985 from William Bradford Reynolds, Assistant Attorney General, to *William F. Weld,* U.S. Attorney in Boston, Massachusetts at that time. Hamilton had authenticated the document through Donald Carr, who showed it to Bradford Reynolds in 2005. Carr was writing a biography of Elliot Richardson and served with Reynolds in the Meese and Thornburgh Justice Departments as a Republican political appointee. Reynolds authenticated the document. He told Carr that Lowell Jensen's secretary brought the letter to him for signature because

Jensen was out of the building, the letter needed to be sent that day, and it needed to be signed by someone in Meese's inner circle. He said he signed the letter but did not draft it. Reynolds said he had a vague recollection that Meese recused himself on PROMIS when he became Attorney General in February 1985 and Jensen had, therefore, to handle PROMIS. Reynolds told Carr that he had an independent memory of Richard Armitage, Adnan Khashoggi, and Manucher Ghorbanifar working together on PROMIS.

Hamilton said it was a very important letter. The source who sent it to him in November 2004 told him that all copies were supposed to have been destroyed but obviously were not. The letter read as follows:

> *Dear Mr. Weld:*
>
> As agreed Messrs. Manichur [sic] Ghorbanifar, Adnan Khashoggi, and Richard Armitage will broker the transaction of Promise software to Sheik Klahid bin Mahfouz for resale and general distribution as gifts in his region contingent upon the three conditions we last spoke of. *Promise* must have a soft arrival. No paperwork, customs, or delay. It must be equipped with the special data retrieval unit. As before, you must walk the financial aspects through Credit Suisse into National Commercial Bank. If you encounter any problems contact me directly.
>
> Sincerely,
> WM. Bradford Reynolds,
> Assistant Attorney General,
> Civil Rights Divison.

Bill Hamilton had subsequently sent me another document, written by *William Weld*, Assistant Attorney General by that time, to Stephen S. Trott, Associate Attorney General, dated February 29, 1988. The subject of the letter was:

> Allegations by INSLAW, Inc. against Attorney General Meese, Deputy Attorney General Burns, and former Deputy Attorney General Jensen – [re:] Closing of Independent Counsel Matter.

Weld wrote as follows: (excerpt)

> The Public Integrity Section has reviewed allegations by INSLAW, Inc. that Attorney General Meese, Deputy Attorney General Burns, and/or former Deputy Attorney General Jensen com-

> mitted 'procurement fraud' and/or obstruction of justice. The public Integrity Section concluded that the information submitted is not sufficiently specific to constitute grounds to initiate a preliminary investigation. The Section, however, recommended that the materials provided by INSLAW be supplied to the office of Professional Responsibility, which has been conducting its own investigation of the INSLAW matter as to persons not covered by the Independent Counsel statute ---

This letter, declining to investigate INSLAW's allegations, was written by William Weld on February 29, 1988. Weld resigned from the DOJ one month later, on March 29, 1988. It appeared to be a conflict of interest to me, i.e, Weld is asked by Bradford Reynolds to facilitate the financial aspects of the PROMISE software to Sheik Klahid bin Mahfouz in 1985, then in 1988, one month before he resigns, Weld declines to investigate INSLAW's charges against the DOJ based on insufficient evidence!

At that time, Adnan Khashoggi, named in the above 1985 letter to Weld, had been implicated in the Iran-Contra affair as a key middleman in the arms-for-hostages exchange along with Iranian arms dealer Manucher Ghorbanifar, and in a complex series of events, was found to have borrowed money for these arms purchases from the now-bankrupt financial institution the Bank of Credit and Commerce International (BCCI) with Saudi and US backing. In 1988, Khashoggi was arrested in Switzerland, accused of concealing funds, held for three months and then extradited to the United States where he was released on bail and subsequently acquitted. http://en.wikipedia.org/wiki/Adnan_Khashoggi

When I asked Bill Hamilton at INSLAW what his thoughts were on the two "Weld" documents, he wrote this:

> Elliot Richardson said to us that we are all patriots, why wouldn't the government approach one of our lawyers or Nancy or me if it was a legitimate national security issue?
>
> One of our lawyers in the U.S. Court of Federal Claims litigation in the late 1990s was Major General Hugh Overholt. When he came to see Elliot, Nancy and me in 1995, Elliot said the following: 'General Overholt, you are a patriot. What are you going to do if you conclude that the allegations are true that the government has misappropriated PROMIS for sensitive national security projects?'

> General Overholt answered Elliot by saying that he would tell the government that INSLAW and its lawyers have no interest in embarrassing the United States but the government must either compensate INSLAW for the harm it has done, or face the music.
>
> Elliot responded to General Overholt by saying that he has gone over the same question in his own mind on a number of occasions and always reached the same conclusion."

I sent the two "Weld" documents to Rudnick, Stavin and Moldea to compare them side by side, asking them if Weld was a good guy or a bad guy? All three of them unanimously defended Weld and defined him as a "good guy." Dan Moldea pointed out that Weld had left the DOJ at least a year before either Rudnick or Stavin had left, and therefore may not have known about the DOJ stonewalling their respective MCA investigations. Wrote Moldea: (excerpted)

> Here's what I think: At the time of my interview with Weld in April 1988, the details of your nightmare were not on the public record ... My story in *Regardie's*, which was in the July issue, came out in late May, and it was the first to provide those details while placing Hundley, Margolis and DeFeo – and even Baker – on the spot for the first time ---
>
> --- When Weld heard the rumors about what we now know was a blatant attempt to shut you down, he, no doubt, went to his own people for answers, namely Margolis and DeFeo, and perhaps even Hundley. Of course, they spun the story of their bad behavior their way, placing themselves in the most positive light.
>
> Bottom line, I think you're right. Weld was completely in the dark about what was happening to you and was intentionally misled by his subordinates. Simultaneously, Reagan, [Howard] Baker, and Meese were certainly in the right place at the right time to know exactly what was going on. And in the end, I believe, they corrupted the process – without the knowledge of William Weld, who was gone by the time of the denouement."

In July 1988, Howard Baker had left his White House chief of staff job and returned to MCA's board of directors in March 1989, just in time to help Lew Wasserman celebrate his seventy-sixth birthday. Baker had previously served on the MCA board from January 4, 1985 to March 2, 1987 at which time he had resigned to accept the position of chief of staff to President Reagan. (http://www.highbeam.com/doc/1G1-7087634.html)

At a glimpse, looking at the timeline of the FBI investigation and wiretaps, it appeared that Baker was in a unique situation during the probe of MCA. He had left the MCA board to work for Reagan in March 1987, three months after Stavin and Gates' began their investigation (December 1986), and returned to MCA's board of directors in March 1989, just months after the FBI wiretaps had been shut down (in the Fall of 1988).

Edwin Meese submitted his resignation on July 5, 1988. William Weld had already resigned from the DOJ four months earlier, on March 29, 1988. It appeared that there was a wholesale exodus occurring at the Justice Department in 1988 when Arnold Burns, deputy attorney general, also resigned along with four top aides. More on this later ---

FBI agent Thomas Gates had mentioned the story written about Marvin Rudnick in *The American Lawyer* to John Cohen. Cohen had noted it in one of his memorandums that were stored at the National Archives. I subsequently obtained a copy of the story, July/August 1988 issue, entitled "Death of a Mob Probe – MCA Charges a Prosecutor with Misconduct, and Justice Kills a Two-Year Investigation. Why?" by Michael Orey.

The American Lawyer story came out approximately one month *after* Dan Moldea's *Regardie's* story hit the streets, so it noted in the last sentence of the article, in a postscript, that " --- Newcomer had recommended to his superiors that Rudnick be fired."

Marvin Rudnick was depicted in the story as a hard-hitting, aggressive prosecutor who played hard-ball with MCA when he doggedly refused to eliminate MCA from his investigation of Salvadore Pisello. Pisello was convicted of tax evasion in March 1985, but while prosecuting that case, Rudnick learned about Pisello's income from MCA and that launched yet another investigation, at the urging of the IRS.

On May 10, 1985, William Knoedelseder, Jr., a business reporter for the *Los Angeles Times*, had broken a story revealing that Pisello's involvement with MCA had been more extensive than Rudnick had realized. Knoedelseder had obtained a copy of a report prepared by internal corporate auditors of MCA for presentation to the company's board of directors which detailed MCA's payments to Pisello. The press revelations rekindled government interest in Pisello's involvement with MCA.

In a section with the heading "Rudnick Unleashed," *American Lawyer* described the ensuing battle royal that ultimately lost Rudnick his job. When a grand jury indicted Pisello on a second round of tax charges on July 9, 1987, Rudnick "opened fire on MCA." His press release announcing the indictment documented MCA's payments to Pisello's company, Consultants for World Records, which Rudnick made sure to point out was "shared" with New York organized crime figures who he named openly in the release.

"By the Fall of 1987, MCA had had enough," wrote *American Lawyer*. "The company turned its guns on the person it considered to be the root of its problems: Rudnick." Enter MCA's lawyer William Hundley, former chief of the Justice Department's Organized Crime and Racketeering Section, who was well known in Justice. The rest of Marvin Rudnick's story is already outlined in the above *Regardie's* article.

Rudnick commented that with Richard Stavin's resignation from the DOJ, it proved that the DOJ was involved in a cover-up, not a personnel action as they tried to use in his termination. "I knew they were under tremendous pressure from above," he said. In an e-mail to Stavin, Rudnick wrote: *"I remember Bill Wagner telling me that your wiretaps included a call that went right into the White House.* I figured you either had a great case or you, too, would be fired."

Stavin responded: "They spoke to me about having just passed the California bar exam [he had previously worked out-of-state], and hoped that I would stay with the Strike Force. They knew there would be hell to pay if they had fired me after the maelstrom with Marvin."

The e-mail exchanges between the two former prosecutors had awakened long-forgotten memories. Wrote Stavin: "I am starting to get incredibly angry over this again. What happened to Marvin and the derailing of my career was truly a travesty. The DOJ had two veteran hard-charging prosecutors who simply wanted to do their jobs and root out the Mob wherever it be found, be that at MCA or anywhere. Well, I guess that old saying held true on a grander scale, 'You can't fight city hall!'"

Stavin had listened to almost every call made when the wiretaps were in effect, spent countless hours at the listening post alongside numerous agents who were assigned on a shift basis to monitor the wiretap.

The intercepted conversations captured Giaquinto referring to Robert Booth Nichols as a "super sleuth" and other similar terms. Martin Bacow boasted to Giaquinto about LAPD-OCID detective John St. John, and Giaquinto would boast back about his "government man" (Robert Booth Nichols) "being higher than the CIA."

One intercepted conversation, taken from the FBI wiretaps, revealed a conversation in which Giaquinto told Martin Bacow that the computer printouts being delivered to him by his "government man" would show connections to companies they owned, stockholders, and other companies as well as *indictments and other ongoing investigations.* Giaquinto also discussed the printouts in the context of an ongoing IRS case. (Marvin Rudnick had been investigating Salvador Pisello for tax evasion of income derived from MCA. Again, it appeared that the prosecutors' internal reports to the DOJ were circling back to Giaquinto via Robert Booth Nichols).

On July 15, 1987 FBI surveillance agents observed Giaquinto exit Le Dome Restaurant on Sunset Boulevard with RBN and walk to Giaquinto's vehicle. RBN was photographed by the surveillance team as he retrieved a box from Giaquinto's trunk, then drove to the Beverly Hills Hotel and entered the Polo Lounge Restaurant. The surveillance was terminated at that time because they believed the subject was attempting to determine if he was being followed.

In an interview, Richard Stavin remembered the incident. He said that he and Thomas Gates "were astounded by the comments Giaquinto made about Robert Booth Nichols as to what information he could get from the federal government."

I sent Stavin an FBI report on Nichols, and he responded: "I had seen other intelligence reports on RBN similar to this one. We had thought that he might have been involved in another Ollie North Iran-Contra deal through MCA and the Reagan/Wasserman connection. John Cohen intimated that we might have been on to something there." Stavin added: "I guess we'll never know how my investigation would have turned out had it not been sabotaged. Nichols was/is very mysterious."

I asked Stavin if he ever came across any mention of Nichols' involvement with the Wackenhut/Cabazon Joint Venture in his investigation? He answered, "I seem to recall the Cabazon reservation deal and Wackenhut popping up with RBN. We had so much else on our plates it was just another un-followed up lead."

He said he had not heard anything relating to PROMIS in his investigation.

I sent Stavin a copy of the Peter Zokosky interview from February 14, 2001, and he wrote back: "My, my. Gates and I really did stumble onto something more than MCA and the Mob, didn't we!" He added later, "Well 18 years later it looks like some justice will be done."

I had contacted Dan Moldea in October 2008 because he had authored the book *Dark Victory,* and I planned to use some of that information in my book.

During subsequent conversations on the phone, I had asked Dan if he had information on the FBI wiretaps of MCA, i.e., Eugene Giaquinto, Robert Booth Nichols, the mob, et al? I outlined to Dan what I had obtained relative to the wiretap information and he suggested that I contact Richard Stavin and Marvin Rudnick for comments. He provided me with their phone numbers.

Dan had been invaluable to me in various aspects of my book, and I am most grateful to him. He is also an incredibly talented writer and investigator and I am a devoted fan of his. Without Dan, I doubt that Stavin or Rudnick would have talked to me. Thus Dan had been copied on all the e-mail exchanges and concluded with the following letter:

> Dear Cheri:
>
> Congratulations for the gold mine of information you have created by putting these two good and decent men together. I never knew a lot of what they have been discussing in their exchanges.
>
> You know my feelings about both of them. They were honest prosecutors who were doing their jobs well, determined to prevent what became a *Chinatown* ending.
>
> Keep up the great work. And please do these guys proud in your upcoming book. Your friend, Dan."

There was no need to "do these guys proud," they did themselves proud when they made a decision of conscience at the height of their careers and kept the faith. I am simply proud to know them.

♦♦♦♦♦♦♦♦

I was subsequently provided with information from a 2004 book which I'd had no knowledge of until after my interviews with Stavin,

Rudnick and Moldea were concluded, but it's worth getting on the record because it substantiates much of what they told me in 2009.

The book is titled *Mr. and Mrs. Hollywood: Edie and Lew Wasserman and their Entertainment Empire* by Kathleen Sharp. On pages 475 – 478, author Sharp wrote:

> Burns, Weld and others complained about their boss [Meese] to Howard Baker, the President's chief of staff. Weld said that his superiors often asked if he couldn't close pending investigations of Meese's friends: "Hasn't that [case] been hanging around a long time? It's really hurting [the person or company under investigation]." In more than one case, the subjects of those investigations were in California, Weld said later. He and [Arnold] Burns were growing frustrated at being undermined and sidestepped in Meese's office.

Another excerpt read as follows:

> --- Nevertheless, Baker urged the two well-respected lawyers to remain on staff. They did, briefly. But the situation worsened, and, a week later, on March 30, 1988, Burns, Weld, and four top aides resigned from the Justice department. It was an unprecedented mass exit, the signal of a complete loss of faith in the U.S. Justice Department. *The Justice Department was now seen as so corrupt that Senator Robert C. Byrd (D.-W. VA) called Meese 'the crown jewel of Reagan's sleaze factor,' and demanded his resignation.* Even so, the exodus left Meese unbowed and still in charge."

The *Boston Globe* exposed the revolt inside Justice in an article on March 30, 1988 entitled, "Top Meese Aides Quit, Reportedly in Act of Conscience Weld, Burns were said to Urge Boss' Resignation" by Stephen Kurkjian, Globe Staff. (excerpted)

> WASHINGTON – Two top Justice Department officials, including William F. Weld, the former US attorney for Massachusetts, abruptly resigned yesterday, reportedly in acts of conscience over the refusal of Attorney General Edwin S. Meese 3rd to step down amid continued questions about his conduct in office.
>
> Weld, head of the Justice Department's criminal division, and Arnold I. Burns, deputy attorney general and Meese's second in command, submitted their resignations in letters to President Reagan after meeting with the White House

> chief of staff, Howard Baker, at his home at 7 A.M [and submitted their resignations] ---" http://www.encyclopedia.com/doc/1P2-8055592.html

The following excerpt credited to Kathleen Sharp's 2004 book, *Mr. and Mrs. Hollywood* included this passage which corroborated Thomas Gates' and Richard Stavin's information to the Judiciary Committee in March 1992: (Provided to author Sharp by a source who wished to remain anonymous)

> In May 1988, Giaquinto learned about the government investigation of him. "He went ballistic," said my source. MCA's executive Giaquinto had had enough. "I'm calling Meese and getting this thing stopped right now," he said.

"Sure enough," wrote Sharp, "after Giaquinto dropped Meese's name, the three cases against MCA – the payola, videocassettes, and record investigations – began to lose steam." Years later, Marvin Rudnick told Sharp that "*this is a cover-up that goes all the way to the top*." Other attorneys and investigators told Sharp they believed that "Wasserman and Meese had covered up a larger case of mob infiltration *and CIA influence at MCA*." "It's just not happenstance that two of MCA's presidents of two of their major divisions are doing business with the Mob," said Stavin.

I wondered if the "CIA influence at MCA" mentioned above was Robert Booth Nichols and his corporate partners in FIDCO and/or Meridian International Logistics? Both of these corporations were comprised of CIA-related board members.

Bill Hamilton believed, after more than two decades of research, that the modified version of his PROMIS software had been used for money laundering of drug profits to fund unauthorized intelligence operations, and he was convinced that part of the reason that the FBI wiretaps of MCA executives connected with the Mob and Robert Booth Nichols were shut down was because the FBI and prosecutors had bumped into an intelligence operation involving PROMIS. Hamilton believed that when the operation began to unravel due to the FBI probe, resignations followed at various levels within the Justice Department and the White House. To prove his point, Hamilton offered a chronology of the events as follows: (Excerpted from an e-mail from Hamilton)

> Just two weeks after William Weld signed the memo to Steven Trott declining INSLAW's request for an independent counsel, i.e., on March 16, 1988, Weld and Arnold Burns went to the White House to meet with Chief of Staff Howard Baker in a bid to force the ouster of Meese as Attorney General. After it became clear that President Reagan would not fire Meese, Weld and Burns went to [Howard] Baker's home on March 29, 1988 at 7:30 in the morning and submitted their resignations.
>
> On May 6, 1988, the Department of Justice announced to the public that it had declined INSLAW's request for the appointment of an independent counsel to investigate the roles of Attorney General Meese, Deputy Attorney General Arnold Burns, and former deputy Attorney General D. Lowell Jensen to drive INSLAW out of business and award a massive sweetheart Project EAGLE procurement to their friends to install PROMIS on new computers in every litigation and investigative office of the Justice Department, and that the Department had cleared Meese of any wrongdoing.
>
> One week later, on May 13, 1988, Ronald LeGrand telephoned me with information about the INSLAW case from his trusted Criminal Division source who made it clear to LeGrand that he was coming forward in reaction to the public statement by the Department on May 6, 1988 and who implicitly made clear his familiarity with the memorandum Nancy and I had submitted to the Public Integrity Section of the Criminal Division on the subject in early 1988.
>
> [This memorandum would have been the allegations that William Weld responded to in his letter to INSLAW on February 29, 1988 in which he wrote, *"The Public Integrity Section has reviewed allegations by INSLAW, Inc. that Attorney General Meese, Deputy Attorney General Burns, and/or former Deputy Attorney General Jensen committed 'procurement fraud' and/or obstruction of justice. The public Integrity Section concluded that the information submitted is not sufficiently specific to constitute grounds to initiate a preliminary investigation---."*]

On page 9 of the Summary section of *The Inslaw Affair* Investigative Report by the House Judiciary Committee, dated September 10, 1992, it was reported that sworn statements had been obtained from former Federal prosecutors Richard Stavin and Marvin Rudnick on March 13 and 14, 1992. After initial resistance from the Bureau, a sworn statement was taken from FBI Special Agent Thomas Gates on March 25 and 26, 1992.

Special Agent Gates stated that,

> Mr. [Danny] Casolaro claimed he had found a link between the INSLAW matter, the activities taking place at the Cabazon Indian Reservation, and a Federal investigation in which Special Agent Gates had been involved regarding organized crime influence in the entertainment industry.

The depositions of Rudnick and Stavin detailed their Strike Force findings. On page 478 of Kathleen Sharp's 2004 book, *Mr. and Mrs. Hollywood,* she wrote:

> Stavin discussed the ties between Giaquinto and Robert Booth Nichols. *Stavin believed that MCA was helping the government by offering the cover of its offices around the world.*

As of this writing, David Margolis is still serving in the Attorney General's office, according to an article entitled, "David Margolis –Why He Matters" at the WhoRunsGov.com/*Washington Post* website which reminded readers that Margolis' current position in 2010 was Associate Deputy Attorney General under Attorney General Eric Holder. Margolis was described as " *--- the Justice Department's highest-ranking career official*" under Eric Holder. (Holder assumed the office of U.S. Attorney General serving under President Barack Obama beginning in February 2009). (http://www.whorunsgov.com/Profiles/David_Margolis)

An excerpt from the article read as follows:

Why He Matters

> Margolis is the Justice Department's highest-ranking career official and something of an institution unto himself at the department. A 45-year veteran of DOJ, he has served under 18 attorneys general and navigated sensitive cases throughout his tenure. He figured prominently in the Whitewater investigation during the Clinton administration and the U.S. attorney scandal under President George W. Bush.
>
> "In 2010, Margolis drew scrutiny for his decision to spare from punishment two Bush administration lawyers who authored memos justifying the use of enhanced interrogation methods on suspected terrorists. After criticism from civil libertarians, Margolis was defended in a letter signed by 17 former top Justice De-

partment officials, including attorneys general from both political parties dating back to the administration of President George H.W. Bush. Palazzolo, Joe, "Former Justice Officials Rally Around Margolis," MainJustice.com, March 5, 2010.[(1)]Palazzolo, Joe, "Former Justice Officials Rally Around Margolis," MainJustice.com, March 5, 2010.

"As associate deputy attorney general, Margolis serves as a key adviser to the department's senior political appointees. He also fills other roles, including overseeing the interview process for potential U.S. attorneys, disciplining federal prosecutors when necessary and vetting FBI officials. According to a lengthy 2006 *Legal Times* profile, Margolis once described his "eclectic" role to an incoming attorney general in this way: *"I'm the department's cleaner. I clean up messes."* McLure, Jason, "Margolis Is the DOJ's Ultimate 'Inside Man,'" *Legal Times*, Sept. 18, 2006.(2)*McLure*, Jason, "Margolis Is the DOJ's Ultimate 'Inside Man,'" *Legal Times*, Sept. 18, 2006.

Margolis's career history as listed at the website included "Deputy Assistant Attorney General (1990 – 1993); Senior official, Organized Crime Section, Criminal Division (1976-1990)."

— 23 —

The Wiretaps

I had purchased some of the FBI wiretap affidavits from the Western Historical Manuscript Collection at the University of Missouri-Columbia in 1994. They had been sent there by Dr. Tony Casolaro, Danny's brother. Danny had obtained them from Bill McCoy, who had obtained them from Peter Zokosky (RBN's close friend and mentor). Zokosky had sent the wiretap affidavits to McCoy on January 17, 1991. McCoy was a retired Chief Warrant Officer from the U.S. Army's Criminal Investigation Division who had become involved in the Casolaro investigation of the PROMIS software. He died at home in 1997.

Presumably the FBI wiretap affidavits that Richard Stavin provided to the Judiciary Committee on Inslaw, as noted on page 72 of the Inslaw Affair Investigative Report, were the same affidavits that I had purchased from the University of Missouri-Columbia in 1994.

While re-reading the FBI wiretap affidavits, I found myself chuckling aloud as I envisioned Richard Stavin, Thomas Gates, and numerous other agents sitting for hours at a listening post as they absorbed the full impact of what they had stepped into.

In 2000, I had also been provided with reports originating from Robert Booth Nichols' (RBN) file at FBI headquarters in Los Angeles which, when combined with the wiretap affidavits, presented a broad mosaic of the organized crime apparatus in the entertainment industry at that time.

Thomas Gates could not have guessed as he sat at the FBI listening post, that the target of his investigation, RBN, might have been an undercover operative working for the NSA and/or the DOJ, or that he would subsequently be sued by his target as a result of his investigation.

One of the most revealing and comical comments I came across in RBN's documents, was made by a judge in a Los Angeles court when Nichols was suing FBI Special Agent Thomas Gates for allegedly going out of his jurisdiction in February 1989 to contact several Australian Federal Police departments and individuals in Tokyo, Japan, and during his inquiry informed them that RBN and officers of his corporation, Meridian International Logistics (MIL), were "*involved with the Gambino crime family and the Yakuza.*"

The lawsuit, filed in the Los Angeles Superior Court on June 16, 1989 alleged that Agent Gates defamed RBN and interfered with his ability to do business overseas, especially in Australia and Japan. "MIL was engaged in the funding and support of innovative medical research and technologies," according to the statement of the case.

RBN's lawyers, Mark Robinson and John Rowell, demanded that the government produce the evidence that was obtained during its investigation of RBN. The government responded that the evidence was "under seal" and no discovery could be allowed because it was a covert investigation.

The judge replied, "*I don't know, if this investigation was so covert, how did the Plaintiff learn about it?*"

Indeed, how did he learn about it? (RBN's lawsuit was dismissed by the court). Only through hindsight and the knowledge of Robert Booth Nichols' relationship with the Department of Justice, the NSC/NSA, and powerbrokers worldwide at the time of the wiretaps, can the full scope of this story be appreciated. Nichols even insinuated at one time that he worked for the "Illuminati," a secret society that theorists say controls and manipulates world events and is comprised of notable world leaders.

Thomas Gates had been investigating organized crime, labor racketeering and stock fraud since 1981 and in the course his investigations he had become familiar with the machinations of La Cosa Nostra (LCN) and its corrupt influence on companies and individuals. Thomas Gates and Richard Stavin had written the wiretap affidavits and Stavin had submitted them in support of an application to intercept for periods of thirty days each wire communications over the telephones of various LCN-related individuals.

The affidavits of particular interest to me related to Robert Booth Nichols and his business partner, Eugene Giaquinto, who was also the President of MCA Home Entertainment Division in Los Angeles. Giaquinto's friend, Martin Bacow, and his alleged uncle, Edward Sciandra, as well as Michael Del Gaizo and Angelo Commito, were all under investigation in 1987 for various suspected offenses including extortion, insider trading (MCA/Universal), the purchase and sale of narcotics/controlled substances, and the allocation and use of the proceeds of its trafficking.

But in particular, the conversations that Stavin and Gates sought to be intercepted related to "conversations regarding grand jury investigations and criminal investigations being conducted by law enforcement agencies; conversations regarding the furnishing of criminal intelligence and general background of companies and individuals; conversations concerning times and places of covert meetings to *disseminate confidential federal law enforcement information*; and the manner and means in which *computer printouts are obtained from federal law enforcement agencies* and how they are disseminated."

The wiretap applications and affidavits submitted by Stavin and Gates evidenced a belief that Robert Booth Nichols was providing government information and printouts to Giaquinto, MCA and/or the Mob.

The subsequent wiretaps were so spectacularly successful that they were dismantled and the investigation was shut down when DOJ headquarters received pressure from "above." Nevertheless, some aspects of those voluminous wiretaps will be illuminated here for the first time, as follows:

In the wiretaps, Martin Bacow was described as "the back door liaison Teamsters connection to the movie industry." Edward Sciandra, also known as The Conductor, was alleged in FBI files to be "the Underboss of the Russell Bufalino La Cosa Nostra (LCN) family." Michael Del Gaizo operated Northstar Graphics in New Jersey. The targets of the wiretaps generally talked to each other in coded language, but the agents who intercepted them understood their language, and provided explanation in the affidavits.

On June 30, 1987 Eugene Giaquinto told his friend Marty Bacow that Irving Azoff, in charge of the record division of MCA, "was planning to take over the whole thing." Bacow told Giaquinto to wait, "it's warfare."

On July 7, Giaquinto and Bacow discussed the internal situation at MCA. Bacow told Giaquinto to bide his time and they would see what could be done.

In the meantime, Bacow informed Giaquinto that some people wanted to produce a film about Meyer Lansky with the actor, Jimmy Caan. The intercept indicated that the LCN from either Florida or New York was attempting to get involved in the Lansky film.

Giaquinto didn't want to give a piece of the film to them, and told Bacow that if they want war, that he had a meeting in New York and he had anything he wanted and it came from "number one" (John Gotti, the boss of the Gambino family in New York, and the most powerful of the five LCN families in New York City and the country).

Giaquinto talked about his close relationship with John Gotti, and Bacow responded that his "guy downtown" was tied up with them, he is their friend (Gotti's friend). (The guy downtown was Detective John St. John at the Los Angeles Police Department in charge of LAPD's Organized Crime Intelligence Division. Bacow was St. John's direct contact with Giaquinto).

Giaquinto was also communicating with Michael Villano in New York City who was associated with John Gotti.

Giaquinto had awarded a multi-million dollar contract to Northstar Graphics in New Jersey operated by Michael Del Gaizo, and Sidney Sheinberg, President of MCA/Universal, was critical of Giaquinto giving the contract to Northstar. Giaquinto expressed concern that Del Gaizo might carry out some type of threat or violence against Sheinberg to retain the contract.

On July 8, Giaquinto told Bacow that his government man was coming to meet with him next week and they had a master plan. He said that Bacow wouldn't believe what they have in those machines (computers), companies we own, stockholders. He said he would show him reports coming out of Washington D.C. – that he had them just working on his company. Giaquinto said he had carte blanche with "G" (John Gotti) in New York and that he had known him (Gotti) and his friend (Michael Villano) all his life.

Bacow indicated that Eddie Sciandra said he wanted to go to Lew Wasserman and Sidney Sheinberg (Pres. of MCA) and tell them who they were up against. Giaquinto replied that maybe Sheinberg would break a toe and end up in the hospital for a couple of days, "maybe he'll break a leg."

The intercept narration outlined that this stemmed from the problem with the Northstar Graphics contract and the LCN believed Sciandra was being irrational and should be "retired." If Sciandra threatened MCA executives, it would cause trouble for his nephew, Giaquinto, who worked for MCA. Sciandra was also trying to get a piece of Giaquinto's share of the Lansky film.

On July 12, Bacow asked Giaquinto if Azoff had something on Sidney Sheinberg? Giaquinto said it had been bandied about and he would know more when those other documents came in. The explanation for this was interpreted in the intercept as Giaquinto obtaining confidential government information from some government agency personnel in Washington D.C. (They didn't know at that time that it was Robert Booth Nichols who was Giaquinto's "government man.")

The FBI reports on Nichols, originating from FBI headquarters in Los Angeles, dated October 24, 1987, corroborated the affidavit and offered even more details: "Giaquinto has described Robert Booth Nichols as his 'government man.' L.A. intercepted a conversation wherein Nichols told Giaquinto that he had 'Treasury identification.'"

The FBI report further noted that Eugene Giaquinto was associated with John Gotti, boss of the Gambino LCN family, and he (Giaquinto) was intercepted telling Martin Bacow that the computer printouts being delivered to him by his "government man" would show connections to other companies as well as *indictments and other ongoing investigations.* Giaquinto also discussed the printouts in the context of an ongoing IRS case. (Marvin Rudnick had been investigating Salvador Pisello for tax evasion of income derived from MCA. Again, it appeared that the prosecutors' internal reports to the DOJ were circling back to Giaquinto via Robert Booth Nichols).

On July 15, 1987 FBI surveillance agents observed Giaquinto exit Le Dome Restaurant on Sunset Boulevard with an unidentified male and walk to Giaquinto's vehicle. The unknown individual was photographed by the surveillance team as he retrieved a box from Giaquinto's trunk, then drove to the Beverly Hills Hotel and entered the Polo Lounge Restaurant. The surveillance was terminated at that time because they believed the subject was attempting to determine if he was being followed. The surveillance agents obtained the license plate number of the Cadillac Coup DeVille driven by the unidentified male and learned through Department of Motor Vehicles records that the car was registered to Harold Okimoto at an address in Hawaii.

A subsequent cross-check of the Hawaii address by agents with the Honolulu Division of the FBI showed that a man named Robert Booth Nichols (RBN) also used that same address. A photograph was produced through the California law enforcement teletype system (CLETS) along with another address for RBN at Marina Del Rey, California. (This was the address that Nichols and pals referred to as the "007" apartment which was used as a listening post for the Lebanon operation noted in previous chapters).

The photograph was compared with the photo taken in the parking lot of the Le Dome restaurant on July 15 and it was determined that the unidentified male handing computer printouts to Eugene Giaquinto was Robert Booth Nichols.

The law enforcement computer and inquiries to the California Department of Justice further indicated that Nichols had fingerprints on file for applications to carry a concealed weapon submitted in 1975 with the San Diego sheriff's office and other agencies throughout California, including a 1991 application to posses, sell and/or transport machine guns. His Meridian Arms license listed the purpose of the business was for the sale, demonstration, research and development of new machine guns.

The FBI team also learned about the FBI investigation initiated in March 1978 which alleged that RBN *was an internationally known money-launderer for narcotics traffickers and organized crime figures.* He was reportedly well known and influential in the sale of armaments to foreign governments, including the former Marcos regime in the Philippines. *Nichols had made claims of having access to highly sophisticated computers in Switzerland with detailed information on any number of subjects.* Nichols was allegedly moving large sums of money from the Marcos government and concealing it in Swiss bank accounts.

Nichols further claimed to have highly placed sources in numerous foreign government agencies which can detect any investigation initiated against him. One of these individuals was supposedly a United States Senator with much seniority whom Nichols claimed to utilize in the trafficking of narcotics and money laundering. Nichols was also reportedly used by the Carlos Gambino family to launder "family money," according to the FBI report.

(I wondered if Nichols was using the PROMIS software to launder money? Bill Hamilton had said that RBN told him that there was a major repository in Switzerland of documents relating to the Iran/Contra scandal and that his "guess" was that the repository would contain documents relating to the government's misappropriation of PROMIS. Hamilton said he never managed to obtain any documents through RBN, however).

(The original 1978 FBI case against RBN was allegedly closed in December 1982 because they couldn't obtain enough evidence for prosecution. This closing of FBI cases against RBN was echoed throughout the years in all subsequent investigations of him, though the reasons for closing them varied. It appears that the FBI was being kept out of the loop by the agencies that contracted with Nichols).

On July 23, 1987 the FBI wiretaps captured Eugene Giaquinto gossiping to RBN about a money laundering operation for heroin money that involved restaurants owned by LCN people in New York and [allegedly] the record division of MCA.

On July 24, phone conversations took place in which Irving Azoff, Sal Pisello and the investigation of the record division of MCA was discussed. Giaquinto said he was considering sending the MCA board of directors an incriminating letter prepared in 1985 on behalf of Pisello sent to Azoff which would conflict with Azoff's testimony at the trial.

One FBI report detailing an investigation of RBN revealed that Nichols had contacted banks throughout the United States and advised them that they had access to various *substantial Foundation or Trust Fund money* and he could provide loans up to a billion dollars. At one point Nichols approached Union Bank in Los Angeles regarding *Meridian Arms Corporation opening an account at Union Bank asking them to receive a $25 Billion dollar wire transfer from an unidentified bank in New York.* Union Bank declined because they were afraid that the wire transfer might involve some type of fraud by wire violation. The case was closed administratively by the Los Angeles office of the FBI because no violation could be established.

A background investigation of Meridian Arms revealed that in 1981 Nichols indicated he was an "*international financial consultant with numerous government contacts throughout the world.*" This included arranging loans with foreign governments. He said he had been employed in this type of work for ten years.

Robert Booth Nichols

— 24 —

Robert Booth Nichols

I lost track of Robert Booth Nichols until July 15, 2008 when a Bloomberg News article appeared on the Internet entitled "Bayou's Israel Cheated in Scam," by court reporters David Glovin and Bob Van Voris. http://www.bloomberg.com/apps/news?pid=20601127&sid=aLCwdJsx0V3M&refer=law

The article talked about Samuel Israel of Bayou Management Group LLC being cheated by Robert Booth Nichols, "who in a 1993 lawsuit claimed to have worked for the U.S. Central Intelligence Agency for 20 years. Nichols was also the target of a 1987 probe by the Federal Bureau of Investigation of organized crime in the entertainment industry," wrote Bloomberg.

An excerpt of the article read as follows:

> As Samuel Israel grew desperate to raise money in 2004 to save his Bayou Group LLC hedge fund firm, he turned for help to a Hawaii man who promised a windfall and then conned him out of $10 million, said a U.K. investigator.
>
> Robert Booth Nichols cheated Israel, later convicted in his own $400 million theft, in a 'prime bank' fraud, a scheme used by con-artists promising quick riches in secret markets, the U.K. investigator said in a document filed in June in federal court in New York. U.S. prosecutors seeking to recover funds for Bayou investors won a British judge's ruling in November freezing $1 million Nichols held there, and they may be pursuing millions more in Singapore, Nichols's lawyer said.

Robert Booth Nichols, 65, denied wrongdoing and sought to retain the $1 million in London. He said in court papers that he helped Israel invest in a legitimate, though unspecified "project" involving U.S. government obligations. Nichols said he had no reason to believe Israel was engaged in fraud.

"He was asked to find something, and he found it," Nichols's lawyer, Joseph Bainton, told Bloomberg, declining to elaborate. "There are very few people capable of performing this service, for which he was paid a lump sum of $10 million."

Nichols said in court papers that he believed the investment was on behalf of Israel personally, that Nichols was told his services "involved matters of national interest," and that a first cousin of President Bush, John P. Ellis, vouched for the legitimacy of the transaction. Nichols said the deal required him to contact representatives of foreign governments that he knew, according to court documents.

Nichols' lawyer told Bloomberg that "Mr. Ellis attended some meetings and gave Mr. Nichols some assurance with respect to the approval of the United States." Ellis worked at GH Venture Partners in 2004, according to Nichols' court documents.

The criminal case is U.S. v. Israel, 05cr1039, U.S. District Court, Southern District of New York (Manhattan).

The bankruptcy case is Bayou Group LLC, 06-22306, U.S. Bankruptcy Court, Southern District New York (White Plains).

The missing link in the above story is the $250 Billion Treasury Note secured by 2,500 metric tons of gold at the Atlanta Federal Reserve, Serial Number SC 3040-20. Robert Booth Nichols' lawyer described this to Bloomberg as an unspecified "project" involving U.S. government obligations. However, the reporters had no knowledge at the time they wrote the story that the "project" for which Nichols was paid $10 million allegedly involved Nichols locating and obtaining the Treasury Note for Samuel Israel and depositing it at the London Safe Deposit Box Company Ltd. http://londonsafedeposit.co.uk/

In early July 2008 Samuel Israel was already in custody for conspiracy and fraud, including misappropriation of millions of dollars in investor funds for his personal use http://www.cnbc.com/id/25495282 and, according to court documents, he had provided details of the secret "project" to the FBI at some point in time. As a result of his cooperation, the FBI, with the assistance of the City of London Police, reportedly retrieved the Treasury Note documents at the London Safe Deposit Company and returned to the U.S.

Samuel Israel sued Robert Booth Nichols demanding the return of the $10 Million. Nichols responded in lengthy court filings that exposed the $250 Billion "project" and alleged that George Bush's first cousin, John P. Ellis, provided confirmation of the legitimacy of the "project" and that the U.S. government sanctioned it. (Case 1:08-cv-06036-CM Document 1-8 filed 7/2/2008, Page 15 of 19).

Interestingly, nothing was published as of this writing in mainstream media relative to the $250 Billion Treasury Note ("project") discussed in Nichols' letter/court filing to Judge Colleen McMahon (Case 1:08-cv-06036-CM Document 32-2 Filed 12/23/2008, Page 1 of 5 at the United States Courthouse in New York) in which his lawyer wrote:

> On September 12, 2008 we served the enclosed Rule 30(b)(6) Notice in an attempt to quickly obtain clarification on this $250 Billion issue. The Government contends that the notice is overbroad, burdensome and oppressive. In making this assertion, the Government has yet to state plainly whether these instruments are authentic. If they are not authentic, then how burdensome could it be to produce a witness to say: 'Sam told us he had this stuff and we finally got around to collecting it last summer.' On the other hand, if these instruments are authentic, then this case – indeed the entire Bayou bankruptcy case – changes quite dramatically. We would like to get to the bottom of this issue quickly. The Government's delay in producing documents has forced the parties to defer the commencement of depositions. So even if Your Honor can quickly break the logjam on the $250 Billion issue, it nonetheless appears some adjustment to the schedule is necessary.

It is noteworthy that on July 2, 2008, just days after Samuel Israel, 48, walked into the police station in Southwick, Mass. and said he was a fugitive wanted by the federal government, Robert Booth Nichols's lawyer filed a "Demand for Trial by Jury" at the court in New York. (Document 1-9).

In effect, it appears Nichols was blackmailing the powers that be because a public trial would have exposed a scandal far exceeding the Bernie Madoff fiasco. This was not the first time Nichols had used this tactic. On March 21, 1993 the *Los Angeles Times* had published a story entitled, "Trial Offers Murky Peek into World of Intrigue" by Henry Weinstein and Paul Feldman which reported that Nichols presented himself during testimony as a globe-trotting businessman and intelligence operative. Armed with letters on White House stationary and snapshots of himself posing with foreign political and military dignitaries, Nichols told jurors that he toiled quietly and selflessly for nearly two decades on behalf of the CIA in more than 30 nations from Central America to Southeast Asia.

The *Los Angeles Times* reported that Nichols was investigated by the FBI for international money laundering in 1978. In a 1987 federal court wiretapping affidavit, prepared by FBI Agent Thomas G. Gates, it stated that "FBI investigative files further reveal that Nichols may have been associating with the Gambino La Cosa Nostra organized crime family in New York." The court case in Los Angeles ended in a mistrial, wrote the *Times.*

Nichols' demand for a Trial by Jury in the Bayou case was effective. In January 2009 Bayou Management and Nichols came to an agreement to settle out of court for an undisclosed amount of money. The court gave Nichols 45 days to come up with the money, which would have been March 6, 2009, his birthday.

However, on Valentines Day, February 14, 2009 Robert Booth Nichols reportedly died in Geneva, Switzerland. Nichols and a friend, Mark Soltz, a New York stockbroker, had been staying at a hotel near the airport while conducting business in Geneva. When Nichols failed to show up at a meeting in the morning, his friend found him dead and identified the body to authorities. The exact cause of death was not determined, but authorities believed he died of a massive heart attack. There was also a blow to the head, but police assumed that was caused when he fell to the floor. The friend reportedly arranged to have the body cremated in Geneva and the U.S. Embassy in Bern notified Nichols' wife, Ellen, in California. (Embassy of the United States Bern, Sulgeneckstrasse 19, CH-3007 Bern, Switzerland, (031) 357-7011). http://bern.usembassy.gov/contact.html

Detective John Powers of the Riverside Sheriff's Department in California had been communicating with me on a 28-year-old cold-case file relating to a triple homicide in Rancho Mirage which he was working on, so I asked him as a favor if he could confirm the death of Robert Booth Nichols. Detective Powers subsequently wrote back that he had confirmed Nichols' death through the FBI and also through Ellen Nichols, Robert's wife. Ellen's lifelong love affair with her husband had ended abruptly with his death in Geneva, and she was devastated. She told Detective Powers that she believed if she had been with him in that Geneva hotel room, she might have been able to save him, but she had been recuperating from surgery on her leg and had stayed behind with her father in Los Angeles.

At the time of Nichols' death, there were numerous factions chasing the Treasury Note in an attempt to learn if it was authentic, or not? According to one source, a copy of the $250 Billion Treasury Note was attached to Samuel Israel's original court filings against Robert Booth Nichols, but that exhibit had apparently been redacted from the Internet court records. http://dockets.justia.com/docket/court-nysdce/case_no-1:2008cv06036/case_id-328683/

Meanwhile, it appeared that all references to the Treasury Note were being systematically erased from the court and the Internet. As of April 15, 2009 the Bayou case had reportedly not been vacated, though Nichols' lawyer had notified the court that his client was deceased, according to Bob Van Voris, the Bloomberg reporter who covered the case.

Theories abound as to whether Nichols actually died and took his secret to the grave, or simply disappeared into the international netherworld where aging spies and intelligence operatives go to retire. As of this writing, it is unknown whether Nichols paid the settlement money to Bayou before his death, or if it remains unpaid. Some theorize he was murdered to keep him from testifying in court about the "project" and John P. Ellis. Others believe the government came to his rescue and he was in a Witness Protection program with a new identity – for reasons that only Nichols and his handlers would know.

As of this writing, there were already "Nichols sightings" in Europe. One person said a lawyer had told him that Nichols was sighted in Liechtenstein.

According to Detective John Powers, the FBI was investigating the circumstances of Nichols' death and they asked him not to interview the witness, Mark Soltz, until they (the FBI) had completed their investigation. In the meantime, the Treasury Note was a mystery that had a history and a paper-trail, and the question remained, was it authentic? One Bloomberg reporter said Prosecutor Jeff Alberts filed a letter to the court stating the Treasury Note was not authentic, but he was unable to produce a copy of the letter.

One retired banker in Europe provided some history on the Treasury Note. He wrote:

> Having spoken with a banker friend in Switzerland, he related to me that the 2500 m/t of Au [gold] used to secure the TN was originally 10,000 m/t. And that in 1983 four TN's were created secured by 25% of the Au in the depository. In other words the TN in question is 1-of-4 created in 1983.

The banker followed up with:

> You are absolutely correct in that there were 5 TN, whereas, I originally related there were 4; the 4th was split into 2 TN's, thereby creating 5 TN's secured by the 10 m/t of Au. Also confirmed that the names of the TN's, as stated within your e-mail is correct.
>
> The run on the bank that you referred to occurred when the bank holding the lien called in their loan(s) for apparently $550B, which shook the financial foundations around the world. What I am unable to find out is 'WHICH' bank called in their marker?? Basically, it is an obligation of the Treasury. Apparently, the Judge ordered the attorney's to find out if the TN was real or not... that started the snowball that's bout' to 'blow the socks off' of the entire game.

After further investigation, the banker wrote:

> I called a banker friend in Zurich this morning to see what he might know? He related that Au held in US Fed depositories have heavy liens/encumbrances, of which, many may be fraudulent. Asking what he knew, or had heard about the leverage liens currently in the Fed depository in Atlanta? And asked if he knew anything specifically about 2500 metric tons of Au at the Atlanta facility? His remark was stunning, quote: "The word is that US held assets may have debenture liens in excess of 4x its value."
>
> I asked: 'You mean 4x its value at $400+ p/oz. 10 years ago, or 4x its value today?' He answered: 'At today's strike prices' Asked how he knew? He said, 'They'd received several memos beginning

months ago and that Swiss banks haven't traded in US Fed deposits (either, liened or leveraged) for over a year.' Further, 'They will only advance cash or credits to 80% of current market value (in lieu of) clean collateral.' (Meaning no liens and/or encumbrances).

Based on what has been related by what I consider a creditable source, it is possible the paper in question [Treasury Note] may well be fraudulent."

The Bernie Madoff ponzi scheme reportedly amounted to less than $50 Billion http://www.time.com/time/business/article/0,8599,1866689,00.html yet it received overwhelming media coverage. If the Treasury Note in question was a $250 Billion ponzi scheme perpetrated by Robert Booth Nichols against Samuel Israel, then why all the secrecy surrounding it? That question remains to be answered. One writer, Guy Lawson, is seeking to find the answer to that question. He has reportedly spent countless hours interviewing Samuel Israel in prison, and what a story he will have when his book goes into print! In a phone interview, Lawson said he has seen photos relating to the "project" (obligations of the U.S. government) and confirmed that the photos were indeed removed from Israel's case file.

We exchanged information about Robert Booth Nichols, I sent him some RBN documents, and he sent me a 300-page Deposition taken by Assistant U.S. Attorney Jeff Alberts in New York on December 16, 2008. Also present at the deposition were three representatives from the Federal Bureau of Investigation (FBI); Jay F. Kramer, Christopher Kim, and S.A. Carl A. Catauro.

Within the lengthy Deposition document, I found mention of John Ellis, the first cousin of President George W. Bush, whom Nichols described as Samuel Israel's "best friend" (p. 61) and dozens of U.S. intelligence people named in the document whom Nichols said worked for the CIA. I noticed that some of them were closely connected to Wackenhut, such as Frank Carlucci (p. 39) and Harry Fair.

Interestingly, I noticed that Nichols refrained from providing most of the names of people he worked closely with that are listed extensively on his personal and corporate documents, as well as in the FBI reports on him. Clearly he was withholding a great deal of information from the Deposition.

He gave a clue to this when he explained why he never paid income taxes. He said he was told [by his handlers]: "You will never be bothered by your government, period. Your job is to keep this information ... in secure locations. It is a very sensitive matter, very sensitive to this country, and under no circumstances can this reach the public ---"

Nichols added," And my files, they said they never wanted my files at any time to be public, at any time, under any circumstances." He said he was told that what was taking place today (the Deposition), would not happen to him. He clearly felt he'd been left out in the cold. "I do what I'm told to do. I am a facilitator. I am a person who is tasked to undertake something, achieve an objective --- that's what I do. There is no paperwork in my world, except the results of achieving an objective."

With regard to FIDCO, Nichols said, "I was involved with them jointly and several other parties in the development of the 'fuel air explosive.'" (This was in addition to the alleged redevelopment of areas in Lebanon, near Beirut). Nichols said his code-name, as used by the directors of FIDCO and the British, was "mongoose." His code name for the fuel air explosive project was "Eel."

Within the Deposition, Nichols said he had met with the Chinese about the U.S. government obligations to the Maiwah family, a prominent entity in Luxembourg, which are the lineage and the offspring of Chiang Kai-shek.

He was told the documents were legitimate by a number of people, one of which was allegedly an advisor to the President of the United States, and another by the name of Tansri Teong, a liaison officer for the Maiwah family, whom he communicated with as well as members of the Maiwah family.

Nichols stated that he was hired by Samuel Israel to perform a service for which he was paid $10 million. He described the service as follows:

"To obtain a sealed treasury box that originated from the Chinese, from the Chinese that he [Israel] said he was quite familiar with, and it could not be opened ... it had to be a hundred million dollars box, a hundred million dollars in a certain series or the series was irrelevant, but no more than a hundred million dollars on the plate and identification." (If it contained different figures, higher figures, then it would be bogus).

He (Nichols) was supposed to provide to Samuel this box unopened, to provide him the names of the principles with whom he could speak to negotiate the redemption of that box and many other boxes of the same nature; to provide him photocopies precisely of Federal Reserve notes and U.S. government silver (and gold) certificates, their location, and what security vaults and security house they were located in and with whom negotiations could take place to settle that. Nichols explained:

"The Chinese didn't say, give this to Samuel Israel. They said, 'sit down with the correct credentials in the Treasury or the Executive Branch with this if that's necessary. These are legitimate documents. This is a legitimate debt.' So Samuel Israel said that's what he's gonna do. They didn't say, 'work this out with someone in an alley or something of that nature.' They said sit down with the correct parties and the United States government. Sam Israel said, I am going with my best friend, John Ellis, and proceeding. They [the Chinese] said they'd settle for eight cents on the dollar ---."

Nichols said he was told that these were "financial instruments that Israel believed to be bona fide obligations (debt) of the U.S. Department of the Treasury; that *five* of those instruments had already been taken and settled on by the United States government. The Chinese told him that they were settled with payments from Chase Morgan.

Nichols ultimately provided Samuel Israel with an "original etching" of a $100 million Note, and Israel paid him $10 million which he deposited in banks in London, Liechtenstein, and Singapore. Nichols said the bank called the Note currency, but he (Nichols) called it an "etching" because the U.S. government says they never printed a bill over $10,000. Nichols reportedly told this to Israel, but Israel told him it was not his affair. Nichols said he obtained the note from (name withheld) who took it out of a security vault in Switzerland (where many more notes existed), and brought it to him and said, here is your etching.

Guy Lawson advised me to read the 2003 book *Gold Warriors: America's Secret Recovery of Yamashita's Gold* by Sterling and Peggy Seagrave. He said it gives an outstanding history of the looted treasury of Chiang Kai-shek in China by the Japanese, who stored it in the Philippines.

I wondered if Robert Booth Nichols had read this book in 2003, one year before he scammed Samuel Israel (in 2004) out of $10 million dollars? Assistant U.S. Attorney Jeff Alberts in New York reportedly filed a letter with the court stating the Treasury note was a fraud.

In the Deposition, Nichols had addressed this issue. He felt the U.S. government should have had witnesses present when the box was opened in the U.S., after it was seized in London. "I think that it should have been opened in the presence of counsel and parties from the other side. It's like asking the Federal Reserve, is this a legitimate box – and if they say yes, that means they could owe a trillion dollars, and if they say no, they owe nothing. I just think there should have been someone else present to give another opinion."

Jeff Alberts had asked, "Is that because you think the federal government might lie about whether or not they are legitimate financial certificates so they don't have to pay [the] money?"

Nichols answered, "It's a possibility." No one will ever be able to question Nichols further on this issue, because he was found dead in Geneva two months after the Deposition was taken.

Every government official I talked to, every journalist, told me that nothing can be done to dismantle the Octopus, there is no one in office in this great nation that has the power to prosecute the Octopus criminals because the tentacles have become an integral, and accepted culture within our society, and indeed within our economy.

I began my investigation of the Octopus in the late 1980's and ended it in December 2009. I called it the never-ending-story. But during that two decades, I gained a perspective. Sooner or later, the pendulum always swings back. In the year 2009 a number of events occurred which indicated that, through attrition, the pendulum was in fact swinging back.

••••••••

— 25 —

Rachel's Resolution

On August 6, 2008 I had contacted Rachel Begley, the daughter of Ralph Boger who had been killed in a Cabazon-related triple homicide in June 1981. After speaking with Rachel, it became apparent that there is a new generation on the horizon, the cowboys are aging and on the way out, and their legacy of war, corruption and greed will be left to the history books. Because the Octopus and its tentacles cared nothing for the future, it is unlikely that their machine will survive them. Rachel believed that through attrition, America will survive this page in its history, and emerge wiser. In the following months Rachel proved that one woman can make a difference in clipping the tentacles of the Octopus.

For 28 years Rachel Begley waited for the murderer(s) of her father, Ralph Boger, 42, Fred Alvarez, 32, vice-chairman of the Cabazon Indian Tribal Council, and Patricia Castro, 44, to be brought to justice.

For three of those years, Begley actively investigated the execution-style triple slaying while gathering documents and secretly taping interviews with suspects and placing them on her website.

The executions took place on June 29, 1981 while Alvarez, Boger and Castro relaxed in the back patio of Alvarez's rented home on Bob Hope Drive in Rancho Mirage, California. The three victims each were shot with a single .38 caliber bullet to the head, according to an autopsy report. There were no visible signs of a struggle. Their bodies were discovered on July 1 by former tribal chairman Joe Benitez and Cabazon member William Callaway.

Fred Alvarez, along with Benitez and Callaway, were scheduled to meet at 10 A.M. on July 1 with Steve Rios, an attorney in San Juan

Capistrano, to initiate an investigation of Cabazon tribal affairs, according to the *Indio Daily News* dated 7-1-81.

Alvarez, Benitez, and Calloway had previously divulged their findings to Paul Zalis at the *Daily News* in May 1981 (currently known as the Desert Sun), asserting to the reporter that they were marked for death, but their story never got published.

The *Indio Daily News did* report the subsequent killings of Alvarez, Boger and Castro however. Staff writer Paul Zalis wrote that Indio City Manager Phillip Hawes confirmed that William Cole, a Los Angeles-based attorney, had been hired to investigate possible links between the triple slayings and the Cabazon Casino. Cole said his office was coordinating efforts with the Riverside County Sheriff's Department in investigating the murders. He noted that "sheriff's deputies had confiscated papers from the Alvarez home and he expected officials to turn those over to his office."

"Detective Gordon Hunter said the sheriff's department was 'investigating leads' into the Alvarez slayings, but said he had no 'knowledge' of whether deputies had confiscated any of Alvarez's papers," wrote Zalis.

Alvarez's mother, Phyllis, told the *Indio Daily News* that "she believed the murders were the result of a 'Mafia contract.' She also said her son was killed because he was trying to get the Cabazon Casino shut down."

Rachel Begley was 13 years old when her father, Ralph Boger, and his friends were murdered. She never gave up hope that the killers would be prosecuted, and consistently prodded local jurisdictions over a span of years to get the case re-opened. Her efforts were rewarded when Detective John Powers at the Riverside Sheriff's department was assigned to the cold-case file in 2007.

Their respective findings resemble the stuff of spy novels, comprised of all the malevolent dynamics of clandestine government agents and organized crime figures involved in murder, money laundering and covert arms deals while exploiting Indian sovereignty (independent of most U.S. laws) at the Cabazon reservation.

The triple-homicide case was originally investigated by Deputy Attorney General Sanford Feldman and Special Agent Frank E. Brock respectively, both from the special investigations unit of the state Department of Justice, San Diego, California. Decades later,

Detective Powers re-opened the case based on the information provided by Rachel Begley in November 2007.

••••••••

The public background to the story began with the Cabazon Band of Mission Indians, located 25 miles east of Palm Springs, California. According to public historical data, on May 15, 1876, President Ulysses S. Grant issued an executive order which officially created the Cabazon Reservation, consisting of 2,400 acres over three parcels of desert (later reduced to 1,700 acres).

After more than a century in the desert, the tribal nation began blazing the path for Native American gaming in California. http://www.indiangaming.com/istore/Dec08_Cabazon.pdf

According to a *San Francisco Chronicle* article entitled, "Tiny California Tribe's Huge Clout," dated September 4, 1991, in 1980 a rundown warehouse was transformed into the "Cabazon Indian Casino," the first Indian card room in the nation. Tommy Marson, described in congressional hearings as a known associate of the Gambino crime family, "lent the Cabazon tribal administrator, John Philip Nichols, $50,000 to start the casino, according to Nichols' son, John Paul. The manager of the casino was Rocco Zangari, a former bookie later indicted on racketeering charges."

Citing local ordinances forbidding gambling, Indio police staged a series of raids on the casino in 1981, but Cabazon lawyers fought back, winning a court injunction that not only prohibited local law enforcement from interfering with gambling activities on the reservation, but ultimately led to a Supreme Court ruling on February 25, 1987 that neither the State of California nor Riverside County could regulate the bingo and card game operations of the Cabazon Band of Mission Indians. This landmark case, known as the "Cabazon Decision," made them the *first* tribe in California to establish non-regulated gaming and resulted in the creation of the Indian gaming industry. The Cabazon tribe had established high-stakes bingo that same year, in 1987.

The National Indian Gaming Commission was subsequently established pursuant to the Indian Gaming Regulatory Act of 1988. http://www.nigc.gov/ The purpose of NIGC was to "shield Indian tribes from organized crime and other corrupting influences; to ensure that Indian tribes are the primary beneficiaries of gaming revenue; and to assure that gaming is conducted fairly ---"

As of this writing, there are fewer than 55 members of the Cabazon Band. http://www.fantasyspringsresort.com/cbmi/index.html As owners and operators of Fantasy Springs Resort Casino in Indio, the Cabazon tribe oversees the 12-story, 250-room hotel, Vegas-style casino with nearly 2,000 slots, 40 table games, an off-track betting room, and virtual poker room as well as five restaurants.

The darker, more obscure aspects of this success story bubbled to the surface in 1980 when Fred Alvarez, vice-chairman of the Cabazon Indian Tribal Council, wrote a letter to Ronald Reagan outlining criminal enterprises that he had uncovered at the reservation. This was one month prior to the Presidential election. It is unknown why Fred wrote to Reagan during a time when Reagan held no political position. All copies of the letter disappeared after Fred's murder, but a response, signed personally by Ronald Reagan, dated October 6, 1980 was subsequently found in which Reagan said he found Alvarez's comments to be "very interesting."

Authorities explain that the cash nature of Indian gaming made it an ideal business to launder money. That same lack of accountability made it easy for an *outside management* company to skim the vast majority of an operation's income. "Someone will come in and manage the operation, when in fact the purpose is to skim the profits," said one FBI supervisor.

Reagan was elected president of the United States in November 1980, and took office in January 1981, almost six months before the Alvarez, Boger, Castro triple homicide occurred. With all *resistance eliminated* at the Cabazon reservation, it marked the beginning of government exploitation of the tiny band of Indians when "outside management" in the form of Cabazon tribal administrator John Philip Nichols formed a joint venture with Wackenhut International, a Florida-based security firm run by former FBI, CIA, NSA and military officials.

Police reports indicate that Nichols previously did business in Saudi Arabia, South Africa, Panama, Nicaragua, Guatemala, Mexico, Chile, Brazil, the Netherlands, England, Canada, France, Spain, Japan, Korea and Taiwan. In 1960 Nichols became the manager of a Coca-Cola bottling plant in Sao Paolo, Brazil, then he became a Pentecostal leader of the Chilean Pentecostal movement and attended several evangelical and gospel congresses in Bolivia.

When Nichols was hired in 1978, he wrote himself a 10-year contract with the Cabazon tribe that gave him 50 percent of the profits of any business he brought to the reservation. In the summer of 1980 and during the next three years, Nichols embarked on a series of international security and military ventures to provide security for Crown Prince Fahd's Saudi Arabia palace, proposals to manufacture 120mm combustible cartridge cases on the reservation and in Latin America, along with 9mm machine pistols, laser-sighted assault weapons, sniper rifles and portable rocket systems. At one point he even sought a contract to develop biological weapons on the reservation.

In January 1985, John Philip Nichols was arrested for hiring a man to solicit the murder of five people for drug-related reasons, but the murders were not carried out due to his arrest. He was convicted of felony murder solicitation. (While serving 18 months in the California Institution for Men in Chino, John Philip Nichols' son, John Paul Nichols, took over his position as acting administrator of the Cabazon tribe. In 1989, Mark Nichols inherited the position of administrator from his brother, John Paul Nichols).

A *Los Angeles Times* article entitled, "Indian's Aide Held in Alleged Slaying Plot," dated January 19, 1985 reported that Indio Police Capt. Carl Kennedy was unable to connect the murder-for-hire proposal leading to Nichols' arrest with the unsolved July, 1981 execution murders of Fred Alvarez, Ralph Boger, and Patricia Castro in Rancho Mirage. "The killings were investigated without success by the Riverside County Sheriff's office," according to the *Times*, "but official interest in the murders was renewed last year [1984] when Jimmy Hughes, a 27-year-old ex-Army Ranger, told authorities that he had been the payoff man in the Alvarez case." (As noted in the Peter Zokosky interview, he had convinced Jimmy Hughes to talk to authorities and had driven him to Indio for the meeting).

Hughes, security director of the Cabazon band's casino and bingo operations for four years until early 1984, reported that he had been instructed in [John Philip] Nichols' presence to take $5,000 to the mountain community of Idyllwild in the summer of 1981 and give the money to a man there as partial payment for the Alvarez killings.

The *Los Angeles Times* reported that the Riverside County sheriff's office and the state Department of Justice initiated an investigation, but after months without announced results, [Jimmy] Hughes went public with his information in October 1984, then moved out of Riverside County. Coincidentally, at that same time (1984), Jimmy Hughes' cousin, Rod Pacheco, worked as a prosecutor at the Riverside County District Attorney's Office.

Indio Police Chief Curtis R. "Sam" Cross, who worked on the murder-solicitation case against John Philip Nichols, told the *Press Enterprise* in Riverside, California in March 1985 that he sent a letter to Rep. Jim Bates, D-San Diego, requesting a congressional investigation of the Cabazon Indians' business ventures.

Nothing ever came of all the investigations in the 1980's.

Despite all the allegations set forth over the years, Senator John McCain, R-Ariz., vice chairman of the Senate Select Committee on Indian Affairs, refused to intercede in Cabazon affairs, noting, " --- By solemn treaty with the Indian tribes, recently affirmed by President Bush, we must treat Native Americans as sovereign nations."

••••••••

On the tenth anniversary of the triple-murders, Barbara Clark, the aunt of Fred Alvarez, sent a 4-page letter to the Cabazon Nation in Indio. The letter was dated June 28, 1991. Clark wrote that her nephew, Fred Alvarez, had visited with her in Truckee, California two weeks prior to his death. While they ate breakfast she said Fred discussed things that were going on at the Cabazon reservation, such as "dealings with the Contras, plans for weapons sales, and mismanagement of the tribal business."

Fred told his aunt that he planned to meet with an attorney "to get everything documented." He added that "the management of the tribal business wanted him out of the way --- He knew they had placed a contract out on him, and he even knew who the hit man was." Clark didn't ask the name of the hit man because she didn't take Fred seriously at the time.

Clark, who is a Native American member of the Maidu Indian Nation/Pitt River in Northern California, wrote that a year after her nephew's murder, a woman came to the delicatessen that she managed and mentioned that she was from Rancho Mirage. Clark noted that her nephew had been murdered there. As the conversation progressed, Clark said the woman told her, "Oh! I knew that the big Indian was going to be killed two weeks *before* he was killed."

The woman explained that her boyfriend's sister had been dating a "high roller" in Palm Springs who talked about the upcoming murder of the "big Indian." Clark provided the information to the California Attorney General's office, and was subsequently informed by investigators from the DOJ that the "high roller" was John Paul Nichols, Jr.

Clark said she flew to Riverside to testify before a Grand Jury, noting that it was about the same time that John Philip Nichols, Sr. was being charged with solicitation of murder of five other men. Clark wrote that "the Grand Jury failed to act on the evidence at hand – she was told later by a reliable source that there were too many big names involved, and the case was to be dropped. The case was then closed."

••••••••

In 1991 a series of events, including the death of Washington D.C. investigative journalist Danny Casolaro on August 10, brought the Cabazon-related triple homicide back into national scrutiny. Casolaro had been preparing to visit Indio to investigate the Cabazon/Wackenhut connections to a cabal of spooks, arms dealers, drugs and organized crime figures which he dubbed "The Octopus."

In July 1991, one month prior to Danny Casolaro's death, Anson Ng, a reporter for the *Financial Times* of London, was shot and killed in Guatemala, according to a 1991 *TC Technical Consultant* story. "He [Ng] had reportedly been trying to interview an American there named Jimmy Hughes, a one-time director of security for the Cabazon Indian Reservation secret projects."

A *San Francisco Chronicle* article entitled, "Tiny California Tribe's Huge Clout," dated September 4, 1991, best summarized the failure of the justice system at every level to unlock the mystery of Cabazon's forbidden secrets. Reporter Jonathan Littman mused:

> "In all, federal and state agencies [have helped] to finance nearly $250 million worth of projects on the 1,700-acre reservation. That is particularly impressive in light of the tribe's size – the entire Cabazon population numbers no more than 30.
>
> To observers in and out of government, these undertakings pose an obvious question: How did a tiny band of Indians, one of the smallest in the nation, give rise to a multimillion-dollar

> network whose influence reaches into all quarters of the U.S. government?
>
> The answer lies in a maze of politicians, military officers, organized-crime figures, intelligence agents, foreign officials ranging from Saudi sheiks to Nicaraguan Contras – and John Philip Nichols, a globe-trotting evangelical social worker with an uncanny ability to win federal grants, who once served 18 months in state prison for solicitation to commit murder.
>
> Although the full story of the Cabazon reservation is still unfolding, there are indications that this network reaches far beyond the borders of the tribe's land.

♦♦♦♦♦♦♦♦

In early August 2008 Rachel Begley introduced me to Detective John Powers at the Riverside Sheriff's department. Powers had been working with Rachel on the Alvarez triple-homicide cold-case file since 2007, but the few remaining law enforcement people who had worked the case had dim memories of the details 28 years later.

I wanted to help John and Rachel if I could, but by then I had acquired so much information that it would require a book to explain it all to them. I didn't know where to begin, so I decided to send them a 77-page Matrix Link Analysis that I had compiled in 2000 for Kelly O'Meara which provided significant names in my manuscript and the linkages to each other, a name-base of sorts in alphabetical order. Along with the Matrix I sent a 10-page outline of all the corporate structures, joint ventures and operations that related to the individuals in the Matrix.

I then began sending them material from the RCMP investigation and Detective Sue Todd's findings during their joint 8-month probe of the Octopus in 2000. In particular I encouraged Detective Powers to get copies of the Paul Morasca Homicide Investigation File – Case No. 82-1052505 and the Di Giorgio Extradition File – Case No. CR89-0603 VRW, U.S. verses Di Giorgio. The Morasca file reportedly contained over a thousand pages dating back to the early 1980's and referenced the Alvarez murders.

The e-mails were flying back and forth for months, then one day, on October 20, 2008 I received an e-mail from Powers that he had traveled to San Francisco and obtained copies of the Paul Morasca file. He said, "Everything you said would be there was there," and he wanted copies of my notes or typewritten memorandums from the Morasca file referencing a transcript of a conversation between Robert Booth Nichols (RBN) and Patrick Kenneally, the investigator at the Riverside District Attorney's office in the early 1980's at the time of the Alvarez murders.

I called Powers and read him a portion of my notes on the phone as follows: "A Riverside investigator named Patrick Kenneally [investigator for the Riverside D.A.'s office] spoke to Robert Booth Nichols. A transcript of the conversation indicated that Kenneally and Nichols jousted back and forth for a while, then Nichols asked Kenneally for a copy of the FBI report on himself. Kenneally refused. So RBN asked Kenneally what HE wanted? Kenneally said he wanted evidence against Dr. John Philip Nichols at the Cabazon Indian reservation in Indio. Shortly thereafter, Dr. Nichols was arrested and convicted on attempted murder and related charges."

In the transcript, it is clear that the conversation between RBN and Kenneally was recorded from a telephone call that RBN made to Kenneally. It begins with Kenneally answering the phone and RBN saying, "Hi Pat, how are you? Peter [Zokosky] said I should call you." The two men are very familiar with each other and you can tell from the conversation that they talk often. It is also clear that Kenneally had no idea he was being tape-recorded, though anyone who knew RBN knew he tape recorded all his calls, and his wife, Ellen, transcribed them.

Kenneally made unflattering comments about the FBI's investigation and said that he was ordered to turn everything he learned over to FBI Agent Rudy Valadez, whom he didn't trust. (Valadez worked with FBI agent Robert Barnes, who "handled" Philip Arthur Thompson and Michael Riconosciuto). This indicated that the FBI was not just assisting in the investigation, but took over control of the whole thing.

The typewritten transcript of this conversation was sent to Detective Ed Erdelatz in San Francisco, who worked the Paul Morasca homicide case, from the Sheriff's station in Indio, according to the original mailing envelope that contained the transcript. The postmark on the envelope was too faded to be read, but Dr. John Philip Nichols was arrested on January 16, 1985, just six months after that conversation took place.

On October 21, 2008, Detective Powers wrote that he would like to obtain copies of all my memorandums/notes on the Paul

Morasca homicide file. Powers said he believed that the document that Kenneally was offering RBN was the three-page FBI Report on RBN dated 12-02-82 that Zokosky showed Kelly O'Meara and me at our interview at his home in February 2001. Since Dr. Nichols was arrested within months of that phone call, it appeared that Kenneally gave the memo to RBN, who then provided a copy to his friend Zokosky, which I subsequently photographed at Zokosky's house. However, Zokosky had told Kelly and me that RBN obtained that FBI report from the DOJ.

Powers explained that the reason he was interested in the RBN/Kenneally phone conversation and *who recorded it* was because at that point, the FBI and DOJ had denied any knowledge of the Alvarez triple murder case to him. They claimed they didn't have a case file or any documentation that they were ever involved in the case.

Powers wrote: " --- Now, this doesn't necessarily mean I'm being lied to, but it's possible the people I'm talking to on the telephone are not in a position to have access to this file. I simply haven't asked the right person yet. I have a ton of documentation to prove that the FBI and DOJ were both assisting us in this investigation. DOJ Agent Frank Brock conducted several interviews and I have two of his reports with a DOJ report number written at the top. DOJ has no record of that report number and Agent Brock died ten years ago, so he can't verify it for me."

According to legend and rumor, Patrick Kenneally abruptly left the Riverside District Attorney's office and moved to another state at some point after that conversation with Robert Booth Nichols (RBN) took place. Reportedly, no one who had worked the Alvarez homicide case ever heard from him again. In 2008, John Powers located Kenneally and interviewed him, as did reporter Nathan Baca at KESQ-TV in Riverside County who was always breathing down Powers' neck.

Kenneally never knew that conversation with Robert Booth Nichols had been tape-recorded until Powers told him in 2009. Kenneally denied that the meeting with RBN and the exchange of documents ever took place. Maybe Zokosky was correct when he said RBN obtained the FBI report from the DOJ? (Nearly two years later, I learned from a former D.A. investigator and other sources who recently interviewed Kenneally that the motivating factor behind his retirement and departure from Indio was because two men in suits had allegedly shown him photos of his children getting off the school bus).

I had sent Detective John Powers my notes on Kelly O'Meara's 2-14-01 interview with Peter Zokosky in which Zokosky had said that Jimmy Hughes came to him for help and Zokosky convinced Hughes to talk to authorities and had driven Hughes to the Riverside District Attorney's office to report what he knew about the Alvarez triple-homicide. On June 20, 1984, Hughes had met with Deputy Attorney General Sanford Feldman (Special Investigations Unit, California DOJ), Special Agent Frank E. Brock (Special Investigations Unit, California DOJ), Patrick Kenneally (investigator for the Riverside D.A.'s office), officers from the Fresno Police and several others, according to Peter Zokosky. Hughes had been given a polygraph at that time. (According to police reports, Gene Gilbert was not present at this meeting. In June of 1984 he was a Sergeant at the Indio Police Department. He subsequently became involved in the Alvarez triple-homicide case when he went to work at the D.A.'s office as an investigator.)

Detective Powers followed up with a visit to Zokosky's home in March 2009 and not only interviewed Zokosky for four hours, but obtained a 11" wide by 20" long bankers box labeled "Inslaw" containing some of Zokosky's accumulated documents over the years. A DOJ liaison that Powers worked intermittently with on the Alvarez case had accompanied Powers to the Zokosky interview. Zokosky had offered the box of documents to Powers and Powers agreed to borrow it to make copies and he would return it at a later date.

In speaking with a source close to the investigation, I learned that some old cassette tapes had been provided to Powers by Zokosky, one of which was the same tape that Zokosky had played for Kelly and me at our interview with him regarding the Morasca homicide in which Michael Riconosciuto had narrated his version of the events leading up to the death of Paul Morasca which involved a money laundering and drug operation in which the Fresno chapter of the Hells Angels were allegedly used.

Another tape recording contained the conversation between Patrick Kenneally and Robert Booth Nichols relative to the "exchange" of documents, i.e, the *transcript* that Powers had found in the Paul Morasca file from S.F.P.D. RBN had taped that phone conversation on July 10, 1984, Ellen Nichols had transcribed it, and both had been given to Zokosky for safekeeping. Obviously Zokosky had provided that transcript to (name-withheld) who sent it to authorities in Indio, who then forwarded it to Detective Ed Erdelatz in San Francisco. (The initials "J.L" and a date at the top of the Kenneally/RBN transcript in the Morasca file had indicated who Zokosky gave the transcript to).

In communicating with John Powers about this turn of events, he commented, " --- thank God for Gene Gilbert and his foresight [in the 1980's] to make copies and send them to San Francisco to protect them." Powers suggested that portions of the RBN/Kenneally taped conversation might play a significant role in a future trial.

It is noteworthy that Paul Morasca was found dead (murdered) in his condo on January 14, 1982 by Detective Ed Erdelatz just six months after the Alvarez murders. Morasca had been appointed to become the manager of the new Cabazon Casino prior to his death. This might explain why so many of the Alvarez triple-homicide reports were included into the Paul Morasca file.

One report written by Gene Gilbert dated September 17, 1991, sent to the House Judiciary Committee on Inslaw, stated that the Cabazon Indians had computer access to law enforcement programs such as NCIC and NADDIS. Another section stated that "Wayne Reeder paid Jimmy Hughes between $200,000 and $250,000 to leave the area." Gilbert had told Kelly O'Meara that Peter Zokosky and Wayne Reeder were investors in the Cabazon Casino and a skeet range. But he said the Mob built the Casino for the Cabazons.

In a letter sent to Jimmy Hughes, dated April 13, 1982, Phyllis Riconosciuto, Michael's previous wife, had contracted with Hughes (and Steven Bates) to provide professional body-guard services for her husband, Michael, for the period of April 14, 15, and 16 to fly to Fresno, California to assist Michael to "get his affairs in order and to protect Michael during this period until he goes into protective custody with the FBI at the Oakland [California] office."

The letter noted that Michael Riconosciuto was to meet with FBI Special Agent Robert Barnes, and after Agent Barnes assumed protection for Riconosciuto, then Hughes and Bates could return to Palm Springs. The agreed upon flat fee for rendering this service was $1,300 including air fare, hotel costs and meals. The letter was signed by both Phyllis Riconosciuto and Jimmy Hughes.

This letter would indicate that Jimmy Hughes had either met or knew FBI agent Robert Barnes. According to Detective Sue Todd, who had interviewed Agent Barnes in 2000, he confirmed that he had been the "handler" for both Michael Riconosciuto and Philip Arthur Thompson in a large drug/sting operation in San Francisco (mentioned in the Di Giorgio file).

This letter was also written during the time (1982) that Michael Riconosciuto was involved with Dr. John Philip Nichols, administrator at the Cabazon Indian reservation, who was a partner at that time in the Cabazon/Wackenhut Joint Venture to develop weapons on the reservation with Robert Booth Nichols and Peter Zokosky.

The date on this letter to Jimmy Hughes (April 1982) also coincided with Riconosciuto's claim that he had worked undercover (on loan from the FBI) for Fresno prosecutor Brian Leighton who was instrumental in prosecuting 29 members of a drug/arms organization called "The Company." The Company had been written up in the *San Francisco Chronicle* on April 28, 1982 under the heading "Story of Spies, Stolen Arms and Drugs." According to reporter Bill Wallace, The Company consisted of (quote) "about 300 members, many of them former military men or ex-police officers with nearly $30 million worth of assets, including planes, ships and real estate."

The article went on to say that "federal drug agents said the organization had imported billions of dollars worth of narcotics from Latin America, and was also involved in gunrunning and mercenary operations." Specialized military equipment consisting of nine infrared sniperscopes, a television camera for taking pictures in darkness, 1500 rounds of small arms tracer ammunition for night combat, a five-foot remote-control helicopter, and secret components from the radar unit of a Sidewinder guided missile had been stolen from the U.S. Naval Weapons Station at China Lake in the Mojave Desert.

Detective John Powers mentioned in an e-mail communication on November 27, 2009 that he had found a hand-written "Time Line" in Peter Zokosky's box of documents, created by Zokosky, which outlined a chronology of events beginning in 1981 and ending in 1985. This was the same document that I had provided to Rachel Begley months earlier which Zokosky had given me years ago.

Powers said the time-line was very helpful: "Peter used his wife's day-by-day calendar and wrote down all of the important dates that he could find. I now have the date that Wayne Reeder drove Jimmy to the airport so he could flee to Central America. I have the date that Peter accompanied Dr. Nichols to Canada for the Valleyfield meeting, which proves Nichols was out of the country during the Alvarez murders. There are some other very important dates that helped me to figure out when certain things happened," wrote Powers.

In looking at the Zokosky time-line in my file, I found that Zokosky and Nichols had traveled together to the Valleyfield meeting in Canada from June 22 to June 30, 1981. Another notation in Zokosky's time-line labeled, "The $30,000 Caper," indicated that in May 1984 a large sum of cash in the amount of $30,000 was withdrawn from the Bingo Palace 1st Trust Bank account.

In looking at Kelly O'Meara's notes from an interview with John Belton in Canada, who had been Detective Sue Todd and RCMP Sean McDade's mutual "source," I noticed a statement made by Belton regarding the trip to Canada by Dr. John Nichols and Peter Zokosky in which they were involved in the purchase of Valleyfield Chemical Corporation in Canada in May 1981. Belton had said, " *--- Dr. Nichols used people in Canada to make sure he had an alibi when the Alvarez people were murdered on Bob Hope Drive.*"

This was an interesting statement because the Canadian meetings were outlined in a Wackenhut Inter-Office Memorandum I had found in Michael Riconosciuto's files in the desert, dated May 25, 1981, from Robert Frye, a Vice President of Wackenhut in Indio, to Robert Chasen, a Vice President of Wackenhut in Coral Gables (and former Commissioner of U.S. Customs). A notation in the Wackenhut memorandum referred to the proposed purchase of Valleyfield Chemical Products Corporation in Valleyfield, Quebec, near Montreal, Canada.

Valleyfield had gone into receivership when its owner, Gerald Bull, was jailed in the United States for illegally shipping weapons to South Africa. (Bull had developed the original Project Babylon super rail gun for the Iraqi government and was reportedly assassinated by the Israeli Mossad in March 1990). The Canadian government took possession of Valleyfield and sold it to a consortium headed by Welland Chemicals Ltd. of Mississauga on April 7, 1981.

The Wackenhut memorandum outlined an interest to purchase Valleyfield Chemical by Dr. John Nichols with a Barry Zuckerman and Charles F. Agar, both Canadian citizens, who were involved in a Canadian firm called Mineral Resources International Limited, as well as both being involved in Canadian financial institutions.

"Dr. [John] Nichols envisions that the role of the Cabazon/Wackenhut Joint Venture should the Zuckerman-Agar group be successful in purchasing this plant, would be to serve as the foreign marketing representative for the plant; to have this group possibly finance the establishment of the casing/loading facility on the Cabazon reservation; and to have the capability to conduct R&D [Research and Development] for the group in the armament industry," noted the memorandum.

A meeting had been set up in Ottawa, Canada at 9:00 A.M., May 26, 1981 involving Dr. John Philip Nichols, Frank Agar, F. Thornburg, A.R. Frye and members of the Canadian Munitions Board to discuss capital investment in the Valleyfield plant, according to the memorandum.

In Peter Zokosky's handwritten "time-line," he noted a trip to Canada with Dr. John Nichols on June 22 through June 30, 1981. Directly next to that notation were the words in capital letters, "FRED KILLED." Zokosky later explained that Dr. Nichols had stayed back in Canada, rather than return to California on June 30th with Zokosky. Nichols' excuse for staying in Canada was weak and made no sense to Zokosky at the time.

Fred Alvarez, Ralph Boger and Patti Castro were executed on June 29, 1981, so Dr. Nichols had an alibi for his whereabouts at the time of the murders.

♦♦♦♦♦♦♦♦

Over the years I had accumulated a file of documents pertaining to Jimmy Hughes' activities in the 1980's, which I subsequently provided to Rachel Begley and she presumably provided them to John Powers. Some of these documents provided a window into Hughes' alternating relationship with Dr. John Nichols, Wayne Reeder, and other individuals involved with the Cabazons at that time.

On April 4, 1983, John Paul Nichols, Dr. Nichols' son, who was by then the Cabazon Arms – Cabazon/Wackenhut Joint Venture "Project Manager," wrote a letter to the Army Discharge

Review Board asking for Hughes' military record because he required security clearances to work in the Cabazon/Wackenhut Joint Venture.

Wrote Nichols: "Mr. James Hughes Jr. has been in our employment for over three years. He has been instrumental in developing our reservation security force as well as providing superior training in law enforcement techniques, safety and sundries to our employees. He was a key person in developing, organizing and security financing for a successful trap and skeet range on the Cabazon Indian reservation."

Nichols further wrote that Hughes had shown himself to be a man of superior qualities and unusual maturity for someone his age. In addition, Hughes was becoming more and more involved in the Joint Venture with Wackenhut Services and would soon become "involved in matters where a security clearance is necessary involving government contracts." Hughes' military record would have a direct bearing on whether he would qualify for the needed security clearances. Arthur Welmas, the Tribal Chairman, had also signed the letter on Hughes' behalf.

However, Hughes' career took a dive in 1984. By February 1984, Jimmy Hughes had left Nichols' employment and went to work for Wayne Reeder. By June 1984, Hughes had been terminated by Reeder and Reeder was suing him in a Riverside Superior Court Civil Action (Indio No. 41885) for allegedly threatening his life.

Hughes responded in a court document that he had simply been attempting to collect a debt owed to him by Reeder on September 13, 1984 at a meeting with Reeder and Peter Zokosky.

Hughes said in his court Declaration that the probable purpose for Reeder's injunctive relief against Hughes was to "*discredit and destroy my prospective testimony in criminal cases currently under investigation which are to be brought against a business associate of the plaintiff's [Dr. John Philip Nichols] and quite probably against the plaintiff himself should sufficient data be generated in the future to establish his knowing participation in these criminal activities* ---" On page six of his Declaration, Hughes said he expected to testify against Dr. Nichols in a court of law on charges against him of "conspiracy to commit murder."

Hughes outlined that he was employed at the Cabazon Indian Casino and Bingo Palace concurrently from approximately February 1980 through February 1984. "During this period of my employment by these two entities, Dr. John Philip Nichols alleged that they were, in part, fronts for United States government sanctioned covert military activities and arms shipments to Central and South America." " --- over a period of time I became aware of a series of activities by Dr. John Philip Nichols and other members of his family (who are also employed there) which made me realize that their activities were criminal (including issuing contracts to commit murder) and were not governmental in nature as Dr. Nichols had alleged---," he declared.

Hughes further stated that when he reached a full realization of what Dr. Nichols was involved in at the Cabazon Indian Casino and Bingo Palace, he severed his connection with them and accepted employment from Wayne Reeder, who through his corporation Bingo Pavilion, Inc. had made a $230,000 investment in the Cabazon gambling enterprise. Reeder promised Hughes that he would set him up in a security business to be owned jointly by Reeder and Hughes, including a promise that he would secure contracts for the new company with the Indian Palms Country Club which was owned by Reeder.

Reeder had allegedly confided to Hughes that "Dr. Nichols and family were 'skimming' profits off the top of the gambling enterprise in order to avoid taxes and avoid making the contracted payments to Bingo Pavilion, Inc." owned by Reeder. Reeder asked Hughes to return to the Cabazon gambling operations at the reservation so he (Hughes) could monitor the gross receipts and report back to Reeder.

However, Hughes subsequently learned that Nichols and Reeder had made a deal in which Reeder would "get rid" of him (Hughes) so that he couldn't make Nichols' illegal activities known. An attached Exhibit B was written by John Paul Nichols (Dr. Nichols' son) to Wayne Reeder and his attorney reminding Reeder that he had made an agreement with the Nichols family that Jimmy Hughes "would be gone" sometime between May 12, 1984 and May 14, 1984, and that Hughes was going to open a security business somewhere. Arthur Welmas, Tribal Chairman, had reported to Nichols that Hughes was seen coming out of his apartment on May 17, and their (the Tribal Council) patience was wearing thin. John Paul Nichols concluded the letter by saying, "I suggest that you stick to your deal with the officers of Cabazon Bingo, Inc."

John Patrick McGuire had also worked for Wayne Reeder and provided a Declaration on Hughes' behalf. One paragraph in McGuire's Declaration noted that he had spoken with Reeder's lawyer, Clay Weed, on or about May 23, 1984 and Mr. Weed had said: "It's not in Mr. Reeder's interest to do anything about the Nichols's or their illegal activities at the Bingo operation because to do so would jeopardize Mr. Reeder's investment." (Reeder had allegedly invested $230,000 in the Cabazon gambling enterprise at that time).

Hughes stated in his court Declaration that he remained in Reeder's employ until about June 1984, then Reeder terminated him at Nichols' insistence. Hughes had already initiated a series of contacts with various law enforcement agencies to report what he knew concerning Nichols' illegal activities, including solicitation of murder. Hughes said the day after he visited the Riverside District Attorney's office in April 1984, he received a death threat in the form of a gruesome photograph (in an envelope) attached to the windshield of his car. The photograph was provided as an Exhibit C.

On April 15, Hughes had been told by a friend that there was a "contract on his life." Shortly thereafter, Peter Zokosky received a phone call to the same effect. Hughes also discovered that a $30,000 withdrawal had been made by John Paul Nichols from the Bingo Palace's account by check payable to cash at that same time.

Hughes stated that since that time, *the California Department of Justice had offered him participation in their Witness Protection Program due to the threats and his cooperation with them.* Reeder had terminated him in June 1984 and he had since moved to Los Angeles.

On September 13, 1984 Hughes had a meeting with Wayne Reeder and Peter Zokosky at Reeders' office at the Indian Palms Country Club. Hughes demanded that Reeder make good on his promises, but Reeder said that wasn't feasible anymore. Hughes pointed out that Dr. Nichols had placed a contract on his life, as well as Reeders: " --- You know there are contracts on both of us. If I die, so will you." Wayne Reeder took that as a threat and sued Jimmy Hughes for allegedly threatening his life.

Hughes subsequently talked to Keith Carter, the *Indio Daily News* Managing Editor, about his dissatisfaction with the various law enforcement agencies he and Zokosky had provided information to during the past four months. "I'm not going to say anything else to them," he explained. "All they (the local and state law enforcement agencies) care about is their own jurisdiction. The case is too big for them to see the whole picture. They can't handle it." Hughes said that he had been in contact with federal officials in Washington D.C., who were interested in the case. "I'm not at liberty to say who I'm talking to, but it's obvious the state of California needs help," he said.

••••••••

Detective John Powers had the foresight in 2009 to scan and copy the entire Alvarez investigation and the entire Paul Morasca file onto the Sheriff Department's main file server, back it up onto an external hard drive, and also copied to CD's.

Jimmy Hughes was still in California as of June 1985, he was staying with Peter Zokosky and keeping a low profile. Hughes had testified against Dr. John Philip Nichols at a Grand Jury hearing in Riverside in May 1985, but subsequently moved to Guatemala and did not testify at Dr. Nichols' trial in Indio.

Pat Kenneally, the investigator for the Riverside D.A., allegedly left Riverside unexpectedly. Some speculated that he left because the prosecutor working in the Riverside County District Attorney's office at that time was Rod Pacheco, Jimmy Hughes' cousin. Others speculated that it was because of Kenneally's conversation with Robert Booth Nichols and/or a subsequent FBI probe of the matter. It is possible, looking at the time frames, that while Robert Booth Nichols was tape-recording his conversation with Kenneally on July 10, 1984, he (Nichols) was being wiretapped by the FBI!

••••••••

On February 27, 2009, Rachel Begley arrived at my home in California to make copies from eight boxes of documents that I had acquired during the past 18 years. (I had acquired more boxes after the RCMP investigation). During the eight days that she stayed at my home, she made thousands of copies of documents, including old Cabazon and Wackenhut documents dating back to the early 1980's. We drove out to Bob Hope Drive in Rancho Mirage and she placed a flower at the site where her father had been murdered in 1981. The house had been bulldozed shortly after the murders, so the only thing that remained was an empty lot.

Less than a block away, at the northwest corner of Bob Hope Drive and Frank Sinatra Drive, was the "Sunnylands" winter estate of Walter Annenberg, a Reagan protégé. Annenberg had led a lavish lifestyle and Fred Alvarez could have observed it from his porch. Sunnylands had hosted gatherings with such notables as Frank Sinatra, Bob Hope, Bing Crosby, President Ronald Reagan and First Lady Nancy Reagan. The Reagans often celebrated New Year's Eve with the Annenbergs, the Bloomingdales, and Edie and Lew Wasserman, chairman of MCA Corporation. Walter Annenberg subsequently gave his home located at 668 St. Cloud Road in Bel Air (Los Angeles) to the Reagans as a gift upon Ronald Reagan's departure from the Presidency of the United States.

From there Rachel and I drove to the Cabazon Tribe's Fantasy Springs Casino in Indio and had dinner at the Casino buffet while musing about the history of the Cabazons in the early 1980's and the effect it had on her life.

Rachel has vivid memories of the last time she saw her father. Her thoughts are frozen in time to the week before his death, when she was 13 years old: "I was excited; my dad was coming to pick me up for a day out on the town. I sat, waiting impatiently for him to pull up. I loved when my dad would pick me up for days out. Today would be a little different though, Gail, my step-mom, wasn't coming with him but this was okay, it would just be me and my dad together that day. I heard the loud roar of his Harley pull up and I ran out to greet him, soon, we were off to the mall."

Rachel becomes stoic when she recalls the ice cream parlor. Her soulful blue eyes look inward to some private place when she talks about her father: "We went into an ice cream shop and he ordered two pistachios. I explained that I liked mint and he said, 'You'll like this, I promise. It's green like the mint,' so I acquiesced.

"When we sat down to eat our ice cream, dad said, 'I have to talk to you about something.' He sounded very serious. 'Okay, what's wrong?' I asked. 'I'm helping Fred stop some bad guys,' he said as he took a bite of his ice cream. 'What's going on, dad?' I asked. 'There are some shady things going on down at the reservation. Fred and I are trying to stop it.' I remember he studied my face closely, to see my reaction. 'Don't worry, we'll be OK,' he added, as if saying it would make it true.

"Fred Alvarez and my dad were best friends," Rachel recalled. "I knew Fred as an uncle. He and my dad had partied together, rode their motorcycles together, and had done business together in the past. When my dad told me that they were trying to stop some bad things at the reservation, it came as no surprise. It didn't cross my young mind, at the age of 13, that there was any real danger involved in what they were doing. Besides, my dad told me they would be okay. Looking back in retrospect, I realize that dad wasn't sure at all that they would be okay. We finished our ice cream and began talking about how I was doing in school ---"

On March 2, Detective John Powers from the Riverside County Sheriff's Department arrived at my home to meet with Rachel face-to-face and update her on the progress of his investigation. I was allowed to sit in on the meeting and take notes. Powers also allowed me to photograph him with Rachel for my book.

Powers was not at all what I had expected. He was young, good-looking, dressed in casual clothes and he had traveled to my home from Riverside on a motorcycle. His eyes smiled, his demeanor was relaxed and friendly, and he had a sense of quiet about him that I learned over time was a built-in patience and ability to listen carefully, even when you didn't think he was listening. By contrast, his e-mails had been written scrupulously, as if he had considerable writing experience, and he was so detail-oriented that I guessed that was why he worked in the cold-case division of the homicide unit. In truth, he was one of the most intrepid investigators I had encountered in my experience, yet if you met him on the street you'd never guess he was a homicide detective. Rachel was devoted to him because he had worked so hard on her case.

Powers said he had requested an arrest warrant for Jimmy Hughes from Mike Murphy, the Deputy Attorney General, California Dept. of Justice, San Diego. The DOJ advised Powers that they would approve the arrest warrant for Jimmy Hughes, but they wanted Powers to arrest "all the suspects simultaneously." They said when Powers was ready to perform all the arrests, then all the warrants would be released together.

Detective Powers related the names of the subjects that he had been investigating and interviewing. Much of the information that Powers provided at our meeting can't be included here because it would compromise the DOJ's case against Jimmy Hughes in the upcoming court trial, which is not anticipated to take place until at least two years from now, according to Detective Powers.

However, some of the key people that Powers interviewed were former Hells Angels bikers headquartered in San Diego at the time of the triple-homicide in 1981. It is noteworthy that at the time of the murders, both Fred Alvarez and Ralph Boger were also members of a biker club in the Riverside County area. Also of note, though Powers didn't mention this aspect, were Michael Riconosciuto's earlier claims that the Hells Angels were used by The Company for drug trafficking operations in Fresno. Riconosciuto had named the people involved in that operation in a letter to Dr. John Phillip Nichols when he was attempting to obtain security clearances for his participation in the Cabazon/Wackenhut Joint Venture, created in April 1981, less than three months *before* the Alvarez triple-homicide.

Detective John Powers was nearing the end of his two-year investigation. With the full support and backing of the Riverside County sheriff, he had examined thousands of old documents across the state, resurrected police reports from forgotten archives (which were not computerized 28 years ago), and interviewed dozens of hostile witnesses who feared to come forward in 1981. He'd done his job, he solved the case, but he had to involve a prosecuting agency in order to get an arrest warrant.

The Riverside D.A.'s Office had a conflict of interest with District Attorney Rod Pacheco, who was Jimmy Hughes' cousin, so Powers was forced to take the case to the California State Attorney General's Office to seek an arrest warrant and charges filed. This was the first time the DOJ had become involved in the case during Powers' two year investigation. They had no involvement in the investigation, only the prosecution. It was now up to the DOJ to bring justice to the victims and their families, as well as closure to the dozens of investigators who worked the case during the past 28 years.

Three months later the warrant still hadn't been issued on Jimmy Hughes. On June 22, 2009, Rachel Begley called the California Attorney General's office to learn the status of the arrest warrants. She had learned that FGBMFI [Full Gospel Business Men's Fellowship International] of which Jimmy Hughes was a high-standing member, would be holding a convention in Florida during the upcoming

4th of July weekend. She believed Hughes would be attending this convention and she wanted the arrest warrant implemented before Hughes departed Florida and returned to Honduras.

With no positive response from the DOJ, Rachel launched a desperate campaign with media, Internet websites, and political figures, including California Attorney General Jerry Brown, to motivate the DOJ to move forward with the warrant immediately. Rachel's campaign, along with some prodding from John Powers, got the ball rolling on the warrant. However, it turned out that Jimmy Hughes never attended the FGBMFI conference in Florida after all. Possibly because his friends in the military and FGBMFI co-member, Gen. Daniel López Carballo, were busy designing a coup that very same weekend in Honduras. Jimmy Hughes Ministries (FGBMFI) is located in the village of Zambrano, north of Tegucigalpa, where Hughes ministered to the military and trained military personnel as well.

On June 28, 2009, the president of Honduras, Manuel Zelaya, was rousted from his home in Tegucigalpa and exiled at gunpoint to Costa Rica. The *Wall Street Journal* reported on June 29 in an article titled, "Coup Rocks Honduras" by Paul Kiernan, Jose De Cordoba and Jay Solomon, http://online.wsj.com/article/SB124619401378065339.html, that Honduras's Supreme Court gave the order for the military to detain the president. Later, Honduras's Congress formally removed Mr. Zelaya from the presidency and named congressional leader Roberto Micheletti as his successor until the end of Mr. Zelaya's term in January.

Mr. Zelaya called the action a kidnapping, and said he was still president. The U.S. and other countries condemned the coup. President Barack Obama said he was "deeply concerned" and called on all political actors in Honduras to "respect democratic norms." Venezuela President Hugo Chávez, a close ally of Mr. Zelaya and nemesis of the U.S., said he would consider it an "act of war" if there were hostilities against his diplomats. "I have put the armed forces of Venezuela on alert," Mr. Chávez said.

"Retired Honduran Gen. Daniel López Carballo justified the move against the president, telling CNN that if the military hadn't acted, Mr. Chávez would eventually be running Honduras by proxy ---." President Chávez had close ties to Iran and reportedly offered to commit his Venezuelan troops to Iran if war broke out between Iran and the United States.

General Daniel Carballo was named in a Spanish publication, Publico.es, as being the "designer of the military strategy of the coup d'etat." This is an excerpt from Publico.es (translated from Spanish to English)

Title: "Micheletti Purges the Police of the Still Loyal Controls to Zelaya." 7-21-09.

> " --- In the new regime there are people in charge of tortures and disappearances. Behind the changes of the last days, it is the hand of Billy Amendo Jewel and Daniel Lopez Carballo, *both men who designed the military strategy of the coup* d'etat of the 28 of June [2009]." http://babelfish.yahoo.com/translate_url?doit=done&tt=url&intl=1&fr=bf-home&trurl=http%3A%2F%2Fwww.publico.es%2Finternacional%2F240159%2F&lp=es_en&btnTrUrl=Translate

••••••••

Finally, on September 26, 2009 self-described Mafia hit-man James "Jimmy" Hughes, 52, was arrested as he boarded a plane destined for Honduras at Miami-Dade International Airport. The fugitive warrant from the California DOJ listed three counts of murder and conspiracy to commit a crime for the 1981 execution-style murder of Cabazon Tribal Council Vice-Chairman Fred Alvarez, his friend Ralph Boger, and Patricia Castro in Rancho Mirage, California.

Detective John Powers at the Riverside County Sheriff's Department in California, Central Homicide Unit – Cold Case Division, was officially present at the arrest scene to confirm Hughes' identity. He'd been notified the day before by authorities in Miami that Jimmy Hughes was in the U.S. and preparing to depart for Honduras.

Media reports were confused or misleading about the details of the arrest. This is how it went down according to John Powers: Powers flew to Miami and subsequently met authorities at the airport. He went to the gate where the passengers were boarding the plane and quickly scanned the crowd for Jimmy Hughes. He was the only person who could pick Hughes out of the crowd, so the other officers awaited his signal.

When Powers motioned to the other officers that Hughes was not in the crowd, two Customs Officers boarded the plane and located Hughes' assigned seat. They found Hughes on the plane with his wife and after identifying him by his passport, took him into custody. Two uniformed Customs Officers escorted Hughes off the plane in handcuffs. When they came down the ramp, Det. Powers confirmed they had the right man.

Three agencies assisted Powers with the arrest. US Customs and Border Protection were the primary agency making the arrest. They processed Hughes in their facility at the airport and then turned custody over to Miami-Dade County Police Department - Airport District. The police department took custody of Hughes on the warrant and booked him into the County Jail located at 1321 N.W. 12th Street in Miami. An officer with Department of Homeland Security / I.C.E was also present and provided some assistance.

Although Powers was there, he was not the arresting officer because he didn't have jurisdiction in Miami. His purpose for being there was to make sure Hughes did not slip through their fingers and make it out of the country. Powers was the only person who could identify Hughes on site and he provided photographs of Hughes to the other officers. Powers also wanted to attempt an interview with Hughes once he was arrested but Hughes invoked his Miranda rights and refused an interview. Powers also was hopeful that Hughes would waive extradition so he could bring him back to California, but Hughes chose to fight extradition.

One of the arresting officers who assisted Powers and wrote the report was CBP (Customs Border Patrol) Officer Dale Munson. One of the two Miami-Dade Police Officers who assisted was Detective Richard Wilkinson. Both were uniformed officers assigned to the Airport District.

Powers was forced to obtain a Governor's Warrant to have Jimmy Hughes brought back to California. He filed a Felony Complaint for Extradition in Indio Court on October 1, 2009, case number INF-066719. The California State Attorney General is prosecuting the case because the current Riverside County district attorney, Rod Pacheco, is a second cousin of the defendant.

Hughes had reportedly left Riverside County in 1984, stayed with Peter Zokosky for a while in 1985, lived in Los Angeles for a while, visited his mother in Guatemala, then joined FGBMFI in 1987 and subsequently founded Jimmy Hughes Ministries – Free the Oppressed in Honduras.

Inexplicably, at the FGBMFI website Hughes admitted he was a Mafia hit-man before he found God: http://www.fgbmfivoice.com/stories/996hughes.htm

An excerpt reads as follows:

> --- *After a six-year hitch in the military, I became a professional hit man for the Mafia. I collected money, hurt a lot of people and saw a lot of blood. I know what it's like to cut the throat of a man, see a man die, or throw a man in the trunk of a car and take him to his death. I did many horrible things. I allowed myself to do whatever was necessary.*
>
> One day I had a contract on a man. They had paid me a lot of money to kill this person. I travelled over many states, and walked into the man's house one day, pulled out my pistol, and put a bullet in everybody's head.
>
> There were many people there that day because he was having a party. As I stood there with the gun in my hand, I suddenly realized that all those people were dead. They had died instantly. I had been paid to kill one man, but had killed half a dozen people. The rest had just been in the wrong place at the wrong time ---

Nineteen months *before* Jimmy Hughes' arrest, Rachel had confronted Hughes at a FGBMFI dinner event on February 22, 2008 at the Banker's Ball Room – Fresno Fulton Mall in California. The billing for the event advertised "World Renowned Evangelist Jimmy Hughes of Honduras" and "Former Commanding General Daniel Lopez Carballo of Honduras" as the keynote speakers. http://fgbmfi-sjvc.org/FGBMFI-Fresno-Flier.pdf

Rachel walked up to Jimmy Hughes, with General Carballo present, and introduced herself as the daughter of Ralph Boger. She was accompanied by Fred Alvarez's son, Mikel Alvarez. She said to Hughes, "You were the 'bagman' in our father's murder. I'd like to talk to you about that." She wanted Hughes to say he was sorry for the murder of her father, Fred Alvarez and Patti Castro, but he didn't.

Hughes refused to speak to her at first, but returned when he saw her crying. He didn't want to talk about his past.

> I have nothing to say about that. Can't say anything about that.

Nevertheless he confided,

> Your parents got killed in a Mafia hit. That's life. That's what happened.

Hughes added:

> --- I don't care about my past. My past is my past. It's none of your business. It's nobody's business. I don't care who died. I don't care who got killed. I was trained in the military. I killed people all over the world, right or wrong, because the government ordered me to. Your dad and I were friends. He touched somebody --- they gave an order and that's what happened to him. It's a lot bigger than the murder of this guy or the murder of that guy. It's big --- you're talking political people ---

Hughes was apparently unaware that Rachel had her camcorder turned on and everything he said was recorded. The recording can be viewed at her website: http://www.youtube.com/watch?v=eyjVd10w59I

After viewing the video, I dubbed Rachel "Danger Girl," which she scoffs at, but which aptly describes her Indian/Irish fearlessness and hard-headed disregard for her own mortality. Despite that, she emanates a kind of mother-earth kindness and depth that charms everyone who meets her. Throughout the 16 months that I observed, up-close, her relentless pursuit of the killers of her father, and indeed, other related criminal types who regularly monitored her website, some of whom issued threats, I wondered when I awakened in the morning if my friend Rachel would still be in this world, or in the next realm of the happy hunting grounds?

♦♦♦♦♦♦♦♦

After Jimmy Hughes' arrest, Rachel Begley was besieged with media requests for interviews, as was John Powers. John generally deferred the media to Rachel, so her story became widely known to the *Los Angeles Times*, Associated Press, NBC News, *Good Morning America*, and some local media such as KESQ-TV in Palm Desert and The Desert Sun newspaper which covered the area where the triple homicide occurred. Rachel was approached by television producers (*Dateline* and the Lifetime channel) for the story of her life, a la Erin Brockovich-style, and last known, she was trying to negotiate with a big-screen film promoter without a Literary Agent to represent her. Oddly, the agents she had approached didn't take the time to respond to her queries.

In addition, the news stories left out one of the most significant contributions that Rachel made to the investigation, which was her extraordinary computer expertise. John Powers once wrote that her ability was "awesome," he had grown to appreciate her tracking skills. On more than one occasion I had asked her to locate individuals that I needed to interview (which I had already spent hours trying to locate on the Internet), and within minutes she provided their home, work and e-mail addresses, including phone numbers. She could even send a satellite photo of what their house looked like.

During her investigation, *before* Jimmy Hughes' arrest, Rachel's website at Desertfae.com attracted observers from all points of the spectrum. She has a large family which keeps her busy during the day, but late at night we communicated back and forth and I was astonished at what she was able to track through her website. The Department of Justice had visited on numerous occasions, members of the Cabazon tribe and related casino people, known members of organized crime, police departments, friends of Jimmy Hughes, including Hughes himself, the Federal Reserve Bank, attorney's for people being investigated, the Saudi government, multiple military bases, various state government offices (CA, NV, AZ, NY) along with a variety of reporters and other interested folks who spent hours surfing through her documents and videos.

In mid-October, after Jimmy Hughes' arrest, Rachel began receiving threats from people who seemed to have been close to Hughes or were members of his organization in Honduras. However, a side benefit of the substantial news coverage came in the form of an e-mail from a Honduran source who revealed that Hughes was a close friend and "asesor" (Spanish for "advisor") of Romeo Vásquez Velásquez, who was allegedly also a member of FGBMFI. The source added that Jimmy Hughes had assisted with the planning of the Honduras coup.

It was true, according to news accounts, that the interim defacto president of Honduras, Roberto Micheletti, had been placed in office by coup leaders General Romeo Vásquez Velásquez and General Daniel Lopez Carballo, both friends of "hit-man" Jimmy Hughes, and at least two of these men, possibly all three, were in fact members of FGBMFI. Both of the above Honduran generals had also been trained at the School of the Americas. http://soaw.org/pressrelease.php?id=144

An Internet search of Velásquez produced a Wikipedia site that said Romeo Vásquez Velásquez was a Brigadier General and head of the armed forces of Honduras who was sacked by President Manuel Zelaya on June 25, 2009 for refusing to allow the armed forces to help in conducting an referendum on a constitutional change proposed by President Zelaya. "He attended the School of the Americas (SOA/WHINSEC) at least twice, in 1976 and 1984 and expands the number of SOA/WHINSEC graduates who have overthrown heads of state." http://en.wikipedia.org/wiki/Romeo_V%C3%A1squez_Vel%C3%A1squez

In looking up "School of the Americas," I came upon the following: The School of the Americas (SOA), in 2001 renamed the "Western Hemisphere Institute for Security Cooperation," is a combat training school for Latin American soldiers, located at Fort Benning, Georgia. Initially established in Panama in 1946, it was kicked out of that country in 1984 under the terms of the Panama Canal Treaty. Former Panamanian President, Jorge Illueca, stated that the School of the Americas was the "biggest base for destabilization in Latin America." The SOA, frequently dubbed the "School of Assassins," has left a trail of blood and suffering in every country where its graduates have returned.

Over its 59 years, the SOA has trained over 60,000 Latin American soldiers in counterinsurgency techniques, sniper training, commando and psychological warfare, military intelligence and interrogation tactics. These graduates have consistently used their skills to wage a war against their own people. Among those targeted by SOA graduates are educators, union organizers, religious workers, student leaders, and others who work for the rights of the poor. Hundreds of thousands of Latin Americans have been tortured, raped, assassinated, "disappeared," massacred, and forced into refugee by those trained at the School of Assassins. http://www.soaw.org/type.php?type=8

As noted earlier, former Commanding General Daniel Lopez Carballo of Honduras, a member of FGBMFI and keynote speaker with Jimmy Hughes that day in February 2008, was subsequently written up in a Spanish speaking newspaper as the "*designer of the military strategy of the coup*" that took place in Honduras in June 2009.

From the Honduran military's point of view, the U.S. had a stake in the coup as well. Retired General Daniel López Carballo told

CNN that the coup was warranted because "Venezuelan President Chávez would be running Honduras by proxy if the military had not acted." The ousted president of Honduras, Manuel Zelaya, had been in the process of forming a friendship or alliance with Venezuelan president Hugo Chávez, who according to news reports, had already formed an alliance with Iran and offered military support to Iran in the event that Iran went to war with the U.S.

The U.S. operates an airbase in Honduras (see The Soto Cano Air Base below) which it is continuing to expand with major upgrades in 2009. The infrastructure of the Soto Cano Air Base is such that the Honduran Constitution does not permit a permanent foreign presence in Honduras. A "handshake" agreement between the United States and Honduras allows the U.S. military's Joint Task Force (JTF-Bravo) to remain in Honduras on a "semi-permanent" basis. This agreement, an annex to the 1954 military assistance agreement between the United States and Honduras, can be abrogated with little notice.

If president Zelaya had sided with Hugo Chávez militarily, then the U.S. could have lost that airbase in Honduras. (Oliver North once used this air base as a base of operations for the U.S. backed Contras in the 1980s).

The Soto Cano Air Base (commonly known as Palmerola Air Base) is a joint Honduras and United States military base near Comayagua in Honduras, about 60 miles (97 km) from the Honduran capital of Tegucigalpa. A large concentration of U.S. troops and the Honduran Air Force academy use the airbase. The airbase became operational in 1981. Now the U.S. military uses Soto Cano as a launching point for its war on drugs efforts in Central America as well as humanitarian aid missions throughout Honduras and Central America.

In addition, the US military's Joint Task Force Bravo (JTF-B) is headquartered at Soto Cano. JTF-B consists of Medical Element – Military Hospital, Army Forces, Air Force Forces, Joint Security Forces, and the 1st Battalion-228th Aviation Regiment (consisting of some 18 aircraft, a mix of UH-60 Black Hawk helicopters and CH-47 Chinook helicopters). http://en.wikipedia.org/wiki/Soto_Cano_Air_Base

The influential Full Gospel Business Men's Fellowship International (FGBMFI) has a history all its own. Prominent right-wing activists, such as Joseph Coors (Heritage Foundation) and Sanford McDonnell (McDonnell Douglas Corporation) were members of FGBMFI. Former President Ronald Reagan had close ties with FGBMFI. In 1970, five FGBMFI members, including Pat and Shirley Boone, Harold Bredesen, and George Otis, prayed with then-California Governor Reagan at his home in Sacramento. Otis, a former Lear executive, was overcome with the Spirit and began to speak in the voice of God. He compared Reagan to a king, and prophesied that Reagan would "reside at 1600 Pennsylvania Avenue" if he continued to walk in God's way. Reagan reportedly took the prophecy very seriously. A Reagan Aide who later worked on Pat Robertson's presidential campaign, invited Nita Scoggan, the wife of a FGBMFI member, to form a prayer group in the White House. Reportedly, Col. Oliver North attended the prayer meetings. http://www.cephas-library.com/church_n_state/church_n_state_profiles_of_u.s.private.gov_organizations_and_churches.html

The strong FGBMFI military connections had a wide-ranging effect on foreign policy in Central America under the Reagan administration. Since 1964, FGBMFI had held regular military prayer meetings in the Washington D.C. area. At one point there were three chapters there, including one in the Navy Officers' Club, and the Secretary of Defense even arranged to have two prayer rooms built in the Pentagon. A 1986 FGBMFI brochure listed over a dozen military names, a few of which were the Chairman of Joint Chiefs of Staff, the Commandant of the Marine Corps, the Chief of Naval Operations, the Chief of Staff of the Army, and the Chief of Staff of the Air Force.

In Central America, President Reagan supported General Ríos Montt, a Pentecostal "true believer," who became president of Guatemala in an army coup in March 1982, and was aided and supported by Full Gospel businessman John Carrette, a former Army Ranger in Vietnam and vocal supporter of Rios Montt. According to Carrette, the then presidents of Guatemala, El Salvador and Honduras were all Full Gospel.

Carrette later became the Executive Vice President of FGBMFI and helped set up Jimmy Hughes in Honduras. Hughes, also a former Army Ranger, wrote at his FGBMFI website that Carrette flew from Guatemala to meet him in Los Angeles. " --- In 1987, John Carrette 'god-fathered' me into the Full Gospel Business Men's

Fellowship, and I have been in the Fellowship ever since. I live in Honduras. I have a wife and two children, and we have a ministry called 'Free the Oppressed' ----." http://www.fgbmfivoice.com/stories/996hughes.htm

Ríos Montt's ties to the United States military went back to 1950 when he graduated as a cadet at the School of the Americas in the Panama Canal Zone, which at that time educated students in counterinsurgency tactics for the purpose of combating potential "communist" influence in the region. The FGBMFI fellowship entered Guatemala in 1952; its directors were leading businessmen, media people and military officers, including a former minister of defense.

By 1982 General Ríos Montt was best known outside Guatemala for heading a military regime (1982–1983) that was involved in some of the worst atrocities of Guatemala's 36-year civil war. Given Ríos Montt's staunch anticommunism and ties to the United States, the Reagan administration continued to support the general and his regime, paying a visit to Guatemala City in December 1982. During a meeting with Ríos Montt on December 4, Reagan declared: "President Ríos Montt is a man of great personal integrity and commitment. ... I know he wants to improve the quality of life for all Guatemalans and to promote social justice."

Reagan later agreed, in January 1983, to sell Guatemala millions of dollars worth of helicopter spare parts, a decision that did not require approval from Congress. In turn, Guatemala was eager to resurrect the Central American Defense Council, defunct since 1969, in order to join forces with the right-wing governments of El Salvador and Honduras in retaliations against the leftist Sandinista government of Nicaragua. http://en.wikipedia.org/wiki/Efra%C3%ADn_R%C3%ADos_Montt.

But Rios Montt's extreme version of Christian fundamentalism was hurtling out of control, even by Guatemalan standards. In August 1983, Gen. Oscar Mejia Victores seized power in another coup. In 1984 retired General Montt spoke at a FGBMFI world convention, and Ronald Reagan succeeded in pressuring Congress to approve $300,000 in military training for the Guatemalan army.

♦♦♦♦♦♦♦♦

In a Spanish article from the Honduran newspaper *La Prensa,* Hughes openly discussed his bloody past. It was an astounding story. Clearly he felt well insulated in Central America, given his ties to military generals and the powerful FGBMFI in that area of the world. It appears that most of the quotes in the *La Prensa* article were derived from a *Vertice, Newspaper of Today* (El Salvador) article published on July 6, 2003.

> Title: "*Jimmy Hughes – From CIA operative and mafia hitman to evangelical pastor,*" by Jessica Figeroa. (Translated from Spanish to English below).
> From *La Prensa* in Honduras – 10/5/09: (excerpted)
>
> > Talking about his dark past was always part of his testimony as a conference speaker. Despite the new life that he found in God, he yet seems to have unsettled scores with justice. Things caught up with him 28 years later.
> >
> > The Rev. Jimmy Hughes is the founder of the 'Gateway of Hope'(Puerta de Ezsperanza) Rehabilitation Center, which rescues youth gang members in Honduras, and is also president of "Free The Oppressed Ministries," established in Zambrano.
> >
> > He was arrested last Saturday at the Miami International Airport as he prepared to travel to Honduras.
> >
> > He is accused of being involved in the 'Octopus Murders' that occurred in 1981 in California.
> >
> > The victims of an execution-style shot to the head were: Fred Alvarez, 32, Patty Castro, 44, and Ralph Boger, 42, according to the Riverside County Sheriff, Dennis Gutierrez. Hughes had arrest warrants.
>
> **The CIA trained him, the FBI protected him**
>
> > The Salvadorian newspaper *El Diario de Hoy* published on July 6 of 2003, an interview with Hughes, in which he described his life before joining the ranks of the CIA. He also mentions how he ended up being an elite military-trained hitman for the Mafia, 'until God rescued him.'
>
> **Excerpts from Jimmy Hughes 2003 interview:**
>
> > *The end of the Vietnam War in 1973 marked the beginning of my military career. My instructors and teachers were American fighters who survived operations against the Vietcong. I was 17 years old and aspired to climb the ladder in the military.*

I enrolled in each course no matter how hard it was. I attended schools in parachuting, scuba diving, escape and rescue operations, as a prisoner of war, resistance and survival in jungle, sea and desert environments. I specialized in plastic explosives and as a sniper. In six years, the military training that I received, including the Rangers and Delta Force, transformed me into an elite soldier.

At the age of 23, I began working for the CIA in covert missions outside the United States. In Asian countries, Europe and South America, I fought to defend the rights of others. I helped people who wanted to be free and to fight dictators. The US Army did not train me to be a cold-blooded killer, but to defend my country and the enemies of democracy and freedom.

After several secret missions, I left the CIA, and four years later (1984), I left the Army and went to live a quiet life in California, never imagining that my bloodiest were yet to come.

Collecting tributes

While serving in the military, I had an Italian friend who often spoke to me about a 'Padrino' (Godfather), and I never paid much attention; I thought those were just things you see in the movies.

My first job in the mob was collecting money from those who did not pay their bills, and that included broken legs, arms and heads with baseball bats.

Although the Army I had already gotten a taste of what it was like to kill, with the mob, I offered my talent for gifts or money. I would murder someone for five, ten, twenty, thirty, forty thousand dollars. The most I got paid for killing somebody was fifty thousand dollars, because it was professionally done. This was how at age 27, I sold myself to evil.

I became the confidant of the Godfather, who was in the business of casinos. I was the bodyguard for his children. I became a famous hitman for the mafia; everybody in the United States asked for Jimmy Hughes.

By that time I was addicted to cocaine. I loved cocaine. I had a terrible addiction; I would always carry the drug in my pockets. I drank hard liquor all day. I always had terrible nightmares because I had shed enough blood to fill a pool.

Free Death

One day, the Godfather called me and gave me an order to kill a suspect for thirty thousand dollars. To my surprise, I knew this guy; we used to be friends. But in the mafia, [illegible] is business.' When I arrived at the guy's home, I was n[illegible] normal person; I had been exposed to so much violence [illegible] become a demon. I said hi to the guy and went into his [illegible]

He never imagined that he had just opened the door to de[illegible] But inside the mansion, there were five other people who were drinking and snorting cocaine. I thought, 'I must get this done for the $30,000 that I was being paid;' however, I did not know who the other five were. Then I thought to myself that I would do a service to society by doing them all. The other five would be added to the contract... for free.

The night began to fall and when I took my gun out, no one noticed it because they were too drugged and drunk. They were all talking nonsense, so I began: "Bang, bang, bang..."

Everyone around me was dead within seconds; no one moved. They were totally unprepared; no one was expecting to die. I had shot all of them in the head. But right after it all happened, and as I was still holding the gun in my hand, between a pool of blood, I would see shattered face of the man that I was paid to kill, and it would feel as though I would see my reflection in a mirror.

The hairs in the back of my neck stood up as I saw my own bloody image. At the same time, I began to hear a voice say, "Jimmy: You know that I love you and I forgive you." I said to myself: "Oh God, I'm either going crazy or I did too many drugs and I had killed so many people in my life."

In that horrific scene, I somewhat laughed, but then big chills came down my spine.

My heart almost stopped. Then I heard the same voice again: "Jimmy: You know that I love you and I forgive you." Then, I ran out of the place, leaving half a dozen dead for thirty thousand dollars.

Trapped in the solitude of my home, I took the phone and decided to call my mother, who was as a Christian missionary in Guatemala.

"Listen," I said to her, "I do not know if the FBI is going to catch me or if I should turn myself in. I don't know if I'm going to go to jail or if the mafia is going to kill me, but I want you to pray for me. I will not die or go to jail without setting things right with God."

She prayed intensely for me over the telephone line from Guatemala, with me in California, and God in heaven. It was

...irst experienced the immense power of prayer, a ...eater than any weapon ever held in my hands.

...n the mafia to the FBI

The next day, I went to see the Godfather and told him I wanted to quit, and that I would never kill anyone anymore and wanted to be alone.

He looked like he was seeing a mad man. He paid me the $30,000, but immediately said: "Jimmy, you know the rules, you know you're putting your own life in danger."

I replied: "Yes, I know, but if something happens, we all die." The FBI, the Justice Department and the Police had already been after me. They wanted to pick my brain to see how much information they could get about the mafia. But they had no evidence against me; I was a professional and never left a fingerprint at the crime scenes. I was proud of that. I was very careful with that, because of my training, I was very professional.

When they realized that there was no evidence against me to take me to court, I went into the Witness Protection Program of the FBI in exchange for giving the authorities some information.

I then devoted myself to God; I studied theology and graduated as a reverend and now, I serve the mafia of good, led by the Godfather of salvation and eternal life, Jesus Christ.

Projects in Honduras

Jimmy Hughes Ministries operates in Zambrano (Honduras) through his foundation Free the Oppressed, which in Spanish is called 'Ministerio Liberen a los Oprimidos.'

Other organizations include:

- The Prince of Peace Children's Home.
- The Rainbow House.
- Casa Santiago catering services for missionary teams.
- Gateway of Hope Rehabilitation Center for Young People.

All of these centers are located in the village of Zambrano, north of Tegucigalpa, where he lived with his family.

Link to original article in Spanish ---
http://www.laprensahn.com/Sucesos/Ediciones/2009/10/05/Noticias/De-maton-de-mafia-italiana-a-pastor-evangelico

Can also be read at this website (in English) ---
http://deadlinelive.info/2009/10/05/jimmy-hughes-%E2%80%93-from-cia-operative-and-mafia-hitman-to-evangelical-pastor-2/

••••••••

So this is what Rachel Begley and Detective John Powers were up against when they chased an Octopus assassin through the labyrinth and brought him to justice 28 years after the fact. The angels had answered their prayers.

Reporter Nathan Baca at KESQ-TV, News Channel 3, won a regional Emmy for his 35-part series entitled "The Octopus Murders." From the podium at the San Diego Hilton as he accepted his Emmy Award, Nathan Baca announced: (excerpted)

> I do this in memory of murder victims Ralph Boger, Fred Alvarez and Patti Castro. I hope and pray that justice, a justice that has been delayed for far too many years, will soon be had by the families of these victims. Thank you.

One of the former Hells Angels that Det. Powers named during our meeting on March 2nd was subsequently identified on October 1st in a KESQ- TV news story entitled "Founder of Coachella Valley Judo Named in Murder Conspiracy" by Nathan Baca, News Channel 3 reporter. http://www.kesq.com/Global/story.asp?s=11241586

> Excerpts from the story read as follows:
> RIVERSIDE – Glen Heggstad is a well-respected local businessman. He founded Coachella Valley Judo and Jiu-Jitsu in Palm Desert. Now, the California Attorney General's Office is accusing Heggstad of conspiring to murder Cabazon Indian vice chairman Fred Alvarez.
>
> Alvarez was murdered at a Rancho Mirage home on July 1st, 1981. His friend, Ralph Boger, and Alvarez's girlfriend, Patty Castro, also died.
>
> The state Attorney General's office says former Cabazon Indian security chief Jimmy Hughes offered to hire Heggstad to murder Alvarez.
>
> Fred Alvarez was going to blow the whistle on illegal weapons manufacturing deals signed off by Cabazon tribal leadership.
>
> It was Jimmy Hughes, arrested Saturday in Miami, who actually pulled the trigger, according to detectives. Hughes was on his way to Honduras where he runs Jimmy Hughes Ministries.
>
> Investigators believe Heggstad knew about the murder plot but did nothing to stop it.

> News Channel 3 talked to Glen Heggstad on the phone Monday night before he was accused of murder conspiracy. He claimed he cooperated with detectives, telling them Hughes told him that he had murdered Alvarez. Heggstad also claimed he had nothing to do with the plot to kill three people.
>
> The National Geographic Channel aired a segment last year on his 2001 escape from Colombia. Rebels took Heggstad hostage and tortured him during a cross-continent motorcycle ride.
>
> Heggstad claims to be a former Hells Angel. Though he's accused of murder conspiracy, Glen Heggstad is not under arrest for any crime at this time.
>
> News Channel 3 tried repeatedly Thursday to reach Heggstad on the phone and in person. He did not return calls.
>
> This information comes from the felony complaint filed at Larson Justice Center in Indio Thursday morning. The warrant affidavit written by Riverside County Sheriff's detectives is currently sealed at the Riverside Courthouse ---".

Heggstad subsequently provided a book he had written to reporter Nathan Baca. Inside the cover page, he autographed the book with the following notation:

> "Nathan: If you are seeking to report the truth, please remember that there are two sides to every story. Just because a cop or prosecutor says something, doesn't make it true. You are going to be very surprised when you finally hear what I have to say. In the meantime, given the track record for integrity in the police dept. and prosecutor's office, I ask that in the interest of justice, that you keep an open mind. All the Best, Glen Heggstad. 11-17-09.

Heggstad was in fact a Hells Angel biker in San Diego at the time of the murders. He operated a Martial Arts Do Jo in Palm Desert, California and in the intervening years he lived in a luxury condo in Mazatlan and worked for *National Geographic* magazine. At a website: http://www.lukeswab.com/2009/03/wwwstrikingvikingnet/

"Luke," a friend of Heggstad's, wrote the following:

> "I meet up with a guy named Glen Heggstad. He is a well known adventure rider who wrote the book *Two Wheels Through Terror*. He is working on his second book right now. Long story short, he was captured by Colombian Rebels on a ride from California to Tierra Del Fuego. His first book is about that experience and how

> he got out as well as the rest of the ride. It is an amazing read. It was a privilege to be able to stay with him for a few days and talk about travel. You can check out his site at: www.strikingviking.net
>
> Staying at Striking Vikings pad was a treat. It was a welcome change from sleeping next to the ants, roaches, coyotes and cow pies. I am glad I got a lead for me to look him up. He is down with the motorcycle cause and helps those out when he can. He lives in the penthouse of one of the tall rises on the Malicon. The view from my balcony. The camera was setup on the hot-tub---"

By his own admission, Jimmy Hughes was contracted to "stop Fred Alvarez." John Paul Nichols had also reportedly offered money to Glen Heggstad to stop Fred Alvarez from attending the Cabazon Tribal meeting to oust Dr. John Phillip Nichols, the tribal administrator at that time. The Tribal Council meetings were always held on the first Wednesday of each month. Thus Fred Alvarez had to be stopped before he could attend the meeting to vote against Dr. Nichols.

In a 1995 book, *Return of the Buffalo* by Ambrose Lane, the author wrote that the minutes of the tribe's General Council meeting noted that Fred Alvarez had been "voted out of office as a tribal officer" (1st Vice Chairman) on June 6, 1981 and replaced by Brenda James. (pp. 91-92). The vote was reportedly held by secret ballot and counted by Glenn Feldman, tribal attorney at that time. The newly elected officers for the next four years were: Arthur Welmas, tribal chairman; Brenda James, 1st vice chairman; Charles Welmas, 2nd vice chairman; John James, secretary-treasurer.

If this is true, then it conflicts with most of the current claims that Fred Alvarez needed to be stopped from voting at the upcoming Council meeting. Nevertheless, that would not have precluded Fred from bringing charges against Dr. Nichols, et al, at a tribal meeting, as Fred was still a member of the Cabazon tribe prior to his death on June 29, 1981.

••••••••

On October 5, 2009, I wrote to Detective John Powers asking him what documents in my files pertaining to the Mob could I publicize in an article or in my book that would *not* interfere with or jeopardize his case?

Powers responded that he could only speculate what will or will not be used in the trial against Jimmy Hughes, since the trial is probably two years away. He said the Attorney General's Office has very little information about any of the possible Mob connections, and the affidavit he (Powers) put together for Hughes' arrest warrant didn't go into any Mob connections. But Powers cautioned: "That doesn't mean it won't come out in the trial ... the 'Mob angle' comes into the story when people ask for motive. That's when the entire Octopus falls out of the sky and complicates everything. When people ask, 'Why did the Nichols family want Fred [Alvarez] out of the picture?' Then we have to start talking about what the Nichols family was getting into. I would love to avoid all of that in a trial but I don't think it's possible. It's all over the Internet if you know what to look for --- ."

Powers concluded: "The best answer I can give you at this point is that you have uncovered all of this Mob information long before I became involved in the case and you have every right to publish it and talk about it with anyone. At this point in the case none of that information is evidence against Jimmy, so I can confidently say that you are not exposing evidence of the case."

I could not imagine how the DOJ prosecutors were going to keep the Mob out of their case? Throughout my research, I had repeatedly bumped into the Mob connections at the Cabazon reservation in the early 1980's. Dr. John Philip Nichols and his son had been observed by Indio police meeting with Tommy Marson, a Gambino organized crime associate, at Marson's sprawling mansion in Rancho Mirage, California. Marson had provided the seed money for the first Cabazon Casino (the first Indian Casino in California), and by his own admission, Jimmy Hughes had been a "Mafia" hit-man.

Within the Morasca Homicide Case File No. 82-1052505 (at S.F. Police Dept.) was a report entitled, "Interim Overview ---," dated February 1982, which included a document from the Indio Police Dept. dated August 21, 1981, relating to the investigation of the Cabazon Indians in Indio. This document included a surveillance report in which Dr. John Nichols was observed communicating, visiting and meeting with various La Cosa Nostra (LCN) crime figures such as Tommy Marson, Irving Shapiro, Vincent Caci Bolognia, Anthony Fratianno, Daniel Magano, and other LCN underworld figures.

It doesn't take a stretch of the imagination to surmise that Dr. Nichols and his LCN friends were involved in some manner of financial transactions, they weren't having tea parties, and that LCN could conceivably have provided money to Dr. Nichols for nefarious purposes as well as business objectives. Dr. Nichols appeared, for all intents and purposes, to be the intermediary between the Cabazons and the Mob, and the Mob needed that infiltration.

This was all speculation based on my own findings, so in an effort to clarify the Riverside Sheriff department's *final* position at the end of their two-year investigation, I asked Detective John Powers to summarize his perspective in relation to the various criminal enterprises he had encountered during his probe. What was the real motive for the triple-homicide, and was it related to the Octopus?

His response was pragmatic, and somewhat anticlimactic, but as I explained to him later, the truth is the truth, and that is the purpose of writing the book. Nevertheless, from a law enforcement point of view, including the California DOJ, it is their job to remove conspiracy entanglements from the case, because that would play into the hands of the defense lawyer.

This is Detective Powers' straightforward reply to my question, received on November 9, 2009:

> Cheri: In reference to your questions for *The Last Circle*.
> (1) The Motive: I've heard many people say that Fred [Alvarez] was killed because of what he knew. I don't actually believe that. I think Fred knew very little about what was really going on at Cabazon. I believe Fred suspected the money was being mishandled and / or stolen from the Indians by the Nichols family. I believe Fred was going to bring this to the attention of the tribal council at the upcoming meeting and possibly introduce evidence of profit skimming.
>
> If Fred convinced the tribal council that the Nichols family was stealing Indian money, it could have resulted in the Nichols family being fired and sent packing. I don't think Fred had any idea how devastating that would have actually been to the Nichols family.
>
> There were three major things going on that Fred didn't know anything about. At least I've never been given any proof that Fred knew about it. One of those things was the Mafia connection. The Mafia was directly connected to the start-up capital in the Cabazon Casino. Tommy Marson gave them a $50,000 loan and Rocco Zangari was the first casino manager. The Mafia would not have invested this kind of money if they didn't believe this was a potential gold

mine. Everybody believed the Cabazon Casino could potentially bring in millions of dollars.

If the Nichols family was fired, the casino would have continued on without them. There were plenty of investors who believed in it and plenty of lawyers willing to take it to the Supreme Court and fight for the right to gamble on Indian land. The Cabazon Casino was going forward with or without Dr. John Philip Nichols. The only people who stood to lose any money by Fred coming forward with his information were the Nichols family. They were the only people with a motive to stop Fred.

Another thing that Fred probably didn't know about was the extent of the business proposals that Cabazon Arms was trying to get off the ground. There was nothing illegal about what Cabazon Arms was trying to do. The manufacturing of weapons for the US Government is a huge industry with millions of dollars available in government contracts. You have to submit your bid proposals of what you are capable of doing and you have to be able to win your bid.

Cabazon joined with Wackenhut because Wackenhut had a great reputation and long history with the US Government. Wackenhut joined with Cabazon because Doc Nichols had a long history of successfully obtaining grants and government contracts. The two forces complimented each other. Cabazon Arms obtained the financial backing of investors (like G. Wayne Reeder) and found an ammunition manufacturer (Peter Zokosky) and they had the perfect location to build and test large caliber weapons on the Cabazon Reservation.

This was a no-brainer great idea and everyone saw the potential to make millions of dollars if they obtained the contracts. It was also completely legal and there was nothing for Fred to blow the whistle on.

Fred coming forward with accusations about the Nichols family stealing Indian money would have caused problems. The government would not have awarded the contract to Cabazon Arms if the allegations turned out to be true. Most likely, the government would have insisted that the Nichols family be removed from the equation before any contract was awarded.

With the amount of money at stake, I have no doubt that Wackenhut, the Cabazon tribe, G. Wayne Reeder and everyone else would have insisted that the Nichols family be removed from the deal. The only people who really stood to lose any money by

Fred coming forward with his information would have been the Nichols family. As it turned out, the Nichols family was accused of a number of other nefarious deeds and Cabazon Arms never obtained a single government contract.

The third major thing going on at Cabazon that Fred probably didn't know about, were the events surrounding the infamous Lake Cahuilla Incident.

In September of 1981, the CIA had the full authority and backing of the Presidency to invest in, train, and support the anti-Sandinista movement of the Contras in Nicaragua. This was well known and well documented as you know.

The Contra rebels needed a lot of weapons and training on how to use them. Weapons manufacturers were climbing over each other to win the government contracts worth millions of dollars to manufacture cheap guns in massive quantities. And retired US servicemen with combat experience were being hired to train the Contras in their headquarters in Honduras.

The Lake Cahuilla Incident is a perfect picture of how these things occurred. You only have to look at those in attendance to figure out what was happening. You had representatives from Cabazon Arms, representatives from weapons manufacturing facilities, financial investors, and Contra Generals and procurement members from Nicaragua. The City Manager was there because the city of Indio owned this facility and there were foreign dignitaries visiting. The city police were there to protect everyone present. There were some very important people present and a lot of weapons being fired. This kind of security is very common.

In 1981, this was very common and completely legal. The US Government doesn't deny supporting, training and arming the Contras. Cabazon Arms was just trying to tap into another government contract that was potentially worth millions. I won't bother repeating myself but this is the same as above. It would have continued with or without the Nichols family and only the Nichols family would have lost money by Fred's accusations.

In a nutshell, I believe Fred was preparing to bring a case against the Nichols for embezzlement and / or mismanagement of funds. Fred had no idea how damaging his accusations actually were and how much money he was going to cost the Nichols family. This is why I believe Fred was killed and why I believe the Nichols were the only ones with the motive to do it.

(2) Yes, you provided me with a lot of material that helped in my investigation. I couldn't say immediately what specific docu-

ments or information were the most helpful without going back and reviewing everything. But I did read the Internet version of *The Last Circle* at the very beginning of this investigation and I learned a great deal about what I was getting myself into.

Oh, I just remembered something incredible that I learned from you. You told me that I would find previously unknown documents and notes connected to the Alvarez investigation hidden inside of the Paul Morasca file in San Francisco. I thought there was no chance in Hell that was possible and you must have bogus information.

"I couldn't take the chance of being wrong so I went to San Francisco and looked for myself. My jaw hit the floor when I searched the Morasca file and found a dozen police reports from the Riverside County Sheriff's Dept. and Riverside County DA's Office, and Indio Police Department and they were all about the Alvarez murders. These were reports I had never seen before and for some reason were missing from the Alvarez murder file.

"Some of these reports were very helpful in solving this case and I would never have known about them if it weren't for you. Thank you."

JP

••••••••

As of December 1, 2009 the extradition of Jimmy Hughes from Miami to Riverside, California was being stalled by Hughes' Miami lawyer, Rene Sotorrio. Hughes had been arrested on September 26, 2009 and by December 1st he still hadn't been extradited and remained in the Metro West Detention Center in Miami. The next extradition hearing was scheduled for December 3rd.

The wheels of justice grind slowly, but the history of DOJ prosecutions on anything related to the Octopus to date in California was essentially zero. I had concerns that at some point the federal government might attempt to step into the case as they had in the past, but Powers explained that the California DOJ planned to narrow the prosecution of Jimmy Hughes to a simple case that excluded any exculpatory evidence relating to the Octopus conspiracies, i.e, the Mob, Wackenhut, etc., which could be used by the defense. I presumed this was also why Detective Powers chose not to mention my name or my research contributions to any of the media people who interviewed him after the Jimmy Hughes arrest.

In the meantime, Rachel Begley was monitoring the progress of the extradition of Jimmy Hughes through media reports and making inroads at the clerk's office in Miami. On November 20, she sent an e-mail to Deputy Attorney General Mike Murphy at the DOJ's office in San Diego. I roared when I read it, and realized that the DOJ didn't have a chance with "Danger Girl" on their backs, nor did Jimmy Hughes. This is the e-mail that she sent:

> **From:** Rachel Begley
> **Sent:** Friday, November 20, 2009 6:16 PM
> **To:** Mike Murphy – DOJ CA.
> **Subject:** Jimmy Hughes Continuance?
>
> Hi,
>
> I did some checking around today and found out about Hughes' atty asking for a continuation. The way one of the news sources makes it sound is that Hughes' atty was in contact with you (or your office) about this continuation?
>
> I'm just curious if that is true? And if so, why stall it? Let's get him back to California and make his attorney actually work to come to California, let's not help them with their defense ya know? Rachel Begley.

Jimmy Hughes waived extradition in court on December 3, and will be brought back to California by Detective John Powers and booked into the Riverside County jail. Rachel Begley will likely be a key witness at Hughes' trial in a couple of years, along with other individuals introduced in *The Last Circle*. Over the years, the investigation of the Octopus took on a life of its own, so I followed it where it took me, like a leaf on a river. My story ended with the arrest and extradition of Jimmy Hughes, but there will be plenty of media coverage at the trial, and the Octopus saga will find its own ending.

••••••••

NEWS FLASH – Addendum 2010: Seven months later a surprising twist occurred in the Jimmy Hughes homicide case. Deputy Attorney General Mike Murphy, who was prosecuting the case out of the San Diego office, notified Rachel Begley that he planned to drop the charges against Hughes at a felony settlement conference hearing in Indio on July 1, the 29th anniversary of the triple homicide in which Begley's father, Ralph Boger, had been found murdered.

Hughes had been arrested on September 26, 2009 and charged with three counts of murder (with special circumstances) and one count of conspiracy. Inexplicably, the case was suddenly being dismissed, despite the fact that Jimmy Hughes had been in custody for nine months.

Rachel wanted to speak at the court hearing, under Marcy's Law, in which the victim can give a statement to the court and to the accused. I accompanied her to the District Attorney's office prior to the hearing in her effort to obtain assistance from the Witness/Victim Advocate Services Division of the D.A.'s office, Indio branch.

Rachel spoke with Lorena Serrano, victim services advocate, who was the first person we had encountered in the court system who listened attentively to Rachel's story and promised to follow through on Rachel's behalf.

That evening, on June 30th, while we ate dinner with Andrew Rice who was interviewing us for a story in *Wired* magazine, a surprise call came in from Lorena advising Rachel to call Robin Sax, a high profile victim's advocate attorney in Los Angeles. Sax was a former Riverside County prosecutor and former Los Angeles County Deputy District Attorney.

Robin is also an in-house NBC News legal analyst and regular guest commentator for several national television shows, analyzing many hi-profile cases including CNN's *Larry King Live,* HLN's Nancy Grace, NBC's *Today Show, Dr. Phil,* Tyra Banks, *CBS Early Show, Issues with Jane Velez Mitchell,* HLN's *Prime News,* Fox's *Geraldo at Large, Insider* and many others. She has commentated on high profile cases including Jaycee Duggard, Amber Dubois, Chelsea King, Anthony Sowell, Roman Polanski, Charlie Sheen, Michael Jackson, Casey Anthony, Natalee Holloway, Drew Peterson, OJ Simpson and many others.

Sax offered to represent Rachel free of charge and immediately filed a motion with the superior court in Indio to Preserve Victims Rights under Marcy's Law and Proceed to Preliminary Hearing relative to the Jimmy Hughes case # INF066719.

At the hearing on July 1, media from all over California swarmed the courthouse with TV cameras and jostled to get into the courtroom. At 1:30 P.M. Deputy Attorney General Mike Murphy requested that the case against Jimmy Hughes be dismissed under Penal Code 1385.

Murphy told the court that the Attorney General's office originally accepted the Riverside Sheriff's package for prosecution last summer, but after his office reviewed and interviewed key witnesses, they developed *new* information that was not known to law enforcement at the time that the Riverside sheriff's department filed the charges. Based on this new information, Murphy said they reassessed the case and dropped it. There was also a problem with the "procedural history" of the case; Murphy did not define what it was or reveal what the *new* information was. He said, "We have lost confidence in our ability to proceed with the prosecution of this case."

Judge Dale R. Wells denied Robin Sax's motion to retain Jimmy Hughes in jail and proceed to a preliminary hearing where evidence could be presented, but he allowed Rachel to give her statement.

Judge Wells also granted the prosecutor's request to drop the case, and Jimmy Hughes was set free that day.

At the conclusion of the hearing, Detective John Powers told the Associated Press that he still believes Hughes is guilty and hoped to someday resubmit the case with new evidence.

On July 2, 2010 NBC TV News, Los Angeles (NBC-LA), aired coverage of the court hearing in Indio: A segment of the newscast included a 25-year-old interview in which Jimmy Hughes said that the Fred Alvarez triple homicide in 1981 was an "ordered assassination," but he was only the bagman. Hughes told the reporter, Patrick Healy, in the 1985 news clip that the hit was an "authorized, backed, government covert action." See video of the news clip at this website: "http://www.nbclosangeles.com/station/as-seen-on/Victim_s_Daughter_Decries_Dismissal_of_Murder_Charges_Los_Angeles.html"

The *Desert Sun* in Indio wrote the following on July 2, 2010:

"Octopus Murders' Case Dropped: Officials Refuse to Divulge New Evidence that Led to Dismissal" by Brian Indrelunas: (excerpted)

> ... Begley said she doubts that Murphy and the attorney general's office had discovered new evidence.
>
> "I frankly don't believe that he found any new (information)," she said. "The evidence that we found was more than sufficient and handed to him on a silver platter."

Begley left the courtroom in tears but said she isn't done fighting.

"It's not the end, definitely not the end," she said. "We have a legal strategy."

Frustrated with prosecutors' handling of the case, Begley hired her own attorney, Robin Sax, late Wednesday.

Sax filed a motion asking Wells to keep the case active long enough for a preliminary hearing to be held, but the judge rejected the motion, saying that a victim did not have the necessary standing to make such a request in a criminal case.

Sax said she would continue working on Begley's behalf but declined to detail her next steps.

Wells dismissed the case against Hughes without prejudice, meaning prosecutors could refile the case in the future, said Westrup, the attorney general's spokesman.

Powers, the sheriff's detective, said he would continue to actively investigate the case and would consider resubmitting it to prosecutors.

But with Hughes released Thursday, Begley said she fears for the safety of herself and others---"

The statement that Rachel Begley articulated in the courtroom (for the record) before the judge dismissed the case. As follows: (excerpted)

Statement to the Court and Honorable Judge Dale R. Wells

July 1, 2010

Your Honor,

May I request that this statement, per Marcy's Law, be made a permanent record of this court.

My name is Rachel Begley. My father, Ralph Boger, was murdered in an execution style triple homicide in Rancho Mirage 29 years ago. The anniversary of his murder is today, July 1st.

The defendant, James Hughes, who is sitting in this court today, admitted his involvement in my father's murder years ago, and has published at various websites in the US and in Latin American newspapers that he was a professional mafia hit man before he found God. I will gladly provide you with these articles at your request.

I am not here today to present the abundance of evidence against Jimmy Hughes; I am here to plead with you *not* to release

Mr. Hughes because I and numerous other victims and witnesses will live in fear for the rest of our lives if Mr. Hughes is set free to return to his home in Honduras where he is politically connected with both the government and the military. If future harm comes to me or other witnesses by Hughes or his followers, I believe there would be no cooperative effort between the United States and Honduras to bring Mr. Hughes to justice.

Indeed, he is being released today in the US despite the fact that he is a self confessed hit man who has cold bloodedly murdered numerous innocent people during his career as a hit man.

This case is paralleling the Joran Van Der Sloot case in which he was released in Aruba and subsequently killed a girl in Lima, Peru. I ask this court, how many people must die or suffer at the hands of James Hughes before he is brought to justice? He has literally gotten away with murder if he is released today. This is a demoralizing lesson to the general public who regained their faith in the justice system when Mr. Hughes was arrested in September 2009.

It is also demoralizing to the law enforcement people in Riverside who risked everything to reopen this case and solve it when no one else cared---despite the fact that there is no statute of limitations on the murder of three people in 1981.

I don't know the law, Your Honor, but I pray that you will do the right and honorable thing in this court today, regardless of whether Mr. Mike Murphy of the Dept of Justice in San Diego chooses not to prosecute this case for personal reasons, or because of a technicality relating to due process that occurred 29 years ago, or because this case is complicated and could be an embarrassment to the Justice Department at this late date.

I request, Your Honor, that the record state that I believe there should be a preliminary hearing so that the court can determine the evidence in this case. Nothing has changed since the filing of this case, so either it was an unethical filing or an unethical dismissal-even according to Mr. Murphy's own words, this case should have been tried 25 years ago. Due to the diligence of Det. John Powers and my own independent investigations, and lack of the statute of limitations, there has been no due process violation. Instead, only an abuse of prosecutorial discretion. This case is not just a personal setback, but a setback for the system as a whole.

While I expect the defense attorneys to fight on behalf of their client, I am astounded by the lack of victim advocacy and society protection by the prosecution in this case. Frankly, it amounts to prosecutorial misconduct and a miscarriage of justice.

I do not understand how Attorney General Jerry Brown could support the release of Mr. Hughes. How can he be elected Governor of California if he can't manage his staff competently in San Diego?

Please be advised that the only request I am making for myself and on behalf of the family members of the other murder victims, is that the evidence against Mr. Hughes be presented in a court of law and that Mr. Hughes face his accusers here in the United States rather than hiding out in Honduras where he is untouchable.

He preaches publicly in Latin America and in the US that God has forgiven him for his murders, yet I question whether he has truly repented. He has never shown any remorse for his crimes of murder, never apologized to me or the other victims, so how could he have repented?

I ask that James Hughes remain in custody at least until another DOJ prosecutor who is less timid can be assigned to prosecute this case. Or perhaps the case can be handed over to another jurisdiction or a special prosecutor. My own attorney, Robin Sax, has offered to prosecute this case as a special prosecutor, should the court allow this. There must be a way, Your Honor, with the power and wisdom of this court, that you can find a way to protect the lives and rights of Hughes' victims.

To Jimmy Hughes I say: I hope your short time in jail has given you time to truly repent. Be advised that even if the court and the Attorney General fail me today, I will never give up seeking truth and justice for my dad, Fred, and Patty.

— *fini* —

EPILOGUE

As of this writing, December 3, 2009, Bill Hamilton has hired attorneys Boyden Gray and Roderick Hills to jointly represent INSLAW in an effort to influence President Barack Obama's Administration to compensate INSLAW for the misappropriation of the modified version of the PROMIS software by previous administrations.

Hamilton has become "the Keeper of the Flame" in this never-ending legal saga, and now pursues the plausible angle that PROMIS was used for "other" purposes, i.e., "*the unforgivable use of the unauthorized NSA bank surveillance version of PROMIS to launder profits from drug trafficking so some of them could be used to finance covert intelligence projects.*"

Former homicide detective Sue Todd, and former Insight reporter Kelly O'Meara had gathered so much information on the Octopus respectively that they compiled a 46-page proposal entitled, "Proposed Investigation into the Theft of Promise Software, Illegal Drug Trafficking and Money Laundering" which was submitted to a wealthy benefactor for funding. I was invited to join them in this proposal/investigation and I readily agreed.

The proposal contained the history of their respective investigations along with their distinguished resumes, and a page entitled, "*Purpose of the Investigation,*" which listed some of the following goals: " ... To determine whether the alleged modified PROMIS software had been utilized for money laundering – To determine whether the alleged modified PROMIS software had been utilized for drug trafficking – To obtain documented evidence that high-ranking officials of the Reagan/Bush administration, including members and paid operatives of the Department of Justice, Central Intelligence Agency, National Security Council, and possibly U.S. Customs, allegedly were directly involved in drug trafficking, money laundering, illegal arms sales, organized crime, espionage, and murder – and to obtain the necessary evidence to expose and hold accountable those parties involved." Thirty names were listed as potential witnesses to be interviewed.

The proposal sought a total of $217,500 for estimated costs for a six-month investigation which included salaries for three investigators, travel within the U.S. and Australia, Canada and Russia, car rentals, airline tickets, hotels, food and telephone expenses. The money would be placed into an investigation escrow account and drawn upon as needed. In the end, the proposal was withdrawn from the benefactor because an agreement could not be reached relative to the use of the information at the conclusion of the proposed investigation.

Attorney George Granby in Long Beach, California, with 34 years in law practice, has successfully represented Michael Riconosciuto for two years and is currently working to overturn his conviction with documents that were withheld from his original trial in Washington State.

Documents & Photographs

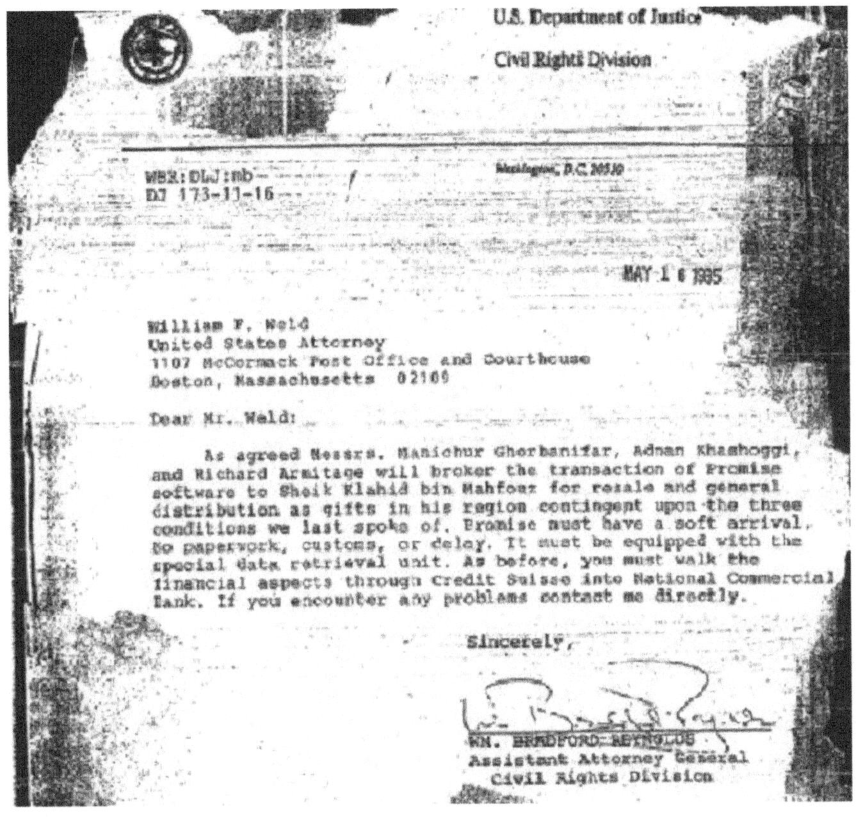

U.S. Department of Justice

Civil Rights Division

WBR:DLJ:mb
DJ 173-11-16

Washington, D.C. 20530

MAY 16 1985

William F. Weld
United States Attorney
1107 McCormack Post Office and Courthouse
Boston, Massachusetts 02109

Dear Mr. Weld:

As agreed Messrs. Manichur Ghorbanifar, Adnan Khashoggi, and Richard Armitage will broker the transaction of Promise software to Sheik Klahid bin Mahfouz for resale and general distribution as gifts in his region contingent upon the three conditions we last spoke of. Promise must have a soft arrival. No paperwork, customs, or delay. It must be equipped with the special data retrieval unit. As before, you must walk the financial aspects through Credit Suisse into National Commercial Bank. If you encounter any problems contact me directly.

Sincerely,

WM. BRADFORD REYNOLDS
Assistant Attorney General
Civil Rights Division

May 16, 1985: U.S. Attorney William Weld is instructed by Assistant Attorney General Bradford Reynolds to handle financial aspects of PROMIS distribution to the Arabian Sheik. Adnan Khashoggi, Richard Armitage and Manichur Ghorbanifar will broker the deal.

U.S. Department of Justice

Criminal Division

WFW:JCK:GEMcD:WK:SMK:dcb

Office of the Assistant Attorney General

Washington, D.C. 20530

FEB 29 1988

MEMORANDUM

TO: Stephen S. Trott
Associate Attorney General

FROM: William F. Weld
Assistant Attorney General

SUBJECT: Allegations by INSLAW, Inc. Against
Attorney General Meese,
Deputy Attorney General Burns, and former
Deputy Attorney General Jensen -
Closing of Independent Counsel Matter.

The Public Integrity Section has reviewed allegations by INSLAW, Inc. that Attorney General Meese, Deputy Attorney General Burns, and/or former Deputy Attorney General Jensen committed "procurement fraud" and/or obstruction of justice. The Public Integrity Section concluded that the information submitted is not sufficiently specific to constitute grounds to initiate a preliminary investigation. The Section, however, recommended that the materials provided by INSLAW be supplied to the Office of Professional Responsibility, which has been conducting its own investigation of the INSLAW matter as to persons not covered by the Independent Counsel statute. The Office of Professional Responsibility will be requested to immediately refer to the Public Integrity Section any evidence it may develop relating to possible criminal misconduct by persons covered by the Independent Counsel statute, so that the Section may consider whether the evidence is sufficient to trigger a preliminary investigation. The Section is also considering a request by INSLAW to open a perjury investigation as to persons not covered by the Independent Counsel statute.

I concur with this recommendation and am so closing this matter.

OK 3/2/88

February 29, 1988: Assistant Attorney General William Weld from the Public Integrity Section of DOJ writes that the allegations by INSLAW against A/G Edwin Meese, et al, are not "sufficiently specific [enough] to constitute grounds to initiate a preliminary investigation." INSLAW charged that Meese, et al, committed "procurement fraud and obstruction of justice" in the theft of the PROMIS software.

CABAZON ARMS

WACKENHUT SERVICES INCORPORATED
3280 PONCE DE LEON BLVD.
CORAL GABLES, FLORIDA 33134
(305) 445-1481

A CSC/WSI JOINT VENTURE

CABAZON SECURITY CORPORATION
83-180 REQUA AVENUE
SUITE #9, INDIO, CALIFORNIA 92201
(714) 342-5155

January 20, 1983

Dr. Harry Fair
Tactical Technology
1400 Wilson Blvd, Rm. 1014
Arlington, VA 22209

Dear Harry:

The clearance documents that were submitted for Cabazon Arms to DOD were found to be acceptable by the Los Angeles DOD Office and have been forwarded to Washington D.C. for final approval.

On February 15, 1983, I will be forwarding to you a unique list of agents and production techniques related to biological warfare. The Stormont Laboratories, Inc., business plan I mailed you was to prepare you for what we are sending you in this area. Their products could be utilized in small countries bordering Albania or large countries bordering the Soviet Union. You will be amazed at the scope.

The reason I sent you the Viper small machine gun 9MM parabellum was for cost comparison. Even though Peter Zokosky has the British interested, it can not be compared with the Cabazon Arms CA 9 SMG. We have not included the drawing of the laser sighting and laser guidance systems which is an optional low cost attachment. The laser attachment is in the final stages of development in San Diego. The CA 9 SMG can be produced for $75.00 per unit on the reservation and sold for $100.00 to $125.00. It meets all needs of the small poor democracy for 9MM parabellum. They can afford to purchase this one. We have fired over 50,000 rounds with the test model using South Korean ammunition without jamming. We could begin manufacturing within two weeks in a country like Guatemala, Chile, etc., utilizing USA produced dies and Swedish extrusion machinery. The gun is in a family series and can utilize different barrels for example equipped with silencers, etc., or it can be made into a rifle.

Peter Zokosky has fired both the Viper and the CA 9 SMG and was impressed with both, but particularly with the CA 9 SMG. Kuwait has been particularly interested in financing the production of the CA 9 SMG. We have USA financing available.

January 20, 1983: Cabazon Arms writes to Dr. Harry Fair at the Picatinny Arsenal about forwarding a "unique list of agents and production techniques related to biological warfare --"

We would initially manufacture on the reservation. We can purchase an existing small company with all the licenses to manufacture and export. We are ready.

We are continuing to experiment with the combination sniper rifle (9MM) equipped with micropressor vision enhancement (no tubes) (night vision). Micheal Riconosciuto and some friends of the reservation have been working cooperatively on this project. Within another 90 to 120 days we should have a working model to use on the CA 9 SMG and the sniper rifle.

The on going projects in research and development are as follows:

1. The immediate development of a second 9MM calibre machine pistol that will have a adjustable cycle rate of fire.

2. An assault rifle with selective fire, with the option of incorporating laser sighting in the foregrips.

3. A long distance sniper rifle.

4. A small portable rocket system, cartridge activated off the end of a disposable adaptor which would attach to the assault rifle.

Time frames for the first three above projects (to production) would be three months and six months for the fourth. This is subject to my securing additional working capital.

As we discussed in Dover and Washington, D.C., we continue to work on closed circuit lasers and other areas of research.

I have the only existing working model in my office of the electronic communication system we discussed. I personally am not satisfied with it. We should have it functional by the time the night vision is ready.

We have been re-working the cooling and stabilizing device for projectiles fired from space re-entry vehicles.

We are continuing to pursue the 120MM contract. A definite decision has not been made to date by the US government.

Sincerely,

John P. Nichols

JPN/JJ
Enc.

January 20, 1983: Continuation of letter: John P. Nichols, Cabazon Arms, writes that Michael Riconosciuto and some friends of the Cabazon reservation are working on the experimental combination sniper rifle equipped with microprocessor vision enhancement ---"

WACKENHUT

INTER-OFFICE MEMORANDUM

TO: R.E. Chasen
S & S Group

DATE: May 25, 1981

FROM: A.R. Frye

DIV/AREA: WSI

SUBJECT: Trip Report (May 11-22, 1981)

During the above period, the writer traveled to New Jersey, Indiana and Washington, D.C., accompanied by Dr. John Nichols, Administrator for the Cabazon Indians. The threefold purpose of the trip was as follows:

(1) To explore the apparent potential for the Cabazon-WSI Joint Venture to enter into the manufacture of 120 mm. combustible cartridge cases and other related armament activities -- using Cabazon land as the site for such actions.

(2) To contact appropriate U.S. Government agencies in Washington, D.C., with a view to insuring the Joint Venture is placed on pertinent Bidder's Lists re security services involving small business, socially disadvantaged firms, and set-asides for Indian firms.

(3) To contact the appropriate U.S. Government agencies associated with the possible export of items on the Munitions List (specifically the night vision goggles), as well as to contact several recommended attorneys who are experienced in processing of requests for export licenses, etc..

Re Item (1):

During this part of the trip we were also accompanied by Peter Zokosky, the former President of Armtec Defense Products, Inc., Coachella, Calif. Zokosky is a close friend of Dr. Nichols, and he has indicated an interest in working with the Joint Venture in this regard.
Based upon Zokosky's prior business relationship with Army personnel at the Pickitinny Arsenal, we spent a considerable amount of time on May 12 & 13 at the Arsenal (U.S. Army Armament Research & Development Command, Large Caliber Weapon Systems Laboratory, Dover, N.J. 07801 --"ARRADCOM").
Personnel contacted at the Arsenal included Mr. R. Scott Westley, Army Project Officer and Dr. Harry D. Fair, Chief, Propulsion Technology, Applied Sciences Division, as well as Ken Russell, Project Officer.
Predicated upon these contacts, the following potential activities merit consideration as business to be initiated by the Joint Venture:

o Construction of a facility for the manufacture of 120 mm. combustible cartridge cases for sale to the U.S. Army, under Army contracts; with sales also to NATO, especially to the Federal Republic of Germany, who are adopting the use of such cases in their Leopard tanks. (The obvious key to any such endeavor is Zokosky. He is reportedly one of only 6-7 personnel in the world who have had

PAGES 453-457: May 25, 1981: Wackenhut Inter-Office memorandum – From A.R. Frye, V.P. in Indio to R.E. Chasen, V.P. in Coral Gables, related to the Joint Venture between the Cabazon Indian Tribe and Wackenhut Inc. to develop arms on the reservation.

any significant experience in the development and manufacture of the slurry process involved in combustible cartridge cases. He is under a present non-compete agreement with Armtec, his former company, until August, 1981. Armtec is the present sole source supplier of 120 mm. combustible cartridge cases to the U.S. Govt. Zokosky is also serving as a consultant to the British Govt.)

It should be noted that several key ingredients necessary for the successful manufacture of such cases are available through the use of land on the Cabazon Reservation in Calif., namely, an arrid climate, a large quantity of water, remote location, available work force, closeness to major transportation routes, and lack of opposition by adjacent governing bodies and "irate citizens" over the siting of such a facility.

o Developing a companion facility on the reservation for the complete assembly of shell casings, to include the assembly of propellants, war heads, fuses, etc.; as well as an R&D facility for the development of new combustible cartridge cases for other weapons systems.

o Use of adjacent Indian tribal lands as a location for a large caliber weapons range test site. (The Cabazons have already been granted the right to such use of land under the control of their sister tribes, the Torres Martinez, involving some 30,000 acres of very remote and desolate land near the Salton Sea.)

o Potential use of a test firing range for the U.S. Government on the Santa Rosa Mountain. (During our discussions with Dr. Fair at the Pickitinny Arsenal, he indicated the Govt. was interested in locating a site near the main power grid on the West Coast, which was also at an elevation of at least 8000 feet for possible testing of the railgun. These requirements are met on the Santa Rosa mountain - under the control of the Santa Rosa Indians, who have also pledged the use of this land to the Cabazons.) Note attached Time Magazine article of 12/1/80 on the railgun.

On May 13, 1981, we also met with a former Army associate of Zokosky's, Mr. Victor Guadagno, Vice President, Flinchbaugh Products, Product Development Center, Wharton, N.J., a Division of General Defense Corp. This Flinchbaugh facility manufactures warheads and related items under Army contracts for the 105/120/155 mm. projectiles. Guadagno advised that since he retired as a Colonel from the Picktinny Arsenal in 1978 and was placed in charge of the Flinchbaugh effort at Wharton, he has increased the business from an annual volume of under $300,000 to more than $3 million in 1980, with an anticipated volume of $6 million in 1981, at an expected profit margin of 10%. Guadagno said that Flinchbaugh would be most interested in forming some kind of joint venture relationship with Cabazon-WSI regarding the production of warheads,etc; and that he would be personnaly interested in working for the Cabazon-WSI Joint Venture in developing such a production capability.

On May 14, 1981, we met with personnel at the Indiana Army Ammunition Plant, Charlestown, Ind. This is a GOCO plant operated under Army contract by ICI Americas Inc., and currently employs some 1500 workers. Per a recent news release, ICI Americas Inc. was awarded a $60 million contract by the Army to so operate this facility -- although the contract period was not specified

We were afforded the opportunity of being escorted on a tour of the loading operations at the plant involving production of bag charges for 155 mm. shells. It was apparent that this facility is very labor intensive; uses production methods that are not highly automated; and continues to use the Government plant originally built for World War I.
During our discussions with the Chief Buyer, Mr. Fred L. Marquis, he advised that he was aware that a Canadian munitions plant, which was involved in the production of propellants for both the Canadian and U.S. Governments, was having some sort of financial difficulties with the Canadian Government, and was sought to be purchased by several international firms, including Welland Chemicals, SNPE, and Mucen Machine. The name of this Canadian firm is Valleyfield Chemical Products Corp., P.O. Box 5520, Valleyfield, Quebec, Canada J65 4V9; and the plant is located in Valleyfield, near Montreal.
Mr. Marquis advised that due to a desire by the U.S. Army authorities that ICI Americas Inc. overhead costs in operating the GOCO plant should be reduced by foreign military sales or other foreign commercial sales, ICI Americas Inc. was interested in whether the Cabazon-WSI Joint Venture might be interested in becoming involved in a marketing arrangement with ICI Americas Inc. to handle such foreign sales. We advised we would probably be so interested and would accordingly respond to them shortly.

On May 15-21, in several discussions with officials of the Valleyfield Chemical Products Corp. and a representative of the Canadian Munitions Board, it was ascertained that the Valleyfield plant was in fact under receivership by the Canadian Government due to the default on a Canadian Government loan; that the default was primarily due to a judgmental error of the first order in not meeting a loan repayment schedule solely in order to not have an adverse appearing quarterly P&L statement, which prompted the Canadian Government to take over the plant under receivership; that the plant had an estimated capital value of about $18 million, but due to an anomaly in the Canadian law applicable to this instance, purchasers could bid to take over the plant for only some $6 million; and that it was the expressed desire of pertinent Canadian officials that the takeover be accomplished solely by Canadian interes without any foreign representation. Moreover, should there not be any qualifyir parties, the Canadian Government was prepared to nationalize the plant in order to continue with the production of propellants under Canadian and U.S. Government contracts.

Through personal contacts of Dr. John Nichols with a Barry Zuckerman and Charles F. Agar, both Canadian Citizens, who are involved in a Canadian firm called Mineral Resources International Limited, as well as both being involved in Canadian financial institutions, it was ascertained that they are interestec in the possibility of acquiring this plant, using their own financial capabili Dr. Nichols envisions that the role of the Cabazon-WSI Joint Venture, should the Zuckerman-Agar group be successful in so purchasing this plant, would be to serve as the foreign marketing representative for the plant; to have this group possibly finance the establishment of the casing/loading facility on the Cabazon Reservation; and to have the capability to conduct R&D for the group in the armanent industry. (It is to be noted that the Cabazon Indians have also set up a Joint Venture with Mineral Resources International Limited wherein this Joint Venture will conduct oil and gas exploration on Indian lands throughout the U.S. This entity is under the aegis of the Cabazon Oil an Gas Company.)

A meeting has been set up in Ottawa, Canada at 9:00 a.m., May 26, 1981 involvi Dr. Nichols, Frank Agar, F. Thornburg, the writer and members of the Canadian in any manner of capital investment in this Valleyfield plant.

Re Item (2):

While in Washington, D.C., personal contact was made with the offices of Senators Hayakawa and Cranston of California; the Bureau of Indian Affairs; the Department of Commerce; and the General Services Administration. Follow -up will be made with other appropriate agencies by Robert Meskunis, for and on behalf of the Cabazon-WSI Joint Venture, to ensure the J-V is placed on bidder's list, etc. (Meskunis was formerly associated with an intelligence activity of the Government; served as a Deputy Director of a CAP agency involved in overseeing many grants and contracts to minority firms; is presently a Vice Pres. of a firm called Environmental Group, located in Washington, D.C.; and is a long term friend of Dr. Nichols. Because of his proficiency in writing proposals as well as his knowledge of the Executive Branch activities in Washington, D.C., it is envisioned that he will be retained at some time in the future as an employee of the Cabazon-WSI Joint Venture. All of his present activities for the J-V are basically reimbursed only for out-of-pocket expenses.)

Re Item (3):

Through arrangements made between Senator Hayakawa's office and the Department of State, we were able to have an appointment on May 18, 1981 with Mr. Jos. P. Smaldone, Chief, Arms Licensing Division, Office of Munitions Control(PM/MC), U.S. Department of State. We were thoroughly briefed about the general aspects of the International Traffic in Arms Regulations; the fact that all items contained on the Munitions List under the ITAR are processed by his office when approval is sought to export such items from the U.S. to a non-barred country (only communist bloc countries are so barred by the ITAR, as well as present shipments to Iran-IRAQ due to their war); and were provided with a copy of the pertinent ITAR and other explanatory data in the form of MC Letters. Mr. Smaldone confirmed that the night vision goggles are items set forth under Category XIIa of the munitions list, which required approval by his office for export; and that the prerequisite for obtaining any such license was to file an Application for Registration. He also advised that his office coordinated with the Department of Defense on the granting of any license to permanently export any munitions list item; and that all other items which are not set forth on the Munitions List are handled by the Department of Commerce re approval to export.

Meetings were subsequently held with several attorneys in the Washington area who were recommended to Dr. Nichols as being eminently qualified to handle the processing of the Cabazon-WSI Joint Venture Application for Registration with the Department of State; the subsequent processing of application/licenses for the export of night vision goggles to foreign buyers; and the possible utilization of the Joint-Venture in other business opportunities involving clients of these attorneys, as well as representing the Joint Venture on specific projects of significant magnitude, such as the establishment of the Army test sites on the Cabazon lands, etc. These attorneys are Mr. William M. Briggs, 910 Seventeenth St., N.W., Wash.,D.C. 20006 and Mr. Glade F. Flake, 5530 Wisconsin Ave, Washington, D.C. 20015.

RECOMMENDATIONS: (Immediate Near-Term Only)

1. Predicated upon discussions with Dr. Nichols, and the obvious need to bring in revenue to the Cabazon-WSI Joint Venture at the earliest possible date, it is highly desirous that the sale of the projected amount of 300 night vision goggles to Guatemala be expedited. (Dr. Nichols assures that an authorized representative of the Guatemalan Government has stated his firm intent to procure 300 of these goggles as soon as they become available through the Joint Venture; with an additional 600 required subsequently. The anticipated sales price for the initial order is about $2.4 million. Dr. Nichols has also advised that the Jordanian Government desires to obtain some 3,000 of the goggles.)
To facilitate these transactions, it is necessary to:

   o File an application for registration by the Joint Venture with the Department of State. This registration will cost $350 for a three year period.
   o Firm up the deal between the Joint Venture and John Vanderwerker, President of Intersect Corporation, Irvine, Calif., who has the apparent exclusive rights for foreign marketing with the Litton Electron Tube Division in third world countries; also most important is to ensure a firm arrangement is worked out with Litton on behalf of Intersect/Joint Venture re pass through of warranties. (This firming up of the arrangements with Vanderwerker and Litton should occur in meetings in Tempe, Ariz. within the next 2-3 weeks.)
   o Obtain letters of commitment from the Guatemalan representative on the order for 300 goggles; and after the Registration is approved by the State Department, and pending approval by the State Dept. on the license approval, contractually obtain up-front monies which will permit the ordering of the modular facilities for use in assembling the goggles on the Cabazon Reservation.
   o The processing of the registration and license application will necessitate an agreement is worked out with one of the above mentioned attorneys, ostensibly Mr. Glade Flake, who has indicated he would be initially willing to so assist on an hourly basis.

4. It is crucial for any anticipated involvement of the Joint Venture in the manufacture/assembly of combustible cartridge cases and loading of shells, etc. to have the talents of Peter Zokosky as the Joint Venture representative in charge of these activities. Peter Zokosky has considerable personal wealth and is highly thought of by those persons whom we met at the Arsenals. We will hopefully be able to secure his services on the basis of equity participation. He will be instrumental in the planning for and obtaining Government contracts, based upon unsolicited proposals.

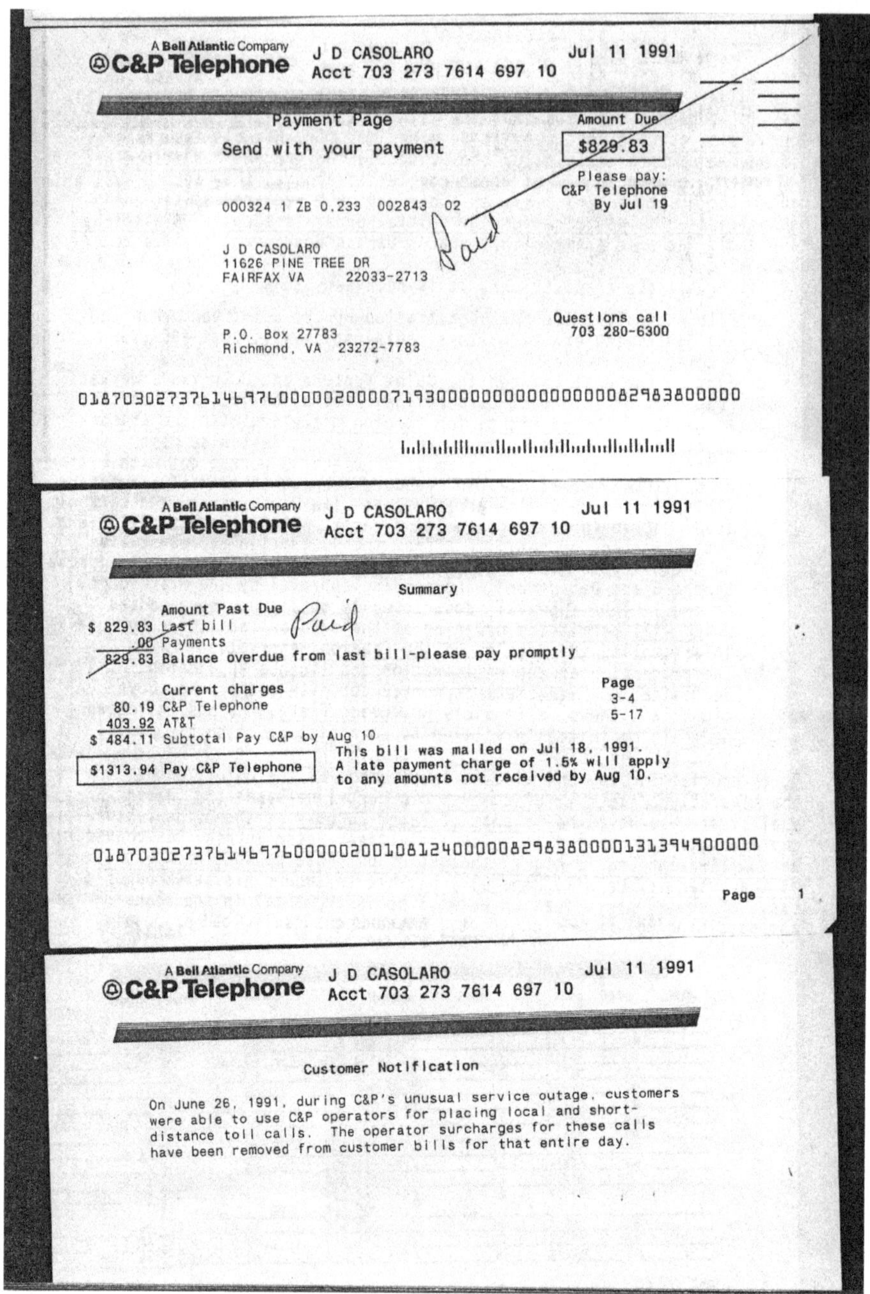

A Bell Atlantic Company
C&P Telephone
J D CASOLARO
Acct 703 273 7614 697 10
Jul 11 1991

Payment Page
Send with your payment
Amount Due
$829.83
Please pay:
C&P Telephone
By Jul 19

000324 1 ZB 0.233 002843 02

Paid

J D CASOLARO
11626 PINE TREE DR
FAIRFAX VA 22033-2713

Questions call
703 280-6300

P.O. Box 27783
Richmond, VA 23272-7783

0187030273761469760000020000719300000000000000000829838 00000

A Bell Atlantic Company
C&P Telephone
J D CASOLARO
Acct 703 273 7614 697 10
Jul 11 1991

Summary

Amount Past Due
$ 829.83 Last bill
.00 Payments
829.83 Balance overdue from last bill-please pay promptly

Paid

Current charges
80.19 C&P Telephone
403.92 AT&T
$ 484.11 Subtotal Pay C&P by Aug 10

Page
3-4
5-17

$1313.94 Pay C&P Telephone

This bill was mailed on Jul 18, 1991.
A late payment charge of 1.5% will apply
to any amounts not received by Aug 10.

01870302737614697600000200108124000008298380000131394900000

Page 1

A Bell Atlantic Company
C&P Telephone
J D CASOLARO
Acct 703 273 7614 697 10
Jul 11 1991

Customer Notification

On June 26, 1991, during C&P's unusual service outage, customers were able to use C&P operators for placing local and short-distance toll calls. The operator surcharges for these calls have been removed from customer bills for that entire day.

Danny Casolaro's phone bill for July 11, 1991, one month before he died. The actual phone numbers that Danny called were withheld here to protect the privacy of the recipients of the calls.

BEHOLD, A PALE HORSE

A True Crime Narrative

by Daniel Casolaro
©, 1990

Behold, a pale horse and its rider's name
was death and Hades followed him, and they
were given power over a fourth of the earth
to kill with sword and with famine and with
pestilence and by wild beasts of the earth

PAGES 459-463: Danny Casolaro's typewritten book proposal for "Behold, A Pale Horse."

BEHOLD, A PALE HORSE

A True Crime Narrative

An international cabal whose freelance services cover parochial political intrigue, espionage, sophistocated weapon technologies that include biotoxins, drug trafficking, money laundering and murder-for-hire has emerged from an isolated desert Indian reservation just north of Mexicali.

While this cabal continues today, its origins were spawned thirty years ago in the shadow of the Cold War. In recent months, however, some of its members have emerged from the trenches like scarecrows to take gratuitous credit for their roles in delaying the release of the hostages in Iran until after the 1980 presidential election, scuttling and resettling the dope and dirty money schemes of the notorious, Australian-based Nugan Hand Bank, assisting Super Gun maker Gerald Bull who was assassinated last spring in Brussels and for the development and distribution of the Fuel Air Explosive which can pack the power of a nuclear weapon in a shoebox.

I propose a series of articles and a book, a true crime narrative that unravels this web of thugs and thieves who roam the earth with their weapons and their murders, trading dope and dirty money for the secrets of the temple.

BEHOLD, A PALE HORSE will be a haunting odyssey that depicts a manifesto of deceit, decisions of conscience, good and evil, intrigue and betrayal.

John Philip Nichols found his promised land just north of Mexicali on the wild grasses above the Salton Sea.

He was sixty years old then and the Cabazon Indian reservation on the edge of Sonora was an ideal place for him to nurse his secret self. This is the vast desert emptiness where the yucca reaches nearly forty feet high, where the Mormons saw it as a symbol pointing to the promised land and they called it the Joshua Tree. But the Joshua Tree is an ugly, unsymetrical lily with burly arms crooked at the elbow and it points everywhere, not unlike John Philip Nichols, as if asking itself "what shall I do next?"

There is a point on the ridge of the Little San Bernardino mountains known as Salton View where you are more than five thousand feet above the desert and where, to the north, you can see the great escarpmen of Mount San Jacinto and, to the south, the man-made Salton Sea, the orchards of the Coachella valley and, on a clear day, old Mexico.

It is always clear in Indio and with the clarity of the warbler in the cottonwood grove, John Philip Nichols knew that he could bring his box office charity and all his earthly possessions into the reservation of the Cabazon Band of Mission Indians.

With no more than two dozen Indians and nearly two thousand acres of desert solitaire, cactus and cottongrove, the Cabazon reservation was a suitable home for gambling, dope, dirty money and gun running and all the fugitive visions that line the edge of oppression.

John Philip Nichols didn't howl under twelve full moons before the gambling was underway and, in the desert night, people flocked from all over to Indio Bingo and to the poker casino at the fork of Highway 10 and Highway 86.

Under a major corporation's umbrella subsidiary, later to be named Cabazon Arms, the gun runners and the money traders soon arrived, the weapon makers and the generals from Babylon, contra resuppliers, covert operatives from both the East and the West and, in what one source calls "a marriage of necessity," the dope dealers, the mobsters and the murderers.

Whatever John Philip Nichols saw in the dark cathedral of those desert nights in silence and certainty cracked and came unglued. After a number of still unsolved execution-style murders and a solicitation-for-murder charge for which he was jailed, the dark vision of John Philip Nichols eroded. Although he's been released from a short stint in prison, he's a one-eyed Jack now since only Indio Bingo gambling -- managed by his sons, the Las Vegas-managed poker casino, the Indians and the most formid creatures of the desert remain.

Several of the Cabazon Arms associates during the 1980s are coming out of the shadows to take top billing for the actual participation in the multi-million dollar laundered payment to the Iranians to delay the release of the hostages, in shutting down the dope and dirty money schemes of Nugan Hand and resurfacing its activities, in assisting Gerald Bull in the refinements and distribution of his weapon arsenal including his Super Gun and in the development of the Fuel Air Explosive technologies -- though to be responsible for the Beirut bomb which killed 241 U.S. servicemen.

While rumors of the hostage release delay circulated for years after the election of Ronald Reagan, it wasn't until 1988 that testimony was offered by two covert operatives in two different courts regarding their knowledge and participation of a hostage-release stall managed by then Reagan campaign chief William Casey. But now, two more covert operatives have emerged from that desert reservation in the journey of this story effort to confirm that previous testimony and provide richer details regarding the laundered payment by the Saudis and other particularities in order to prevent what Casey feared the most, a surprise release of the hostages before the election almost guaranteeing windfall votes for President Jimmy Carter. The alleged reward to another Reagan insider for that mission to Iran in the summer of 1980 has been almost wholly responsible for the leaks leading to this odyssey. For it was in that reward in the form of a multimillion dollar government contract that technologies were found to have been stolen by the government from another company. In that other company's recovery from bankruptcy, its CEO has been the real life star and gumshoe in this drama that continues to unfold each day.

In 1982, the body of thirty year old Paul Morasca was found hog-tie and fatally strangled in his condominium on San Francisco's Telegraph Hill. Morasca, who had been working among the Cabazon Arms confidantes reportedly had the access codes for offshore accounts containing hundreds of millions of dollars in drug money ostensibly for covert operations. Morasca's partner, who is one of the key sources for this story, claims to have scuttled Nugan Hand's operations and assumed control over all of the funds. Two years earlier, abou ninety miles inland from Sydney, Frank Nugan's body was found slumped over in

With a little more than a handful of Indians and nearly 2000 acres of desert solitaire, cactus ~~and~~, cotton grove and sweeping views, the Cabazon ~~mission~~ reservation was a suitable home for gambling and gun running. John Philip Nichols wouldn't haul under twelve moons before the gambling was underway and, in the desert night, people would come from all over to the fork at Highway 10 and Highway 86 and into Indio Bingo and the poker casino. Under a Wackenhut ~~international~~ security subsidiary umbrella,

Soon the gun-~~makers~~ runners soon arrived, chemical warfare developers, new weapons ~~to be headed~~ makers for Babylon, contra resuppliers, covert intelligence operatives from both East + West, bikers, (as well as) international dope dealers, mobsters and S+L looters, and murderers — "the marriage of necessity," as one source called the ~~the mottley~~ crew.

The ~~fullness of the~~ whole spectrum of ~~Nichol~~ view from John Philip Nichols is a Kalaidoscope is known only to him, while a few things are ~~known~~ clear

Danny Casolaro's hand-written notes for "Behold, A Pale Horse."

The Octapus.

Eight people who have changed the course of the world, a real life "Mission Impossible" Team whose gifts exploited the secret empires of rogue spy networks, BIG oil and organized crime

→ Span the events on all continents over a quarter of a century

Danny Casolaro's hand-written note about "The Octopus" regarding the secret empires of rogue spy networks, big oil and organized crime.

DEATH OF THE POET

A book proposal by Daniel Casolaro

An international cabal whose services cover parochial political intrigue, espionage, the trade of weapon technologies including biotoxins, drug trafficking, money laundering and murder has emerged from an isolated desert Indian reservation just north of Mexicali.

While this cabal continues today, its origins were spawned thirty years ago in the shadow of the Cold War. In recent months, however, its members have come out of the trenches like scarecrows to take gratuitous credit for the purposeful delay of the release of the hostages in Iran until after the 1980 election, scuttling and resettling the schemes of the notoric Australian-based Nugan Hand Bank, involvement with Gerald Bull -- assassinat last spring in Brussels and the development and distribution of the fuel air explosive which has reportedly been used in Managua, South Africa and in Beirut.

I propose a series of articles and a book, a true crime narrative, that unravels this cabal which roams the earth with its intrigue of injustic its weapons and its murders, trading dope and dirty money for the secrets c some phantom temple.

DEATH OF A POET will be a haunting odyssey to depict a manifesto c deceit, decisions of conscience, good and evil, intrigue and betrayal.

Danny Casolaro's typewritten book proposal for "Death of a Poet" regarding an international cabal involved in political intrigue, espionage, bio-toxins, drug trafficking, money laundering and murder emerging from an isolated desert Indian reservation.

Proposal.

– Richard Helms ← Quick Dancer Helms silence and betrayal

Ray Cline – George Pender –

close to Howard Hunt

In the mid 1950s, returning

In 1945 J. Edgar Hoover worried that the creation of a super secret agency beyond the cops at the FBI would could endanger

a general intelligence service

DEATH OF A POET.

John Nichols – How could a

Loosely structured in the years after WW II by a confederation of triumphant veterans,

Edwin Wilson –

Frank Terpil –

Felix Rodriguez –

Howard Hunt –

Al C. Holbert –

John Delarocque – —Major Barbara—

Delarocque Dowland → Pender →

Ari Ben Menashe –

Al C. Holbert –

Hiddy +

Richard Brenneke –

Michael Riconosciuto –

Haverhill, Ohio – Customs agents.

Paul Moranca –

Drew Thornton.

The Crunch –

Dr. John Nichols
– San Luis Obispo –

extention

What are the boundaries of new Burmese state.

Creative Artists Agency
(212) 334-9169

Danny Casolaro's hand-written notes for "Death of a Poet." Provides names of the characters to be used in the book.

(8)

I propose a series of articles and a book, either in fictionalized form or a true crime narrative, that unravels a 1990 web of thugs and thieves who roam the earth with weapons and espionage, trading in dope, dirty money and murder for the secrets of the temple.

Since possession of a secret is no guarantee of its truth, THE MANIFESTO OF DECEIT promises to be a haunting odyssey of the decisions of conscience, good and evil, intrigue and betrayal.

I expect the first chapters of a ~~book~~ to be ~~underway as soon~~ complete ~~within~~ ~~60 days~~ three months of the initial advance and each subsequent chapter to be delivered ~~at the rate of~~ every ~~few weeks~~ month in order for the completed book to be finished by the summer of 1991.

Danny Casolaro's hand-written notes for "The Manifesto of Deceit --- a haunting odyssey of the decisions of conscience, good and evil, intrigue and betrayal."

1) This is the story of a ~~tiny~~ group of people ~~less than a dozen~~ of them -- whose cloak and dagger intrigue, from Albania in the 50s to Kuwait in 1990, has ~~spawned~~ dominated key events that have spanned the globe for nearly a half century.

This is the story of eight men whose cloak and dagger intrigues have dominated key events ~~that have spanned~~ spanning the globe for nearly a half century. They make up the octopus and their story will help to unravel

They are not government officials but their tentacles can reach into any part of government in almost any country including both legitimate intelligence agencies and rogue spy networks. They are not notable industrialists but they can pull the strings of the worldwide oil industry at will. They are not well known criminals but they have successfully penetrated all factions of organized crime including the Mafia, the Japanese Yakuza, the secret Chinese Triads and the Terrorist underground. This is the octopus and the telling of this story will help to unravel the most compelling puzzles of the 20th century.

With tag team compartments

~~THE OCTOPUS~~ — A RENEGADE FORMIDABLE GROUP RUNNING GUNS, DRUGS & MURDERS

THIS IS THE STORY OF EIGHT MEN WHOSE REAL LIFE "IMPOSSIBLE MISSION", CLOAK + DAGGER INTRIGUES HAVE DOMINATED KEY EVENTS SPANNING THE GLOBE FOR NEARLY A HALF CENTURY, THEY are the individuals who MAKE UP THE OCTOPUS AND ~~THEIR EXPOSURE~~ AND ITS EXPOSURE WILL HELP TO UNRAVEL THE MOST COMPELLING PUZZLES OF THE 20TH CENTURY.

THEY ARE NOT GOVT OFFICIALS BUT THEIR TENTACLES CAN REACH INTO ANY PART OF GOVT IN ALMOST ANY COUNTRY. THEY ARE NOT NOTABLE INDUSTRIALISTS BUT THEY CAN PULL THE STRINGS OF THE OIL & BANKING INDUSTRIES AT WILL. THEY ARE NOT WELL KNOWN CRIMINALS BUT THEY HAVE SUCCESSFULLY PENETRATED ALL FACTIONS OF ORGANIZED CRIME INCLUDING THE MAFIA, THE JAPANESE YAKUZA, THE SECRET CHINESE TRIADS, (HONG) AND THE TERRORIST UNDERGROUND.

Danny Casolaro's hand-written notes relating to "eight men whose real life 'mission impossible' intrigues have dominated key events spanning the globe for nearly a half century ---"

Exploiting FOREIGN POLICY OBJECTIVES WITH THE CONTRAS IN NICARAGUA ~~LATIN AMERICA~~ IS ONE THING BUT WHY WAS THE CREATION OF A LATIN AMERICAN EQUIVILENT TO THE GOLDEN TRIANGLE SO IRRESISTABLE TO THE OCTOPUS?

A HUGE AMOUNT OF MONEY -- SEVERAL BILLION DOLLARS -- WAS RAISED FOR THE AFGHAN FREEDOM FIGHTERS. WHAT HAPPENED TO MOST OF THE MONEY? THE FREEDOM FIGHTERS DIDN'T GET IT. EVEN THE OCTOP. HAD TO FIGHT FOR THIS OPERATION. WHO ELSE STARTED TO PLAY ~~THE GLASS BEAD~~ GAME? HOW WAS IT STOPPED?

WAS IT JUST A CLEVER HAND THAT THE OCTOPUS PLAYED WITH KUWAIT ~~OPEC DECISIONS?~~ AND IRAQ? WHAT ABOUT KUWAIT'S OPEC DECISIONS WHICH GOADED SADDAM HUSSEIN INTO HIS TAKEOVER. WHAT ROLE DID THE OCTOPUS PLAY.

BEFORE THE REINS OF THE OCTOPUS ARE ~~BEING~~ TURNED OVER TO SEVERAL YOUNGER PLAYERS, THE GAME CONTINUES NOW — JULY, 1991 — ON THE TINY CARIBBEAN ISLAND NATION OF DOMINICA. POSSESSING THE LARGEST BOILING DEEPWATER LAKE IN THE WORLD, DOMINICA'S GEOTHERMAL POTENTIALITY IS UNMATCHED. IT IS HERE THAT THE OCTOPUS MAY BE MAKING ITS BOLDEST AND MOST DANGEROUS MOVE YET. WHAT'S GOING TO HAPPEN THERE?

#

Danny Casolaro's hand-written notes about questions he needed answered relating to the Octopus. He wrote, "The reins of the Octopus are turned over to several younger players, the game continues now – July 1991 – on the tiny Caribbean Island nation of Dominica ---."

Office of the Attorney General — John K. Van de Kamp

News Release

Duane Peterson (213) 736-2298
Press Secretary
3580 Wilshire Blvd.
Los Angeles, CA 90010

Alan Ashby (916) 324-5440
Chief Public Information Officer
1515 K Street
Sacramento, CA 95814

Kati Corsaut (916) 739-5239
Public Information Officer
Division of Law Enforcement
4949 Broadway
Sacramento, CA 95820

WORLD'S LARGEST METHAMPHETAMINE SEIZURE ANNOUNCED

Contact: Jerry Smith
Special Agent in Charge
Bureau of Narcotic Enforcement
(415) 557-2955

November 17, 1989

SAN FRANCISCO -- An eighteen-month long investigation into drug trafficking in the Bay Area has resulted in the seizure of 1,022 pounds of methamphetamine, believed to be the world's largest seizure of that drug, Attorney General John Van de Kamp announced today.

Last month, agents from the Attorney General's Bureau of Narcotic Enforcement with agents of the Drug Enforcement Administration and local police agencies served a search warrant on a storage locker in Hayward where they found the half ton of methamphetamine, worth almost $100 million on the street. Also seized was $1 million in cash which will now pay for enhanced narcotics enforcement.

The seizure followed the arrest of Ben Kalka, 40, of Oakland; James Vencill, 47, of Los Angeles, John Yenches, 45, of Martinez' and Richard Schwartz, 57, of Kenwood.

Kalka and Vencill have been charged in federal court with conspiracy to manufacture and sell methamphetamine and the sale of a controlled substance. Yenches and Schwartz have been charged with possession of methamphetamine with the intent to distribute.

November 17, 1989: News Release from the Office of the California Attorney General announcing the "World's Largest Methamphetamine Seizure" in San Francisco in which Ben Kalka, et al, were arrested.

REMARKS BY JOHN VAN DE KAMP
CALIFORNIA ATTORNEY GENERAL
NEWS CONFERENCE ANNOUNCING
RECORD METH SEIZURE
NOVEMBER 17, 1989
SAN FRANCISCO, CALIFORNIA

Final
1030

Behind me you see more than one thousand pounds of methamphetamine, the largest seizure of this illegal drug ever made. And this more recognizable material is cash, about $1 million that we seized along with the dope.

Agents from my Bureau of Narcotic Enforcement, along with DEA and local narcotic officers, seized this stash from a storage locker in Hayward just three weeks ago, and the Drug Enforcement Administration assures me this is the world's record.

Before I tell you about the people who made and planned to sell this deadly dope, let me tell you what this means in hard cash.

One pound of methamphetamine is told by the "cooker" for between $6,000 and $10,000 dollars, so this haul would bring him between six and ten million. Then we have the wholesalers, who stand to see between sixteen and twenty thousand dollars per pound -- or in this case between 16 and 20 million. From there, the street dealers, who sell quarter gram doses to users for $25 each, could realize anywhere from 40 to 58 million dollars,

PAGES 472-474: November 17, 1989: Official script of remarks made by California Attorney General John Van De Kamp to news media relative to the one thousand pounds of meth and $1 million in cash that was seized from Ben Kalka.

That's a tremendous amount of money, but in these days of multi-ton drug seizures, we almost become blase about another $50 million. Put in perspective though, the entire annual budget of the San Francisco Police Department is $180 million.

But this half ton of methamphetamine represents more than just profits in a dope sellers pocket.

Consider for a minute the real cost of methamphetamine to society. Economists have estimated that methamphetamine abuse costs California at least $348 million a year. That's reflected in reduced productivity, an insidious loss that eats away at the health of our economy. Then there are lost jobs, treatment and support, crime, accidents, and social welfare. And for some, death. Meth cost many, Californians their lives each year.

Happily, this half ton of meth will not reach our streets. And the men who made this stuff have been arrested. Instead of raking in the big bucks they're looking at doing some big time behind bars.

Ben Kalka of Oakland, considered the mastermind of this organization faces a life sentence in federal prison. He'll be in good company as we'll be asking for stiff prison terms for his fellow "cookers" and traffickers James Vencill, Richard Schwartz and John Yenches. They face maximum prison sentences of 30 to 40 years.

We began this case early last year on a tip and have been following this bunch since then, determining where they cooked, stored and sold the dope. Our agents made some multi-kilo buys and during subsequent search warrants executed at an estate in Kenwood, we seized lab equipment, some of this cash and dope. We then searched a Hayward storage locker controlled by Kalka and took the bulk of this huge dope haul.

Announcement of the seizure and arrests were delayed to allow our agents time to track down some additional leads.

Today, a San Francisco police narcotics officer is being buried after being struck down during a drug deal. John Blessing was only 36 years old, and he left behind his wife and eight-year-old twins. His death is a reminder that our narcotics officers put their lives on the line every day to rid our state of illegal drugs.

This seizure will not dry up entirely the meth supply in the Bay Area. But it does send a message. And our capacity has increased year after year after year. But there is much more to do.

# # # # #

SEALED
BY COURT ORDER

MICHAEL J. YAMAGUCHI
United States Attorney

STEPHEN G. CORRIGAN
Chief, Drug Task Force

WILLIAM I. SHOCKLEY
Assistant United States Attorney

450 Golden Gate Avenue
San Francisco, California
Telephone: (415) 436-6805

Attorneys for the Plaintiff

Nov 4 9 AM '97

UNITED STATES DISTRICT COURT

NORTHERN DISTRICT OF CALIFORNIA

IN THE MATTER OF JOHN DI GIORGIO,	No. CR-89-0603 VRW DECLARATION OF ASSISTANT UNITED STATES ATTORNEY WILLIAM I. SHOCKLEY

The undersigned, Assistant United States Attorney William I. Shockley, hereby declares under penalty of perjury that on Monday November 3, 1997 the undersigned spoke with Orrin Grover, attorney for John Di Giorgio, who stated that he has no objection to the granting to the motion to unseal the file for examination and copying.

Subscribed to this 3rd day of November, 1997, at San Francisco, California.

WILLIAM I. SHOCKLEY
Assistant United States Attorney
DECWIS.jd2

Document No. 368

District Court
Criminal Case Processing

November 3, 1997: Court filing - Declaration of Assistant U.S. Attorney William Shockley granting a motion to unseal the Ben Kalka, John Di Giorgio, et al, case file.

CHRISTOPHER J. CANNON
Bar No. 88034
Sugarman & Cannon
600 Harrison Street
Suite 535
San Francisco, CA 94107
(415) 957-1144

ORIGINAL
FILED
APR 23 1997
RICHARD W. WIEKING
CLERK, U.S. DISTRICT COURT
NORTHERN DISTRICT OF CALIFORNIA

Attorneys for BEN KALKA

UNITED STATES DISTRICT COURT

NORTHERN DISTRICT OF CALIFORNIA

BEN KALKA, Petitioner, v. WARDEN, JOSEPH CRABTREE.	No. CR-89-0603 VRW SUPPLEMENTAL PETITION FOR A WRIT OF HABEAS CORPUS

Petitioner, Ben Kalka, through counsel, Christopher J. Cannon hereby petitions for a Writ of Habeas Corpus under 28 U.S.C. § 2255, and by this verified petition states:

I.

PETITIONER'S CUSTODIAL STATUS

Petitioner is presently in the custody of the Attorney General at Jesup F.C.I., following his conviction for criminal offenses in the Northern District of California.

\ \

\

SUPPLEMENTAL PETITION FOR A WRIT OF HABEAS CORPUS

PAGES 476-479 : April 23, 1997: Court filing – Supplemental Petition for a Writ of Habeas Corpus by Ben Kalka, Petitioner, based on his claim that "the government had provided the precursor chemicals for the drugs" [that he manufactured and sold].

II.

TRIAL COURT PROCEEDINGS

On August 17, 1990, Petitioner, Ben Kalka entered a guilty plea to one count charging a violation of 21 U.S.C. § 846 Conspiracy to Distribute Methamphetamine and another count charging a violation of 21 U.S.C. § 841(a)(1) Possession of Methamphetamine with the Intent to Distribute. On February 6, 1991, he was sentenced to a term of 20 years in the custody of the Attorney General. Kalka is presently serving that sentence.

III.

APPEAL

Petitioner did not file any appeals and was not advised of his right to appeal.

IV.

OTHER APPLICATIONS FOR POST CONVICTION RELIEF

This is Petitioner's supplemental application for a Writ of Habeas Corpus. A petition addressing only double jeopardy claims was filed on June 6, 1995. That petition is still pending.

V.

GROUNDS FOR PETITION

In this case, Ben Kalka was convicted for his participation in a huge methamphetamine conspiracy. Not until long after that plea, however, did he learn that the government had provided the precursor chemicals for the drugs. One of the reasons he failed to learn that information is that the government a filed to disclose it. The other reason the source of the drugs remained secret is that his attorney had a direct conflict of interest which prevented him from conducting an appropriate investigation of the case.

Following "negotiations" Kalka entered a plea agreement and cooperated.

At sentencing, Kalka's guidelines were grossly overstated because the attorney never forced the government to prove whether the methamphetamine was D or L methamphetamine; the Court failed to rule on Kalka's claims he was not an organizer, supervisor or manager and he was being penalized from the results of his self incriminating disclosures, despite guideline provisions which would have allowed Kalka to admit his behavior with out increasing his penalties. The Court also failed to advise Kalka of his right to appeal his sentence.

Finally, counsel's advice led to serious errors in Kalka's performance under his agreement to cooperate.

The Fifth and Sixth Amendments to the United States Constitution require that this Kalka be released from custody.

VI.

COUNSEL AT TRIAL AND ON APPEAL

Petitioner was represented in the District Court by Marvin Cahn Esq. Kalka was not advised of his right to appeal and did not file an appeal.

PETITIONER RESPECTFULLY REQUEST THAT THIS COURT: 1. Issue a writ of habeas corpus ordering petitioner's release from custody, and/or 2. Grant any other relief to which petitioner may be entitled.

Dated: April 23, 1997

Respectfully submitted,

Christopher J. Cannon
Attorney for Ben Kalka

\chris\
g.fnt\
255pet.004

SUPPLEMENTAL PETITION FOR A WRIT OF HABEAS CORPUS

FILED

APR 20 2000

RICHARD W. WIEKING
CLERK, U.S. DISTRICT COURT
NORTHERN DISTRICT OF CALIFORNIA

UNITED STATES DISTRICT COURT

NORTHERN DISTRICT OF CALIFORNIA

UNITED STATES OF AMERICA, Plaintiff,

v.

BENJAMIN KALKA, Defendant.

No. CR 89-0603 VRW

ORDER FOR RELEASE FROM CUSTODY

IT IS ORDERED that the United States Marshal release from his custody Banjamin Kalka, the defendant in the above entitled action.. Immediately following defendant's release from custody, he shall report in person to the United States Probation Office in the district to which he is released. The defendant may travel to Los Angeles upon notification to the Probation Office. The defendant may reside in Los Angeles pending transfer of defendant's supervision to the Central District of California.

Dated: 4.20.2000

VAUGHN R. WALKER
United States District Judge

UNITED STATES MARSHAL RETURN

I hereby certify and return that in response to the within Order for Release from Custody, received at San Francisco, California, this ________ day of ________________, 2000, I release the within named defendant ______________________ from my custody, on ____________________, 2000.

JAMES J. MOLINARI
United States Marshal

by: ____________________
Deputy Marshal

April 20, 2000: Court filing – Order for Release of Custody in which the U.S. Marshall released Ben Kalka from custody. Kalka had been sentenced to 20 years in prison, but was released on April 20, 2000 because he agreed to sign a declaration dated 4/20/2000 to "waive all claims against the government arising out of [his] claim that the government provided or participated in the provision of precursor chemicals to [him]." Case No. CR 89-0603-VRW.

Calvin L. Robinson
83327-011 J-1
FDC Pleasanton
5701 - 8th Street, Camp Parks
Dublin, CA 94568

Claimant in Pro Per

The "Drug Tug" was seized in S.F. Bay in the Spring of 1988 and was found hauling a barge containing 157 TONS OF HASHISH AND MARIJUANA

UNITED STATES DISTRICT COURT

NORTHERN DISTRICT OF CALIFORNIA

UNITED STATES OF AMERICA,
PLAINTIFF,
-Vs-
$292,888.04 IN U.S. CURRENCY,
DEFENDANT,
CALVIN L. ROBINSON,
CLAIMANT.

Case No. C-90-2839-VRW-JPV

AFFIDAVIT OF CALVIN L. ROBINSON FOR THE RECUSAL OF DISTRICT COURT JUDGE JOHN PAUL VUKASIN, JR.

Date: December 12, 1991
Time: 10:00 A.M.
Courtroom: Two

I, Calvin L. Robinson, hereby declare under penalty of perjury, based upon my own personal knowledge, information, and belief, that:

1. I am the claimant in the above entitled matter.

2. I am a layman at law and untrained in the law.

3. On June 6, 1988, I alleged in pro per, in a "Motion for Preliminary Hearing and Declaration in Support", to Magistrate Joan Brennan of this Court, that United States Attorney General, Edwin Meese III, was engaged with United States Customs Service (USCS), DEA, IRS, and other government agents and agencies, in a "scheme and conspiracy" of "Federal

(1)

AFFIDAVIT FOR RECUSAL

Pages 481-482: December 12, 1991: Court filing – Affidavit of Calvin Robinson for the Recusal of District Court Judge John Paul Vukasin. Calvin Robinson was the captain of a tug boat, dubbed the "Drug Tug" by news media. His tug was seized in San Francisco Bay in 1988 and was found hauling a barge containing 157 tons of hashish and marijuana. Robinson maintained in his court affidavit that Judge Vukasin was conspiring against him under the orders of Edwin Meese. On Page 13 of the affidavit, Robinson says his lawyer, David Mayer, died of a gunshot wound the day before he was to appear in court to represent Robinson. Robinson said he believed his lawyer was killed to silence him about his attorney/client files relating to Ben Kalka, who had been Mayers' client at one time.

Nichols. Mayer discovered that Weichman was giving information from Kalka's and my attorney/client files to government agents. I believe Mr. Mayer made the connection between Dougherty and Nichols; and made the connection between Meese and Vukasin.

31. On February 6, 1989, Mr. Mayer died from a gun shot wound. A suicide tape was found. His death was ruled suicide. I learned of Mr. Mayer's death on the morning of February 7, 1989, the day Mayer was suppose to appear to defend me. The trial in case No. CR-88-0336-JPV was in process. The government attorney Assistant U.S. Attorney Laurie Kloster-Gray, had called the first government witness. I was dumb struck with disbelief. I was in shock. When I talked with Mr. Mayer on Sunday, February 5, 1989, he appeared very involved in the prospect of defending me at trial, and the logistics it presented. Mayer told me he was trying to get a second attorney to help him during the trial, to "brain storm" it as it unfolded. I felt in my heart that Mr. Mayer had not committed suicide, but I was unaware then of what I now know today. I did not learn until late in October of 1991, that Mayer's files contained a link to Dougherty through Nichols. I also learned of the link between Brian, Meese, and Vukasin. That information opened the link to the INSLAW pirated PROMIS DOJ software through Riconosciuto and Brian. That information established a link between a number of people in addition to Mr. Mayer, who have met suspicious untimely deaths, often ruled suicide, with information about the various people or facts linked to Riconosciuto, Brian, Nichols, the INSLAW pirated PROMIS DOJ software, MEESE, and the DOJ. I believe that Mr. Mayer was murdered to silence him. I am

FIRST INTERCONTINENTAL DEVELOPMENT CORP.
909 · 15TH STREET, SUITE 6
SANTA MONICA, CA 90403 USA
TEL (213) 451-4652
(310)

January 11, 1983

Robert B. Nichols
5100 Via Dolce, Suite 107
Marina del Rey, California
90291

Dear Bob,

Please find, enclosed, for your records, a copy of the resolution, resulting from a meeting of the Board of Directors of First Intercontinental Development Corporation via conference call on January 8, 1983.

Very truly yours,

George K. Pender,
President

GKP/mmi
Enclosure

January 11, 1983: FIDCO (First Intercontinental Development Corporation) letter from George Pender, President to Robert Booth Nichols.

FIRST INTERCONTINENTAL DEVELOPMENT CORPORATION

First Intercontinental Development Corporation (FIDCO) is a corporation of California, U.S.A.

The principals of the corporation are as follows:

ROBERT A. MAHEU - Senior Vice President and Director. Former Chief Executive for Howard Hughes Operations. Senior Consultant and Associate in Leisure Industries and Management Consultant to other major U.S. companies.

* GEORGE K. PENDER - Chairman and Director. Former Director of Pacific Ocean area of Burns and Roe, Inc., an international engineering and construction corporation with active projects on all seven continents of the world. Senior Engineer Consultant to Burns and Roe, Inc.

KENNETH A. ROE - Director. Chairman and President of Burns and Roe, Inc., International Engineers and Constructors, a family corporation owned by Kenneth Roe and his family. Major current project of the company is the engineering design and construction of the U.S.A. Fast Breeder Nuclear Reactor Plant in conjunction with Westinghouse Electric Corporation which is responsible for the nuclear system supply of steam. Construction value of present business backlog of Burns and Roe, Inc. is in excess of six billion U.S. dollars.

FRANCIS T. FOX - Vice President and Director. Former General Manager of Los Angeles International Airport. Former Director of Aviation for Hughes Nevada Operations (now Summa Cprporation). City Manager of San Jose, California (third Largest city in California). President of Foundation for Educational Services, Los Angeles, California.

CLINT W. MURCHISON, JR. - Director. Chairman, President and Owner of C. W. Murchison Companies worldwide. Owner of Dallas Cowboys NFL football team, headquartered in Dallas, Texas.

* ROBERT B. NICHOLS - Director, Senior Vice President and Chairman of Investment Committee. Chief Executive Officer of R.B.N. Companies International, a holding company, which through its various subsidiaries, is engaged in, among other things, one of the largest retail operations in the Pacific Basin; the manufacturing and development of high technology electronics; real estate development; construction; and international finance.

WILLIAM M. PENDER - Director and Seniour Vice President, Finance. Licensed Contractor, State of California.

* MICHAEL A. McMANUS - Director, Vice President and General Counsel. Assistant to the President of the United States at the White House, Washington, D.C.

* GLENN R. SHOCKLEY - Director. Consultant to Fortune 500 Companies in Business Management. Internationally known as Financial Consultant in Funding.

FIDCO list of Principles of the corporation which include Robert Booth Nichols, Michael McManus (assist to the president of the United States at the White House), Robert Maheu (Howard Hughes Operations) and other notables including Clint Murchison, Jr. of Dallas, Texas

ORI

THE WHITE HOUSE
WASHINGTON

June 29, 1983

Dear George:

It was good to see you again. I appreciate the update you and your associate gave me concerning the status of your efforts in the rebuilding of Lebanon.

Without question FIDCO seems to have a considerable role to offer particularly in the massive financial participation being made available to the Government of Lebanon.

As you are aware, the United States Government is providing financial aid. We are very interested in the success of the rebuilding effort in Lebanon.

I will appreciate your continuing to keep me posted.

Best personal regards.

Sincerely,

Mike

Michael A. McManus, Jr.
Assistant to the President

Mr. George K. Pender
President, FIDCO
908 15th Street
Suite 6
Santa Monica, California 90403

June 29, 1983: Letter on White House stationary from Michael McManus, Assistant to the President [Ronald Reagan], to George Pender, President of FIDCO, regarding FIDCO's role in "the massive financial participation being made available to the government of Lebanon."

JUL-20-1994 16:09 FROM TO 18189543237 P.003/1

FIRST INTERCONTINENTAL DEVELOPMENT CORP.

909 · 15TH STREET, SUITE 6
SANTA MONICA, CA 90403 USA
TEL. (213) 451-4662

July 12, 1983

President Amin Gamayel
Presidential Palace
Beirut, LEBANON

Dear Mr. President,

I had visited Beirut in February and May, 1983 to discuss FIDCO participation in the redevelopment of Lebanon. These meetings were held with the Chamouns, Maurice Ghanem and Mourad Baroudy. Of particular interest is the fact that FIDCO offered to arrange the financing of projects considered, provided they were in the government sector. Unfortunately, the response, to date, is dragging and a golden opportunity for Lebanon is slowly dying.

I had made no effort to see you at that time as I thought it more prudent to delay until I had something more tangible to present. I expressed specific interest in the rebuilding of Damour and Alkhyam. FIDCO has presented these projects to an international Trust with whom we have a close relationship, and we are very confident that we can arrange the funding under International Chamber of Commerce format, provided FIDCO can negotiate turn-key contracts on both projects. We are ready, willing and able to proceed immediately on this basis.

I understand you will be at the White House on July 22nd. Would it be possible for me to meet with you in Washington, D.C. on July 21st briefly so that I may personally present our interest in Lebanon? As per copy of attached letter, the White House is actively interested in our efforts.

For your personal information, I was a good friend of Bechir. I was with him in Beirut in 1976 when the Syrian Army came in to police. When he later visited the United States on a speaking tour, my wife and I went to Framingham, Massachusetts to meet with him. I miss him tremendously.

I would appreciate your reply as soon as possible. You can also reach me via telex 652483 RBN ASSOCS LSA. Thank you for your time and consideration.

Sincerely yours,

George K. Pender

George K. Pender,
President

GKP/eh
Enclosure

July 12, 1983: Letter from George Pender, President of FIDCO, to Amin Gamayal, the President of Lebanon at the Presidential Palace in Beirut, regarding FIDCO financing the redevelopment of Lebanon. Pender advises President Gamayal to respond via telex 652483 RBN ASSOCS LSA, which is Robert Booth Nichols' telex number at his apartment in Marina Del Rey, California. (This was actually a NSC/NSA listening post for the operation in Lebanon to get a hostage released, according to Nichols' partner, Peter Zokosky).

JUL-20-1994 16:09 FROM TO 16189543237 P.004/004

Arab Bank Limited
Established in 1930
General Management: Amman, Jordan
P.O. Box 68
Cable Address: BANKARABI
Telex: ARABNK 21230
Telephone: 38161-9

Chairman - General Manager

Amman: 23rd Nov, 1983
Ref. : 649/31/9

Mr. George K. Pender,
Chairman and Director,
First Intercontinental
Development Corp.
908 - 15 St. Suite 6,
Santa Monica - CA 90403
U. S. A.

Dear Mr. Pender,

Mr. Ahmad has talked to me about the fund to reconstruct Lebanon and we the Arab Bank together with a group of other banks will be glad to cooperate with you concerning this respect.

We shall discuss, in future, how this cooperation will be made and on what conditions and plans.

You have mentioned in your letter to Mr. Ahmad on Sep. 27th that this fund amounts US$ three billion or more. There is no problem to take care of this by the Arab Bank and the other group of banks as stated above. The terms and conditions will be discussed with you provided the condition is clear in Lebanon and subject to the approval and counter guarantees of the Lebanees Authority.

Yours sincerely,

Abdul Majeed Shoman
Chairman
General Manager

TOTAL P.004

November 23, 1983: Letter from Abdul Majeed Shoman, General Manager of the Arab Bank Limited in Amman, Jordan, agreeing to cooperate and accept "US$ Three Billion dollars or more" adding that "there is no problem to take care of this by the Arab Bank and the other group of banks ---"

871867

FILED
In the office of the Secretary of State
AUG 22 1978

ARTICLES OF INCORPORATION

OF

FIRST INTERCONTINENTAL DEVELOPMENT CORPORATION

I

The name of this corporation is FIRST INTERCONTINENTAL DEVELOPMENT CORPORATION.

II

The purpose of this corporation is to engage in any lawful act or activity for which a corporation may be organized under the General Corporation Law of California other than the banking business, the trust company business or the practice of a profession permitted to be incorporated by the California Corporations Code.

III

The name and address in the State of California of this corporation's initial agent for service of process is: George K. Pender, 908 15th Street, Suite 6, Santa Monica, Ca. 90403.

IV

This corporation is authorized to issue only one class of shares of stock; and the total number of shares which this corporation is authorized to issue is 100,000.

DATED August 22, 1978

GEORGE K. PENDER

GEORGE K. PENDER

I hereby declare that I am the person who executed the foregoing Articles of Incorporation, which execution is my act and deed.

GEORGE K. PENDER

August 22, 1978: Articles of Incorporation filed for FIDCO by George Pender, President of FIDCO.

SPECIAL OPERATIONS REPORT

Subject's Name: CABAZON INDIANS	Residence Address		City	File No. 6-2 / Residence Phone
Aliases	P.D. No.	County No.	F.B.I. No.	C.I.I. No.
Sex / Descent / DOB:	POB:	Height / Weight	Hair	Eyes
Occupation	Business Address		City	Business Phone
Vehicle - Year / Make	Model	Color	License No.	State / Year
Vehicle Registered to	Address		Subject's Wife or Husband	

Resume of, and/or Reason for making, report:

Nicaraguans and Earl Brian at Lake Cahuilla - 09/10/81

Details of Report:

Validity: 1
Reliability: B

Approved	Date & Time Typed	Clerk	Reporting Officer (s)
	10/10/91	sb	9500-91-008

228-70 (2/82)

PAGES 489-491: September 10, 1981: Special Operations Report entitled, "Nicaraguans and Earl Brian at Lake Cahuilla – 09/10/81" written by Gene Gilbert, former investigator for the Riverside District Attorney's office, Indio branch, and sent to the House Judiciary Committee on INSLAW. The report lists the names of those who attended the meeting at the gun range at Lake Cahuilla where sniper rifles and night vision goggles were demonstrated to Contra leaders for future manufacture and sale by the Cabazon/Wackenhut Joint Venture at the reservation. According to the report, Contra leaders Edin Pastora Gomez (Commander Zero) and Jose Curdel (Commander Alpha) attended this meeting. The permits for the demonstration were obtained by Meridian Arms, headed by Robert Booth Nichols and Michael Riconosciuto.

Special Operations Report
Page 2
Subject: Cabazon Indians

Intelligence:

Lake Cahuilla Gun Range with Nicaraguans - 09/10/81

People Present:

1. Phil Hawes - City Manager, City of Indio

2. Peter Zokosky - President of Armtech - Coachella

3. Wayne Reeder - Builder/Developer

4. Jimmy Hughes - Security Chief - Cabazon Indians

5. Michael Riconosciuto - Researcher for Cabazon Indians

6. Two Nicaraguan Generals

   a. Edin Pastora Gomez - Commander Zero
   b. Jose Curdel - Commander Alpha

7. Representative from Browning Arms - Identity Unknown

8. John Phillip Nichols - Cabazon Indian Manager

9. John Paul Nichols - Son of John Phillip Nichols

10. Art Welmas - Tribal Chairman of Cabazon Indians

11. Indio Police Department Officers Present:

    a. Chief Cross - Parking Lot - Indio Police Department
    b. Dave Baird - Range with Hawes
    c. Jim Carney - Range surveillance, surrounding hills
    d. Bill Talley - Range surveillance, surrounding hills
    e. Ted Fish - Range surveillance, surrounding hills
    f. Terry Miller - Range surveillance, surrounding hills

12. Scott Wesley - United States Army

13. Honduran Telephone Company (Military connection network in Southern Hemisphere)

14. John D. Vanderworker and couple of his friends - Vanderworker C.I.A. Research Director - for C.I.A. 8 Years.

Special Operations Report
Page 3
Subject: Cabazon Indians

15. Raul Aranna - Central Caribbean research procurement front for liberation of Nicaragua (Pre Contra days).

16. Earl Brian - Wisconsin businessman and C.I.A. employee.

On 09/10/81, the above two groups were at the Cahuilla Range. The officers, except Cross, were placed around the surrounding area in a surveillance/protection type mood.

The other group arrived at the range between 2200 and 2300 hours. Some arrived as follows:

1. James Hughes and Michael Riconosciuto
   1973 Buick Station Wagon
   CA 876JLG
   Car was filled with automatic weapons (i.e. AR15 and MP5'S. Also contained numerous night vision equipment.

2. John Phillip Nichols
   1981 White Cadillac
   CA 1BOA990

3. John Paul Nichols
   1981 Datsun
   CA 1CHB714

4. Wayne Reeder/Earl Brian
   1981 White Rolls Royce
   OK 2XG2302

5. Two Military Generals
   1981 Honda
   AZ AFM877

6. Peter Zokosky
   1980 Volkswagen
   CA 198ZUF

Purpose of the meeting was to test a new night vision device and weapons. All weapons tested were semi-automatic. New sniper rifle tested was a 50 caliber with a 308 bullet.

Some automatic weapons were present, but all had necessary permits through Meriden Arms. Meriden Arms owned by Michael Riconosciuto, Robert Booth Nichols (no relation to John Phillip Nichols), and Don Oliver - former Under Sheriff for San Diego

Special Operations Report
Page 4
Subject: Cabazon Indians

County.

Meeting and testing took about one hour, then all parties left

END REPORT

Central American connection?

Details surface on Nichols' role in security test

By JOHN HUSSAR
Desert Sun Special Projects Editor

LAKE CAHUILLA — Three men dressed in gaudy sports shirts sat at a table, speaking in Spanish, while they examined night-vision goggles and a rifle with a night-vision sniper scope.

The only sound that shattered the warm evening of Sept. 10, 1981, was the staccato gunfire at the county-owned police firing range.

Several men were wearing the mask-like goggles while others fired semiautomatic rifles with special night scopes at man-shaped paper targets. The night-vision goggles and scopes gave them illuminated green vision in the desert darkness.

One man firing was John Philip Nichols, consultant to the Cabazon Indians in Indio.

Another was rumored to be Eden Pastora, otherwise known as Commander Zero, an anti-Sandinista rebel who broke with the new Nicaraguan government after helping to overthrow dictator Anastasia Somoza in 1979.

The demonstration also drew Peter Zokosky, former consultant to the Indian-owned Cabazon Arms Co.; Indio City Manager Phil Hawes; Cabazon Tribal Chairman Art Welmas; local developer Wayne Reeder; Nichols' sons, John Paul and Mark; former tribal security chief James Hughes Jr.; and John Van Dewerker, whose Orange County Intersect business then was involved in security services.

The entourage also included Michael Riconosciuto, a high-tech electronics engineer, who said he had been working in a joint business venture with Nichols on various projects, including night-vision goggles.

AP Laserphoto

WAS HE HERE? — Nicaraguan rebel leader Eden Pastora may have witnessed security testing in the Coachella Valley in 1981.

A third partner was Paul Morasca, who was found murdered in a San Francisco apartment in 1982. San Francisco police detectives said Riconosciuto discovered the body, then drove to Indio to confer with Nichols before contacting police. The murder has not been solved.

Nichols, now 60, had set up the demonstration for the benefit of the three mystery military-types from Central America, according to several sources.

To this day, the identity of the three men remains a puzzle. Nichols, who is to be sentenced Wednesday on murder solicitation charges in an unrelated incident (see related story, Page A-2), may be the only one who knows.

Nichols had planned on selling the

(Continued on Page A-2)

Nichols' murder solicitation sentence due

1985

INDIO — A Cabazon Indian consultant will be sentenced Wednesday in Superior Court on two counts of solicitation to commit murder.

In an agreement with prosecutors, John Philip Nichols, 60, a non-Indian consultant to the local Cabazon Band of Mission Indians, entered no-contest pleas to those charges in return for a promise of a sentence of not more than four years. The maximum sentence possible is six years.

Nichols, who has been in Riverside County Jail since his Jan. 16 arrest at an Indio motel, was accused of plotting an unsuccessful murder-for-hire scheme.

Indio police allege that Nichols asked two Indio residents to kill five other people. However, the supposed "hit men" were police informants who cooperated in a subsequent investigation.

Three of five murder solicitation counts against Nichols were dropped after the agreement that he would plead no contest to the remaining two counts. Junior Rodriguez, 25, and Lydia Tapia, 28, both of Indio, were the alleged intended targets of the crime, prosecutors said.

Nichols is the business adviser to the small band of Indians. The incident is not related to Indian business, police said.

Nichols' attorney, Gary Scherotter of Palm Springs, said he has prepared a report to Superior Court Judge Noah Ned Jamin that could lead to a reduced sentence. Nichols, who suffers from diabetes, is being held in lieu of $500,000 bail.

Law enforcement officers have not released a motive for the alleged murder solicitation except to say it revolves around the use of narcotics. Nichols does not use narcotics, police said.

★ ★ ★

1985 *Desert Sun* newspaper article entitled, "Details Surface on Nichols' Role in Security Test," which names the people who attended the Lake Cahuilla demonstration. In addition to Cabazon Administrator John Phillip Nichols, others included Peter Zokosky, Jimmy Hughes [tribal security chief], Wayne Reeder [local developer], Michael Riconosciuto [a high tech electronics engineer], John Van Dewerker, Phil Hawes [Indio City Manager], and others. Also mentions the death of Paul Morasca.

LOS ANGELES TIMES / ★ THURSDAY, MAY 16, 1991 A17

Noriega Papers Claim CIA Sent Him Millions

By MIKE CLARY
SPECIAL TO THE TIMES

MIAMI—Gen. Manuel A. Noriega, Panama's former strongman leader, was paid more than $11 million from a Central Intelligence Agency slush fund, according to a Noriega defense document released Wednesday.

And despite federal charges that Noriega was heavily involved in drug smuggling, the document contends that he once warned the CIA to put an end to cocaine shipments to the United States that were being used to raise funds for the Contras in Nicaragua.

Those assertions—and others suggesting Noriega was a CIA operative under extreme pressure from U.S. officials to overlook many instances of American-sponsored illegal actions—were included in a 107-page document prepared by lawyers defending Noriega against the charges here.

The rambling, highly censured document released by a federal court also recounts a secret meeting with former National Security Council staff member Oliver L. North and claims that Noriega helped the CIA supply Argentina with Exocet missiles for use against Britain during the Falkland Islands War. The CIA "was concerned that Argentina's forces . . . would be crushed," the document states.

The filing from defense attorneys Frank A. Rubino and Jon A. May was reviewed and edited by the Justice Department under provisions of the Classified Information Procedures Act, which requires the defense to make known any defense strategy that could involve the disclosure of classified information. Noriega is scheduled to go on trial July 22.

The Justice Department deleted key sections of the document, including details of Noriega's contacts with President Bush.

Among other allegations in the filing, which is unsupported by documentation:

—Noriega knew that planes carrying arms to Nicaraguan rebels returned to the United States loaded with illegal drugs. He understood that the U.S. government "clearly was involved in a guns for drugs policy" and warned the CIA against it.

—When Noriega refused to assist the Contras in an invasion of Nicaragua, John M. Poindexter, Ronald Reagan's national security adviser, "responded by threatening Noriega specifically and Panama in general." Later, after meetings with North on a yacht in the Potomac and in a London hotel room, Noriega was pressured to order Panamanian commandos to take part in Contra operations. "Noriega just listened," the defense document says.

—Less than eight weeks before he was indicted on drug charges, in February, 1988, Drug Enforcement Administration chief John C. Lawn reported there was insufficient evidence to charge Noriega.

—Noriega served as a conduit for cash payments from the CIA to onetime anti-Sandinista leader Eden Pastora.

May 16, 1991: Los Angeles Times newspaper article entitled, "Noriega Papers Claim CIA sent Him Millions," which reported in the last paragraph of the article that "Noriega served as a conduit for cash payments from the CIA to onetime anti-Sandinista leader Eden Pastora."

No. 90-55281
CV 89-4383 RG (KX)

United States Court of Appeal

For the Ninth Circuit

MERIDIAN INTERNATIONAL LOGISTICS, INC., a Nevada Corporation,

Plaintiff and Appellant,

vs.

THOMAS G. GATES,

Defendant and Respondent.

APPEAL FROM

UNITED STATES DISTRICT COURT

CENTRAL DISTRICT OF CALIFORNIA

APPELLANT'S OPENING BRIEF

MARK P. ROBINSON
JOHN D. ROWELL
ROBINSON, ROBINSON & PHILLIPS
1000 Wilshire Boulevard, Suite 1950
Los Angeles, California 90017
Telephone: (213) 485-1798
Attorneys for Appellant,
MERIDIAN INTERNATIONAL LOGISTICS, INC.

Court filing: United States Court of Appeal - For the Ninth Circuit, Meridian International Logistics, Inc., Plaintiff, verses Thomas G. Gates, Defendant and Respondent.

AFFIDAVIT IN SUPPORT OF APPLICATION

I, Thomas G. Gates, being first duly sworn, depose and say:

I

INTRODUCTION TO INVESTIGATION:

1. I am a Special Agent (SA) for the Federal Bureau of Investigation (FBI). As such, I am an "investigative or law enforcement officer...of the United States" within the meaning of Title 18, U.S. Code, Section 2510(7), th[illegible] an officer of the United States, who is auth[illegible]ct investigations of, a [illegible] enumerated in Title 18, U.S. Cod[illegible]

Bill McCoy from Peter 1/17/91

2. I have be[illegible] 10 1/2 years. Since 1981, I h[illegible]ation of organized criminal activ[illegible] approximately 18 investig[illegible]onic surveillance, both as a mo[illegible]n charge. During those inves[illegible]epted communications, prepared tra[illegible]taken part in physical surveillances prompted by intercepted communications, and directed other agents as to these activities. I have spoken with numerous other law enforcement personnel, who have special expertise in the investigation of labor racketeering and stock frauds. Through my experience and training, my contacts with investigators who have experience in labor racketeering and stock fraud investigations, my debriefing of informants and other individuals knowledgeable about these matters, and my own

EXHIBIT C

Court filing: This is Exhibit C in the above case, in which Meridian International Logistics (MIL) owned by Robert Booth Nichols, et al, sued FBI Special Agent Thomas Gates for allegedly going out of his jurisdiction overseas to investigate Robert Booth Nichols and his partners. Exhibit C is a discovery document, Affidavit in Support of Application, in which Thomas Gates requested authority to wiretap Robert Booth Nichols and his partners in MIL. Gates states in the Affidavit that he has been investigating organized crime activities since1981. This document was sent to Bill McCoy for informational purposes by Peter Zokosky on 1/17/91. Bill McCoy then provided it to Danny Casolaro.

investigations, I have become familiar with how some union officials, alleged labor consultants and La Cosa Nostra (LCN) members and associates manipulate, extort, and corruptly influence companies and/or individuals associated with the production of films and television shows and how stockbrokers associated with the LCN, LCN members and associates use deceptive and fraudulent practices in the buying and selling of stocks.

3. This affidavit is made in support of an application to continue to intercept, for a period of thirty (30) days, wire communications over the telephones numbered (213) 278-3538, and (213) 273-3906 located at 412 South Arnaz Drive, Apartment 304, Los Angeles, California of MARTIN BACOW, EUGENE GIAQUINTO, ANGELO T. COMMITO, EDWARD SCIANDRA, MICHAEL DEL GAIZO, JOSEPH GAROFALO, ROBERT NICHOLS and others as yet unknown.

4. This investigation is being conducted by SAs of the FBI, and other law enforcement agents and officers. I am the FBI case agent, and as such, I am responsible for directing the participation of FBI Agents in this investigation. The facts set forth in this affidavit are known to me due to my participation in the investigation, my conversations with other law enforcement personnel regarding various aspects of this and related investigations, my reading of official reports and notes, and my review of tape recordings and transcripts of other court authorized wire interceptions and consensually monitored conversations.

5. Based upon the information set forth in the affidavit, and my experience, I believe that:

Court filing: This document is a continuation of Thomas Gates' Affidavit (above) in which Gates names those people to be wiretapped [intercepted] by the FBI. Two of the names listed are Robert Booth Nichols and Eugene Giaquinto, a Board member of MIL at that time and President of MCA/Universal Home Entertainment Division. (MCA= Music Corporation of America).

2) The source, type and quantity of the narcotics/controlled substances;

3) The methods and means of delivery of the narcotics/controlled substances and the locations from which and to which the deliveries are made, including the identities of purchasers, couriers and sellers; and

4) The source of funding for the purchasing of narcotics/controlled substances and the allocation and use of the proceeds from its trafficking.

6. Normal investigative procedures have been tried and have failed to obtain the goals of this investigation, or appear reasonably unlikely to succeed if tried as more fully described herein.

II. TELEPHONE FACILITIES OVER WHICH WIRE COMMUNICATIONS ARE TO BE INTERCEPTED

7. FBI Special Agent (SA) Thomas G. Gates obtained information, pursuant to a Federal Grand Jury subpoena, from the Pacific Bell Telephone Company that telephone number (213) 278-3538 is listed to Charles Hairston, 412 South Arnaz Drive, Apartment 304, Los Angeles, California, that telephone number (213) 273-3906 is listed to EUGENE GIAQUINTO, 412 South Arnaz Drive, Apartment 304, Los Angeles, California.

III. PERSONS WHO MAY BE INTERCEPTED

8. This affidavit is made in support of an application for authorization to intercept wire communications over the telephones numbered (213) 278-3538, subscribed in the name of Charles Hairston, true name EUGENE GIAQUINTO, located at 412 South Arnaz Drive, Apartment 304, Los Angeles, California, and

Court filing: This document is a continuation of Thomas Gates' Affidavit (above) in which Gates requests authority for the wiretaps based on his belief that the wiretaps will reveal "the source of funding for the purchasing of narcotics/controlled substances and the allocation and use of the proceeds from its trafficking."

(213) 273-3906, subscribed to by EUGENE GIAQUINTO, located at 412 South Arnaz Drive, Apartment 304, Los Angeles, California. Based on the information contained in this affidavit, I believe that wire interceptions of the following persons and others yet unknown which are evidence of violations of Title 18, U.S.C. 371, 1343, 1503, and 1951, and Title 21, U.S.C. 841, 844 and 846 will be overheard if authorization for wire interceptions is granted:

(a) EUGENE FRANK GIAQUINTO, also known as (aka) Charles Hairston, 412 South Arnaz Drive, Apartment 304, Los Angeles, California. Residence telephones: (213) 278-3538 and (213)273-3906. Business telephone: (818) 777-4302. Date of birth (DOB): May 21, 1941. Employment: President of Home Entertainment, a division of MCA/Universal, Inc. GIAQUINTO is believed to be the nephew of EDWARD SCIANDRA (See Exhibit G, paragraphs 61, 65, 66, 72 and 75 for the basis of affiant's belief). GIAQUINTO is also a close associate of MICHAEL DEL GAIZO and many La Cosa Nostra (LCN) members and associates, hereinafter described.

(b) MARTIN BACOW, aka William Martin, is recognized as the "back door liaison Teamsters connection to the movie industry" (see Exhibit D, paragraph 53). DOB: August 1, 1921; address: 4135 Laurel Canyon, Apartment 5, Studio City, California; telephone: (818) 760-3897. Employment address: none. MARTIN BACOW has no known criminal record.

(c) ANGELO T. COMMITO, aka Angie. DOB: June 16, 1945. Address: One Fawn Ridge Road, Fairfax, California 94930, telephone (415) 456-2933. Employment address: Labor Health and Benefit Plans, Inc., 730 Franklin, Chicago, Illinois. Employment

- 8 -

Court filing: This document is a continuation of Thomas Gates' Affidavit (above) in which Gates provides some names from the movie industry to be wiretapped [intercepted] such as Eugene Giaquinto, Martin Bacow, and others in related pages.

MINUTES

MERIDIAN INTERNATIONAL LOGISTICS, INC.

An emergency meeting of the Board of Directors of Meridian International Logistics, Inc., a Nevada corporation, was held on Wednesday, May 25th, 1988 at 15270 Sutton Street, Suite 103, Sherman Oaks, California 91403.

Present, were Robert B. Nichols, Ellen M. Hopko and Gene F. Giaquinto. Contact by telephone was made with Donald R. Oliver in El Cajon, California, and with Barry A. Smith in Cupertino, California.

The purpose of the impromptu meeting was to accept the resignation of Eugene F. Giaquinto as a Director of the corporation, at the request of Robert Nichols. Mr. Giaquinto's resignation, (which he has stated will be written, signed, and received by the corporation by Friday, May 27th, 1988), was due to the current investigation of MIL, initiated by FBI Agent Thomas G. Gates (which MIL became aware of on March 1st, 1988 when he contacted Mr. Nichols by telephone and requested a meeting). Upon meeting with Agent Gates on March 8th, 1988, our legal counsel, Judge Mark Robinson, interpreted the line of questioning of Agent Gates as having a main focus on the relationship between Robert Nichols and MCA, Inc. (of which Mr. Giaquinto is an Officer). This concerned the Board at the time, but Mr. Giaquinto had stated he has never had any involvement whatsoever that would jeopardize MIL, or MCA (which is presently being investigated by the Organized Crime Task Force, as is widely publicized in the media). However, when MIL's Officer in Charge of Transfers, David Stanley, received a subpoena for documentation on stock issuance and transfers of MIL in his possession on May 16th, 1988, delivered by Agent Gates, Mr. Nichols felt that Mr. Giaquinto's involvement with MCA has brought about this investigation.

Therefore, due to Mr. Nichols concern, which Mr. Giaquinto understood and thus stated he would submit written resignation within two days; it was the unanimous decision of the Board to remove Mr. Giaquinto from the position of Director of MIL forthwith.

The Board has decided to leave this position of Director vacant at this time, with the intention of filling this vacancy in the near future with a qualified individual who would best serve the interest of the corporation.

There being no further business to come before the Board, the meeting was duly adjourned with a Waiver of Notice being attached to memorialize these minutes.

- 43 -

Pages 499-500: May 25, 1988: Minutes of Meridian International Logistic (MIL) Inc. – The minutes state that the purpose of the impromptu meeting was to accept the resignation of Eugene Giaquinto as a Director of the MIL corporation at the request of Robert Booth Nichols. The minutes read as follows (Excerpt): "Upon [RBN] meeting with [FBI] Agent Gates on March 8, 1988, our legal counsel, Judge Mark Robinson, interpreted the line of questioning of Agent Gates as having a main focus on the relationship between Robert Nichols and MCA Inc. of which Mr. Giaquinto is an officer.

MERIDIAN INTERNATIONAL LOGISTICS, INC.

WAIVER OF NOTICE

We, the undersigned, being all Directors of Meridian International Logistics, Inc., do hereby certify that we waive notice of the emergency meeting held on May 25th, 1988, at 15270 Sutton Street, Suite 103, Sherman Oaks, California 91403, and consent to and approve of the resolutions passed and occurring at said meeting.

Dated this 25th day of May, 1988.

Signed: ______________________
Robert B. Nichols

Signed: ______________________
Ellen M. Hopko

Signed: ______________________
Donald R. Oliver

Signed: ______________________
Barry A. Smith

HOME ENTERTAINMENT

Gene F. Giaquinto

President

May 31, 1988

To Whom It May Concern:

I hereby submit my resignation as a Director on the Board of Meridian International Logistics, Inc. effective immediately.

Sincerely,

Gene F. Giaquinto

GG/mc

May 31, 1988: Signed letter on MCA Home Entertainment stationary from Eugene Giaquinto, President of MCA Home Entertainment Division, to the Board in which he submits his resignation as a Director of the Board of MIL effective immediately.

Gene F. Giaquinto

September 9, 1988

Dear David:

This letter concerns my letter of resignation and your desire to have me keep the 10,000 shares of stock in Meridian International Logistics, Inc. Upon reflection of your generosity and in view of the short tenure I had with Meridian, I do not feel it is appropriate for me to retain the stock so generously issued to me by Robert Nichols as a gift.

Enclosed is Stock Certificate Number M6105, issued to me representing 10,000 shares of Meridian, properly transferred to you.

Sincerely,

Eugene F. Giaquinto

Enclosure

cc: Richard P. Crane, Jr.

Mr. David Stanley
1666 San Onofre Drive
Pacific Palisades, California 90272

PAGES 502-504: September 9, 1988: Letter from Eugene Giaquinto to David Stanley in Pacific Palisades in which he returns the 10,000 shares of stock in MIL issued to him by Robert Booth Nichols as a gift.

The following abbreviations, when used in the inscription on the face of this certificate, shall be construed as though they were written out in full according to applicable laws or regulations:

TEN COM --as tenants in common

TEN ENT as tenants by the entireties

JT TEN as joint tenants with right of survivorship and not as tenants in common

UNIF GIFT MIN ACT ...... Custodian ...... (Cust) (Minor) under Uniform Gifts to Minors Act ...... (State)

Additional abbreviations may also be used though not in the above list.

For Value received I *hereby sell assign and transfer unto*

PLEASE INSERT SOCIAL SECURITY OR OTHER IDENTIFYING NUMBER OF ASSIGNEE

ROBERT NICHOLS

15270 Sutton Street, Apartment 10, Sherman Oaks,

(NAME AND ADDRESS OF TRANSFEREE SHOULD BE PRINTED OR TYPEWRITTEN)

California 91403

Ten thousand (10,000) ****************** *Shares of the Capital Stock represented by the within Certificate and do hereby irrevocably constitute and appoint*

ROBERT NICHOLS *Attorney to transfer the said stock on the books of the within-named Corporation with full power of substitution in the premises.*

Dated July 8, 1988

SIGNATURE

INCORPORATED UNDER THE LAWS OF THE STATE OF NEVADA

M6105

10,000

MERIDIAN INTERNATIONAL LOGISTICS, INC.

SEE REVERSE FOR CERTAIN DEFINITIONS

This Certifies that --EUGENE F. G[illegible]QUINTO--

is the owner and holder of --TEN THOUSAND--

FULLY PAID AND NON-ASSESSABLE SHARES OF THE CAPITAL STOCK OF

Meridian International Logistics, Inc., transferable on the books of the Corporation by the holder hereof in person or by duly authorized attorney upon surrender of this Certificate properly endorsed. This Certificate is not valid until countersigned by the Transfer Agent and registered by the Registrar.

Witness the facsimile seal of the Corporation and the facsimile signatures of its duly authorized officers.

MERIDIAN INTERNATIONAL LOGISTICS, INC. INCORPORATED MARCH 27 1961 NEVADA

Dated: December 4, 1987

Secretary

President

Countersigned and Registered:
MERIDIAN INTERNATIONAL LOGISTICS, INC.
Transfer Agent and Registrar
By
Authorized Officer

U.S. Department of Justice

Federal Bureau of Investigation

Los Angeles, California

In Reply, Please Refer to
File No.

December 2, 1982

ROBERT BOOTH NICHOLS,
also known as
Robert Bert Nichols,
Robert Nelson,
Robert Nioon
ANTI-RACKETEERING

On March 16, 1978, information obtained through a confidential source alleged that Robert Booth Nichols, also known as Robert Bert Nichols, Robert Nelson, and Robert Nioon, was reportedly an internationally known launderer of money from both narcotics and organized crime activities. In addition, Nichols was well-known in the sale of armaments to various countries throughout the world. Nichols is alleged to be very influential in the sale of armaments to the Philippine Government, and has been tied closely with Ignacio Paz, Deputy Chief of Staff, Intelligence, Philippine Government. Nichols informed Los Angeles' confidential source that Nichols had assisted officials of the Philippine Government in removing large sums of money from the Philippines, thereafter, investing the money with Nichols, who was placing the money in Swiss bank accounts. Based upon the information developed by Los Angeles confidential source, Los Angeles initiated an Anti-Racketeering investigation.

Nichols is described as follows:

Name	Robert Booth Nichols
Aliases	Robert Bert Nichols, Robert Nelson, Robert Nioon
Sex	Male
Race	White
Date of Birth	March 6, 1943
Place of Birth	Loma Linda, California
Height	6'2"
Weight	200 pounds
Hair	Black
Eyes	Brown
Social Security Account Number	[redacted]

This document contains neither recommendations nor conclusions of the FBI. It is the property of the FBI and is loaned to your agency; it and its contents are not to be distributed outside your agency.

SEARCHED
INDEXED

Pages 505-507: December 2, 1982: FBI report emanating from FBI headquarters in Los Angeles which states that information was received from a confidential source on March 16, 1978 indicating that Robert Booth Nichols was reportedly an "internationally known launderer of money from both narcotics and organized crime activities." The report also states that Nichols was assisting officials of the Philippine government with removing large sums from the Philippines and placing the money in Swiss bank accounts. Page three of the report stated that "Nichols' name was associated with the illegal transportation of narcotics through the 'Golden Triangle,'" and Nichols should be considered "armed and dangerous." This report was obtained from Peter Zokosky, Nichols' friend and partner, who said he received it from Robert Booth Nichols.

ROBERT BOOTH NICHOLS

Marital Status	Married
Wife	Ellen Marie Nichols
Nee	Dolinshek
Also Known As	Ellen Marie Hopko
Residences	14055 Tahiti Way Apartment Number 115 Marina Del Rey, California
	P.O. Box 1501 Terme, Italy

Information developed by Los Angeles confidential source indicated that Nichols resides in the Los Angeles, California, area approximately three months out of the year, and conducts all of his business transactions from his apartment, 14055 Tahiti Way, Apartment Number 115, Marina Del Rey, California, where Nichols maintains several telephones and one telex, number 652483. The remainder of the year Nichols resides in a 3.5 million dollar villa, further described on a business card of Nichols' as Tenuta Monterosso, Casella, Postale N. 20, 15011 Acqui, Terme, Italy, telephone number 01442177.

Through investigation conducted by the Federal Bureau of Investigation (FBI), Los Angeles, the following profile was developed on Nichols:

Nichols is the son of a Los Angeles surgeon and ran away from home at the age of approximately seventeen. Nichols proceeded to Hawaii where he became involved with organized crime figures, one of which who is identified as Harold Tadao Okimoto. Okimoto, who does business in Hawaii under the corporate name of Musi-Vend of Hawaii, Incorporated, 743 Waiakamilo Road, Honolulu, Hawaii. Okimoto has numerous anti-racketeering references dating back to 1962, and in addition to his firm in Hawaii is alleged to own an electronics company in Japan. Okimoto has been a frequent traveler with Nichols and has been seen in Nichols company in Las Vegas, Nevada, Los Angeles, California, Manila, Philippines, and various cities throughout Europe. Nichols has applied through the state of California for numerous permits to possess and/or transport weapons. Nichols currently possesses a concealed weapons permit which was issued by the Sheriff for San Diego County, San Diego, California, Permit Number GP15764, which permit allows Nichols to carry a Walther semiautomatic nine millimeter pistol, Serial Number 188924S. Nichols is listed as an officer for Meridian Arms Company, 3540 Wilshire Boulevard, Suite 817, Los Angeles, California; and under that business name has applied for a permit to possess and/or transport machine guns. On December 19, 1977, Nichols was issued a permit to possess and/or transport machine guns in the state of California, under Permit Number 513 issued by the state of California-Department of Justice,

ROBERT BOOTH NICHOLS

Sacramento, California. The permit was issued to Nichols for the purpose of manufacturing and demonstrating one sub-machine gun prototype identified as a G-77. Nichols was limited to demonstrate the sub-machine gun to law enforcement agencies, other licensed dealers, and foreign countries approved by the United States State Department.

Nichols' employment record consists of the following:

Nichols was employed for the Preventer Security Center and Electronics Company in Hawaii, United States of America, between 1969 and 1971. Nichols terminated his employment with Preventer Security as he did not get along well with his immediate supervisor, Tony Cunimura. No employment was identified for Nichols between 1971 and 1973. In 1973 Nichols began a four year apprenticeship program with a Swiss company dealing in finance and representing various portfolios of mid-East companies. Nichols indicated that, with respect to that position, he dealt closely with a Ms. Cecelia Ottolenghi, who resides in Italy, telephone number 91444-2177. According to information developed by the Federal Bureau of Investigation, Los Angeles, Nichols claimed that his apprenticeship program was completed in 1977, at which time he became an active partner presenting financial portfolios all over the world. In 1975 Nichols became associated with Manila International Tours and Travel, 3540 Wilshire Boulevard, Suite 817, Los Angeles, California. During one inquiry by a state of California police agency, Nichols was asked what his position was at Manila International Tours and Travel; and Nichols turned to a fellow employee inquiring of that employee what Nichols did for the company, and the employee responded, "You are the president?"

Throughout the investigation conducted by the Federal Bureau of Investigation, Los Angeles, Nichols' name was associated with the illegal transportation of narcotics through the "Golden Triangle." Although Nichols uses a great number of code words, it appears that the code words relate to drug trafficking.

In view of the fact that Nichols has secured at least one gun permit which permits Nichols to carry a nine millimeter handgun, Nichols should be considered armed and dangerous.

FORMS.TEXT HAS 0 DOCUMENTS
CANNOT FIND THE FORM

INBOX.1 (#1922)

TO: HQ2 @ EMH2, SF @ EMH1, HN @ EMH1

FROM: LA @ EMH1

SUBJECT: 296/0042 PRIORITY

DATE: 24 OCT 87 05:01:06 GMT

CC:

TEXT:

VZCZCLA0042

PP HQ SF HN BERN TOKYO

DE LA #0042 2960004

ZNR UUUUU

P 230255Z OCT 87

FM LOS ANGELES [illegible] (OC-2) (P)

TO DIRECTOR PRIORITY

[illegible]

TO SAN FRANCISCO PRIORITY

ATTN: SA LOUIS GEORGE (ORA)

TO HONOLULU PRIORITY

[illegible]

TO LEGAT BERN PRIORITY

TO LEGAT TOKYO PRIORITY

BT

UNCLAS

ROBERT BOOTH NICHOLS, AKA; RICO, OO:LA

RE LA TELETYPE TO FBIHQ OCTOBER 20, 1987.

EUGENE FRANK GIAQUINTO DEPARTED LOS ANGELES ON OCTOBER [illegible],

1987 TO ATTEND MCA INTERNATIONAL MEETINGS IN HOLLAND AND ITALY.

GIAQUINTO IS SCHEDULED TO RETURN TO LOS ANGELES ON NOVEMBER 2,

SEARCHED ___ INDEXED ___
SERIALIZED ___ FILED ___
OCT 24 1987
FBI — SAN FRANCISCO

INDEXING
YES ___
NO ___
PAGE NOS. ___

Noel ___
Hopkins ___
Carlon ___

October 24, 1987: FBI teletype report (cover page) on Robert Booth Nichols.

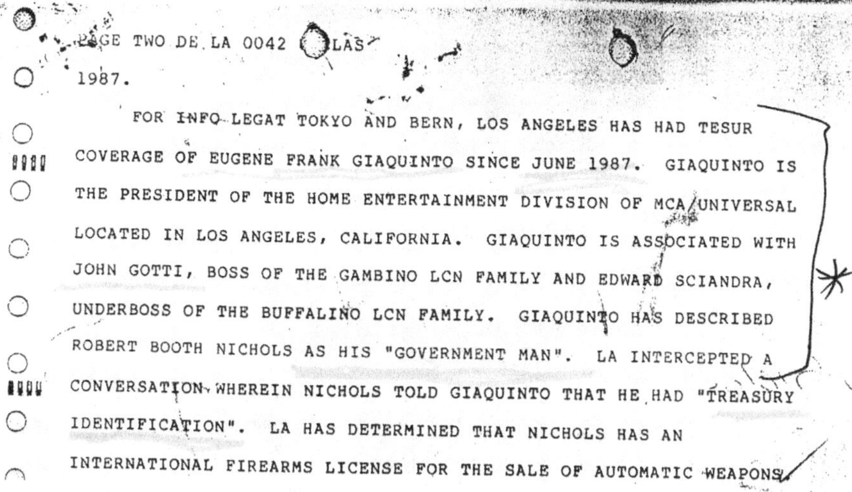
PAGE TWO DE LA 0042 LAS
1987.

FOR INFO LEGAT TOKYO AND BERN, LOS ANGELES HAS HAD TESUR COVERAGE OF EUGENE FRANK GIAQUINTO SINCE JUNE 1987. GIAQUINTO IS THE PRESIDENT OF THE HOME ENTERTAINMENT DIVISION OF MCA/UNIVERSAL LOCATED IN LOS ANGELES, CALIFORNIA. GIAQUINTO IS ASSOCIATED WITH JOHN GOTTI, BOSS OF THE GAMBINO LCN FAMILY AND EDWARD SCIANDRA, UNDERBOSS OF THE BUFFALINO LCN FAMILY. GIAQUINTO HAS DESCRIBED ROBERT BOOTH NICHOLS AS HIS "GOVERNMENT MAN". LA INTERCEPTED A CONVERSATION WHEREIN NICHOLS TOLD GIAQUINTO THAT HE HAD "TREASURY IDENTIFICATION". LA HAS DETERMINED THAT NICHOLS HAS AN INTERNATIONAL FIREARMS LICENSE FOR THE SALE OF AUTOMATIC WEAPONS.

October 24, 1987: Continuation of FBI teletype report (above) on Robert Booth Nichols. This page states that Eugene Giaquinto has been monitored since June 1987; that "Giaquinto is associated with John Gotti, boss of the Gambino LCN [La Cosa Nostra] family and Edward Sciandra, underboss of the Bufalino LCN family." The report states that "Giaquinto has described Robert Booth Nichols as his 'government man.'" The report further states that "Nichols told Giaquinto that he had 'Treasury Identification.'"

The Washington Post

FINAL

Inside: Health
Today's Contents on Page A2

TUESDAY, JUNE 6, 1995

Prices May Vary in Areas Outside Metropolitan Washington (See Box on A2)

25¢

Ex-Prosecutors Indicted in Cali Case

Former Top Justice Dept. Official Among 59 Drug Cartel Racketeering Defendants

ASSOCIATED PRESS

xplaining Cali drug cartel . attorney's office in Miami.

By Jim McGee
Washington Post Staff Writer

Three former federal prosecutors, including one who served as a top-ranking Justice Department official, were named in an indictment yesterday in Miami along with 56 others as part of a broad racketeering case against the Colombia-based Cali cartel, a group charged with running a $2 billion cocaine distribution enterprise since 1983.

The indictment incorporates evidence gathered over a decade about the cartel's activities in the United States, where it allegedly controls about 80 percent of the cocaine supply and is believed to have smuggled in at least 210,000 tons of the drug. It describes the cartel as a multinational corporate-style enterprise that has effectively used U.S. lawyers to protect its financial interests and help disrupt investigations here and in Colombia.

Among the defense attorneys indicted in the case is D.C. practitioner Michael Abbell, who once headed the Justice Department's Office of International Affairs. Abbell, who left the department in 1984, had participated in federal efforts to investigate one of the Cali cartel's cofounders, Jose Santacruz Londono. Donald Ferguson, who had been an assistant U.S. attorney in Miami, also was charged. Former assistant U.S. attorney Joel Rosenthal has pleaded guilty in the case to charges of money laundering.

Abbell and other lawyers face charges of money laundering, drug conspiracy and racketeering. The indictment charges them with obstructing justice, preparing false affidavits and conveying warnings to arrested cartel members that they should not cooperate with the government. It also details hundreds of thousands of dollars in legal fees and other payments to the cartel's lawyers.

The case against the lawyers is unusual because it calls into question the generally protected nature of at-

See CALI, A16, Col. 1

■ *Probe is a blow to attorney-client confidentiality, lawyers say.* *Page A16*

June 6, 1995: *Washington Post* front page article entitled, "Ex-Prosecutors Indicted in Cali Case," which reported that "Michael Abbell, who once headed the Justice Department's Office of International Affairs" was among the defense attorneys that were indicted in the Cali Cartel case. (Excerpt): "Abbell and other lawyers face charges of money laundering, drug conspiracy and racketeering ---"

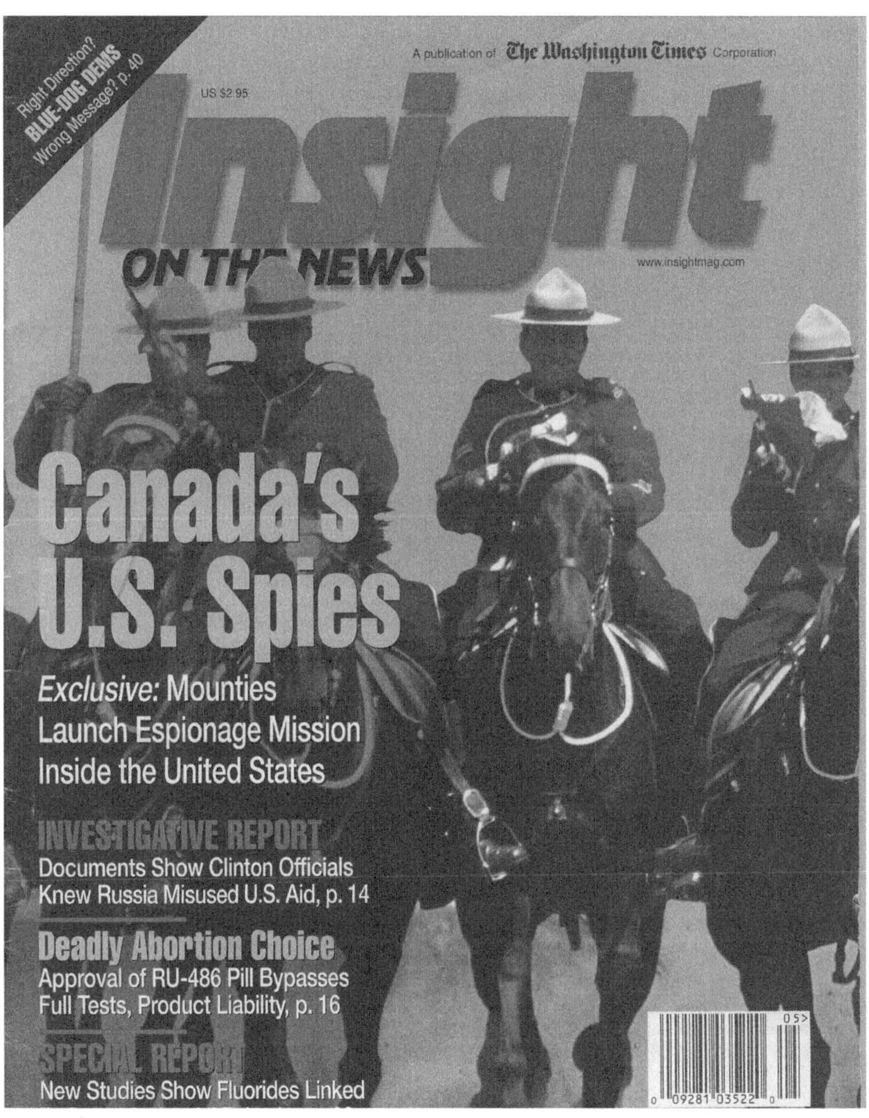
Right Direction?
BLUE-DOG DEMS
Wrong Message? p. 40
A publication of The Washington Times Corporation
US $2.95
Insight
ON THE NEWS
www.insightmag.com
Canada's U.S. Spies
Exclusive: Mounties Launch Espionage Mission Inside the United States
INVESTIGATIVE REPORT
Documents Show Clinton Officials Knew Russia Misused U.S. Aid, p. 14
Deadly Abortion Choice
Approval of RU-486 Pill Bypasses Full Tests, Product Liability, p. 16
SPECIAL REPORT
New Studies Show Fluorides Linked

January 29, 2001: Insight magazine publishes Part 1 of a four-part series about the secret RCMP investigation in the United States.

Royal Canadian Mounted Police | Gendarmerie royale du Canada

FICHE

FACSIMILE / MESSAGE TRANSMITTAL
ENVOI D'UN MESSAGE PAR TÉLÉCOPIEUR

Security Classification/Designation - Classification/désignation sécuritaire	
PROTECTED/PROTÉGÉ "B"	
Precedence - Priorité	Date 2000-02-08
Our File - Notre n° de dossier 1999-2313	Your File - Votre n° de dossier
Reference No. - N° de référence	

TO / À — Insp. Mike Lemay - RCMP Liaison Officer Washington

INFO. / RENS. — I.P.L.O. CID - Attn: Cpl. O'Neil — HQ Please send to ILPO

FROM / DE — Sgt. Mike Stanistreet - OIC Special Projects - ANSIS; Cst. Sean McDade - ANSIS

SENDER - EXPÉDITEUR		RECIPIENT - DESTINATAIRE	
Fax. No. - N° de télécopieur	Telephone No. - N° de téléphone	Fax. No. - N° de télécopieur	Telephone No. - N° de téléphone
(613) 993-4044	(613) 990-9134	(202) 682-1254	(202) 682-7723

COMMENTS / COMMENTAIRES — Total number of pages including this one / Nombre total de pages, y compris celle-ci ▶ 2

Request for consent for investigative travel to San Francisco, California from Ottawa, Ontario

Consent is herby requested for Cst. McDade to travel to San Francisco to meet with Hercules Police investigators to assist in the review of documents and information which may be pertinent to a homicide investigation currently being conducted by Hercules Police.

The investigator believes that the documents may also corroborate information related to an investigation being conducted in Canada by the RCMP, National Security Investigations Section, under Project "ABREVIATION".

Cst. McDade will provide assistance in the interpretation and understanding of the documents to be researched which are currently in the possession and control of a source known to the Hercules Police Department.

The arrangements for McDade to attend and review the documents has been agreed to by Commander Tom Muehleisen Hercules Police. In order to take advantage of the best economic means, a mutually acceptable itinerary has been arranged as follows;

Travel via US Air from Ottawa to San Francisco on 2000-02-18 (departure: 06:24 hrs, arrival: 11:51 hrs). Return to Ottawa on 2000-02-22 - San Francisco (departure: 12:20 hrs, arrival 22:50 hrs).

Could consent of U.S. authorities be obtained as expeditiously as possible in order to take advantage of the current extremely low cost travel available.

Travel of Cst. McDade authorized by C/Supt. Antoine Couture, OIC "A" Division, RCMP, Criminal Operations.

This message is intended for the use of the addressee. Disclosure of message content may breach one or more laws. If you have received this communication in error, notify the sender immediately by telephone.

Cette communication est exclusivement destinée à la personne à qui elle est adressée. La divulgation de son contenu peut constituer une infraction à une ou plusieurs lois. Si vous avez reçu cette communication par erreur, veuillez en aviser immédiatement l'expéditeur par téléphone.

Operator - Opérateur			Telephone No. - N° de téléphone	Daily No. - N° quotidien
TO BE DELIVERED BY / À LIVRER D'ICI LE	Date	Time - Heure	Authorizing Signature / Signature de l'approbateur	Date 2000-02-08
REPLY REQUIRED BY / RÉPONDRE D'ICI LE			C/Supt. Antoine Couture OIC "A" Div. CROPS	Time - Heure 15:17

2875 (1995-12) (FLO) — 1 — Canada

February 8, 2000: This is a classified document originating from the National Security Division of the Royal Canadian Mounted Police (RCMP) in Canada. This document authorizes RCMP investigator Sean McDade to visit Cheri Seymour in California to review (and copy) her documents. (Project Abbreviation = PROMIS).

Subj: **future phone conversation**
Date: 1/19/00 11:19:16 AM Pacific Standard Time
From: simorp@yahoo.com (dear hunter)
To: stormbird8@aol.com

Good afternoon. I'm looking to contact Carol (Cherie) regarding a matter that has surfaced in the past. If this email account is still active, please reply and I will in turn forward a Canadian phone number and explain my position and reason for request.

Regards...

Do You Yahoo!?
Talk to your friends online with Yahoo! Messenger.
http://im.yahoo.com

———— Headers ————
Return-Path: <simorp@yahoo.com>
Received: from rly-yd03.mx.aol.com (rly-yd03.mail.aol.com [172.18.150.3]) by air-yd02.mail.aol.com (v67.7) with ESMTP; Wed, 19 Jan 2000 14:19:16 1900
Received: from web3403.mail.yahoo.com (web3403.mail.yahoo.com [204.71.203.57]) by rly-yd03.mx.aol.com (v67.7) with ESMTP; Wed, 19 Jan 2000 14:19:03 1900
Message-ID: <20000119190248.18027.qmail@web3403.mail.yahoo.com>
Received: from [206.172.244.201] by web3403.mail.yahoo.com; Wed, 19 Jan 2000 11:02:48 PST
Date: Wed, 19 Jan 2000 11:02:48 -0800 (PST)
From: dear hunter <simorp@yahoo.com>
Subject: future phone conversation
To: stormbird8@aol.com
MIME-Version: 1.0
Content-Type: text/plain; charset=us-ascii

Wednesday, September 20, 2000 America Online: Stormbird8 Page: 1

January 19, 2000: This is the first e-mail sent from Sean McDade to Cheri Seymour, pseudonym of Carol Marshall on *The Last Circle* Internet version. Sean identified himself as Dear Hunter using simorp@yahoo.com which is PROMIS spelled backward.

Subj: **Re: Response to: Future phone conversation**
Date: 1/22/00 3:36:15 AM Pacific Standard Time
From: simorp@yahoo.com (dear hunter)
To: Stormbird8@aol.com
CC: simorp@yahoo.com

Thanks Carol.

Sean McDade - Investigator with the National Security
Investigation Section of the R.C.M.P. I'm located in
Ottawa, Ont. (613) 990-9134 - bs (613) 598-9434 -
pg
Reference past matters in which Micheal Riconosuito
may have been involved with, in which there are
allegations of Canadian involvement (knowing or
unknowingly).
I would just like to discuss any knowledge you may
have to assist with my investigation.
Message sent Saturday 0630 EST.
I will be working Monday-Friday and can be reached at
any time during those days.

Regards......Sean (I would appreciate Carol if any
contact we have can be kept confidential for time
being)

— Stormbird8@aol.com wrote:
>
>
> Friday eve.
>
> TO: Dear Hunter
>
> Give my regards to Sue Todd. Please send your phone
> number and I'll call
> you. I currently live in Southern California and
> will meet with you at your
> convenience. What is your name and what are you
> investigating? What
> information do you seek from me?
>
> Best,
> Stormy
> (Carol)
>

> In a message dated 1/21/00 8:25:47 AM Pacific
> Standard Time, simorp@yahoo.com
> writes:
>
> << Subj: Re: Response to: Future phone
> conversation
> Date: 1/21/00 8:25:47 AM Pacific Standard Time
> From: simorp@yahoo.com (dear hunter)
> To: Stormbird8@aol.com
>
> Thank you for replying......
>

Wednesday, September 20, 2000 America Online: Stor

January 22, 2000: E-mail response from Cheri Seymour and response back from Sean McDade identifying himself as "investigator with the National Security Investigations Section of RCMP," and requesting to discuss author's knowledge to assist with his investigation.

Ottawa-Carleton
Regional Police Service

Service de police régional
d'Ottawa-Carleton

Sean R. McDade
Investigator
National Security Investigation Section
R.C.M.P. - Ottawa
713-155 McArthur Avenue
Vanier, Ontario K1A 0R2

Office: (613) 990-9134
Pager: (613) 598-9434
Fax: (613) 993-4044

SUE TODD
Police Detective

Hercules Police Department
111 Civic Drive
Hercules, CA 94547
Phone: (510) 799-8260
Private: (510) 799-8269
Fax: (510) 799-8281

February 19, 2000: These business cards were presented to author Cheri Seymour at her home by RCMP investigator Sean McDade and Detective Sue Todd from Hercules Police Department.

Case 1:08-cv-06036-CM Document 32-2 Filed 12/23/2008 Page 1 of 5

26 BROADWAY
SUITE 2400
NEW YORK, NY 10004-1840
(212) 480-3500 TELEPHONE
(212) 480-9557 FACSIMILE
WWW.BAINTONLAW.COM

October 2, 2008

J. JOSEPH BAINTON
(212) 480-2529
bainton@baintonlaw.com

BY HAND

Honorable Colleen McMahon
Daniel Patrick Moynihan
United States Courthouse
500 Pearl St., Room 640
New York, NY 10007

Re: Petition for Relief of Forfeiture
U.S. v. Israel III, 05 Cr. 1039 (CM);
Bayou Management LLC v. Robert B. Nichols, et al.
08 Civ. 6036 (CM)

Dear Judge McMahon:

We are the attorneys for Robert and Ellen Nichols. We write to request a conference with the Court for the purpose of discussing adjusting the Scheduling Order entered in these consolidated proceedings in light of the following developments. (A copy of that order is enclosed.)

Your Honor will likely recall that at the initial conference I showed you a photograph of a box bearing the seal of the United States Federal Reserve and the serial number SC 3040-20 that Mr. Israel paid Mr. Nichols $10 Million to locate. I told you that Mr. Nichols never opened the box and that he delivered it to Mr. Israel in a safety deposit facility in London. I have since learned that the name of that facility is the London Safe Deposit Company.

While the Government reports that it is weeks away from producing all of the documents we have requested, their initial production contained what purports to be obligations of the United States Federal Reserve in the aggregate sum of $250 Billion secured by the deposit in the Atlanta Federal Reserve of 2,500 metric tons of gold. We enclose documents bearing Bates Nos. NICHOLS-USA 000072 through 000082. All of these documents bear the same serial number as appears in the photograph of the box Mr. Nichols obtained for Mr. Israel.

STAMFORD, CONNECTICUT ♦ CENTRAL ISLIP, NEW YORK ♦ NEWARK, NEW JERSEY

PAGES 516-517: December 23, 2008: Court filing of Petition for Relief of Forfeiture in Bayou Management verses Robert Booth Nichols, et al. This October 2, 2008 letter to Judge Colleen McMahon provides details relative to a $250 Billion treasury note secured by 2,500 metric tons of gold at the Atlanta Federal Reserve. Samuel Israel of Bayou allegedly paid RBN $10 million to locate the treasury note and place it in a box at the London Safe Deposit Company in London, England. However, the FBI seized the box and Samuel Israel sued RBN for the return of his $10 million.

Hon. Colleen McMahon
October 2, 2008
Page 2

The Government has also stated in response to Interrogatory No. 14 that in or about July 2008 -- roughly three months after commencement of this proceeding -- the FBI, with the assistance of the City of London Police, retrieved these documents from the London Safe Deposit Company in London, England. The Government has not advised us if they were in the box that Mr. Nichols handed to Mr. Israel in this very same facility or if the Government has the box of which we showed you pictures.

The Government has not provided us with any other information, including what, if anything, it was told about these documents and their location by Sam Israel. It does seem curious that given the length of time that we understand Mr. Israel has been cooperating with the Government that the Government would wait until only a few months ago to reduce to possession what purports to be a $250 Billion obligation.

On September 12, 2008, we served the enclosed Rule 30(b)(6) Notice in an attempt to quickly obtain clarification on this $250 Billion issue. The Government contends that the notice is overbroad, burdensome and oppressive. In making this assertion, the Government has yet to state plainly whether these instruments are authentic. If they are not authentic, then how burdensome could it be to produce a witness to say: "Sam told us he had this stuff and we finally got around to collecting it last summer."

On the other hand, if these instruments are authentic, then this case -- indeed the entire Bayou bankruptcy case -- changes quite dramatically. We would like to get to the bottom of this issue quickly.

The Government's delay in producing documents has forced the parties to defer the commencement of depositions. So even if Your Honor can quickly break the logjam on the $250 Billion issue, it nonetheless appears some adjustment to the schedule is necessary.

With best regards, I am,

Respectfully yours,

J. Joseph Bainton

Enclosures

cc: Sharon Cohen Levin, Esq. (via first-class mail w/o enclosures)
Barry A. Bohrer, Esq. (via first-class mail w/o enclosures)
Gary J. Mennitt, Esq. (via first-class mail w/o enclosures)

Case 1:08-cv-06036-CM Document 1-8 Filed 07/02/2008 Page 15 of 19

19. Mr. Nichols believes that the services that he provided to Israel involved matters of national interest. Mr. Nichols was advised by Israel and others that Israel's pursuit of the Project was known to and had been sanctioned by the Government.

20. Confirmation of the Government sanction and the general legitimacy of the Project was communicated to Mr. Nichols by Mr. John P. Ellis, who at the time was affiliated with GH Venture Partners of New York, New York, a company that enjoyed (and enjoys) an honorable reputation.

21. Mr. Ellis is the first cousin of President George W. Bush and his material involvement with President Bush's 2004 political campaign (particularly in Florida) was reported in the general press.

22. It was therefore reasonable for Mr. Nichols to rely upon the statements made to him by Mr. Ellis about the legitimacy of both the Project and Israel.

23. Mr. Nichols only became aware of the criminal allegations against Israel after this action became public in or about September 2005, which was long after all of the events giving rise to this Petition had occurred.

24. Accordingly, the interest of Petitioners in the Account is prior, paramount, and superior to any interest of any other party

PAGES 518-519: JULY 2, 2008: This court filing, page 15 of 19, states that Robert Booth Nichols (RBN) was advised by Samuel Israel and others that Israel's pursuit of the "project"(above) was sanctioned by the U.S. government, and confirmation of the legitimacy of the "project" was communicated to RBN by Mr. John P. Ellis who is the first cousin of President George W. Bush.

WHEREFORE, Petitioners Robert B. Nichols and Ellen M. Nichols respectfully demand that this Court:

1. Enter a judgment for restitution to the full extent of their interest in the Account;

2. Declare that their interest in the property is prior, paramount, and superior to any interest of any other party; and

3. Render such other, further or different relief as it may deem just and proper.

Dated: New York, New York
April 17, 2008

BAINTON MCCARTHY LLC

By: ______________________
J. Joseph Bainton (JB-5934)

Attorneys for Petitioners
Robert B. Nichols and Ellen M. Nichols
26 Broadway, Suite 2400
New York, NY 10004-1840
(212) 480-3500
(212) 480-9557 (facsimile)

TO: Michael J. Garcia, Esq.
United States Attorney
Southern District of New York
One Saint Andrews Plaza
New York, New York 10007
Attn: Sharon Cohen Levin, Esq.
Chief, Asset Forfeiture Unit

-- and --

Barry A. Bohrer, Esq.
Morvillo, Abramowitz, Grand, Iason,
Anello & Bohrer, P.C.
565 Fifth Avenue
New York, New York 10017
Attorneys for Defendant Samuel Israel III

01/20/2009 17:40 FAX 12129079700 002/004

Suite 1900
250 Park Avenue
New York, New York 10177
Tel: 212 907-9700
Fax: 212 907-9800
www.sgrlaw.com

MEMO ENDORSED

SMITH, GAMBRELL & RUSSELL, LLP
Attorneys at Law

J. Joseph Bainton
Direct Tel: 212-907-9702
Direct Fax: 212-907-9802
jbainton@sgrlaw.com

USDS SDNY
DOCUMENT
ELECTRONICALLY FILED
DOC #:
DATE FILED: 1/21/09

January 20, 2009

1/21/09 all deadlines extended 45 days all pending motions to be held in abeyance. CM

VIA FACSIMILE

Hon. Colleen McMahon
United States District Judge
Daniel Patrick Moynihan
United States Courthouse
500 Pearl St., Room 640
New York, NY 10007-1312

Re: Petition for Relief of Forfeiture, U.S. v. Israel III, 05-Cr-1039 (CM);
Bayou Management, LLC. v. Nichols, et ano., 08-Civ-6036 (CM)

Dear Judge McMahon:

We are the attorneys for Robert B. Nichols and his wife, Ellen M. Nichols (collectively the "Nichols").

We write to advise the Court that the Government, Bayou Management and the Nichols have reached an agreement in principle to compromise all matters pending before Your Honor. The only open issue is the Nichols' ability to fund the compromise.

We write pursuant to Your Honor's Individual Practice Rule 1, E, to request that all existing deadlines be enlarged by 45 days in order to afford the Nichols an opportunity to raise the sum of money that will resolve all matters before Your Honor. While the Nichols are not presently capable of funding the compromise, they believe in good faith that within 45 days they will be able to raise the necessary funds.

Atlanta, Georgia | Frankfurt, Germany | Jacksonville, Florida | New York, New York | Washington, D.C.

PAGES 520-521: January 21, 2009: Court filing - Attorney for Robert Booth Nichols, et al, requests an extension of the deadline to pay Bayou Management a sum of money stipulated in a settlement agreement reached by both parties outside the court. The Judge gave RBN, et al, a 45-day extension and placed all pending motions in abeyance until the next deadline.

Hon. Colleen McMahon
Page 2

At the end of this 45 day period (if not hopefully sooner) the parties will present the Court with either (a) a stipulation of dismissal or (b) a pre-trial order that complies in all respects with Your Honor's Individual Practice Rule 3, D.

With best regards, I am,

Respectfully yours,

J. Joseph Bainton

cc: All Counsel (via e-mail)

USDS SDNY
DOCUMENT
ELECTRONICALLY FILED
DOC #: ___
DATE FILED: 5/4/09

UNITED STATES DISTRICT COURT
SOUTHERN DISTRICT OF NEW YORK

-- X

UNITED STATES OF AMERICA : 05 Cr. 1039 (CM)

-against-

SAMUEL ISRAEL III,

Defendant.

-- X

ROBERT B. NICHOLS and
ELLEN M. NICHOLS,

Petitioners.

-- X

BAYOU MANAGEMENT, LLC,

Plaintiff, : 08 Civ. 6036 (CM)

-against-

ROBERT B. NICHOLS, ELLEN M. NICHOLS,
SAMUEL ISRAEL III, and JOHN DOES 1-5,

Defendants.

-- X

STIPULATION AND ORDER OF SETTLEMENT AND EXTINGUISHMENT OF CLAIM

WHEREAS, on or about July 8, 2004, Samuel Israel III ("Israel") caused $120 million (the "$120 Million") to be transferred from Bayou Management, LLC ("Bayou Management") to a bank account in Israel's name at Deutsche Postbank in Germany (the "Israel Postbank Account");

WHEREAS, on or about July 19, 2004, Israel transferred $10 million of the $120 Million from the Israel Postbank Account to Robert B. Nichols ("RBN") and Ellen M. Nichols ("EMN," and together with RBN, the "Nichols"), which transfer shall be referred to herein as "the Nichols Transfer";

WHEREAS, on May 30, 2006, Bayou Management, Bayou Group, LLC, Bayou Advisors, LLC, Bayou Equities, LLC, Bayou Fund, LLC, Bayou Superfund, LLC, Bayou No Leverage Fund, LLC, Bayou Affiliates Fund, LLC, and Bayou Accredited Fund, LLC (collectively, the "Debtors") filed separate voluntary petitions for relief under Chapter 11 of the

PAGES 522-523: May 4, 2009: Court filing – Stipulation and Order of Settlement and Extinguishment of Claim. This document states that on March 5, 2009, the attorneys for Robert Booth Nichols, et al, informed the Government and Bayou Management that "RBN died on February 15, 2009" before the settlement deadline occurred. The Nichols' counsel provided a death certificate stating that Robert Booth Nichols died in Geneva, Switzerland on February 15, 2009.

WHEREAS, on March 5, 2009, counsel for the Nichols informed the Government and Bayou Management that RBN died on February 15, 2009;

WHEREAS on March 8, 2009, counsel for the Nichols provided the Government and Bayou Management with a death certificate stating that "Robert Booth Nichols" died in Geneva Switzerland on February 15, 2009;

WHEREAS RBN's asserted interest in the forfeited assets at issue in the above captioned criminal ancillary proceeding, which is disputed by the Government, cannot legally be transferred to any estate beneficiary because such transfer would neither convey a right, title or interest in the property that vested before the commission of the acts which gave rise to the forfeiture of the property, *see* 21 U.S.C. § 853(n)(6)(A), nor be a bona fide purchase for value, *see* 21 U.S.C. § 853(n)(6)(B);

WHEREAS, EMN, admitting no wrongdoing, has agreed to settle these matters, upon the terms and conditions set forth herein;

April 13, 1982

Mr. Jim Hughes
Cabazon Security Corp.
83-180 Requa Ave., #9
Indio, CA 92201

Dear Jim:

Michael Riconosciuto and his wife Phyllis want to retain your professional services along with those of Mr. Steven Bates for the period of April 14, 15 and 16, 1982, to fly to Fresno, California to help Michael Riconosciuto get his affairs in order and to protect Michael during this period until he goes into protective custody with the F.B.I. at the Oakland office.

Michael Riconosciuto is to meet with special agent Robert Barnes. After Mr. Barnes has assumed the protection for Mr. Riconosciuto you and Mr. Bates can return to Palm Springs.

The agreed upon flat fee for rendering this service shall be $1,300.00 including air fare, hotel costs and meals. Incidentals will be paid in addition to the $1,300.00 flat fee.

Sincerely,

Phyllis Riconosciuto

Phyllis Riconosciuto

Agreed and accepted by

James Hughes

James Hughes

April 13, 1982: Letter to Jimmy Hughes, Cabazon Security Corporation, from Phyllis Riconosciuto hiring Hughes to body-guard her husband, Michael Riconosciuto, until MR could be taken into protective custody with FBI Special Agent Robert Barnes from the Oakland, California FBI office.

APR 03 '91 16:05 DESERT SUN PUBLISHING P02

CABAZON ARMS

WACKENHUT SERVICES INCORPORATED
3280 PONCE DE LEON BLVD.
CORAL GABLES, FLORIDA 33134
(305) 445-1481

A CSC/WSI JOINT VENTURE

CABAZON SECURITY CORPORATION
83-180 REQUA AVENUE
SUITE #9, INDIO, CALIFORNIA 92201
(714) 342-5155

9

April 4, 1983

TO: Army Discharge Review Board

FROM: 1. John Paul Nichols, Project Manager
2. Cabazon Band of Mission Indians
3. Cabazon Indian Casino
4. Bingo Palace, Inc.
5. Cabazon Security/ WSI Joint Venture

Mr. James Hughes Jr. has been in our employment for over three years. He has been instrumental in developing our reservation security force as well as providing superior training in law enforcement techniques, safety and sundries to our employees.

He was a key person in developing, organizing and security financing for a successful trap and skeet range on the Cabazon Indian Reservation.

At all times Mr. Hughes has shown himself to be a man of superior qualities and unusual maturity for someone his age.

Mr. Hughes is becoming more and more involved in our joint venture with Wackenhut Services and will become involved in matters where a security clearance is necessary involving government contracts. His military record will have a direct bearing on whether he will qualify for these security clearances.

Your decision will affect his personal life directly and our Band's enterprises by perhaps not allowing us to use a trusted employee. Please consider Mr. Hughes request. He has always shown the highest quality character in any duty performed for us.

Thank you.

Sincerely yours,

John Paul Nichols
Project Manager

Arthur Welmas
Tribal Chairman

April 4, 1983: Letter from John Paul Nichols, Cabazon Arms, to the Army Discharge Board outlining Hughes' exemplary employment record and attempting to obtain security clearances for Hughes to work in the Cabazon/Wackenhut Joint Venture.

(619) 342-5000
(619) 342-1530

May 17, 1984

To: Gary Packham
Wayne Reeder

From: John-Paul Nichols

Subject: Credibility

Wayne, the last time we spoke you stated Jim Hughes Jr. would be gone las weekend (May 12, 1984 to May 14, 1984) and that he was going to open a security business somewhere.

He is obviously still there as of today May 17, 1984 as his car is still there and he was seen by Arthur Welmas coming out of his apartment.

We have been told every week for a month that Jim Hughes Jr. would be leaving the property the "next" weekend and that he was terminated. This has not happened.

Arthur Welmas' comment to me was that patience lasts only so long as we are honestly dealt with. How can I put the Board of Directors of Cabazon Bingo, Inc. off if I have no answers for them?

You made an agreement with them relative to Jim Hughes Jr., I suggest that you stick to your deal with the officers of Cabazon Bingo, Inc.

Sincerely,

John-Paul Nichols,
General Manager

cc: Cabazon Bingo, Inc. Board of Directors
Dr. John Philip Nichols
Mark Nichols
Philip Nichols

JPN/dn

EXHIBIT B

May 17, 1984: Letter from John Paul Nichols, General Manager of Cabazon Casino, to Wayne Reeder and Gary Packham strongly urging Reeder to "stick to his deal" and terminate Hughes' employment as security chief at Reeder's Indian Palms Country Club.

A ATTORNEY OR UNREPRESENTED PARTY (NAME AND ADDRESS) TELEPHONE NO

SUZANNE L. HARRIS, ESQ. (818) 2431292
SUZANNE L. HARRIS, A PROFESSIONAL CORP.
4121 Wilshire Boulevard, Suite 412
Los Angeles, California

ATTORNEY FOR (NAME)

FOR COURT USE ONLY

#45303

B SUPERIOR COURT OF CALIFORNIA, COUNTY OF RIVERSIDE

46-634 Highwau 111
Indio, CA 92202

C PLAINTIFF WAYNE REEDER

D DEFENDANT JAMES HUGHES

E RESPONSE TO PETITION FOR INJUNCTION PROHIBITING HARASSMENT

CASE NUMBER INDIO 41885

1. a. [X] Defendant denies doing all of the acts alleged in paragraph 4 of the Petition (See declarations)
b [ ] Defendant denies doing some of the acts alleged in paragraph 4 of the Petition (Specify the acts that you den doing).

2. [ ] Defendant has done some or all of the acts alleged, but the actions are justified or excused for the following reasons
a. [X] Defendant's acts served a legitimate purpose (Give details)

See declarations, no threats were made. Defendant attempted to discu a debt which was owed to him by the plaintiff on Sept, 13, 1984

b. [ ] Defendant's acts were constitutionally protected (Give details).

c [ ] Other (Give details)

3 a. [X] Plaintiff has not suffered substantial emotional distress (Explain)

Defendant did not threaten the plaintiff. Plaintiff could not have and did not suffer any emotional distress. (see declarations.)

b [X] A reasonable person in Plaintiff's position would not have suffered substantial emotional distress (Explain)

Defendant did not threaten the plaintiff. A discussion was had concerning plaintiff's debt to the defendant. All remarls were clearly understood to threaten nothing - except possibly legal actic

4 [X] Plaintiff's distress is not the result of Defendant's alleged acts (Explain).

Plaintiff believes himself to be under a death threat from another person and has so stated on a number of occasions to witnesses. (See declarations attached hereto.)

5 [ ] Defendant's acts, if any, did not amount to a course of conduct knowingly and wilfully directed against Plai (Explain)

6. [X] Defendant has other defenses (Give details).

Defendant made a reasonable and legitimate effort to resolve a business dispute in the presence of a witness. (See declarations.)

7. [X] Defendant consents to entry of the following order(s) (Set forth in detail).

Defendant requests that no order issue because no order will alter or deter the conduct of the person who is threatneing both plainti and defendant.

READ "INSTRUCTIONS FOR LAWSUITS TO PROHIBIT HARASSMENT" BEFORE FILLING OUT THIS FORM. 17

(Continued on Reverse)

Form Approved by the Judicial Council of California Effective January 1 1979

RESPONSE TO PETITION FOR INJUNCTION PROHIBITING HARASSMENT

76R445M 4.84
RD035

CCP

1984: Court filing – Response to Petition for Injunction Prohibiting Harassment. This is the cover page for Jimmy Hughes' declaration that he did not issue a death threat against Wayne Reeder.

DECLARATION OF JAMES G. HUGHES, JR.

I, JAMES G. HUGHES, Jr., declare and state as follows:

I am the defendant in the within action for injunctive relief filed by the plaintiff Wayne Reeder. (WAYNE REEDER vs. JAMES HUGHES, Superior Court of the State of California, County of Riverside, civil action no: Indio 41885.) In order for this court to understand that I have been the victim of harassment, threats, and intimidation, and not the perpetrator or initiator of such activity, and that the probable purpose of the plaintiff's petition for injunctive relief is to discredit and destroy my prospective testimony in criminal cases currently under investigati which are to be brought against a business associate of the plaintiff's (and quite probably against the plaintiff himself should sufficient data be generated in the future to establish his knowing participation in these criminal activities), it is necessary that I provide this court with some background information concerning my association with the plaintiff, Wayne Reeder, and his business associate John Philip Nichols, Ph.D., as that association developed over the past several years.

MY EMPLOYMENT BY CABAZON INDIAN CASINO AND BINGO PALACE, INC.:

I am a former employee of Cabazon Indian Casino and Bingo Palace, Inc. I was concurrently employed by these two entities from approximately February of 1980 through February of 1984. These two entities run and maintain the Cabazon Indian Casino and Bingo Palace (which are gambling enterprises operated on the Cabazon Indian Reservation under the principal direction of John Philip Nichols, Ph.D. and his son John-Paul Nichols.

-1-

PAGES 528-534: September 25, 1984: Court filing – Declaration of James G. Hughes, Jr.. Jimmy Hughes alleges in this Declaration that Dr. John Phillip Nichols, Cabazon Administrator, told him that the gambling enterprises on the reservation were fronts, in part, for U.S. government sanctioned covert military activities and arms shipments to Central and South America. Hughes subsequently concluded that Dr. Nichols was involved in various criminal activities, including murder, so he left the reservation and went to work for Wayne Reeder. He received death threats and complained to the District Attorney's office.

During the period of my employment by these two entities, Dr. John Philip Nichols alleged that they were, in-part, fronts for United States government sanctioned covert military activities and arms shipments to Central and South America. [I attach thereto and incorporate herein by reference Exhibit A which is a true and correct copy of some 'routine' correspondence concerning these alleged covert activities which was shown to me by Dr. Nichols at or near the date stated (i.e., September 1, 1981) which I assume was provided to me in order to gain my trust and confidence and which I can state was prepared by Dr. Nichols at the Cabazon Reservation during the course of my employment there.] Over time I became aware of a series of activities by Dr. John Philip Nichols and other members of his family (who are also employed there) which made me realize that their activities were criminal (including issuing contracts to commit murder) and were not governmental in nature as Dr. Nichols had alleged (or at minimum, Dr. Nichols was perverting quasi-governmental activities entrusted to him for his own profit and in disregard of the consequences to the security of the United States which ensued from his actions.)

When I reached a full realization of what Dr. Nichols was really doing and why, I severed my connection with them (i.e., with the Cabazon Indian Casino and Bingo Palace, Inc.) At that time, I accepted employment from Wayne Reeder, who through his corporation Bingo Pavilion, Inc. had made a $ 230,000.00 investment in the gambling enterprise.

Mr. Reeder made a variety of promises to me as an inducement to my employment with him (including: a promise to set me up in my own security business and to invest at least $ 15,000.00 in a new security company to be owned jointly by Mr. Reeder and myself, five per cent of his share of Bingo Pavillion, Inc., a promise of security contracts for my new company with the Indian Palms Country Club of which Mr. Reeder is an owner, a promise to relocate myself and my new business in the future at one of the other facilities which he owned in another part of the U.S. or in any othe location of my own choosing at the termination of my first project for him in Indio.) Mr. Reeder told me that his company Bingo Pavillione Inc. had made an approximately $ 230,000.00 investment in the gambling enterprise on the reservation and that he did not feel that he was being repaid properly and that he thought that Dr. Nichols and family, were 'skimming' profits off the top of the gambling enterprise in order to avoid taxes and avoid making the contracted for payments to Bingo Pavillion, Inc.

Mr. Reeder stated that he wanted me to return to the casino and bingo palace as a representative of Bingo Pavillion, Inc. in order to monitor the gross receipts of the gambling operations in order to determine why his corporation's (Bingo Pavillion) inves ment and agreed to per centage of gross receipts had not been paid. [Unknown to me at that time, Nichols and Reeder had made somekind of deal through which Reeder was to get rid of me so that I could not make Nichols' illegal activities known. See Exhibit B which is attached hereto and incorporated herein by reference which Mr. Reeder turned over to me reluctantly and partly by accident when I appeared at his office and demanded documentary data to assi in my co-operation with law enforcement authorities [see infra.]

I agreed to work for Mr. Reeder, in part, because I belie ved his story and I had sympathy with his plight since I, too, had gradually come to the realization that something criminal in nature was going on at the gambling enterprise.

I remained in Reeder's employ from February of 1984 to about June or July 1984. Reeder severed our relationship claiming that my presence was unacceptable to Nichols but reaffirming his promise to place me in a new security company of my own (and reaffirming his other promises as well. See lines 26 -28, page 2 and lines 1-9, page 3, infra.)

CONTACTS WITH LAW ENFORCEMENT AGENCIES:

During my employment with Reeder, I initiated a series of contacts with various law enforcement agencies to report to them what I knew concerning Nichols' illegal activities, including a contract to commit murder.

The day after I first went to the Riverside District Attorney's Office (approximate date April 11, 1984) I received a death threat in the form of a gruesome photograph attached to the windshield of my car on the day after my meeting with the D.A.'s office. [See Exhibit C which is attached hereto and incorporated herein by reference, which is a true and correct copy of the photograph which I found attached to my car's windshield in an envelope.]

On or about April 15, 1984, I was told that there was a contract on my life by a friend. Shortly thereafter Peter Zokosky received a phone call to the same effect. I also discovered that a $ 30,000.00 withdrawal had been made by John-Paul Nichols from the Bingo Palace's account by check payable to cash at this same time. [Note: since cash withdrawals are the means by which hits are paid for (as I learned from Dr. Nichols) I had every reason to believe that an attempt to kill me was going to be made.

Since that time, the Department of Justice of the State of California has offered me participation in their witness protection program due to these threats and my co-operation with them.

I assumed and Wayne Reeder assumed too (or at least told me that he assumed) that he (Reeder) was also targeted with a contract to kill by Nichols in order to keep him (Reeder) from securing repayment of Bingo Pavillion's loan and its agreed to share of the profits of the gambling enterprise. However, unknown to me at that time, Reeder appears to also be involved in criminal activities.

MEETING OF SEPTEMBER 13, 1984 AMONG WAYNE REEDER, PETER ZOKOSKY, AND MYSELF:

On September 13, 1984 I had a meeting with Wayne Reeder and Peter Zokosky (which I had requested months before) to discuss my business arrangement with Mr. Reeder (see pages 2 and 3, *supra*.) and his future fulfillment of his promises to me. (Peter Zokosky attended this meeting at Wayne Reeder's request.)

Before I started talking, Peter Zokosky and Wayne Reeder discussed the fact that they both thought that the $ 30,000.00 bank withdrawal (see page 4, lines 24-28) was to pay for contracts to kill against Wayne Reeder and myself.

I then said:

> " You've made me promises. But in looking at these papers [Referring to Exhibit B], I see that you are making deals with my life. "

Reeder said something. I do not recall his exact words, but he said something evasive.

I said:

" You've made promises."

Reeder said:

" We've looked at a couple of things [proposed plans for the security company] but things didn't look feasible."

I said:

" You've made deals behind my back. You care more about you fucking money than you do about people's lives. Don't you realize we're both in the same fucking boat. You know there are contracts on both of us. If I die so will you. "

I left and waited for Peter Zokosky outside. It was clear in the context of our discussions (see page 5, lines 5-11) that I was not threatening Mr. Reeder's life. On the contrary, I was referring to the fact that Nichols had evidently placed contract on both of us.

REQUEST FOR RELIEF AND ANALYSIS OF THE UNDERLYING MOTIVATION BEHIND THIS COMPLAINT FOR INJUNCTIVE RELIEF:

I assume that this injunctive relief proceeding which is not founded on fact or any reasonable interpretation of fact, has arisen for the following reasons:

1) To discredit my testimony in advance before I actually testify against Nichols in a court of law on charges against him of conspiracy to commit murder;

2) That Reeder has made up with Nichols in an effort to protect his investment (and/or has initiated this proceeding in orde

to avoid later disclosure of his own criminal activities and probable knowledge of and collusion with Nichols' criminal activities.)

At no time have I ever threatened Mr. Reeder or intended to injure him in any manner. I am considering filing suit against Mr. Reeder for breach of contract but plan no other action against him. I do not live in the jurisdiction at this time and I have no intention of coming into contact with Mr. Reeder except through appropriate judicial processes.

I request that no injunction issue herein. Or in the alternative, if this court feels that an injunction is appropriate, that mutual restraining orders issue ordering Wayne Reeder and John Philip Nichols, Ph.D. and the Nichols family and their agents, servants and employees be restrained from harassing, molesting, injuring or annoying me in any manner whatsoever. (With the express exception that I shall have the right to have a process server approach Mr. Reeder for service of summons and complaint if I decide to file suit against him.)

I declare under penalty of perjury that the foregoing is true and correct. If sworn as a witness herein, I could and would competently tstify to the matters stated herein.

Executed at Los Angeles, California on September 25, 1984.

JAMES G. HUGHES, JR.

Full Gospel Business Men's Fellowship International

San Joaquin Valley Chapters
Cordially invites you to a Very Special Dinner Event
Featuring: Two Very Special Speakers
Friday Feb. 22, 2008 @ 6:00 PM at the
Famous Bankers Ball Room - Fresno Fulton Mall

Former Commanding General Daniel Lopez Carballo of Honduras
World renowned Evangelist Jimmy Hughes of Honduras
Come and hear the testimony of Joshua Hughes, on his miraculous and continuing recovery from death.

Both of our guests have powerful testimonies of how God came into their lives just at the right time, and transformed them into Soldiers of GOD!!!
If you know someone that needs a miracle, Please bring them!

This event is for everyone: Bring your Wife, Brother, Sister, or a Friend
Cost of Dinner $35.00 per person

For More Information or Directions, Please Call:
Mike Alarcón 559 260-0098 - Bruno Quintana 559 273-7238 - Rey Mejía 559 318-9080
Gabe Jacquez 559 901-2216 - Lucio Gómez 559 799-8923 - Quentin Unruh 559 227-3087
Carl Alemania 559 351-0413 – Armando Bañuelos 559 805-6511

Visit us at www.fgbmfi-sjvc.org

February 22, 2008: Flyer advertising the Full Gospel Business Men's Fellowship International (FG-BMFI) dinner event in Fresno, California. Keynote speakers were Jimmy Hughes from Honduras, and Commanding General Daniel Lopez Carballo of Honduras. Rachel Begley confronted Jimmy Hughes at this event and recorded his response to her accusations that he was the bag-man in the 1981 triple homicide in which her father, Ralph Boger, was murdered. (See Chapter 25 for this story).

http://www.fgbmfivoice.com/stories/996hughes.htm

FOR MORE TRUE STORIES CLICK HERE

A Hit Man with a New Mission

Jimmy Hughes, Honduras

After a six-year hitch in the military, I became a professional hit man for the Mafia. I collected money, hurt a lot of people and saw a lot of blood. I know what it's like to cut the throat of a man, see a man die, or throw a man in the trunk of a car and take him to his death. I did many horrible things. I allowed myself to do whatever was necessary.

One day I had a contract on a man. They had paid me a lot of money to kill this person. I travelled over many states, and walked into the man's house one day, pulled out my pistol, and put a bullet in everybody's head.

There were many people there that day because he was having a party. As I stood there with the gun in my hand, I suddenly realized that all those people were dead. They had died instantly. I had been paid to kill one man, but had killed half a dozen people. The rest had just been in the wrong place at the wrong time. Satan has no mercy. He has no mercy whatsoever.

Eventually the Mafia put a contract of $30,000 out on my life. The FBI wanted to make deals with me because of all the information I had after so many years of working for organized crime. I didn't know from one day to the next if I would go to prison or if I would die. That's the way I lived, but like with the nation of Israel when God brought them out of Egypt and opened up the Red Sea before them, God opened up my Red Sea, I crossed over, and He closed up the past. Now I won't fear the past; I only look forward to the future with God. At that time, though, there was still turmoil in my life. My $30,000-a-month cocaine habit, along with the gallon of liquor I drank every day, meant I needed money.

PAGES 536-539: FGBMFI website in which Jimmy Hughes tells his story about being a "Mafia Hit-Man" before he found God. Hughes talks about killing half a dozen people at a party, despite the fact he was paid to kill only one individual.

Then one day God sent a Full Gospel Business Man into my life. His name was John Carrette. He was the Executive Vice President of the FGBMFI. He flew from Guatemala to meet me in Los Angeles. My mom was his pastor in Guatemala. He met me at the Hyatt Hotel and began to share with me about the FGBMFI.

There was something neat about this business man. He had authority in his mouth. He had the presence of God within him. The brightness of Jesus was in his eyes. I saw Jesus in his face. He spoke with power, and said, "Jimmy, God needs you in Central America. He needs you as the soldier that you were. He needs you in His army. He calls you to ministry." I wanted to do what God told John, but I couldn't because I had to take care of a lot of details, but he prayed for me; that business man prayed for me. I felt the power of God come over me.

About a year passed and one day I sat down on the chair where my grandmother had died the year before. The best friend I had ever had was my grandma. I sat down on the chair where she had died, picked up a .357 magnum and stuck it in my mouth till that barrel touched my throat. At that time in my life, I was very weak. I was skinny and sickly, and had no friends. The drugs, liquor and violence had totally destroyed my life.

I pulled the hammer back, and was ready to pull the trigger. God must have looked down at my situation, just shaking His head, "Oh, Jimmy, Jimmy, Satan will take your life today. There's nothing I can do because of your rebellion. I've given you opportunity after opportunity, and you've bound my hands."

Thank God for the Lamb of God! Somewhere in heaven, Jesus was interceding for me, and the Holy Spirit came to Guatemala. My mother was preaching in her service on a Sunday morning, and John Carrette was present. Full Gospel Business Men were present in that church service. The Holy Spirit came there and said, "Pray for Jimmy now." My mother stopped the service, and told everybody to pray for Jimmy. She didn't tell them the details. She just said, "Let's pray for my son today."

God gave the command and said, "Save Jimmy's life," even though I was in the United States and my mom and her church were in Guatemala, thousands of miles away.

I pulled that trigger. Boom! The gun went off and the bullet came out of the barrel, but before it hit the back of my throat, that bullet disappeared. I heard Jesus say, "I am the same today as I was yesterday, and the same as I will be for you tomorrow, Jimmy, for you are loved." My life was given back to me. I began to weep and to cry, and from that time on, I have been serving the Lord. That was in 1985.

In 1987, John Carrette "god-fathered" me into the Full Gospel Business Men's Fellowship, and I have been in the Fellowship ever since. I live in Honduras. I have a wife and two children, and we have a ministry called, "Free the Oppressed." We work with gang leaders and gang members. We work with the youth from all of Central America. On the military bases, we have seen the power of God change gang members, and gang leaders – violent men – into God-fearing and loving men of God.

I remember one time the guerilla fighters came into my mother's Children's Home in Guatemala, which had about 75 children. The Holy Spirit woke me at one in the morning. The guerillas had surrounded the Children's Home. I was taking care of the boys' house, which was way in the back of the property. I went downstairs, and a gunman put a rifle in my face through the window.

They had masks on their faces, but I could see the hate and violence in their eyes. I could see a man running from the river. They had surrounded the houses with their machine guns, rifles and pistols. They told me to open the door, that they were the police and they wanted in. I woke up the rest of the adults and all the children. I told them to start praying because these men had come to kill us, rape the women and steal everything. The men began to hit the door with a tree trunk. The door only had a little latch.

As I walked upstairs to go into my bedroom to pick up my Japanese sword, the Lord reminded me that He fought our battles for us. He asked me, "If I'm with you, who can be against you?" I picked up a little boy in my arms and began to cry out to God, "Oh Lord, tonight I'll give you my life, and let my blood be a sacrifice unto you for these children. If You'll promise me that these children will not be hurt and the women won't be raped, I'll give my life to these men, and they can kill and do whatever they want with me. Let them be satisfied with my blood."

One of the gunmen broke all the windows downstairs with his rifle, and came into the house. I saw his shadow go right by me. I went back upstairs to grab my Samurai Sword. He turned on all the lights in the bottom part of the dormitory so he could see the front door to open it.

Out of the corner of my eye, I could see big angels holding the door shut. That gunman jumped right back out the window where he came in and they started shooting at the house. Bullets were flying all over. It was a wooden house. One bullet hit me, and one of our fifteen-year-old boys had a hole blown through his pant leg. He flew back and knocked five boys over. When he stood up that bullet had come out of his pant leg. He didn't lose a drop of blood, nor was any bone broken.

You see, Satan had taken three contracts out on my life. He had written my name on three bullets. The first bullet was when I had tried to commit suicide and pulled the trigger on the .357 Magnum. The second was the bullet which had just hit me. And there was still the third contract – the third bullet with my name on it.

As I walked into my bedroom, I picked up my sword and the Holy Spirit came upon me. I began to break all the glass in the windows with the sword, speaking in tongues as I did. It just flowed from my belly. The men started shooting at me from both sides at point blank range! A man shot his pistol right at my heart, right at my chest. He pulled the trigger and that bullet came right at my chest from about ten feet away.

The angels of the Lord came down and that bullet was simply diverted in clear view. Instead of hitting my chest, it hit the metal of the window. It just moved in the air. The man started losing his mind, shooting in the air. I grabbed the Bible and opened the door, and chased the man to the river with the Word of God. They ran away and disappeared into the night. That was a powerful testimony of how God delivers.

When you are walking with the Lord, He delivers. He said, "I'll give my angels charge concerning you." For those who fear God, He will give His angels charge concerning them. He gave His angels charge concerning the Children's Home that night.

In 1995, we went to Honduras. I had $20.00 in my pocket when God told me to leave Guatemala. I went by faith to serve the Lord. That's where the ministry really took off. I had been asking God for a four-wheel drive vehicle. My wife just laughed, and said, "Be humble. Don't ask for what you can't afford." My response was, "I don't serve a little God. My God is big, and He has no borders."

In November of 1995 I was on a highway in Honduras, praising the Lord as I drove to a special event at the Chulateca Chapter. A semi-truck was coming from the other direction. There wasn't a cloud in the sky and nobody else was on the road – just me and the semi-truck. I was worshipping the Lord when all of a sudden the lights went out. Dark clouds came over my car, and I could feel great evil. It was just for a few seconds. I couldn't see anything in front of me. When the cloud lifted, there was a car in front of me, coming at great speed as it tried to pass the semi-truck.

Apparently he had seen me and he hit the brakes of his big old truck. It was just a matter of seconds; there was no time to make decisions. I saw death coming, but not to the man in the oncoming car. I went the other way, hitting the bumper of that semi-truck; it opened up my car like a can of tuna. It flipped over in the air, and when it hit the pavement, my left arm was outside the window of that vehicle.

The weight of the car fell on top of my arm, and dragged my arm 50 meters on pavement and about 20 meters on gravel before the car stopped. My collar bone was broken and my face had shattered the whole windscreen. The car came to rest upside down. I couldn't see out of the corner of my eye, but I was sure I had lost my arm.

The pain was great, and I cried out to God, saying, "Lord, take away the pain." His presence came into the car just like that. I heard the voice of the Lord say, "I have called you to warfare. I want more intimacy with you." Then my bones began to move, and the pain left instantly. When I got out of that car, there wasn't a drop of blood from my body. My bones were completely healed, and my left arm was intact, as if nothing had happened.

Once again God had shown Himself faithful to me. It was really awesome! Sometimes we go through difficult, and even scarey circumstances, but in your fear, as you cry out to God, He will prove Himself faithful.

July 6, 2003

CHRONICLE

"Murderer of five thousand dollars"

The United States Army made him a deadly weapon. It was a key figure in the covert operations of the CIA (Central Intelligence Agency) in Asia, Europe and South America dictators and overthrowing regimes helping people struggling to be free, until Jimmy Hughes becomes a murderer hired by the tentacles of the Italian Mafia in the United States. The Justice Department failed to put him behind bars and the FBI (Federal Bureau of Investigation) had to give him protection in exchange for information. Today tells his story to EL DIARIO DE HOY.

Texts: Mauricio Acosta Vásquez
Photos: Omar Carbonero
vertice@elsalvador.com

COMPARTELO CON UN AMIGO/A

Jimmy Hughes, who was an expert in terrorizing and killing another, is now an international evangelist

The end of the war in Vietnam, in 1973, marked the beginning of my military career. My instructors and teachers were American soldiers who survived the fire from the Vietcong. He was 17 years old and coveted positions in the military scale.

I enrolled in each course no matter how hard it was. I attended schools in parachuting, scuba diving, escape and rescue operations, as a prisoner of war resistance and survival in jungle, sea and desert. I specialized in plastic explosives and a sniper. In six years, military schools like the Rangers or Delta Force turned me into an elite soldier.

In my 23 years spent working for the CIA on covert missions outside the United States. In countries of Asia, Europe and South America fought to defend the rights of others. I helped people who wanted to be free and to fight dictators regimes. This means that the United States Army trained me not to be a damn, but to defend my country and the enemies of democracy and freedom.
After several secret missions left the CIA and, four years later (1984), I left the army and went to California to live quietly, never imagining that my actions were to come bloodiest.

A crack head

The military ranks had an Italian friend told me about a certain Godfather and never paid much attention because I thought those were things seen only in movies. But one day I met him in California, we went out for drinks and remember the experiences we in the Army. In the heat of the drinks I asked him about "The Godfather" and I said I could work with the Family. A few days later we met again and introduced me to Dr. Nichols, who was interested in me, to know my military career. I was the man he needed to do their dirty work. The mafia had recruited me, the Godfather was Dr. Nichols.

From bullets to the public

- Jimmy Hughes is currently an

PAGES 540-543: July 6, 2003: Vertice newspaper article in which Jimmy Hughes is interviewed and describes his career as a Mafia hit man, his involvement in covert operations for the CIA, and how the FBI gave him protection in exchange for information.

My first job in the Mafia was to collect the money from those who did not pay their bills and that included broken legs, arms and heads with baseball bats. So I began to unleash a spiral of street violence that grew more and more. I was not afraid of anything or anyone. Mafia families from other states subcontracted me for not using their own murderers and thus evade the authorities. There was a sort of agreement between the families and so I traveled to other parts of America as a murderer. That became my job: to kill for money.

Although the army had already tasted what was to kill, with the mob came to offer my talents and my gifts of money, to the ticket. Murderer of five, ten, twenty, thirty and forty thousand dollars. The most I got paid for killing a being was fifty thousand dollars, and I was a professional job.'s How the 27 years I sold into prostitution of evil.

I became the confidant of the Godfather, who was engaged in the casino business. I was the bodyguard of her children. Became so famous as that when the Mafia hit man throughout the United States asked Jimmy Hughes, the family sent me because they knew they could rely on my work completely.

international evangelist.

- Is the founder of Gateway Rehabilitation Center of Hope, which rescues youth gangs in Honduras.

- Is the president of "Free The Oppressed Ministries (Ministry Free the Oppressed).

- On July 12, at the Amphitheatre of the International Fair, Jimmy give his testimony in Congress called Save Multitudes 2003 from 6:30 pm.

- Admission is free.

- For more information call 242-3333.

I arranged the situations of violence and whether to kidnap someone to threaten him I was a professional to terrorize a human being. He was an expert in that area.

By that time I was addicted to cocaine, I loved cocaine. He had a terrible addiction, drug always carried in my pockets. He drank liquor all day. But one thing leads to another and the addiction began to rob me of sleep and only slept two times a week because they always suffered from severe nightmares. With so much blood shed would fill a pool.

Free Death

One day the Godfather called me and gave the order to kill a guy for $ 30,000. To my surprise, this guy I knew, we were friends. But between the mafia, "are bussines bussines' (business is business).

When I got home from the subject, I was not a normal person, I see so much violence had become a demon. He greeted me with a greeting: "How are you, how are you, nice ..." and went into his house.

He never imagined that he had opened the door to death. But within the mansion, had five other people who were drinking and snorting cocaine. I thought, 'I have to kill it by 30 000, but the other five do not know who they are. " The others did not see them as important people and I even thought that made him a favor by removing them from society as well. I said, 'Well, the other five are free in the contract. "

The night began to fall and when I got my gun no one noticed because they were drugged, drunk and talking nonsense. He began: "Bum, bum, bum ...'.

All around me were dead within seconds, no one could react. They were unprepared, no one expected to die. The shot they dropped on his head.

But it happens that even having the gun in my hand, in the middle of the pool of blood, I see his face shattered by a bullet from this man she would pay me $ 30,000. In the face undone, I see myself reflected in a mirror.

I bristle hairs and froze me to see that I am. At the same time I begin to hear a voice say 'Jimmy you know today that I love you and I can forgive you. " I said then, 'what happens. Either God is mad or I'm losing the sense so much drugs, so much blood, so much violence. "

In this macabre scene, half laughed, but then I fell into a big chill.

I felt almost paralyzed me the heart and back again to hear his voice: 'Jimmy you know today that I love you and I can forgive you. " Then I ran away from that place, leaving half a dozen dead by $ 30,000.

On reaching the house was desperate and looking for how to relieve the distress, which continued to haunt me. For the first time I felt inside me a sort of repentance. I felt I could do no more, everything was a hell.

Trapped in the solitude of my home, picked up the phone and decided to call my mother, who was as a Christian missionary in Guatemala.

When he answered my call, immediately said, 'Mom, I'm in trouble. " She said, 'Jimmy, you've always been in trouble. "

"Listen," I said, I do not know if the FBI is going to catch me or if I surrender. I do not know if I am sent to jail or kill me if the mafia, but I want to pray for me. I will not die or go to jail without first making passes with God. "

She prayed intensely for me. Through the telephone line could join my mother in Guatemala, I, in California, and God in heaven. I first experienced the immense power of prayer, a power greater than any weapon ever had in my hands.

From the mafia to the FBI

The next day I showed where the Godfather and told him I wanted to quit, they would no longer kill anyone and wanted to be at peace.

he looked like someone who is faced with a madman. I paid the $ 30,000, but I immediately said: 'Jimmy, you know the procedure, you know you put your life in danger. "

I replied: 'Yes, I know, but you know that if something happens we all perish. "

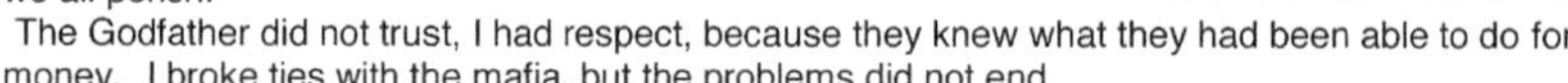

The Godfather did not trust, I had respect, because they knew what they had been able to do for money. I broke ties with the mafia, but the problems did not end.

The FBI, the Justice Department and the Police as I had booked. They were behind me, wanted to know what was what I had in the brain, what they knew about the Mafia.

But in the United States met to the letter so that you are innocent until you prove otherwise.

Before take you to court, prosecutors claim to have evidence against you. So I, being a professional, never left a fingerprint on the crime scenes. That was like a pride for me. I was very careful with that, because my training was very professional.

When they realized that there was no evidence against me to take me to court, I included in the Witness Protection Program of the FBI, in exchange for giving the authorities some information. I knew the law, had studied hard and knew what to expect. FBI agents knew that they dealt with a gross, but I reached the limit of having a hand in hand with the FBI and told them I had already worked enough. That he had no information to give.

My life was troubled. Every time I climbed into my car, afraid that in turn broke the Mafia or send me a couple of thugs to my house. He was cornered and was at the dead end when I made my covenant with God: to live or die. And he decided that I would live to give my testimony to anywhere where He leads me. To tell people that if God forgave the apostle Paul, who persecuted Christians to kill them, and he has forgiven me so many times my hands stained with blood, may also forgive everyone who has sinned. There is no wrong to that the power of God can not forgive.

In 1997 I came to my mother in Guatemala. Since we are brought together into an intense hug. She regained her lost son and I was a mother who never had abandoned me in your prayers. I gave myself completely to be an instrument of God, I studied theology and graduated from Reverend and now serve the mafia of good, led by The Godfather of salvation and eternal life, Jesus Christ.

Copyright 2002 El Diario de Hoy - All Rights Reserved. vertice@elsalvador.com

Reproduction in whole or part without written permission from the owner.

http://www.elsalvador.com/vertice/2003/060703/cronica.html

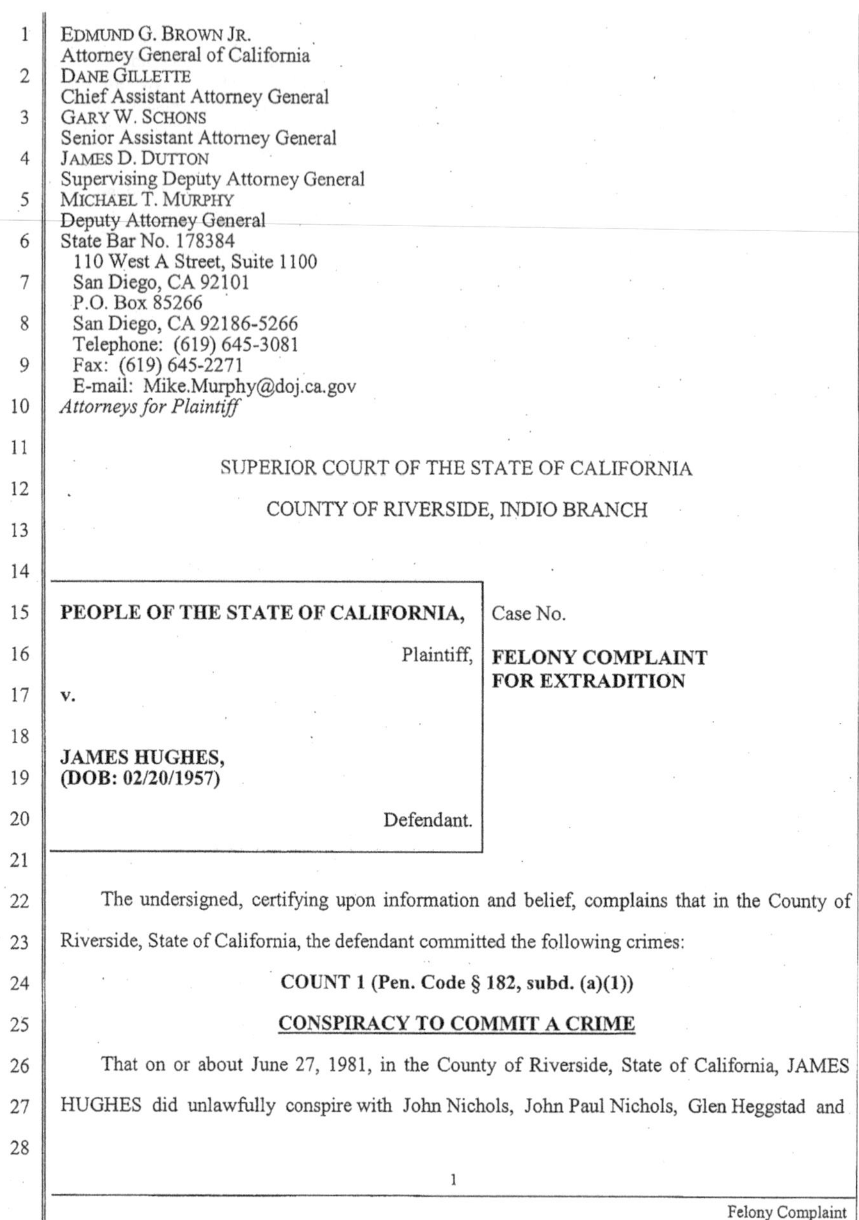

EDMUND G. BROWN JR.
Attorney General of California
DANE GILLETTE
Chief Assistant Attorney General
GARY W. SCHONS
Senior Assistant Attorney General
JAMES D. DUTTON
Supervising Deputy Attorney General
MICHAEL T. MURPHY
Deputy Attorney General
State Bar No. 178384
110 West A Street, Suite 1100
San Diego, CA 92101
P.O. Box 85266
San Diego, CA 92186-5266
Telephone: (619) 645-3081
Fax: (619) 645-2271
E-mail: Mike.Murphy@doj.ca.gov
Attorneys for Plaintiff

SUPERIOR COURT OF THE STATE OF CALIFORNIA

COUNTY OF RIVERSIDE, INDIO BRANCH

PEOPLE OF THE STATE OF CALIFORNIA, Plaintiff, v. **JAMES HUGHES,** **(DOB: 02/20/1957)** Defendant.	Case No. **FELONY COMPLAINT FOR EXTRADITION**

The undersigned, certifying upon information and belief, complains that in the County of Riverside, State of California, the defendant committed the following crimes:

COUNT 1 (Pen. Code § 182, subd. (a)(1))

CONSPIRACY TO COMMIT A CRIME

That on or about June 27, 1981, in the County of Riverside, State of California, JAMES HUGHES did unlawfully conspire with John Nichols, John Paul Nichols, Glen Heggstad and

1

Felony Complaint

PAGES 544-546: 2009 Court filing – Felony Complaint for Extradition. Jimmy Hughes was arrested in Miami on September 26, 2009 and extradited in December to Indio, California. The Complaint states he was charged with three counts of murder and one count of conspiracy.

other persons whose identities are unknown to commit the crime of Murder, in violation of Penal Code section 187, subdivision (a), a felony.

The object of the conspiracy was to prevent Fred Alvarez from exposing illegal activities of John Philip Nichols, occurring at the Cabazon Indian Reservation.

Thereafter, in the County of Riverside, pursuant to the above conspiracy and in furtherance of the object thereof, the following overt acts were committed:

OVERT ACT NUMBER 1

On or about June 27, 1981, James Hughes asked a friend to introduce John Paul Nichols to Glenn Heggstad, for the purpose of hiring Heggstad to prevent Fred Alvarez from exposing illegal activities of John Philip Nichols, occurring at the Cabazon Indian Reservation.

OVERT ACT NUMBER 2

On or about June 27, 1981, John Paul Nichols met with Glenn Heggstad, for the purpose of hiring Heggstad to prevent Fred Alvarez from exposing illegal activities of John Philip Nichols, occurring at the Cabazon Indian Reservation.

OVERT ACT NUMBER 3

On June 29, 1981, James Hughes went to Fred Alvarez's residence to prevent Fred Alvarez from exposing illegal activities of John Philip Nichols, occurring at the Cabazon Indian Reservation.

COUNT 2 (Pen. Code § 187, subd. (a))

<u>MURDER</u>

That on or about June 29, 1981, in the County of Riverside, State of California, the crime of Murder, in violation of Penal Code section 187, subdivision (a), a felony, was committed by JAMES HUGHES, who did unlawfully, and with malice aforethought murder FRED ALVAREZ, a human being.

NOTICE: The above offense is a serious felony within the meaning of Penal Code section 1192.7, subdivision (c).

COUNT 3 (Pen. Code § 187, subd. (a))

MURDER

That on or about June 29, 1981, in the County of Riverside, State of California, the crime of Murder, in violation of Penal Code section 187, subdivision (a), a felony, was committed by JAMES HUGHES, who did unlawfully, and with malice aforethought murder PATRICIA CASTRO, a human being.

NOTICE: The above offense is a serious felony within the meaning of Penal Code section 1192.7, subdivision (c).

COUNT 4 (Pen. Code § 187, subd. (a))

MURDER

That on or about June 29, 1981, in the County of Riverside, State of California, the crime of Murder, in violation of Penal Code section 187, subdivision (a), a felony, was committed by JAMES HUGHES, who did unlawfully, and with malice aforethought murder RALPH BOGER, a human being.

NOTICE: The above offense is a serious felony within the meaning of Penal Code section 1192.7, subdivision (c).

Executed this 29th day of September, 2009, at San Diego, California.

Michael T. Murphy

MICHAEL T. MURPHY
Deputy Attorney General

Based on the foregoing Complaint, and the Affidavit in Support of Arrest Warrant filed by Detective John Powers on August 28, 2009, I find there is probable cause for the issuance of a warrant of arrest for the above-named defendant.

____
Judge of the Superior Court,
State of California

Former Cabazon employee shuns further work with law agencies

By KEITH CARTER
Daily News Managing Editor

A former Cabazon Bingo Palace employee who claims he was the target of a murder-for-hire plot said Friday he will no longer cooperate with county and state law enforcement officials investigating the case.

James Hughes Jr., who reportedly has been providing information to authorities about businesses operated by the Cabazon Band of Mission Indians, said he reached the decision because of apparent lack of progress in the investigation.

Hughes made the comments to the Daily News in a telephone interview from the Los Angeles area, where he has been for the past two weeks.

Court documents filed Thursday on behalf of the former Cabazon employee charge that John Philip Nichols, consultant to tribe, earlier this year attempted to put out a murder contract on Hughes and Indio developer Wayne Reeder.

Hughes had left his job with the tribe in February of this year to take a job as security consultant with Reeder's Indian Palms Country Club, but he said he was fired in June by Reeder at Nichols' insistence.

The court declaration was filed in response to a suit filed two weeks ago by Reeder accusing Hughes of threatening his life. Hughes has denied the charges.

Also submitting a statement to the court Thursday was Peter Zokosky, an Indio resident and retired armament company executive who has done consulting work for both the tribe and Reeder.

Zokosky said in his statement that a "watchdog" audit of bingo parlor financial records showed numerous financial "irregularities" and the "skimming" of profits. He said he had been asked by Reeder, who had invested $230,000 in the bingo parlor operation but had received no return on his investment, to conduct the audit.

Zokosky said he was present at the Sept. 13 meeting at which Hughes allegedly threatened Reeder during a dispute over finances, but he denied that any threat was voiced by Hughes.

Both Hughes and Zokosky said they have been

(Continued on Page 2)

providing information about operation of the Cabazon tribe's businesses to the Riverside County District Attorney's office and the state Attorney General's office for the past four months.

Neither the State Department of Justice nor Tom Douglass, Riverside County assistant district attorney, would confirm or deny that they were involved in an investigation of the Bingo operation.

Hughes said Friday that his dissatisfaction with the way in which the investigation of Nichols and the tribe has been handled led him to sever his contacts with representatives from two agencies.

In his response to the lawsuit, he had indicated that because of the information he had provided, he had been offered assistance under the government's witness protection program.

"I'm not going to say anything else to them," he explained. "All they (the local and state law enforcement agencies) care about is their own jurisdiction. The case is too big for them to see the whole picture. They can't handle it."

In addition to the allegations concerning the murder-for-hire plot, Hughes in his declaration also charged that the tribe's bingo and casino businesses were fronts for U.S. government-sanctioned covert military activities and arms shipments to Central and South America.

He also charged that there had been "skimming" from bingo parlor profits by the Nichols family.

Hughes said Friday that he had been in contact with federal officials in Washington, D.C., who are interested in the case.

"I'm not at liberty to say who I'm talking to, but it's obvious the state of California needs help," he said.

Despite the alleged threat to his life, Hughes said he planned to return to Indio Tuesday for a court hearing on the lawsuit filed by Reeder.

"I won't run from Nichols, Reeder or anyone else," he said. "Right now, it's an all-out war. I don't fear them."

Zokosky Friday echoed Hughes' criticism of the law enforcement officials who have been investigating the allegations of the two men.

"The really discouraging part of this whole situation is the way it has been handled by the law enforcement people," he said. "The whole system is riddled with the same problem. This case would have died 50 times if someone had not taken a special interest and pushed it. Nobody wants to take charge and look at the overall picture."

He said that although he is "a firm believer in the system," the conduct of local, state and federal law enforcement officials in the case has left him disillusioned.

"It's hard to believe that after four months of providing information, the object of the investigation has not even been questioned," Zokosky said.

1984 *Daily News* interview with Jimmy Hughes entitled, "Former Cabazon Employee Shuns Further Work with Law Agencies." Hughes severed contact with the State Attorney General and moved over to the FBI.

LAW OF ROBIN SAX
BY: ROBIN SAX (KATZENSTEIN)
ATTORNEY AT LAW
STATE BAR #190105
1434 WESTWOOD BLVD SUITE 17
LOS ANGELES, CA 90024
(310) 470-9955
EMAIL: ROBIN@ROBINSAX.COM

FILED
SUPERIOR COURT OF CALIFORNIA
COUNTY OF RIVERSIDE
JUL 01 2010
N. LARES

SUPERIOR COURT OF THE STATE OF CALIFORNIA

IN AND FOR THE COUNTY OF RIVERSIDE

THE PEOPLE OF THE STATE OF CALIFORNIA, Plaintiff, v. JAMES HUGHES, Defendant.	Case No.: INF066719 **MOTION TO PRESERVE VICTIMS' RIGHTS UNDER MARSY'S LAW AND DEMAND THAT CASE PROCEED TO PRELIMINARY HEARING**

TO: TO THE HONORABLE JUDGE PRESIDING, ATTORNEY GENERAL EDMUND BROWN OF THE STATE OF CALIFORNIA AND HIS AUTHORIZED REPRESENTATIVES AND AGENTS INCLUDING BUT NOT LIMITED TO DEPUTY ATTORNEY GENERAL MICHAEL MURPHY ALL LAW ENFORCEMENT AGENCIES INVOLVED IN THE INVESTIGATION OF THE CASE, AND COUNSEL RENE SOTTORIO, STEVE HARMON, AND DEAN BENJAMINI

PLEASE TAKE NOTICE, pursuant to California Constitution article I, §28, section (b) also known as Marsy's Law, RACHEL BEGLEY will move this court to insure the victim's rights are met in this case.

This motion will be based on this notice of motion and motion, the files and pleadings in the above entitled matter, the attached points and authorities, and argument made in court.

Pages 548-557: July 1, 2010: Court filing - Motion to Preserve Victim's Rights under Marcy's Law and Demand that Case Proceed to Preliminary Hearing; filed by victim's advocate attorney Robin Sax on behalf of Rachel Begley. Case No. INF066719. The language in the Motion addresses the possible reason that the A/G dropped the case as follows: " --- The only conclusion, though speculative, is that something or someone has scared the Attorney General's office ---." The Motion also includes excerpts from newspaper articles in which Jimmy Hughes gave details of the murders he says he committed.

STATEMENT OF THE FACTS

On June 24, 2010 Rachel Begley received notice from the Attorney General's Office after numerous of her own calls that the case above entitled case would be dismissed on July 1, 2010 the proposed date for felony settlement conference. Despite the insanely short notice and living thousands of miles away, Begley got on a plane to come to Riverside County California in order to have her voice heard in this courtroom.

Whether its coincidental, ironic, or corrupt Deputy Attorney General Mike Murphy from San Diego, the assigned prosecutor, notified Rachel Begley on June 24th that he planned to drop charges against Hughes on the twenty-ninth (29th) anniversary of the triple homicide in which Begley's father, Ralph Boger, was murdered. While citing two reasons to Begley and the press, there is no legitimate legal reason for the dismissal.

Boger, Fred Alvarez and Patty Castro were found dead on July 1, 1981 in Rancho Mirage; each had been shot execution style in the back of the head. Rachel Begley was only 13 at the time. In 1984 James "Jimmy" Hughes claimed to authorities and reporters that he was the bag-man in the murders, that he delivered the money for the hit and the Cabazon Indian tribe's administrator, John Philip Nichols, had contracted the hit.

Hughes left the United States before he could testify and built a new life in Latin America where he has lived for 28 years. The triple homicide case had never been solved until Detective John Powers of the Riverside County Sheriff's Department took control of the cold case file on November 27, 2007.

From 2007 until 2009, Detective Powers, interviewed all available witnesses which included witnesses from the past plus new witnesses. From the new evidence from witness statements including a still existing fresh confession witness, new impeachment evidence, the defendants own written accounts of the crime, prosecutors believed there was beyond ample evidence to file charges in 2009 and seek extradition of the defendant from Florida.

From filing of the case until July 1, 2010 there has been not one single substantive hearing in the case with the only motions filed being that from the media requesting entry to the proceedings. There has been no preliminary hearing to determine if there is sufficient evidence to hold the defendant to answer to trial, no filing of due process or the like from the defense, and therefore no reason for this case to be dismissed.

ARGUMENT

WHILE PROSECUTORS ENJOY WIDE LATITUDE IN FILING DECISION, PROSECUTORS DO NOT HAVE THE SOLE AUTHORITY TO DIMSISS A CASE

The mission statement of the California Attorney General's Office states, "It is our duty to serve our state and work honorably every day to fulfill California's promise. The Attorney General and our Department's employees provide leadership, information and education in partnership with state and local governments and the people of California to:

- Enforce and apply all our laws fairly and impartially.
- Ensure justice, safety, and liberty for everyone.
- Encourage economic prosperity, equal opportunity and tolerance.
- Safeguard California's human, natural, and financial resources for this and future generations."

(www.http://ag.ca.gov/ag/mission.php)

Consistent with the public mission statement, the Attorney General's Office has internal requirements for filing cases. And while, the internal requirements for the filing of criminal case are not publicly accessible other prosecutor offices (including the Los Angeles and Riverside County District Attorneys offices) both cite in their policy manuals that a decision to file rests on the initial decision that the case is prosecutable beyond a reasonable doubt (Source: Riverside and Los Angeles County Policy Manuals). In the instant case, not only was the case filed presumably consistent with policy and mission standards but Deputy Attorney General Murphy indicated to Detective Powers (at the time notice was being delivered to the Sheriff's Department that the case was going to be dismissed) that there was more than ample evidence to file and prove this case not just now but twenty five years ago and said that because the case was not filed earlier the lack of due process requires a dismissal in the case.

Recognizing that the defendant has due process rights, it must be pointed out that the filing of the case in 2009 was based on additional and new information probative evidence provided by law enforcement to the prosecutor in this case. Probably most damaging of all, was the new statements by defendant Hughes himself made to "El Diario de Hoy' published on July 6, 2003 where the defendant, in his words, described his life, mission, and crimes as Mafia hitman specifically the crime in the instant case. Excerpts from the 2003 interview include the following:

> **Collecting tributes**
> *While serving in the military, I had an Italian friend who often spoke to me about a 'Padrino' (Godfather), and I never paid much attention; I thought those were just things you see in the movies. My first job in the mob was collecting money from those who did not pay their bills, and that included broken legs, arms and heads with baseball bats.*
>
> *Although the Army I had already gotten a taste of what it was like to kill, with the mob, I offered my talent for gifts or money. I would murder someone for five, ten, twenty, thirty, forty thousand dollars. The most I got paid for killing somebody was fifty thousand dollars, because it was professionally done. This was how at age 27, I sold myself to evil.*
>
> *I became the confidant of the Godfather, who was in the business of casinos. I was the bodyguard for his children. I became a famous hitman for the mafia; everybody in the United States asked for Jimmy Hughes.*
>
> *By that time I was addicted to cocaine. I loved cocaine. I had a terrible addiction; I would always carry the drug in my pockets. I drank hard liquor all day. I always had terrible nightmares because I had shed enough blood to fill a pool.*
>
> **Free Death**
> *One day, the Godfather called me and gave me an order to kill a suspect for thirty thousand dollars. To my surprise, I knew this guy; we used to be friends. But in the mafia, 'business is business.' When I arrived at the guy's home, I was no longer a normal person; I had been exposed to so much violence that I had become a demon. I said hi to the guy and went into his house.*
>
> *He never imagined that he had just opened the door to death. But inside the mansion, there were five other people who were drinking and snorting cocaine. I thought, 'I must get this done for the $30,000 that I was being paid;' however, I did not know who the other five were. Then I thought to myself that I would do a service to society by doing them all. The other five would be added to the contract…for free.*
>
> *The night began to fall and when I took my gun out, no one noticed it because they were too drugged and drunk. They were all talking nonsense, so I began: "Bang, bang, bang…"*

Everyone around me was dead within seconds; no one moved. They were totally unprepared; no one was expecting to die. I had shot all of them in the head. But right after it all happened, and as I was still holding the gun in my hand, between a pool of blood, I would see shattered face of the man that I was paid to kill, and it would feel as though I would see my reflection in a mirror.

The hairs in the back of my neck stood up as I saw my own bloody image. At the same time, I began to hear a voice say, "Jimmy: You know that I love you and I forgive you." I said to myself: "Oh God, I'm either going crazy or I did too many drugs and I had killed so many people in my life."
In that horrific scene, I somewhat laughed, but then big chills came down my spine.
My heart almost stopped. Then I heard the same voice again: "Jimmy: You know that I love you and I forgive you." Then, I ran out of the place, leaving half a dozen dead for thirty thousand dollars.

(Article from the Honduran newspaper La Prensa, written by Jessica Figeroa
Translation by Mario Andrade, July 6, 2003)

It is well settled law that crime-charging power is vested in the public prosecutor by Government Code section 26501. "Prosecutors have a great deal of discretion in this crime-charging function. Charging discretion takes three basic forms: (1) evidentiary sufficiency-a determination of whether the evidence warrants prosecution; (2) charge selection-a determination of the appropriate charge or charges; and (3) discretion not to prosecute-a determination of whether there is an alternative to formal criminal prosecution." (Prosecutorial Discretion (Cont.Ed.Bar 1979) § 11, p. 5.) This prosecutorial discretion, though recognized by statute in California, is founded upon constitutional principles of separation of powers and due process of law. (*People v. Sidener* (1962) 58 Cal.2d 645, 650, 651, 25 Cal.Rptr. 697, 375 P.2d 641, overruled on other grounds in *People v. Tenorio* (1970) 3 Cal.3d 89, 89 Cal.Rptr. 249, 473 P.2d 993.) The district attorney's unlimited discretion in the crime-charging function has been uniformly recognized. (See, e.g., *Boyne v. Ryan* (1893) 100 Cal. 265, 34 P. 707; *People v. Adams* (1974) 43 Cal.App.3d 697, 117 Cal.Rptr. 905; *People v. Municipal Court (Bishop)* (1972) 27 Cal.App.3d 193, 103 Cal.Rptr. 645; *Ascherman v. Bales* (1969) 273 Cal.App.2d 707, 78 Cal.Rptr. 445; *Taliaferro v. City of San Pablo* (1960) 187 Cal.App.2d 153, 9 Cal.Rptr. 445; *Taliaferro v. Locke* (1960) 182 Cal.App.2d 752, 6 Cal.Rptr. 813.)

In the instant case, the decision to file this case was made by the Attorney General's Office (the Riverside County District Attorney's Office declared a conflict after determining that the defendant was second cousins with the elected District Attorney Rod Pacheco whose terms ends this year). Presumably and consistently with the new evidence in the case, the new witness statements, the re-interview of all integral witnesses, including the statements of key and material witnesses, a review of the defendant's statements made from 2003 and on, the Attorney General's Office exercised their prosecutorial function and filed the case.

While trial court has broad statutory discretion to dismiss, power is not absolute but is limited amorphous concept that dismissal be "in furtherance of justice," which requires consideration of both constitutional rights of defendant and interests of society represented by People; dismissal not in furtherance of justice is abuse of discretion requiring reversal. West's Ann.Cal.Penal Code § 1385.

As of today there has been no written reasons why this case is being dismissed, the only clues have been offered to Detective Powers, Rachel Begley and the press. In each of these arenas there has been inconsistent reasoning. To Begley and the press, the attorney general cites due process (despite the new evidence and no statute of limitations for murder) and to the Detective we get a slew of different reasons. The only conclusion, though speculative, is that something or someone has scared the Attorney Generals office in preceding with the case as a review of the evidence not only substantiates the Attorney General's original decision to file but there has not even been a preliminary hearing in the case where the court can determine if there is enough evidence to proceed. Since the case has been filed, the court has the opportunity to weigh in and determine whether a dismissal is appropriate. The victims, the decedent's heir, and society encourages this court to allow for the case to go to preliminary hearing to determine whether sufficient cause exists in order to hold the defendant to answer to trial.

The State of California has adopted Marsy's Law in order to preserve and recognize the rights of victims. The law in relevant portion as listed on the Attroney General's own website states the following: "On November 4, 2008, the voters of the State of California approved Proposition 9, the Victims' Bill of

Rights Act of 2008: Marsy's Law, a measure to provide all victims with rights and due process. This webpage is for informational purposes only and is an overview of some of the key sections of Marsy's Law. A full copy of the text of the Victim's Bill of Rights Act of 2008: Marsy's Law (Proposition 9) is available from the California Secretary of State at http://voterguide.sos.ca.gov/past/2008/general/text-proposed-laws/text-of-proposed-laws.pdf#prop9. Relevant portions and summary have been provided by the Attorney General's website and states:

Marsy's Law significantly expands the rights of victims in California. Under Marsy's Law, the California Constitution article I, § 28, section (b) now provides victims with the following enumerated rights:

1. To be treated with fairness and respect for his or her privacy and dignity, and to be free from intimidation, harassment, and abuse, throughout the criminal or juvenile justice process.
2. To be reasonably protected from the defendant and persons acting on behalf of the defendant.
3. To have the safety of the victim and the victim's family considered in fixing the amount of bail and release conditions for the defendant.
4. To prevent the disclosure of confidential information or records to the defendant, the defendant's attorney, or any other person acting on behalf of the defendant, which could be used to locate or harass the victim or the victim's family or which disclose confidential communications made in the course of medical or counseling treatment, or which are otherwise privileged or confidential by law.
5. To refuse an interview, deposition, or discovery request by the defendant, the defendant's attorney, or any other person acting on behalf of the defendant, and to set reasonable conditions on the conduct of any such interview to which the victim consents.
6. To reasonable notice of and to reasonably confer with the prosecuting agency, **upon request**, regarding, the arrest of the defendant if known by the prosecutor, the charges filed, the determination whether to extradite the defendant, and, **upon request**, to be notified of and informed before any pretrial disposition of the case.
7. To reasonable notice of all public proceedings, including delinquency proceedings, **upon request**, at which the defendant and the prosecutor are entitled to be present and of all parole or other post-conviction release proceedings, and to be present at all such proceedings.
8. To be heard, **upon request**, at any proceeding, including any delinquency proceeding, involving a post-arrest release decision, plea, sentencing, post-conviction release decision, or any proceeding in which a right of the victim is at issue.
9. To a speedy trial and a prompt and final conclusion of the case and any related post-judgment proceedings.
10. To provide information to a probation department official conducting a pre-sentence investigation concerning the impact of the offense on the victim and the victim's family and any sentencing recommendations before the sentencing of the defendant.
11. To receive, **upon request**, the pre-sentence report when available to the defendant, except for those portions made confidential by law.

12. To be informed, **upon request**, of the conviction, sentence, place and time of incarceration, or other disposition of the defendant, the scheduled release date of the defendant, and the release of or the escape by the defendant from custody.
13. To restitution.
    A. It is the unequivocal intention of the People of the State of California that all persons who suffer losses as a result of criminal activity shall have the right to seek and secure restitution from the persons convicted of the crimes causing the losses they suffer.
    B. Restitution shall be ordered from the convicted wrongdoer in every case, regardless of the sentence or disposition imposed, in which a crime victim suffers a loss.
    C. All monetary payments, monies, and property collected from any person who has been ordered to make restitution shall be first applied to pay the amounts ordered as restitution to the victim.
14. To the prompt return of property when no longer needed as evidence.
15. To be informed of all parole procedures, to participate in the parole process, to provide information to the parole authority to be considered before the parole of the offender, and to be notified, **upon request**, of the parole or other release of the offender.
16. To have the safety of the victim, the victim's family, and the general public considered before any parole or other post-judgment release decision is made.
17. To be informed of the rights enumerated in paragraphs (1) through (16).

Throughout the course of the precedings some of these rights have been violated including the manner in which the Deputy Attorney General informed Rachel Begley as to the status of the case. When pointed out to Mr. Murphy, he responded that Begley was not a victim under Marsy's Law. Marsy's Law defines who a victim is and again according to the Attorney General's own website, "Prior to the passage of Proposition 9, "Victim" was defined under the Penal Code "as the person against whom a crime had been committed." With the passage of Proposition 9, "victim" as used in the California Constitution article I, § 28 is defined as "a person who suffers direct or threatened physical, psychological, or financial harm as a result of the commission or attempted commission of a crime or delinquent act. The term 'victim' also includes the person's spouse, parents, children, siblings, or guardian, and includes a lawful representative of a crime victim who is deceased, a minor, or physically or psychologically incapacitated.

The term 'victim' does not include a person in custody for an offense, the accused, or a person whom the court finds would not act in the best interests of a minor victim." (Cal. Const., art. I, § 28(e).)

Since, Begley under the above definition, qualifies as a victim, and is demanding that her rights under Marsy's law be protected. As such, the manner by which Begley has been informed of the dismissal, the reasons for the dismissal, the treatment by the Attorney's General Office since the inception of the case have all violated these protections. Ms. Begley is asking that the court insure that Marsy's Law is adhered to and at the minimum allow for a continuance so that a meeting with counsel and Begley is possible to understand the basis for the dismissal of the case as well as a determination be made as to whether Marsy's Law has been vilated.

CONCLUSION

Based on the above reasons and reasons given in court, the victim in this case is requesting that the case proceed to preliminary hearing and that a meeting occur between the Attorney General's Office, counsel, and Ms. Begley to insure that all information under Marsy's law is provided to the victim

Respectfully submitted,

By ____________________________
ROBIN SAX KATZENSTEIN

Attorney for RACHEL BEGLEY

Dated: ______________________________

____
JUDGE OF THE SUPERIOR COURT

101235866.1

Danny Casolaro with briefcase – Photos taken in July 1991, one month before his death. The briefcase was missing after his death and never found. Photo provided by Rachel Begley from her research files.

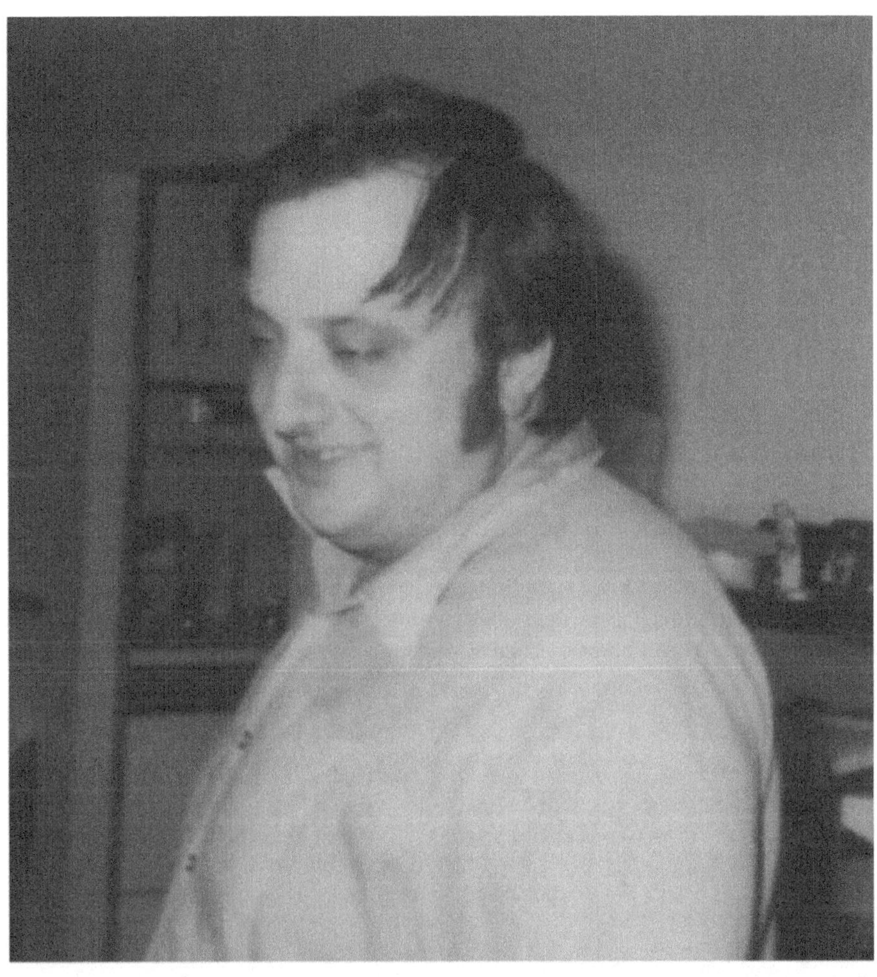

Photo of Michael Riconosciuto - From his files in the desert.

Above: Road to Trona (California Desert) 2000. Below: Dave Hendrix and Kelly O'Meara en-route to Trona, CA. Photos by Cheri Seymour.

Riconosciuto's trailer in the Desert (Trona, California) This is where Riconosciuto hid his documents. Photos taken in 2000 by Cheri Seymour.

Former *Insight* magazine reporter Kelly O'Meara (2001)

Above: Homicide Detective Sue Todd (L) and reporter/author Kelly O'Meara (R) (2001.
Below: Homicide Detective Sue Todd (2001).

RCMP (Royal Canadian Mounted Police) National Security Investigator Sean McDade at author's home on February 21, 2000. Photo by Cheri Seymour.

Above: Ted Gunderson at his FBI office desk in Los Angeles. Right: Ted Gunderson, Retired FBI.

Robert Booth Nichols with wife, Ellen Nichols, in costume on movie set for "Under Siege." (Nichols had a cameo appearance in the movie).

Former Commanding General Daniel Lopez Carballo of Honduras at FGBMFI Dinner Event – 2/22/08 – Bankers Ballroom – Fresno Fulton Mall. Keynote speaker with Jimmy Hughes of Honduras. http://fgbmfi-sjvc.org/FGBMFI-Fresno-Flier.pdf

Fax image of young James "Jimmy" Hughes.

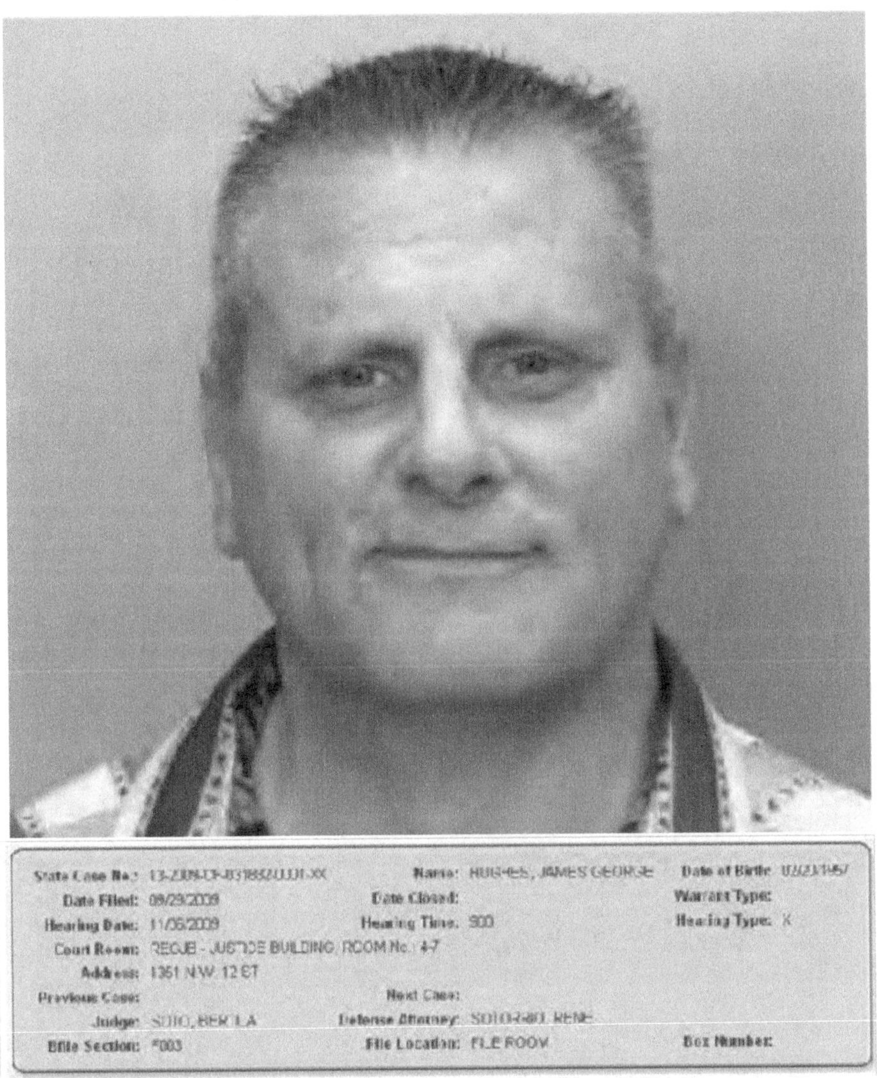

James "Jimmy" Hughes Miami-Dade Booking Photo. Arrested on 9-26-09

Jimmy Hughes of Honduras at FGBMFI Dinner Event – 2/22/08 Bankers Ballroom – Fresno Fulton Mall, California (Rachel Begley confronted Hughes at this event) http://fgbmfi-sjvc.org/FGBMFI-Fresno-Flier.pdf

Jimmy Hughes with John Carrette, Exec. V.P. of FGBMFI (taken from Jimmy Hughes Ministries.org/FGBMFI website). http://www.jimmyhughesministries.org/fgbmfi.html

http://www.fgbmfivoice.com/stories/996hughes.htm

A Hit Man with a New Mission

Jimmy Hughes, Honduras

EXCERPTED:

"After a six-year hitch in the military, I became a professional hit man for the Mafia. I collected money, hurt a lot of people and saw a lot of blood. I know what it's like to cut the throat of a man, see a man die, or throw a man in the trunk of a car and take him to his death. I did many horrible things. I allowed myself to do whatever was necessary.

"One day I had a contract on a man. They had paid me a lot of money to kill this person. I travelled over many states, and walked into the man's house one day, pulled out my pistol, and put a bullet in everybody's head.

"There were many people there that day because he was having a party. As I stood there with the gun in my hand, I suddenly realized that all those people were dead. They had died instantly. I had been paid to kill one man, but had killed half a dozen people. The rest had just been in the wrong place at the wrong time ---"

~~~~~~~~~~~~~~~~~~~~~~~~~~~~~~
~~~~~~~~~~~~~~~~~~~~~~~~~~~~~~

Jimmy Hughes in El Salvador. Photo from Vertice in El Salvador – July 6, 2003. http://babelfish.yahoo.com/translate_url?doit=done&tt=url&intl=1&fr=bf-home&trurl=http%3A%2F%2Fwww.elsalvador.com%2Fvertice%2F2003%2F060703%2Fcronica.html&lp=es_en&btnTrUrl=Translate

Above: Rachel Begley with her dad, Ralph Boger, a week before his murder in June 1981. This is the last time that Rachel saw her dad when they went for ice cream. Photo provided by Rachel Begley.

Below: Fred Alvarez was Vice-Chairman of the Cabazon Tribal Council until he was voted out as a tribal officer on June 6, 1981. He was murdered twenty-three days later, on June 29.

Above: Rachel Begley at home – 2009. (Photo by David R. Lutman). Below: Rachel Begley, warrior –2009.

Above: Rachel Begley with Detective John Powers from Riverside County Sheriff's Department, Central Homicide Unit – Cold Case Division (California). At author's home on 3-2-09. Below: Detective John Powers: Informal visit on 3-2-09 from Riverside County Sheriff's Department, Central Homicide Unit – Cold Case Division (California). Photos by Cheri Seymour

Above: Fantasy Springs Casino, Cabazon 3-4-09. Below: Site of 1981 triple homicide on Bob Hope Drive, Rancho Mirage, California (Murders of Fred Alvarez, Ralph Boger, and Patti Castro) Rachel Begley placed a flower at this site on 3-4-09. Photos taken by Cheri Seymour on 3-4-09

Above: KESQ-TV (News Channel 3) reporter Nathan Baca and Rachel Begley. Nathan won a regional Emmy for his 35-part series entitled "The Octopus Murders." Photo by Cheri Seymour on 3-4-09. Below: This note was inscribed on a book and given to Nathan Baca at KESQ-TV by Glen Heggstad.

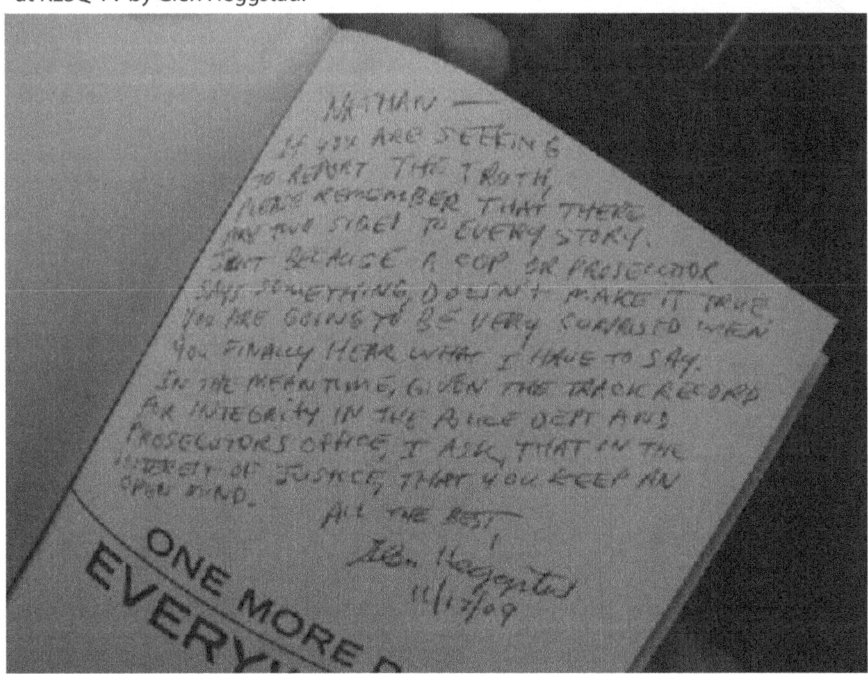

NATHAN —
IF YOU ARE SEEKING
TO REPORT THE TRUTH,
PLEASE REMEMBER THAT THERE
ARE TWO SIDES TO EVERY STORY.
JUST BECAUSE A COP OR PROSECUTOR
SAYS SOMETHING DOESN'T MAKE IT TRUE.
YOU ARE GOING TO BE VERY SURPRISED WHEN
YOU FINALLY HEAR WHAT I HAVE TO SAY.
IN THE MEANTIME, GIVEN THE TRACK RECORD
FOR INTEGRITY IN THE POLICE DEPT AND
PROSECUTORS OFFICE, I ASK, THAT IN THE
INTEREST OF JUSTICE, THAT YOU KEEP AN
OPEN MIND.
ALL THE BEST,
11/17/09

Above: Gilberto Rodriguez, Cali Cartel. Source: South Florida Sun-Sentinel Date: November 24, 2004. http://www.cocaine.org/colombia/cali.html

Below: The Cali Drug Cartel Leaders – L to R, Miguel Rodriguez-Orejuela,, Gilberto Rodriguez-Orejuela, Jose Santacruz-Londono. http://www.justice.gov/dea/pubs/history/1990-1994.html

Above: Frank Sinatra and the Mob by J.D. Chandler. Frankie and the Boys 1976 - Left to right: Paul Castellano, Gregory DePalma, Sinatra, Tommy Marson, Carlo Gambino, Aladena Fratianno, Salvatore Spatola, Seated: Joseph Gambino, Richard Fusco
Below: Adnan Khashoggi (with wife), Paris, France on November 4-6, 2008.

Author Cheri Seymour at beginning of her investigation, working as a reporter.

Author's file boxes for *The Last Circle*.

The Last Circle
Corporate Structures - Joint Ventures
[Overview - Not Detailed]

CORPORATE STRUCTURES:

FIDCO - [First Intercontinental Development Corporation]
Board of Directors: *See 1/11/83 FIDCO list of Directors

1. Robert Booth Nichols [also on MIL & Meridian Arms]
2. Michael A. McManus
3. Robert A. Maheu
4. Clint W. Murchison, Jr.
5. George K. Pender
6. Glenn Shockley [also on MIL]
7. Others not pertinent

MIL - [Meridian International Logistics]
Board of Directors: *See MIL documents

1. Robert Booth Nichols [also on FIDCO & Meridian Arms]
2. Eugene Giaquinto [also MCA Corp.]
3. Glenn Shockley [also on FIDCO]
4. Peter Zokosky [also Meridian Arms] *See FMC agreements
5. Harold Okimoto
6. Donald Oliver [also Meridian Arms]
7. Ellen Hopko [Nichols' wife]
8. Barry Smith
9. Others not pertinent

Meridian Arms - [A subsidiary of MIL]
Board of Directors: *See SOP Contra Report & other doc's.

1. Robert Booth Nichols [also on MIL and FIDCO]
2. Michael Riconosciuto [briefly for 1 year]
3. Donald Oliver [also on MIL]

4. Peter Zokosky [also on MIL] *See FMC agreements.

HERCULES RESEARCH CORP.

Board of Directors: *See Hercules doc's.

1. Michael Riconosciuto [also Meridian Arms - Recovery Technology, Inc. - Inter/Ocean Trading Co.]
2. Marshall Riconosciuto [also on PyroTronics Corp.]
3. Patrick Moriarty [also on PyroTronics Corp. & Red Devil Fireworks - other corporations not pertinent]

RECOVERY TECHNOLOGY, INC.

Board of Directors: *See [Riverside] *Press Enterprise* 1985.

1. Michael Riconosciuto [see above]
2. Paul Morasca

INTER-OCEAN TRADING CO.

Partners: *See *The Last Circle*

1. Michael Riconosciuto [see above]
2. Ted Gunderson

WACKENHUT CORPORATION

Board of Directors: *See Sept. 1992 *SPY* article on Wackenhut [Information below also taken from Wackenhut brochures]

1. George Wackenhut - President
2. Robert E. Chasen - Executive Vice President, Coral Gables
3. A.R. [Robert] Frye - Vice president, Indio, Calif.
4. John S. Ammarell - Executive Vice President
5. Clarence M. Kelley - Officer
6. Frank Carlucci - Officer
7. Admiral Bobby Ray Inman - Officer
8. William Casey - Outside legal counsel
9. Others not pertinent

PYROTRONICS CORPORATION

Board of Directors: *See corporate doc's

1. (1) Patrick Moriarty [also Hercules & Red Devil Fireworks]

2. (2) Marshall Riconosciuto [also Hercules Research Corp.]
3. (3) Robert A. Ferrante [others not pertinent]

JOINT VENTURES

Cabazon/Wackenhut Joint Venture [April 1981 - April 1983]

**See 5/25/81Wackenhut Inter-Office Memorandum. *See 1/31/92 Wackenhut letter from lawyer.*

Contracted Participants:

1. A.R. [Robert] Frye [also Wackenhut Corp.]
2. Robert Chasen [also Wackenhut Corp.]
3. Peter Zokosky [also MIL - Meridian Arms - Armtech Inc.]
4. John Vanderwerker [also Intersect Corp.]
5. Ex-Senator James Abourezk - South Dakota [handled legal affairs for the Cabazon Tribe in the Joint Venture]
6. Arthur Welmas - Cabazon Tribal Chairman since 1978

Non-Contracted Participants:

1. Dr. John Philip Nichols [also Sertec]
2. Robert Booth Nichols [also FIDCO - MIL - Meridian Arms]
3. Michael Riconosciuto [also Meridian Arms - Hercules - etc.]

Sertec Joint Venture [Began in October 1981]

Participants: *See [Riverside] *Press Enterprise* 1985.

1. Dr. John Philip Nichols [also Cabazon/Wackenhut Joint Venture]
2. Paul Morasca [also Recovery Technology, Inc.]
3. Michael Riconosciuto [also Recovery Technology, Inc. - Meridian Arms - Hercules]
4. Beryl. L. Barber [also Sonoma Engineering and Research]

FMC Joint Venture [FMC = Food Machinery Corporation of America]

[Began in July 1983] Deal was not consummated to my knowledge ---

*See July 27, 1983 letter from William Frasch to Col. Tom Bamford at FMC re: joint venture.

Contracted Participants:

1. Michael Riconosciuto [Meridian Arms - Hercules, etc.]
2. Robert Booth Nichols [Meridian Arms - FIDCO - MIL]
3. William Frash [Lilac Corporation]
4. Col. Tom Bamford [FMC Corp.]

Non-Contracted Participants:

1. Peter Zokosky [Meridian Arms - MIL]
2. Patrick Moriarty [Hercules - PyroTronics]

Index

Symbols

20/20 24, .195

A

Abbell, Mike 6, 12, 13 79, 82, 84-89, 161, 197, 202, 211-213, 252, 267-269, 292, 333
ABC News 47
ABC Nightline News 347
Abernathy, Neal 285, 294, 298, 299, 317, 330, 337
Abourezk, James 41, 45
Ackerman, Harold 213, 292
Adler, David 244
Agar, Charles F. 407
Age of Surveillance, The Aims and Methods of America's Political Intelligence System, The 45
Air America 243
Al-Kassar, Monzer 109, 110
Alberts, Jeff 388, 389, 392
Ali & Fahd Shobokski Group 203
Alighieri, Dante 214, 283
Al Saud, Fahd bin Abdul Aziz 175
Al Saud, Abdullah bin Abdulaziz 45, 397
Alvarez, Fred 305, 306, 323, 393, 394, 396-407, 411-418, 425, 429-436, 439, 442,
Alvarez, Phyllis 394
American Cytogenetics 156
American Lawyer 349, 366, 367
American Stock Exchange 43
Ammarell, John 47, 125, 127, 132
Ancient Mariner, The 275
Andrews, Andy 237
Annenberg, Walter 412
Aquino, Michael A. 234-237
Arab Bank Limited 7, 291
Arana, Raoul 131, 147
Armitage, Richard 363
Ashmore, Robert 33
Asmar, Tony 76, 77, 110
Assad, Hafez 75, 108, 109
Assad, Rifat 75, 77
Australasian and Pacific Holdings 244
Aviation Week & Space Technology 239
Aviv, Juval 108, 154

B

Baca, Nathan 402, 429, 430
Bacow, Martin 348, 350, 358-360, 368, 377-379
Bailey, F. Lee 35
Bainton, Joseph 384
Baker, Bobby 97, 98
Baker, Howard 9, 349, 354, 355, 361, 365, 366, 370-372
Baker, James 108
Bamford, James 68, 69, 312, 313
Bank of Credit and Commerce International (BCCI) 110, 111, 113, 209, 364
Bank of Irvine 117
Barber, Beryl 585
Barber, Earl 152, 306
Barnes, Robert 300, 301, 309, 340, 401, 404, 405
Barnett, Tracy 90
Baroudy, Mourad 100
Bason, George 154, 155, 251
Bates, Jim 398, 404
Baumzweiger, William 232
Bayou Group LLC 383, 384
Bazargan, Mehdi 155
B. Dalton Bookseller 24
Beavers, Dave 18-20, 23, 24, 29, 30, 34
Begley, Rachel ix, 393-395, 400, 405-407, 411-415, 418-420, 429, 436-441, 535, 559, 569, 573-576, 578
"Behold, A Pale Horse" 41, 92, 459, 464
Bejcek, Donald 22
Bell, Bruce 276-280

Benitez, Joseph R. (Mike) 303, 393, 394
Ben-Menashe, Ari 65, 154, 155, 250
Berckmans, Bruce 47
Berkowitz, Paul 19
Bickel, Bob 6, 52, 84, 85, 87, 91
Bingaman, Jeff 328
Bio-Rad Laboratories, Inc 149-152, 156
Biotech Capital Corporation of New York 156, 249
Black, Edwin F. 245, 422
Blanton, Tom 267
Bloomberg News 383, 384, 387, 388
Blue Grass Conspiracy, The 65
Blum, Jack 91
Bodine, Keith 347
Boegner, Jean Pierre 126
Boger, Ralph 305, 393-397, 407, 414, 416, 418, 425, 429, 437, 440
Bolles, Don 90
Bologna, Vincent Caci 306
Bonner, Rob 359
Boone, Pat and Shirley 423
Booth, Wade 119
Boston Globe 370
Botnar, Octav 151
Boyak, Alan 92, 103-105, 205-209, 322, 323, 347
Branch Davidians 235
Bredesen, Harald 423
Brent, Shaula 24
Brewer, C. Madison "Brick" 251
Brian, Earl 38, 56, 57-64, 91, 146, 147, 149, 153-156, 173, 174, 180, 182, 249, 269, 298, 321, 345, 489
Brisker, Henry 237
Brock, Frank E. 340, 394, 402, 403
Brooks, Jack 247, 272, 351, 352
Brown, George W. 610
Brown, Jerry 415, 441
Bryan, Richard 328
Bryant, William Jr. 251, 253
Bua, Nicholas J. 329
Bufalino crime family 347, 355
Bufalino, Russell 377
Buffam, Randy 307-311, 322, 324, 326, 331, 334, 335
Bull, Gerald 406
Bureau of Alcohol, Tobacco & Firearms (BATF) 74, 93
Burmese Trade Council 342
Burns, Arnold I. 363, 366, 370, 372
Burns & Roe, Inc 95, 96
Bush Administration I & II 373
Bush, George 4, 38, 84, 108, 155, 237, 245, 255, 257, 268, 272, 327, 373, 374, , 444
Bush, George W. 373, 384, 385, 398, 518
Bush family 351
Bush, Neil 52
Butler, Curt ix
Byrd, Robert C. 370

C

Cabazon tribe 38-42, 96, 121, 125, 128, 130, 133, 135, 139-142, 146, 147, 150, 158-162, 204, 255, 302-306, 310, 311, 319, 322, 323, 326, 331, 332, 340, 341, 345, 368, 373, 393-401, 404-416, 420, 429, 431-435
Caffrey, Ronald 109
Cali Cartel vii, 6, 12, 13, 79, 83, 84, 87, 89, 161, 197, 211, 212, 267, 268, 289, 292, 333
Callaway, William 393
Canadian Security Intelligence Service (CSIS) 5, 58, 59, 286, 287,293, 297, 327
Cannan, Patrick F. 11, 41, 42
Cannon, Chris 299, 300, 311
Capitol News Service 30, 34
Carballo, Daniel 415-421
Carlucci, Frank 38, 47, 75, 145
Carr, Donald 362, 363
Carroll, Joseph 47
Carter administration 83, 145
Carter, Jimmy 83, 229, 248, 254, 257,
Carter, Joye 263
Carter, Keith 410
Cartinhour, E. B. 54, 65
Casey, William E. 38
Casino du Liban 77
Casolaro, Anthony 3, 50, 89, 90, 135, 243, 347, 350, 375

Casolaro, Danny v, vii, ix, 1, 3-14, 36, 37, 40, 41, 49, 50-60, 65, 66, 73, 84-93, 111-115, 118, 128, 134, 135, 139, 144, 153, 167, 168, 172, 185, 190, 191, 195, 197, 202-208, 211, 220, 221, 239, 243, 247, 252, 257-261, 264, 270, 278, 283, 296, 326, 342, 343, 346-348, 350, 361, 373, 375, 399, 458, 459, 464-470, 495
Castle Bank 78
Castro, Fidel 222, 225,
Castro, Patricia 305, 393-397, 407, 416, 418, 425, 429
Catauro, Carl A. 390
Catena, Gerardo 97
Central Intelligence Agency (CIA) 4, 5, 7, 10, 14, 38-41, 46, 47, 53-56, 60, 73, 75, 77, 83, 84, 88, 91, 92, 98-104, 107, 109, 112, 118-121, 124, 133, 135, 138, 139, 142-148, 153, 162, 168, 172, 173, 180, 182, 204, 205, 209, 210, 221-230, 238, 239, 243-245, 250, 254, 258, 260, 262, 265, 266, 270, 276, 277, 283-286, 289, 291, 292, 318-321, 327, 341, 368, 371, 383, 386, 396, 425, 426, 435, 444
Chasen, Robert 47, 62, 92, 141, 161, 162, 406
Chávez, Hugo 415, 422
China Lake Naval Weapons Center 64, 67, 405
Chinatown (movie) 369
Chomsky, Noam 267
Cicippio, Joseph 203
Clark, Barbara 398, 399
Clearing House Interbank Payment System (CHIPS) 10, 11, 78, 198
Cline, Ray 92
Clines, Thomas 244, 245
Clinical Sciences, Inc. 156
Clinton administration 272, 278, 353, 373
Clinton, William J. 211, 257, 272
CNN 40
Cocaine Politics 83
Coelho, Tony 19, 20
Coeur d'Alene Press 276
Cohen, John ix, 10-13, 146, 148, 169, 195-199, 211, 247, 272, 289, 319, 321, 326, 346-353, 358, 366, 368
Colby, William 244, 245
Coleman, Lester 101, 102, 110, 111, 293, 297, 305
Cole, William 394
Colhoun, Jack 267
Commito, Angelo 90, 356, 377
Committee of the States 325
"The Company" 36, 37, 64- 68, 74, 81, 82, 121-123, 127, 148, 161, 169, 197, 199, 294, 405, 414
Compton, Karl T. 218
Connolly, John 46, 132, 179, 198, 202-205
Consolidated Savings and Loan 117, 205
Coors, Joseph 423
Corbett, William 47
Cornell University 280, 281
Corson, Robert 120
Coyle, Robert E. 22, 24
Credit Suisse 363
Crimes of Patriots 245
Cross, Curtis R. "Sam" 398
CRYPTX (software) 319
Cuellar, Joseph 60, 66, 264
Curdel, Jose 321
Curry Company 19, 22, 134
Cusic, Rod 18, 20, 23
Cutter Biological 157

D

Dahlem, Arthur 22, 25
DALITE (software) 270
Dankel, Mark Peter 160
Dark Victory: Ronald Reagan, MCA and the Mob, 14, 353, 369
Davis, Norman 151
Decency in Government [D.I.G.] 29-31, 34
De Cordoba, Jose 415
Defense Electronics 239

Defense Intelligence Agency (DIA) 110, 111, 250, 342
Defense News 239
DeFeo, Michael 354, 356-362, 365
De Gaulle, Charles 126
Del Gaizo, Michael 90, 356, 377, 378
Denton, Sally 65
Desarno, James V. 262
Desert Sun 394, 419, 439
DeSilva, Jim 37, 131, 344
Deukemejian, George 30
Di Giorgio, John 300, 301, 400, 405
Dole, Bob 276
Donner, Frank J. 45
Donovan, William "Wild Bill" 221, 222, 234
Drug Enforcement Administration (DEA) 11, 42, 47, 67, 75-77, 83, 84, 101, 103, 108-112, 197, 205-207, 213, 250, 292, 310, 323, 346, 347
Dunbar, Steve 19
Dwyer, John C. 333

E

Earman, John 226
Easterly, Clay 237
ECHELON 14, 311-313, 319
Eckerson, Bruce 19, 23
Eismann, Dennis 191
Eitan, Rafi 265, 292, 315
Electronic Data Systems (EDS) 130
El Khouri, Sami 99, 139
Ellis, John P. 384-387, 390, 391
Emmert, Chuck 306
Erdelatz, Eddy 305, 320, 401, 404
Estep, Gary 18
Euramae Trading 74, 75, 77, 101, 107, 111, 112, 166
Executive Intelligence Review 103
Eye, The 245
Eysenck, H.J. 227

F

Fair, Harry 41, 42, 69, 91, 139, 140, 141, 146, 150, 158, 293, 310, 345
Federal Bureau of Investigation (FBI) 6-14, 19-23, 29, 30, 33, 35, 38, 44-47, 54, 60, 65, 67, 71, 73, 80, 84, 86, 88, 90, 95, 97, 104, 117, 125, 133, 135, 139, 153, 167, 173, 174, 177-179, 191, 196-205, 208-211, 250, 260-264, 276, 293, 295, 300, 301, 304, 306-311, 314, 318, 322, 330, 333, 334, 338-340, 346-351, 355-361, 366-381, 383-387, 390, 396, 401-405, 411, 425, 427, 428
Feldman, Glen 41, 431
Feldman, Paul ix, 210, 386
Feldman, Sanford 340, 394, 403
Ferrante, Robert 117, 205
FIDCO (First Intercontinental Development Corporation) 71, 74, 75, 77, 90, 95-107, 142, 145, 165, 166, 180, 212, 220, 291, 338, 339, 371, 390
Financial Crimes Enforcement Network (FinCen) 13, 78-82, 93, 129, 198, 347
Financial News Network 298
Financial Post 153
Financial Times 399
Finger, Milt 237
Finley, Steve 131, 344
Finz, Stacy 119
Firebird Lake Airstrip 81
FMC Corporation 68-70, 192, 345
FOIMS (software) 80, 93, 94, 207
Forbes, Michael 315
Forster, William H. 237
Fort Detrick 216-222, 225, 230, 232
Fox, Frances T. 96
Frash, William 68, 69
Fratianno, Anthony 306, 432
Freeman, Dan 352
Frezeli, Charlie 110
Fricker, Mary 117, 153, 269
Friece, Ned M. 346, 350
Frye, Robert 12, 41, 42, 127, 141, 142, 146, 161, 162, 294, 310, 406, 407
Full Gospel Business Men's Fellowship International (FGBMFI) 412-425, 533, 534, 567-569

G

Gable, Clark 9, 172
Gale, Ted 349
Gamayel, Amin 7, 98-100, 137, 289, 338
Gamayel, Bashir 97, 98
Gamayel family 97
Gambino, Carlos 378, 577
Gambino family 9, 63, 86, 88, 90, 136, 204, 255, 306, 320, 321, 347, 348, 350, 353, 355-358, 376-380, 386, 395, 432
Ganem, Maurice 77, 101
Gannon, Matthew Kevin 110
Garofalo, Joseph 90, 356
Gates, Thomas 8, 9, 12, 13, 133-137, 167, 174-177, 198-204, 210, 211, 318, 346-352, 356, 358-360, 366, 368-377, 386
Genovese crime family 97
Geschickter, Charles 225
Ghanem, Maurice 100, 101
Ghorbanifar, Manucher 52, 53, 363, 364
GH Venture Partners 384
Giancana, Sam 98
Giaquinto, Eugene 8, 9, 90, 91, 134-137, 168, 177, 204, 346, 348-351, 356, 358-360, 368-373, 376-381
Gideon's Spies 292
Gila Indian Reservation 81
Gilbert, Gene ix, 13, 79-84, 197, 198, 203, 289, 307, 309, 319-323, 340, 403, 404, 489
Glovin, David 383
Goddard, Donald 101
Goldberg, Jerry 30, 31, 34
Gold Coin Saloon 17, 18, 30
Gold Warriors: America's Secret Recovery of Yamashita's Gold 392
Gomez, Edin Pastora 321
Gorchynski, Julie 159, 160
Goss, Larry 232
Gotti, crime family 321
Gotti, John 91, 204, 320, 350, 378, 379
Gottlieb, Sidney 222-230
Granby, George ix, 444
Grant, Tom 232, 395
Grant, Ulysses S. 395
Gray, C. Boyden 255, 443
Green, Nile 607
Grimaldi, Massimo 284
Gritz, Bo 55, 92, 237
Gunderson, Ted ix, 35-37, 71-73, 91, 92, 104, 105, 120, 123-127, 136, 150, 165, 166, 169, 177, 181, 183, 187, 190, 199, 205, 206, 233, 237, 566, 584

H

Habib, Danny 77
Hadron, Inc. 62, 63, 149, 154, 155, 156, 174, 249
Hager, Steve ix
Hamilton, Bill (BH) ix, 4, 6, 11, 12, 38, 52-57, 62, 65-68, 82, 84-86, 89, 91, 93, 105, 111, 130, 135, 154, 155, 173, 185, 221, 229, 247-249, 252-255, 258, 264-273, 284, 285, 289, 308, 323, 324, 328, 329, 344, 352, 362-364, 371, 381, 443
Hamilton, James 229
Hamilton, Nancy 4, 11, 38, 56, 247, 249, 284, 323, 328, 329, 364, 372
Hammond, Lonnie 19
Hand, Michael 55, 56, 207, 243-245
Hanna, Richard 21
Hardy, Ed 19
Hashem, Mohammad Jameel 45
Hawes, Phillip 394
Hawkins, Willis 47
Hayes, Chuck 92
Healy, Patrick 439
Heggstad, Glen 429-431, 577
Hells Angels 340, 340, 403, 414, 429
Helms, Richard 92, 222, 224, 245
Hendrix, Dave ix, 315, 317, 561
Henry, Brian 262
Hersh, Seymour 267
High Times (magazine) ix, 3, 99, 107, 108
Hills, Roderick 443
Himmler, Heinrich 236
Hitler, Adolf 175, 221, 222, 236, 237

Holbert, Al 121-127, 132, 207, 301, 306, 340
Holder, Eric 373
Holmes, Julian 267
Honegger, Barbara 110
Hoover, J. Edgar 7, 97
Hotel Del Charro 7, 97
Hot Zone, The 163, 164
Hougan, Jim 266
Houghton, Bernie 244, 245
Hubbell, Webster 272
Hughes, Howard 7, 51, 95, 96, 98, 105, 153, 203, 291, 347, 484
Hughes, Jimmy 147, 340, 345, 397, 398, 399, 403-441, 442, 492, 524-528, 535, 536, 540-549, 568-572
Human Ecology Fund HEF 227, 228
Hundley, William 349, 357, 358, 365, 367
Hunter, Gordon 394
Hunt for Red October 69
Hunt, H.L. 96, 97
Hunt, Howard 92
Hunter, Gordon 394
Hurley, Michael T. 75-77, 101, 102, 111, 112, 205

I

Imbrogno, Roger 192
Indio Daily News 394, 410, 547
Indo-China Project, The 13
InFerGene Company 156, 157
Inman, Bobby Ray 38, 47
Insight (magazine) ix, 14, 315, 316, 319, 323-334, 338, 351, 443, 511, 564
Inslaw viii, 4, 10-12, 37, 39-42, 51-64, 67, 71, 79, 84, 85, 91, 105, 111-113, 139, 146, 148, 153-155, 160, 169, 173, 195, 202, 204, 205, 211, 221, 247-255, 258, 264-269, 270, 272, 278, 284, 287-289, 323, 329, 334, 345, 346, 351-353, 356, 362-365, 372, 373, 375, 403, 404, 443, 450, 489
"Inslaw Affair, The" 247-251, 268, 269, 346, 353, 372
Interfor 108, 109
Interprobe 116
In These Times 108
Investigative Reporters and Editors 90
ISCOM (Intelligence Security Command) 207
Ishii, Shiro 217-219
Isikoff, Michael 268
Israel, Samuel 383-392
ITAR (International Trafficking of Armaments) 153, 348

J

Jahota, Skip 206
James, Brenda 431
James, John 431
Jenkins, Raymond 19, 21, 26, 36, 192
Jensen, Bill 122, 132
Jensen, Lowell 53, 249-252, 269, 270, 362, 363, 372
"J.H." (source) 66, 67, 73-82, 93, 94, 101, 117, 143, 177, 193, 242, 333
Jimenez, Felix 108
"J.M." (witness) 286
John Birch Society 46
Johnson, Lyndon (LBJ) 97, 98, 168
Jordan, Lucky 20
Josiah Macy, Jr. Foundation 225

K

Kai-shek, Chiang 390, 392
Kalka, Ben 121- 124, 127, 131, 132, 169, 170, 182, 299-309, 319, 340, 344
Keeney, Jack 361
Kelley, Clarence 38, 47
Kelley, Paul X. 47
Kelly, John (Tim) ix, 14
Kendall, Denis 88, 149-151, 174
Kenneally, Patrick 340, 401- 404, 411
Kennedy, Carl 397
Kennedy, Edward 230
Kennedy, John F. 179, 192, 229
Kennedy, Robert 357
Khashoggi, Adnan 52-54, 363, 364, 449, 579
Kiernan, Paul 415

Kim, Christopher 390
King, Stephen 35
Klenk, Ann 91
Knoedelseder, William Jr. 9, 356, 366
Knozzi, Richard 207
Komitet gosudarstvennoy bezopasnosti (KGB) 126
Kramer, Jay F. 390
Kressop, Cap 103
Kussman, Russell S. 159
Kwitney, Jonathan 245

L

LaBarge, George P. 22
La Cosa Nostra (LCN) see Mafia
Lansky, Meyer 98, 378, 379
Last Circle, The ix, 1, 4, 5, 66, 263, 271, 273, 275, 280-285, 288, 293, 298, 326, 433, 436, 437, 513, 582, 583, 584
Lavas, Raymond 79, 91, 120, 169, 170, 181, 182
Law Enforcement Assistance Administration (LEAA) 247, 248, 270
Lawrence, Scott ix, 13, 14, 38, 55, 70, 121, 127, 160, 161, 168, 211, 237, 289, 320, 334, 337
Law Review 273
Lawson, Guy 389, 392
Lawton, Valerie 330
Lederberg, Joshua 159
Legal Times 374
Leiden, Jeffrey 233
Leighton, Brian 64-68, 74, 81, 169, 405
Leon, Garby ix, 130, 192, 257-260, 263-267, 270-273
Levi, David F. 30
Levinson, Edward 98
Lewin, Jim 247, 346
Lewis, Astrid 237
Lidell, Mason O. Jr 261, 262
Life (magazine) 151
Lilac Corporation 68
Lilly, John 227
Littman, Jonathan 118, 127, 128, 133, 134, 168-172, 177-193, 199, 270, 310, 347, 399
Londono, Jose Santacruz 12, 13, 79-84, 197, 212, 289, 333
London Times 109, 110
Los Angeles Times ix, 65, 116, 133, 147, 210, 356, 366, 386, 397, 419, 493
LSD 224-227, 340
Lumumba, Patrice 222

M

M16 5, 286
MacArthur, Douglas 7, 96, 97, 215, 218-220
MacLean, Pam 300
Madoff, Bernie 385, 389
Mafia (La Cosa Nostra/Mob) 8, 9, 209, 225, 290, 293, 322, 324, 346, 349, 353-356, 366- 371, 376-381, 394, 404, 416, 418, 425, 431-433, 436, 536, 540, 571
Magano, Daniel 306, 432
Maheu, Robert 7, 74, 95, 98, 120, 291, 338, 347, 351
Mahfouz, Klahid bin 363, 364
Mailer, Norman 267
Manchurian Candidate, The (movie) 263, 273
Manor, Leroy J. 245
Man Who Knew Too Much, The 96, 98, 162, 192, 215
Marcos, Ferdinand 105, 307, 380
Margolis, David 348, 349, 354-361, 365, 373, 374
Mariposa Gazette 17, 18, 21, 23, 24
Mariposa Guide 20, 23, 195, 326
Marks, John 221, 225-230
Marmack, Jim 120
Marshall, Carol (Cheri Seymour) 275, 281, 326, 513
Marshall, Jonathan 83
Marson, Tommy 306, 395, 432, 433
Massey, Dave ix, 195, 267
Mattheys, Ken 19, 20, 24
Maxwell, Robert 272
May, Alan Michael 120, 121, 123, 127, 191
Mayer, David 302

MCA Home Entertainment Division 177, 351, 376, 501
McCain, John 276-279, 398
McCarthy, Joseph 7, 97
McClendon, Sarah 257-263, 267
McCoy, Bill 91, 375
McCoy, Frank 19
McDade, Sean ix, 4-6, 13, 14, 284-290, 295-302, 307-319, 322-335, 406, 512-515, 565
McFarlane, Robert C. "Bud" 155
McGuire, Patrick 342, 410
McKean, Rod 21
McKee, Charles Dennis 110
McKee, Seth 47
McKinney, Julianne 238
McMahon, Colleen 385
McManus, Michael A. 7, 95, 98, 99, 101, 145, 172, 176, 291, 338
Medellin Cartel 104
Meese, Edwin 155, 156, 249-252, 268-272, 302, 345, 348-353, 355, 358-366, 370-372
Merced Sun Star 119
Meridian Arms 68, 69, 71, 74, 135, 137, 140, 146, 147, 174, 203, 292, 380, 381
Meridian International Logistics (MIL) 8, 9, 11, 13, 71, 90, 134-138, 142, 149, 168, 174, 204, 341, 351, 356, 371, 376
METC (Modular Energy Transfer Catalyzer) 116
Meyer, Edward C. 68, 238
Micheletti, Roberto 415, 416, 420
Miller, Bud 132
MK-Delta 224
MK-Naomi 225
MK-Ultra 182, 221, 224-230, 234, 237
Mob see Mafia
Moldea, Dan ix, 14, 54, 352-357, 361, 362, 365, 366, 369, 370
Montt, Rios 423, 424
Moon, Sun Myung 351
Morasca, Paul 122, 123, 128-133, 178, 191, 207, 243, 301, 304-306, 309, 310, 319, 320, 340, 344, 400-404, 411, 432, 436
Moriarty, Patrick 116, 117, 170, 181, 183, 301, 303, 311
Mossad 5, 108, 250, 270, 286, 297, 327, 406
Moushey, Bill 303
Mr. and Mrs. Hollywood: Edie and Lew Wasserman and their Entertainment Empire 370, 371, 373
Murchison, Clint Jr. 7, 96, 98, 180, 291, 484, 583
Murchison, Clint Sr. 7, 96-98, 180, 220
Murphy, Daniel 254, 255
Murphy, Mike 413, 436-438, 441
Murphy, Thomas C. 210
Music Corporation of America (MCA) 8, 9, 14, 19, 22, 23, 36, 54, 81, 90, 134, 136, 137, 177, 204, 293, 346-362, 365-373, 376-381, 412

N

Naito, Ryoichi 216
Napa Sentinel 120
Narcotics and Dangerous Drugs Information System (NADDIS) 94, 404
National Aeronautics and Space Administration (NASA) 61
National Center for Supercomputer Applications (NCSA) 275
National Commercial Bank 363
National Crime Information Center (NCIC) 94, 309, 404
National Drug Policy Board 353
National Institute of Health 350
National Rifle Association (NRA) 276, 280
National Security Agency (NSA) 10, 14, 38, 65, 77, 250, 254, 255, 265, 311, 312, 322, 337, 338, 341, 343, 375, 376, 396, 443
National Security Council (NSC) 7, 8, 12, 14, 74, 75, 77, 102, 103, 138, 145, 337, 376
Newbold, Richard 346, 347
Newcomer, John 357, 359, 366
Newsweek 267, 268

Ng, Anson 399
Nichols, Ellen 124, 130, 171, 172, 177, 178, 344, 386, 387, 401, 404
Nichols, Jim 103, 105
Nichols, John Paul 395, 399, 409, 410
Nichols, John Philip (JPN) 152, 186, 310, 311, 319, 322, 345, 395- 402, 405- 411, 414, 431- 435, 492, 525, 526, 528
Nichols, Mark 397
Nicholson, Garth 232
Nichols, Robert Booth (RBN) 6-14, 41, 42, 45, 47, 56, 66-71, 74-96, 100-105, 121-149, 152, 154, 161, 162, 165- 192, 197-210, 212, 215, 220, 221, 233, 239, 240, 241, 247, 265, 267, 270, 271, 273, 289, 291, 292, 302, 306, 309-314, 318, 319, 322, 333, 337, 338-348, 351, 356, 360, 368- 389, 395-410, 431-436, 452, 483, 484, 486, 489, 492, 495, 496, 499, 502, 505, 508, 509, 516, 518, 520, 522, 525, 526, 528, 567, 583, 585, 586,
Nixon, Donald and Edward 120
Nixon, Richard 7, 97, 98, 120, 252, 254, 266
Noriega, Manuel 84, 147, 148, 235
North, Oliver 51, 108, 109, 119, 144, 150, 235, 368, 422, 423
Northside Bank of Miami 83
Northstar Graphics 377, 378
Nugan, Frank 243, 244, 245, 341
Nugan Hand Bank 207, 208, 243, 244, 245, 341
NUSAC 44

O

O., Steve 220, 238, 261, 291, 344
Obama, Barack 373, 415, 443
Oceanside Blade Citizen 119, 120
October Surprise (book) 110
October Surprise (scandal) 41, 155, 257, 258
Office of Naval Intelligence (ONI) 343
Office of Research and Development (ORD)[CIA} 230
Office of Strategic Services (OSS) 221, 222, 223, 229, 234, 245, 320
Okimoto, Harold Tadoo 75, 77, 80, 104, 105, 136, 137, 140, 168, 204, 206, 210, 215, 339, 342, 380
Olberg, Ralph 72, 73
Olga (Casolaro's housekeeper) 50, 51, 52, 85, 86
Olmstead, Thomas 61-64, 67, 93, 170, 181-183
Olson, Craig 262
O'Meara, Kelly ix, 315-320, 323, 333, 334, 337, 338, 343, 400-406, 443, 561, 564
OPERATION ARTICHOKE 221, 223
Orey, Michael 349, 366
Osaka Chemical Research Institute 217
Osman, Tim 72, 73
Otis, George 423
Outbreak (movie) 164
Overholser, Winfred 221
Overholt, Hugh 364, 365
Overoye, Arnold O. 32

P

P2 110
Pacheco, Rod 398, 411, 414, 417
Paige, Paul 18, 19, 20
Palazzolo, Joe 374
Pan Am 108-110
Parry, Bob 91, 267
Patterson, Tony 169, 170, 181, 182
Payne, Donald 276
Paz, Ignacio 10, 339
Pender, George 7, 74, 77, 95-102, 105, 210, 291, 338, 483-488, 583
Pender, William M. 96
Perot, Ross 258, 271, 338
Peterson, Wolfgang 164, 438
Philby, Kim 92
Phoenix Program 153
Pirushki, Anthony 20
Pisello, Salvatore James 353-357, 361, 362, 366-368, 379, 381
Pittaway, George & Jim 342

Pollard, Jonathan 286, 287, 327
Popular Front for the Liberation of Palestine-General Command (PFLP-GC) 108-110
Porath, Phil 130, 131, 132
Powers, John ix, 216, 386, 387, 394, 395, 400- 407, 411- 417, 419, 420, 429-433, 436-441, 575
Preloznik, Joseph F. 96, 140, 141
Press Enterprise (Riverside) 315, 398
Preston, Richard 164
Project ABBREVIATION. 295
Project EAGLE 250, 372
PROMIS ix, 4-6, 10-14, 38, 40, 51-54, 58, 59-65, 74, 80, 94, 111-113, 120, 130, 153-155, 161, 173, 197, 198, 247-255, 264-272, 284-299, 307-309, 314, 318, 319, 322-335, 345, 347, 352, 355, 363, 364, 369-372, 375, 381, 443, 449, 450, 512, 513

Q

Quarton, Greg 119
Queen Elizabeth II (see Windsor, Elizabeth Alexandra Mary)
Quick, Mary 128-131, 178, 191, 243, 340

R

Ramirez, Gloria 160
Rankin, Henry 116
Rawley, James 47
R.B.N. Companies, International 95
Reagan Diaries 356
Reagan, Nancy 355, 412
Reagan, Ronald 4, 7, 14, 29, 31, 34, 38, 39, 54, 56, 57, 65, 72, 84, 95, 99, 110, 120, 145, 146, 153, 155, 198, 249, 250, 253, 255, 257, 258, 268, 269, 270, 272, 276, 278, 303, 320, 327, 349, 353, 354, 355, 356, 358, 361, 362, 365, 366, 368, 369, 370, 372, 396, 412, 423, 424, 444
Reeder, Wayne 120, 147, 322, 342, 404, 406, 407, 408, 409, 410, 411, 434
Regardie's 353, 357, 365, 366, 367
Renkin, Al 69, 70, 173
Reno, Janet 237, 238, 257, 258, 263, 272, 329
Reynolds, William Bradford 362, 363, 364
Ric, Bobby 115, 117, 118, 119, 128, 129, 150, 160, 169, 170, 174, 181, 182, 183, 184, 185, 186, 187, 188, 189, 190, 191, 192, 193, 199, 206, 240, 307, 309, 316, 318, 323
Richardson, Elliot 253-255, 258, 264-268, 362-365
Riconosciuto, Marshall 116, 118, 119, 170, 183, 184, 205, 307, 311
Riconosciuto, Michael ix, 11-13, 37- 42, 55-57, 61, 64-72, 76, 81, 84-88, 92-94, 101, 103-107, 112, 115-135, 139, 140, 142, 144-156, 160, 162, 165, 169, 170, 173-185, 189-193, 197-199, 205-207, 209, 213, 220, 221, 233, 238-240, 243, 247, 250, 262, 264, 267, 269, 284, 285, 289-294, 297- 311, 316-319, 322, 323, 326, 330-333, 340, 341, 344, 350, 401, 403-406, 414, 444, 452, 489, 492, 524, 560, 562, 583-586
Ridgeway, James 85, 115
Rios, Steve 393, 423, 424
Ristau, Bruno 82, 83
Ritter, Kay 29, 33, 34
Robb, Charles 328
Robinson, Calvin 302, 376
Robinson, Donald 22
Rockefeller Institute for Medical Research 216
Rodriguez, Gilberto 211, 212
Gilberto 6, 12, 13
Ocampo 83
Rodriguez, Miguel 212, 289, 333
Rodriguez, Paul ix, 6, 12, 13, 79, 81, 82, 83, 84, 86, 87, 89, 197, 203, 211, 212, 289, 316, 332, 333, 579
Roland, Tiny 151, 263, 273, 276, 277, 314, 317
Rosenbaum, Ron 87, 88, 89, 220, 221
Rosenthal, Joel 212

Rositzke, Harry 223
Rosselli, Johnny 98
Rothstein, Jimmy ix, 267, 334
Rowell, John 176, 376
Rowley, James 38
Royal Canadian Mounted Police [RCMP] viii, 4, 5, 6, 13, 14, 42, 58, 59, 283, 284, 287-290, 293, 295-299, 305-309, 313-317, 322-335, 400, 406, 411, 511, 512, 514, 515, 565
Rudnick, Marvin ix, 8, 9, 134, 346-361, 365-373, 379
Rupp, Heinrich 92
Russbacher, Gunther Karl 257, 258
Russell, Dick 96-98, 162, 192, 215, 216, 267
Russell, Seymour 229

S

Safar, Fahim 91
Salerno, Ralph 353
Samper, Ernesto 83, 212
Sanders, Murray 218, 220
Sanford, Terry 156, 174, 340, 394, 403, 423
San Francisco Chronicle 64, 118, 127, 128, 133, 134, 156, 188, 189, 193, 236, 237, 243, 270, 299, 309, 310, 395, 399, 405
San Francisco Daily Journal 300
San Francisco Examiner 157
San Jose Mercury News 276
Sara Priest Indian reservation 134
Sawyer, Wilbur 216
Sax, Robin 438-442
Schalow, Arthur 11, 115
Schilly, Bob 21
School of the Americas (SOA) 420-424
Sciandra, Edward 90, 356, 377-379
Scientific Engineering Institute 230
Scoggan, Nita 423
Scott, Peter Dale 83, 91, 147, 160, 211, 264, 289, 320, 334, 337
Seagal, Steven 9
Seagrave, Sterling and Peggy 392
Seale, John 232
Search for the Manchurian Candidate, The 180, 221, 225, 239
Segal. Jakob 232
Segal, Lilli 232
Serrano, Lorena 438
Seymour, Cheri ix, 301, 325-331, 334, 337, 351, 512-515, 561, 562, 565, 575-578, 581
Shackley, Ted 244, 245
Shannon, Ted 151
Shaw, Joe 322
Sheinberg, Sidney 378
Shockley, Glen R. 13, 96, 137, 140-144, 172, 197, 291, 300, 338, 341
Shoman, Abdul Majeed 102, 291
Silver Pictures 270
Sinatra, Frank 271, 273, 412, 579
Sinatra, Tina 263, 271, 273
Sinclair, Roderick 21-26, 31
Smith, Barry 207, 583
Smith, Ed 213
Smith, Jason (see Phillip A. Thompson)
Snell, Joe 151
Society for the Investigation of Human Ecology 227, 230
Society for Worldwide Interbank Financial Telecommunication (SWIFT) 10, 11, 198
Soltz, Mark 386, 387
Sonenshine, Tara 347
"Source" 345, 346, 350
Spiro, Ian Stuart 119, 120
Spokesman-Review (Spokane) 159
SPY (magazine) 46, 47, 86, 132, 133, 198, 203, 204, 205, 206
Stalling, Danielle 85
Stanford University 231, 293, 343
Stavin, Richard ix, 8, 9, 134, 137, 204, 346, 349-352, 356-361, 365-377
Steinberg, Jeffrey 103
Stephens, Jackson 272
Stern, Carl 257
Stiffed: A True Story of MCA, The Music Business, and the Mafia 9, 356, 357
St. John, John 359, 360, 368, 378

Strategic Software Planning Corporation 4, 284
Strauss, Robert S. 349, 354, 357
Strecker, Robert 232
Suchesk, Art 103, 104
Summa Corporation 96, 203
Systematics 272

T

Tactical Technology 239
TC Technical Consultant 399
Technical Services Staff (TSS, CIA) 224-229
Teller, Edward 121, 237
Temple of Set 236
Teong, Tansri 391
Texas Observer 244
Thabet, Raymond 213
Thompson, Allan 330
Thompson, Arvo 220
Thompson, Julio 273
Thompson, Phillip Arthur PAT 131, 132, 301, 303, 305, 307, 309, 322, 344, 401, 405
Thornburgh, Richard 253
Thornton, Andrew "Drew" 65
Thrasher, Don 24, 25, 195, 326
Tibbetts, Samuel 155
Time 83, 159, 162, 163, 212
Todd, Sue ix, 4-6, 14, 285-287, 293, 296-326, 329-331, 335, 400, 405, 406, 443, 515, 563
Toohey, Brian 245
Toronto Star 14, 297, 308, 315, 318, 330
Torrijos, Omar 83
Tower, John 155
Tracy, Spencer 17
Trafficante, Jr., Santos 98
Trail of the Octopus 101
Trefry, Richard G. 237
Trott, Mike 340, 363, 372
Truman, Harry 96
Turner, Stansfield 38, 83, 229
Turner, William 51, 54, 66, 153
Tyme Share Inc. 129, 130, 207, 208, 309

U

Under Siege 9
Union Bank 381
Unit 731 216, 217
United Press International (UPI) 153, 156, 298
Urnovitz, Howard 231
U.S. Customs 6, 13, 14 , 42, 61, 62, 76, 83, 84, 141, 160-162, 169, 211-214, 288, 289, 302, 320, 324, 332-334, 337, 406, 416, 417, 444
U.S. Department of Energy's [DOE] Office of Counterintelligence 328
U.S. Department of Homeland Security 417
U.S. Department of Justice (DOJ) 6, 8, 9, 11, 13, 14, 62, 82, 84, 154, 155, 161, 197, 202, 206, 208, 211, 212, 213, 250, 252, 257, 267, 268, 269, 272, 284, 285, 288, 289, 292, 301, 309, 324, 333, 3339, 340, 342, 345, 346, 347, 348, 349, 353, 355, 356, 358, 360, 364, 365, 366, 367, 368, 373, 374, 375, 376, 377, 379, 380, 394, 397, 399, 402, 403, 410, 413, 414, 415, 416, 420, 432, 433, 436, 437, 442, 444
U.S. National Archives and Records Administration 346, 350, 351, 366
U. S. Secret Service 38, 66, 67, 127
U. S. State Department 73, 75, 83, 122, 322, 334

V

Valenti, Jack 134, 168
Vallely, Paul E. 234
Valleyfield Chemical Products Corporation 406, 407
Van de Kamp, John 30-33, 300, 303
Vanderwerker, John 91, 142-147, 172, 341
Vanity Fair 87, 89
Van Meter, Leslie 18-20
Van Meter, Ron 18-21
Van Vlet , Teresa 214
Van Voris, Bob 383, 387

Vaughan, Doug 85, 115
Velásquez, Romeo Vásquez 420, 421
Videnieks, Peter 13, 14, 56-66, 154, 160-162, 173, 174, 251, 269, 288, 289, 307, 332-334
Village Voice 85, 115, 139
Vinson, George 30, 33
Vukasin, John Paul Jr. 302

W

Wachowski, Larry & Andy 263
Wackenhut Corporation 37-47, 56-58, 61, 62, 78, 83, 91, 96, 117, 120, 121, 125, 127, 130-133, 135, 139-142, 144-151, 157-162, 175, 186, 198, 204, 207, 229, 255, 269, 293, 310, 311, 319, 321, 331-333, 341, 344, 345, 396, 399, 405-408, 411, 412, 414, 434-437
Wackenhut Electronic Systems Corporation 44
Wackenhut, George R. 43-47, 131, 132, 162, 344
Wager, Don DW 344
Wagner, Ben 29-31, 34, 35
Wagner, Bill (Walt) 347, 367
Wagner, Vivian L. 29-31, 34
Wa Latteral 165, 166
Wallace, Bill 64, 236, 405
Wallace, David 216
Wall Street Journal 239, 245, 415
Walsh, Tom 19, 22
Warner Brothers 257, 270, 273
Warner, James H. 276-280
Washington Jewish Week 108
Washington Post 212, 213, 239, 373
Washington Report 257
Washington Times 231
Wasserman, Edie 355, 370, 412
Wasserman, Lew 9, 349, 355-358, 361, 362, 365, 368, 370, 371, 378, 412
Waters, Maxine 275, 276, 279
Weaver, Wendy 88
Webb, Gary 275
Webster, William 258
Weed, Clay 410
Weinberg, Bill 99, 107, 109
Weinberg, Charlie 124
Weinstein, Henry ix, 133, 134, 210, 386
Weiss, Brian 128, 131, 132
Weld, William 360-366, 370, 372
Wells, Dale R. 439, 440
Welmas, Arthur 91, 147, 162, 408, 409, 431, 585
Welmas, Charles 431
Westinghouse Electric Corporation 95
West, Louis Jolyon 225
White, George 226-229
White, James 22-24
Whitehurst, Frederick 308
Whittinger, John 236
Wilcher, Paul 257-263
Wilkinson, Richard 417
Williams, Michael 119
Williams, Peter 216
Williams, Ron 24, 25
Willoughby, Charles 97, 215, 216, 218
Wilson, Dick 162
Wilson, Edwin 92, 244
Windsor, Elizabeth Alexandra Mary 21-26, 31
Wired 153, 269, 438
Wynogradsky, Janice 181, 183

Y

Yakuza 88, 90, 104, 105, 174, 204, 209, 348, 376
Yamamoto, Michael 193
Yates, Earl "Buddy" 245

Z

Zalis, Paul 394
Zangari, Rocco 395, 433
Zelaya, Manuel 415, 416, 421, 422
Zipperstein, Steve 211
Zokosky, Peter ix, 41, 69, 91, 102, 103, 127, 130, 137, 140-142, 146-149, 152, 161, 162, 168-179, 185-191, 203, 271, 310, 321, 322, 337-345, 369, 375, 397, 401-411, 417, 434, 486, 492, 495, 505, 583-586
Zuckerman, Barry 407